The Marshall Plan

P9-CFB-980

SEP 11 1998

STUDIES IN ECONOMIC HISTORY AND POLICY
THE UNITED STATES IN THE TWENTIETH CENTURY

Edited by
Louis Galambos and Robert Gallman

The Marshall Plan
America, Britain, and the reconstruction of Western Europe, 1947–1952

MICHAEL J. HOGAN
The Ohio State University

CAMBRIDGE UNIVERSITY PRESS

Published by the Press Syndicate of the University of Cambridge
The Pitt Building, Trumpington Street, Cambridge CB2 1RP
40 West 20th Street, New York, NY 10011-4211, USA
10 Stamford Road, Oakleigh, Melbourne 3166, Australia

© Cambridge University Press 1987

First published 1987
Reprinted 1988
First paperback edition 1989
Reprinted 1989, 1994, 1995

Printed in the United States of America

Library of Congress Cataloging-in-Publication Data is available.

A catalogue record for this book is available from the British Library.

ISBN 0-521-25140-0 hardback
ISBN 0-521-37840-0 paperback

An earlier version of the Introduction appeared as "Revival and Reform: America's Twentieth-Century Search for a New Economic Order Abroad," in *Diplomatic History* 8 (Fall 1984).

An earlier version of Chapter 1 appeared as "The Search for a 'Creative Peace': The United States, European Unity, and the Origins of the Marshall Plan," in *Diplomatic History* 6 (Summer 1982).

An earlier version of Chapter 2 appeared as "Paths to Plenty: American Marshall Planners and Debate over European Integration, 1947–1948," in *Pacific Historical Review* 53 (Autumn 1984).

Portions of several chapters appeared as "American Marshall Planners and the Search for a European Neo-Capitalism," in *American Historical Review* 90 (February 1985).

HC
240
H614
1995

For my Mother and Father,
Sisters and Brothers

Contents

Editors' preface

THE DECADE OF THE 1940S was a decisive moment in modern American history, as important for developments at home as for changes in U.S. relations with the rest of the world. The Second World War pulled the economy out of its worst depression, and in subsequent years the federal government for the first time in the nation's history took explicit responsibility for controlling the aggregate level of economic activity in the United States. A new style of foreign policy also emerged during and after the war. A nation that had in the 1930s turned its back on the European powers and belligerently proclaimed its neutrality, now became the leading power in the Allies' wartime coalition and in the postwar phalanx of Western, non-communist nations. These remarkable developments have received a great deal of attention from scholars – and deservedly so. But few historians have stressed the causal links between foreign and domestic events during these decisive years; of those who have, none has done so as convincingly as Michael Hogan.

Hogan's *The Marshall Plan: America, Britain, and the reconstruction of Western Europe, 1947–1952*, places this important policy innovation in a framework that he traces back to the 1920s, when Americans began to develop their particular brand of "associative state." This new style of commonwealth brought organized interests into the state. Competition was qualified by new patterns of cooperation designed to shape the state as well as the capitalist system. As Hogan demonstrates, this was the vision that American planners attempted to impose on Western Europe through the Marshall Plan.

But of course the European powers had their own internal problems and external interests. Hogan's meticulous research in foreign and domestic sources enables him to describe the manner in which tensions developed between the United States and its allies and to analyze the outcome of these struggles. His rich historical account of this significant economic policy provides an excellent introduction to the whole field of postwar economic diplomacy. We are especially pleased to add this outstanding volume to the

Cambridge University Press series on "Economic History and Policy: The United States in the Twentieth Century."

LOUIS GALAMBOS
Professor of History
The Johns Hopkins University

ROBERT GALLMAN
Kenan Professor of Economics
   and History
University of North Carolina at
   Chapel Hill

Preface

I BEGAN THIS BOOK shortly after finishing a volume on Anglo–American economic diplomacy of the 1920s. That volume, which dealt in part with the diplomacy of European reconstruction following the First World War, stimulated my interest in the Marshall Plan to rebuild Western Europe after the Second World War.[1] A history of the Marshall Plan seemed appropriate for other reasons as well. Although the plan was widely regarded as one of the most important international initiatives of the recent period, no thoroughgoing account of it existed at that point, only studies that treated its origins in 1947 and 1948. Then too, documents pertaining to the plan were just becoming available in the United States and in Great Britain. The availability of British documents was particularly important, in part because of my continuing interest in Anglo–American relations, in part because the British played a role second only to the Americans in the operation of the plan. These documents, notably the Bevin and Attlee papers, the Cabinet records, and the multiple files of the British Treasury and Foreign Office, have made it possible to write with some assurance about Whitehall's policy toward Western Europe, thereby filling a gap in the postwar history of British diplomacy. Much the same can be said of the memoirs, diaries, and published accounts by participants in the continental countries as well as in Great Britain. Together, they enriched my understanding of the political, economic, and security imperatives that influenced America's partners in Western Europe. They also revealed more clearly the search for institutional mechanisms that could reconcile these imperatives with the common goals of an international community. The result, I hope, is a book that comes almost as close to an international history of the Marshall Plan, especially an Anglo–American history, as it does to a history of American diplomacy.

Another reason for launching this project was the hope that my earlier work on European reconstruction would enable me to put the Marshall Plan in historical perspective and to draw some interesting comparisons between the two postwar eras. This turned out to be the case, although not in the way I had anticipated at the start of my research. Like many scholars

[1] The Marshall Plan included countries outside of Western Europe. But these countries were peripheral to the plan as well as to the region, which explains my focus on Western Europe throughout the narrative.

of recent history, I had thought of the Second World War as a great divide that separated the postwar era from all that preceded it. Other historians had begun to challenge this notion, of course, but their conclusions were embryonic and tentative. They understated the linkages between the two postwar eras, which I began to appreciate only as I read the archival and manuscript material available on both sides of the Atlantic. These linkages inspired my Bernath Lecture of 1984, parts of which are included in the Introduction to this book. The purpose of this Introduction is to put the Marshall Plan in a larger historical setting.

One aspect of this setting should be mentioned here. In my work on the 1920s, I had tried to adapt to the study of diplomacy the corporatist model of analysis then being developed by scholars of the domestic scene. Joan Hoff-Wilson, Melvyn P. Leffler, David S. Painter, and others would later use much the same model to good effect in their own books on American diplomacy. I define corporatism in the Introduction. The point to note here is that I had not thought of it as a useful model for analyzing the Marshall Plan, in large part because I anticipated a sharp contrast between the first and second postwar periods. My thinking changed only when research pointed toward continuity as the dominant motif. At that point, in other words, I began to think of the Marshall Plan as an outgrowth of organizational, economic, and political forces that had been working to forge an American brand of corporatism long before the second postwar era. What follows, then, is not simply an analysis of the plan from its inception in 1947 through its termination at the end of 1951, but one that sees it as an international projection of the corporative political economy that had evolved in the United States.

My thinking on the nature of the modern political economy, like the economy itself, has evolved over time. For this I am indebted to the documents, which force all of us to adapt our thinking to historical reality, but also to Ellis W. Hawley, Charles S. Maier, Thomas Ferguson, Robert M. Collins, Robert Griffith, Kim McQuaid, and other scholars whose work added immeasurably to my own analysis. Fellowships from the Harry S Truman Library Institute and the Woodrow Wilson International Center for Scholars facilitated a good deal of the research, as did financial assistance from the American Philosophical Society, the George C. Marshall Research Foundation, and the Miami University Faculty Research Conference. A grant from the Ohio State University College of Humanities helped in the final preparation of the manuscript. I also benefitted from access to the private papers of W. Averell Harriman, clearly one of the best collections for the postwar period, and from a long and stimulating interview with Governor Harriman four years before his death. Other participants in the Marshall Plan, especially Lincoln L. Gordon, Harold Van Buren Cleveland, Charles

P. Kindleberger, and Henry Labouisse, also shared their insights in a colloquium at the Wilson Center and a conference at Harvard University.

A number of scholars read parts of the manuscript, which is improved by their advice, including Lawrence S. Kaplan, John Lewis Gaddis, Charles Maier, Thomas J. McCormick, John Gimbel, Alan S. Milward, Werner Link, Charles P. Kindleberger, Forrest C. Pogue, Klaus Schwabe, Werner Abelshauser, Knut Borchardt, Manfred Knapp, and Thomas A. Schwartz. I owe a double debt to Alan Milward, who will object to some of the conclusions reached in this study but who contributed to it through his own work and through his diligence in sending me the many fine papers produced by scholars at the European University Institute in Florence, Italy. This list would not be complete without a special thanks to Ellis Hawley and Lawrence E. Gelfand, former mentors who have been unflagging in their support and advice, and Melvyn Leffler, whose willingness to read large parts of the manuscript with a very critical eye makes him the best of friends.

The excellent and helpful staffs of the Public Record Office and the National Archives made my long stay in both facilities comfortable and productive. I am indebted to them, especially to Ronald E. Swerczek, Gerald K. Haines, and Sally M. Marks of the Diplomatic Branch of the National Archives. I am also indebted to officials of the Treasury Department and the Agency for International Development who declassified thousands of documents for my use. Dr. Benedict K. Zobrist and his staff at the Harry S Truman Library deserve special mention, particularly Philip D. Lagerquist, Dennis Bilger, Erwin Mueller, and my old friend Elizabeth Safly. I spent a very hot summer in the Truman Library. The air conditioner did not work, the main reading room was being remodeled, and the researchers were consigned to a windowless basement we called the bunker. This should have been a prescription for disaster, but was not. Not only did all members of the staff aid in my research, they created a happy and friendly environment in which to work. So did the late Grace Carvin, with whom I stayed while in Independence, and Robert H. Ferrell, who shared with me his knowledge of the Marshall Plan and of the impressive holdings of the Truman Library.

In addition, Karen Clift was tireless in tracking down much of the published literature I needed for this project. Jack Temple Kirby provided moral and intellectual support over the many years of research and writing. Louis Galambos and Frank Smith, my editors, helped to clean up the last draft of the manuscript. Pamela Messer typed so many versions of each chapter that she began to call it her book, as in many ways it is. I want to thank her for being a good friend as well as an efficient and patient typist. Alice Jablonsky was a warm and wonderful host during many of my research trips to Washington, D.C., taking me into her home and into her family. I have the fondest memories of those days and am deeply grateful for her friendship and generosity. I am also grateful to several graduate students who aided with the research, including Ken Kan and Vivian Tan. Two others, Ann Heiss and Kurt Schultz, were particularly helpful, not just in their research assistance but in their many thoughtful suggestions and in their zeal to make my prose more readable. Working with them was one of the most rewarding and happiest parts of this enterprise. My wife, Virginia, and our children, Christopher, David, Joseph, and Ann, already know how much they have contributed to this book. It is a lucky writer who has the patient support of such a family, for which I am grateful beyond measure.

First and last I thank the wonderful gang at 1434 Rainbow Drive, where I grew up: my father and mother, Gene and Donna Hogan, and my brothers and sisters, Denny, Sally, Pat, and Donnaree. They continue to provide much of the inspiration for the work that I do, not to mention an endless stream of encouragement and more love than I deserve. This book is dedicated to them, though it can never repay all that they have given to me.

M. J. H.
Columbus, Ohio

Introduction

Toward the Marshall Plan: from New Era designs to New Deal synthesis

I

ORIGINAL ACCOUNTS of the Marshall Plan, or the European Recovery Program as it was known officially, hailed this celebrated enterprise as evidence of America's assumption of world leadership after the Second World War.[1] Together with the North Atlantic Treaty and other instruments of Cold War diplomacy, the Marshall Plan supposedly marked the end of the isolationist era and the beginning of what Henry Luce called the "American Century." This interpretation paralleled that found in older works on

---

[1] The relevant literature includes Harry B. Price, *The Marshall Plan and Its Meaning* (Ithaca, NY, 1955); Joseph M. Jones, *The Fifteen Weeks (February 21–June 5, 1947)* (New York, 1955); Robert H. Ferrell, *George C. Marshall* (New York, 1966); Louis J. Halle, *The Cold War as History* (New York, 1967); Joyce Kolko and Gabriel Kolko, *The Limits of Power: The World and United States Foreign Policy, 1945–1954* (New York, 1972); Thomas G. Paterson, *Soviet–American Confrontation: Postwar Reconstruction and the Origins of the Cold War* (Baltimore, 1973); Adam B. Ulam, *Expansion and Coexistence: Soviet Foreign Policy, 1917–1973*, 2d ed. (New York, 1974); John Gimbel, *The Origins of the Marshall Plan* (Stanford, CA, 1976); and Walter F. LaFeber, *America, Russia, and the Cold War, 1945–1975*, 3d ed. (New York, 1976). More recent works have begun to break new ground in the study of the Marshall Plan, including the plan's bureaucratic dimension, its economic accomplishments, and its emphasis on integrating economies and increasing productivity. See Hadley Arkes, *Bureaucracy, The Marshall Plan, and the National Interest* (Princeton, NJ, 1972); Charles S. Maier, "The Politics of Productivity: Foundations of American International Economic Policy after World War II," *International Organization* 31 (Autumn 1977): 607–33; Maier, "The Two Postwar Eras and the Conditions for Stability in Twentieth-Century Western Europe," *American Historical Review* 86 (April 1981): 327–52; Armin Rappaport, "The United States and European Integration: The First Phase," *Diplomatic History* 5 (Spring 1981): 121–49; Imanuel Wexler, *The Marshall Plan Revisited: The European Recovery Program in Economic Perspective* (Westport, CT, 1983); and Alan S. Milward, *The Reconstruction of Western Europe, 1945–1951* (London, 1984).

I

domestic history. These works viewed the New Deal as a second American revolution, the domestic equivalent of the revolution in American diplomacy engineered by Cold War policymakers in the 1940s. More recent works, to be sure, have begun to overturn the older interpretation. Those on domestic history have portrayed twentieth-century developments as part of a larger historical process by which Americans adjusted their economic and political institutions to the profound transformations brought on by industrialization. In these works, the liberal critique embedded in older scholarship, which separated the New Deal of the 1930s from the New Era of the 1920s, has given way to interpretations that consider both eras related parts of the modern American search for a new economic and political order.[2]

Scholars of American diplomacy have been slow to pursue this theme. Recent works in this field have failed to connect the trends in domestic history to those in the history of foreign relations or to note how institutional adaptations at home influenced the direction of policy abroad.[3] In these works, to put it differently, the Marshall Plan remains essentially cut off from the nation's previous history. This lack of connection explains why the present volume begins with an essay that departs from the norms of a standard introduction – one that starts by tracing the evolution of American domestic and foreign policies from the New Era through the New Deal, ends by sketching the lines of continuity and change that link these decades to the Marshall Plan for Western Europe, and thus sets the stage for the narrative that follows.

The purpose here is to cast the Marshall Plan in the context of America's twentieth-century search for a new economic order at home and abroad, and to do so by subsuming the three decades after the First World War under an interpretative framework that is new to the study of American diplomacy. This framework is a variant of one that recent historians of the domestic scene have used to understand modern efforts to create what some have called an associative state, others a corporative neo-capitalism.[4] By

---

[2]   The new interpretations emerge in works by a divergent group of organizational, institutional, and revisionist historians of both the Left and the Right. See, for example, Grant McConnell, *Private Power and American Democracy* (New York, 1966); Robert H. Wiebe, *The Search for Order, 1877–1920* (New York, 1967); James Weinstein, *The Corporate Ideal in the Liberal State, 1900–1918* (Boston, 1969); Ronald Radosh and Murray N. Rothbard, eds., *A New History of Leviathan. Essays on the Rise of the American Corporate State* (New York, 1972); Kim McQuaid, "Corporate Liberalism in the American Business Community, 1920–1940," *Business History Review* 52 (Autumn 1978): 342–68; Ellis W. Hawley, *The Great War and the Search for a Modern Order: A History of the American People and Their Institutions, 1917–1933* (New York, 1979); and Robert M. Collins, *The Business Response to Keynes, 1929–1964* (New York, 1981).

[3]   For convenient summaries of the literature on American foreign relations, see the historiographical essays in Gerald K. Haines and J. Samuel Walker, eds., *American Foreign Relations: A Historiographical Review* (Westport, CT, 1981).

[4]   For a discussion of this framework, see Ellis W. Hawley, "The Discovery and Study

these I mean an American political economy founded on self-governing
economic groups, integrated by institutional coordination ar-
ket mechanisms, led by by
limited but positive go' ~~stable currencies~~ /th
in which all could share :ed
with the localized and :n-
tury, including individu ~~fixed exchange~~ he
twentieth-century trenc by
national economies of ~~nondiscrimination~~ ve
regulation. The result a ie-
thing of a hybrid econc ~~trade~~ o-
capitalism that went be :al
theory but stopped sho
This trend fundamei y,
which for all practical iy
along lines similar to ie
United States. To the i-
sioned in classical theor in
and comparative advar s,
and nondiscriminatory trade — American leaders would add new mechanisms of economic planning, new institutions of coordination and control, and new partnerships between public and private elites in the
collective administration of world trade and development. These new elements were to be the bricks and mortar in a multilateral framework, a
new system in which multinational arrangements put a limit on competitive nationalisms, market forces and coordinating mechanisms worked to
integrate economies, and economic integration cleared a path to stable
growth and international harmony.

This framework was a comprehensive design for American foreign policy,
and viewing it as such allows us to conceptualize the whole period from
the First World War through the Marshall Plan in terms of a single process,
bracketed at either end by major efforts to rebuild the devastated economics
of war-torn Europe. This is not to deny the reality of historical change. Far
from it. One of the major purposes of this introduction is to delineate the
important policy innovations of the 1930s and show how they influenced
the Marshall Plan. But it is to argue that the most important changes grew
out of an evolutionary progression, that New Dealers and Marshall Planners
would take the nation further down a road well traveled by their Republican
predecessors in the 1920s.

of a 'Corporate Liberalism,' " *Business History Review* 52 (Autumn 1978): 309–30.
Thomas J. McCormick has discussed the prospect for a corporatist synthesis in his
"Drift or Mastery? A Corporatist Synthesis for American Diplomatic History" *Reviews
in American History* 10 (December 1982): 318–30.

II

Recent scholarship has undercut the original interpretation of the 1920s as a reactionary decade squeezed between two dynamic reform periods. Elements of a business progressivism survived and were personified in the policies of Secretary of Commerce Herbert C. Hoover, whose brand of associationalism envisioned an organic political economy in which public and private elites cooperated in the job of economic and social management. Hoover's associationalism built on the policies of Theodore Roosevelt and Woodrow Wilson, on the writings of men like Herbert Croly and Walter Lippmann, and on the patterns of public–private cooperation and power sharing that had marked the War Industries Board and other agencies of wartime mobilization. It linked these prewar and wartime developments to the New Deal policies of the 1930s, and it had the support of important elements in the private sector, particularly of those progressive business leaders who had earlier formed the National Civic Federation, and of those labor leaders whose business unionism looked to a labor–management partnership based on increased productivity and bread-and-butter gains for workers.[5]

Hoover's associationalism, as Ellis W. Hawley has shown, accepted the economic collectivism and interdependence that came out of industrialization, the rise of organized and bureaucratized concentrations of private economic power, the concomitant decline of market forces, and the consequent need to supplement these forces with institutional regulating and coordinating devices. It tried to reconcile this need with nineteenth-century traditions by locating the most important parts of the regulatory apparatus in the private sector, specifically in the growing network of trade associations, professional societies, farm cooperatives, and labor unions. Enlightened functional elites, rather than public authorities, were to act as agents of economic rationalization by working within and between their groups

[5] See especially Ronald Radosh, "The Corporate Ideology of American Labor Leaders from Gompers to Hillman," *Studies on the Left* 6, no. 21 (1966): 66–88; Weinstein, *Corporate Ideal in the Liberal State*; Murray N. Rothbard, "War Collectivism in World War I," in Radosh and Rothbard, *A New History of Leviathan*, 66–110; Robert D. Cuff, *The War Industries Board: Business–Government Relations during World War I* (Baltimore, 1973); Ellis W. Hawley, "Herbert Hoover, the Commerce Secretariat, and the Vision of an 'Associative State,'" *Journal of American History* 61 (June 1974): 116–40; Joan Hoff Wilson, *Herbert Hoover: Forgotten Progressive* (Boston, 1975); Robert H. Zieger, "Labor, Progressivism, and Herbert Hoover," *Wisconsin Magazine of History* 58 (Spring 1975): 196–208; Robert D. Cuff, "Herbert Hoover, the Ideology of Voluntarism, and the War Organization during the Great War," *Journal of American History* 64 (September 1977): 358–72; and David Burner, *Herbert Hoover: A Public Life* (New York, 1978). See also the essays by Hawley, Zieger, and Wilson in Ellis W. Hawley, ed., *Herbert Hoover as Secretary of Commerce: Studies in New Era Thought and Practice* (Iowa City, 1981), 43–79, 80–114, 115–47.

to eliminate waste, allocate resources efficiently, tame the business cycle, and optimize output. In performing these tasks, they were to be guided by the dictates of modern science. They were to rely on the new tools of scientific management and industrial sociology and look for assistance to those disinterested engineers and professional managers who supposedly possessed the knowledge and experience required to solve complex economic problems without the waste and inefficiency inherent in an older, competitive individualism or in an oppressive and bureaucratic statism.[6]

Although the emphasis was on private self-regulation by the groups, government had a positive role to play in the new associative order. It could provide useful information and services, defend legitimate group interests, promote associational activities, and champion the cause of countercyclical stabilization. It could collaborate with private elites in an organized system of power sharing, working through this system to mediate disputes, eliminate destabilizing competition, encourage scientific management, and foster enlightened group action and self-regulation. Through these and other initiatives, public and private leaders would join forces to achieve the greater productivity and higher living standards that were needed to avoid the redistributive conflicts and the pressure for greater government control that would supposedly result from economic stagnation and retrenchment. In Hoover's system, then, market forces and parliamentary forums would be reinforced with institutional coordinators, private economic governments, and new modes of public–private power sharing. Political solutions would give way to technocratic formulations and redistributive battles would be replaced by a corporative collaboration based on what Charles S. Maier has called the "politics of productivity."[7]

In dealing with the international economy, Hoover and other Republican policymakers also tried to blend private and public power, market incentives, and new forms of regulation in a way that foreshadowed the mixed economic policies of a later day. Some aspects of their policy reflected a lingering commitment to the older traditions of antistatism and antimonopoly. The Republicans waged a sustained campaign against European proposals to supplement the market with public planning or private cartels. They rejected European calls for government financing of economic recovery, British suggestions for preferential commercial and shipping arrangements, French proposals for intergovernmental control over key raw

[6] Hawley, "Herbert Hoover, the Commerce Secretariat, and the Vision of an 'Associative State.' " See also Hawley, *Great War and the Search for a Modern Order*. My interpretation also draws on two unpublished papers by Professor Hawley: "Neo-institutional History and the Understanding of Herbert Hoover" (author's files); and "Techno-corporatist Formulas in the Liberal State, 1920–1960: A Neglected Aspect of America's Search for a New Order," paper presented at the Conference on Twentieth-Century Capitalism, Harvard University, Cambridge, MA, September 1974.
[7] In addition to the sources cited in note 6, see Maier, "The Politics of Productivity."

materials, and British, French, and German efforts to establish government-sanctioned resource monopolies. In their view, these and similar initiatives pointed toward a statism that would prevent the most efficient use of resources, hamper productivity, and lead to war. The Republicans relied instead on private finance to underwrite recovery and sought, through monetary stabilization and currency convertibility, to remove the constraints on individual initiative and create a climate in which private enterprise and the price mechanism could foster growth and integrate markets.[8]

Yet these aspects of policy did not mean that Republican leaders relied solely on an unregulated privatism to rebuild Europe and reorganize the world economy. In these areas, as on the home front, government had a positive if limited role to play and one it could best perform in collaboration with private elites whose expertise and commitment to business over politics supposedly made them more reliable managers and less likely than their public counterparts to transform economic issues into dangerous political controversies. In these areas, moreover, Republican policymakers promoted business collectivism and self-regulation, devised transnational coordinators to supplement market forces, and then offered these strategies and their faith in private expertise as the best way to resolve disputes, prevent excessive government intervention, and encourage a rational and productive integration.

On the American side, for example, Hoover divided the Bureau of Foreign and Domestic Commerce into commodity divisions. He staffed these divisions with experts drawn from the leading export industries and trade associations, tied them to groups in the private sector through a network of cooperating committees, and worked through the resulting system to disseminate information, study trade and investment trends, and promote overseas resource development.[9] In addition, Hoover envisioned the World War Foreign Debt Commission as an agency for adjusting claims on a scientific basis. He urged a technical management of tariff rates by a commission of experts who were to stand above political considerations and congressional logrolling. He also helped to establish a loan-control mechanism through which public leaders and private bankers were to share the responsibility for directing capital exports into reproductive channels. And together with Secretary of State Charles Evans Hughes, he urged business and banking leaders to collaborate in promoting foreign trade, worked through a private

---

[8]   Joseph Brandes, *Herbert Hoover and Economic Diplomacy: Department of Commerce Policy, 1921–1928* (Pittsburgh, 1962), 63–147; Brandes, "Product Diplomacy: Herbert Hoover's Anti-monopoly Campaign at Home and Abroad," in Hawley, *Hoover as Secretary of Commerce*, 185–214; and Michael J. Hogan, *Informal Entente: The Private Structure of Cooperation in Anglo–American Economic Diplomacy, 1918–1928* (Columbia, MO, 1977).

[9]   Brandes, *Hoover and Economic Diplomacy*, 5–21; and Hawley, "Herbert Hoover, the Commerce Secretariat, and the Vision of an 'Associative State,' " 123–4.

financial consortium to develop the China market, and organized oil developers, raw-materials importers, and cable and radio builders to fight foreign cartels and open the door to American expansion.[10]

At the same time, Hoover and other Republican policymakers tried to impose their associative system on the international economy. In dealing with European reconstruction, they asserted the primacy of economics over politics and sought to resolve outstanding issues by applying technocorporative formulations. They encouraged banking leaders in Europe and the United States to join in constructive schemes of monetary stabilization and viewed the reparations imbroglio as a technical problem amenable to scientific solution by nonpolitical business experts. In promoting resource development, expanding communications facilities, and financing modernization, they abandoned their initial plans for competitive action, worked with private American and European leaders to construct cooperative structures, and then redefined the Open Door principle to accommodate the new forms of "cooperative competition." Through the network of private and central bank institutions, through the oil, financial, and radio consortiums, and through the loan-control procedure, the Agent General for Reparations, and the Bank for International Settlements, they organized new frameworks of transnational action, new mechanisms of public–private cooperation, and new instruments for a stable development of the world economy.[11]

For Republican policymakers, of course, the world was not a blank slate on which they could draw their blueprint for a corporative order. This was particularly true of the Old World. Here, the Republicans envisioned an interdependent community linked by unfettered commerce and superintended by nonpolitical agencies of economic coordination and control. They would assist in this endeavor by funding war debts on a capacity-to-pay basis and by joining business leaders to manage the flow of productive capital. They would also back the Agent General for Reparations, encourage private experts to put the reparations settlement on a businesslike basis, and organize networks of private- and central-bank cooperation. But the Europeans were to do their part as well. They were to make currencies

[10] Hogan, *Informal Entente*, 78–208; Melvyn P. Leffler, "Herbert Hoover, the 'New Era,' and American Foreign Policy," in Hawley, *Hoover as Secretary of Commerce*, 148–79; and Hawley, *Great War and the Search for a Modern Order*, especially 100–17.

[11] Frank Costigliola, "The Other Side of Isolationism: The Establishment of the First World Bank, 1929–1930," *Journal of American History* 59 (December 1972): 602–20; Hogan, *Informal Entente*; Melvyn P. Leffler, "American Policy Making and European Stability, 1921–1933," *Pacific Historical Review* 46 (May 1977): 207–28; Leffler, *The Elusive Quest: America's Pursuit of European Stability and French Security, 1919–1933* (Chapel Hill, NC, 1979); Hogan, "Thomas W. Lamont and European Recovery: The Diplomacy of Privatism in a Corporatist Age," in Kenneth Paul Jones, ed., *U.S. Diplomats in Europe, 1919–1941* (Santa Barbara, CA, 1981), 5–22; and Leffler, "Herbert Hoover, the 'New Era,' and American Foreign Policy."

convertible, reduce reparations, and negotiate debt-funding agreements with one another and with the United States. Initiatives of this sort would break the financial chains that shackled the European economies and allow market mechanisms and enlightened business concerts to integrate markets, expand trade, and stimulate growth. In American eyes, the interdependent community that resulted would also help to control German nationalism, making it possible to revitalize Germany's productive power without restoring its prewar hegemony.[12]

Building the new order meant overcoming resistance in Europe, where most leaders were trying to shift the financial burden of the war to the backs of their neighbors, where the French sought economic and military dominance at the expense of Germany's recovery, and where the British aimed to retain their prewar leadership in critical sectors of the world economy. The Americans used their financial leverage, particularly their control over private loans and debt reductions, to overcome much of this opposition. They pressured the Europeans to fund war debts, reduce reparations, and reform finances. Together with their collaborators in the private and central banks on both sides of the Atlantic, they also engineered the Dawes Plan, arranged successful schemes of monetary stabilization, managed bond sales, and negotiated stabilization loans – all of which enabled the Europeans to handle their balance of payments and achieve a fragile equilibrium in the years after 1924.[13]

Republican policymakers used the same leverage to bring the British and French into line with their corporative formulations. Between 1921 and 1923, British and American leaders resolved many of their initial postwar differences and formed a partnership to develop international oil resources and regulate world communications. To bring this partnership about, public officials in the United States had to forego early plans to develop independent systems. Instead, they organized oil, radio, and cable consortiums under Anglo–American leadership, and did so to avoid a wasteful duplication of existing systems, accommodate the realities of international business as defined by private leaders, and create institutional mechanisms for the orderly development of the world economy. The British made similar sacrifices for similar reasons. By substituting cooperation for competition, they hoped

[12]   Hogan, *Informal Entente*, 38–105.
[13]   The various parts of this story can be followed in ibid.; Herbert Feis, *The Diplomacy of the Dollar: First Era, 1919–1932* (Baltimore, 1950); Lester V. Chandler, *Benjamin Strong, Central Banker* (Washington, DC, 1958); Stephen V. O. Clarke, *Central Bank Cooperation, 1924–1931* (New York, 1967); Joan Hoff Wilson, *American Business and Foreign Policy, 1920–1933* (Lexington, KY, 1971); Jon Jacobson, *Locarno Diplomacy: Germany and the West, 1925–1929* (Princeton, NJ, 1972); Charles S. Maier, *Recasting Bourgeois Europe: Stabilization in France, Germany, and Italy in the Decade after World War I* (Princeton, NJ, 1975); Stephen A. Schuker, *The End of French Predominance in Europe: The Financial Crisis of 1924 and the Adoption of the Dawes Plan* (Chapel Hill, NC, 1976); and Leffler, *Elusive Quest*.

to tap American financial resources and strap the United States with a share of the responsibility for defending mutual interests.[14]

A similar story unfolded in the financial arena, where the Anglo–American partnership that took shape had the additional advantage of forcing the French to bow before American policy objectives in Germany. As Frank Costigliola has argued, the Anglo–American financial partnership was fragile and was superimposed on a struggle for national advantage. For key British leaders, however, success in this struggle actually required a high degree of cooperation with the Americans, particularly after the British abandoned early hopes for a general cancellation of war debts and negotiated the 1923 debt-funding agreement with Washington. To manage their balance of payments, protect their leadership of the sterling area, and recapture London's historic position as financial center of the world, the British were compelled to rely on American financial support to stabilize sterling and to adopt the American position on war debts and reparations. The Americans reciprocated by underwriting sterling, working with the British to bring other countries into the gold fold, and forsaking plans to construct an overseas banking system that would rival the British system. Out of these arrangements emerged a creditor entente. Both countries defended the gold standard, called for the prompt settlement of war debts, demanded the reduction of reparation payments, and backed their demands with what amounted to a ban on loans to the French government. The results isolated the French and led directly to the Dawes Plan, which together with the Locarno agreements, the Young Plan, and the Anglo–American schemes of monetary stabilization, seemed to point toward the defeat of prewar autarchies and to Germany's reintegration into an interdependent European community. A new day of peace and plenty seemed just around the corner.[15]

As it turned out, the Republican approach was flawed and failed to bring enduring stability at home or abroad. In the realm of economic diplomacy, Republican policymakers were unable to harmonize differences between bankers and manufacturers, between opposing wings of the business community, or between free-trade champions and defenders of the home market. They attacked foreign cartels but supported American participation in oil, radio, and financial consortiums that amounted to multinational monopolies. They wanted American banks to take responsibility for underwriting European recovery and refused to reverse course when private resources proved inadequate or when the loan-control mechanism failed to guarantee the productive investment of private capital. They celebrated an impartial

---

[14] Hogan, *Informal Entente*, 105–85.

[15] Frank Costigliola, "Anglo–American Financial Rivalry in the 1920s," *Journal of Economic History* 37 (December 1977): 911–34; Hogan, *Informal Entente*, 38–77; and Dan P. Silverman, *Reconstructing Europe after the Great War* (Cambridge, MA, 1982).

expertise yet often ignored "expert" advice when it contradicted precon-
ceived notions or political expediencies. They applied the capacity-to-pay
principle in debt settlements even though the creditor position of the United
States demanded a more enlightened policy. The need for greater generosity
was especially important in light of the American tariff, which, Hoover's
arguments notwithstanding, was seldom adjusted "scientifically" and was
never low enough for the Europeans to manage their balance of payments
without serious deflationary consequences. In the end, Hoover himself remained an ambivalent internationalist whose commitment to the home market and to the principle of privatism ruled out more effective action to
rebuild Europe and reorganize the world economy.[16]

In the United States as well, Hoover's associationalism failed to bring
different groups together in a new community founded on permanent
growth and social harmony. It failed to appease the supporters of McNary–
Haugenism, satisfy the exponents of public power development, and discipline the spokesmen for antitrust. Nor did it elicit support from conservative business leaders, who refused to forge partnerships with labor or join
in constructive efforts to balance America's accounts with the rest of the
world.[17] Indeed, public policy throughout the Republican Ascendancy was
pulled in opposite directions by promoters of an organized capitalism and
defenders of an older, more conservative order. The result was a stalemate
that would not be broken until New Dealers finally moved the nation farther
down the road toward a corporative neo-capitalism than their Republican
predecessors had been able to go in the 1920s.

This stalemate arose fundamentally from the disintegration of what
Thomas Ferguson and others have called the "System of '96," by which
they mean the political alignment that took shape in the United States at
the end of the nineteenth century. The Republican Party presided over this
system. The GOP organized a dominant political coalition that included at
its core a nearly homogeneous community of business and banking leaders.
By the 1920s, however, changes in the industrial structure had begun to
split the business community into two camps. A group of large-scale, science-
based, capital-intensive firms had emerged as world leaders in their industries. These modern, multidivisional enterprises had relatively few workers,
high profit margins, and a generally sophisticated management that was
amenable to the latest developments in technology, to Taylorite strategies

---

[16] For an excellent brief critique of New Era foreign policy, see Leffler, "Herbert Hoover,
     the 'New Era,' and American Foreign Policy." See also Hogan, *Informal Entente*,
     209–27.

[17] In addition to the works cited in note 6, see the essays by Hawley, Wilson, and Zieger
     in Hawley, *Hoover as Secretary of Commerce*; Hawley, "Herbert Hoover and Amer-
     ican Corporatism, 1929–1933," in Martin L. Fausold and George T. Mazuzan, eds.,
     The Hoover Presidency: A Reappraisal (Albany, NY, 1974), 101–19; and Hawley's
     essay in Hawley et al., *Herbert Hoover and the Crisis of American Capitalism* (Cam-
     bridge, MA, 1973), 3–33.

of scientific management, and to the new techniques of industrial relations. They also enjoyed considerable influence in the executive branch of government and had just begun to organize and promote their views through important private foundations such as the Institute of Economics, of which the modern-day Brookings Institution is the lineal descendant.[18]

The interests of this group were fundamentally different from those of a bloc of labor-intensive firms, largely, but not exclusively, small and medium-sized enterprises that enjoyed commanding influence in Congress and were well represented in such agencies as the National Association of Manufacturers and the United States Chamber of Commerce. Labor and trade policy brought these differences into sharp focus. On the labor question, capital-intensive firms adopted a conciliatory approach similar to the one urged by Hoover; out of this came support for employee-representation schemes, for corporate programs of welfare capitalism, for the new science of industrial relations, for the eight-hour day in the steel industry, and for the Railway Labor and Norris–LaGuardia acts. Labor-intensive firms remained wedded to the antilabor policies of the past. Unable to afford the price in higher wages, better benefits, and improved working conditions that it would take to buy a more cooperative labor force, they launched a virulent assault against the trade-union movement, resorted to the "big stick" in dealing with labor strikes, led the crusade for the open shop, and applauded the use of antilabor court injunctions by the Justice Department.[19]

So far as international trade was concerned, the firms in this second group made up the nationalist wing of the business community and the Republican Party. Labor-intensive firms, especially large-scale firms, could and often did expand into international markets and collaborate in campaigns to lower American tariffs. To a large extent, however, their collaboration depended on the degree of government assistance they could muster, on whether they faced more efficient foreign competitors in the American and world markets, and on whether they could join together in larger, more competitive combinations of the kind the Webb–Pomerene Act of 1918 had sought to encourage. Without guarantees of this sort, they were likely to retire to the

[18]   Thomas Ferguson, "From Normalcy to New Deal: Industrial Structure, Party Competition, and American Public Policy in the Great Depression," *International Organization* 38 (Winter 1984): 41–94. See also Walter Dean Burnham, "The System of 1896: An Analysis," in Paul Kleppner et al., *The Evolution of American Electoral Systems* (Westport, CT, 1981), 147–202.

[19]   Ferguson, "From Normalcy to New Deal." Support for the case that Ferguson makes as outlined in this and the next paragraph of the text can be found scattered in the literature on American domestic and foreign economic policies. See, for example, Hawley, *Great War and the Search for a Modern Order*; Hogan, *Informal Entente*; Leffler, *Elusive Quest*; Mira Wilkins, *The Maturing of Multinational Enterprise: American Business Abroad from 1914 to 1970* (Cambridge, MA, 1974), 139–63; and William H. Becker, *The Dynamics of Business–Government Relations: Industry and Exports, 1893–1921* (Chicago, 1982).

home market, seek to protect their position behind a wall of restrictions, and generally complain about reducing war debts and thus raising taxes in order to underwrite the recovery of foreign competitors. Their position on such issues set them at odds with the highly competitive capital-intensive firms for which the world was an oyster to be enjoyed without penalty in the home market. These outward-looking firms, together with their allies among the great international investment houses, led the campaign to reduce war debts, lower tariffs, and organize a more open system of world trade.[20]

Fragmentation at the center of the dominant political coalition, fragmentation growing naturally out of fundamental transformations in the industrial structure, thus helps to account for the schizophrenia of public policy in the New Era. But the failure of New Era designs should not obscure Hoover's belief in positive, if limited, government, his commitment to economic planning and self-regulation, or his efforts to organize enlightened concerts of group action. Nor should it conceal the important transitional role that Hoover and other Republican leaders played in a larger historical process that led from earlier progressive visions and wartime experiments to the organizational and economic adaptations of the 1930s and 1940s. The Republicans had contributed to a new brand of corporative neo-capitalism in the United States and had sought to reorganize the international system along similar lines. New Dealers would bring additional components into the associative structure. They would also devise new forms of government action at home and abroad. To a large extent, however, both they and their successors would live in a world shaped by historical forces, and not only by the powerful American commitment to privatism and the tradition of antimonopoly, but also by the frameworks of group action and public–private power sharing coming out of the progressive period and the New Era of the 1920s. Indeed, these frameworks and others like them would often be used, as they had been in the 1920s, to contain government and reconcile its new role with the older traditions of laissez-faire.

III

The System of '96 rapidly disintegrated in the aftermath of the stock market crash in 1929. This disintegration did not lead immediately to a major political realignment, but to continued stalemate in the early New Deal. Labor-intensive firms supported the National Recovery Administration (NRA) so long as it emphasized private planning, industrial cartelization, and business self-regulation under the benign supervision of a cooperating government. But they broke with their collaborators in the public sector

---

[20]   As Ferguson points out, support for lower tariffs and an open, multilateral trading system that gave vent to the principle of comparative advantage invariably came from firms that were comparatively advantaged. See Ferguson, "From Normalcy to New Deal," 94.

when New Deal policy pointed toward international expansion and a more active role for the state in such areas as economic regulation and social-welfare policy. Nor would they accept the New Deal decision to recognize labor as a legitimate partner in the American political economy. After the collapse of the NRA, this group retreated to private systems of economic planning and rejected representation for organized labor and consumer groups.[21]

As Robert M. Collins, Kim McQuaid, and Thomas Ferguson have shown, however, economic depression and New Deal activism led spokesmen for the capital-intensive bloc and great investment banks to redefine New Era formulations in a way that left more room for organized labor, conceded a larger role for the state, and included Keynesian strategies of aggregate economic management. These were the men – such men as Clarence Francis, W. Averell Harriman, Paul G. Hoffman, and Charles E. Wilson – who organized the Business Advisory Council, staffed the NRA's Industrial Advisory Board, and formed the American Policy Commission. Given their organic view of society, their faith in private expertise, their flexible attitude toward labor, and their support for modest social programs, economic planning, and overseas expansion, these men were destined to play a pivotal role in America's twentieth-century search for a new economic and political order. Their outlook linked them backward to the technocorporatism of the National Civic Federation and the associationalism of Herbert Hoover, and forward to what Robert Griffith has called the "corporate common-wealth" of the Eisenhower years.[22]

This group exerted only occasional influence during the early days of the New Deal, when public programs for stimulating recovery oscillated between protecting the home market, breaking monopolies, promoting little NRAs, and expanding public-sector spending. In the NRA and other forums, its leaders waged a ferocious but inconclusive battle with private and public officials who supported strictly statist or free-market solutions to the economic depression and who rejected reciprocal trade in favor of economic nationalism. After 1934, however, the gradual convergence of public policy and progressive opinion in the business community led to a major political realignment. Out of this process came the dominant political coalition –

[21] For New Deal politics and the NRA experience, see Ellis W. Hawley, *The New Deal and the Problem of Monopoly* (Princeton, NJ, 1966).

[22] McQuaid, "Corporate Liberalism in the American Business Community"; Robert M. Collins, "Positive Business Responses to the New Deal: The Roots of the Committee for Economic Development," *Business History Review* 12 (Autumn 1978): 369–91; Collins, *Business Response to Keynes*, 53–73; McQuaid, *Big Business and Presidential Power: From FDR to Reagan* (New York, 1982), 18–61; Ferguson, "From Normalcy to New Deal"; and Robert Griffith, "Dwight D. Eisenhower and the Corporate Commonwealth," *American Historical Review* 87 (February 1982): 87–122.

the so-called New Deal coalition – that would set the political agenda in the United States over the next four decades.

The convergence occurred on three critical issues: economic and social policy, labor–management relations, and multilateral trade. Through the Committee for Economic Development, progressive business leaders eventually fashioned a strategy of stabilization that harnessed Keynesian theory to Hoover's vision of an associative state. One variant of this theory had been tested in the recession of 1937, when the Roosevelt administration resorted to planned deficits and public works in order to prompt recovery. Another test would come in the Second World War and a third in the immediate postwar period. By that time, business opinion had crystallized behind a conservative version of Keynesian theory, according to which an active and flexible monetary policy and the largely automatic fiscal stabilizers of a full-employment budget would regulate the business cycle, limit government expenditures, and promote growth in the private rather than the public sector. Something very close to this strategy was incorporated in the Employment Act of 1946.[23]

Business and government leaders wedded this strategy to Hoover's New Era formulation and used the combination to define anew the basis for a public–private partnership. Neglected under this arrangement were those antitrusters who wanted to halt the trend toward industrial concentration, break up large-scale enterprises, and rely solely on natural market forces to regulate the economy. Defeated were those left-wing liberals whose gloomy predictions of economic stagnation had led them to demand more centralized planning, greater government direction of the economy, and permanent programs of public works. The new liberalism looked instead to a collectivist commonwealth in which government power would be enlarged, delimited, and shared. Following this vision, government planners would bring into the public sector much of the welfare capitalism pioneered by their corporate counterparts in an earlier day. They would organize and give representation to previously unrecognized labor, agricultural, and professional groups, including them in the corporative community and working with them to shape social and economic policy. By blending market forces with the new tools of macroeconomic management and with such new planning mechanisms as the Council of Economic Advisors, they would also work to influence aggregate economic performance without disputing the right of private leaders to make fundamental decisions regarding production, allocation, prices, and wages. And through new frameworks of group action and power sharing, they would collaborate with private officials to achieve

[23] Collins, "Positive Business Responses to the New Deal"; McQuaid, "Corporate Liberalism in the American Business Community"; Collins, *Business Response to Keynes*, especially 78–152; Hawley, "Techno-corporatist Formulas in the Liberal State"; and Herbert Stein, *The Fiscal Revolution in America* (Chicago, 1969), 91–130, 169–205.

an economic growth that contained state power and prevented redistributive conflicts.[24]

Capital-intensive firms led the way to a similar accord between business and labor. They grudgingly accommodated the Wagner Act of 1935 and worked closely with government and labor partners in such wartime agencies as the War Production Board and the War Labor Board, which reconstituted the government–business–labor detente that had been achieved under the War Industries Board twenty-five years earlier. This was followed in 1945 by the National Labor–Management Conference, which signaled management's willingness to join government in recognizing the new status of independent trade unions. All sides looked to a three-cornered partnership as the basis for industrial stability and abundance. The central question involved the terms of this partnership, with Walter Reuther and other labor progressives urging worker codetermination in areas traditionally reserved for management. During the war years, they had called for national economic planning through industrial councils in which government, labor, and business would jointly organize war industries and direct the process of postwar reconversion. After the war, they demanded a voice for workers in industrial decisions relating to prices, profits, technological change, and plant location.[25]

Such demands went further than progressive corporate officials were willing to go. These officials rejected the idea of industrial councils, relegated labor to the role of a subordinate partner in the wartime mobilization agencies, and later refused to bend under trade-union pressure for labor participation in pricing and profit policy. Yet neither did they resort to the big-stick policy that Hoover had deprecated in the 1920s. Progressive business leaders in the capital-intensive bloc, particularly those active in the Business Advisory Council, the Committee for Economic Development, and the National Planning Association, accepted trade unions and agreed to collective bargaining on issues of immediate interest to workers. Unlike their counterparts in the National Association of Manufacturers, the Chamber of Commerce, and the labor-intensive bloc, these leaders had no desire to strangle the trade-union movement. They sought instead to limit its economic and political power while preserving the basis for an effective detente, a goal they accomplished in the Taft–Hartley Act of 1947. With the acquiescence of government and the support of most trade-union leaders, they also succeeded in defeating Reuther's demands and limiting the scope of labor–management conflict to basic bread-and-butter issues.[26] The result

[24] Collins, *Business Response to Keynes*, especially 115–52.
[25] McQuaid, *Big Business and Presidential Power*, 99–107; and David Brody, *Workers in Industrial America: Essays on the Twentieth-Century Struggle* (New York, 1980), 173–214.
[26] McQuaid, *Big Business and Presidential Power*, 145–9; Brody, *Workers in Industrial America*, 173–214; and Paul A. C. Koistinen, "Mobilizing the World War II Econ-

was a labor–management partnership that tied economic gains for workers to the rock of productivity and exchanged labor recognition of traditional managerial prerogatives for management recognition of independent trade unions.

International trade was the last area in which public policy and progressive private opinion gradually converged. The policy that resulted committed public officials more firmly to the principles of multilateralism and made the government more responsible for organizing the international economy. But it also integrated these innovations into a larger corporative synthesis that included ideas similar to those Hoover had championed in the 1920s, specifically the reliance on private management and expertise, on supposedly neutral coordinating institutions, and on frameworks of group action and power sharing that tended to limit and divide state power. This synthesis did not emerge immediately after Roosevelt's electoral triumph in 1932. It came out of policy debates in the early New Deal and only after the stalemate between nationalists and multilateralists had made American economic diplomacy appear even more wildly contradictory than it had been in the era of Republican ascendancy.

In the early New Deal, the Treasury Department's quest for monetary stabilization and the State Department's search for trade liberalization recalled the liberal internationalism of an earlier era. Both looked to a world system in which fixed exchanges, lower tariffs, and multilateral trade would enable free-market competition and comparative advantage to stimulate growth and integrate economies. At the London Conference of 1933, however, this strategy suffered a major defeat at the hands of New Dealers who sought domestic economic recovery through policies that combined economic isolationism with a crude neo-mercantilism.[27] The controversy that followed the London Conference was similar to the one surrounding the NRA's approach to domestic economic management, just as the compound of free-market and statist strategies that resulted would follow the lines of accommodation reached on the home front after 1934.

The famous battle between Secretary of State Cordell Hull and foreign-trade advisor George N. Peek revealed one dimension of this controversy. Peek favored an autarkic commercial policy in which government would control, direct, and finance American commerce and seek national self-sufficiency through bilateral trade, barter agreements, and policies of preference. For Hull, on the other hand, neither economic self-sufficiency nor

omy: Labor and the Industrial–Military Alliance," *Pacific Historical Review* 42 (November 1973): 443–78.

[27]   Lloyd C. Gardner, *Economic Aspects of New Deal Diplomacy*, 2d ed. (Boston, 1971), 24–33; Dick Steward, *Trade and Hemisphere: The Good Neighbor Policy and Reciprocal Trade* (Columbia, MO, 1975), 14–18; and James R. Moore, "Sources of New Deal Economic Policy: The International Dimension," *Journal of American History* 41 (December 1974): 728–44.

state trading and bilateralism were desirable, since they would further frag-
ment the world economy, perpetuate the depression, lead to international
conflict, and imperil private enterprise and political freedom in the United
States. Hull called instead for reciprocal trade and nondiscrimination, stressing in his plea how such policies would allow unfettered market mechanisms
and private enterprise to stimulate growth without the economic and political pitfalls that inhered in state trading.[28]

Hull scored an important victory in mid-1934, when Congress passed the
Reciprocal Trade Agreements Act. This victory was the first step in breaking
the stalemate that had characterized economic diplomacy in the New Era
and the early New Deal, and it was followed by other victories that routed
the economic nationalists and welded the capital-intensive bloc to the New
Deal coalition. By 1936, Hull was negotiating reciprocal trade agreements
under the authority conferred by Congress, Secretary of the Treasury Henry
Morgenthau, Jr., was arranging the tripartite currency accord with Britain
and France, and both men were steering a course that would lead – from
the Lend-Lease Agreement through the Bretton Woods agreements – to a
postwar world economy based on multilateral trade and full convertibility.
In the process, however, they accommodated the views of Harry Dexter
White and other public and private leaders whose middle way between
Hull's free-trade doctrine and Peek's neo-mercantilism elaborated the strategy that Hoover had tried to follow in the 1920s. This strategy of the middle
way combined free-market incentives and private enterprise with modern
forms of technical management, government aid, and public–private cooperation. Following these guidelines, American policymakers helped to
organize private bondholders into the Bondholders Protective Association
and cooperated with the group to negotiate debt-funding agreements with
foreign governments. They established the Export–Import Bank, linked it
through advisory committees to the business and banking communities, and
used it to underwrite private trade and overseas development. They also
supported such international stabilizers as the World Bank, the International
Monetary Fund, and the Inter-American Development Commission. And
through these and other agencies, they sought to banish restrictive policies
and state trading, integrate the world economy along multilateral lines, and
supplement market forces and private enterprise with institutional regulators
and government aid.[29]

[28]   Gardner, *Economic Aspects of New Deal Diplomacy*, especially 24–46; Steward,
       Trade and Hemisphere, 1–61; and Frederick C. Adams, *Economic Diplomacy: The
       Export–Import Bank and American Foreign Policy, 1934–1939* (Columbia, MO,
       1976), 68–97.
[29]   In addition to the works cited in note 28, see Benjamin M. Rowland, "Preparing the
       American Ascendancy: The Transfer of Economic Power from Britain to the United
       States, 1933–1944," in Benjamin M. Rowland, ed., *Balance of Power or Hegemony:
       The Interwar Monetary System* (New York, 1976), 195–224; Thomas G. Paterson,
       "Foreign Aid under Wraps: The Point Four Program," *Wisconsin Magazine of History*

This approach went beyond the simple antistatism in Hull's laissez-faire bible. But it also stopped short of the autocratic state trading that Hull and other New Dealers saw as a fundamental threat to peace and prosperity. It blended government action and institutional coordinators with private enterprise and free-market regulators and then tried to harmonize these two lines of policy by carefully delineating the government's role and building new networks of group action and public–private power sharing. Behind these components of the New Deal's foreign-policy formulation united the leadership of a powerful multilateral bloc. Great investment banks and capital-intensive firms headed this coalition, which also included allies in the trade unions, in organized agriculture, in liberal academic circles, and in private foundations and business associations. Included as well, at least in the immediate postwar years, were labor-intensive firms that enjoyed comparative advantage at a time when European industry was being rebuilt. Together these groups would throw their weight behind the Reciprocal Trade Agreements Act, the Bretton Woods institutions, the General Agreement on Tariffs and Trade, and the other instruments of a postwar world system founded on full convertibility and multilateral trade.

The political realignment of the 1930s thus made it possible for American policymakers to eliminate some of the contradictions that had characterized Republican economic diplomacy in the 1920s. The New Deal coalition was able to launch initiatives that ushered in a prolonged period of international economic growth, a goal that had not been attained after the First World War. Yet this success should not obscure the important contribution Republican leaders made to a foreign-policy formulation that essentially added new dimensions to the corporative design that Hoover and others had started to draft in the 1920s. Out of this synthesis of New Era designs and New Deal inventions came the Marshall Plan to rebuild Western Europe.

IV

Viewed from this perspective rather than in the context of the Cold War, the Marshall Plan can be seen as a logical extension of domestic- and foreign-policy developments going back to the first American effort to reconstruct war-torn Europe. Indeed, the second generation of American recovery planners confronted problems very similar to those that had confounded the Republicans earlier and devised solutions that elaborated and formalized

56 (Winter 1972/73): 119–26; James M. McHale, "National Planning and Reciprocal Trade: The New Deal Origins of Government Guarantees for Private Exporters," *Prologue* 6 (Fall 1974): 189–99; Fred L. Block, *The Origins of International Economic Disorder: A Study of United States International Monetary Policy from World War II to the Present* (Berkeley, CA, 1977), 32–55; and Richard N. Gardner, *Sterling–Dollar Diplomacy: The Origins and Prospects of Our International Economic Order*, 2d ed. (New York, 1969), 71–144.

the stabilization strategies pioneered by their predecessors in the first post-war period. If the Marshall Planners succeeded where the Republicans failed, this success was due in part to policy innovations growing first out of the New Deal and then out of the Cold War. Nevertheless, these innovations must not conceal the lines of continuity that linked the two generations and mark both postwar eras as part of an American effort to remake the Old World in the image of the New.

In the chapters that follow, I argue that American Marshall Planners, like the Republicans before them, tried to transform political problems into technical ones that were solvable, they said, when old European ways of conducting business and old habits of class conflict gave way to American methods of scientific management and corporative collaboration. Marshall Planners were far more interested than their predecessors in cutting the web of exchange controls, quotas, and import licenses and the tangled network of over two hundred bilateral trade and payments agreements that stifled intra-European commerce and prevented the most efficient use of local resources. But they echoed the arguments of their predecessors in attacking these and other restrictions as tantamount to the sort of economic autarky that generated conflict and discouraged growth. The Marshall Planners also repeated earlier demands for European self-help and redoubled efforts to reduce reparations, fix exchange rates, and make currencies convertible. They claimed, as the Republicans had claimed earlier, that these measures and those to liberalize trade would permit individual initiative and normal market mechanisms to integrate economies and stimulate growth. And much like the first generation of recovery planners, they sought to reconcile their faith in private enterprise with the institutional imperatives of an integrated order, employing as the agents of reconciliation public–private partnerships and supposedly neutral authorities similar to those Hoover had envisioned in the 1920s.

In the United States, for example, the Marshall Plan carefully delimited the government's role in the stabilization process. This role was perceived as a national-security imperative and as an aid to private enterprise. It was to be performed so far as possible in collaboration with private elites. Policymakers ruled out a government aid corporation to administer the recovery program and established instead an independent agency, staffed it with managerial talent from the private sector, and linked it to private groups through a network of advisory committees. Marshall Planners then urged participating countries to replicate this administrative system. The result was a series of partnerships that blended public and private power, much like the Marshall Planners tried to fuse free-market forces and institutional coordinators to clear the obstacles to a single market in Western Europe. This strategy inspired their plan for a European payments union through which a supervisory board of experts was to use both administrative controls and market incentives to adjust national monetary and fiscal policies in the

But we cannot, of course, deny the influence of intervening developments. In the second postwar period, heightened fears of Soviet expansion led the State Department and the Pentagon to match economic aid with military commitments. These agencies also broke new ground with the North Atlantic Treaty and the related efforts to integrate Western European defense systems, efforts that complemented those of the Marshall Planners to the extent that integration became the conceptual link between strategic and economic goals.

Students of strategic planning have missed this linkage. By focusing on American attempts to build a bipolar equilibrium, they have also slighted parallel efforts to forge a viable balance of power among the Western European states and have failed to note how integration became the key to both objectives. That is, in American thinking, integration was the way to reconcile Germany's recovery with France's security and bring both together in a unit of sufficient scale to contain the Soviets. Integration as a strategic concept forms an important subtheme in the following chapters, which necessarily focus on the Marshall Plan as an instrument of economic, not military, integration. This theme runs parallel in the narrative to related American efforts to bring Britain into Western Europe, make it a counterweight to the former Reich, and thus win support in Paris for Germany's recovery and reintegration.

On the economic side, as we will see, Marshall Planners enlarged New Era conceptions to include a number of important policy innovations. They abandoned the earlier reliance on private credits in favor of a major government aid program that enabled the Europeans to rehabilitate their economies and manage their balance of payments without crippling deflation or excessive reparations. They also went beyond earlier notions of an interdependent European economic community of essentially independent states, envisioning now a structural integration that entailed some limitations on the exercise of sovereign power. In addition, Marshall Planners promoted the new strategies of macroeconomic management, broadened the networks of corporative collaboration to include organized agriculture and labor, and sought labor's support by encouraging modest programs of social welfare. These innovations reflected the impact of Keynesian thinking and New Deal experiences on American policy. They added significant increments, as it were, to the rudimentary strategies that Republican leaders had started to develop in the first postwar period.

Out of the blend of old and new came what I call the New Deal synthesis, a policy formulation that guided American efforts to remake Western Europe in the likeness of the United States. Its central component was the principle of federalism as embodied in the American Constitution and subsequently modified by the trend toward an administrative state that had peaked recently in the New Deal. Translated into European terms, federalism meant the fusion of separate economic sovereignties into an integrated market capped by supranational institutions of economic planning and administration. The idea of supranationalism, captured in what the following chapters call the planners' approach to European recovery, was another component of the American policy synthesis. It coexisted with a third component, which the chapters denote as the free-traders' approach and which embodied the older American faith in making currencies convertible, eliminating bilateral barriers, and allowing the normal mechanisms of a free economy to forge a single market. The result was both a strategy of integration that relied on administrative and automatic regulators, and a vision of a mixed capitalist economy in Europe similar to the one that had grown up in the United States. Supplementing the planners' and traders' approaches was a commitment to Keynesian techniques of macroeconomic management, to national and transnational networks of corporative collaboration and public–private power sharing, and to American methods for engineering a productive abundance in which all could share.

Greater productivity, itself a key component of the New Deal synthesis, would adjourn the redistributive struggles that fueled extremist political parties in Western Europe. It would also put participating countries on a self-supporting basis and thus facilitate their entry into the multilateral system of world trade that American leaders considered to be a prerequisite to economic prosperity and democratic freedom in the United States. Virtually all other components of the American synthesis attempted to attain these goals by building a European economic order conducive to recovery and sustained growth. Economic integration would create a framework for enlisting Germany in the cause of recovery while at the same time bringing the gains in resource utilization, specialization, and economies of scale that were needed to balance Western Europe's accounts with the dollar area. Supranational agencies would guide local elites down the road to integration; transnational networks of corporative collaboration would corral labor, management, and government in common programs for productive abundance; and both would turn the old diplomacy of national rivalry into bureaucratic bargaining, and the old politics of class conflict into the politics of administration. Similar benefits would come from translating the problem of economic growth into a technical problem soluble by adopting American methods of private production, including American engineering, manufacturing, and marketing techniques and American strategies of labor–management teamwork.

The task was formidable, the opposition strong. As we will see, Marshall Planners had to convince some European governments to reduce public expenditures, others to increase them. They had to defeat Communists in the trade-union movement, win British support for Europe's integration, and get the French to go along with Germany's reintegration. They also had to undercut rivals in the Army Department whose Germany-first orientation threatened efforts to reconcile Franco–German differences within the framework of a comprehensive recovery plan and an integrated Western Europe. This battle had been won by 1950, only to be replaced by another with the Treasury Department, where policymakers were more conservative than the Marshall Planners and less inclined to support a recovery strategy that ran the risk of organizing Western Europe into an economic bloc ringed with restrictions against the dollar.

In addition, Marshall Planners faced challenges from conservatives in Congress who had long been critical of the Truman administration's foreign policies. Although conservatives, particularly in the Republican Party, scored important gains in the congressional elections of 1946, these gains had been reversed by Truman's surprising victory at the polls two years later. At the same time, Truman's call for a Fair Deal at home and a liberal reconstruction abroad rallied many of the liberals who had earlier been disillusioned by the administration's apparent indifference to the economic and social policies emerging from the New Deal. Trade-union leaders followed the same path trod by liberals. At first put off by Truman's anti-inflationary policies and his criticism of labor's postwar strikes and wage demands, they had been won back by his veto of Taft–Hartley and his pledges of support in the 1948 campaign. By the start of that year, Truman had resuscitated the political coalition – the New Deal coalition – that would support the objectives of the administration's foreign policies in the months ahead.[30]

Within three years, however, the political balance would begin to shift in both the United States and Western Europe. The outbreak of fighting in Korea, and particularly the Chinese intervention of November 1950, would add to the pressure on American resources and force the Truman administration to reverse its policy of using economic rather than military power to fortify Western Europe. This policy, which initially had relegated rearmament to a secondary strategy and then to a position of parity with recovery, now gave way to one that placed it above reconstruction. Out of this shift came a massive expansion of defense expenditures on both sides of the Atlantic. The economic dislocations that followed, together with greater American pressure to rearm Germany, led to a wave of anti-Americanism in Western Europe and, in some countries, to a political fragmentation that pitted the forces of the Left against those of the Right. Something similar occurred in the United States. Congressional opponents attacked the administration's military commitments to Western Europe, formulated a conservative critique of the Keynesian policies being used to underwrite the

[30]   For these developments, see Alonzo L. Hamby, *Beyond the New Deal: Harry S Truman and American Liberalism* (New York, 1973); Robert J. Donovan, *Tumultuous Years: The Presidency of Harry S Truman, 1949–1953* (New York, 1982); and Richard H. Pells, *The Liberal Mind in a Conservative Age: American Intellectuals in the 1940s and 1950s* (New York, 1985).

economic aid and rearmament programs, and finally combined forces to
bring the Marshall Plan to a premature conclusion.

V

The themes outlined in this introductory section open one after another,
like the folds of an expanding accordion, in the chapters that follow. The
first three chapters discuss the Marshall Plan from conception through
congressional enactment; subsequent chapters analyze the plan in operation.
Chapters 4 and 5 develop the recurring themes of American recovery policy,
the emphasis on European integration, German reintegration, and supranationalism, and the efforts to overcome British and French opposition.
Chapter 5 also notes the growing emphasis on the traders' approach to
European integration, that is, on liberalizing trade, fixing realistic exchange
rates, and organizing a monetary union. The triumph of the traders' approach marked a turning point in the history of the Marshall Plan, a point,
moreover, when the United States embarked on a particular strategy of
integration approximately six months earlier than previous accounts have
recognized.

The sterling crisis marked another turning point and is the subject of
Chapter 6, which describes the relationship between the sterling and dollar
blocs and the first steps toward an Anglo–American accommodation that
exempted Great Britain from the process of European integration. Chapter
7 elaborates themes developed earlier while paying particular attention to
the crisis of confidence that gripped the Western alliance in early 1950, the
negotiations looking toward an institutional mechanism to coordinate national policies, and the formation of the European Payments Union. Chapters 8 and 9 deal with the final turning point in the last eighteen months
of the Marshall Plan. They discuss the origins of the Schuman Plan, the
efforts to reconcile recovery and rearmament imperatives in the wake of
the Korean War, and the demise of the American aid program. The Conclusion offers my evaluation of the complex and bold American plan to
build a new economic and political order in the Old Country, a plan whose
ramifications are still shaping events today.

1

Searching for a "creative peace": European integration and the origins of the Marshall Plan

I

THE MARSHALL PLAN rested squarely on an American conviction that European economic recovery was essential to the long-term interests of the United States. These interests were interdependent and mutually reinforcing, so much so that public officials saw little need to rank them in the order that subsequent historians have tried to establish. They included economic interests. Policymakers in the Truman administration were convinced that a "dynamic economy" at home required American trade and investment abroad, which in turn required the reconstruction of major trading partners in Europe and their reintegration into a multilateral system of world trade. These requirements summed up a world view rooted in political conviction as well as in economic interests. American leaders envisioned an open international economy founded on the principles of liberal capitalism, such as free trade and equal opportunity. But they also equated these principles with democratic forms of government, associated autarkic economic policies with totalitarian political regimes, and assumed that "enemies in the market place" could not be "friends at the council table." "The political line up followed the economic line up," as Cordell Hull once put it.[1]

Strategic interests paralleled those of an economic and political nature. American policymakers viewed European markets, sources of supply, manpower resources, and industrial capacity as strategic assets that must not be controlled by a hostile power or coalition. The recent war had demonstrated the threat to American security inherent in such a development and

---

[1] U.S., Office of the Federal Register, *Public Papers of the Presidents of the United States: Harry S Truman, 1947* (Washington, DC, 1963), 37; Paterson, *Soviet–American Confrontation*, 4 (for the second quotation); and Cordell Hull, *The Memoirs of Cordell Hull*, 2 vols. (New York, 1948), 1: 364.

the concomitant need to preserve American access to Europe's resources while denying them to potential rivals. Postwar developments reinforced wartime lessons. The defeat of Germany and the exhaustion of Britain and France had left a power vacuum in Central and Western Europe into which the Soviet Union might expand unless the United States assembled the components of a viable balance of power. This meant filling the vacuum by rebuilding economic and political systems strong enough to forestall aggression and defeat Communist parties, whose rise to power seemed the most likely way for the Soviets to extend their influence.[2]

American interests dictated an active role in rebuilding Europe, but enumerating these interests explains neither the full range of American goals nor how American policymakers hoped to achieve them. American ambition subsumed economic, political, and strategic interests in a larger design much like the one that had guided Republican policymakers in the 1920s. The Marshall Planners would replace the old European state system with what they saw as a more viable framework for achieving their policy objectives on the Continent. They would do so by applying the American principle of federalism and using it to create an integrated European economy similar to the one that existed in the United States. The strategic assumptions behind this policy held that an integrated economic order, particularly one headed by supranational institutions, would help to control German nationalism, reconcile Germany's recovery with France's economic and security concerns, and thus create a balance of power in the West sufficient to contain Soviet power in the East. The economic assumptions grew fundamentally out of the American experience at home, where a large internal economy integrated by free-market forces and central institutions of coordination and control seemed to have laid the groundwork for a new era of economic growth and social stability. An economic United States of Europe would bring similar benefits, or so the Americans believed, and in the process would realize all of their goals on the Continent. Besides creating a framework for controlling the Germans and containing the Soviets, it would limit Communist inroads, dissolve class tensions through a shared abundance, and set the continental countries on the path to a multilateral system of world trade.

Although recovery planners would develop other strategies to re-create the American system in Europe, these additional strategies were the beams and buttresses of a grand design that began with the idea of integration. This idea was not new, either in Europe or in the United States. The Europeans had organized a number of unification movements, some of which called for immediate political federation, others for a loose confederation of semiautonomous states, still others for a gradualist approach that would

---

[2] Melvyn P. Leffler, "The American Conception of National Security and the Beginnings of the Cold War, 1945–1948," *American Historical Review* 89 (April 1984): 346–81.

begin with technical cooperation and economic integration in selected lines
of industry and agriculture.[3] In the United States, similar visions had inspired
a coterie of enthusiasts who championed the cause of economic integration
and political federation as two of the keys to peace and prosperity in postwar
Europe. In 1939, the American journalist Clarence K. Streit published *Union
Now*, which became one of the most popular books on the subject. During
the war years, Count Richard Coudenhove-Kalergi, head of the Pan-
European Union, took up exile in New York, where he organized a seminar
on the subject of European federation, published a variety of works on the
same topic, and established important contacts with sympathetic opinion
leaders. The Council on Foreign Relations prepared a paper entitled "American Interests in the Economic Unification of Europe with Respect to Trade
Barriers." Former Ambassador William C. Bullitt gave President Franklin
Roosevelt a memorandum on Allied war aims that, among other things,
envisioned some form of political unification in postwar Europe. And in
response to growing congressional interest in the subject, the Library of
Congress circulated a paper discussing European unification as a method
of controlling postwar Germany.[4]

Such proposals at first received only sporadic consideration in Washington, where officials were preoccupied with the war effort or otherwise worried that regional blocs might undercut their plans for a worldwide system
of multilateral trade. This situation changed in 1947, however. After initial
attempts to stimulate recovery had failed and alternative reconstruction
policies had been rejected, American leaders gave the idea of European
unification, or at least European economic integration, a prominent place
in their policy planning. At that point, economic conditions in Europe had
started to deteriorate. The victorious powers had been unable to negotiate
a final peace settlement, the wartime alliance was breaking down, and the
Soviets were beginning to consolidate their control over Eastern Europe.
These developments, which are so familiar to historians of the early Cold
War, led American policymakers to see economic integration as the best
way to achieve the interrelated economic, political, and strategic goals on
their agenda for postwar Europe.

[3] Arnold J. Zurcher, *The Struggle to Unite Europe, 1940–1958* (Washington Square,
    NY, 1958), 3–9, 19–35; George Lichtheim, *Europe and America: The Future of the
    Atlantic Community* (London, 1963), 16–21; Michael Curtis, *Western European In-
    tegration* (New York, 1965), 10–11; Roger Morgan, *West European Politics since
    1945: The Shaping of the European Community* (London, 1972), 77–8; Robert C.
    Mowat, *Creating the European Community* (London, 1973), 14–27; and Richard
    Vaughan, *Twentieth-Century Europe: Paths to Unity* (London, 1979), 25–56.
[4] Zurcher, *Struggle to Unite Europe*, 10–18; Vaughan, *Twentieth-Century Europe*, 46,
    65–6; and Max Beloff, *The United States and the Unity of Europe* (Washington, DC,
    1963), 1–6. See also Clarence K. Streit, *Union Now: A Proposal for a Federal Union
    of the Democracies of the North Atlantic* (New York, 1939).

II

At the end of the war, American officials had optimistically assumed that the road to European recovery could be smoothed by limited bilateral loans, currency stabilization through the International Monetary Fund, and the largely American-financed relief and reconstruction activities of the International Bank for Reconstruction and Development and the United Nations Relief and Rehabilitation Administration (UNRRA). They continued to fund UNRRA's relief operations, won congressional approval for American membership in the Bretton Woods institutions, increased the lending capacity of the Export–Import Bank, and negotiated a $3.75-billion loan to Great Britain. These forms of piecemeal assistance supplemented their efforts to stimulate recovery by building a multilateral system of world trade and by encouraging the most efficient use of European resources.[5] The latter included German reparation payments and coal transfers. These were to play an important part in underwriting reconstruction in the liberated areas and in safeguarding European security against a resurgent German militarism. Indeed, both the Morgenthau Plan and JCS 1067 had assumed that the liberated areas would replace Germany as the industrial centers in a new European economy.[6]

American policymakers had discarded the Morgenthau Plan by the time of the Potsdam Conference, and over the next year the State Department took the first steps toward the new policy that would crystallize in 1947. Alarmed by the spread of economic and social disorder in the occupation zones and the lagging pace of recovery elsewhere, policymakers in the State Department made a greater effort to revive the German economy. They still counted on the transfer of German resources to ensure security and promote recovery in other areas of Europe, as well as on a four-power treaty to guarantee Germany's disarmament and demilitarization. But the hope was that these initiatives would ease French security concerns, make it possible for the Soviets to abandon their claims in Eastern Europe, and mobilize the victorious powers behind new efforts to revive and unify the German economy. These new efforts were evident in proposals by American policymakers to restore coal production in the Ruhr; in their defense of the so-called first-

[5] Gardner, *Sterling–Dollar Diplomacy*, 71–164, 188–253; Paterson, *Soviet–American Confrontation*, 75–98, 147–73, 207; Alfred E. Eckes, Jr., *A Search for Solvency: Bretton Woods and the International Monetary System, 1941–1947* (Austin, TX, 1975), 165–209, 214.

[6] On the Morgenthau Plan and JCS 1067, and the controversy surrounding both, see John Lewis Gaddis, *The United States and the Origins of the Cold War, 1941–1947* (New York, 1972), 118–23; Ernest F. Penrose, *Economic Planning for the Peace* (Princeton, NJ, 1953), 245–6, 268–70; John M. Blum, *From the Morgenthau Diaries: Years of War, 1941–1945* (Boston, 1967), 338; and Bruce Kuklick, *American Policy and the Division of Germany: The Clash with Russia over Reparations* (Ithaca, NY, 1972), 49–51.

charge principle, by which German imports rather than reparation payments would have first claim on current German production; and in their support for the reparation and level-of-industry plan that Allied leaders worked out in March 1946. In theory, at least, this plan would provide the liberated countries with the reparations they needed to support their own recovery and yet leave Germany with sufficient plant and capital equipment to maintain a standard of living equal to, but not higher than, that of its neighbors.[7]

The 1946 plan envisioned a balanced revival of the German and European economies. It would put Germany on a self-supporting basis without threatening the economic requirements and military security of its former victims and would thus clear the path to a stable political accommodation on the Continent. In addition, Germany's economic recovery would contribute to recovery in Europe as a whole, which, together with piecemeal assistance from the United States, the World Bank, and the International Monetary Fund, would lead to a general restoration of the world economy and a multilateral system of world trade.

As 1947 dawned, however, there were few signs that American strategies were promoting a stable recovery in Europe. By that time, the United States had expended over $9 billion in a variety of aid programs on the Continent. But European industrial and agricultural production still lagged behind prewar levels. Despite strenuous efforts by some European countries, capital equipment and plant facilities remained hopelessly obsolete or in need of wholesale repair from war damage. A shortage of manpower and of basic resources, especially coal and steel, restrained production, while food shortages and the erosion of wages by inflation discouraged maximum efforts by a demoralized workforce. The depletion of gold and dollar reserves and the network of bilateral trade and payments agreements also hampered efforts to import essential items, prevented the most efficient use of local resources, and made it difficult for the Europeans to join in American plans for a multilateral system of world trade. Making matters worse, the severe winter of 1946–7 aggravated existing shortages, further restrained production, and nearly wiped out earlier economic gains. Translated into cold statistics, agricultural production in Western Europe averaged only 83 percent of its 1938 volume, industrial production only 88 percent, and exports a bare 59 percent. In human terms, these figures added up to widespread fatigue and a pervasive sense of pessimism.[8]

[7]   Daniel Yergin, *Shattered Peace: The Origins of the Cold War and the National Security State* (Boston, 1978), 114, 117; Kuklick, *American Policy and the Division of Germany*, 141–66; Gimbel, *Origins of the Marshall Plan*, 77; Lloyd C. Gardner, *Architects of Illusion: Men and Ideas in American Foreign Policy, 1941–1949* (Chicago, 1970), 241–3; Gaddis, *United States and the Origins of the Cold War*, 240–1, 325; and "Reparations and the Level of Post-war German Economy: Plan of Allied Control Council," U.S., Department of State, *Bulletin* 14 (April 14, 1946): 636–9.
[8]   Paterson, *Soviet–American Confrontation*, 207; Eckes, *Search for Solvency*, 216; Jones, *Fifteen Weeks*, 24–5, 42, 82–5; Price, *Marshall Plan and Its Meaning*, 29–32.

Clearly, American leaders had not appreciated the extent of economic disruption in Europe; nor could much more be expected from the stabilization strategies they were using. UNRRA was due to expire in March 1947, and the Truman administration contemplated only modest post-UNRRA relief assistance. The British were drawing on the proceeds of the Anglo–American loan, which had been expected to meet their needs until 1951, at a rate that would lead to its exhaustion by early 1948. Negotiations for a new multilateral trading system were also moving slowly and neither the World Bank nor the Export–Import Bank had the capital or the authorization to finance a comprehensive recovery program.[9] Added to all of this was the general failure of policy in Germany, where American and Allied leaders had found it difficult to reconcile competing economic and security requirements within the framework of the 1946 level-of-industry plan.

For American leaders, the 1946 plan had held the promise of putting Germany on a self-sustaining basis and increasing its contribution to recovery across the Continent. But economic conditions there remained the worst in Europe. General Lucius D. Clay, the American zone commander, chafed under the restrictions imposed by the level-of-industry plan and by the inability of the Allies to agree on the terms for German unification and central administration. He and other officials in the Army Department complained constantly that reparation transfers, coal exports, and restrictions on German production were saddling the American Army with unnecessary occupation costs, handicapping German recovery, and fostering a popular discontent upon which the Communists and Soviets were capitalizing. Clay had reacted as early as May 1946 by curtailing reparation deliveries from the American zone. He demanded prompt Allied agreement on economic unification and on a higher level of industry. The British also sought relief from the financial burden of occupation, first through bizonal fusion with the Americans and thereafter by pressing Clay's demand for an upward revision of Germany's level of industry.

The French, on the other hand, clung tenaciously to the 1946 agreement.

For a breakdown of American aid to various countries, see Nelson Newton, Assistant to the Secretary of Commerce, memorandum to the Under Secretary of State, August 15, 1947, Records of the Department of State (National Archives, Washington, DC), Record Group 59, file: 840.50Recovery/8-1547 (hereafter cited as RG 59, with file number).

9 Paterson, *Soviet–American Confrontation*, 86–9, 172–3; Gardner, *Sterling–Dollar Diplomacy*, 269–86, 292–9, 348–61; William McC. Martin, Jr., Chairman, Export–Import Bank, letter to President Harry S Truman, December 26, 1946, Harry S Truman Papers (Harry S Truman Library, Independence, MO), President's Official File, folder: 27-B, Export–Import Bank (hereafter cited as OF with folder designation); and John J. McCloy, President, International Bank for Reconstruction and Development, letter to Truman, March 25, 1947, Truman Papers, OF, folder: 85-E, United Nations Monetary and Financial Conference.

Their postwar planning had assumed that France would take Germany's place as the industrial hub of Europe and as the fulcrum in a new European balance of power. The Monnet Plan had been based on this assumption. The plan aimed to make French exports more competitive in the international economy, particularly the European economy, where the goal was to replace German with French products. Doing so was the key to French security and to a level of domestic economic growth that would ameliorate social divisions and end the redistributive battles of the interwar period. To achieve these goals, however, recovery in France had to precede recovery in Germany; French steel producers had to have first claim on the Ruhr's rich deposits of coal and coke; and Germany's steel output had to be limited in order to avoid overproduction in Europe. It was this line of thinking that led the French to claim the Saar and to demand substantial reparations, detachment of the Rhineland, and international ownership of the Ruhr coal and steel industries. Until these demands were satisfied, they refused to permit an upward revision of Germany's level of industry or to accept proposals for German unification and central administration.[10]

Franco–American differences, as well as differences between the Soviet Union and the United States, came to a head at the Moscow Foreign Ministers Conference of March–April 1947. The French delegation rejected the Anglo–American proposals for a higher level of German production and a central administration of the Allied occupation zones. They called again for French annexation of the Saar, guarantees of German coal exports, continued reparation transfers, and international ownership of the Ruhr industries. The Soviets endorsed the last two of these demands. They linked Anglo–American concessions on these points to their support for central administration and revision of the 1946 level-of-industry agreement. And when concessions were not forthcoming, they joined the French to block an American compromise that would exchange a four-power security treaty and limited reparations from current production for economic unification and a higher level of industry in Germany.

Convinced that Soviet leaders hoped to gain politically from the deadlock over German policy, Secretary of State George C. Marshall agreed with British Foreign Secretary Ernest Bevin to proceed with plans for reorganizing the Bizone and raising the level of industry. This approach squared with recommendations coming from General Clay but not with thinking in the State Department, where policymakers were loath to sanction any measures that might arouse anti-German sentiment in France, weaken the government there, and play into the hands of the French Communists. Marshall, in

[10]   Gimbel, *Origins of the Marshall Plan*, 21–2, 38–41, 82–90, 98, 101–21, 128, 155–8, 187; Milward, *Reconstruction of Western Europe*, 126–41; and Frances M. B. Lynch, "Resolving the Paradox of the Monnet Plan: National and International Planning in French Reconstruction," *Economic History Review* 37 (May 1984): 229–43.

deference to such considerations, had joined Bevin in supporting French claims to the Saar and to a higher level of German coal exports.[11] These were modest gestures by comparison to French demands. Nor were they sufficient to conceal the early failure of the State Department's efforts to reconcile economic and security imperatives within the framework of a balanced restoration of the German and European economies.

The German muddle headed a long list of problems that highlighted the failure of American policy. Great Britain's economic plight and withdrawal from Greece generated stark warnings of where current policies could lead and new calls for a more aggressive use of American resources. Truman's decision to aid Greece and Turkey pointed in this direction. But it also brought new attacks on the negative and piecemeal nature of American aid programs and fresh demands for a more positive and comprehensive effort to prevent disaster in Europe and to avert an ugly recrudescence of the narrow economic nationalism that had plagued the interwar years. Adding to these pressures was the mounting political turmoil in France and Italy, where worsening economic conditions brought on by the winter crisis were undermining governmental authority and strengthening Communist parties.[12] Together, these developments led to a major reassessment of American policy.

The War Department led the charge by seizing on the so called Hoover Report to launch a full-scale offensive against the State Department's support for a balanced restoration of the German and European economies. At the behest of President Truman and Secretary of War Robert P. Patterson, former president Herbert Hoover had agreed to investigate the factors slowing recovery in Germany. His report, issued in March 1947, recommended lifting the restraints imposed by the level-of-industry plan, halting the removal of nonmilitary industrial plants, and allowing the Ruhr and the Rhineland to remain parts of Germany. These revisions in policy, it main-

[11] Developments at the Moscow Conference can be followed in U.S., Department of State, *Foreign Relations of the United States*, 1947, (Washington, DC, 1972), 2:234–491 (hereafter cited as *FRUS*). See also Scott Jackson, "Prologue to the Marshall Plan: The Origins of the American Commitment for a European Recovery Program," *Journal of American History* 65 (March 1979): 1043–68; Gimbel, *Origins of the Marshall Plan*, 186–94; Lucius D. Clay, *Decision in Germany* (Garden City, NY, 1950), 174; Charles E. Bohlen, *Witness to History, 1929–1969* (New York, 1973), 262–3; Bohlen, *The Transformation of American Foreign Policy* (New York, 1969), 87–8; and Alan Bullock, *Ernest Bevin, Foreign Secretary, 1945–1951* (New York, 1983), 377–92. For a British record of the Moscow Conference, see Bevin's "Review of the Proceedings of the Council of Foreign Ministers in Moscow, March 10th–April 24th, 1947," General Records of the British Foreign Office (Public Record Office, Kew, England), Ernest Bevin Papers, Record Class FO 800/447/Conf./47/4 (hereafter cited as FO 800, with appropriate filing designation).

[12] Michael J. Hogan, "The Search for a 'Creative Peace': The United States, European Unity, and the Origins of the Marshall Plan," *Diplomatic History* 6 (Summer 1982): 267–85.

tained, would leave Germany with the factories and resources needed to increase production and thus spare American taxpayers the onerous expense of supporting the German population. Together with proper safeguards against a renascence of German militarism, they would also permit Germany to contribute to the peaceful stabilization of Europe as a whole.[13]

Hoover's report clearly assigned priority to reviving German industry as an engine that would drive recovery across the Continent. In doing so, it challenged the State Department's support for a balanced recovery strategy and touched off a mighty debate in the Truman administration. Patterson, Clay, and other officials in the War Department quickly endorsed its findings. In their view, too, Germany should be the locomotive of recovery. At a meeting in mid-March, moreover, Hoover won support from Secretary of Commerce Averell Harriman, Secretary of the Navy James V. Forrestal, and Director of the Budget James E. Webb.[14] Officers in the State Department, on the other hand, drafted a paper attacking the report and emphasizing again the need to balance Germany's recovery against the economic and security requirements of its neighbors.[15] Presidential assistant John R. Steelman expressed fear of reviving the "German colossus along lines suggested by Hoover," and Edwin W. Pauley, former United States representative on the Allied Reparations Commission, denounced Hoover's report as a "major reversal" of American policy. If implemented, Pauley also warned, the plan would revive Germany at the expense of its victims

[13] Patterson Memorandum for the President, January 16, 1947, Truman letter to Hoover, January 18, 1947, Hoover letter to Truman, January 19, 1947, and Hoover letter to Truman, March 18, 1947, with attached report of the President's Economic Mission to Germany and Austria, "The Necessary Steps for Promotion of German Exports, so as to Relieve American Taxpayers of the Burdens of Relief and for Economic Recovery of Europe," Truman Papers, OF, folder: 950-B, Economic Mission as to Food and Its Collateral Problems; Herbert C. Hoover, *An American Epic*, 4 vols. (Chicago, 1959–64), 4:246, 253–5; Gimbel, *Origins of the Marshall Plan*, 180–3; Yergin, *Shattered Peace*, 139; and Louis P. Lochner, *Herbert Hoover and Germany* (New York, 1960), 177–93.

[14] Under Secretary of State Dean Acheson tel. to Marshall, March 20, 1947, *FRUS, 1947*, 2:394–5; Walter Millis, ed., *The Forrestal Diaries: The Inner History of the Cold War* (New York, 1951), 255–6; and Harriman letter to Truman, March 21, 1947, Truman Papers, President's Secretary's File (hereafter cited as PSF with folder designation), folder: Subject File – Cabinet – Commerce, Secy of – Harriman.

[15] J. C. de Wilde memorandum to Willard Thorp and John Hilldring, March 25, 1947, with attachments, E. A. Lightner memorandum to Hilldring, Thorp, and John D. Hickerson, March 27, 1947, and de Wilde memorandum to Walter Rudlin, April 11, 1947, RG 59, file: 740.00119Council/4-1147; F. Kirlin memorandum to Acheson, May 2, 1947, RG 59, file: 740.119Control(Germany)/5-247; Thorp memorandum to Ernest A. Gross, April 29, 1947, Hilldring memorandum to Acheson, May 1, 1947, with attached "Memorandum on Mr. Hoover's Third Report," W. J. Williams memorandum to Rudlin, May 7, 1947, and Hilldring memorandum to Acheson, May 8, 1947, RG 59, file: 840.50Recovery/5-847. See also Jackson, "Prologue to the Marshall Plan," 1063–4.

and raise anew the dark specter of German domination of the Continent.[16]

Despite the acrimony that greeted it, the Hoover Report brought American leaders to the conclusion that "almost any action would be an improvement" on current policy.[17] Even policymakers in the State Department admitted that past initiatives had failed. And though still reluctant to abandon their goal of a balanced recovery, they were thinking now of a new strategy for reconciling national rivalries in Europe and bureaucratic conflicts in Washington. The new approach emerged from their deepening conviction that previous aid programs had failed and would continue to fail so long as American assistance was used in piecemeal efforts to revitalize national economies. The squabbling between the War and State departments was symptomatic of the drawbacks inherent in uncoordinated aid programs. Worse still, the piecemeal approach seemed to be perpetuating the very order that had hampered economic growth and led to German domination in the prewar period.

The new approach promised to resolve all of these problems. It would merge economic sovereignties in a unified and supranational system large enough to control the Germans. It would bring the gains in resource utilization, specialization, and economies of scale needed to generate recovery. Recovery, in turn, would enable the Europeans to balance their accounts with the Western Hemisphere and join the flagging campaign for multilateralism. In theory, at least, an approach that integrated economies would also assuage those officials in Paris and Washington who had been opposing the State Department's efforts toward a balanced restoration. Some policymakers even hoped it might prepare the ground for a great-power accommodation on the Continent, although most saw it as a device to bolster Western Europe against Communist subversion and Soviet aggression. In such considerations lay the origins of the Marshall Plan and the integrationist strategy it embodied. Contrary to the conventional wisdom, moreover, this strategy did not originate with senior officials in the State Department. It first emerged in discussions among officials of junior rank and then began winning converts among top policymakers, leading Republicans, journalists, and congressmen.

III

In the State Department, the thinking of some junior officials had been influenced by the regional planning for European economic recovery undertaken by such United Nations (UN) agencies as the Emergency Economic

[16]   Steelman undated memorandum for the president, Truman Papers, PSF, General File: Hoover, Herbert C.; and Pauley letter to Truman, April 15, 1947, John W. Snyder Papers (Truman Library), Alphabetical File: Germany, general, 1946–1951.

[17]   Steelman undated memorandum for the president, Truman Papers, PSF, General File: Hoover, Herbert C.

Committee for Europe, the European Coal Organization, and the European
Central Inland Transportation Organization. By mid-1946, these organizations had enjoyed reasonable success in distributing scarce commodities,
allocating rolling stock, and eliminating economic bottlenecks. Building on
this success, the United Nations Economic and Social Council (ECOSOC)
had appointed a special subcommission on economic reconstruction in the
devastated areas. Its report concluded that long-term stabilization in Europe
required coordinated economic management on a regional basis. There
should be, it recommended, a permanent economic commission replacing
the existing emergency organizations, and this commission should be
"charged with the task of facilitating concerted action for the economic
reconstruction of Europe, and with initiating and participating in measures
necessary for the expansion of European economic activity and for the
development and integration of the European economy." The UN General
Assembly endorsed this proposal and, in March 1947, ECOSOC established
the Economic Commission for Europe.[18]

There had been strong support for these international initiatives among
junior officers, including Thomas C. Blaisdell, Jr., Paul R. Porter, and Theodore Geiger of the American Economic Mission in London, Charles P.
Kindleberger and Walt W. Rostow of the State Department's German and
Austrian Economic Division, and Harold Van B. Cleveland, assistant chief
of the Division of Investments and Economic Development. These men were
alarmed by the current trend toward the division of Germany and Europe
into exclusive blocs, an outcome they thought would sow the seeds of future
conflict. Nor did they support existing efforts to rebuild independent national economies and thus re-create the sort of fractured structure that had
always been an "important factor" in "retarding" productivity on the Continent. They hoped instead to fashion an all-European political settlement
out of which would emerge an integrated economic and political order. If
organized through supranational institutions of regional coordination, this
approach could harness Germany's power, allay French and Soviet security
concerns, and prevent the division of Europe into rival economic and political blocs. If accompanied by measures to liberalize intra-European trade
and make currencies convertible, it could also unleash the latent productive
power of European enterprise and bring the continental countries into line

[18]   United Nations, General Assembly, Official Records of the Second Part of the First
       Session of the General Assembly, Supplement No. 3, Preliminary Report of the
       Temporary Sub-commission on Economic Reconstruction of Devastated Areas (A/
       147), October 26, 1946, p. 67. See also H. Van B. Cleveland, "The United States
       and Economic Collaboration among the Countries of Europe," Department of State,
       Bulletin 16 (January 5, 1947): 3–8; and Leroy Stinebower, Acting US Representative
       to ECOSOC, "Accomplishments of Fourth Session of the Economic and Social Coun-
       cil," Department of State, Bulletin 16 (April 13, 1947): 655–6. See also Walt W.
       Rostow, The Division of Europe after World War II: 1946 (Austin, TX, 1981),
       70–2.

with American plans for a multilateral system of world trade. The United States, as these junior officers saw it, should take the lead in supporting such an approach. It should make better use of the UN organizations that might serve as instruments of regional association and German reintegration and should encourage the kind of associative planning that would unify the European economies.[19] This was the way to a "creative peace," as Porter explained in a memorandum for his colleagues, and the only alternative to an uneconomic self-sufficiency that would raise the specter of autarky, prevent recovery, and foster the kind of political instability that benefitted the Communists.[20]

By the spring of 1947, more important policymakers were also coming to see European economic integration as a way to resolve outstanding differences over Germany and promote recovery across the Continent. In April 1946, Rostow and other members of the German and Austrian Economic Division had drafted a report similar to Porter's memorandum and had won support for their views from Under Secretaries of State Dean G. Acheson and William L. Clayton.[21] In January of the next year, John Foster Dulles told the National Publishers' Association that when the victorious powers "plan for the future of Germany" they must plan "in terms of the economic unity of Europe." "A Europe divided into small compartments," he thought, could not be "a healthy Europe." But one applying the American idea of federalism could enjoy the benefits of a market "big enough to justify modern methods of cheap production for mass consumption." Dulles also envisaged some form of supranational control over the Ruhr, both as a step toward economic integration and as an institutional mechanism through which the Europeans could harness Germany's resources to the cause of recovery without again becoming its dependents.[22]

Similar thinking permeated the War Department and the American delegation to the Moscow Foreign Ministers Conference. In the War Department, Colonel Charles H. Bonesteel had suggested that international

[19] Cleveland, "United States and Economic Collaboration," 3. See also Blaisdell letter to Thorp, December 20, 1945, Blaisdell letters to Clayton, August 27, October 1, and December 20, 1946, and unsigned "Report on Session of UN Devastated Areas Subcommission in London, July 31–September 14, 1946," Thomas C. Blaisdell, Jr. Papers (Truman Library), box 7, folder: Miscellaneous Documents from the London Mission, 1945–1946; Stinebower, "Accomplishments of Fourth Session of the Economic and Social Council," 655–6; Beloff, *United States and the Unity of Europe*, 10–11; and Rostow, *Division of Europe*, 53–62, 70–2.

[20] Porter letter to Kindleberger, January 16, 1947, with enclosed memorandum by Porter to Ambassador Robert Murphy of January 14, 1947, RG 59, file: 501.BD Europe/1-1647. Porter sent a copy of the same memorandum to Leroy Stinebower of the State Department in a letter of January 17, 1947, RG 59, file: 501.BD Europe/1-1747.

[21] Rostow, *Division of Europe*, 3–8, 51–69, 94–119.

[22] Dulles, "Europe Must Federate or Perish: America Must Offer Inspiration and Guidance," *Vital Speeches of the Day* 13 (February 1, 1947): 234–6.

supervision of the Ruhr could lead first to integration of the French and German economies and then to a wider economic unity in Central and Western Europe. Both he and Secretary of War Patterson saw in such a course the best way to revive production in the former Reich without restoring its prewar hegemony. The same goal led Dulles, Marshall, and other members of the American delegation in Moscow to urge the formation of a supranational agency to oversee the Ruhr. Under their proposal, the Ruhr would remain part of Germany, but Germany's neighbors would have equal access to its resources and such disputes as might arise would be resolved on a "European-wide basis" by the international authority. "What is required," Marshall insisted at Moscow, "is a European solution in a Europe which includes Germany."[23]

This supranational agency fell short of the four-power ownership the French and Soviets demanded, a solution the Americans ruled out lest it weaken Germany, stir irredentist claims, or give the Soviets control over economic and strategic assets of incalculable value. Nonetheless, the American proposal suggests that Marshall had now joined Dulles in viewing some form of economic integration as the best way to revive European production and make Germany's rehabilitation acceptable to the French. The two men said as much in radio addresses delivered shortly after returning from Moscow. Marshall reviewed the conference disputes over unification, central administration, reparations, and security, and accused the Soviets of opposing a balanced revival of the European economy. But he also noted that postoccupation control over the Ruhr was still a matter for debate and stressed the importance of integrating a revived Germany into the European economy.[24] Dulles, for his part, explained how the American delegation had considered the Ruhr to be a European rather than a national asset and had suggested "over-all European" supervision in order to prevent its resources from again becoming "an economic club in the hands of Germany." "As we studied the problem of Germany," he concluded, "we became more and more convinced that there is no economic solution along purely national lines. Increased economic unity is an absolute essential to the well-being of Europe.[25]

By this time, other influential Republicans, congressmen, journalists, and opinion leaders were reaching the same conclusion. According to Joseph

---

[23]   For the views of Bonesteel and Patterson, see Melvyn P. Leffler, "Standing Tough: The Strategic and Diplomatic Aftermath of the Iranian Crisis of March 1946," paper presented at The Lehrman Institute, New York, April 1985. For the discussions of the Ruhr at the Moscow Conference, see *FRUS, 1947*, 2:262–6, 280–1, 323–7, 346–7, 383–4, 417, 437. For Marshall's remarks, see U.S., Department of State, *Germany, 1947–1949: The Story in Documents* (Washington, DC, 1950), 329–30.

[24]   Address by the Secretary of State, Department of State, *Bulletin* 16 (May 11, 1947): 919–24.

[25]   Dulles, "We Cannot Let Ourselves Be Stymied: Report on Moscow Conference," *Vital Speeches of the Day* 13 (May 15, 1947): 450–3.

Jones, Dulles's speech before the National Publishers' Association had been approved in advance by Senator Arthur Vandenberg and Governor Thomas E. Dewey.[26] In Congress, Senators J. William Fulbright and Elbert D. Thomas, together with Congressman Hale Boggs, had introduced a concurrent resolution calling for economic and political federation in Europe.[27] In the *New York Times*, an appeal for a "United Europe" carried the endorsement of eighty-one prominent Americans.[28] Similar appeals appeared in the editorial pages of the *St. Louis Post-Dispatch*, the *Wall Street Journal*, the *Washington Post*, the *Christian Science Monitor*, and the *Washington Star*.[29] In addition, Walter Lippmann devoted two important columns to the need for a massive American aid program that would induce an economic reorganization of Europe. The United States, he stated, should abandon the piecemeal aid policies of the past for a comprehensive recovery plan agreed to by the Europeans themselves and used to support the "unification of Europe."[30]

The idea of European economic integration, even political unification, thus enjoyed growing currency in Washington. One line of thinking emphasized the creation of an integrated single market that would foster the same kind of productivity, high living standards, and political stability that existed in the United States. Another called for supranational institutions of economic coordination and control, both to guide the process of integration and to reconcile Germany's revival with the economic and security concerns of its neighbors. Still another stressed the need to supplement these institutions with additional initiatives (such as liberalizing intra-European trade and making currencies convertible) that would speed the process of integration and square this process with American plans for a multilateral system of world trade. Although no one had advanced a detailed blueprint for an integrated Europe, these and similar arguments were being touted by junior officers in the State Department, by leading newspapers, by Republican spokesmen, and by influential journalists as the keys to peace. They were also becoming central features in policy planning for a new European recovery program.

---

[26] Jones, *Fifteen Weeks*, 220. Republican Harold E. Stassen also endorsed an aid program that would, among other things, encourage the growth of economic integration and a customs union in Europe. See his speech "Production for Peace," in *Vital Speeches of the Day* 13 (June 15, 1947): 521–3.

[27] U.S., Congress, *Congressional Record*, 80th Cong., 1st sess., 1947, 2418–22, 2347. See also Tristram Coffin, *Senator Fulbright: Portrait of a Public Philosopher* (New York, 1966), 101–2.

[28] *New York Times*, April 18, 1947, 12.

[29] For newspaper commentary, see Ernst H. Van Der Beugel, *From Marshall Aid to Atlantic Partnership: European Integration as a Concern of American Foreign Policy* (New York, 1966), 101–3.

[30] Lippmann, "Marshall and Dulles," *Washington Post*, May 1, 1947, 13, and Lippmann, "Cassandra Speaking," *Washington Post*, April 5, 1947, 9.

IV

Early planning for European recovery centered in George Kennan's Policy Planning Staff and in a special agency of the State–War–Navy Coordinating Committee (SWNCC).[31] The SWNCC agency had been established on March 11, following Under Secretary Acheson's request for a study of additional aid needs in various countries.[32] To facilitate its work, Acheson had also set up the Committee on the Extension of U.S. Aid to Foreign Governments. Headed by William A. Eddy, the State Department's representative on the SWNCC agency, the committee undertook an extensive review of European economic problems.[33] Although it tended to be preoccupied with identifying countries in need of aid, and with determining if such aid could be effective and could serve American interests, it also tried to consider how national sovereignties might be transcended. As Joseph Jones, who attended the meetings, recalled, the State Department's economic officers encouraged committee members to think of Europe as a whole and to administer aid in ways that would foster economic unification.[34]

The result, by April 14, was a SWNCC report that, among other things, offered a vigorous endorsement of economic integration and German reintegration as essential features of any stabilization strategy. The report insisted that economic programs in the occupied areas, including Germany, should be coordinated parts of a comprehensive recovery plan, which in turn should seek to build the sort of "regional" trading and production system that would enable recipient countries to become self-supporting.[35]

Soon after the SWNCC study was completed, Joseph Jones, Ben T. Moore, and Harold Van B. Cleveland, all junior officers who had served on the departmental committee, became leading apostles for the cause of European economic integration. Along with Porter, Bonesteel, and Kindleberger, they

---

[31] On the organization of the Policy Planning Staff, see George F. Kennan, *Memoirs (1925–1950)* (New York, 1969), 342–3; and Dean G. Acheson, *Present at the Creation: My Years in the State Department* (New York, 1969), 228.

[32] Acheson letter to Secretary of War Patterson, March 5, 1947, and Memorandum by the State Department Member (Hilldring) of the State–War–Navy Coordinating Committee, March 17, 1947, *FRUS, 1947*, 3:197–8, 198–9; and Acheson, *Present at the Creation*, 226.

[33] *FRUS, 1947*, 3:199, footnote 3; and Acheson, *Present at the Creation*, 226.

[34] Jones, *Fifteen Weeks*, 231. The records of the Committee on the Extension of U.S. Aid to Foreign Governments are located in the Records of Interdepartmental and Intradepartmental Committees (State Department) (National Archives), Record Group 353, Lot 122, box 17, folder: AFG Minutes (hereafter cited as RG 353, Lot 122, with box and folder designations).

[35] Report of the Special "Ad Hoc" Committee of the State–War–Navy Coordinating Committee, April 21, 1947, *FRUS, 1947*, 3:204–19. This report had been approved by the Committee on the Extension of U.S. Aid to Foreign Governments. See the minutes of the committee's tenth meeting, April 14, 1947, RG 353, Lot 122, box 17, folder: AFG Minutes.

insistently pressed this idea on their senior colleagues. Porter repeated his earlier arguments in talks with Under Secretary Clayton.[36] Bonesteel suggested that cooperative development of the cheap foodstuffs and raw materials of northern Africa could help forge European unity and create an economic base for continental recovery.[37] Moore, Kindleberger, and Cleveland told Kennan that the "symbols of nationalism in France and Italy and in Germany are essentially bankrupt and in danger of being captured by reactionary and neo-fascist political elements which we do not wish to support." The great need was for transcending nationalism and developing "the supra-national ideal of European unity," something the United States should do by using its financial "leverage" to support a comprehensive "recovery plan which stresses the raising of European production and consumption through the economic and 'functional' unification of Europe." It should begin, they argued, by promoting currency convertibility, encouraging the immediate lowering of tariff barriers, using the Economic Commission for Europe as an agency of joint programming, and trying to secure the kind of Soviet participation that might lay the groundwork for an all-European settlement.[38]

There is no doubt that these ideas influenced George Kennan and his Policy Planning Staff. In fact, Kennan recruited Bonesteel for his staff and drew heavily on SWNCC's interim report in preparing his own studies of European recovery. This is particularly clear in his memorandum of May 16, and in his recommendations to Acheson on May 23. In these documents, Kennan set forth the principles that should govern any effort to correct the "economic maladjustment" that made Europe vulnerable to communism. He wanted the Europeans to act collectively in framing a comprehensive recovery program and to assume joint responsibility for making their program work. The United States, for its part, would provide "friendly aid" in the drafting process and financial support for the results. Kennan then went on to recommend both short-term measures, including interim aid for Italy and increased production of German coal, and a long-term program designed to encourage "intramural economic collaboration" and "regional political association" in Europe. His insistence on shaping American occupation policies with a view to integrating Germany into the long-term program, together with his emphasis on increasing German coal production, was a clear indication that Kennan was coming to see economic integration, even political federation, as a way to reconcile Germany's revival with the security and economic needs of its neighbors. Indeed, the very procedures

---

[36] Rostow, *Division of Europe*, 73.
[37] Bonesteel Memorandum, May 13, 1947, RG 59, Records of the Office of European Affairs, 1934–1947 (John D. Hickerson and H. Freeman Matthews Files), box 3, folder: Memoranda, January–June, 1947.
[38] Quoted in Beloff, *United States and the Unity of Europe*, 15–18. See also Jones, *Fifteen Weeks*, 243–4.

he outlined for devising a recovery program – the emphasis on a comprehensive plan and collective action – required the kind of cooperation that would help effect the long-term goal of unification.[39]

Due largely to Kennan's recommendations, the work of the SWNCC and State Department committees, and the proselytizing of junior officers, the idea of European integration quickly found its way into the public and private statements of key officials in the State Department. It was Jones, fresh from his work on the department's foreign-aid committee, who drafted speeches for Acheson and Marshall, including Acheson's famous address before the Delta Council in Cleveland, Mississippi, on May 8, 1947. Because Jones borrowed heavily from the SWNCC report and from the advice of Moore, Cleveland, and other junior officers, it was not surprising that these speeches combined current concerns about the breakdown of the Moscow Conference, the European economic crisis, and the vitality of America's export markets, with the idea that recovery in Germany and across Europe could be achieved only by forging the "various parts" of the Continent into "a harmonious whole." A "coordinated European economy," according to Acheson's speech, was a "fundamental objective" to be pursued, if necessary, "without full Four Power agreement." According to Marshall's draft, the United States should encourage the "growth of European unity."[40] As it turned out, Marshall never delivered Jones's draft speech. But Acheson handed a copy of it to the secretary in mid-May, just as Marshall was considering Kennan's report and the recommendations of his under secretary for economic affairs, William Clayton. It thus seemed to reinforce what Marshall was getting from other sources and became one of the several documents that influenced the speech he later delivered at Harvard.

More significant in its immediate impact was the memorandum prepared by Clayton, whose recent European trip and talks with Porter, Rostow, and other junior officials had converted him to the cause of expanded aid to encourage European integration. Written for Acheson and Marshall, the memorandum recommended $6–7 billion in new aid each year over a three-year period. This level of expenditure was necessary to avert "economic, social and political" chaos in Europe, contain communism, prevent the collapse of America's export trade, and achieve the goal of multilateralism. To revive European productivity, moreover, Clayton thought it imperative that aid be used to reorganize an economy that had become "divided into

[39] Kennan to Acheson, May 23, 1947, with attached recommendations of the Policy Planning Staff of same date, *FRUS, 1947*, 3:223–30; and Kennan Memorandum, May 16, 1947, *FRUS, 1947*, 3:220–3. See also Kennan, *Memoirs*, 352–9.

[40] Jones, *Fifteen Weeks*, 206–13, 244–6, 274–81; Acheson, *Present at the Creation*, 228–9; Jones memorandum to Acheson, May 20, 1947, with attached draft speech for Marshall, Joseph M. Jones Papers (Truman Library), box 2, folder: Marshall Plan Speech; and Jones Memorandum for the File, July 2, 1947, Jones Papers, box 1, folder: Miscellaneous Mimeo Speeches.

many small watertight compartments." Like Kennan, he believed that any recovery plan must encourage "a European economic federation."[41]

On May 28, Kennan, Clayton, and the heads of other departmental offices met with Marshall to discuss Clayton's recommendations and the report of the Policy Planning Staff. Clayton reiterated the substance of his memorandum, including his and Kennan's demand for a system of "closer European economic cooperation" that would "break down existing economic barriers." All seemed to agree with this approach, and the goal of "economic federation" became the basis for ensuing decisions. It was decided, for example, to invite the Eastern European countries to participate in the recovery program, but only if they "abandoned [the] near-exclusive Soviet orientation of their economies" in favor of European-wide integration. The Soviets might participate on similar terms, and if they refused, America's goal should be integration in Western Europe alone. Concerning the question of American versus European initiative, the difference of opinion tended to be over where an effective balance between self-help and American prodding could be struck. No one dissented, however, when Marshall's special assistant, Charles E. Bohlen, concluded that American aid should be conditioned on "substantial evidence of a developing overall plan for economic cooperation by the Europeans themselves, perhaps an economic federation to be worked out over 3 or 4 years."[42]

Following this discussion, Bohlen drafted the speech that Marshall delivered at Harvard University on June 5. Based largely on Kennan's report and Clayton's memorandum, the speech emphasized the need for recovery in "Europe as a whole" and invited all European countries to cooperate in this task. It noted the willingness of the United States to give financial support and provide "friendly aid" in drafting a recovery plan. But the initiative must come from the Continent and must result in a "joint" program "agreed to by a number, if not all, European nations."[43] Marshall's speech did not suggest a scheme for achieving European integration. Such a scheme, he had argued in response to the Fulbright resolution earlier,

[41] Clayton Memorandum, May 27, 1947, *FRUS, 1947*, 3:230–2. See also Jones, *Fifteen Weeks*, 241–2, 246–8; Acheson, *Present at the Creation*, 230–1; Acheson Oral Interview, Ellen Clayton Garwood Papers (Truman Library), box 1, folder: Marshall Plan Project; William L. Clayton, "GATT, the Marshall Plan, and OECD," *Political Science Quarterly* 78 (December 1963): 493–503; Clayton's speech before the ECE, May 2, 1947, in Frederick J. Dobney, Jr., ed., *Selected Papers of Will Clayton* (Baltimore, 1971), 195–7; and Dobney's introduction to this edition, 13–14.

[42] Summary of Discussion on Problems of Relief, Rehabilitation, and Reconstruction of Europe, May 29, 1947, *FRUS, 1947*, 3:234–6. See also Acheson, *Present at the Creation*, 231–2; and Kennan, *Memoirs*, 359–60.

[43] For Marshall's speech, see *FRUS, 1947*, 3:237–9. See also Bohlen letter to Ellen St. John Garwood, May 29, 1949, Garwood Papers, box 1, folder: Correspondence of W. L. Garwood and Ellen C. Garwood; Bohlen, *Witness to History*, 263–5; Bohlen, *Transformation of American Foreign Policy*, 88; and Acheson, *Present at the Creation*, 232–3.

should be left to the Europeans. Yet he was "deeply sympathetic" with this general objective and it seems clear that his emphasis on joint programming and on a European-wide plan was intended to promote it.[44]

Marshall's speech left the door open to Soviet participation in the recovery program. At his staff meeting on May 28, it had been decided to "play it straight" and invite the Soviets to collaborate.[45] Marshall himself seemed anxious not to preclude the possibility of participation and even Forrestal believed that "there was no chance of Russia's not joining in this effort."[46] Yet whatever enthusiasm existed for such a prospect came almost exclusively from junior officials on the economic side of the State Department. At least some of these officials were convinced that dividing Germany and organizing Europe into rival blocs would prevent the restoration of East–West trade and lead to future wars. In their view, an all-European recovery program offered the last hope of a peaceful political accommodation. This view stood in stark contrast to the conclusions reached earlier by a group of high-level officials led by Kennan. Kennan assumed that a great-power settlement was impossible and that continued stalemate at the negotiating table would lead to economic collapse in Central Europe and to the expansion of Soviet influence into an area deemed vital to the military security and economic well-being of the United States. To his way of thinking, the United States, Britain, and France must cooperate to prevent these dangers, first by consolidating their zones in Germany and then by integrating them into a Western European complex strong enough to balance the Soviet bloc in Eastern Europe.[47]

By the time of Marshall's speech, virtually all top policymakers had been converted to Kennan's view, a fact that helps to explain their reluctance to include the Soviets in any plan for internationalizing the Ruhr and their decision to join the British in an economic reorganization of the Bizone. Those in the defense establishment had worried for some time that worsening economic conditions in France, Germany, and Italy would enhance Soviet influence in Western Europe at the expense of the American position.

[44]   Marshall letter to Senator Vandenberg, June 4, 1947, Department of State, *Bulletin* 16 (June 22, 1947): 1213.

[45]   Kennan, *Memoirs*, 360.

[46]   See Millis, *Forrestal Diaries*, 279, 288.

[47]   For Kennan's views, see John Lewis Gaddis, "The United States and the Question of a Sphere of Influence in Europe, 1945–1949," in Olav Riste, ed., *Western Security: The Formative Years. European and Atlantic Defence, 1947–1953* (New York, 1985), 60–91. Extrapolating from Gaddis's essay, it seems clear that junior officials on the economic side of the State Department were heirs to the Wilsonian vision of a single world, most recently enshrined in the Atlantic Charter and initially defended by Charles Bohlen and other high-level officials. As Gaddis points out, however, developments in 1946 led these policymakers to accept Kennan's gloomier vision instead, with the result that junior officials were more or less alone in their hope that an all-European recovery program might clear the way to a great-power accommodation within the framework of an integrated European economy.

They were less concerned about the prospect of direct Soviet intervention than about the danger that economic and political turmoil would strengthen indigenous Communist parties, which were, in their eyes, mere instruments of Soviet diplomacy. The triumph of these parties would bring the resources of Western Europe under Soviet control, thereby augmenting the economic recovery and war-making ability of the Soviet Union while weakening the strategic position and defense capabilities of the United States. Such concerns had led General Clay and defense officials in Washington to press for measures to resuscitate the German economy. The same concerns now prompted their support for a massive recovery program.[48]

Similar concerns had influenced policy planning in the State Department. Here, all agreed that recovery and integration offered the best hope for attaining the sort of economic and political order in Europe that the United States had pursued since the 1920s. But whereas junior officials also hoped that integration might become a device for promoting a general European settlement, top policymakers viewed it as a mechanism for bringing western Germany and Western Europe together as a viable counterweight to the Soviet bloc.[49] Officials who attended Marshall's staff meeting on May 28 had talked about the recovery program in these terms. Clayton and Kennan had envisioned it as a vehicle for stabilizing Western Europe against Communist subversion and Soviet expansion. The SWNCC study had emphasized the importance of using American aid to keep strategic areas and key resources in "friendly hands." Staff planning in general had concentrated on a Western European, rather than an all-European, recovery program; Acheson had been determined to go ahead "without full Four Power agreement"; and neither Acheson nor other key officials had seriously considered the threat that a comprehensive and transnational recovery program might pose to Soviet security. At the very least, they wanted the onus for any breakdown of European cooperation to fall on the Russians. Their decision to base American recovery policy on the concept of integration would make it difficult for the Soviets to escape this responsibility. But the same decision would have unintended consequences as well, and of these none would be more important than the seeds of dissension it sowed between Britain and America.

V

Following the Harvard speech, American leaders elaborated the principles that should govern recovery planning by the Europeans. These principles were also included in the instructions that would steer Clayton's talks with the British, who were expected to play the role of brokers for the American

---

[48] Leffler, "The American Conception of National Security," 356–69.
[49] Rostow, *Division of Europe*, 7–8, 38–45, 58–69.

plan with their associates on the Continent.[50] Any recovery program, the Americans now insisted, should transcend national boundaries and should be founded on collective action, the maximum use of European materials, the pooling of information and resources, and the reintegration of Germany. These principles were the keys to putting Western Europe on a self-supporting basis and clearing the way to a fully multilateral system of world trade. Even before Clayton's departure for London, however, it had become clear that British leaders were not particularly keen on the American planning principles or on the integrationist strategy these principles embodied.

Long before Clayton's visit, policymakers in the Foreign Office had been talking about some kind of Anglo–Western European association. One line of British thinking led from wartime planning to the Treaty of Dunkirk in March 1947 and then to the Brussels Pact. It envisioned a British-led Western European security system that operated as a barrier to German or Soviet aggression, reassured the French, and gave the British defense in depth on the Continent. A related line of thinking, more germane to the focus of this volume, contemplated close Anglo–French economic collaboration as the cornerstone of a wider economic association among the states of Western Europe. Representatives of both countries had inaugurated discussions aimed in part at exploring this prospect. Ernest Bevin had urged the Cabinet in late 1946 to launch a full-scale study of the advantages and disadvantages of an Anglo–Western European customs union. He was particularly interested in whether a customs union would be compatible with the principles of multilateralism then being written into the draft charter for the International Trade Organization (ITO) and with the trade and currency agreements between Great Britain and the countries of the Commonwealth and sterling bloc. The Cabinet had agreed to this request and had appointed in January 1947 a special committee of experts to conduct the investigation.

[50]   For reiteration of the American principles, see Marshall tel. to Ambassador Jefferson Caffery, Paris, June 12, 1947, Memorandum of Conversation by the Secretary of State, June 13, 1947, and undated Memorandum of Conversation by the Counselor of the Department of State, *FRUS, 1947*, 3:249–51, 251–3, 260–1; Samuel Reber Memorandum of Conversation, June 20, 1947, and Robert A. Lovett Memorandum of Conversation, June 24, 1947, RG 59, file: 840.50Recovery/6-2047 and /6-2447; and H. Freeman Matthews Memorandum of Conversation, June 20, 1947, RG 59, Records of the Office of European Affairs, 1934–1947 (Hickerson and Matthews Files), box 9, folder: Memoranda for the President, 1947. For Clayton's instructions, see undated Memorandum Prepared for the Use of the Under Secretary of State for Economic Affairs, *FRUS, 1947*, 3:247–9. For the background on Clayton's instructions, see Kennan memorandum for Acheson, June 6, 1947, with enclosed Memorandum of Discussion: Mr. Acheson's Morning Meeting, June 5, 1947, undated memorandum from Marshall to Lovett, Kennan memorandum to Marshall, June 9, 1947, with enclosure, and undated memorandum from Lovett to Marshall, RG 59, Records of the Policy Planning Staff, box 9, folder: Economic Policy (hereafter cited as RG 59, PPS Records).

By that time, however, the issue of a customs union had provoked important differences inside the Labour government, and the Cabinet's decision could neither harmonize these differences nor conceal those that were emerging between British and American policymakers.[51]

On the British side, representatives of the Board of Trade and the Treasury had blocked for two years the efforts of the Foreign Office to examine the merits of an Anglo–Western European customs union. This course entailed the removal of tariffs between participating countries, and taking it, they warned, would disrupt the domestic economy. It would also reduce the Treasury's ability to regulate foreign payments and would compromise the network of preferential trade agreements that linked Great Britain to the Commonwealth countries and the sterling area. Even when the Board of Trade and the Treasury finally consented to a study of the issues involved, they did so on terms that betrayed no slackening of their earlier opposition, or of their parallel conviction that the selective reduction of tariffs and negotiation of new trade agreements were far better ways to expand the scope of Anglo–European cooperation.[52]

For Bevin, of course, it was the political, rather than the economic, gains that made his proposal attractive. Yet even on the political side he faced opposition, in this case from parliamentary backbenchers on the left wing of the Labour Party, whose program, published in the pamphlet *Keep Left*, looked to an Anglo–European association of socialist states that would operate as a "Third Force" in world affairs. For them, this was the way to

[51] John Baylis, "Britain, the Brussels Pact, and the continental commitment," *International Affairs* 60 (Autumn 1984): 615–29; Bullock, *Bevin*, 144–5, 316–18, 358; Bevin, "Proposal for a Study of the Possibilities of Close Economic Co-operation with our Western European Neighbours," January 18, 1947, Cabinet Paper (47) 35 (hereafter cited as CP, with the year and number of the paper), General Records of the British Foreign Office, Record Class FO 3/1, 62398, UE416 (hereafter cited as FO 371, with appropriate folder and document numbers); and Cabinet Minutes (47) 13th Conclusion, January 28, 1947 (hereafter cited as CM, with the year and number of the conclusion), FO 371, 62398, UE416. For more detail on Foreign Office thinking prior to the Marshall Plan, see Victor Rothwell, *Britain and the Cold War, 1941–1947* (London, 1982), especially 406–56; John W. Young, *Britain, France, and the Unity of Europe, 1945–1951* (Leicester, England, 1984), especially 13–62; and Sean Greenwood, "Ernest Bevin, France, and 'Western Union': August 1945–February 1946," *European History Quarterly* 14 (July 1984): 319–38.

[52] The record of these early reservations by the Board of Trade and the Treasury runs from 1946 through June 1947. For opinion in the Treasury, see the documents for September and October 1946 in the Records of the British Treasury, Overseas Finance Division (Public Record Office), Record Class T236/779/OF120/5/1 (hereafter cited as T236, with appropriate filing designation). For the views of the Board of Trade, see its note of June 30, 1947, "Customs Union for Western Europe," attached to Sir Edmund Hall-Patch of the Foreign Office memorandum to Bevin, June 30, 1947, FO 371, 62552, UE5263. See also Hall-Patch's memorandum to Bevin of August 7, 1947, FO 371, 62552, UE7147.

prevent the division of Europe, preserve Britain's independence of the United States, and stop a costly arms race from wrecking the Labour government's social-welfare programs at home.[53]

By late 1947, Bevin would defeat his backbench critics and put his own unmistakable stamp on British diplomacy, including his abiding distrust of the Soviet Union and his deep conviction that Britain's security now depended on close cooperation with the United States as well as with Western Europe. But in spite of this conviction, and the fears of the Board of Trade, the arrangements he had in mind involved a middle course between the recommendations of his opponents in Parliament and the proposals contemplated in Washington. Specifically, Bevin and many of his colleagues in the Foreign Office had been thinking of a Western association that would function not as a rival of the United States but as a vehicle by which Britain might retain its status as a great power. Their plans were still inchoate. They did not think in terms of a United States of Europe that would include the Germans but not the Soviets. Former Prime Minister Winston Churchill had recently proposed such a scheme, which officials in the Foreign Office thought likely to provoke the Soviets or end in German domination of the Continent. These officials aimed instead at an Anglo–Western European group less formal than the one proposed by Churchill yet strong enough to protect their economic and security interests should the Americans withdraw from Europe, coherent enough to control the Germans, and independent enough to make Britain a real partner, rather than a mere appendage, of the United States. An arrangement of this sort required above all that British policymakers reconcile their membership in a Western European group with their ties to the Commonwealth and the sterling area. These ties formed the basis of Britain's world position. Bevin wanted American support for this position, including financial support for Britain's role as banker to the sterling area and diplomatic support for a continental association in which the British could play a leading part without sacrificing their interests elsewhere.[54]

The differences between American and British thinking became clear during Clayton's talks with Bevin and other British leaders in late June. By that time, the British were in the midst of a major financial crisis caused by a drain on their gold and dollar reserves that was bound to grow worse in July, when the terms of the Anglo–American loan agreement would require the British Treasury to make pound sterling fully convertible into dollars. Under these circumstances, the British were finding it difficult to move toward the kind of multilateralism that the Americans were supporting or to afford the cost of their financial commitments to the sterling bloc and

---

[53] Bullock, *Bevin*, 395–8.

[54] Bevin's views and those of his colleagues are developed in the text. For background, see also Rothwell, *Britain and the Cold War*, 406–56; and Greenwood, "Ernest Bevin, France, and 'Western Union,'" 319–38.

other areas of the world. In the ITO negotiations, then underway in Geneva, they were leading the opposition to American demands for the quick removal of preferential trade barriers. They had also withdrawn from Greece. Bevin and other British policymakers reminded Clayton of these facts, using them to build a case for special assistance from the United States outside the framework of the proposed European recovery program. Without such aid, Bevin warned, the British would not be able to stabilize their economy, support American plans for multilateralism, or maintain their commitments in Germany and elsewhere.[55]

The British also objected to the integrationist thrust of American recovery policy, specifically to what appeared to be the American emphasis on a structural integration that did not take account of Britain's position in other areas of the world. After all, they insisted, Great Britain was not "just another European country." It had an empire of its own, conducted a substantial trade with non-European countries, and shouldered a heavy financial burden in Germany. Through the resources of its empire, moreover, it could make a contribution to European recovery second only to that of the United States. For these reasons, Bevin and others thought it inappropriate for Britain to be "lumped" together with the other European countries and thus reduced to a relationship with the United States comparable to the one "between the U.S.S.R. and Yugoslavia." They envisioned instead a "financial partnership" similar to the informal entente through which the two countries had promoted European stabilization after the First World War, but one now requiring special interim assistance from the United States. Anything less, Bevin pleaded, would sacrifice the "little bit of dignity we have left."[56]

Despite the sorrowful elegance of this appeal, Clayton seemed determined to treat Great Britain as "just another European country." He and other American policymakers assumed that Britain lacked the economic resources to be independent. Some, including Kennan, thought in terms of a North Atlantic union that included the United States, Britain, and Canada; most favored Britain's integration into Europe.[57] Clayton belonged to the second

[55] Memoranda of Conversations by the First Secretary of Embassy in the United Kingdom, June 24 (2), 25, and 26, 1947, *FRUS, 1947,* 3:268–83, 288–93; and Ambassador Lewis Douglas, London, tel. to Marshall, June 25, 1947, RG 59, file: 840.50Recovery/6-2547. For the British records of the Clayton talks, see Summary Record of a Meeting in the Prime Minister's Office, June 24, 1947, FO 371, 62405, UE5388; and Note of a Meeting of British and American Officials, June 24, 1947, Records of the Prime Ministers' Office (Public Record Office), Clement B. Attlee Papers, Record Class PREM 8/495 (hereafter cited as PREM 8, with document number).

[56] See the sources cited in note 55. The quotes are from the memoranda of June 24 and 25, 1947, *FRUS, 1947,* 3:268–73, 276–83.

[57] Kennan explained his thinking to John Balfour, the British minister in Washington. See Balfour's letter to Nevile Butler of the Foreign Office, June 10, 1947, FO 371,

group. A weathered veteran of the American campaigns for multilateralism (including the ITO discussions and the Anglo–American loan negotiations), Clayton had an aversion that bordered on mania when it came to the sterling area and the system of imperial preferences. He would not agree that these arrangements distinguished Britain's position from that of the continental countries or merited special assistance from the United States. In a veiled reference to the Anglo–American loan of 1946, he told Bevin that previous measures of piecemeal assistance had failed to work. Congress would now demand a comprehensive recovery program and some degree of European integration. Under this program, American aid would consist largely of commodity assistance rather than long-term modernization loans, and the Europeans would be expected to help themselves by liberalizing trade, curbing inflation, incorporating Germany, and developing joint plans for the efficient use of local resources. These conditions would be embodied in aid agreements between the United States and each of the governments involved. In line with these conditions, Clayton also urged the British to replace their plans to socialize the Ruhr coal mines with an efficient managerial scheme that would enhance production and thus contribute to economic growth across the Continent.[58]

The Ruhr issue was then one of the sorest points in Anglo–American relations. Like the Americans, the British were dead set against French plans to separate the Ruhr from the rest of Germany. They also wanted to hold down occupation costs in the Bizone, increase coal production, and impose some form of international supervision to control the Germans. In their view, however, international supervision was less a step toward a structural integration of the kind the Americans had in mind than a step toward Bevin's plan for a loose grouping of Western European states linked informally to the Commonwealth and the sterling area. This potential source of tension between the two countries was compounded by the more immediate problem stemming from the clash of British and American economic principles. Bevin was convinced that effective control of the Germans required public ownership of the Ruhr industries. The Americans were just as devoted to the principle of private enterprise. As they saw it, moreover, poor British administration in the Ruhr had slowed the production of coal, which was desperately needed to fuel recovery in Germany and elsewhere, and current British plans to nationalize the mines would only make a bad situation worse. In Marshall's words, "time does not permit of experimentation."[59]

Unable to reconcile their views, Clayton and the British turned instead

---

62399, UE4674. See also Balfour to Butler, May 29, 1947, with enclosure, FO 371, 62411, UE4877.

[58] See note 55.

[59] Clayton Memorandum of Conversation with Marshall, June 20, 1947, *FRUS, 1947*, 2:929. American and British thinking on the Ruhr is outlined in Gimbel, *Origins of the Marshall Plan*, 203–11; and Greenwood, "Ernest Bevin, France, and 'Western Union,' " 319–38.

to a working paper that summarized the areas of agreement, obfuscated differences, and made further negotiations possible. Drafted in the Foreign Office, the paper acknowledged that Marshall Plan aid would cover Europe's short-term needs rather than long-term requirements, which would have to be financed through the World Bank. These needs were to be set out by the Europeans in a collective recovery scheme that would also describe the current economic situation on the Continent and commit participating governments to the principles of self-help, mutual aid, and joint programming. The paper admitted that American opinion required "a 'continental' rather than a country approach" to recovery. It stated that such an approach would promote the natural "evolution" of Europe toward a "viable economic unit," but then acknowledged that this line of development posed "special difficulties" for the British. After some discussion and a few revisions, Clayton accepted the Foreign Office paper, which Bevin then agreed to use for "guidance" in discussing Marshall's proposal at a conference with the French and the Soviets.[60]

The tripartite conference opened in Paris on June 27 and quickly became mired in differences over the American demands, particularly the interrelated demands for European integration and German reintegration. Soviet Foreign Minister Vyacheslav M. Molotov, who suspected the British and French of conspiring with the Americans at his country's expense, objected to Germany's participation in the recovery plan prior to four-power agreement on a German peace treaty. He pointedly asked French Foreign Minister Georges Bidault if he was willing to forfeit reparations and raise the level of German industry in order to encourage European recovery. Bidault skirted this question. Along with Bevin, he accused Molotov of trying to undermine the conference, incite French opinion, and avoid concessions that might enable Russia's "hungry satellites" to participate in the American program.[61]

The need for these concessions, more than anything else, disrupted the conference. The Soviets were unwilling to relinquish control over the management of their economy. In operation, Molotov claimed, Marshall's plan would violate national sovereignties and enable the United States to influence the internal affairs of other nations. Molotov wanted the Europeans to draft national recovery plans and negotiate the terms for American aid only after the United States had announced its conditions and guaranteed that congressional funding would be forthcoming. According to Bevin, Molotov's pro-

---

[60] Undated Aide-Mémoire by the British Foreign Office for the Secretary of State for Foreign Affairs, *FRUS, 1947,* 3:284–8.

[61] Caffery tel. to Marshall, June 29, 1947, *FRUS, 1947,* 3:299–301. See also Caffery tels. to Marshall, June 27 and 28 and July 1 and 2, 1947, *FRUS, 1947,* 3:296, 297–9, 303–4, 304–6; Douglas tels. to Marshall, June 28 and July 1 and 2, 1947, RG 59, file: 840.50Recovery/6-2847, /7-147, and /7-247; and Bevin tel. to the Foreign Office (hereafter cited as FO), London, June 28, 1947, enclosed in Bohlen memorandum to Lovett, July 2, 1947, RG 59, file: 840.50Recovery/7-247.

posal amounted to asking the United States for a "blank check." Because it did not meet American requirements for a comprehensive scheme, joint planning, and resource sharing, he and Bidault rejected it. Thus rebuffed, Molotov withdrew from the conference, warning that American policy would divide rather than unify the Continent.[62]

Neither the Americans nor Bevin and Bidault were disappointed by Molotov's departure. The latter two had hoped that Molotov would "refuse to cooperate" – had "wished" for the conference to fail. When this wish came true, they had tried to heap all of the blame on the Soviets.[63] As for the Americans, although they had decided to invite the Soviet Union to share in the burdens as well as the benefits of a comprehensive recovery scheme, most thought the Russians would gain little by going along. The Soviets, Kennan and Clayton had argued, did not have a shortage of dollars or of the foods, fibers, and basic commodities that would make them eligible for short-term credits or relief assistance from the United States. Their failure to join the World Bank had ruled out this source of long-term loans and, pending a general settlement of outstanding issues, Clayton did not think that Congress would be generous in its aid appropriations for the Russians.[64] At best, American officials saw Marshall's plan as a way to break Soviet influence in Eastern Europe; at worst, they were counting on Soviet opposition to galvanize support for the plan in Congress.[65] Anticipating this opposition, both they and the British had decided to organize the recovery program outside the UN's Economic Commission for Europe.[66] The com-

[62] Caffery tel. to Marshall, July 1, 1947, *FRUS, 1947,* 3:301–3. See also Caffery tels. to Marshall, June 28 (2) and 29, 1947, and Douglas tel. to Marshall, July 3, 1947, *FRUS, 1947,* 3:297–301, 306–7; Douglas tel. to Marshall, June 28, 1947, RG 59, file: 840.50Recovery/6-2847; Bevin tels. to FO, June 29 and July 1, 1947, enclosed in Bohlen memorandum to Lovett, July 2, 1947, RG 59, file: 840.50Recovery/7-247; Douglas tel. to Marshall, June 29, 1947, RG 59, file: 840.50Recovery/6-2947; and Caffery tel. to Marshall, July 2, 1947, RG 59, file: 840.50Recovery/7-247. See also Bevin's memorandum on the Tripartite Conference, July 5, 1947, FO 371, 62407, UE5594.

[63] Caffery tels. to Marshall, June 18 and July 1, 1947, *FRUS, 1947,* 3:258–60, 301–4. See also Caffery tels. to Marshall, June 29 and July 2, 1947, *FRUS, 1947,* 3:299–301, 304–6; and Caffery tel. to Marshall, July 2, 1947, and Bevin tels. (2) to FO, July 1, 1947, enclosed in Bohlen memorandum to Lovett, July 2, 1947, RG 59, file: 840.50Recovery/7-247.

[64] Clayton memorandum to Marshall, June 19, 1947, RG 59, file: 840.50Recovery/6-1947; Kennan memorandum to Lovett, June 30, 1947, RG 59, PPS Records, box 33, folder: Chronological, 1947; and Memorandum of Conversation by the First Secretary of Embassy in the United Kingdom, June 26, 1947, *FRUS, 1947,* 3:288–93.

[65] Lord Inverchapel, the British Ambassador in Washington, tel. to FO, June 13, 1947, FO 371, 62399, UE4698. See also Inverchapel tel. to FO, June 14, 1947, FO 371, 62401, UE5010.

[66] In addition to the first document cited in note 65, see Summary of Discussion on

mission included representatives of the Soviet Union and its Eastern European clients and was thus an inappropriate instrument in what American officials were increasingly coming to see as a bipolar world.

Molotov's refusal to cooperate hardly came as a surprise to these officials. They had intended the Marshall Plan to strengthen Western Europe as a counterweight to Soviet power on a divided Continent. But while this was one goal, other objectives had also governed American policy. The principles to which Molotov objected, including shared information and resource pooling, were essential elements in an American plan to promote productivity and abundance through some form of European economic integration. It was the strategy of integration, as much as the strategy of containment, that shaped American policy, wrecked the chances for Soviet (and Eastern European) cooperation, and, ironically, prevented the sort of all-European settlement envisioned by the junior officers who had been the first to champion the cause of European unity.

VI

For American leaders, European integration had become a goal to be pursued with or without Soviet support. From the deadlock over Germany and the wreckage of the administration's early reconstruction programs, it had emerged as part of a grand design for remaking the Old World in the likeness of the New. Although initially some had hoped that economic integration might lay the foundation for an accommodation between the United States and the Soviet Union, high-level officials had not been willing to adjust their thinking to Soviet concerns. In their eyes, integration was a strategy for advancing American interests over Soviet resistance. After the collapse of the Paris conference, all those involved would abandon the idea of East–West collaboration within the framework of an all-European union. They would concentrate on integration in Western Europe alone. But in doing so, as we will see, they would often find their allies as stubborn as the Soviets had been. This problem had been evident in Clayton's talks with the British. It would become even more apparent when representatives of the non-Communist countries met in Paris to draft the "joint" program Marshall had demanded.

Problems of Relief, Rehabilitation, and Reconstruction of Europe, May 29, 1947, *FRUS, 1947*, 3:234–6; and Bullock, *Bevin*, 406.

2

Paths to plenty: European recovery planning and the American policy compromise

I

AT THE TIME of the three-power conference in Paris, the State Department had not devised a concrete *plan* for stabilizing Europe. Instead of a plan, there had emerged an emphasis on European initiative in drafting a recovery program, a determination to provide the Europeans with limited "friendly aid" in the drafting process, and a set of principles to guide European and American action. In addition to maximum self-help, mutual aid, and resource sharing, American leaders were talking about the importance of liberalizing intra-European trade, making currencies convertible, and using central institutions to coordinate national policies. A comprehensive recovery plan founded on such concepts, or so the Americans assumed, would erase the traditional territorial constraints on European enterprise, abolish old habits of bilateralism and restrictionism, and eliminate archaic concerns with national self-sufficiency and autonomy. These attributes were seen as barriers to maximum productivity, and they were to give way now to a large, functionally ordered, and organically integrated economy similar to the one that existed in the United States. This was the American way to stable abundance and social peace in Western Europe and to a fully multilateral system of world trade.

Together with supranational institutions of coordination and control, economic integration would also help to build a viable balance of power among the states of Western Europe and a workable correlation of forces on the Continent. It would create a unit coherent enough to harness Germany's industrial strength without restoring its prewar dominance and strong enough to countervail the Soviet bloc in Eastern Europe. Seen in this light, integration had emerged as both an economic and a strategic concept, and putting this concept into operation had become even more important after the Soviets turned their backs on the second American effort to rebuild Europe in the image of the United States.

Obstacles to the American design existed in other quarters as well, how-ever, and these would become more apparent when non-Communist leaders from both sides of the Atlantic met in Paris and Washington to draft a recovery plan. Indeed, the very process of planning worked like a super-heated crucible to agitate differences only intimated earlier. The Europeans were skeptical of a recovery strategy that meant transcending sovereignties and subordinating national interests to the needs of Europe as a whole. Their recovery planning often aimed to re-create the Continent's segmented prewar economic structure, a development that eventually forced American policymakers to modify their emphasis on European responsibility and play a greater role than expected in drafting the European program. In the Amer-ican camp, on the other hand, there were disagreements over the political constraints on policy, over the best way to optimize output and integrate economies, and over the degree of free-market initiative and supranational control that should be involved. Out of these disagreements finally emerged a composite strategy that relied on both market forces and administrative mechanisms. This strategy would remain a central component of the New Deal policy synthesis that guided American Marshall Planners once the recovery program went into operation. And because previous accounts have failed to describe its development or to explore fully the European and American differences involved, it is important to discuss both issues with care.

II

Following Molotov's retreat from the Paris conference, Western leaders speculated on the motives behind Soviet policy and the meaning of this policy for the future of Europe. Marshall's proposal had been popular, which meant that Molotov's withdrawal had isolated the Communists. Bevin and Bidault wondered if the Soviets had miscalculated. Or did they consider Europe's economic condition beyond repair? Did they believe that congres-sional tardiness, economic recession, or resurgent isolationism would pre-vent the United States from acting swiftly? Were they holding themselves aloof in order to reap the benefits of a failed American initiative? Whatever the answers, Marshall's proposal and Molotov's retreat had divided the Continent into hostile blocs. Policymakers on both sides of the Atlantic now expected the Soviet Union, together with its Communist supporters in the West, to do everything possible to retard recovery and sabotage the Marshall Plan.[1]

[1]   See, for example, Ambassador Jefferson Caffery, Paris, tel. to Marshall, July 3, 1947, and Ambassador Lewis Douglas, London, tel. to Marshall, July 4, 1947, *FRUS, 1947*, 3:308–9, 310–12; Douglas tels. #3719 and #3743 to Marshall, July 8, 1947, RG 59, file: 840.50Recovery/7-847; and Douglas tel. to Marshall, undated (received July 19, 1947), RG 59, file: 840.50Recovery/7-1947. For similar thinking in the United

This realization lent new urgency to policy planning in Europe and the United States. In Washington, President Truman had already appointed three fact-finding committees to investigate the resources available for an aid program and the impact of this program on the American economy. The most important of these was the President's Committee on Foreign Aid, a nonpartisan group headed by Secretary of Commerce Averell Harriman and composed of university experts and representatives from organized business, labor, and agriculture. All three boards established liaisons with the State Department, where policymakers hoped the new committees, especially the so-called Harriman Committee, would help to dissipate public doubts about the capacity of the United States to sustain a massive recovery program and mobilize congressional and public support behind the Marshall Plan.[2]

In the State Department, meanwhile, planning for European recovery went forward in George Kennan's Policy Planning Staff and in the new Committee on the European Recovery Program. The Recovery Committee, known informally as the "Board of Directors" or the "Tuesday–Thursday Group," had been organized in late June to consider Marshall's recent proposal. Chaired by Willard Thorp, the assistant secretary of state for economic affairs, it met every Tuesday and Thursday evening in the Old State Department Building and was composed of representatives from every departmental office concerned with European recovery. Among its members there was broad agreement on the need to integrate economies and put Western Europe on a self-supporting basis over a three- or four-year period. To achieve these goals while limiting the financial burden on American taxpayers, those involved thought the United States should concentrate on short-term commodity assistance, leave the World Bank responsible for long-term modernization loans, retain a veto over the distribution of its aid, and negotiate bilateral agreements binding each of the participating countries to the principles of self-help and joint programming.[3]

States, see Robert G. Hooker, Jr., memorandum for Mr. Thompson, July 14, 1947, RG 59, file: 840.50Recovery/7-1447; and memorandum by the Policy Planning Staff, July 21?, 1947, *FRUS, 1947*, 3:335–7.

2 For the origins and work of these three committees, see PPS/3, "Studies Relating to the Impact of Aid to Foreign Countries on U.S. Domestic Economy and Natural Resources," June 19, 1947, RG 59, PPS Records, box 3, *Reports and Recommendations, 1947*, Vol. 1; Marshall and Harriman Memorandum for the President, June 19, 1947, Truman Papers, President's Confidential File (hereafter cited as CF with folder designation), folder: State Department, 1946–47; Statement Issued to the Press by the White House, June 22, 1947, *FRUS, 1947*, 3:264–6; and Thorp memorandum to Kennan, June 30, 1947, RG 59, PPS Records, box 9, folder: Economic Policy.

3 For the origins and membership of the Recovery Committee, see Ben T. Moore letter to Clair Wilcox, July 28, 1947, Records of the Committee on the European Recovery Program, RG 353, Lot 122, box 26, folder: 5.17.10, ERP Subject File, Board of Directors; and Committee on the European Recovery Program, Minutes of Meeting, June 25, 1947, RG 353, Lot 122, box 26, folder: REP Minutes. For the agreement

Beyond these points, however, there were important disputes between free-traders and planners over the best way to enhance production and foster integration. Advocates of free trade wanted to replace the patchwork pattern of nonconvertible currencies and bilateral commercial agreements with a currency-clearing scheme and a customs union. These reforms would presumably liberate enterprise from the shackles of a segmented economy and allow normal market mechanisms to forge a rational pattern of European production and trade. For the planners, on the other hand, neither a customs union nor a clearing scheme would be practical until production had revived. Negotiating them now would only lead to enervating controversies over the internal financial reforms and national tariff adjustments that would be needed to bring such mechanisms into existence – controversies that could further destabilize Western European politics and work to the advantage of the Communists. To avoid these dangers, the planners wanted to concentrate on restoring Europe's existing industries, increasing production in bottleneck areas, reducing the most flagrant restrictions on intra-European trade and payments, and building supranational coordinators to engineer a functional integration of the European economies.[4]

These debates finally resulted in a compromise that favored the planners' approach – in other words, one that looked to both transnational planning and market incentives to integrate economies and increase production. The United States would support a European customs union and currency-clearing scheme. But these were long-term reforms to be achieved once the present obstacles to production and trade had been removed. In the short term, the United States should insist on a supranational planning authority with the power to allocate resources, set production targets, and foster integration. It should also provide basic grants for essential commodities and capital equipment that would bring immediate gains in production. And as production increased, it should encourage European leaders to permit normal market mechanisms to eliminate uneconomic forms of production and apportion resources on a rational basis.[5]

on substantive issues among members of the Recovery Committee, see the sources cited in notes 4 and 5.

4   This analysis is based on the discussions in the Recovery Committee's first six meetings and on several of the many documents that the committee considered. See Committee on the European Recovery Program, Minutes of Meetings, June 25 and July 1, 3, 8, 10, and 15, 1947, RG 353, Lot 122, box 26, folder: REP Minutes; and Charles P. Kindleberger, "Scope of Secretary Marshall's Suggestion to Europe," July 2, 1947 (REP D-4/8), Thorp undated memorandum to Kennan (REP D-4/12), unsigned, undated "Impediments to Intra-European Trade" (REP D-3/2), and unsigned, undated "Note on a European Customs Union" (REP D-3/5), all in RG 353, Lot 122, box 27, folder: REP Documents.

5   In addition to the Minutes of Meetings cited in note 4, see Committee on the European Recovery Program, Minutes of Meetings, July 24 and 31, 1947, RG 353, Lot 122, box 26, folder: REP Minutes; and undated memorandum by Kindleberger, "Problems of Procedure in U.S. Aid to Europe" (REP D-15, later renumbered as REP D-16/11),

Thinking in the Policy Planning Staff ran along similar lines. By mid-July, the staff had finished a hefty paper entitled "Certain Aspects of the European Recovery Problem from the United States Standpoint." The paper reviewed the causes of Western Europe's distress and the factors that impeded recovery. It noted how continued deterioration there could strengthen the Communists and imperil American interests, explained why these interests made a comprehensive aid program imperative, and went on to offer recommendations that generally paralleled those emerging from the Recovery Committee.[6] The United States, as Kennan had explained earlier, should follow the "functional approach" and concentrate its aid on "key" sectors that lent themselves to "treatment on an overall European basis."[7]

The Policy Planning Staff and the Recovery Committee also adopted similar positions toward Great Britain and western Germany, stressing in each case the familiar themes of production and integration. They agreed that Britain must occupy a unique position in the recovery program, partly because of its great dependence on extra-European trade, partly because it would be difficult to reconcile the British system of imperial preference with American designs for an integrated Europe, and partly because any shortage of outside assistance might compel the financially beleaguered British to adopt restrictive commercial policies that would retard recovery and wreck American efforts to build a multilateral system of world trade. But they also wanted to incorporate the British into a *European* recovery program, taking the position, as Clayton had done earlier, that special assistance or some form of North Atlantic union should be considered only if Marshall Plan aid failed to solve Britain's balance-of-payments problem.[8]

The emphasis on restoring existing industries and increasing output applied with particular force to western Germany, where economic recovery was still deemed essential to recovery in other areas of Western Europe, to political stability in the occupation zones, and to the restoration of a "balance of power" in Europe that Marshall had proclaimed as one of the strategic goals of American policy. The Policy Planning Staff and the Re-

and undated Kindleberger memorandum, "Problems of Procedure in U.S. Aid to Europe" (REP D-15/1, later renumbered as REP D-16/11a), RG 353, Lot 122, box 28, folder: REP Documents.

6 PPS/4, "Certain Aspects of the European Recovery Problem from the United States Standpoint," July 23, 1947, RG 59, PPS Records, box 3, *Reports and Recommendations, 1947*, Vol. 1. See also Kennan memorandum for Under Secretary of State Robert A. Lovett, June 30, 1947, RG 59, PPS Records, box 33, folder: Chronological, 1947.

7 Kennan memorandum to Thorp, June 24, 1947, *FRUS, 1947*, 3:267–8.

8 Kennan memorandum for Lovett, June 30, 1947, RG 59, PPS Records, box 33, folder: Chronological, 1947; PPS/4, July 23, 1947, RG 59, PPS Records, box 3, *Reports and Recommendations, 1947*, Vol. 1; Committee on the European Recovery Program, Minutes of Meetings, July 10, 17, and 24, 1947, RG 353, Lot 122, box 26, folder: REP Minutes; and undated memorandum, "Special Consideration for Britain under the Marshall Plan" (REP D-3/3), RG 353, Lot 122, box 27, folder: REP Documents.

covery Committee therefore stressed the need for new measures to revive production and make the Bizone self-supporting. Although this recommendation corresponded with thinking in the War Department, both groups also thought it important to reverse the army's policy of treating the Bizone as an American "enclave." The United States, they continued to insist, should balance recovery there against recovery in the liberated areas. It should adjust western Germany's production and trade to the requirements of a European recovery program and win support from other participating countries for the "supranational" approach to economic planning favored in the State Department.[9]

In line with this thinking, American leaders launched two important initiatives on the German front during the second half of 1947. The State and War departments finally persuaded the British to suspend temporarily their plans to socialize the Ruhr coal mines, placing them instead under a private German management that American officials found more compatible with their commitment to private enterprise and their plans to raise German production as an aid to European recovery.[10] At the same time, General Clay and his counterpart in the British zone completed work on the new level-of-industry plan that Secretary Marshall and Foreign Secretary Bevin had authorized following the failure of the Moscow Foreign Ministers Conference. Although the plan aimed to put the Bizone on a self-supporting basis, the State Department had tried to tailor this goal to its own approach by persuading General Clay and his superiors in Washington to dovetail bizonal requirements with the general European recovery program being drafted in Paris.[11] Both initiatives grew out of bureaucratic negotiations between the War and State departments, whose relations resembled those between sovereign states and whose compromise represented an uneasy reconciliation of the two directions in American diplomacy: the one toward a self-supporting Germany that would pull the rest of Europe along in the wake of its own recovery, the other toward a stabilization that would

[9] Committee on the European Recovery Program, Minutes of Meeting, June 25, 1947, RG 353, Lot 122, box 26, folder: REP Minutes; and Millis, *Forrestal Diaries*, 341. See also Kennan memorandum for Lovett, June 30, 1947, RG 59, PPS Records, box 33, folder: Chronological, 1947; PPS/4, July 23, 1947, RG 59, PPS Records, box 3, *Reports and Recommendations, 1947*, Vol. 1; Committee on the European Recovery Program, Minutes of Meetings, July 17, 22, 24, and 29, 1947, RG 353, Lot 122, box 26, folder: REP Minutes; Kindleberger, "Problems of Procedure in U.S. Aid to Europe"; and Melvin L. Manfull, Secretary to the Committee, to the Committee on the European Recovery Program, July 2, 1947, enclosing "Questions concerning the Relation of the US–UK Zones in Germany to the General Problem of European Recovery" (REP D-2/1), and the enclosures (REP D-2/2) in Manfull to the Committee, July 9, 1947, RG 353, Lot 122, box 27, folder: REP Documents.
[10] For this story, see the documents in *FRUS, 1947,* 2:924–5, 927–33, 940–2, 946–66; Gimbel, *Origins of the Marshall Plan*, 207–15; and Department of State, *Bulletin* 17 (September 21, 1947): 576–84.
[11] Gimbel, *Origins of the Marshall Plan*, 225–6, 249–50.

integrate German and European requirements within the framework of a comprehensive recovery program.

These successes were tempered by developments in Paris, where both European and American leaders were taking positions opposed to the State Department's strategy. Among the Europeans, there was great reluctance to accept the principles of mutual aid and joint programming or to sacrifice national interest to American plans for an integrated market. In the American camp, on the other hand, Under Secretary of State Clayton and other American officials in Europe did not support the supranational planning called for in the State Department. They put their faith instead in unfettered market mechanisms and, like the free-traders on the Recovery Committee, were more inclined to stress the importance of organizing a European customs and clearing union. These developments, as we will see, led to a showdown between the State Department and its agents in Paris and to a larger American role in recovery planning than accorded with Marshall's original emphasis on European responsibility.

III

On July 12, 1947, British and French leaders convened another conference in Paris to survey European resources and needs and draft a comprehensive recovery scheme. The results were to be presented to the American government no later than September 1.[12] Altogether, sixteen nations – Austria, Belgium, Denmark, France, Great Britain, Greece, Iceland, Ireland, Italy, Luxembourg, the Netherlands, Norway, Portugal, Sweden, Switzerland, and Turkey – were represented.[13] The occupation authorities provided the conference with information concerning the Bizone.[14] The Poles and Czechs, bowing to Soviet pressure, refused to attend. The Scandinavians were present only on condition that the conference not bypass the United Nations, interfere with their trade in Eastern Europe, or compromise their neutrality.[15]

[12] Caffery tel. #2667 to Marshall, July 3, 1947, *FRUS, 1947*, 3:308–9; and Caffery tel. #2668 to Marshall, July 3, 1947, RG 59, file: 840.50Recovery/7-347.
[13] Caffery tel. to Marshall, July 13, 1947, RG 59, file: 840.50Recovery/7-1347.
[14] Caffery tel. to Marshall, July 3, 1947, RG 59, file: 840.50Recovery/7-347; and unsigned Memorandum of Conversation, July 25, 1947, RG 59, file: 840.50 Recovery/7-2547.
[15] The Polish and Czech stories can be followed in the documents in *FRUS, 1947*, 3:313, 313–14, 318–19, 319–20, 320–2, 322, 327; and in Llewellan E. Thompson Memorandum of Conversation, July 11, 1947, RG 59, file: 840.50Recovery/7-1147. On the policy of the Scandinavian countries, see Caffery tel. to Marshall, July 10, 1947, *FRUS, 1947*, 3:316–17; American Embassy, Denmark, dispatch #234 to Marshall, July 11, 1947, RG 59, file: 840.50Recovery/7-1147; American Embassy, Norway, dispatch #1220 to Marshall, July 15, 1947, RG 59, file: 840.50Recovery/7-1547; American Embassy, Norway, tel. to Marshall, July 16, 1947, RG 59, file: 840.50Recovery/7-1647; and Memorandum of Conversation, July 15, 1947, enclosed

The harmonious spirit of the conference's first days soon gave way to acrimonious debate over the nature and purposes of the recovery program. Following an Anglo–French plan, the conferees easily agreed to establish the Committee on European Economic Cooperation (CEEC), composed of all participants, four technical committees to investigate the key economic sectors of food and agriculture, coal and steel, power, and transportation, and an Executive Committee to direct the work of the conference.[16] The British and French dominated the Executive Committee and tried to steer the CEEC toward their version of the recovery program. They urged the conferees to draft a program that concentrated on long-term measures of industrial reconstruction and modernization, arguing that only measures of this kind would put Western Europe on a self-supporting basis within three or four years.[17]

The French were particularly determined to safeguard their security by bringing the Monnet Plan into the continental recovery scheme. This maneuver would give their requirements priority over those of the Bizone and make France, rather than Germany, the economic and political center of an integrated Western European system. As a result, the French delegation in Paris objected strongly when the bizonal authorities provided an estimate of German steel production based on the revised level-of-industry plan. The plan called for increasing Germany's steel production to nearly eleven million tons by 1951, and for production increases ranging from 80 to 95 percent of prewar levels in such industries as metals, heavy machinery, and chemicals.[18] In operation, the French complained, the new bizonal plan would reduce Germany's reparation transfers, curtail its coal exports, and undercut the steel-production targets set in the Monnet Plan. It would revive Germany at their expense, they warned, which in turn would antagonize public opinion in France, strengthen the Communist Party there, and lessen the chances for French cooperation in the European recovery program. To lend weight to these warnings, the French delegation to the CEEC refused to accept the estimates of bizonal steel, coal, and coke production, halting

in American Embassy, Norway, dispatch #1236 to Marshall, July 22, 1947, RG 59, file: 840.50Recovery/7-2247.

[16] Caffery tel. to Marshall, July 13, 1947, RG 59, file: 840.50Recovery/7-1347; Caffery tel. to Marshall, July 14, 1947, RG 59, file: 840.50Recovery/7-1447; and the British Charge letter to Marshall, July 15, 1947, and Caffery tel. to Marshall, July 20, 1947, *FRUS, 1947*, 3:331, 333–5.

[17] Caffery tel. to Marshall, July 18, 1947, RG 59, file: 840.50Recovery/7-1847; Alexander Kirk, American Ambassador to Belgium, tel. to Marshall, July 19, 1947, RG 59, file: 840.50Recovery/7-1947; Caffery tel. #2884 to Marshall, July 20, 1947, RG 59, file: 840.50Recovery/7-2047; and Caffery tel. #2886 to Marshall, July 20, 1947, *FRUS, 1947*, 3:333–5.

[18] Ambassador Robert Murphy, American Political Adviser in Germany, tel. to Marshall, July 15, 1947, *FRUS, 1947*, 2:988–90; and Gimbel, *Origins of the Marshall Plan*, 225.

all work on the conference reports dealing with these commodities until British and American leaders agreed to tripartite talks on Germany's level of industry.[19]

The State Department wanted to meet this demand, although Marshall apparently counted on a British initiative to circumvent opposition from General Clay and his superiors in Washington, who were ready to deny the French even if it meant wrecking the negotiations in Paris. Bevin fell in with this strategy. He persuaded the Cabinet to postpone the level-of-industry plan temporarily and agreed to host a tripartite conference on the German problem. This is not to say that British and American leaders would make substantive concessions when the conference opened in London on August 22. The British had decided against granting the French a voice in bizonal policy, lest they use it to further their own ambitions at the expense of German workers and British taxpayers. The War Department had held the State Department to terms that ruled out concessions on Germany's level of industry. As a result, the American negotiators in London deflected French demands for stricter limits on Germany's steel production and guarantees concerning German coal and coke exports. Nor would they approve the proposal for international control of the Ruhr that now supplemented, if it did not fully supplant, the earlier French demand for international ownership. Their only concessions were renewed promises to integrate Germany's resources into a European-wide recovery program and to consider sympathetically a French plan for international supervision of the Ruhr coal and steel industries. Even these concessions squared less with French hopes for hegemony than with Marshall's statements at the Moscow Conference and the State Department's support for a balanced approach to European recovery and security. They dovetailed, in other words, with an American strategy that relied on economic integration and supranational regulators to harmonize Franco–German differences and build a Western European framework large enough to produce abundance and contain the Soviets.[20]

[19] For French complaints, see "Conversation between M. Bidault, Mr. Harriman, and Ambassador Caffery," July 15, 1947, in Caffery dispatch #9273 to Marshall, July 21, 1947, RG 59, file: 840.50Recovery/7-2147; and Caffery tel. to Marshall, July 11, 1947, French Foreign Minister Georges Bidault letter to Marshall, July 17, 1947, Bidault communication to the State Department, July 17, 1947, Caffery tels. (2) to Marshall, July 18, 1947, and Caffery tel. to Marshall, July 20, 1947, *FRUS, 1947,* 2:983–6, 991–2, 992–3, 993–6, 997–9. For French policy at the Paris conference, see Caffery tel. to Marshall, July 17, 1947, RG 59, file: 840.50Recovery/7-1747; Caffery tel. to Marshall August 6, 1947, RG 59, file: 840.50Recovery/8-647; Caffery tel. to Marshall, August 8, 1947, RG 59, file: 840.50Recovery/8-847; Caffery tel. to Marshall, August 13, 1947, RG 59, file: 840.50Recovery/8-1347; and Caffery tel. to Marshall, July 20, 1947, *FRUS, 1947,* 3:333–5. See also United Kingdom delegation (hereafter cited as UK del.) tel. to FO, August 6, 1947, FO 371, 62579, UE697; and UK del. tel. to FO, August 13, 1947, FO 371, 62416, UE8106.
[20] British Embassy, Washington, tel. to FO, July 22, 1947, Bevin memorandum to the Cabinet, July 22, 1947, and CM (47) 63rd Conclusion, July 23, 1947, PREM 8/495;

The London talks failed to bring France into a three-power consensus on the German problem. The appearance of consultation and the prospect of future concessions on the Ruhr were enough to end French obstructionism in Paris, where the CEEC began using the new level-of-industry plan to calculate the rate of recovery in the Bizone and the part that Germany's resources would play in a comprehensive scheme. But the French still demanded a recovery program that emphasized industrial reconstruction and modernization. They refused to adapt the Monnet Plan to the revised level of German steel production and the concomitant decline of German coal and coke exports that the new level implied. Nor would they endorse a Benelux plan to revive Germany's production and trade, seeking instead, as they had with Anglo–American policy in the Bizone, to remold this plan to fit the contours of French foreign policy.

From the start of the CEEC meeting, the Benelux delegates, with some support from the Scandinavians and the Italians, had complained that French policy amounted to seeking American assistance for national stabilization schemes. It offered little to those countries that counted on increased trade with Germany, to those that had escaped war damage, or to those that had achieved a substantial degree of recovery. On the contrary, they said, it would enable France and other states with ambitious modernization programs to monopolize American assistance and dominate European markets after recovery had been achieved.[21] As an alternative to the French plan, the Benelux delegates wanted to divert American aid to purposes more in tune with their national interests. Their proposals would revive Germany as a market for Benelux exports, yield less support for the Monnet Plan, and postpone the day when modernized French industry could challenge the lead that Belgium enjoyed in intra-European trade.

The Dutch, in particular, hoped to restore their prewar markets in Germany, and the Belgians sought to loosen the whole network of bilateral payments agreements and quantitative import restrictions that governed trade between participating countries. Belgium ran a large surplus in intra-

---

FRUS, 1947, 2:983–1067; and Gimbel, *Origins of the Marshall Plan*, 231–42, 252–3. A State Department memorandum made the connection between the American approaches to the Ruhr and the problem of European economic recovery: "It appears that the basic conception behind the American approach to the Ruhr problem ... may be realized, at least in Western Europe, through the Marshall Plan which aims at a coordinated and equitable utilization of key industrial resources in the interest of European economic recovery." See the memorandum attached to John D. Hickerson's memorandum to Lovett, August 23, 1947, *FRUS*, 1947, 2:1050–4.

21 Kirk tel. to Marshall, July 18, 1947, RG 59, file: 840.50Recovery/7-1847; Kirk tel. to Marshall, July 19, 1947, RG 59, file: 840.50Recovery/7-1947; James Clement Dunn, American Ambassador to Italy, tel. to Marshall, July 29, 1947, RG 59, file: 840.50Recovery/7-2947; and Caffery tel. to Marshall, July 20, 1947, and Caffery tel. to Marshall, July 27, 1947, *FRUS*, 1947, 3:333–5, 338–9. See also UK del. tel. to FO, July 17, 1947, FO 371, 62413, UE6153.

European trade. But the credit margins in most bilateral payments agreements were too narrow to sustain a further expansion and debtors, whose margins were exhausted, sought to safeguard their gold and dollar reserves by raising quantitative restrictions on imports from their creditors. These developments threatened the large intra-European surplus that helped to finance Belgium's recovery. The Belgians therefore wanted to use Marshall Plan dollars to widen bilateral credit margins and make credits transferable from one debtor to another. Initiatives of this sort, they said, would help to reduce quantitative import restrictions and multilateralize intra-European payments, which would then speed the process of economic recovery and hasten the day when participating countries could balance their accounts with the Western Hemisphere. At a meeting of financial experts in London, however, the British and French would go no further than a decision to appoint a special CEEC group that was to study ways of making intra-European trade more flexible.[22]

Although the British, as we will see, had their own reasons for opposing these measures, it was the French who raised the most strenuous objections to the Benelux proposals. The French took a dim view of efforts to divert Marshall aid from the Monnet Plan to the revival of German production and trade, as the Benelux had suggested, and their plan for liberalizing trade pointed away from the Belgian scheme to a strategy of integration more appropriate to the ambitions of the French government.

During and after the war, General Charles de Gaulle, Georges Bidault, Jean Monnet, and a wide range of other French leaders, including Hervé Alphand and a number of key officials in the Quai d'Orsay, had come to believe that a European economic union would be needed to support the French economy and tame the Germans in the postwar period. As we have seen, policymakers in the French government and the British Foreign Office had looked to close Anglo–French economic collaboration as the cornerstone of a wider European association. The two governments had established a committee of officials to study the prospects for such cooperation. Bidault had even gone so far as to predict that an Anglo–Western European bloc would emerge as an independent "Third Force" in world affairs, equal in power to both the United States and the Soviet Union. Similar ideas were

[22]   Caffery tel. to Marshall, July 20, 1947, *FRUS, 1947,* 3:333–5; Caffery tel. to Marshall, August 2, 1947, RG 59, file: 840.50Recovery/8-247; Caffery tels. to Marshall, July 31 (#3044) and August 1, 1947, *FRUS, 1947,* 3:341–3; Caffery tel. #3043 to Marshall, July 31, 1947, RG 59, file: 840.50Recovery/7-3147; and Caffery tel. to Marshall, August 9, 1947, RG 59, file: 840.50Recovery/8-947. See also UK del. tel. to FO, July 17, 1947, FO 371, 62413, UE6153; UK del. tels. to FO, July 18 and August 6, 1947, FO 371, 62579, UE697; Roger Makins, Assistant Under Secretary of State, memorandum to Bevin, July 31, 1947, FO 371, 62632, UE6877; UK del. tel. to FO, July 31, 1947, FO 371, 62579, UE6804; UK del. tel. to FO, August 13, 1947, FO 371, 62416, UE8106; and Milward, *Reconstruction of Western Europe,* 66–7, 76–7.

popular with important policymakers in the British Foreign Office, and with none more so than Ernest Bevin. But Anglo–French differences over how to handle the Germans, together with British concerns about political instability in France and about preserving the Commonwealth conection and close ties to the United States, had forced Bevin to take a more cautious approach toward Anglo–Western European economic integration than the one favored in France. Indeed, the Monnet Plan led many in Paris to the conclusion that only rapid progress toward some form of European economic integration would give France access to the raw materials and labor resources required to modernize French industry. Added to this was their determination to devise a strategy of integration that would enable France to control Germany's recovery, a determination that grew as American leaders laid plans to rebuild the bizonal economy and bring western Germany into the European recovery program.[23]

The direction of French strategy became clear in the early days of the CEEC meeting, when the French delegation urged the formation of a European customs union. It would take years to organize such a union, the French admitted. Nonetheless, they wanted the conferees to commit themselves to this goal and begin negotiations looking toward a harmonization of national tariffs. A customs union, they said, would appeal to integrationist sentiment in the United States, assure congressional support for the Marshall Plan, and bring the gains in trade and production needed to raise living standards and put Western Europe on a self-supporting basis.[24] Left unsaid were the special advantages that would accrue to the French, whose proposals for a customs union and for international control of the Ruhr pointed to a line of policy that would lead from the CEEC meeting of 1947, through the Finebel and Fritalux negotiations of 1949, to the Schuman Plan of 1950. In the case of a customs union, the success of this strategy depended less on international control mechanisms than on two other factors. Through a customs union, the French could work to reduce Germany's prewar tariffs and yet retain the quantitative restrictions on competitive German imports that would be eliminated under the Benelux proposal. This was one way to contain Germany and safeguard the Monnet Plan, the other being a customs union large enough to balance Germany's power against the combined power of Britain, Italy, and the Benelux countries.

If the proposal for a customs union pointed to a persistent strain in the strategy of French policymakers, then the reaction of the other delegations at Paris suggested the difficulties that would dog and finally defeat this proposal in the years ahead. The response of the British, Italian, and Benelux delegations depended inevitably on the extent to which the French proposal dovetailed with their own aspirations. The Italians wanted to negotiate a tariff union with the French, seeing this and the larger project as a partial solution to their economic problems and as a route to Italy's political reassimilation into the Western community. Although the Belgians preferred their own plan for liberalizing payments and eliminating quantitative import restrictions, their decision ultimately turned on the verdict of their Dutch partners. And the Dutch would join a union only if it included Great Britain and western Germany. Such a union would enable the Netherlands to reconstitute its important prewar trade with both countries and prevent France from dominating the group. For different reasons, then, both the Dutch and the French saw British membership as the sine qua non of any union – the key to a viable balance in the West and to a rational pattern of European production and trade.[25]

In the British government, however, there had been no resolution of the earlier disputes over the merits of an Anglo–Western European customs union. Bevin remained alive to the political advantages of this idea, and in August Sir Edmund Hall-Patch, an under secretary in the Foreign Office, suggested that European economic integration along lines "comparable to the vast industrial integration of the United States" might "go far to solve our own economic difficulties."[26] But policymakers in the economic ministries still thought this course more likely to exacerbate current difficulties than to solve them. Repeating arguments rehearsed the previous January, they saw it leading to transnational economic coordination of a kind that would prevent the Labour government from pursuing an independent course at home. Of particular concern was the government's ability to harbor British labor and industry from the competitive currents of the marketplace. This concern had led British policymakers to reject proposals, coming from the CEEC, for the coordination of national production. The same concern prompted sepulchral predictions of the destructive dislocations that would ensue if national tariffs were lowered and British industries, particularly the steel, chemical, and textile industries, faced ruinous competition from lower-cost producers on the Continent.

Adding to these concerns was a solicitous regard for the Commonwealth, with which the British did twice as much trade as they did with Western Europe. According to officials in the Board of Trade and the Treasury, joining a European union would surely bring a decrease in Commonwealth

---

[25] Regarding Italy's position, particularly its proposal for a Franco–Italian tariff union, see the documents in RG 59, file: 651.6531/8-747, /8-1147, /8-1247, /8-1547, and /8-2247; and UK del. tel. to FO, August 8, 1947, FO 371, 62552, UE7090. For the Benelux position, see Caffery tels. to Marshall, August 9 and 14, 1947, RG 59, file: 840.50Recovery/8-947 and /8-1447; UK del. tel. to FO, August 4, 1947, FO 371, 62552, UE6911; and UK del. tel. to FO, August 11, 1947, FO 371, 62552, UE7194. See also Caffery tel. to Marshall, August 20, 1947, *FRUS*, 1947, 3:364–7.

[26] Hall-Patch memorandum to Bevin, August 7, 1947, FO 371, 62552, UE7147.

trade without compensating gains on the Continent, where British exporters faced stiff competition from producers in similar industries. Nor could this situation be avoided by incorporating the whole of the Commonwealth into a European union. Such a course meant scrapping the network of commercial and currency arrangements that tied the Commonwealth into a large multilateral market where British exporters had preferential advantages and where payments were made in sterling rather than in dollars. It meant impeding recovery at home, aggravating the Treasury's already serious dollar drain, and increasing Britain's dependence on American aid. These conclusions, coming from the economic ministries and the Colonial Office, were reaffirmed in a report issued in August by the special committee of experts that Bevin had persuaded the Cabinet to establish the previous January.[27] The Foreign Office would seek to reverse these judgments in the weeks ahead. But given the current opposition, neither Bevin nor the British delegation in Paris could do much to support the French proposal.

This position put the British delegation under heavy pressure from the French, who still viewed European integration as a way to curry favor in Washington and tie Germany's economy to the cause of French hegemony. The British countered by insisting that French policy established the wrong priorities. European recovery planners, they insisted, should concentrate on raising production and controlling inflation before tackling such long-term issues as tariff policy and a customs union. They also tried to steer the CEEC away from the French proposal, first by proposing a customs-union study group that would conduct its work outside the scope of the conference, then by giving qualified support to some variant of the Benelux plan for liberalizing intra-European payments and eliminating quantitative import restrictions. In their view, however, the Benelux plan would have to be guided by the amount of American aid available, by the stability of national price structures, and by what each country could afford to import without dislocating its economy or risking its gold and dollar reserves. The British talked about eliminating import quotas gradually, starting with those on noncompetitive commodities, and about achieving convertibility through a

[27] Tim Martin, British delegation to the Geneva trade talks, letter to L. Barnett, Economic Relations Department, Foreign Office, July 18, 1947, FO 371, 62552, UE6282; Sir Stafford Cripps, Minister for Economic Affairs, memoranda of July 16 and 31, 1947, T236/808/OF265/2/4; UK del. tel. to FO, August 2, 1947, FO 371, 62552, UE6852; UK del. tel. to FO, August 4, 1947, FO 371, 62552, UE6911; UK del. tel. to FO, August 6, 1947, FO 371, 62579, UE697; UK del. tel. to FO, August 10, 1947, FO 371, 62552, UE7116; UK del. tel. to FO, August 13, 1947, FO 371, 62416, UE8106; UK del. tel. to FO, August 16, 1947, FO 371, 62552, UE7405; UK del. tel. to FO, August 18, 1947, FO 371, 62416, UE7440; Commonwealth Relations Office tel. to Dominion Governments, August 21, 1947, FO 371, 62416, UE7798; and Sir Sidney Caine, Deputy Under Secretary, Colonial Office, undated memorandum, "The Colonies and a Customs Union," FO 371, 62553, UE8359. See also Milward, *Reconstruction of Western Europe*, 235–41.

series of stages that would not culminate until 1951. They also warned that American dollars could extend bilateral credit margins, and thus increase intra-European trade, only if France and other countries adopted fiscal and monetary policies that curbed inflation and prevented them from absorbing a disproportionate share of Marshall Plan aid. In this field, as in others, moreover, the British were reluctant to give participating countries as a group the right to dictate national policies.[28]

These reservations hardened as the British economy deteriorated in the second half of 1947. The worldwide scarcity of dollars, the fuel and grain shortages that followed the winter crisis, and the rising cost of imports from the United States combined to slow the pace of British recovery and confront the British Treasury with a major dollar crisis. So did the Treasury's decision in July to abide by the terms of the 1946 Anglo–American loan agreement and make sterling convertible into dollars. By early August, Britain's dollar reserves were dwindling at the rate of $176 million a week, a clip that would exhaust the balance of the American loan by October and force the Treasury to draw down its final reserves. In these circumstances, the British delegation in Paris became more leery than ever of the Benelux proposal. They were in no mood to multilateralize intra-European trade and payments at a time when their own government was considering new bilateral commercial and exchange-control arrangements in order to reverse Britain's trade deficit and protect its shrinking reserves.[29]

By mid-August, progress at the CEEC meeting had been disappointing. The Benelux and French delegations had advanced proposals that came close to some of the recommendations emanating from the State Department, and following their lead the conference had appointed special committees to study the prospects for currency convertibility and a customs union. But these studies would not be finished before the conference adjourned. In the meantime, the British were dragging their feet on trade and payments policy, the French were refusing to modify their Monnet Plan, and the conferees as a group were unable to agree on a comprehensive program that incorporated the American principles of maximum self-help, mutual aid, and resource sharing. Unwilling to subordinate national interests to European needs, the conferees were following the approach Molotov had

[28] Cook minute, August 5, 1947, FO 371, 62552, UE6911; Note by the UK delegation on progress of the CEEC meeting, August 13, 1947, FO 371, 62416, UE8106; UK del. tel. to FO, August 15, 1947, FO 371, 62552, UE7394; UK del. tel. to FO, August 15, 1947, FO 371, 62552, UE7393; UK del. tel. to FO, August 15, 1947, FO 371, 62632, UE7395; FO tel. to UK del., August 15, 1947, FO 371, 62632, UE7282; UK del. tel. to FO, August 18, 1947, FO 371, 62552, UE7394; Commonwealth Relations Office tel. to Dominion Governments, August 21, 1947, FO 371, 62416, UE7798; and UK del. tel. to FO, August 30, 1947, FO 371, 62553, UE8053.
[29] For the British economic situation and American concern, see *FRUS*, 1947, 3:17–49. See also Milward, *Reconstruction of Western Europe*, 260–2.

recommended earlier, compiling uncoordinated lists of separate national requirements and doing so without regard to the resources available.

Given these developments, Under Secretary of State Clayton and other Americans in Europe began urging the State Department to adopt a more aggressive policy toward the CEEC. Because their recommendations did not always fit with thinking in Washington, where policymakers were more sensitive to congressional expectations and less inclined to stress the primacy of a European customs or clearing union, the State Department was compelled to spend much of its time negotiating policy differences with its own representatives abroad. This situation made it difficult for the Americans to give consistent guidance to the Europeans and probably contributed to the lack of satisfactory progress in Paris. Nevertheless, out of these policy disputes eventually came a compromise similar to the one hammered out between free-traders and planners in Washington – one, in addition, that finally set the stage for more vigorous efforts to bring the CEEC's work into line with congressional expectations and American hopes.

IV

Clayton had been on hand for the opening of the CEEC conference and in subsequent talks with European leaders had reiterated arguments first put forward in his meetings with Bevin and other British officials in London. He urged actions that would boost production and put Western Europe on a self-supporting basis within three or four years. The United States would help by providing essential commodities and capital equipment to restore existing industries. But the Europeans would have to do their part by seeking long-term modernization loans from the World Bank and by devising sound production programs, balancing budgets, and abolishing exchange and trade controls. They should also develop "in broad lines a type of European federation" that would "eliminate the small watertight compartments" into which the Continent had become divided, and should begin, Clayton insisted, by agreeing to eliminate all tariffs over a ten-year period.[30] Together with the champions of free trade in Washington and Lewis W. Douglas, the American ambassador to the United Kingdom, Clayton made the same points in a new round of talks with the British. In all of these discussions, the parties involved placed particular stress on the need to reduce tariffs

[30] Clayton tel. to Marshall and Lovett, July 10, 1947, *FRUS, 1947*, 3:317–18. See also Clayton tel. to Marshall and Lovett, July 9, 1947, Caffery tel. to Marshall and Lovett, July 11, 1947, Clayton tel. to Marshall and Lovett, July 29, 1947, and Clayton tel. to Lovett, July 31, 1947, *FRUS, 1947*, 3:315–16, 328–30, 339–41, 341–2; Dunn dispatch #1341 to Marshall, July 25, 1947, RG 59, file: 865.50/7-2547; Clayton tel. to Lovett, July 11, 1947, RG 59, file: 840.50Recovery/7-1147; UK del. tel. to FO, July 30, 1947, FO 371, 62418, UE6666; and UK del. tel. to FO, August 1, 1947, FO 371, 62418, UE6837.

and make currencies convertible, giving the impression that these were immediate items on the American agenda and inspiring the French campaign against Britain's opposition to a European customs union.[31]

The differences between these views and those in the State Department became apparent in early August, when Clayton and Douglas met in Paris with Jefferson Caffery, the American ambassador in France, Robert Murphy, the American political adviser in Germany, and Paul H. Nitze, the deputy director of the State Department's Division of Commercial Policy and a member of its Committee on the European Recovery Program.[32] Nitze summarized the thinking in the Recovery Committee and reviewed the Policy Planning Staff's recent paper, whereupon Clayton and the ambassadors approved the paper but went on to express views not fully parallel with the policy compromise that had emerged in Washington. Clayton and the others placed greater emphasis on the possibility that supranational planning could be used to revive prewar cartels or extend statist controls, and on the need for trade and monetary reforms that would set the stage for a European customs and clearing union. The Europeans, they insisted, should abandon costly social programs, "stabilize their money," fix "proper exchange rates," and agree in principle to reduce and eventually eliminate "all tariffs and trade barriers."[33]

These goals were the remedies for Europe's malaise, and they were the ones that Clayton and the ambassadors thought the United States must now prescribe. European leaders were slighting the American principles, unwilling, so it seemed, to transcend sovereignties and make the "hard-core" adjustments needed to revive production, increase trade, and integrate economies. They were adopting instead the "Molotov approach" and treating American aid as a "pork-barrel." As a result, Clayton and the ambassadors

[31]　In addition to the last two documents cited in note 30, see Balfour tel. to FO, July 31, 1947, FO 371, 62415, UE6810; Makins Record of Conversation [with Ambassador Douglas], August 15, 1947, Hall-Patch minute, August 16, 1947, and UK del. tel. to FO, August 19, 1947, FO 371, 62552, UE7560 and UE7461; and Harold Wilson, President of the Board of Trade, note of a conversation with Clayton, August 18, 1947, FO 371, 62416, UE7709.

[32]　Nitze had been sent over as a result of a recommendation by the Committee on the European Recovery Program. See its Minutes of Meeting, July 24, 1947, RG 353, Lot 122, box 26, folder: REP Minutes. See also Marshall tel. to the American Consulate, Geneva, for Clayton from Nitze, July 30, 1947, RG 59, file: 840.50Recovery/7-3047.

[33]　Memorandum by Wesley C. Haraldson of the Office of the United States Political Adviser for Germany, August 8, 1947, *FRUS, 1947,* 3:343–4, 345–50. See also Clayton, Caffery, Douglas, Murphy, and Nitze tel. to Marshall and Lovett, August 6, 1947, *FRUS, 1947,* 3:343–4; and Nitze's report on his conversations in Paris in Committee on the European Recovery Program, Minutes of Meeting, August 12, 1947, RG 353, Lot 122, box 26, folder: REP Minutes. For a summary of Ambassador Douglas's views, see Douglas tel. to Lovett, July 18, 1947, RG 59, file: 841.51/7-1847.

agreed, the State Department must discard its commitment to European initiative, list the reforms it expected, and make these reforms the *"quid pro quo"* of American aid.[34] For Clayton, in particular, the billions of dollars that the United States was investing in European stabilization gave it the right, even the "duty," to demand the internal adjustments and cooperative action that would lift European trade and production out of the "morass of bilateralism and restrictionism."[35]

Under Secretary of State Robert A. Lovett, who now directed the chorus of recovery planners in Washington, carefully delineated the lines of harmony and discord between his views and those of the Americans in Paris. One of several Wall Street bankers on loan to the government from Brown Bros., Harriman, Lovett knew the terms of a good investment when he saw them. He did not doubt that European leaders were paying too little attention to the integrating principles of self-help, mutual aid, and joint programming. Nor did he quarrel with Clayton's emphasis on a three- or four-year recovery program that would revive production, restrain inflation, and limit the financial demands on the United States. The American people, he believed, could not be expected to support costly modernization schemes or a grab bag of national "shopping lists" that did little to balance European and American accounts by the end of the Marshall Plan period.[36]

At the same time, however, Lovett outlined differences with Clayton that were similar to those between free traders and planners on the Recovery Committee. Like the planners, Lovett did not believe that the CEEC should get bogged down in such complicated issues as a customs union and a clearing scheme. These issues should be considered eventually, but their potential for dislocating economies and exacerbating political divisions made it better to begin by increasing production in bottleneck areas, reforming finances, curbing inflation, and reducing bilateral barriers to intra-European trade. This was a course calculated to halt the economic decline that fostered communism. It was also one on which the Europeans might agree and to which long-term reforms could be appended.[37]

34 Committee on the European Recovery Program, Minutes of Meeting, August 12, 1947, RG 353, Lot 122, box 26, folder: REP Minutes; and Haraldson memorandum, August 8, 1947, *FRUS, 1947*, 3:345–50. See also Clayton, Caffery, Douglas, Murphy, and Nitze tel. to Marshall and Lovett, August 6, 1947, *FRUS, 1947*, 3:343–4.

35 Clayton tel. to Lovett, August 15, 1947, RG 59, file: 840.50Recovery/8-1547.

36 For the quotation, see *FRUS, 1947*, 3:357, footnote 1. For Lovett's views, see Lovett tel. to Clayton and Caffery, July 10, 1947, Lovett tel. to Clayton and Caffery, August 14, 1947, Lovett tel. to Douglas, August 20, 1947, and Lovett tel. to Caffery, August 24, 1947, *FRUS, 1947*, 3:324–6, 356–60, 367–8, 376–7; Lovett Memorandum of Conversation, July 25, 1947, RG 59, file: 840.50Recovery/7-2547; and W. Wallner Memorandum of Conversation, August 21, 1947, RG 59, file: 840.50Recovery/8-2147. For Lovett's concern about the cost of the Marshall Plan, see also Millis, *Forrestal Diaries*, 279, 282.

37 Lovett tel. to Clayton and the Ambassador, July 10, 1947, and Lovett tel. to Clayton and Caffery, August 14, 1947, *FRUS, 1947*, 3:324–6, 356–60.

Lovett and other policymakers in Washington were also more sensitive than Clayton to the domestic political constraints on American initiative. They wanted to preserve the appearance of European responsibility and avoid any impression of dictating to the CEEC, lest this be interpreted as a commitment in advance of congressional action. Behind the scenes, they had discussed methods of providing more American direction and were assembling, "as unobtrusively as possible," a small group of economic experts in Paris. But actual intervention could not come without a formal request from the conference and any discussion of the specific conditions for American aid, or of the reasons that might prompt its termination, must wait until Congress had authorized Marshall funds and the State Department had begun to negotiate bilateral aid agreements with the participating countries. Congress "must not again be presented on a crisis basis with a virtual commitment to any precise course of action," as had happened in the Greco–Turkish crisis. To avoid this, Clayton must stay clear of specific conditions, simply reassert American principles, and count on Europe's need for outside assistance to produce a unified and realistic recovery program.[38]

The results were disappointing. Clayton, Caffery, and Douglas continued to worry that a permanent organization would cartelize the European economy and to insist that American aid be conditioned on measures to reduce tariffs and organize a clearing union. The Europeans, on the other hand, still refused to transcend national sovereignties, permit the CEEC to examine country requirements critically, or adjust national production and investment programs to the needs of Europe as a whole. Neither would they take those measures of self-help that meant reducing living standards below prewar levels and thus risking political difficulties at home. Their work instead amounted to "an assembly job of country estimates," which, as Caffery pointed out, would merely re-create Europe's prewar "economic pattern" with all the "low labor productivity and maldistribution of effort which derive from segregating 270,000,000 people into 17 uneconomic principalities." By mid-August, moreover, the conferees were thinking in terms of a whopping $29 billion in American aid, and, according to their own estimates, even this amount would not make Europe self-supporting at the end of the Marshall Plan period.[39]

[38] Committee on the European Recovery Program, Minutes of Meeting, July 29, 1947, RG 353, Lot 122, box 26, folder: REP Minutes; and Lovett and Wood tel. to Clayton and Caffery, August 11, 1947, *FRUS, 1947,* 3:350–1. See also Hickerson memorandum of August 11, 1947, and Lovett tel. to Clayton and Caffery, August 14, 1947, *FRUS, 1947,* 3:351–5, 356–60; and Committee on the European Recovery Program, Minutes of Meetings, July 10 and 15 and August 7 and 12, 1947, RG 353, Lot 122, box 26, folder: REP Minutes.

[39] Caffery tel. to Lovett, August 26, 1947, *FRUS, 1947,* 3:380–3. See also Caffery and Clayton tel. to Marshall, August 20, 1947, Clayton tel. to Lovett, August 25, 1947, and Caffery tel. to Marshall, August 25, 1947, *FRUS, 1947,* 3:364–7, 377–9, 379–80; Caffery tel. to Marshall, August 22, 1947, RG 59, file: 840.50Recovery/8-2247;

More than anything else, it was this estimate of American aid that prompted a shift in the State Department's strategy. The figure, which equaled the aggregate dollar deficit of participating countries over a four-year period, stunned the Europeans as much as the Americans. Sir Oliver Franks, who led the British delegation to the CEEC, rushed back to London for consultation with Bevin. He subsequently convened a special meeting of the Executive Committee in Paris, discussed the estimate with his colleagues, and finally decided to let the Americans suggest where adjustments might be made. This decision launched the process of "friendly aid." In Paris, Clayton told Franks that the figure was far too high to be acceptable to Congress. He urged the CEEC countries to reduce their food imports, even if doing so meant lowering living standards, and to show greater progress toward European viability by the end of the recovery period. Lovett and other policymakers in Washington made similar points, stressing, in particular, the need for more effective screening and coordination of national requirements by the CEEC. Because meeting this need would involve the kind of supranational planning that Clayton and the Europeans had been opposing, Lovett also sent Clayton and Caffery a long telegram reviewing American policy and dispatched his special assistant, Charles Bonesteel, along with George Kennan, to discuss outstanding issues with the Americans in Paris. The goal was to forge a consensus that would clear the way for a forceful presentation of the American "requirements" to the CEEC.[40]

In his long telegram of August 26, Lovett distilled the main points of agreement between all American officials and then reasserted the key priorities in the planners' approach to European stabilization. The Europeans, he said, should enumerate "concrete proposals for mutual aid," set national production targets, and establish vigorous procedures for screening individual country requirements and for "correlating" these on an "area-wide basis." They should also establish a supranational organization to oversee this work and to coordinate, direct, and modify their plans during the recovery period. Clayton would have to swallow his objections on this score and proceed slowly in pressing for monetary reform, a clearing scheme, and a customs union. The last two would "contribute little to [the] immediate restoration of production," which was the best way to protect participating governments against the danger of Communist subversion. As for monetary

and Caffery tel. (#3452) to Marshall, August 26, 1947, RG 59, file: 840.50Recovery/8-2647.
40   UK del. tel. to FO, August 19, 1947, FO 371, 62580, UE7575; Makins minute, August 23, 1947, and UK del. tels. to FO, August 24 (2), 26 (2), and 27, 1947, FO 371, 62632, UE7796, UE7792, UE7926, and UE7851; Bonesteel memorandum, "Minutes of Meeting on Marshall 'Plan,'" August 22, 1947, and Lovett tel. to Marshall at Petropolis, Brazil, August 24, 1947, *FRUS, 1947*, 3:369–71, 372–5; *FRUS, 1947*, 3:375, footnote 5; Lovett tel. to Caffery, August 25, 1947, and Caffery tel. to Marshall, August 25, 1947, RG 59, file: 840.50Recovery/8-2547; and Lovett tel. to Clayton and Caffery, August 26, 1947, RG 59, file: 840.50Recovery/8-2647.

reform, Lovett argued that Europe's chaotic monetary structure was really a "symptom rather than a cause" of the Continent's distress, that reforms in this area must wait until production had revived, and that any reforms not grounded "in increased production" could actually retard recovery, widen "the cleavages among producer and consumer groups," and play into the hands of the Communists. The importance of securing these reforms would increase "as production expands and economies are stabilized," but for now, Lovett insisted, production was the first priority.[41]

Kennan and Bonesteel repeated the same arguments during their meeting in Paris with Clayton, Caffery, and Douglas, the result this time being a "common position" similar to the compromise worked out earlier between free-traders and planners on the Recovery Committee. The goals were a speedy revival of production and, as production revived, a stabilization of finances, a reduction of monetary barriers, and a "further liberalization of trade." Through the setting and meeting of production targets, the Europeans would reduce their requirements for outside assistance, place their economies on a self-supporting basis, and thus clear the way for long-run modernization projects and for such schemes as a customs or clearing union. Managing this process would require "concerted action" through a continuing European organization with powers to review national programs, adjust these programs to European needs, and direct "production, trade, and manpower in the most efficient and economic manner."[42]

On August 30, the Americans communicated these "essentials" to the Executive Committee of the CEEC. So far, they said, the conference results were "disappointing." The expectations of $29 billion in American aid and of a continued deficit at the end of the aid period reflected both an absence of concerted self-help and mutual aid by the conferees and unrealistic ideas about resource availabilities in the United States and consumer needs in the participating countries. The United States did not wish to dictate to the Europeans, the Americans insisted, but the conferees should realize that anything short of the American "essentials" would "prejudice the success of the entire Marshall program" in the United States.[43] Similar warnings came from the State Department's economic experts, known as the "Friendly Aid Boys," who arrived in Paris during the last week of August. They went over the CEEC's technical reports, found the results "unacceptable," and offered the Europeans a good deal of "very blunt criticism."[44]

[41] Lovett tel. to Clayton and Caffery, August 26, 1947, *FRUS, 1947*, 3:383–9.
[42] Clayton tel. to Marshall and Lovett, August 31, 1947, *FRUS, 1947*, 3:391–6.
[43] Ibid.
[44] Ben Moore letter to William Phillips and Paul Nitze, September 1, 1947, and William Bray letter to Phillips, September 9, 1947, RG 353, Lot 122, box 38, folder: ERP Subject File, Paris Conference – Comments and Correspondence. The "Friendly Aid Boys" from the State Department included Moore, Bray, Victor Longstreet, Harold Speigel, and William Terrill.

Nevertheless, the conferees remained as reluctant as ever to take measures that meant transcending national sovereignties or reducing living standards. The Scandinavians were opposed to a continuing organization that would circumvent the United Nations or create a Western European economic bloc. The British were opposed to action that might subject their internal policies and foreign trade to supranational control. The French were still refusing to adjust the Monnet Plan in the interest of Europe as a whole, and the conferees as a group were still compiling "individual country statements" that added up to more than the Americans thought they could afford.[45]

In the eyes of American leaders, further reliance on European initiative could not produce the ends desired. The Europeans, as Lovett told the Cabinet, were not being realistic.[46] As the Friendly Aid Boys saw it, the conferees were engaged in actions that would lead to "US rejection" of their recovery program or to a prolonged congressional debate that would "embitter European peoples" and cause untoward "repercussions" on the Continent.[47] As Kennan viewed it, the conferees did not have the political strength or "clarity of vision" to draft a new "design" for Europe. The Scandinavians were "pathologically nervous about the Russians," the British were "seriously sick," and all the other delegations in Paris were infected by the same lack of resolve and realism that afflicted the British. The State Department, Kennan concluded, would have to "decide unilaterally" what was best for the Europeans.[48]

This was the argument that Clayton had made earlier, and it was one that Lovett could now accept. Early in September, Lovett helped to establish the Advisory Steering Committee, an interdepartmental group that was to coordinate recovery policy in the executive branch. At its first meeting on September 9, he took the position that the United States could not support the recovery program emerging from the CEEC and must therefore fill the vacuum created by the failure of European leadership. To do so, the Steering Committee established a number of subcommittees to bring the CEEC's

45 Department Economic Advisers tel. to Lovett, Thorp, Ness, and Nitze, September 5, 1947, *FRUS, 1947*, 3:405–8. See also Clayton tel. to Marshall and Lovett, August 31, 1947, *FRUS, 1947*, 3:391–6; Department Economic Advisers tel. to Ness, Nitze, and Kindleberger, September 6, 1947, RG 59, file: 840.50Recovery/9-647; and Department Economic Advisers tel. to Ness and Nitze, September 7, 1947, and Lovett tel. to Clayton and Caffery, September 7, 1947, both in RG 59, file: 840.50Recovery/9-747.
46 Lovett Notes on Cabinet Meeting, August 29, 1947, RG 59, file: 811.5043/8-2947; and Matthew Connelly Notes on Cabinet Meeting, August 29, 1947, Matthew Connelly Papers (Truman Library), box 1, folder: Notes on Cabinet Meetings, Postpresidential File.
47 Department Economic Advisers tel. to Lovett, Thorp, Ness, and Nitze, September 5, 1947, *FRUS, 1947*, 3:405–8.
48 Memorandum by the Director of the Policy Planning Staff, September 4, 1947, *FRUS, 1947*, 3:397–405.

work into line with the American "essentials" and the State Department decided simply to tell the Europeans that greater sacrifices and "some mutual delegation of the exercise of sovereignty" would be necessary to produce a "workable program."[49] The result was a new phase in recovery planning.

V

The assumption seemed to be that the Paris conferees were handicapped by restrictive instructions from their foreign offices. On September 7, therefore, the State Department appealed directly to the home governments, urging them to accept the American "essentials" and instruct their delegates accordingly. They were also urged to postpone their planned reception of the CEEC's report, now scheduled for September 15; to continue the conference long enough to bring the general report, if not its technical supplements, into line with American thinking; and then to transmit the results as a "preliminary" document subject to emendations and corrections by economic experts in Washington and Paris. The conferees, according to the State Department, had not done enough to incorporate national requirements into an integrated recovery plan for Western Europe as a whole. The new procedure would give them an opportunity to correct this shortcoming and avoid the harsh criticism that might otherwise accompany publication of the report in the United States. At the very least, it would enable the State Department to describe the report as "preliminary" in form and "correct in principle," blame its deficiencies on the lack of time, and claim that revisions would render the final document acceptable.[50]

In a related initiative, policymakers in the State Department decided to submit the bizonal level-of-industry plan to critical examination by the CEEC. They had been disappointed when the occupation authorities, in responding to questionnaires from the conference, had failed to adjust Germany's recovery plans to the needs of Europe as a whole or to permit the conferees to alter bizonal requirements. This failure had made it difficult for the CEEC to consider the sort of supranational approaches that the State Department saw as essential steps to a cohesive Western European order capable of maintaining a stable political equilibrium on the Continent. The new initiative was designed to correct this problem. By permitting the CEEC to scrutinize bizonal requirements and make recommendations con-

---

[49] Advisory Steering Committee, Minutes of Meeting, September 9, 1947, RG 353, Lot 122, box 26, folder: ASC Minutes. The quote is from Caffery tel. to Marshall, September 7, 1947, RG 59, file: 840.50Recovery/9-747.

[50] Lovett tel. to Clayton and Caffery, September 7, 1947, *FRUS, 1947*, 3:415–17. In addition to the sources cited in note 49, see Lovett tel. to Marshall at Petropolis, Brazil, August 31, 1947, Department Economic Advisers tel. to Lovett, Thorp, Ness, and Nitze, September 5, 1947, Lovett tel. to Certain American Diplomatic Offices, September 7, 1947, and Lovett tel. to Douglas, September 11, 1947, *FRUS, 1947*, 3:396–7, 405–8, 412–15, 423–5.

cerning the use of facilities, the allocation of scarce materials, and the reactivation of industrial plant, the State Department hoped to encourage other participating countries to submit their own requirements to careful screening. They too should fit their national production plans into a regional recovery program and thus move toward a more efficient system integrated along functional lines.[51]

Opposition to these American proposals came primarily from the British. Although the State Department had hoped for British support in placing the bizonal level-of-industry plan before the CEEC, Bevin told Ambassador Douglas that western Germany had been brought into the recovery program on the same footing as other countries; its requirements had been adequately discussed at Paris and reintroducing them now would amount to criticism of the conference. Bevin had no interest in permitting the CEEC to determine the rate at which German industry would be reactivated. From the American point of view, he was just as reluctant to establish a precedent that might require the British to subordinate their national interest to American demands for European integration. Britain, as Secretary of State Marshall complained, wanted to "benefit fully from a European program . . . while at the same time maintaining the position of not being wholly a European country," a position the United States would justify if it sanctioned special treatment for western Germany.[52]

Despite American pressure, the British refused to budge on the German question and the State Department had to concentrate instead on its larger proposal to extend the Paris conference and revise its general report.[53] Bevin opposed this as well. He told Douglas on September 9 that time did not permit further revisions, that prolonging the conference would be tantamount to admitting its failure, and that neither Britain nor the other participating countries could make the additional sacrifices required to satisfy American demands. Further pressure from the United States, he also insisted, would "impair national sovereignty," lending credence to Molotov's earlier

[51] Hickerson memorandum to Marshall and Lovett, August 11, 1947, Douglas tel. to Lovett, August 21, 1947, Kennan memorandum, September 4, 1947, Marshall tel. to Douglas, September 5, 1947, Caffery tel. to Douglas, September 5, 1947, Lovett tel. to Certain American Diplomatic Offices, September 7, 1947, and Marshall tel. to Douglas, September 8, 1947, *FRUS, 1947*, 3:351–5, 368–9, 397–405, 409–10, 411–12, 415–17, 418–19; Committee on the European Recovery Program, Minutes of Meeting, August 19, 1947, RG 353, Lot 122, box 26, folder: REP Minutes; Bonesteel memorandum to Lovett, August 27, 1947, RG 59, Bohlen Records, box 6, folder: European Recovery, 1947–48; and Murphy tel. to Marshall, September 8, 1947, RG 59, file: 840.50Recovery/9-847.

[52] Marshall tel. to Douglas, September 8, 1947, *FRUS, 1947*, 3:418–19; Bonesteel memorandum of telephone conversation with Ambassador Douglas, September 8, 1947, RG 59, file: 840.50Recovery/9-847; and FO tels. (2) to UK del., September 8, 1947, FO 371, 62580, UE8350.

[53] See Douglas tels. to Marshall, September 9, 12, and 17, 1947, *FRUS, 1947*, 3:420, 429–30, 434–5.

charges and provoking opposition from nationalists and Communists across Europe.[54] British representatives repeated the same arguments to each of the participating governments as both they and the Americans worked frantically to rally the Europeans behind their respective positions. The Dutch and the Norwegians seemed sympathetic to the American proposals, but nonetheless deferred to British leadership. The Italians took the same position, while the French found it "quite intolerable that the Americans should suddenly address themselves in this manner direct to the sixteen participating powers and in this way risk wrecking the whole conference in its final critical stages." Only when the United States "made concrete offers of substantial assistance could they legitimately expect to discuss terms and conditions." Until then, Bidault told the British ambassador in Paris, France would not yield to American "pressure."[55]

Bolstered by the British and French delegates, the Executive Committee confronted Clayton and Douglas at a meeting on September 11. The Americans had by this time scaled down their original "essentials" to several, somewhat milder points. They asked the conference to continue its work and label its report a preliminary document in which participating countries would pledge to form a continuing organization, seek modernization loans from the World Bank, meet established production targets, and take concurrent steps to liberalize trade and stabilize finances. Following the British lead, the Executive Committee repeated the arguments Bevin had made to Douglas earlier, whereupon the meeting adjourned in what appeared to be a hopeless deadlock.

Later that day, however, Bidault suddenly reversed course. Apparently worried that Congress might turn its back on the Marshall Plan, he now urged the conference to continue for another month and to bring all of Clayton's original essentials into its final report. The British, Dutch, and Norwegians continued to oppose this course. But in a second meeting of the Executive Committee on September 11, they were coaxed into a compromise that the Americans then accepted. Under this compromise, the committee promised to continue the conference for another week, modify its report to reflect the points Clayton and Douglas had enumerated earlier in the day, and label the results a provisional document. The committee also agreed to recess rather than adjourn, to review the provisional report with officials in Washington, and then, if necessary, to reconvene the

54 Douglas tel. to Marshall, September 9, 1947, *FRUS, 1947*, 3:420; and FO tel. to UK del., September 9, 1947, FO 371, 62580, UE8385.
55 UK del. tel. to FO, September 11, 1947, FO 371, 62582, UE8451; FO tel. to UK del., September 9, 1947, FO 371, 62580, UE8385; British Embassy, The Hague, tel. to FO, September 10, 1947, British Embassy, Oslo, tel. to FO, September 10, 1947, and UK del. tel. to FO, September 11, 1947, FO 371, 62582, UE8431, UE8432, and UE8443.

full conference and reconsider its report in light of the Washington conversations.[56]

The British were disappointed. Although Bevin agreed to the new procedure, he did so only after delivering an angry denunciation of American meddling and a fresh warning against further "external pressure." The "clumsy American intervention" had created "an unfortunate impression of high-handedness," which he urged Marshall to correct through renewed expressions of confidence in European responsibility.[57] But no such expressions would be forthcoming, if only because they might imply a commitment to a conference report that still fell short of American expectations and might hamper American leaders at a time when they had decided to scuttle the emphasis on European initiative in favor of a more aggressive role in recovery planning.[58]

During the last days of the CEEC meeting, American officials worked as full participants in the deliberations. The Friendly Aid Boys labored with their European counterparts to correct details in the technical reports; Clayton, Caffery, and Douglas discussed major issues with the heads of the European delegations; and with the threat of congressional disapproval hanging like a shadow over the conference, the Europeans now bowed to the American requirements. The conferees agreed to revise the report's preamble, saluting in it the American principles of self-help, mutual aid, and joint programming, and using it to proclaim "a new era of European economic cooperation" in which programs of "concerted action" would ensure full use of available resources and productive facilities. They also agreed to reduce their estimates of trade deficits during the aid period and to finance long-term modernization projects through loans from the World Bank and private commercial channels. As production increased, moreover, "all possible steps" would be taken to restrain inflation, fix realistic exchange rates, and "reduce the tariffs and other barriers to the expansion of trade." Also included in the report was a French declaration proclaiming the benefits

---

[56] American Embassy, Lisbon, tel. to Marshall, September 10, 1947, RG 59, file: 840.50Recovery/9-1047; Caffery tel. to Marshall, September 10, 1947, RG 59, file: 840.50Recovery/9-1047; Dunn tel. to Marshall, September 11, 1947, RG 59, file: 840.50Recovery/9-1147; Caffery tel. to Marshall, September 13, 1947, RG 59, file: 840.50Recovery/9-1347; Clayton, Caffery, and Douglas tel. to Marshall and Lovett, September 11, 1947, Caffery tel. to Marshall and Lovett, September 12, 1947, Caffery tel. to Marshall, September 12, 1947, and Douglas tel. to Marshall, September 12, 1947, *FRUS, 1947*, 3:421–3, 425–8, 428, 429–30. See also UK del. tels. (5) to FO, September 11, 1947, FO 371, 62582, UE8452, UE8487, UE8488, UE8489, and UE8505.

[57] FO tel. to British Embassy, Washington, September 12, 1947, FO 371, 62582, UE8507. See also Douglas tels. (2) to Marshall, September 12, 1947, *FRUS, 1947*, 3:428–9, 429–30.

[58] Lovett tel. to Douglas, September 13, 1947, *FRUS, 1947*, 3:430–1.

of a European customs union and inviting the participating countries to join in such a union once their payments difficulties had been resolved and currencies were stabilized.[59]

The major stumbling block turned out to be Lovett's demand for a supranational organization. The Swiss still worried that a strong, continuing organization would take on the characteristics of a Western European economic alliance and compromise their neutrality. Nor did they or the British want a supranational authority to dictate trade and production policies. Such an authority, they said, would impair national "sovereignty," drive several countries from the recovery plan, and widen the "schism in Europe." To get around these objections, the British delegation suggested a joint declaration calling merely for mutual and voluntary consultation after the recovery program came into operation. Neither this proposal nor the objections behind it carried much weight in Washington. But Clayton, Caffery, and Douglas seized on European concerns in order to make another pitch for the free-traders' approach to economic revival and integration. The Europeans, they warned Lovett, would never consent to a continuing organization that had the power to allocate materials and design a new European industrial pattern without regard for national boundaries. Although the policy compromise emerging in Washington assumed that a permanent organization would work in tandem with free-market mechanisms to forge a regional economy organized along productive lines, Clayton and his colleagues in Europe thought the results more likely to be a "dangerous degree" of "planned" economic activity and new cartelistic arrangements that "frustrate[d] the ultimate restoration of natural economic forces." In view of these dangers, they said, it would be "much wiser" to reduce "trade barriers," fix "appropriate exchange rates," and thus permit natural market forces, rather than supranational regulators, to "bring about a community of economic interests and responsibility."[60]

Given this opposition, the State Department backed away from its initial

---

[59] Caffery tel. to Marshall, September 15, 1947, RG 59, file: 840.50Recovery/9-1547; and Caffery tel. to Marshall, September 18, 1947, RG 59, file: 840.50Recovery/9-1847. See also Caffery tel. to Marshall, September 14, 1947, Caffery tel. to Lovett and Bonesteel, September 17, 1947, *FRUS, 1947*, 3:431–2, 434; Caffery tel. to Marshall, September 19, 1947, RG 59, file: 840.50Recovery/9-1947; UK del. tels. (2) to FO, September 14, 1947, FO 371, 62582, UE8555 and UE8556; UK del. tel. to FO, September 16, 1947, PREM 8/495; and C. T. Crowe of the Foreign Office, "Report of the Commission on European Economic Co-operation," September 18, 1947, FO 371, 62586, UE8966.

[60] Douglas tel. to Marshall and Lovett, September 17, 1947, and Caffery, Clayton, and Douglas tel. to Marshall and Lovett, September 15, 1947, *FRUS, 1947*, 3:434–5, 432–3. See also Caffery tel. to Lovett and Bonesteel, September 17, 1947, and Caffery tel. to Marshall, September 17, 1947, *FRUS, 1947*, 3:434, 435–7; Caffery tel. to Marshall for Bonesteel, September 8, 1947, RG 59, file: 840.50Recovery/9-847; and FO tel. to UK del., September 4, 1947, and UK del. tels. to FO, September 6 (2) and 8, 1947, FO 371, 62580, UE8355, UE8300, UE8309, and UE8349.

position and settled for a weakly phrased provision in the CEEC's report. Under this provision, the participating countries agreed to form a joint organization once the recovery program had been launched. But the new organization would have none of the supranational powers for which Lovett and the planners had called. Instead, it would merely review the progress of the recovery program, make studies, issue reports, and generally "encourage" member states to take those measures required to meet the broad objectives of the program.[61]

On September 22, the CEEC finished its work and sent its provisional findings to the State Department. In addition to the various pledges enumerated in the general report and its preamble, special committees had been appointed by the participating countries to study the feasibility of currency convertibility and a customs union. The conferees had struck a compromise on the German question, one under which Germany's revival was declared essential to European recovery but was to be carefully controlled so as to protect the economic and security interests of its neighbors. They had also agreed to the cooperative development of hydroelectric resources, the pooling of freight cars, and the standardization of certain kinds of equipment, and had established such goals as rebuilding Europe's merchant fleet, restoring prewar levels of agricultural production, boosting the production of fertilizers and agricultural machinery, and achieving increases ranging from 33 to 250 percent of prewar levels, in the output of coal, electricity, refined oil, and steel.

European leaders offset these pledges and projections with numerous qualifications, all of which reflected their inability to reconcile national aspirations with the State Department's goals of economic integration and supranationalism. The general pledges to the American principles and to such objectives as trade liberalization and financial stabilization remained empty declarations grafted on the report in response to pressure from Washington. They were not backed by concrete measures to achieve them nor by a supranational authority that could guarantee compliance. Neither could the compromise on the German question conceal the unresolved tension between the divergent French and American policies toward Germany's role in the recovery program. According to the report, moreover, restoring existing productive facilities would have to go hand in hand with modernizing plant and equipment; fixing realistic exchange rates would require special stabilization loans from the United States; achieving internal financial stability must be balanced against the need to maintain high levels of employment; and realizing production targets would depend on American assistance sufficient to cover Europe's four-year trade deficit with the dollar area. The report estimated the deficit, exclusive of World Bank loans, at

[61] Caffery tel. to Marshall and Lovett, September 19, 1947, RG 59, file: 840.50Recovery/9-1947. See also the official summary of the conference report in Caffery tel. to Marshall, September 20, 1947, RG 59, file: 840.50Recovery/9-2047.

$19.3 billion. This sum was still greater than the Americans considered realistic, yet smaller than what participating governments thought necessary to become self-supporting by the end of the Marshall Plan period.[62]

Despite these shortcomings, the last-minute revisions in the CEEC report were important to policymakers in the Truman administration. At least they acknowledged the American principles and the American vision of an integrated and productive European economy. They also established procedures for continuing consultation between American and European leaders in Washington, which could be used to correct the flaws in the report and further advance American goals. In these ways, the report set the stage for congressional action on an interim aid program that had become increasingly important to American officials in the summer of 1947. Indeed, the importance of this program helps to explain the State Department's intervention in Paris and its subsequent approach to the European–American consultations in Washington. Through both initiatives, the State Department sought to shape a European policy that guaranteed favorable legislative action on a program of interim aid that was widely perceived as the first installment on the Marshall Plan.

VI

As the summer of 1947 drew to a close, policymakers in Washington became increasingly preoccupied with the deteriorating economic and political conditions in Europe. A British negotiating team arrived in Washington in mid-August armed with dire warnings of an imminent collapse of world trade and an immediate retrenchment of Britain's global commitments unless prompt measures were taken to halt the drain on its dollar reserves. The measures they had in mind amounted to suspending the convertibility of pound sterling, an action that would violate the convertibility pledge in the 1946 Anglo–American loan agreement.[63] American leaders, including Lovett and Secretary of the Treasury John Snyder, were sympathetic to Britain's predicament. Although they did not have much faith in the "low grade of [its] leadership" and were reluctant to encourage any "move further to the left" by the Labour government, they nonetheless thought it essential to keep "England in the picture," as Bernard Baruch put it, "in order to hold the rest of the world." Meeting this need meant arresting the decline of

---

[62] See Committee on European Economic Cooperation, *General Report*, Vol. 1, and *Technical Reports*, Vol. 2 (London, 1947). See also the summaries of the reports in Caffery tel. to Marshall, September 20, 1947, RG 59, file: 840.50Recovery/9-2047; Department of State, *Bulletin* 17 (October 5, 1947): 681–7; and "European Proposals for a Recovery Program," *International Conciliation* 436 (December 1947): 803–27.

[63] Meeting of Ministers (GEN.179/12th Mtg.), August 11, 1947, Chancellor of the Exchequer Hugh Dalton, CP (47) 233, "Balance of Payments," August 16, 1947, and CM (47) 71st Conclusion, August 17, 1947, PREM 8/489.

Britain's dollar reserves, because failure to do so would weaken the British position around the world, provide new opportunities for Soviet expansion, and make American "objectives in Western Europe and elsewhere" unattainable.[64] The problem was that suspending convertibility would embarrass the Truman administration in Congress, where elements in both political parties were critical of the Anglo–American loan agreement and hesitant to support further aid to Europe. To circumvent this problem, the tired negotiators finally concluded two days of round-the-clock discussions with an accord that effectively suspended both the obligations and the benefits of the 1946 agreement. Under its terms, the British would postpone further drawings on the American loan and then protect their reserves by suspending convertibility and negotiating exchange-control agreements with their creditors.[65]

Although this accord enabled the British to manage their balance of-payments difficulties, the situations in France and Italy were more intractable and could not be handled without resorting to Congress. The governments in both countries faced chronic inflation, high unemployment, a shortage of grain, and serious trade deficits. Their shrinking reserves would soon be exhausted and both would be forced to curtail imports and further restrict production. Such a course would almost certainly lead to political challenges from the Left and the Right. It might even lead to the collapse of existing governments and the emergence of Communist regimes, a development, in the opinion of policymakers in Washington, that would wreck the Marshall Plan and the related efforts to contain Soviet expansion. Remedial action was essential. But during the summer and early fall, such short-term ex-

[64] Under Secretary of the Treasury A. L. M. Wiggins, Daily Log, August 22, 1947, A. L. M. Wiggins Papers (Truman Library), box 1, folder: Daily Log, 1947, July and August; Connelly Notes on Cabinet Meeting, August 8, 1947, Connelly Papers, box 1, folder: Notes on Cabinet Meetings, Post-presidential File; Baruch memorandum to Snyder, August 21, 1947, Snyder Papers, box 56, folder: International Monetary Fund and Bank – London Trip to Second Annual Meeting, 1947; and Haraldson memorandum, August 8, 1947, *FRUS, 1947*, 3:345–50. See also Policy Planning Staff memoranda of July 21? and August 14, 1947, and Douglas tel. to Marshall, July 25, 1947, *FRUS, 1947*, 3:335–7, 360–3, 43–4; and Douglas tel. to Marshall, August 1, 1947, RG 59, file: 841.50/8-147. American officials did not think the British were doing enough to solve their own problems. See, for criticism of the British, Douglas tel. to Marshall, July 18, 1947, RG 59, file: 841.51/7-1847; Bernard Baruch memorandum for Secretary Snyder, August 21, 1947, Snyder Papers, box 56, folder: International Monetary Fund and Bank – London Trip to Second Annual Meeting, 1947; and Wiggins, Daily Log, July 29 and 31 and August 1 and 4, 1947, Wiggins Papers, box 1, folder: Daily Log, 1947, July and August.

[65] This story can be followed in *FRUS, 1947*, 3:61–9. See also W. S. Surrey, "Discussions with the British with Respect to Section 8 of the Anglo–American Financial Agreement," September 11, 1947, RG 59, file: 841.51/9-1147; Ness memorandum to Lovett, September 10, 1947, RG 59, file: 840.50Recovery/9-1047; British Embassy, Washington, tel. to FO, August 19, 1947, and CM (47) 72nd and 73rd Conclusions, August 19 and 20, 1947 (and tels. attached to 73rd Conclusion), PREM 8/489.

pedients as post-UNRRA relief, Export–Import Bank loans, increased grain shipments, and the return of blocked assets and gold looted by the Germans had failed to stabilize the situation in either country.[66]

The Marshall plan offered a solution, but because it could not begin much before the spring of 1948, the only immediate recourse seemed to be a special program of interim aid during the "Marshall Gap." Such a program had been under consideration in the State Department for some time. In mid-September, Secretary Marshall announced that interim aid would be necessary and would be "correlated into the general [recovery] program." Truman made the same points in a discussion with selected congressional leaders on September 29. Shortly thereafter, he asked a special session of Congress to consider new measures of stop-gap relief for Europe.[67] Congress eventually approved these measures, but the point to be emphasized here is the administration's decision to sell interim aid as the first step in a comprehensive recovery program that embraced American principles. This was deemed the best way to overcome congressional opposition to further measures of piecemeal assistance. To effect this strategy, however, the administration had to present Congress with a European plan that came close to American guidelines. This need helps to explain the State Department's pressure for last-minute revisions in the CEEC report and the decision, taken by the Advisory Steering Committee, to parallel and review the work of the Paris conference. The same consideration also explains the negotiating posture American leaders adopted in their talks with the CEEC delegation that arrived in Washington during the second week of October.[68]

[66] French and Italian developments can be followed in *FRUS, 1947*, 3:716–90 and 920–1000. See also Advisory Steering Committee, Minutes of Meeting, October 10, 1947, RG 353, Lot 122, box 26, folder: ASC Minutes; Lovett memorandum to Truman, October 13, 1947, *FRUS, 1947*, 3:478–81; and Ness memorandum to Lovett, September 10, 1947, RG 59, file: 840.50Recovery/9-1047.

[67] See the documentation in *FRUS, 1947*, 3:344–5, 345–50, 360–3, 410–11, 411 (footnote 2), 415–17, 472–7, 477–8, 478–81. The quotation is from Lovett tel. to Truman, September 6, 1947, *FRUS, 1947*, 3:410–11. For additional thinking in various government agencies and for Truman's initiatives, see Frank Southard, Director, Office of International Finance, Treasury Department, memorandum to Snyder, September 19, 1947, Snyder Papers, box 11, folder: European Recovery Program, Adm. File; Wiggins, Daily Log, October 2, 1947, Wiggins Papers, box 1, folder: Daily Log, 1947, October; Advisory Steering Committee, Minutes of Meetings, September 17 and 25 and October 2, 10, and 14, 1947, RG 353, Lot 122, box 26, folder: ASC Minutes; Committee on the European Recovery Program, Minutes of Meeting, September 18, 1947, RG 353, Lot 122, box 26, folder: REP Minutes; Connelly Notes on Cabinet Meeting, September 24, 1947, Connelly Papers, box 1, folder: Notes on Cabinet Meetings, Post-presidential File; Truman letter to Senator Styles Bridges, September 30, 1947, Truman Papers, OF, folder: 426 (Jan.–Nov. 1947); Charles S. Murphy, Administrative Assistant to the President, undated Memorandum for the President, Truman Papers, PSF, folder: General File – European Emergency; and White House Press Release, October 24, 1947, Truman Papers, OF, folder: 426 (Jan.–Nov. 1947).

[68] See, for example, Committee on the European Recovery Program, Minutes of Meet-

The Washington conversations again brought to the fore the familiar conflict between the integrationist ideals that inspired American policy and the concerns with national sovereignty that motivated so much of European diplomacy. During talks with members of the presidential fact-finding committees and the Advisory Steering Committee, the CEEC delegates sought assurances that the funds of local currency accumulated through their sale of American-provided commodities – the so-called counterpart funds – would not be controlled by the United States and used to impair the sovereign right of participating governments to manage their economies. They also urged the Americans to accept a continuing European organization with advisory rather than executive authority, guarantee aid sufficient to cover their deficits with North America, and provide this aid in the form of dollars, rather than commodities, without restrictions as to its use by the participating countries.

On none of these issues were the Americans very reassuring. They said that aid would consist mainly of commodities. Purchases outside the United States would be limited and restrictions on the local-currency counterpart of American aid would be determined mutually by the United States and each of the participating countries. Although the details of European programming and the functions of a continuing organization would have to wait until Congress decided the form and amount of aid, the Americans also made it clear that a strong organization, with some allocation authority, would be necessary during the recovery period. In addition, they whittled away at the CEEC's aid estimates.[69]

ing, September 18, 1947, RG 353, Lot 122, box 26, folder: REP Minutes; Lovett tel. to Clayton and Caffery, September 20, 1947, and Clayton and Douglas tel. to Lovett, September 23, 1947, *FRUS, 1947,* 3:442–4, 445–6; Advisory Steering Committee, Minutes of Meetings, September 9, 19, and 25, 1947, RG 353, Lot 122, box 26, folder: ASC Minutes; and Committee on the European Recovery Program, Minutes of Meetings, September 11, 16, and 18, 1947, RG 353, Lot 122, box 26, folder: REP Minutes. See also the documents labeled D-16/4, /7a, /8a, in RG 353, Lot 122, box 28, folder: REP Documents; ASC D-1, D-3, D-1/1a, in RG 353, Lot 122, box 24, folder: ASC Documents; Snyder undated memorandum for the President, Truman Papers, CF, folder: State Department, 1946–47; and Lovett memorandum for the President, September 18, 1947, RG 59, file: Memoranda for the President, box 1.

69 Chairman, CEEC del. to Lovett, October 22, 1947, CEEC del. to the State Department, October 27, 1947, CEEC del. to the Participating Governments, October 31, 1947, Lovett to Chairman, CEEC del., November 3, 1947, and Record of a Meeting between Members of the Advisory Steering Committee and the CEEC Delegation, November 4, 1947, *FRUS, 1947,* 3:446–50, 452–70; Mulliken memorandum to Kotschnig and Rusk, October 23, 1947, RG 59, file: 840.50Recovery/10-2347; Memoranda of Conversations, October 15 and 16, 1947, RG 353, Lot 122, box 28, folder: REP Documents; Memoranda of Conversations, October 21, 22, and 23, 1947, RG 353, Lot 122, box 24, folder: ASC Documents; and Paul Nitze letter to Douglas, October 29, 1947, Records of the Foreign Service Posts of the Department of State (Washington National Records Center, Suitland, MD), Record Group 84, London Embassy Records, box 1018, file: 850 Marshall Plan (hereafter cited as RG 84, London Embassy Records, with appropriate box and file designations). For a British

At the same time, American policymakers urged the Europeans to adopt the policy compromise worked out between planners and free-traders on the Recovery Committee and use it to forge the sort of integrated market that had been a factor accounting for the greater productivity and higher living standards in the United States. In addition to an allocation authority, they wanted realistic production targets, a bottleneck approach, and the fitting of national recovery plans into a European pattern of production and exchange – even if it meant, as Lovett told the CEEC delegation, "some sacrifice of national customs and tradition." They also wanted commitments to fiscal reform, currency convertibility, the elimination of quantitative import restrictions, and the eventual reduction of intra-European tariff rates. "American thought," as the CEEC delegates explained to the participating governments, was "much pre-occupied with the extent to which the reduction or elimination of quantitative restrictions and tariffs might bring benefits to Europe through the creation of a larger market and concentration of productive effort."[70]

The Washington talks ended without European–American agreement on such basic issues as the use of counterpart funds, the functions of a continuing organization, the details of trade and payments policy, and the scope of financial and monetary reform. These and other outstanding issues would have to be considered after Congress had acted and the Marshall Plan had been launched. So far as the Americans were concerned, however, the talks had been aimed less at producing a European–American accord on key points than at tailoring the CEEC's report to congressional expectations. With this purpose in mind, the State Department had simply lectured the Europeans on American requirements and had then made the Paris report, as one CEEC official recalled, "as attractive as possible for presentation to Congress."[71]

VII

Like the transatlantic debates during the Paris conference, the Washington talks had served to clarify the divergent American and European views over the nature and purposes of what eventually became the European Recovery Program. American thinking continued to emphasize the related ideas of economic integration and greater productivity. Lovett and the advocates of economic planning assigned priority to making the most efficient use of Europe's existing resources, both to revive production and to block Com-

account of the Washington talks, see the Foreign Office paper "European Reconstruction: Documents Relating to the Washington Conversations on European Economic Co-operation (6th October–7th November)," FO 371, 62675, UE12282.

[70] See the documents cited in note 69. The quotation is from CEEC del. to Participating Governments, October 31, 1947, *FRUS, 1947*, 3:456–61.

[71] Van Der Beugel, *From Marshall Aid to Atlantic Partnership*, 93.

munist encroachments. They urged policies that would break bottlenecks, liberalize trade, and integrate national stabilization schemes along functional lines. Clayton and the advocates of free trade argued for a currency-clearing scheme and a customs union, stressing in their argument how such measures would integrate economies and create a market large enough to stimulate mass production. The former strategy seemed to require supranational controls and economic planning to achieve its goals; the latter would rely on normal market mechanisms. But both converged on the twin concepts of production and integration, and out of this convergence had come a central component of the policy synthesis that would characterize American diplomacy in the years ahead. Although a customs union and clearing scheme would have to wait until production had revived, gains in production were to be accompanied by greater European efforts to stabilize finances and multilateralize intra-European trade. In the emerging American policy synthesis, such free-trade strategies were to work hand in hand with supranational coordinators to create an integrated Western European system.

The Europeans resisted both directions in American thinking. They would not make specific commitments to a customs union or clearing scheme, arguing, as Lovett had, that such reforms would have to come after American aid had revived national production. But neither would they make the sacrifices Lovett considered essential to optimize output. They refused to engage in genuine joint programming, adapt national production plans to European needs, or subordinate national sovereignties to the authority of a supranational organization. Europeans favored the "Molotov approach" and sought a recovery program that would limit the scope of cooperative action, meet their separate requirements, and preserve the greatest degree of national self-sufficiency and autonomy. Americans, on the other hand, wanted to refashion Western Europe in the image of the United States. They urged European leaders to replace old patterns of national competition and autarky with a new economic system in which transnational coordinators and natural market forces would combine to integrate markets, control contested resources, enhance production, and thus lay the foundation for a new era of stable abundance. These were the points of departure in European and American paths to peace and plenty on the Continent, and they would remain so throughout the subsequent history of the Marshall Plan.

3

European union or middle kingdom: Anglo–American formulations, the German problem, and the organizational dimension of the ERP

I

IN THE SPRING of 1948, American officials began framing the Foreign Assistance Act and working with their European partners to implement the cooperative commitments outlined in the preliminary report of the CEEC. Although the forum now widened to encompass congressional and private leaders, including critics on the Left and the Right, most of those involved were able to maintain the earlier consensus on fundamental points. Much of the discussion involved the traders' and planners' approaches, with policymakers still viewing a combination of these as the key to an integrated European order that dovetailed with the strategic and economic goals of the United States. In theory, integration would create a framework large enough to reconcile Franco–German differences in the West, contain Soviet power in the East, and achieve bipolar equilibrium. It would also enhance productivity in Western Europe, as it had done in the United States, without the arbitrary government controls that threatened private enterprise. The commitment to greater productivity was another component of the New Deal synthesis – a neo-capitalist formulation that also included Keynesian economic strategies and new patterns of public–private cooperation and power sharing.

This formulation, as well as balance-of-power considerations, inspired the defense of the Marshall Plan in Congress and guided American policy in Europe. But because it cut across national interests and more conventional categories of economic thought, it also became the subject of considerable controversy on both sides of the Atlantic. In Europe, controversy centered on French objections to Germany's revival and reintegration and on British plans to bring Western Europe and the Commonwealth together in a middle kingdom that would be independent of American or Soviet domination. American, British, and French delegations would press their respective positions at a second meeting of the CEEC in Paris and at a conference on the German problem in London, with one result being efforts by each to build transnational economic agencies that suited the organizational imperatives of its own foreign policy. In the United States, on the other hand, debate focused on the purposes of the Marshall Plan, its impact on the domestic economy, its chances for success in Europe, and the nature of the organizational mechanism that would be used to balance public and private power.

II

The Economic Cooperation Act – Title I of the Foreign Assistance Act that Congress passed in the spring of 1948 – authorized approximately $5 billion to support the first twelve months of the European Recovery Program (ERP). During the congressional hearings that got under way in late 1947, however, it quickly became apparent that the Truman administration and its supporters intended the measure to do more than revive the European economies. Their goal, in part, was to reconstruct the components of a balance of power on the Continent. This had been a goal when senior officials in the State Department dismissed the hopes of their junior colleagues for a great-power accommodation within the framework of an all-European recovery program. These officials had seen the Marshall Plan as an instrument of containment and subsequent events, particularly the Communist coup in Czechoslovakia, had done nothing to change their minds. Secretary of Defense James Forrestal made this clear when he told the Senate Foreign Relations Committee that "we are living in a world today in which there is imbalance" between the "two great powers, the Union of Soviet Socialist Republics and the United States." The ERP would "redress the balance" by rebuilding Western Europe and thereby filling a "vacuum" that otherwise might be filled by the expansion of Soviet power. It would create, he concluded, the political and economic "equilibrium which is requisite to the maintenance of peace."[1] Forrestal's conclusion is worth noting because its presumption of a bipolar equilibrium differed from the British supposition discussed later in this chapter and because the current literature generally ignores the parallel American presumption that containing Soviet power also required a major reformation of the European economy.

As had been the case since the inception of the Marshall Plan, the goal was to refashion Western Europe in the image of the United States. What this meant became clear during the hearings in Congress, where those who defended the ERP called first for the formation of an integrated European economy. Recalling the benefits that had accrued to the United States after

[1] U.S., Congress, Senate, Committee on Foreign Relations, *Hearings, European Recovery Program*, 80th Cong., 2d sess., 1948, 477–80 (hereafter cited as Senate, *ERP Hearings, 1948*). See also Millis, *Forrestal Diaries*, 341, 349–50.

the founding fathers replaced the Articles of Confederation with the Constitution of 1787, Ambassador Lewis Douglas urged the Europeans to follow the American model, abandon separate economic sovereignties, and organize "the type of economic federal union that we now have" in the United States. According to Congressman John Davis Lodge of Connecticut, it would be a mistake to "put Humpty-Dumpty together again" as it had been in 1938.[2] John Foster Dulles also thought the situation "ripe for a really creative act in Europe." Secretary of State Marshall told the House Committee on Foreign Affairs that European economic integration was "one of the most important considerations in the entire [recovery] program."[3]

Few people wanted to condition American aid on the development of an economic or political union, since any attempt to "coerce" integration would surely produce an adverse reaction in Europe.[4] Nevertheless, the consensus seemed to be that American aid should "play a very great part in promoting" European economic unity. The United States should continue to insist on maximum self-help and mutual aid by the participating countries, on a cooperative European organization to manage the recovery program, on resource sharing and joint programming, and on the internal and multilateral commercial and financial reforms to which the Europeans were pledged and which, in operation, would lead to a rational pattern of European integration.[5]

In theory at least, integration would lay the economic foundation for what the Foreign Assistance Act called a new era of "lasting peace and prosperity" in Western Europe.[6] It would create a "counterbalance to the Soviet system of police states," in part by establishing supranational controls over the contested resources of the Ruhr.[7] These controls would defuse the spirit of nationalism that had made Western and Central Europe the "cockpit" of "power clashes" and the "breeder of wars."[8] They would also make

[2]　Senate, *ERP Hearings, 1948*, 208; and U.S., Congress, House, Committee on Foreign Affairs, *Hearings, United States Foreign Policy for a Postwar Recovery Program*, 80th Cong., 1st and 2d sess., 1947–8, 155 (hereafter cited as House, *Recovery Program Hearings, 1947–8*).

[3]　Senate, *ERP Hearings, 1948*, 605; and House, *Recovery Program Hearings, 1947–8*, 108.

[4]　Senate, *ERP Hearings, 1948*, 605. See also Senate, *ERP Hearings, 1948*, 208–9, 900; and House, *Recovery Program Hearings, 1947–8*, 59, 1498.

[5]　Senate, *ERP Hearings, 1948*, 605, 108, 208–10, 212–13, 245, 298, 549–50, 587–8, 756.

[6]　U.S., Congress, House, Committee on International Relations, *Foreign Assistance Act of 1948 (Public Law 472)*, 80th Cong., 2d sess., 1948, Historical Series, *Selected Executive Hearings, Foreign Economic Assistance Programs*, Part 1, 254–72 (hereafter cited as House, *Executive Hearings, 1948*).

[7]　Senate, *ERP Hearings, 1948*, 586.

[8]　House, *Recovery Program Hearings, 1947–8*, 924; and Senate, *ERP Hearings, 1948*, 549.

it possible to revive the German economy, but not the German threat to Western European security, and to reintegrate the former Reich into what Dulles called a "solid front" not "easily reduced even by Soviet Power."[9] In addition, supranational institutions would help to harmonize national economies so that natural market forces could operate across the ERP area as a whole. This would correct what the Americans saw as a "basic" structural flaw in the Western European system – its division into a "multiplicity" of economic sovereignties – and would forge these sovereignties into "a large domestic market with no internal trade barriers."[10] Such a market would ameliorate the economic conditions that might lead desperate European governments to "accept a Soviet-dictated peace." It would also curb bilateral state trading policies that tended to "channelize and politicalize commerce," and would make it possible for participating countries to join a fully multilateral system of world trade.[11]

The attack on state trading was part of a larger contention, widely repeated during the congressional hearings, that European stabilization could help to protect individual initiative and private enterprise both on the Continent and in the United States. In Europe, it could alleviate the economic duress that encouraged experiments with socialist enterprise and government controls, experiments that limited production and hampered recovery.[12] In the United States, it could prevent the political and economic regimentation that would inevitably result from Western Europe's collapse and America's isolation. Without a prosperous and expanding European economy, or so the argument ran, democratic governments would give way to a coalition of totalitarian regimes tied to the Soviet Union, committed to state trading, and controlling major markets and sources of supply. The latter were strategic as well as economic assets. Their control by a hostile

[9] Senate, *ERP Hearings, 1948*, 588–9.
[10] Senate, *ERP Hearings, 1948*, 587; and Foreign Assistance Act of 1948, in House, *Executive Hearings, 1948*, 254–72. For expressions of similar sentiments, see T. C. Achilles, Division of Western European Affairs, "Thoughts on Western European Security," January 20, 1948, RG 59, file: 840.00/1-2048; Senate, *ERP Hearings, 1948*, 208–9, 245, 298, 756, 848–9; House, *Recovery Program Hearings, 1947–8*, 157–9, 322–6, 1442–4; and David Sarnoff, Chairman, Committee on Europe, United States Associates, International Chamber of Commerce, letter to Senator J. Howard McGrath, with enclosure, March 16, 1948, J. Howard McGrath Papers (Truman Library), box 22, folder: Marshall Plan.
[11] Senate, *ERP Hearings, 1948*, 588; and William T. Phillips draft memorandum on a federal corporation to administer ERP, July 25, 1947, RG 353, Lot 122, box 37, folder: ERP Subject File – Federal Corporation. See also Senate, *ERP Hearings, 1948*, 212–13, 245; and House, *Recovery Program Hearings, 1947–8*, 95–6, 322–6, 341.
[12] See, for example, House, *Recovery Program Hearings, 1947–8*, 73, 182, 224–5. See also Secretary Marshall's address to the Pittsburgh Chamber of Commerce, January 15, 1948, Lou E. Holland Papers (Truman Library), box 84, folder: Personal Correspondence, Marshall Plan.

power would imperil the security of the United States and force a degree of economic and political regimentation "incompatible with the liberty" that Americans had always enjoyed.[13]

According to those who testified on behalf of the ERP, the political isolation of the United States would lead to a militarization of American society. In a hostile world, the American people would have to live in an armed camp and bear the burden of skyrocketing defense expenditures. Defense appropriations might increase by as much as 50 percent. This would mean a permanent war economy with a measure of government control that could jeopardize private enterprise and produce a totalitarianism similar to that being opposed in Europe. These were the conclusions of Secretary of Defense Forrestal, Secretary of Commerce Harriman, and other witnesses, with Harriman citing the report of the President's Committee on Foreign Aid and warning of an " 'immediate and sweeping limitation of our economic and political life, perhaps extending even to our very form of government.' "[14]

Similar limitations would also result from the collapse of multilateralism. Allan B. Kline of the American Farm Bureau Federation noted the "close correlation" between "the volume of foreign trade" and the "amount of undesirable regimentation" placed "upon agriculture in the past."[15] Harriman predicted that a loss of overseas markets would compel the United States to make "far-reaching readjustments" in its system of "agricultural and industrial production and distribution."[16] Paul G. Hoffman and Wayne C. Taylor, speaking on behalf of the Committee for Economic Development, lectured the Senate Foreign Relations Committee on the interdependence of the modern world, warning that Americans could not "expect to isolate our free economy and have it work."[17] From Senator Arthur H. Vandenberg and Philip D. Reed of the General Electric Company came similar observations. Vandenberg asked a constituent to contemplate what it would mean "if the greatest creditor and capitalist nation on earth should find itself substantially isolated in a communist world where the competition would

[13]   Senate, *ERP Hearings, 1948,* 76; House, *Recovery Program Hearings, 1947–8,* 75, 224; Senate, *ERP Hearings, 1948,* 478–81; Marshall's address to the Pittsburgh Chamber of Commerce, January 15, 1948, Holland Papers, box 84, folder: Personal Correspondence, Marshall Plan; and Kennan to Lovett, January 22, 1948, enclosing PPS/20, "Effect upon the United States If the European Recovery Plan Is Not Adopted," RG 59, PPS Records, box 3, *Reports and Recommendations, 1948,* Vol. 2.

[14]   House, *Recovery Program Hearings, 1947–8,* 463, 75–6, 229, 382, 738; Senate, *ERP Hearings, 1948,* 478–81, 485, 487–8. See also Marshall letter to Senator A. Willis Robertson, February 11, 1948, RG 59, file: 840.50Recovery/2-1148.

[15]   Senate, *ERP Hearings, 1948,* 1118.

[16]   House, *Recovery Program Hearings, 1947–8,* 465. See also Senate, *ERP Hearings, 1948,* 249. Marshall made the same point in his address to the Pittsburgh Chamber of Commerce on January 15, 1948. See the copy of his speech in the Holland Papers, box 84, folder: Personal Correspondence, Marshall Plan.

[17]   Senate, *ERP Hearings, 1948,* 852.

force us into complete regimentation of ourselves beyond anything we have ever experienced."[18] Reed told the House Committee on Foreign Affairs that "government monopolies" in Europe would require a similar organization of trade in the United States, with the result being total destruction of "our free-enterprise system."[19]

A commitment to privatism thus took its place among the constellation of motives that infused American recovery policy. The goal, as expressed in the Foreign Assistance Act, was a recovery program that encouraged the unification of European economies, promoted peace and productivity, and served the needs of private trade and investment. Nor was it simply that the act contained sops to particular private interests or provisions under which American surpluses could be dumped in Western Europe.[20] Far more significant were the features designed to protect, even internationalize, the very system of private enterprise. Included here were provisions permitting the Agriculture and Commerce departments to control export allocations, on the assumption, in part, that these were the agencies most responsive to private needs and thus most likely to protect the domestic economy; provisions guaranteeing currency conversion for certain American investments in Europe; and provisions requiring the "maximum" possible use of private channels in furnishing technical assistance or in the procurement, processing, storing, transfer, transportation, and allocation of any commodity or service. Even more important were provisions holding the participating countries to their cooperative commitments to stabilize currencies, fix realistic exchange rates, and liberalize trade, all of which, according to American leaders, were essential to unifying Europe and reestablishing a free world trading system.[21]

Yet to stop the analysis here is not particularly helpful, since it is hardly a revelation to say that American leaders envisioned a recovery program that served the interests and met the requirements of their own political economy. The issue involved the kind of political economy they had in mind. It was this issue that stoked a heated controversy between left- and

[18]   Vandenberg letter to Malcolm W. Bingay, December 29, 1947, Arthur H. Vandenberg Papers (Bentley Historical Library, University of Michigan, Ann Arbor, MI), box 3, folder: Correspondence, Nov.–Dec. 1947. See also Vandenberg letter to Colonel Alton T. Roberts, August 12, 1947, Vandenberg Papers, box 2, folder: Correspondence, June 20–30, 1947.

[19]   House, *Recovery Program Hearings, 1947–8*, 578. For a similar argument by William Clayton, see House, *Recovery Program Hearings, 1947–8*, 334–5.

[20]   See Harold Lee Hitchens, "Congress and the Adoption of the Marshall Plan," Ph.D. dissertation, University of Chicago, 1949, 181–94; and Arkes, *Bureaucracy and the Marshall Plan*, 166–71.

[21]   Foreign Assistance Act of 1948, in House, *Executive Hearings, 1948*, 254–72. See also Winthrop G. Brown, Acting Deputy Director, Office of International Trade, letter to Roland L. Kramer of the Foreign Traders Association of Philadelphia, March 5, 1948, RG 59, file: 840.50Recovery/2-2148.

right-wing critics of the Marshall Plan and the Keynesians who supported it. This three-cornered dispute ranged over a variety of matters that must be noted here. Its significance to us, however, lies largely in what it reveals about those who defended the recovery program, about their conception of the American political economy, and thus about the American neo-capitalism they would try to replicate in Western Europe.

Left-wing critics such as Henry Wallace saw the ERP as the work of American monopolists and imperialists who were seeking to promote their interests at home and overseas at the expense of social justice and world peace. Wallace denounced what he saw as the invasion of government by private business and financial leaders who had turned the State Department and other public agencies into servants of monopoly capital. Responding to business concerns, the Truman administration had supposedly reduced the amount of aid to be made available under the ERP, turning that program into a relief operation that would do little to reconstruct Europe and thus end its "semicolonial dependence on the United States." Nor would the program end the alliance of European and American monopolies that dominated the world economy or destroy the great German coal and steel cartels that Wallace considered the major beneficiaries of American aid. On the contrary, its purpose was to crush the progressive political forces in Europe, whose concern with economic growth and social justice posed a threat to reactionary political and economic elites on both sides of the Atlantic. This it would do by enabling Marshall Planners, particularly through their control of counterpart funds, to violate national sovereignties and abolish the social-welfare measures, the government controls on trade, and the programs of nationalization that in Wallace's view were essential in Europe. In addition, Wallace rejected the strategic design behind the Marshall Plan, which he said would "repeat the Truman Doctrine on a European scale." The plan would divide the Continent into rival economic and political blocs and escalate international tensions. It would also disrupt the traditional pattern of East–West trade, thereby slowing the rate of recovery in Western Europe and perpetuating the region's dependence on the United States.

According to Wallace, moreover, the administration's proposal would lead the American people down a trail of ashes no less dangerous to them than to the Europeans. Aside from bipolarizing international politics and risking "World War III," it would endanger economic stability and democratic progress in the United States. It would protect the profits of the food, oil, shipping, and steel "trusts," but only by creating serious shortages, raising prices, and leading to antiinflationary measures, which, in operation, would reverse the New Deal and place an intolerable burden "on the backs of American workers and farmers and independent businessmen." The ERP, said Wallace, would become "the main political and economic weapon of monopoly in its assault upon the American people." It would be the excuse for business control of government and for cutting social services, raising taxes, busting unions, and taking other steps to regiment ordinary people to the demands of the American imperium.

To avoid these dangers, Wallace favored vigorous measures to dismantle the "trusts," regulate prices, and allocate resources in the United States, measures he also urged abroad, where the recovery plan he had in mind involved a $50-billion fund administered by the United Nations and used to support a "new deal" in Europe. The bulk of the aid would go to the victims of Nazi aggression, including the Eastern European states and the Soviet Union, which would overturn what Wallace saw as the "German-first" orientation of the ERP and prevent a dangerous bipolarization of the world arena. In addition, aid would be used to underwrite genuine programs of economic reconstruction and modernization and would be provided without political conditions attached. Together with international control of the Ruhr and the destruction of prewar cartels, these strategies would invigorate the forces of democratic reform and create an "expanding economy of abundance – free of the stifling restrictions of monopoly both at home and abroad."[22]

A conservative coalition of public and private leaders assaulted the Marshall Plan from the Right, proposing a variety of generally unsuccessful amendments that sought to curtail the amount of aid involved, safeguard the American economy, and forestall socialism in Western Europe. Republicans, mostly from the conservative western and midwestern wing of the party, made up the heart of this coalition in Congress. Although easily overwhelmed by a progressive bloc when Congress voted on the Marshall Plan in March, they nonetheless mobilized a dazzling array of arguments that anticipated the objections raised against the administration's foreign policy during the "Great Debate" of 1950. Senator Robert A. Taft of Ohio and former President Herbert Hoover led the conservative coalition. Both endorsed some form of economic aid to Western Europe in order to build what Hoover called "a dam against Russian aggression." They also emphasized that aid must be used to revive production and create an economic unit that included western Germany. Indeed, many conservatives assumed that only an integrated Western Europe could stand without permanent American props, which they saw as entangling commitments that ran the risk of involving the United States in another European war.

At the same time, Taft objected to the view that economic aid would help to sustain American prosperity by subsidizing exports and forging a multilateral system of world trade. He thought it more likely to create a "false prosperity which cannot be permanently maintained," as had been the case in 1929, when the Europeans defaulted on their debts and the export trade collapsed. In addition, both Taft and Hoover assumed that aid on the scale

---

[22] House, *Recovery Program Hearings, 1947–8*, 1581–1625. Wallace's views were endorsed by a spokesman of the American Labor Party. See Senate, *ERP Hearings, 1948*, 934–5.

proposed by the Truman administration would require stringent economic controls in the United States and would impose "serious taxation on our own people." It would create "scarcity and high prices and economic unrest at home" while undercutting the will of "European businessmen, labor unions, and Government officials to rebuild on the basis of their own efforts." Both men therefore wanted to reduce the administration's aid request. In addition to avoiding "coercive" controls in the United States, a reduced level of aid would discourage radical experiments in Europe and give participating governments the incentive to put their own houses in order.[23]

Henry Hazlitt, a conservative economist and commentator for *Newsweek*, elaborated the conservative critique in his testimony before the House Committee on Foreign Affairs. Following the path blazed by Taft and Hoover, Hazlitt denounced the trend in Europe toward nationalization of industry, government control of trade, and social-welfare programs, all of which would restrain production, generate inflation, and worsen Europe's payments deficit with the dollar area. In his view, no amount of American aid would revive Europe without the revival of unfettered private enterprise. The Europeans must therefore cut social programs they could not afford, stabilize internal finances, and end trade and exchange controls. To point them in the right direction, Hazlitt thought American aid should be conditioned on such reforms and should be limited to relief assistance equal to about half the sum requested by the administration. So far as capital goods and nonfood imports were concerned, the Europeans would have to meet most of their requirements through private American banking channels. Government loans might be provided on a limited and temporary basis, but only on businesslike terms, only to private enterprises, and only if European governments promised not to nationalize the enterprises involved, impose new wage and price controls, or prevent the conversion into dollars of any repayment on the loans. Any other course, Hazlitt concluded, would subsidize the statist regimes and socialist experiments that were the real sources of Europe's economic malady.[24]

Hazlitt sought to promote recovery by removing government impediments to private enterprise and exposing European producers to the bracing atmosphere of a free market. In this sense, the Right's critique differed mark-

[23] Senate, *ERP Hearings, 1948.* 707–12 (for Hoover's views); and U.S., Congress, Senate, Senator Taft speaking for an amendment to reduce the first year's appropriation for the Foreign Assistance Act of 1948, S. 2202, 80th Cong., 2d sess., March 12, 1948, *Congressional Record* 94:2641–50. See also Gary Dean Best, *Herbert Hoover: The Postpresidential Years, 1933–1964,* 2 vols. (Stanford, CA, 1983), 2:316–20; and James T. Patterson, *Mr. Republican: A Biography of Robert A. Taft* (Boston, 1972), 388. For a partial description of the conservative coalition in Congress, a discussion of the amendments proposed, and an analysis of voting, see Hitchens, "Congress and the Adoption of the Marshall Plan," especially 147–52, 179–91.
[24] House, *Recovery Program Hearings, 1947–8,* 612–58.

edly from that of Wallace and others on the Left, for whom the ERP was already a map on which Hazlitt's laissez-faire directions were carved in bold relief. Both the Left and the Right agreed on one thing, however: The recovery program submitted by the Truman administration pointed the United States down the road to ruin. It would exacerbate shortages and raise prices, resulting in a restriction of production and a lower standard of living. But whereas Wallace wanted to deal with these threats through government regulations and allocations, Hazlitt saw this course leading up the same blind alley the Europeans had taken. His fears echoed those of Taft, Hoover, Senator James Kem of Missouri, and others who worried that a massive government aid program would actually promote what Senator Walter George of Georgia called "a wholly new system of trade and commerce through state operation." In Hazlitt's political cartography, the best course was to slash several billion dollars from the amount of aid provided as grants. This reduction would limit inflationary pressures and government controls in the United States and force internal adjustments that would allow normal market forces to generate recovery in Europe.[25]

Defenders of the ERP staked out a position between their critics on the Right and the Left, rejecting the free-market nostrums recommended by Hazlitt as well as Wallace's dismal predictions. Some of their arguments, particularly their emphasis on reviving production, stabilizing finances, and liberalizing intra-European trade, had the backing of generally conservative business organizations such as the National Association of Manufacturers (NAM) and the Chamber of Commerce. For the most part, however, the figures who constituted the major source of private-sector support for the administration's recovery program envisioned strategies that went beyond those normally endorsed by the more traditionally oriented associations. The leadership of this group came largely from academic circles, from the major American trade unions, and from such business organizations as the Council on Foreign Relations (CFR), the Business Advisory Council (BAC), the Committee for Economic Development (CED), and the National Planning Association (NPA).

As we have seen, the last three agencies had taken shape during the depression and war years of the 1930s and 1940s. They had joined the CFR to promote the principles of multilateralism identified with the capital-intensive bloc of firms and great investment banks that represented core components of the New Deal–Fair Deal coalition. They also accepted the need for greater economic planning and for Keynesian strategies of fiscal

---

[25] For the quotation from Senator George, see Senate, *ERP Hearings, 1948*, 173. For Hazlitt's recommendations, see the source cited in note 24. For Senator Kem's views, see U.S., Congress, Senate, Senator Kem speaking against enactment of the Foreign Assistance Act of 1948, S. 2202, 80th Cong., 2d sess., March 12, 1948, *Congressional Record* 94:2618–38. See also the testimony of Merwin K. Hart, president of the conservative National Economic Council, Senate, *ERP Hearings, 1948*, 871–96.

and monetary management. In addition, the BAC, CED, and NPA favored corporative collaboration between private economic groups, including organized business and labor, and between these groups and government authorities in framing public policies. The NPA embodied this collaboration in its membership.

All four agencies played an important role in shaping and promoting the ERP. They published briefs on behalf of the program. Their spokesmen testified before the relevant congressional committees. They served on the President's Committee on Foreign Aid, or Harriman Committee, and on the Committee for the Marshall Plan to Aid European Recovery, a private, nonpartisan organization composed of labor, farm, and business leaders who worked closely with government officials to mobilize support behind the ERP.[26] The result was something like a coordinated campaign mounted by an interlocking directorate of public and private figures. Of the nineteen people on the executive board of the Marshall Plan Committee, eight were members of the CFR and two of these eight were also members of the BAC, CED, or NPA. Included in this list were Allen W. Dulles, president of the CFR, and Philip Reed, chairman of the board of General Electric. Former Secretaries of War Henry L. Stimson and Robert P. Patterson, along with former Under Secretary of State Dean Acheson, also served on the executive board.[27] Dulles, Patterson, and Acheson all testified in Congress on behalf of the ERP, the latter two joining William L. Batt, a Philadelphia manufacturer and a member of the BAC, CED, and NPA, to present the case for the Marshall Plan Committee.[28] Aside from testifying on behalf of that organization, Batt presented the similar views of an NPA committee that had investigated the ERP. Wayne Taylor, who had chaired the NPA committee, also chaired a comparable committee established by the CED and then joined forces with Paul Hoffman to present the CED's findings to Congress.[29]

[26] The Harriman Committee will be discussed later in the text. On the Marshall Plan Committee, see Theodore A. Wilson, *The Marshall Plan: An Atlantic Venture of 1947–1951 and How It Shaped Our World* (New York, June 1977), 36; Wexler, *Marshall Plan Revisited*, 32–3; and Price, *Marshall Plan and its Meaning*, 55–7.

[27] A list of the Marshall Plan Committee's membership is printed in Senate, *ERP Hearings, 1948*, 748–55. Those on the executive board who were members of the CFR, BAC, CED, or NPA were Frank Altschul (CFR, NPA), Allen Dulles (CFR), Herbert Feis (CFR), Herbert Lehman (CFR), Frederick McKee (CFR), Hugh Moore (CFR), Philip D. Reed (BAC, CED, CFR), and Herbert Bayard Swope (CFR). Biographical information on these and other individuals mentioned in the paragraph is drawn from the following sources: *Current Biography: Who's News and Why*; *National Cyclopaedia of American Biography*; *The International Who's Who*; and *Who Was Who in America*.

[28] House, *Recovery Program Hearings, 1947–8*, 687–711, 1625–43; and Senate, *ERP Hearings, 1948*, 746–77, 1205–11.

[29] House, *Recovery Program Hearings, 1947–8*, 1133–63; and Senate, *ERP Hearings, 1948*, 847–53. See also Senate, *ERP Hearings, 1948*, 731–40.

Hoffman was a founder of the CED and, along with Philip Reed of the Marshall Plan Committee, a prominent member of that organization and of the BAC. He was also one of the industry representatives on the Harriman Committee, approximately half of whose business, labor, farm, and academic members can be identified with the BAC, CED, or NPA. Also on the Harriman Committee was Owen D. Young, Reed's predecessor as board chairman of General Electric and a leading spokesman for economic internationalism and business progressivism in the first postwar period.[30] Although not a founding member of the CED, Young had encouraged Hoffman in this venture and served, on the Harriman Committee and in other capacities, as a living link between the business progressivism of an older generation and those individuals, like Hoffman, who preached a somewhat revised gospel in the second postwar era.[31]

The Brookings Institution provided a different sort of linkage – that between business leaders and their allies among professional specialists in public administration, economics, law, international relations, and other fields. The Brookings board of directors included, in addition to Dean Acheson, who was then on the executive board of the Marshall Plan Committee, three members of the CFR and one member of the BAC. Its president, Harold G. Moulton, served as a member of the Harriman Committee and its report on the ERP, as we will see, reinforced recommendations coming from the Harriman group, the CED, and the NPA.[32]

During the congressional hearings, these private leaders joined their government partners in a formidable defense of the ERP. They rejected unilateral American control over counterpart funds. They thought that recipient countries should balance budgets, fix realistic exchange rates, and multilateralize trade, but said that these steps should coincide with, not precede, the revival of production. This last argument squared with the policy compromise worked out between free-traders and planners in the State Department, as did their emphasis on the kind of indicative planning and economic coor-

---

[30] The membership of the Harriman Committee is printed in its report *A Report on European Recovery and American Aid* (Washington, DC, November 7, 1947), iv. In addition to Hoffman and Harriman, the BAC, CED, and NPA members included Hiland Batcheller, president of the Allegheny-Ludlum Steel Corporation (CED); James B. Carey, secretary-treasurer of the Congress of Industrial Organizations (NPA); John L. Collyer, president of the B. F. Goodrich Company (BAC, CED); Chester C. Davis, president of the Federal Reserve Bank of St. Louis (CED); R. R. Deupree, president of Procter & Gamble Company (BAC); William L. Myers, dean, College of Agriculture, Cornell University (CED); and Robert Gordon Sproul, president, University of California, Berkeley (CED).

[31] See Josephine Y. Case and Everett N. Case, *Owen D. Young and American Enterprise: A Biography* (Boston, 1982), especially 755.

[32] A list of the Brookings Institution's directors and officers is printed in its volume *Major Problems of United States Foreign Policy, 1948–1949* (Washington, DC, 1948). The directors referred to were Robert Perkins Bass (CFR), Karl T. Compton (BAC), Huntington Gilchrist (CFR), and Lessing Rosenthal (Chicago CFR).

dination that Hazlitt and other conservatives so strenuously opposed.[33] In their view, the very nature of the recovery program, and particularly the goal of integration, required a measure of economic planning on both sides of the Atlantic. In Europe, it had already led to American demands for the harmonization of national production and investment decisions, the collective allocation of resources, and the formation of a supranational authority. In the United States, it had led to the formation of three presidential fact-finding committees, the Advisory Steering Committee, and a host of other planning agencies. The most important of these agencies was the President's Committee on Foreign Aid. Its executive secretary, Richard M. Bissell, Jr., was a professional economist schooled in Keynesian theory and its report, which became the bible of those who defended the ERP in Congress, reverberated with the neo-capitalist formulations that would guide much of American policy in Europe.

Of interest here is the report's assault on the gloomy economic forecasts issued by Wallace, Hazlitt, and others on the Left and the Right. The report surveyed American resources and deemed them adequate to underwrite a major foreign-aid program without imposing substantial hardships on the American people. Net American exports to Europe under the program would actually be less than in the two previous years and would constitute only a small percentage of aggregate production. Although aggregate production was equal to the task, however, the recovery program would aggravate current shortages of certain commodities, especially foodstuffs, and this situation could set off "a chain of inflationary reactions" across the whole economy. To prevent inflation, the report said, it might become necessary to fasten government controls on the domestic consumption and allocation of items in short supply. But these controls were not the primary means of holding down prices and regulating the economy.

The report placed greater emphasis on licensing exports, on voluntary measures of conservation, and on the kind of fiscal management that would reduce the need for more direct methods of intervention. The recovery program would have to be financed within the framework of a balanced budget, rather than through government borrowing, which would expand bank credit. This approach would inspire European governments to follow the American example. It would restrain inflation and lessen the need for direct controls, but would not lead to a heavier tax burden on the American people as Wallace and Hazlitt feared. Indeed, the report projected a budget surplus large enough to absorb the cost of the recovery program and at the same time reduce the national debt or cut taxes.[34] As other Keynesians

---

[33] See the citations to the Senate and House hearings in previous notes, especially notes 7 through 17, 27, and 28.

[34] *European Recovery and American Aid*, especially 95–105. These pages treat the economic impact of the ERP on the American economy and were almost certainly drafted by Richard Bissell, who, in addition to acting as executive secretary of the

noted, moreover, once inflationary pressures receded, government borrowing could be used to finance the recovery program and prime the pump of the American economy.

According to the Harriman report, scientific fiscal management would combine with free-market forces to guarantee stability in the United States and Western Europe. This combination constituted one element of the New Deal synthesis, which also included supranational planning and efficient administration by cooperating public and private experts. Contrary to Wallace and the other left-wing critics who attacked the invasion of government by business, proponents of the Marshall Plan touted public–private collaboration and power sharing as two of the keys to a successful recovery program. For them, the main difficulties came in settling on a proper mix of public and private power in the United States and in reconciling European aspirations with the free-market and planning imperatives embedded in their administrative strategy. These difficulties formed the organizational dimension of recovery policy.

III

In the United States, the early debates over administrative strategy revolved around the relative merits of entrusting the recovery program to an independent government corporation or to a separate agency of the State Department. Secretary of Agriculture Clinton Anderson had already won support from a cabinet committee for a government export corporation empowered to expedite the marketing of American surpluses by providing loans to foreign importers, negotiating barter transactions, accepting payment in blocked currencies, and selling in foreign markets at prices below those prevailing in the United States.[35] Support for a corporate device to administer the ERP subsequently came from the Treasury Department and from Congressman Christian Herter's Select Congressional Committee on Foreign Aid. The Herter Committee, in particular, called for an independent government corporation with a single administrator, a policy council, and a bipartisan board of directors.[36] According to its advocates, a corporate

Harriman Committee, served as chief secretary of its Economic and Financial Analysis Subcommittee. Owen D. Young was chairman of the subcommittee. I am indebted to Professor Charles P. Kindleberger for insight into the significance of the Harriman Committee's report. According to Professor Kindleberger, it was one of the first published government documents to embody a Keynesian analysis.

35 Anderson letter to Truman, July 19, 1947, and Phillips draft memorandum, July 25, 1947, RG 353, Lot 122, box 37, ERP Subject File, folder: Federal Corporation.
36 Herter's proposal (H. R. 4579), printed in House, *Recovery Program Hearings, 1947–8*, 1–6; and Wexler, *Marshall Plan Revisited*, 30. See also Bureau of the Budget, "Staff Memorandum concerning Administration of the Program for European Recovery," November 4, 1947, James E. Webb papers (Truman Library), box 14, folder: European Recovery Program, Items 1–3.

organization would relieve the State Department of operational responsibilities for which it lacked experience and personnel. It would enjoy a large measure of operational flexibility, attract competent managerial talent from the private sector, and make possible a bipartisan administration of the recovery program. All of these advantages in turn would guarantee a businesslike operation and appease those in Congress who were hostile to the State Department.[37]

Opposition to a corporate device came from officials in the State Department and in the Bureau of the Budget. These officials worried that such an agency would diminish the president's authority in the area of foreign affairs and prevent the unity of command essential to the execution of a coherent foreign policy. These concerns with bureaucratic jurisdiction were paralleled by the conviction that a corporate device, such as the one favored by Secretary Anderson, entailed the sort of state trading that the United States opposed in Europe and that tended to politicize international economic relations. Any massive government procurement operation, as Marshall explained, would "constitute a threat to private enterprise in this country and to sovereign governments in Europe."[38]

Instead of an independent corporation, these officials were calling for a new administrative unit inside the State Department, specifically for an office of foreign programs headed by a new assistant secretary of state. The office would be responsible for the recovery program, as well as for post-UNRRA relief, relief to occupied areas, and aid to Greece and Turkey. This was the arrangement urged by Under Secretary of State Robert A. Lovett and supported by the Committee on the European Recovery Program and the Bureau of the Budget. Under it, there would be interdepartmental coordination and some sharing of administrative tasks with the Agriculture and Commerce departments. But the State Department would act as the major operating agency in the United States and in Europe, as sole claimant for participating countries, and as the central authority in matters relating to foreign policy. Presumably, such an approach would eliminate the need for an independent

[37] Phillips draft memorandum, July 25, 1947, and Bramble memorandum to Phillips, August 11, 1947, RG 353, Lot 122, box 37, ERP Subject File, folder: Federal Corporation; Assistant Secretary of State John E. Peurifoy and Assistant Secretary of State Charles E. Saltzman memorandum to Lovett, September 22, 1947, enclosed in Manfull to the Committee on the European Recovery Program, October 3, 1947, RG 353, Lot 122, box 28, folder: REP Documents/9-16a; Budget Bureau staff memorandum, November 3, 1947, attached to Anderson letter to Webb, November 7, 1947, Truman Papers, OF, folder: 426 (December 1947).

[38] Marshall cited in Arkes, *Bureaucracy and the Marshall Plan,* 67. See also Bramble memorandum to Phillips and Nitze, July 18, 1947, Phillips draft memorandum, July 25, 1947, and Bramble memorandum to Phillips, August 11, 1947, RG 353, Lot 122, box 37, ERP Subject File, folder: Federal Corporation; Jacques Reinstein of the Policy Planning Staff memorandum to Kennan, August 6, 1947, RG 59, file: 800.51/8-747; and Committee on the European Recovery Program, Minutes of Meeting, September 30, 1947, RG 353, Lot 122, box 26, folder: REP Minutes.

corporation and ensure that operational decisions were tailored to foreign-policy objectives.[39]

The State Department began to shift course even before the Truman administration submitted its foreign-aid program to Congress. Officials in that agency grew less inclined to accept operational responsibilities if doing so would alienate congressional critics and lead to legislative restrictions that might hamper the program's success. They were willing to consider an independent operating agency, so long as it avoided the pitfalls inherent in a corporate device and protected their prerogatives in the area of foreign policy. This kind of agency, they also conceded, would attract outside managerial talent and guarantee a businesslike administration. With these considerations in mind, Lovett appointed a special committee under the chairmanship of Lincoln Gordon to draft a new plan for administration of the recovery program.[40]

The committee's report, finished by late October, embraced the State Department's revised position on the question of organization. It called for a new agency, the Economic Cooperation Administration (ECA), to handle domestic and foreign operational responsibilities under the direction of a single administrator in Washington, a special representative of ambassadorial rank in Europe, and a team of recovery experts in each of the participating countries. In matters of policy, the ECA's role would be narrowly circumscribed. The Agriculture and Commerce departments would still control export allocations and, together with the State Department, exercise a veto over specific country programs, division of aid, and termination of assistance. The special representative in Europe would report directly to the State Department, and the ECA's overseas recovery experts would be recruited jointly by both agencies, placed in the foreign service, housed in the State Department's overseas missions, and directed by the chiefs of mission under instructions formulated jointly by the secretary of state and the administrator. In addition, the State Department, not the ECA, would make all decisions relating to foreign policy.[41]

39 Committee on the European Recovery Program, Minutes of Meetings, August 12 and September 30, 1947, RG 353, Lot 122, box 26, folder: REP Minutes; Saltzman memorandum to Lovett, with attached chit sheets, August 13, 1947, RG 59, file: 840.50Recovery/8-1347; Peurifoy and Saltzman memorandum to Lovett, September 22, 1947, RG 353, Lot 122, box 28, folder: REP Documents/9-16a; F. J. Lawton, Acting Director, Budget Bureau, memorandum for the President, October 28, 1947, Truman Papers, OF, folder: 426-L (1945–May 1948); and Webb memorandum for the President, November 3, 1947, Webb memorandum for the Secretary of State, November 3, 1947, and Budget Bureau, Staff Memorandum, November 4, 1947, Webb papers, box 14, folder: European Recovery Program, Items 1–3.

40 Gordon memorandum to Bonesteel, September 23, 1947, RG 353, Lot 122, box 28, folder: REP Documents/9-16a; Committee on the European Recovery Program, Minutes, October 7, 1947, RG 353, Lot 122, box 26, folder: REP Minutes.

41 Committee on the European Recovery Program, Minutes of Meeting, October 16, 1947, RG 353, Lot 122, box 26, folder: REP Minutes; Report of the Committee on

Through such arrangements, the State Department hoped to protect itself while disarming congressional critics. Doubters in the Bureau of the Budget thought the Gordon plan would so limit the ECA's autonomy that operational efficiency might be impaired. Besides, they argued, it was unrealistic to believe that operational and policy matters could be separated when, in practice, operational decisions would often determine policy and rob the State Department of the very authority it sought to safeguard. In their view, it would still be better for the State Department to administer the program and coordinate both policy and operations with other agencies.[42]

Having endorsed the Gordon plan, the policymakers at Foggy Bottom gave no ground to these arguments. The plan, they repeated, would protect their prerogatives in foreign policy. It would expedite "recruitment of the most capable and experienced personnel" from the private sector and guarantee "greater flexibility" in the legislative conditions attached to the aid program.[43] Nor would these policymakers concede when Budget Director James E. Webb secured Truman's tentative support for the bureau's proposal. Lovett arranged his own meeting at the White House, where he reiterated the department's position, persuaded the president to reverse his decision, and secured presidential approval for an administrative scheme much like the one outlined by the Gordon committee.[44]

The results could hardly have been different. As Donald C. Stone of the bureau complained, Truman could not assign operational responsibilities to a department unwilling to accept them.[45] Nor could the bureau count on bureaucratic allies elsewhere. Harriman had warned that administering the program through the State Department would lead to crippling legis-

Organization for ERP, October 20, 1947, RG 353, Lot 122, box 28, folder: REP Documents; Correlation Committee on ERP, "Plan of Organization for ERP," October 30, 1947, RG 353, Lot 122, box 25, folder: ASC Documents; and Correlation Committee on ERP, Log, October 30, 1947, RG 353, Lot 122, box 26, folder: C.C. Logs.

42   Advisory Steering Committee, Subcommittee on Organization, Minutes of Meetings, October 23 and 24, 1947, RG 353, Lot 122, box 26, folder: ASC Subcommittee on Organization; Correlation Committee, Log, October 29, 1947, RG 353, Lot 122, box 26, folder: C.C. Logs; and undated Webb memorandum to the Secretary of State, and Webb memorandum for the President, November 30, 1947, Webb Papers, box 14, folder: European Recovery Program, Items 1–3.

43   Marshall letter to Webb, November 7, 1947, Truman Papers, OF, folder: 426 (December 1947), and Webb memorandum for the President, November 10, 1947, Webb Papers, box 14, folder: European Recovery Program, Items 1–3. See also Advisory Steering Committee, Subcommittee on Organization, Minutes of Meeting, October 23, 1947, RG 353, Lot 122, box 26, folder: ASC Subcommittee on Organization.

44   Lovett tel. to Marshall, November 28, 1947, RG 59, file: 840.50Recovery/11-2847. Lovett's arguments were supported by Secretary Marshall in a telegram he sent to Truman from London. See Marshall to Lovett for the President, December 1, 1947, RG 59, file: 840.50Recovery/12-147.

45   Stone memorandum to Webb, December 3, 1947, Webb Papers, box 14, folder: European Recovery Program, Items 1–3.

lative restrictions, and both he and Anderson seemed ready to go along with any administrative scheme that protected their authority in the area of export allocations and control.[46] In addition, once officials in the State Department had conceded the need for operational management by experts from the private sector, it seemed imperative that they turn to an organizational framework that entailed some form of public–private power sharing and try, within this framework, to keep operational decisions in line with foreign-policy goals.

During congressional hearings on the Foreign Assistance Act, spokesmen for the Truman administration continued to distinguish between operational and policy decisions. The ECA, they said, would handle operational matters on a businesslike basis, would be headed by managerial talent recruited from the private sector, and would be free of unwarranted political interference. But they also thought it important to coordinate the business and political aspects of the recovery program in order to protect the domestic economy and ensure a coherent foreign policy. The prerogatives of executive agencies responsible for domestic economic management must be preserved; the ECA must be under the State Department's "direction and control" in matters relating to foreign policy. Although Secretary Marshall insisted that such control would not extend to the business aspects of the program, neither he nor other policymakers could explain where business stopped and foreign policy began. The "whole procedure," as Marshall frankly admitted, "affects the foreign relations of the United States."[47]

It was this admission that aroused much concern in Congress and among the flock of witnesses who testified on the ERP. In operation, they worried, Marshall's proposal would reduce the ECA's administrator to an "assistant secretary" for other executive officers, impairing the new agency's autonomy and making it difficult to recruit the "best brains" from the worlds of business, agriculture, and labor. Still worse, it would subject essentially business decisions to political control by policymakers in the State Department who had not been successful in managing previous aid programs and were too easily swayed by political considerations and the machinations of foreign governments. Such an administrative arrangement, the critics charged, could neither safeguard the domestic economy nor achieve the program's broad goals in Europe.[48]

For Senator Arthur Vandenberg and other critics, the primacy of private

46   Ibid.; Anderson letter to Webb, November 7, 1947, and Webb memorandum for the President, November 10, 1947, Truman Papers, OF, folder: 426 (December 1947); and Arkes, *Bureaucracy and the Marshall Plan*, 66.
47   Senate, *ERP Hearings, 1948*, 8–22, 150–7, 266–7, 314; and House, *Recovery Program Hearings, 1947–8*, 31, 39–41, 46, 47, 48, 50, 214–15, 153, 474–6.
48   House, *Recovery Program Hearings, 1947–8*, 273, 247, 86, 257, 274, 276, 416, 570, 665–7, 810–11, 1386; Senate, *ERP Hearings, 1948*, 21, 22, 74, 150, 155, 173–5, 806–9, 849–52.

management followed logically from their emphasis on the ERP's economic objectives in Europe. These critics were no less interested than Marshall in relieving suffering and containing communism. Achieving these goals, however, meant stabilizing currencies and exchange rates, reviving industry, liberalizing trade, and, through these and other reforms, fostering integration and boosting productivity. Steering this course, they agreed, required expert administration by men with a practical knowledge of the complicated problems involved. But it also required an administrative structure that permitted these men to apply their knowledge without political interference from the State Department. It required, in other words, a truly independent agency managed by private leaders who controlled operational decisions and shared with public officials the responsibility for making policy.[49]

Those testifying could cite numerous precedents for this kind of public–private power sharing. Some noted the wartime control arrangements worked out by public and private leaders under the aegis of the War Production Board. Others pointed to the President's Committee on Foreign Aid as an example of the benefits to be derived from public–private cooperation. Still others, including Secretary Harriman, cited the Commerce Department's success with its Business Advisory Council and voluntary agreements with industry. Secretary of the Interior J. A. Krug was equally enthusiastic about his department's collaboration with such groups as the National Petroleum Council. "Government–industry action" and "maximum" cooperation, he told the Senate Foreign Relations Committee, would satisfy European and American requirements without "centralizing authority" in Washington.[50]

During the congressional hearings, witnesses suggested a variety of proposals for achieving this kind of public–private cooperation. From business and farm leaders came calls for a policy board composed of government officials and representatives of private economic groups. From labor leaders came proposals under which public policymakers would be guided by the views of private advisory committees. From a variety of other witnesses came schemes for a blend of direct and indirect representation to be achieved by staffing the ECA with representatives from private economic groups, establishing private advisory committees, and preserving some role in the recovery program for those governmental departments, particularly the Commerce and Agriculture departments, that were closely tied to private groups through a network of cooperating committees.[51]

[49]   House, *Recovery Program Hearings, 1947–8*, 247, 257, 810–11; Senate, *ERP Hearings, 1948*, 751, 806, 808.

[50]   Senate, *ERP Hearings, 1948*, 366, 279, 359–60, 365, 851, 1394; House, *Recovery Program Hearings, 1947–8*, 569, 1445. Even Marshall had noted earlier the successful work performed "by a number of government agencies in cooperation with business, agriculture, and labor groups." Cited in Arkes, *Bureaucracy and the Marshall Plan*, 67.

[51]   Senate, *ERP Hearings, 1948*, 728, 734–5, 807–8, 835, 851, 1039, 1115–17, 1127,

One organization embracing the last strategy was the Brookings Institution. Itself one link in the pattern of public–private collaboration that had already taken shape around the ERP, Brookings now wanted that pattern formally embedded in the program's organizational arrangements. The Brookings report, solicited by Senator Vandenberg, acknowledged the "special character of the task" involved in reconstructing Europe, which entailed "economic and business" responsibilities the State Department was not equipped to assume. Needed was a "new and separate agency" headed by a single administrator who had cabinet rank, direct access to the president, and "primary responsibility for the formulation of operating policies and programs." The agency should also be exempt from various federal regulations, particularly those limiting salaries, in order to attract managerial talent from the private sector. In addition, it should have a public advisory board and private advisory committees to maintain regular consultation between its administrator and representatives of "industry, labor, agriculture, and...other private citizens." Because the ERP was not "a purely business job," the new agency must not encroach on roles properly played by government departments. The Commerce and Agriculture departments were to retain their authority over export allocations, the State Department was to negotiate bilateral aid agreements with the participating countries, and the National Advisory Council on International Monetary and Financial Problems was to determine specific financial policies. These were often "political," as opposed to "business," responsibilities. Although it was assumed that the two could be harmonized through consultation and cooperation, each had its own institutional requirements.[52]

Similar recommendations came from the President's Committee on Foreign Aid, the Committee for Economic Development, and the National Planning Association, all of which, like the Brookings Institution, were committed to public–private cooperation and power sharing. Because these agencies envisioned an administrative arrangement that would formalize the pattern of corporative collaboration Hoover had done so much to establish in the 1920s, it is not surprising to find the former president endorsing their views. With support also coming from congressional leaders such as Vandenberg, the recommendations of the Brookings Institution eventually found their way into the Economic Cooperation Act of 1948.[53]

1293, 1346–7, 1394; House, *Recovery Program Hearings, 1947–8*, 582, 590, 594, 810–11, 941–2, 1311–12, 1386–7, 1413, 1445–6.

[52]   The conclusions of the Brookings report are printed in Senate, *ERP Hearings, 1948*, 855–60. On Vandenberg's solicitation of the report, see Senate, *ERP Hearings, 1948*, 74.

[53]   Foreign Assistance Act of 1948, in House, *Executive Hearings, 1948*, 254–72. For the recommendations of the National Planning Association, the Committee for Economic Development, and the President's Committee on Foreign Aid, see Senate, *ERP Hearings, 1948*, 731–40, 847–53; and *European Recovery and American Aid*, 105–14. Taft, as well as Hoover, made similar recommendations. For their views, see the first two sources cited in note 23.

The act included provisions making the ECA an independent agency with a single administrator who was to have cabinet status and direct access to the president. The administrator was to cooperate with other cabinet officials, with private advisory committees, and with the Public Advisory Board in formulating policy and making operational decisions. Included as well were provisions ensuring the bipartisan nature of the Public Advisory Board, allowing the ECA to establish its own missions abroad, and making both the mission chiefs and the special representative directly responsible to the administrator. Through such provisions, Vandenberg and others hoped to ensure the ECA's autonomy. They sought to substitute for the State Department's political control a bipartisan public–private partnership in which essentially private leaders would make operational decisions and collaborate with their public counterparts in the formulation of policy. The administrator would be a "public" official appointed by the president with the consent of Congress. But he was to be recruited from the private sector and run his agency like a "business enterprise." In Vandenberg's words, he was to be the "business head of a business operation."[54]

Vandenberg made his views clear when he vetoed the appointments of Dean Acheson and William Clayton to the job of ECA administrator. Because the post required a man with "particularly persuasive economic credentials unrelated to diplomacy," he told Secretary Marshall, it was "the overriding Congressional desire that the ERP Administrator come from the outside business world...and *not* via the State Department." In the end, Vandenberg himself selected the administrator, choosing Paul G. Hoffman, president of the Studebaker Corporation, one of the industry representatives on the Harriman Committee, and a prominent member of those business agencies, such as the BAC and CED, that had long championed the idea of corporative collaboration between business and government.[55]

In the congressional debates, then, the goals pursued in recovery policy were inextricably linked to the administrative structure that would be employed. Marshall and other policymakers were at a disadvantage in these debates precisely because they shared with their critics a conviction that recovery policy should revive industry, liberalize commercial and currency arrangements, and encourage integration – goals, they admitted, that were best pursued through public–private cooperation and businesslike forms of management undertaken by the "best brains" from the private sector. Their concessions in this regard left them in no position to resist the view of those for whom the "special character of the task" made it imperative to limit

[54] Vandenberg letter to Carl M. Saunders, January 2, 1948, Vandenberg papers, box 3, folder: Correspondence, January 1948; and Arkes, *Bureaucracy and the Marshall Plan*, 84.

[55] Vandenberg letter to Marshall, March 24, 1948, Truman Papers, PSF, folder: Subject File – Cabinet: State, Secy of – George C. Marshall; and Arkes, *Bureaucracy and the Marshall Plan*, 100.

the State Department's authority. Consequently, the administrative structure adopted was one that deliberately dissolved the distinction between the public and private spheres and did so as part of a strategy for advancing the goals of American public policy.

The same goals were also shaping the organizational dimension of American diplomacy in Europe, although in this case the politics of administration masked a deeper, more profound struggle over the larger objectives of the recovery program. One aspect of this struggle revealed itself in disagreements between the Marshall Planners and their counterparts in London — disagreements that highlighted their differing proposals for Western European recovery. American policy gave considerable sweep to free-market forces. British policy relied more heavily on economic controls. American policy called for a European organization that transcended sovereignties. British policy favored a more conventional mechanism of intergovernmental cooperation. American policy assumed a bipolar world of rival Soviet and American blocs. British policy envisioned Western Europe as a middle kingdom under British, rather than Soviet or American, leadership. Before I get to these battles, however, it is important to review British recovery planning, which continued to evolve until it produced a policy synthesis different from the one hammered out in Washington.

IV

British policy toward European integration grew out of Ernest Bevin's earlier proposal for an Anglo–Western European customs union. Bevin and others in the Foreign Office had extolled the political advantages of such a union, whereas officials in the economic ministries had dwelt on the dangers it posed. The Cabinet had commissioned a board of experts to resolve the dispute, and its report of August 1947 had reaffirmed thinking in the economic ministries. Thus stymied, the Foreign Office had been unable to go further than a decision to participate in a Customs Union Study Group, which was to meet in Brussels the following November.

In the meantime, Bevin had continued to push his own proposal with the tireless zeal of a man unaccustomed to defeat. A former trade-union leader whose working-class veneer overlaid a shrewd and imaginative intellect, Bevin by this time commanded the heights of British foreign policy. His ambition, perhaps as oversized as the man himself, stopped at nothing less than the preservation of Great Britain as a major power in a world increasingly dominated by the United States and the Soviet Union. Shared by the European experts on his staff at the Foreign Office, this ambition explains Bevin's persistent efforts to promote the idea of a customs union. In a speech at Southport on September 3, he again called for British membership in such a union. In a note to Prime Minister Clement R. Attlee two days later, he urged the formation of a "high-level" committee to investigate the merits of his proposal. And in a meeting of the Cabinet on September 26, he secured the appointment of an interdepartmental group to consider the relative advantages of a customs union that would include the United Kingdom and the Commonwealth or Empire, the United Kingdom and the Western European countries, or some combination of these groups.[56]

Bevin could expect little from the interdepartmental committee, whose members shared the general antipathy toward a customs union that was still widespread in the economic ministries and the Colonial Office.[57] The committee's report, finished in early November, concluded that a Western European customs union would lead inevitably to full-fledged economic union under the central direction of a supranational authority. Such a union would help to rationalize industry, expand trade, and strengthen the Continent politically. Certain British industries would also improve their position in the European market, and both the United Kingdom and the union as a whole would be in a stronger position to compete with the United States in the international economy. These long-term gains, however, would do little to solve Britain's pressing economic problems, which, according to the report, would actually be exacerbated by the "substantial" internal dislocations that accompanied the elimination of tariffs between members of the union. The Labour government would be unable to implement its "policy of stable prices and assured markets for United Kingdom agriculture" or to shelter key industries, especially the iron and steel industries, against damaging competition from European producers. The diversion of British exports to the Continent would also drain the Treasury's gold and dollar holdings, while the coordination of national fiscal and monetary policies would "conflict with the Sterling Area connection," wreck Britain's "preferential arrangements with the Commonwealth," and further imperil reserves.

The report ruled out various strategies for dealing with the worst of these repercussions. Although the steel and iron industries might be protected by excluding western Germany from the group, the report considered this course politically unacceptable to Britain and economically unacceptable to the Benelux. Nor could serious problems be avoided if Britain remained aloof from a European union, participated in separate European and Commonwealth unions, or formed a single union embracing both areas. The

---

[56] In addition to the discussion in the previous chapter, see Bevin to Attlee, September 5, 1947, FO 371, 62553, UE8360; and Milward, *Reconstruction of Western Europe*, 241–2.

[57] Following Bevin's Southport speech, the Treasury, Board of Trade, Ministry of Supply, and Colonial Office repeated in more detail all of their earlier objections to a customs union. See, for example, undated Caine memorandum, "The Colonies and a Customs Union," FO 371, 62553, UE8359; Harold Wilson memorandum, September 6, 1947, FO 371, 62553, UE8529; and Hall-Patch, "Customs Union," November 8, 1948, FO 371, 62555, UE11531.

first alternative would risk the growth of large-scale European industries more competitive in third markets than British producers. Indeed, the same economic interests that militated against an Anglo–Western European union seemed to dictate Britain's opposition to a strictly continental group. As for the last two alternatives, the report argued that these and similar strategies would weaken Britain's ties to the Commonwealth. They would also cost the Commonwealth countries their preferential position in the British market, make it difficult for them to protect domestic industry and agriculture, or entail other penalties unacceptable to the parties involved. Under these circumstances, the report concluded, the British delegation to the Customs Union Study Group should avoid any action that might be interpreted as a commitment to a European union.[58]

The report was clearly "disappointing from the point of view of the Foreign Office," which Bevin reiterated when the cabinet-level Economic Policy Committee considered the document on November 7. "It was essential," he told the committee, "that western Europe attain some measure of economic unity," including collective control over colonial resources, "if it was to maintain its independence as against Russia and the United States." This had been his position from the start, but it was one that failed to persuade Harold Wilson, president of the Board of Trade, and Sir Stafford Cripps, minister for economic affairs. Wilson and Cripps put the highest priority on safeguarding Britain's special economic links to the Commonwealth. Cripps saw some advantages in bringing the United Kingdom and the Colonies together in a customs union. But when it came to enhancing economic ties to Western Europe, both he and Wilson thought the more conventional mechanism of trade liberalization would give the Labour government greater control over commerce and pose fewer dangers to the network of imperial preferences. Although Bevin wanted more time to study the issues involved, particularly the strategic and political dimensions that formed the basis of his thinking and that the interdepartmental committee had largely ignored, it was clearly impossible to postpone the meeting of the Customs Union Study Group without appearing to obstruct progress. Accordingly, the Economic Policy Committee instructed the British delegation to participate fully in the group's deliberations. But it was to avoid any commitment to European union and seek, so far as possible, to focus the group's work on the advantages of liberalizing intra-European trade.[59]

---

[58] Economic Policy Committee (47) 11th Report, "Customs Union: Interim Report of the Interdepartmental Study Group," November 6, 1947, (hereafter cited as EPC with year and number of report), FO 371, 62732, UE10816. See also Under Secretary of State Roger Makins minute to Bevin, November 6, 1947, FO 371, 62732, UE10817.

[59] Economic Policy Committee (47) 6th Meeting, November 7, 1947, FO 371, 62732, UE10878.

These instructions defined the British approach to European economic integration at the end of 1947.[60] Despite the emphasis on full cooperation with the Study Group, deep divisions in the Cabinet made a truly positive policy impossible. The economic ministries were also convinced, as Wilson told the Economic Policy Committee, that American support for a customs union was waning. This conviction was correct. American enthusiasm had declined with the closing days of the CEEC meeting and Clayton's subsequent retirement from the State Department. But these developments spelled no slackening of American support for European integration. The Foreign Office and economic ministries admitted as much in the great concern they showed lest any appearance of obstructing progress alienate important elements in Washington at a time when Congress was beginning to debate Truman's foreign-assistance proposal.

Under these circumstances, British policy amounted to a holding operation. When the Customs Union Study Group convened in mid-November, the British delegation won support for a comprehensive investigation of the practical and theoretical implications of standardizing European tariffs – a study, in other words, that would preoccupy the group for months and postpone the day of reckoning for the Labour government.[61] This is not to say that Bevin and his colleagues abandoned the field to their opponents. They were determined to convert the economic ministries to the Foreign Office point of view. And by the spring of 1948, their initiatives had finally combined with dismal economic and political news to break the deadlock in the Cabinet.

A new policy synthesis emerged. It began to take shape in December and January 1947–8, when the Foreign Office launched a major assessment of the strategic and political implications of an Anglo–Western European customs union, in effect an evaluation of factors more or less ignored by the interdepartmental committee. The initial assessment took the form of minutes by officials in the Northern and North American departments of the Foreign Office, by Roger Stevens, who was the chief British representative on the Customs Union Study Group, and by Under Secretaries of State H. M. Gladwyn Jebb and F. R. Hoyer-Millar. All were vigorous advocates of greater European unity, and their views can be treated collectively.

As these officials saw it, an Anglo–Western European customs union promised long-term gains that far outweighed the risks involved. They frankly admitted that membership would disrupt the British economy in the short term, weaken the Commonwealth connection, and involve the loss of sovereign rights to a supranational agency. It would lead, in short,

---

[60] The London Committee essentially reaffirmed this approach in late December. See its report EPC (47) 33, "The United Kingdom and the European Recovery Programme," December 22, 1947, FO 371, 62418, UE12696.

[61] In addition to the source cited in note 59, see Milward, *Reconstruction of Western Europe*, 247, 255.

to full-scale economic union. Yet this very prospect, which so worried the economic ministries, exhilarated policymakers in the Foreign Office. In the eyes of the latter, Anglo–Western European unification would increase productivity, raise living standards to a level comparable to that in the United States, and bring impressive political advantages, most notably the containment of Soviet expansion and the creation of a framework for controlling the Germans. Britain, of course, would have to abandon its historic policy of playing European blocs off against one another and throw its weight squarely into the balance. But it would dominate the European union and this position would enhance the power of the British Empire at a time when it was in danger of being "outclassed" by the Soviet bloc and becoming wholly dependent on the United States for the kind of economic and military support that had already seen it through two world wars. Great Britain, as R. M. A. Hankey noted, "cannot survive" as a world power by "hoping to sponge on American aid." Given the current direction of policy, Jebb agreed, "we shall eventually have to make the dismal choice between becoming a Soviet satellite state or the poor dependent of an American plutodemocracy." Through unification, however, Britain, the continental countries, and their overseas territories could forge a "completely new balance of power in Europe, and indeed the world." They could create a middle kingdom capable of playing an "important role in world affairs" and of restoring a "world equilibrium" that was "gravely imperiled," as Jebb put it, "by a 'bi-polar' system centering around what Mr. Toynbee calls the two 'semi-barbarian states on the cultural periphery.'" Any other course, according to P. M. Crosthwaite, would reduce the United Kingdom and the European countries to mere "pigmies between two giants, dependent on one for protection from the other and living in constant expectation of being trampled underfoot when they quarrel."[62]

These views formed the substance of a paper Bevin presented to the Cabinet on January 8, when he once again urged an Anglo–Western European "*bloc* which, both in population and productive capacity, could stand on an equality with the western hemisphere and Soviet *blocs*." This time, moreover, Bevin scored a major triumph. The Cabinet decided to "consolidate the forces of the Western European countries and their Colonial possessions."[63] This decision set the stage for Bevin's celebrated Western-union speech to the House of Commons on January 22. "I believe,"

[62] Stevens touched off the flurry of comments with a minute of December 22, 1947, entitled "Politico-strategic Implications of a European Customs Union," FO 371, 62555, UE12502. See also the minutes by Crosthwaite of December 31, 1947, Hankey of January 3, 1947 [sic, 1948], W. G. Hayter of January 5, 1948, F. B. A. Rundall of January 6, 1948, Jebb of January 8, 1948, and Hoyer-Millar of January 10, 1948, all in FO 371, 62555, UE12502.

[63] CM (48) 2nd Conclusion, January 8, 1948, CAB 128, Cabinet Minutes, Conclusions, and Confidential Annexes (Public Record Office), 12 (hereafter cited as CAB 128, followed by the volume number).

he told a packed audience, "the time is ripe for a consolidation of Western Europe.... We are thinking now of Western Europe as a unit." This consolidation would include the United Kingdom, which could no longer "regard her problems as quite separate from those of her European neighbours" and which must therefore take the lead in forging a "self-reliant" union composed of the British Commonwealth, the Western European states, and their overseas territories in Africa and Asia.[64]

The Cabinet's decision of January 8 grew out of a combination of factors too familiar to merit elaboration here. In addition to ongoing pressure from the Foreign Office, these included the failure of Soviet and Western leaders to reach agreement on the German problem at the London Foreign Ministers Conference of November–December 1947. This failure was followed by a dramatic escalation of East–West tensions, which then combined with mounting economic and political turmoil in France and Italy to convince Bevin and other British officials that further measures were needed to fortify Western Europe against the dangers of Communist subversion and Soviet intimidation. Adding urgency to this conviction was their growing appreciation of the political implications for Western Europe if Marshall aid, as the CEEC report had concluded, failed to put the participating countries on a self-supporting basis.[65] These factors explain why the economic ministries were ready to consider new strategies for promoting a Western union, although the strategy eventually selected would reduce somewhat the scope of Bevin's initial triumph.

With a view to framing a strategy suited to this new environment, the Foreign Office established a working group of Roger Stevens, Edmund Hall-Patch, and Assistant Under Secretary Ivone Kirkpatrick. By mid-February, Stevens had produced a draft paper entitled "Economic Aspects of Western Union." The paper noted the current negotiations that would lead to the Brussels Pact in March, negotiations that extended Bevin's earlier effort, begun with the Treaty of Dunkirk, to build a Western European security system. It then went on to argue that defense arrangements must be supported by an integrated European economic system capable of welding the participating countries together and ending their financial dependence on the United States. It rejected an approach that relied solely on multilateral undertakings to liberalize trade and payments, arguing that such undertakings were inherently feeble and would have to be subsumed under a comprehensive and binding "System." The system would include a customs union and eventually a full-scale economic union of France, western Germany, Italy, the Benelux, and the United Kingdom. It would also include an organizational mechanism to administer the affairs of the union, although

---

[64]   Great Britain, Parliament, *Parliamentary Debates* (Commons), 5th series, 446 (1947–8): 383–410.
[65]   On the combination of factors noted in the text, see, in addition to the sources cited in the preceding three notes, Bullock, *Bevin*, 483–97.

in this case the draft ruled out the CEEC and other institutions that were tied to the United States and thus unable to pursue uniquely British and European goals. Building this system would entail some sacrifice of self-interest and sovereignty. It would mean lowering tariff barriers, disrupting imperial preferences, and reducing the government's ability to regulate foreign competition in the home market. But the "crisis in our affairs," the paper concluded, called for "radical solutions" that in the long run would guarantee "security in Western Europe" and ensure Britain's survival as a world power.[66]

At a meeting of the Cabinet on February 23, Bevin presented a paper summarizing some of the themes outlined by Stevens. He told his colleagues that it would be best to collaborate with the CEEC or its successor unless "a more intimate type of machinery" became necessary to deal with the "detailed and precise issues of integration."[67] This limiting condition referred to economic arrangements among the five powers that would constitute the Brussels Pact, specifically to the need for an economic organization that would supplement their defense arrangements and manage the worsening payments crisis being brought on by Belgium's demand for dollars and France's staggering deficit with the sterling area. Aside from threatening Britain's reserve position and export trade, this crisis had reaffirmed Bevin's conviction that defense arrangements were worthless unless the countries involved formed a tightly woven economic and organizational fabric. Following the cabinet meeting of February 23, Bevin told Cripps that it was imperative to prevent the key partners in a Western union from pursuing divergent economic policies and suggested a "Western union economic bank" as the best mechanism for this purpose.[68]

Bevin's thinking reflected themes that had been common currency in the Foreign Office for some time. Like his associates, Bevin envisioned a regional mechanism that suited the goals of British, not American, diplomacy, in particular the goal of a balance of power that turned on a united and self-supporting Europe. The point to bear in mind is that Bevin was thinking of a union with supranational powers. Only an organization of this kind could weld Western Europe into what the Foreign Office called a "System" and what I have termed a middle kingdom. This point is important because it was not the idea of integration so much as the means of achieving it that met with unflinching opposition in the Cabinet, where the reliance on supranational institutions and the room accorded free-market forces made

---

[66]   "Economic Aspects of Western Union," undated, attached to Stevens minute to Makins, February 11, 1948, FO 371, 71766, UR9.

[67]   CP (48) 57, "Machinery for Furthering the Project for a Western Union," February 18, 1948, PREM 8/980; and CM (48) 16th Conclusion, February 23, 1948, CAB 128/12.

[68]   See the minute by Frank Roberts, Bevin's Personal Private Secretary, to Hall-Patch and Makins, February 24, 1948, FO 371, 71766, UR603.

Bevin's proposal for a customs union particularly unacceptable to Sir Stafford Cripps.

Cripps had become chancellor of the Exchequer in late 1947. A university scientist and barrister turned left-wing laborite for a time in the 1930s, his career had also included stints as president of the Board of Trade and ambassador to the Soviet Union, the latter position doing much to alter the mixture of pacifism and Marxism that had earlier characterized his views on foreign policy. But there had been no diminution of his commitment to economic planning. Together with related concerns over Britain's reserve position and ties to the Commonwealth, it was this commitment that set Cripps and his colleagues in the Treasury at odds with Bevin and his associates in the Foreign Office.

As noted in the Cabinet's decision of January 8, Cripps and other policymakers in the economic ministries had come to support some form of Western union. Their support rested largely on economic rather than political or strategic considerations, specifically on the conviction that Marshall aid alone could not correct Europe's payments deficit with the Western Hemisphere. Europe could become self-supporting only through "a substantial modification of its industrial and agricultural structure." Britain itself would have to take this "leap in the dark," adjust its economic structure to fit a European-wide pattern, and accept some sacrifice of national sovereignty in favor of transnational economic planning and coordination. To effect this leap, however, officials in the Treasury favored an "empirical" approach that stopped short of true supranationalism. They rejected a European central bank and common currency, claiming that gold and dollar reserves were insufficient to support either proposal. Nor did they favor a "grandiose 'general' plan like a customs union," which, in operation, would eliminate tariffs and trade preferences and expose British industry to the unbridled forces of a free market. They called instead for transnational economic planning on an ad hoc, project-by-project basis with a view to intergovernmental and interindustrial agreements aimed at maximizing dollar earnings and savings in the ERP area as a whole. When coupled with an intra-European payments plan that conserved hard-currency reserves, the empirical approach supposedly would create an integrated economic order large enough to enhance productivity, restore equilibrium with the dollar area, and reconcile Franco–German differences. But it would also permit British leaders to direct the process of integration. It would dovetail with the principles of socialist planning employed at home and enable the Labour government to limit the damage to Britain's economic structure and system of imperial preferences.[69]

[69]   Sir Wilfrid Eady, Second Secretary of the Treasury, memorandum to Cripps, February 27, 1948, and Eady memorandum to Sir Edward Bridges, Permanent Secretary of the Treasury, and B. F. St. J. Trend, Assistant Secretary of the Treasury, March 1, 1948, T236/1892/OF265/1F.

Cripps and his colleagues, to put it summarily, wanted to move toward Bevin's goal of a Western union along a path that assured greater control than would be possible through a framework in which free-market forces and supranational regulators might override British interests. This summation foreshadows the terms of a compromise hammered out by the London Committee (an interdepartmental group that coordinated British recovery policy), subsequently ratified by Cripps and Bevin at a meeting of the Economic Policy Committee, and finally approved by the Cabinet on March 8.

The compromise looked to a continuing European recovery organization that would direct all of its efforts toward solving the Continent's payments deficit with the Western Hemisphere. Equilibrium could be achieved by increasing production in the participating countries and their overseas territories, liberalizing trade and improving payments arrangements, and integrating agricultural and industrial lines of production on a project-by-project basis. The last method, according to the London Committee, would be more compatible with Britain's system of imperial preferences, impose fewer restraints on the government's freedom of action, and promise greater rewards and fewer internal adjustments than would be the case with a fully "*automatic* policy of European co-operation" through a customs union. Nor was there any question of central direction by a supranational authority. The continuing organization was to operate as a planning agency. Ultimate control was to be in the hands of national delegations. Specific industrial and agricultural projects were to be arranged through intergovernmental agreement.

If these arguments revealed the Treasury's contribution to the compromise, the final documents also displayed the unmistakable influence of the Foreign Office. The compromise called for a "modified Western European economy," a single "economic entity" to replace the "several uncoordinated economies which exist today." Pursuing this goal might entail "radical changes" in Britain's economic structure and some modification of its ties to the Commonwealth. It certainly would involve reversing Britain's traditional diplomacy with regard to the Continent. The British would have to link their fate to that of a Western European group and take all of the economic and political risks that such a course entailed. But this was the only alternative to becoming "permanent pensioners" of the United States or seeking to survive alone "in a state of continuous economic uncertainty and poverty with all the disintegrating political and social results that would follow." If achieved, moreover, Anglo–Western European economic integration would guarantee strategic security within the framework of a new balance of power. This had been Bevin's goal all along, although it would now be pursued in a way that gave the British government greater control over natural market forces and limited the scope for real supranationalism. The Cabinet captured the fusion of Treasury and Foreign Office strategies when it approved the compromise policy on March 8. According to the minutes of the meeting, the policy represented "an extension to western Europe of the principles of economic planning which the Government had adopted for the United Kingdom, and it was the only means by which the United Kingdom and the other participating countries could establish themselves in a position in which they were economically dependent neither on the Soviet Union nor on the United States."[70]

By the spring of 1948, then, both the British and American governments had brought forth policy compromises that seemed appropriate to their respective national interests and aspirations. Hall-Patch summarized the differences between these policies in a Foreign Office minute of March 9. In Washington, he warned, the sterling area was viewed as a "manifestation of evil," a "barrier" to Anglo–Western European union and thus to an integrated framework large enough to enhance productivity, reconcile Franco–German differences, and contain Soviet power. American officials therefore spoke of the "sort of 'integration' " that would bring Great Britain into Western Europe at the cost of its "economic links" to the sterling area and the Commonwealth. In London, however, the sterling area was seen as the "economic foundation" of a vast multilateral trading system, the dissolution of which would "spell the end of the United Kingdom as a World Power." British officials therefore spoke of an integration that would reconcile their commitments to the sterling area and the Commonwealth with their interests in Western Europe.[71] If the Americans would achieve integration in a way that sacrificed Britain's status as a world power, the British would do so in a way that enhanced that status. If the Americans envisioned a bipolar world dominated by two hegemonic powers, the British envisioned a world in which the Empire, the Commonwealth, and the Western European states would come together in the middle kingdom. This is not to argue that Hall-Patch, Bevin, and others imagined Western Europe as a neutral third force in world affairs, an idea still dear to elements in the left wing of the Labour Party. Bevin was convinced that Western Europe could not survive without American support and was then preparing the ground for negotiations that would lead, in 1949, to the North Atlantic Treaty. But I am arguing that he and other British leaders conceived of the middle kingdom as a self-supporting and equal partner in this larger alliance of Western states – a kingdom, moreover, that operated under British rather than American leadership.

[70] CP (48) 75, London Committee, "The Continuing Organization," undated, CAB 129, Cabinet Papers (Public Record Office), 25 (hereafter cited as CAB 129, followed by the volume number); Economic Policy Committee (48) 9th Meeting, March 4, 1948, PREM 8/980; CP (48) 75, Bevin and Cripps memorandum to the Cabinet, March 6, 1948, CAB 129/25; and CM (48) 20th Conclusion, March 8, 1948, CAB 128/12.
[71] Hall-Patch minute of March 9, 1948, FO 371, 71851, UR873.

Different goals required different economic strategies and organizational forms; hence, the Americans and British went to battle over the nature of a continuing European recovery authority. Against a background of new European initiatives to liberalize trade and payments, initiatives that complemented the free-trade approach touted by some officials in the State Department, American leaders renewed their drive for a strong, supranational authority. This was the planners' part of the American equation for a European neo-capitalism, what the British ambassador in Washington called "the ark of the covenant."[72] As earlier, the British resisted both lines of American policy.

V

Following the CEEC's adjournment in September 1947, there were hopeful signs of further progress toward European economic integration. The Benelux countries negotiated a tariff union; Greece and Turkey established a customs-union study commission; France and Italy followed a similar course, as did the Scandinavian nations; and the French suggested a merger between the Benelux group and the proposed Franco–Italian union.[73] At the same time, the Customs Union Study Group laid plans to standardize tariffs and the Committee on Payments Agreements (CPA) drafted the First Agreement on Multilateral Monetary Compensation. The agreement was signed in November 1947 by France, Italy, and the Benelux, with eight other countries adhering as "occasional members." It was the first step toward eliminating the network of bilateral agreements that hampered the expansion of intra-European trade. Under its terms, so-called second-category compensations (those that pushed deficits beyond existing credit margins and thus required payment in scarce gold or dollar reserves) could be settled only with the consent of the countries party to the transaction. But first-category compensations (those that reduced deficits) would now be arranged automatically by the Bank for International Settlements.[74]

As it turned out, neither the Americans nor the Europeans could make these initiatives succeed. The National Advisory Council endorsed the idea of an intra-European clearing scheme while the State Department sent observers to the CPA meetings and agreed to bizonal Germany's full mem-

[72] British Embassy, Washington, tel. to FO, March 12, 1948, FO 371, 71809, UR335.
[73] William Diebold, Jr., *Trade and Payments in Western Europe: A Study in European Economic Cooperation* (New York, 1952), 320, 383, 377–8, 354–5, 141. See also Waldemar J. Gallman, Charge in the United Kingdom, London, tel. to Marshall, for W. A. Walmsley from Don C. Bliss, January 17, 1948, RG 59, file: 655.5631/1-1748; Caffery tel. to Marshall, January 19, 1948, RG 59, file: 655.5631/1–1948; and Hugh Millard, Charge in Belgium, Brussels, tel. to Marshall, February 6, 1948, RG 59, file: 840.50Recovery/2-648.
[74] Diebold, *Trade and Payments*, 303–7, 24–5; Van Der Beugel, *From Marshall Aid to Atlantic Partnership*, 124–5.

bership in the First Agreement on Multilateral Monetary Compensation.[75] In addition, American leaders expressed "keen interest" in the Franco–Italian tariff negotiations and in the work of the Customs Union Study Group. They also supported Germany's participation in the Study Group and France's efforts to merge the Benelux with the proposed Franco–Italian union.[76] Nevertheless, progress toward a full economic union between the Benelux countries kept foundering on the problems involved in aligning prices, wages, and costs.[77] The French and Italian governments signed a customs-union protocol, but the French seemed less than enthusiastic about the agreement while the Benelux governments dragged their feet on any merger between the proposed union and their group.[78] In each case, considerations of national interest divided the parties and slowed progress, just as they wrecked the Study Group's chances for an early reduction of European tariffs.[79]

[75]   *FRUS, 1948*, 3:380, footnote 1; Caffery tel. to Marshall, November 25, 1947, RG 59, file: 102.1/11-2547; State Department dispatch #508 to American Embassy, London, December 29, 1947, with enclosure, RG 84, London Embassy Records, box 1018, file: 850 Marshall Plan; Warren M. Chase, Acting Political Adviser in Germany, tel. to American Embassy, London, March 1, 1948, RG 84, London Embassy Records, box 1035, file: 850 Marshall Plan; Caffery tel. to Marshall, March 16, 1948, RG 59, file: 840.50Recovery/3-1648; G. F. Luthringer memorandum to Secretary Snyder, September 6, 1947, Snyder Papers, box 11, folder: European Recovery Program, Adm. File. See also "Proposals for an Intra-European Clearing Pool: Report of the Informal Inter-Agency Working Group," no date, RG 353, Lot 122, box 32, folder: 5.17.5 European Recovery Program Committee, C. ERPC Documents/80-99; and Manfull memorandum to William Y. Elliot et al., September 1, 1947, with enclosure, in the Records of the President's Committee on Foreign Aid, 1947 (Truman Library), box 11, folder: General File – State Department Memos with Respect to OEEC Meetings.

[76]   Marshall tel. to American Embassy, Brussels, March 10, 1948, RG59, file: 640.002/2-448. For the American response to the Franco–Italian negotiations, see the documents in RG 59, file: 651.6531/12-947, /1-1248, /1-1648, /1-2448, and /1-2848. See also Raymond Vernon memorandum to Nitze, January 14, 1948, RG 59, file: 840.50Recovery/1-1448. For the State Department's position on the French efforts, see Marshall tel. to American Legation, Luxembourg, January 29, 1948, RG 59, file: 655.5631/1-2948. For American efforts on behalf of the Western occupation zones, see the documents in RG 59, file: 640.002/ 1-2948, /1-3048, /2-1848, /2-1948, /3-1648, and /3-1948. See also Millard tel. to Marshall, November 14, 1947, RG 59, file: 655.5631/11-1447; and Millard tel. to Marshall, February 9, 1948, RG 59, file: 840.50Recovery/2-948.

[77]   Diebold, *Trade and Payments*, 378–83, 341–3.

[78]   Caffery tel. to Marshall, January 19, 1948, RG 59, file: 655.5631/1-1948; and American Embassy, Rome, dispatch #520 to Marshall, March 25, 1948, RG 59, file: 651.6531/3-2548.

[79]   Diebold, *Trade and Payments*, 306–7; Basil D. Dahl, American Commercial Attaché, Copenhagen, dispatch #404 to Marshall, December 18, 1947, RG 59, file: 640.002/12-1847; Philip W. Bonsal, The Hague, tel. to Marshall, January 16, 1948, RG 59, file: 640.002/1-1648; Bliss dispatch #353 to Marshall, February 11, 1948, RG 59,

Similar considerations influenced negotiations over the adjustment of exchange rates and the operation of the intra-European clearing agreement. In January 1948, French devaluation of the franc touched off a stormy controversy. The British disapproved, in large part because the French decision put British exporters at a disadvantage in world markets and increased the pressure for a competitive devaluation of pound sterling. For similar reasons, the British bitterly complained when French officials decided to establish a system of flexible exchange rates that would increase France's earnings of hard currency. On the American side, the State Department seemed sympathetic with the French decision. But the National Advisory Council, together with the International Monetary Fund, denounced the flexible system as blatantly discriminatory and as an example of the competitive nationalism that retarded European economic recovery and integration.[80] The same kind of nationalism hampered the clearing arrangement worked out under the First Agreement on Multilateral Monetary Compensation. In this case, net debtors to the group as a whole proved reluctant to authorize second-category compensations that might jeopardize their reserves, preferring instead to settle their accounts through bilateral deals over which they had more control. Because of this and other limitations, the first clearing, arranged in January 1948, amounted to only $1.7 million, or about 2 percent of the total indebtedness among participating countries.[81]

Although European trade was strangling in a web of exchange controls, American policymakers were in no position to help. They could not, as the Belgians suggested, support a monetary reserve fund or make ERP dollars directly available to a European clearing agency. Nor could they go along with a British proposal whereby creditors on intra-European account would use the local-currency counterpart of American aid to settle balances. These proposals had not been authorized by Congress. Nor were they likely to be unless ERP officials in Washington retained control over the American funds involved.[82] This kind of control was possible by using off-shore procurement, under which a portion of the ERP funds designated for purchases outside the United States would be used to balance accounts on intra-European trade. Some officials in the State Department favored this tech-

file: 640.002/2-1148; and Douglas Airgram #473 to Marshall, February 24, 1948, RG 59, file: 640.002/2-2448.

[80] This story can be followed in *FRUS, 1948*, 3:592, 597–613, 1069–77. See also Charles E. Bohlen letter to Congressman John Davis Lodge, February 10, 1948, RG 59, file: 840.50Recovery/2-1048; and Secretary Snyder letter to Lodge, February 10, 1948, Snyder Papers, box 18, folder: France – general 1946–1948, Alphabetical File.

[81] Diebold, *Trade and Payments*, 25–6; Van Der Beugel, *From Marshall Aid to Atlantic Partnership*, 125.

[82] Lovett tel. to Douglas, September 25, 1947, RG 59, file: 840.50Recovery/9-2647; Marshall tel. to Caffery, February 20, 1948, RG 59, file: 840.50Recovery/2-748; Marshall tel. to Caffery, February 26, 1948, RG 59, file: 840.50Recovery/2-1948; and Lovett tel. to Caffery, April 1, 1948, RG 59, file: 840.50Recovery/3-848.

nique and it was eventually employed by the ECA after passage of the Foreign Assistance Act. But in this case, as in the others, nothing could be done until Congress acted.[83] Even then, real progress depended on how far the British would go toward active collaboration in a European framework. According to early indications, this would not be as far as the Americans had hoped.

Until March 1948, as we have seen, divisions in the Cabinet had prevented British policymakers from pushing ahead with Bevin's plans for an Anglo–Western European economic union or from adopting a positive policy on matters relating to intra-European trade and payments. Britain had signed the Agreement on Multilateral Monetary Compensation as an occasional member, a status that permitted it to veto clearings involving sterling.[84] The British had conditioned their participation in the Customs Union Study Group on special arrangements to protect their system of imperial preferences.[85] Indirectly at least, they had also played a part in scuttling French proposals for merging the Benelux tariff group with the proposed Franco–Italian union.[86] By March, disputes between the Foreign Office and the Treasury had given way to a settlement that looked to the "consolidation" of Western Europe. But this consolidation was to be achieved in a way that left little room for the blend of free-market forces and supranational co-ordinators that characterized the American policy compromise. It thus set British policymakers at odds with their allies in Washington and with the

---

[83] Lovett tel. to Caffery, December 15, 1947, RG 59, file: 840.50Recovery/12-1047; State Department dispatch #508 to American Embassy, London, December 29, 1947, with enclosure dated December 10, 1947, RG 84, London Embassy Records, box 1018, file: 850 Marshall Plan; Marshall tel. to Caffery, February 20, 1948, RG 59, file: 840.50Recovery/2-748; and Lovett tel. to Caffery, April 1, 1948, RG 59, file: 840.50Recovery/3-848. See also Diebold, *Trade and Payments*, 29.

[84] Van Der Beugel, *From Marshall Aid to Atlantic Partnership*, 125.

[85] Britain's reluctance to go ahead without special arrangements also made the Benelux countries hesitant. See Josiah Marvel, Jr., Ambassador in Denmark, Airgram #351 to Marshall, November 6, 1947, RG 59, file: 640.002/11-647; Millard tel. to Marshall, November 14, 1947, RG 59, file: 655.5631/11-1447; Dahl dispatch #404 to Marshall, December 18, 1947, RG 59, file: 640.002/12-1847; Bliss dispatch #128 to Marshall, January 19, 1948, RG 59, file: 640.002/1-1948; Bonsal tel. to Marshall, January 16, 1948, RG 59, file: 640.002/1-1648; Bliss dispatch #353 to Marshall, February 11, 1948, RG 59, file: 640.002/2-1148; Douglas Airgram #473 to Marshall, February 24, 1948, RG 59, file: 640.002/2-2448; and Charles J. Little, First Secretary, American Embassy, Brussels, dispatch #239 to Marshall, April 12, 1948, RG 59, file: 640.002/4-2248.

[86] In this case as well, the Benelux would only join a union that included Britain. Caffery tel. to Marshall, January 31, 1948, RG 59, file: 651.652/1-3148; Kirk tel. to Marshall, February 4, 1948, RG 59, file: 655.5631/2-448; Herman B. Baruch, Ambassador in the Netherlands, tel. to Marshall, February 7, 1948, *FRUS, 1948*, 3:379-80; Millard tel. to Marshall, February 8, 1948, RG 59, file: 655.5631/2-848; and Bliss dispatch #353 to Marshall, February 11, 1948, RG 59, file: 640.002/2-1148.

ERP countries whose national aspirations coincided to some degree with the American design for a European neo-capitalism.

On the European side, British and Belgian leaders tangled over the economic arrangements that would supplement the Brussels Pact. As late as April 1948, Bevin was still talking about a common central bank through which the Brussels Pact powers could prevent competitive economic policies from scuttling their defense agreements. But he now insisted that this and other steps toward European unification must come gradually, must take the form of intergovernmental agreements approved by a continuing European recovery authority, and must be administered on an ad hoc basis. He refused to gird the Brussels Pact with a strong organization composed of ministerial officials and equipped with real executive authority and a powerful secretariat. The Belgians, with initial support from the French, had wanted such an organization to manage the economic and political aspects of the pact. Under pressure from Whitehall, however, the five powers decided instead to establish a consultative council of ambassadors who lacked the power to act independently. The decision did not provide for a strong secretariat or a separate organization to oversee economic arrangements. These were to be organized instead on an "ad hoc" basis through regular diplomatic channels and periodic meetings between economic experts and finance ministers.[87] By following this strategy, the finance ministers of the five powers managed France's deficit through an extension of bilateral credits and then completed work on a new payments plan that would operate within the framework of the ERP, not the Brussels Pact.[88]

Nor were the French more successful than the Belgians when it came to organizing a permanent European recovery organization. Negotiations over the nature of a continuing organization began in January 1948, largely as a result of American pressure for greater progress toward the cooperative commitments outlined in the CEEC report of the previous fall. The French wanted to centralize authority, including authority over national recovery and production plans, in a strong organization that could transcend sov-

[87] Bevin conversation with Bidault, March 17, 1948, and Bevin conversation with the Foreign Ministers of France, Belgium, Netherlands, and Luxembourg, March 17, 1948, FO 800/460/EUR/48/16; and Bevin conversation with Bidault, April 17, 1948, Record of a Meeting of the Foreign Ministers of the United Kingdom, France, Belgium, Netherlands, and Luxembourg, Paris, April 17, 1948, and Bevin conversation with French President Vincent-Auriol, April 17, 1948, FO 800/447/Conf./48/3.

[88] Makins minutes to Bevin, April 26 and 30, 1948, British Embassy, Brussels, tels. to FO, April 28 and 29, 1948, and Treasury note to the London Committee, April 30, 1948, with attached Annexes A–F, FO 371, 71767, UR1212, UR1287, UR1234, UR1250, and UR1269. See also Report by the UK Delegation on the Five Power Official Discussion in The Hague, April 23, 1948, Records of the British Treasury, Economic Cooperation Committee (London Committee), Record Class T232/24/EEC16/8/04 (hereafter cited as T232, with appropriate filing designation).

ereignties. Defended as a step toward European economic unity, their proposal (as in the case of a Ruhr authority and a customs union) aimed at an
organizational framework through which they could bring bizonal requirements into line with those of the Monnet Plan. But British diplomacy had
its own organizational imperatives. British policymakers favored a decentralized structure composed of an assembly, specialized subcommittees, and
a secretariat limited to purely administrative functions. Their plan would
vest ultimate authority over matters of policy in national delegations. It
would protect the sovereignty of the participating countries and enable the
British to resist integrationist schemes that threatened their economic planning or ties to the Commonwealth and sterling area.[89]

Thinking in Washington paralleled the French position. Policymakers in
the State Department favored a vigorous European organization with representatives "of standing," with an "active secretariat" under the leadership
of an "outstanding man," and with the power to organize technical committees, mediate disputes between participating countries, review national
requirements, and develop a "joint agreed program" for Western Europe
as a whole. Such an organization would also advise on the most efficient
use of American aid and maintain continuous contact with the United States
Special Representative in Europe. It, rather than the individual governments,
would be the partner with which American recovery officials worked. In
this role, it would become the "major instrument" for "fostering European
cooperation and further integration."[90] This thinking, moreover, won
congressional endorsement in the Economic Cooperation Act of 1948, which
conditioned American aid on the establishment of a strong "continuing
organization" in Europe.[91]

The structure and power of the continuing organization had not been
decided when the CEEC reconvened in March. But Ambassador Lewis
Douglas had conveyed American thinking to British and French leaders and
the State Department had decided to send a team of experts, led by Henry
Labouisse of the Western European Division, to provide friendly aid on this
and other issues to the CEEC meeting.[92] The new organization, Americans

[89]   Caffery tel. to Marshall, January 30, 1948, and Gallman tel. to Marshall, February
       9, 1948, *FRUS, 1948*, 3:377–8, 381–2; Caffery tel. to Marshall, February 6, 1948,
       RG 59, file: 840.50Recovery/1-648; and Lovett tel. to Certain Diplomatic Offices in
       Europe, December 31, 1947, *FRUS, 1948*, 3:352.
[90]   Marshall tel. to Douglas, February 29, 1948, *FRUS, 1948*, 3:384–6; Douglas tel. to
       Marshall, March 3, 1948, RG 84, London Embassy Records, box 1035, file: 850
       Marshall Plan; Marshall tel. to Caffery, March 9, 1948, RG 59, file: 840.50Recovery/
       3-948; and Marshall circular tel., March 10, 1948, RG 59, file: 840.50Recovery/3-
       1048. See also "Proposed U.S. Position Paper on Structure and Functions of Con-
       tinuing CEEC Organization," in Manfull to the European Recovery Program Com-
       mittee, March 10, 1948, RG 353, Lot 122, box 31, folder: ERP Documents.
[91]   Foreign Assistance Act of 1948, in House, *Executive Hearings, 1948*, 254–72.
[92]   Douglas tel. to Marshall, March 4, 1948, RG 59, file: 840.50Recovery/3-448; Warren

agreed, must not degenerate into a "review and discussion group" that simply paid "lip-service" to "true economic cooperation."[93] It must play a "major role" in developing "all phases of ERP," including the "closer integration and cohesion of Western Europe which events call for."[94] This was the judgment of Secretary of State Marshall and of a long memorandum Labouisse circulated among the CEEC delegations in Paris.[95]

By this time, however, the British Cabinet had approved the paper by the London Committee that called for a continuing organization that would function essentially as a planning agency without executive authority or a strong secretariat. The appointment of Sir Oliver Franks, a leading figure in the CEEC's earlier deliberations, to the British ambassadorship in Washington signaled Bevin's decision to support this policy, bypass the European organization, and deal bilaterally with the United States. At the CEEC meeting in Paris, Bevin and Hall-Patch also restated their opposition to the French demand for a strong organization. Hall-Patch warned that an independent secretariat might well become the instrument of American, rather than European, policy. Bevin linked Britain's opposition to its traditional relationship with the Commonwealth. The British delegation, he told the French, must be able to "harmonize our desire to meet the needs of Europe with our special commitments to the Commonwealth."[96] Attaining this goal required an organization in which decisions would be reached through mutual agreement and real control would reside in home governments. There might be a secretary general, the British said. But to avoid any threat to their sovereignty, they wanted to limit this office to routine administrative functions. They also intended to capture it, along with other key posts, for their own nationals.[97]

Despite the French and American opposition, two factors strengthened

Kelchner memoranda to Peurifoy through Scott, March 2 and 15, 1948, RG 59, file: 840.50Recovery/3-2448; minutes of the Policy Committee on the European Recovery Program, March 5, 1948, RG 353, Lot 122, box 36, folder: PCE Minutes/1-2; Marshall tel. to Caffery, March 9, 1948, RG 59, file: 840.50Recovery/3-948; and Marshall tel. to Caffery, March 12, 1948, RG 59, file: 840.50Recovery/3-1248.

[93] Memorandum by William T. Phillips of the International Resources Division to Nitze, March 4, 1948, *FRUS*, 1948, 3:387–8.

[94] Marshall tel. to Caffery, March 22, 1948, *FRUS, 1948*, 3:400–1. See also Marshall circular tel., March 10, 1948, RG 59, file: 840.50Recovery/3-1048.

[95] A copy of the American (Labouisse) memorandum is attached to Hall-Patch letter to Makins, March 18, 1947, FO 371, 71809, UR509.

[96] British Embassy, Paris, tel. to FO, from Hall-Patch, March 13, 1948, FO 371, 71809, UR348; Bevin conversation with Bidault, March 15, 1948, FO 800/460/EUR/48/16; Caffery tel. to Marshall, March 15, 1948, RG 59, file: 840.50Recovery/3-1548; and Caffery tel. to Marshall, March 20, 1948, *FRUS, 1948*, 3:395–8.

[97] Caffery tel. to Marshall, March 9, 1948, RG 59, file: 840.50Recovery/3-948; Gallman tel. to Marshall, March 12, 1948, *FRUS, 1948*, 3:391–3; Caffery tel. to Marshall, March 15, 1948, RG 59, file: 840.50Recovery/3-1548; and Caffery tel. to Marshall, March 17, 1948, RG 59, file: 840.50Recovery/3-1748.

the British position. For one thing, the British gained leverage when they
agreed to locate the new organization in Paris rather than in London. For
another, the French lacked allies among the other CEEC delegations. Although the Benelux had supported the French position initially, this support
began to wither as they and the other smaller countries grew apprehensive
about their prospects in a supranational organization that might be dominated by the great powers.[98] The results became apparent in the CEEC's
instructions to the working party that was to draft a charter for the continuing organization. These instructions grew out of Anglo–French negotiations in which the British had used all of their "artillery on the vital need
for strong national delegations and the need for limiting the role of the
General Secretary." They were designed to circumvent the "unpalatable
items" contained in the American proposal and earlier put forward by the
French as a result of their talks with Labouisse and other American officials
in Paris and Washington.[99] The instructions envisioned a body composed
of a general assembly, executive committee, and secretariat, but one in which
authority would derive from the assembly and the secretariat would be
limited to administrative responsibilities. As the British had proposed, all
decisions were to be reached through "mutual agreement."[100]

These instructions foreordained the draft character that the working party
eventually produced. It provided for a secretariat of international character,
headed by a secretary general, but with routine duties. Administrative responsibility would reside in an executive committee and ultimate authority
in a council of national representatives acting through mutual agreement.
The new organization could "promote," "investigate," "consider," and
"recommend." But it could not act independently of home governments.
As the British had hoped, it would be little more than a conduit for conventional, intergovernmental cooperation, not an autonomous, supranational authority.[101]

The draft charter hardly matched American expectations. The Europeans
had incorporated provisions enabling the proposed organization to assume
additional powers if the need arose and the participating governments

[98] Caffery tel. to Marshall, March 17, 1948, RG 59, file: 840.50Recovery/3-1748. See
      also Caffery tel. to Marshall, March 16, 1948, RG 59, file: 840.50Recovery/3-1648.
      For American representations at the CEEC meeting, see Caffery tels. (#1420 and
      #1430) to Marshall, March 17, 1948, RG 59, file: 840.50Recovery/3-1748. See also
      British Embassy, Paris, tel. to FO, March 13, 1948, FO 371, 71809, UR349.
[99] Hall-Patch letter to Makins, March 18, 1948, FO 371, 71809, UR509.
[100] Caffery tel. to Marshall, March 18, 1948, RG 59, file: 840.50Recovery/3-1848. See
      also CP (48) 98, Bevin memorandum, "The Second Meeting of the Committee of
      European Economic Co-operation Held in Paris from 15th to 18th March," April
      1, 1948, FO 800/447/Conf./48/2.
[101] Caffery tel. #1578 to Marshall, March 24, 1948, RG 59, file: 840.50Recovery/3-
      2448. See also Caffery tel. to American Embassy, London, March 29, 1948, RG
      84, London Embassy Records, box 1035, file: 850 Marshall Plan.

agreed. They had also drafted a multilateral accord, which, among other things, called for further integration in Europe and for maximum efforts to develop production and modernize equipment, use resources efficiently, multilateralize payments, and "eventually" eliminate all "abnormal restrictions" on the exchange of goods, services, and labor.[102] These provisions, as Ambassador Caffery noted, created a "framework" for future collaboration. But neither Caffery nor the "friendly aid" team were sanguine about "the probabilities for prompt and effective economic cooperation and integration." There was nothing in the draft charter or multilateral accord binding the participants to "full cooperative action" if they thought their national interests dictated otherwise, which seemed to be the case for the British. The British clearly preferred to protect their gold and dollar reserves and maintain their ties to the Commonwealth. They had no plans "to go beyond traditional means of cooperation between governments." Certainly they did not "envisage any transfer of sovereignty to a supra-national body." And so long as they remained timid on this score, it would also be difficult to bring the other CEEC countries into a "unit of efficient economic dimensions."[103]

Nevertheless, the Americans were still determined to make the new organization a "focal point around which closer Western European economic cohesion can be built."[104] In mid-April, after the European foreign ministers had approved the draft charter and the Organization for European Economic Cooperation (OEEC) came into existence, American policymakers began urging participating countries to appoint men of ministerial rank to the new body. Such appointees supposedly would assert their autonomy of foreign offices and transform the OEEC into a strong and independent authority. This was exactly what the British wanted to avoid, of course, and once again they thwarted American hopes. Despite American entreaties that Bevin or another cabinet minister head Britain's OEEC delegation, this job went to Edmund Hall-Patch, an under secretary in the Foreign Office, who also became chairman of the OEEC Executive Committee. The only European of cabinet rank to occupy an executive position in the new organization was Belgian Prime Minister Paul-Henri Spaak, whose determination to prevent an Anglo–French monopoly of top posts had caused a minor skirmish among the Europeans. Spaak became chairman of the Council, while Robert Marjolin of France took charge of the Secretariat.[105]

[102]   Caffery tel. to Marshall, March 23, 1948, *FRUS, 1948*, 3:401–3; Caffery tel. to Marshall, March 24, 1948, RG 59, file: 840.50Recovery/3-2448; Caffery tel. to Marshall, March 25, 1948, RG 59, file: 840.50Recovery/3-2548; and Caffery tel. to Marshall, March 27, 1948, RG 59, file: 840.50Recovery/3-2748.

[103]   Caffery tel. to Marshall, March 28, 1948, and Douglas tel. to Marshall, April 2, 1948, *FRUS, 1948*, 3:404–8, 1079–82.

[104]   Lovett tel. to Caffery, April 8, 1948, *FRUS, 1948*, 3:414–17.

[105]   For American and British policy on this issue, and for the European skirmish over top posts in the OEEC, see the documents in *FRUS, 1948*, 3:412, 414–17, 425;

Defeated on this issue, the Americans had greater success when it came to the German problem, which remained essentially a problem of reconciling economic and security imperatives. Germany's revival had to be harnessed to the causes of European recovery and Soviet containment without restoring its prewar hegemony or reinvigorating the economic autarky that had twice led to world war. The solution to this problem, so far as American leaders were concerned, still lay in their design for an integrated European economy. Although British opposition threatened to wreck this design in the long run, in the short run American leaders could count on more support from Whitehall than had been the case in other areas. Aside from their differences over the dismantling of German industrial plants, which Whitehall supported and Washington opposed, British and American leaders were able to join in efforts to create the rudiments of a West German government, introduce a new German currency, and increase the level of German industrial production.[106] It was the French who raised the greatest resistance, and securing their support became one of the major missions of American diplomats at the CEEC meeting in Paris and the concurrent meeting of foreign ministers in London.

VI

The German problem remained a source of some controversy in the United States. During hearings on the Foreign Assistance Act, many congressional leaders had been critical of the dismantling and removal of German plants and capital equipment at a time, in their view, when Germany needed to be strengthened as a barrier to Soviet expansion and as a contributor to European recovery. The Harriman Committee had expressed similar views, as had a group of cabinet officials who were calling for a full-scale investigation of the reparations program. The State and War departments had

Millard tel. to Marshall, April 3, 1948, RG 59, file: 840.50Recovery/4-348; Achilles memorandum of conversation, April 5, 1948, Clayton-Thorp Office Files (Truman Library), box 15, folder: Reading File, Misc. Memoranda of Conversations; Caffery tel. to Marshall, April 5, 1948, RG 59, file: 840.50Recovery/4-548; Baruch tel. to Marshall, April 8, 1948, RG 59, file: 655.5631/4-848; Douglas tel. to Lovett, April 8, 1948, RG 59, file: 840.50Recovery/4-848; Baruch tel. to Marshall, April 12, 1948, RG 59, file: 655.5631/4-1248; Caffery tel. to Marshall, April 13, 1948, RG 59, file: 840.50Recovery/4-1348; Lovett tel. to Douglas, April 14, 1948, RG 84, London Embassy Records, box 1035, file: 850 Marshall Plan; Caffery tel. to Marshall, April 14, 1948, RG 59, file: 840.50Recovery/4-1448; Caffery tel. to Marshall, April 15, 1948, RG 59, file: 840.50Recovery/4-1548; and Douglas tel. to Marshall, April 16, 1948, and Caffery tel. to Marshall, April 16, 1948, RG 59, file: 840.50Recovery/4-1648. See also Under Secretary of State William Strang minute to Makins, April 16, 1948, FO 371, 71861, UR1066; and Bevin conversation with Bidault, April 16, 1948, and Bevin conversation with the Benelux Foreign Ministers, April 16, 1948, FO 800/447/Conf./48/3.

106   For British policy on the German question, see Bullock, *Bevin*, 514–16.

defended the program, which they said was compatible with Germany's recovery and with interallied security agreements that Britain and France would defend. Nevertheless, Truman had appointed a cabinet-level working group and technical committee to study the reparations program and Congress had included in the Foreign Assistance Act a provision ordering the ECA to conduct a similar review. The goal was to identify those plants that could best contribute to European recovery if retained in Germany.[107]

Although these disputes tended to highlight the persistent tension between the economic and security imperatives that were inherent in a German settlement, they should not obscure the State Department's efforts to reconcile these imperatives within the framework of a comprehensive recovery program. Secretary of State Marshall made this point in his testimony before the Senate Foreign Relations Committee in January. By that time, the Foreign Ministers Conference of late 1947 had failed to reach agreement on German unification and central administration. British and American leaders had begun to reorganize the Bizone and secure French support through three-power consultation, promises of increased German coal exports, and recognition of French economic claims in the Saar. Marshall summarized some of these developments in an exchange with Senator Vandenberg, agreeing as he did that Germany's revival and reintegration were essential to recovery and security in Western Europe. The United States, he said, must move ahead with measures to unify the Western zones and make them an "integral" part of the ERP.[108]

Indeed, bringing western Germany into the associative structure of a unified European economic order had been an American goal since the CEEC negotiations in the summer of 1947. With this goal in mind, the State Department had tried to integrate bizonal resources into the general European recovery program and had agreed in principle to consider some mechanism for overseeing the coal and steel industries of the Ruhr. It had also made bizonal Germany a signatory of the First Agreement on Multilateral Monetary Compensation and had brought bizonal representatives into the working parties that the CEEC appointed to study the merits of a European customs union, draft a multilateral accord, and draw up the charter for a continuing recovery organization. Although the French would not permit German leaders to join the foreign ministers who signed the OEEC protocol in April 1948, under pressure from the United States they had incorporated in the multilateral accord an American-inspired provision placing German trade on a most-favored-nation basis, had abandoned attempts to condition Germany's membership on new level-of-industry arrangements, and had agreed to trizonal representation in the continuing

---

[107] See the documents in *FRUS, 1948,* 2:711–17, 721, 726–8, 730–3, 738–43. See also House, *Recovery Program Hearings, 1947–8,* 77–8, 560, 562; and Senate, *ERP Hearings, 1948,* 1–74, 444–77.

[108] Senate, *ERP Hearings, 1948,* 11–12.

organization.[109] The last agreement emerged from the first session of the London Conference on Germany, which met intermittently between February and June 1948. Out of this session also came a package of understandings that brought the French more into line with American policy.

Marshall struck the keynote of American policy at the London Conference when he wrote Ambassador Caffery that French security and European recovery ultimately depended on the formation of an integrated framework. Because he saw trizonal economic coordination as "the first immediate step required for [the] furtherance of Western European integration," the American delegation in London threatened to withhold ERP aid in order to win France's agreement to an arrangement that put the external trade of its zone under the control of the American-dominated Joint Export–Import Agency.[110] The Americans also demanded prompt establishment of a provisional German administration and rapid progress toward the formation of a permanent government with sufficient authority to play an "appropriate" role in the ERP. Delay, they argued in this case as well, would prevent a "maximum German contribution to European recovery" and slow the "desired process of integrat[ing] Western Germany into Western Europe." These demands collided with a French policy that opposed the formation of a provisional regime, political centralization in Germany, and abandonment of Allied occupation controls. But out of this conflict eventually emerged a compromise that American leaders could accept. The American delegation withdrew its demand for a provisional regime; the French advanced the timetable for the formation of a permanent German government; and together the conferees outlined the principles that would guide the process of constitution making by a German constituent assembly that was to convene in September. In deference to the French, the conferees also enumerated the powers to be reserved by the Western Allies after the formation of a new German government. These included the powers to regulate Germany's foreign trade, guarantee compliance with the new constitution, and enforce various agreements relating to the Ruhr, demilitarization, and level of industry.[111]

In negotiating the Ruhr agreements, policymakers in the State Department had been guided by the interrelated goals of European integration and

[109] See the documents in *FRUS, 1948*, 2:78–9, 112–17, 141–3. See also Marshall tel. to Certain Diplomatic Offices, February 29, 1948, and Marshall tel. to Douglas, February 29, 1948, *FRUS, 1948*, 3:383–6; Douglas tel. to Marshall, March 1, 1948, RG 59, file: 840.50Recovery/3-148; and Douglas tel. to Marshall, March 2, 1948, RG 84, London Embassy Records, box 1035, file: 850 Marshall Plan.

[110] For Marshall's views, see his tels. to Douglas, March 2, 1948, and to Caffery, February 19, 1948, *FRUS, 1948*, 2:113, 70–1. See also the documents in *FRUS, 1948*, 2:87–9, 101–2, 112–13, 114–16, 216–19, 242–4, 289–90.

[111] Marshall tel. to Caffery, May 26, 1948, *FRUS, 1948* 2:283–4. See also the documents in *FRUS, 1948*, 2:107–10, 151–2, 158–60, 175–6, 207–10, 223–6, 240–1, 260–2, 270–2, 305–6.

German reintegration. They still believed, as they had since the Moscow Conference of 1947, that international supervision of the Ruhr would help to control the Germans, ensure French security, and promote European union. Ambassador Douglas, who headed the American delegation to the London Conference, even suggested at one point the formation of a truly international regime that would integrate the coal and steel industries of France, the Benelux countries, and the Ruhr. French policymakers, of course, had their own reasons for supporting integration. They wanted an international regime invested with the attributes of sovereignty, including independent membership in the OEEC and managerial control over the Ruhr coal and steel industries. Arrangements of this nature would give French officials a voice in basic production and investment decisions and in the allocation of German coal resources between domestic consumption and foreign export. They would safeguard France's security and Monnet Plan, but at the cost of offending the Germans and denying the United States a voice in basic management and allocation decisions commensurate with its financial contribution to Germany's recovery. Nor could such arrangements possibly win support from General Clay.

Citing these arguments, the American delegation in London proposed instead an international authority that would advise the occupation officials on economic policies in the Ruhr and harmonize these policies with the OEEC's program for European recovery. The conferees eventually approved an agreement to this effect. The understanding exceeded Clay's wishes, fell short of French expectations, and left unresolved such questions as the power of the new authority and the ownership of the Ruhr coal and steel industries. From the State Department's point of view, however, it brought French and American policy closer to the balanced and supranational approach that it was urging on both the Army Department and the Marshall Plan countries.[112]

The same approach shaped American policy on the security question. In this case, the American negotiators at the London Conference ruled out French proposals for postoccupation rights and permanent limits on German production. These proposals, they said, would hamper Germany's revival and slow the process of European integration. In addition, the Americans never tired of telling the French how measures of this sort ran the risk of alienating the Germans and driving them into the hands of a Soviet government that now posed the greatest threat to European security. This is not to argue that American negotiators were deaf to French economic and security concerns. They were willing to discuss permanent prohibitions and limitations on war-related industries and take steps to guarantee Germany's disarmament and demilitarization. They also accepted international super-

[112] *FRUS, 1948*, 2:92–4, 97–100, 124–8, 135–8, 197–205, 235–7, 244–5, 251–3, 285–8.

vision of the Ruhr and agreed to maintain American troops in Germany until a final peace settlement had been concluded, withdraw these troops only after consultation with France and the other Western Allies, and renew this consultation in the event of a resurgent German threat to European security. At their urging, these concessions were incorporated into another agreement that also established Allied working parties to list the prohibitions and limitations on German industry and draw up the terms for a military security board that would advise on measures to prevent Germany's re-militarization. The agreement, in addition, promised the French a consul-tative voice in matters relating to Germany's overall level of industry. It also kept open the possibility of permanent economic restrictions and limited occupation rights in the period following a peace settlement.[113]

The London accords were an ambiguous accomplishment. Coming just as the Marshall Plan countries were organizing the OEEC and beginning work on the first annual recovery program, they seemed to point toward Germany's revival and reintegration into the sort of economic union that American leaders saw as one of the keys to peace and prosperity on the Continent. Yet these very successes raised new obstacles to further progress. Moscow was critical of accords that it said violated wartime agreements and divided Germany. When the London accords were followed by the German currency reform of June, the Soviets responded by blockading Ber-lin. The Germans were also reluctant to sanction a division of their homeland or to approve measures, such as those establishing a Ruhr authority and listing reserved powers, that might reduce their proposed government to little more than an agent of Allied power. And the French, who ultimately reserved their position on international ownership of the Ruhr until the London Conference reconvened in the fall, were soon wondering if the accords looked to a Franco–German rapprochement within the framework of a European union or to a deflation of their pretensions and a revival of the German behemoth.[114]

The French already could point to disturbing signs that American policy placed Germany's interests ahead of their own. American officials had re-fused to "delegate executive power" over Germany to the OEEC, in part because they were unwilling to trust Germany's fate to its former victims, in part because neither Congress nor the Army Department would relinquish its prerogatives in this area.[115] They also worked out special arrangements whereby the occupation authorities, rather than the ECA, would administer the recovery program in the Bizone, even though these authorities had

---

[113]   *FRUS, 1948*, 2:94–5, 101–2, 110–11, 122–3, 230–1, 232, 233–4, 248, 256–68, 279–80, 291–4.
[114]   John C. Campbell, *The United States in World Affairs, 1948–1949* (New York, 1949), 76–9, 97; and John Gimbel, *The American Occupation of Germany: Politics and Military, 1945–1949* (Stanford, CA, 1968), 204–9.
[115]   Marshall circular tel., March 10, 1948, RG 59, file: 840.50Recovery/3-1048.

consistently resisted the State Department's strategy of balancing Germany's revival against France's security.[116] Making matters worse from the French point of view was General Clay's apparent determination to treat the Bizone as an American enclave. Clay opposed the Ruhr authority and the long list of reserved powers, arguing that both reduced his autonomy and gave the French new opportunities to retard Germany's recovery. He also demanded dollars for Germany's exports, refused to pay dollars for its imports, and blocked efforts to reestablish Germany's foreign trade through the ports of Antwerp and Rotterdam. All of this heightened French fears that Clay, as the State Department itself complained, was not balancing bizonal requirements against those of other areas or "integrat[ing] Germany into the European economy."[117]

Clay's attitude was one of several problems that weakened the general thrust of American policy on the whole question of supranationalism. Despite the State Department's opposition to special arrangements for Britain and the Commonwealth, it had refused to grant the OEEC "executive power" over Germany. Nor had it been willing to give the OEEC the right to make final decisions concerning the use and distribution of American aid. Washington, as Clayton had said earlier, wanted to *"run this show,"* which meant retaining ultimate control over aid decisions in American hands.[118] Yet this policy was likely to relegate the OEEC to an advisory role, undermine its prestige, and lessen its utility as an instrument of integration. It could also justify Britain's opposition to a collective authority and encourage France to seek organizational mechanisms more suited to its own economic and security objectives.

VII

Despite these shortcomings, some of the key elements of American recovery policy were now clear and would remain so in the years ahead. Building on the compromise worked out by free-traders and planners in the State Department – on their fusion, that is, of market mechanisms and institutional regulators – American policymakers were urging their European beneficiaries to revive industry and reform finances, liberalize trade and payments, and build central organizations of economic planning and coordination. They would later supplement these lines of policy with parallel

[116] For the agreement (between Clay and Ambassador Harriman), see the documents in RG 59, file: 840.50Recovery/7-448, /10-2048, /10-2748, /12-348, and /12-1448.

[117] ECA and State Department officials recited the litany of complaints against Clay at a meeting in July. See Policy Planning Staff, Minutes of Meeting, July 1, 1948, RG 59, PPS Records, box 32, folder: PPS Minutes of Meetings, 1948. For Clay's thinking on the London accords, see *FRUS, 1948*, 2:205–6, 216–29, 235–7. See also Campbell, *United States in World Affairs, 1948–1949*, 185; and Clay, *Decision in Germany*, 196–7.

[118] Clayton, "The European Crisis," *FRUS, 1947*, 3:230–2.

plans to export American production know-how and build an alliance of cooperating public and private officials in Europe similar to the one that took shape around the ECA in Washington. These plans, as well, would become important elements in the American design for a European neo-capitalism. But if these were the plans, they differed somewhat from those of the participating countries, whose own aspirations would continue to combine with contradictions on the American side to frustrate the Marshall Planners.

4

Strategies of transnationalism: the ECA and the politics of peace and productivity

I

IN THE SECOND HALF of 1948, the European scene was almost as foreboding as it had been when Marshall announced the recovery program a year earlier. The Berlin crisis, the Communist disruptions and labor unrest, the German economic revival, and the morass of nonconvertible currencies, trade restrictions, and low productivity were serious problems that required concerted action if Western Europe was going to look forward to a new day of peace and prosperity. Amid all of these difficulties, many turned again to the idea of unification as a way to control the Germans, contain the Soviets, and revive the European economies. Some looked to military unification through the Brussels Pact and a North Atlantic defense community. Others pointed to the OEEC as a hopeful sign of economic integration. Still others wanted to bring the new forms of economic and military collaboration under the aegis of a European political federation. Whatever their differences, all shared a vision of redemption through unification. Through greater unity, they saw Western Europe emerging from the rubble and the ruin of war, arising, like Lazarus from the grave, with new life and vitality.

American leaders did what they could to encourage this hope. The Republican Party platform of 1948 urged "sturdy progress toward unity in western Europe." Republican luminaries like Dulles and Dewey called again for "European unity." The Democrats issued a similar proclamation and the State Department announced its strong support for "the progressively closer integration of western Europe." Although the goal was integration in the economic, political, and military fields alike, those making policy were generally pessimistic about the prospects for immediate political federation.[1] They concentrated instead on practical plans for a functional in-

---

[1] The quotes are from Campbell, *United States in World Affairs, 1948–1949*, 518–19.

tegration along economic and military lines. Guided by the New Deal synthesis as it had emerged thus far, they continued their search for a European neo-capitalism, launching new initiatives to liberalize intra-European payments and reform finances, calling again for central institutions of economic planning and coordination, and making new efforts to bring private leaders into a pattern of corporative collaboration with government. American policymakers also adapted the "ERP analogy" to the military field, where they urged the Europeans to unify defense systems "through standardization, integration, and coordination of production and supply" and then tried to incorporate the results into a North Atlantic defense community.[2] Much the same was true of their approach to the German problem. This was a problem that straddled the economic and military fields and one the Americans still hoped to solve by bringing the Germans into an integrated and supranational system.

In all of these areas, American policy retained an essential continuity, as did the difficulties that slowed progress. There still existed the problems of drawing Britain into Europe, of winning France's support for Germany's revival and reintegration, and of bringing the Army Department into line with strategies favored in the State Department and the ECA. American leaders made some progress in dealing with these problems. But gains came slowly and only as a result of hard-fought battles that left a residue of ill-will on both sides of the Atlantic.

II

One of the hallmarks of the New Deal synthesis was an emphasis on co-operating links between private economic groups and between these groups and government authorities. By forging such links, American Marshall Planners hoped to build a transnational alliance behind the ERP, equip participating countries with American production skills, fashion American patterns of labor–management teamwork, and, in these and other ways, maximize the chances for economic integration and social peace on the Continent. The networks of corporative collaboration they created thus formed part of the larger effort to organize a neo-capitalist order similar to the one in the United States. Indeed, these networks started on the American side, where the ECA became the hub in an elaborate system of public–private power sharing.

Once the Foreign Assistance Act had passed, the ECA and the other

See also the memorandum by Ben T. Moore to George Kennan et al., October 25, 1948, Records of the Agency for International Development (ECA Records) (Washington National Records Center), Record Group 286, Acc. 53A405, box 33, folder: Program – European Payments Union (hereafter cited as RG 286, with accession, box, and folder designations).

[2] Department of State Policy Statement, June 11, 1948, *FRUS, 1948,* 3:1091–1108.

agencies involved acted quickly to establish what became an extensive system of corporative collaboration with economic groups in the private sector. They met with the leading commercial banks to arrange credit facilities and held conferences with industry and farm groups to prepare programs for the shipment of goods to Europe. Much of the early consultation was undertaken through the Commerce and Agriculture departments, both of which had well-established liaisons with the private sector. In the Commerce Department, for example, the secretary met periodically with the Business Advisory Council on "matters of broad public policy" while the divisions of international trade and industry cooperation employed a variety of commodity panels and industry advisory groups to consult with private businessmen on matters ranging from export-licensing procedures to the allocation of scarce commodities.[3]

An even more extensive network took shape around the ECA. Under the Foreign Assistance Act, the ECA had a Public Advisory Board, to which Paul Hoffman appointed representatives of business, labor, and agriculture. To assist the administrator with specific aspects of the recovery program, there were also a host of private advisory committees, including an Oil Price Committee and similar groups for overseas development, reparations, and fiscal and monetary problems. Each committee consisted chiefly of prominent figures from the world of business and finance. The Advisory Committee on Reparations, established to assess the "production results" of retaining in Germany more than three hundred plants still slated for removal as reparations, was headed by George Humphrey of the Hanna Company and included such "top-flight" industrialists as Charles Wilson of General Motors, Gwilyn Price of Westinghouse, John McCaffrey of International Harvester, and Frederick Geier of the Cincinnati Milling Machine Company. The Advisory Committee on Fiscal and Monetary Problems included George Harrison of the New York Life Insurance Company, Edward Brown of the First National Bank of New York, Walter Stewart of the Rockefeller Foundation, and Joseph Dodge of the Detroit Bank. Harrison had served earlier as president of the New York Federal Reserve Bank and Dodge had been one of General Clay's major financial advisors in Germany. In addition, Hoffman cooperated with the Council on Foreign Relations, commissioning that group to report on American goals in Europe and the means for achieving them; he also had the "benefit of advice informally given by men such

[3] U.S., Department of Commerce, *Thirty-Sixth Annual Report of the Secretary of Commerce, 1948* (Washington, DC, 1948), xii, 27–32, 168–78. See also George McGhee, Special Assistant to the Under Secretary of State, letter to Wayne C. Taylor of the ECA, April 13, 1948, RG 59, file: 840.50Recovery/4-1348; Arthur Gardiner, State Department Trade Advisor, tel. to William Jacobs of the American Cotton Manufacturers' Association, April 26, 1948, RG 59, file: 840.50Recovery/4-2648; and unsigned memorandum of telephone conversation, May 4, 1948, RG 59, file: 840.50 Recovery/5-448.

as Russell Leffingwell and Bernard Baruch"; and he worked closely with the business leadership of the Anglo–American Council on Productivity, which the ECA helped to establish in 1948.[4]

Similar men – "Wall Street wolves" according to Hoffman's critics – dominated the top positions in the ECA during its first year of operation.[5] Although a number of important slots were occupied by professionals and career public servants such as Richard M. Bissell, Jr., assistant deputy administrator in Washington, and Milton Katz, who became general counsel at the ECA's headquarters in Paris, men with corporate backgrounds similar to Hoffman's were far more typical of the agency's leadership. Averell Harriman, the special representative in Europe, was a senior partner in the Wall Street firm of Brown Bros., Harriman. Howard Bruce, the deputy administrator in Washington, was director and board member of several large business firms, and William Foster, the deputy administrator in Europe, was president of a steel-products company. Business representation was particularly strong in the ECA's industry divisions. The one in Washington was headed by Samuel Anderson, a partner in several large investment companies. In Paris, George W. Perkins of Merck and Company served in a similar capacity.[6] And reporting to Perkins were Clarence Randall, a vice-

---

[4]   Hoffman letter to Clarence Francis of General Foods Corporation, October 1, 1948, Paul G. Hoffman Papers (Truman Library), box 21, folder: ECA, Correspondence, 1948; Richard Heindel, staff associate, Senate Committee on Foreign Relations, letter to Senator Vandenberg, August 24, 1948, Vandenberg Papers, box 3, folder: Correspondence, August 1948; Hoffman letter to C. A. MacDonald, MacDonald-Cook Company, August 23, 1948, Hoffman Papers, box 1, file: Chronological File; Hoffman torep (to representative) 1495 to American Embassy, Paris, October 15, 1948, Records of the Agency for International Development (ECA Telegram Files) (Agency for International Development, Washington, DC), Acc. 53A278, box 45 (hereafter cited as ECA Files, with box number); and Council on Foreign Relations, "Studies on Aid to Europe," November 30, 1948, Clayton Papers, box 73, folder: Council on Foreign Relations.

[5]   The quote is from Hoffman's letter to Frank Gannett, July 15, 1948, Hoffman Papers, box 1, file: Chronological File. By "top positions" I mean the administrator, special representative, their deputies and assistants, the general counsel, comptroller, ECA mission chiefs, and the directors of the key divisions as identified in the text. The directors of the divisions of Administration and Administrative Services, Statistics and Reports, China Program, Organization and Management, Personnel, and Security have not been considered. Information on the directors of the divisions of Operations, Strategic Materials, Procurement Operation, and Program Coordination has not been located. The information that follows in the text is based on the roster of personnel listed in the second edition of ECA's pamphlet *American Business and European Recovery* (Washington, DC, 1948). Except where otherwise noted in the text, biographical information on the men listed on this roster comes from *Who's Who in America, Who Was Who in America, Current Biography: Who's News and Why, National Cyclopaedia of American Biography,* and *Biographical Dictionary of American Labor Leaders.*

[6]   Perkins actually succeeded Langbourne Williams, who served briefly as division head in 1948, and whom Harriman probably recruited from the Business Advisory Council.

president of Inland Steel Company; Cecil Burrill, an executive with Standard Oil of New Jersey; George Green, formerly a vice-president of General Motors; Walter Cisler, a vice-president of Detroit-Edison; and Godfrey Rockefeller, "a director of quite a number of corporations."[7]

Prominent business leaders also headed most of the ECA's overseas missions in 1948: in the United Kingdom, Thomas K. Finletter of Coudert Brothers; in Italy, James Zellerbach, board chairman of Crown Zellerbach Corporation; in Belgium, James G. Blaine, president of the Midland Trust Company of New York; and in France, David K. E. Bruce, a wealthy Baltimore businessman with ties, through marriage, to the Mellon family of Pittsburgh. In addition, the mission chiefs in Norway, Denmark, Turkey, Austria, Greece, and Sweden were, respectively, August Staley, an Illinois banker; Charles Marshall, a prominent New York attorney; Russell Dorr, another New York attorney who had earlier served as one of the State Department's representatives on the Inter-Allied Reparations Agency; Westmore Wilcox, a partner in various New York investment firms; John Nuveen, a Chicago businessman; and John Haskell, a financial executive.[8]

Although it is not surprising that college graduates occupied virtually all top positions in the ECA, it is worth noting that ten of these positions were held by Harvard graduates and over half by graduates of such other blue-chip institutions as Yale, Princeton, Brown, MIT, Swarthmore, Johns Hopkins, and the University of Pennsylvania. Noteworthy too is the previous government service of most of the business leaders and the fact that many belonged to one or more of the prestigious private associations – especially the Business Advisory Council (BAC), the Committee for Economic Development (CED), and the Council on Foreign Relations (CFR) – that routinely

---

In addition to the ECA officials mentioned in the text, Alexander Henderson, a partner in the law firm of Cravath, Swaine, and Moore, Eric Kohler, an accounting executive, and Norman Taber, an investment and financial consultant, served respectively as general counsel, comptroller, and budget director. Bryan Houston, a vice-president of the Pepsi-Cola Company, directed the ECA's Office of Information. And among the chief assistants to the administrator in Washington were Wayne C. Taylor, a Chicago banker before entering government service in the 1930s; Maurice Moore of Cravath, Swaine, and Moore; Samuel Richards, an executive with the Studebaker Corporation; and C. Tyler Wood, a former partner in the law firm of Gilbert, Elliot, and Company, who moved to ECA from his position as deputy to the assistant secretary of state for economic affairs.

7   "Summary of Conference of Hoffman, Harriman, Members of ECA-Paris Staff, and Country Mission Representatives," Paris, July 23–24, 1948, RG 286, Acc. 53A405, box 1, folder: Paris Conference, July 22–28.

8   The remaining four mission chiefs listed in *American Business and European Recovery* were Harriman, who officially headed the ECA mission in the Bizone; Joseph Carrigan, a former dean of the Agriculture School at the University of Vermont, who was chief of mission in Ireland; Alan Valentine, president of the University of Rochester and a director of various firms, who headed the ECA mission in the Netherlands; and Roger Lapham, board chairman of the American Hawaiian Steamship Company and a member of the Business Advisory Council, who led the ECA mission in China.

advised public officials and served as recruiting pools for government positions. As noted earlier, these agencies were closely linked with the multilateral bloc of capital-intensive firms that constituted a critical component of the New Deal–Fair Deal coalition. They had given substantial support to the domestic and foreign policies of the Roosevelt and Truman administrations and had played an important role in overcoming conservative opposition to the ERP in Congress. Hoffman had helped to found the CED, and he and Harriman were leading figures in the BAC. Both men could agree that "top people from every industry" were needed to manage the recovery program efficiently and to solve the difficult economic and technical problems involved in stabilizing finances, liberalizing trade, and boosting production.[9] Harriman recalled turning to the BAC for this talent when staffing his office in Paris, and he also thought it likely that Hoffman had used the CED for similar purposes.[10]

In addition to business leaders, Hoffman tried to incorporate other economic groups into schemes of corporatist collaboration. The major farm groups were represented on the ECA's Public Advisory Board, cooperated with its overseas missions, and worked closely with its food and agriculture divisions. Organized labor played an important part as well, not only in countering Communist attacks on the Marshall Plan but also in persuading European workers to work harder, defer consumption for the sake of investment, accept temporary unemployment, and make the other sacrifices necessary to raise production and achieve "effective European collaboration and economic integration."[11] In Europe, it was argued, "deep-seated union policies and worker habits" had to give way to the "[p]roductivity stress" so typical of the United States.[12] European labor leaders had to recognize the need to narrow wage and price differentials between countries, reduce the barriers to labor migration, and replace the old system of national "self-sufficiency with more efficient production through specialized industries" operating in a European-wide market. To expedite this process, union officials in the United States had to start sharing with "European labor and management" some of their ideas on the best way to organize industry and increase productivity.[13]

Nor were union officials reluctant to play such a role, which essentially meant adapting to the European arena the accommodation already hammered out between progressive labor, government, and business leaders in

[9] "Summary of Conference...," Paris, July 23–24, 1948, RG 286, Acc. 53A405, box 1, folder: Paris Conference, July 22–28.
[10] Interview with W. Averell Harriman, January 6, 1982 (author's files).
[11] Val Lorwin of the State Department, "Labor Participation in the Organization for European Economic Cooperation," April 30, 1948, RG 59, file: 840.5043/5-1448.
[12] Lovett tel. to Caffery, December 8, 1948, RG 59, file: 840.50Recovery/11-2448.
[13] Nitze, "Labor's Role in the European Recovery Program," a speech given to the Philadelphia Labor Education Association, August 14, 1948, copy in RG 59, PPS Records, box 50, folder: Nitze, Paul (Speeches & Articles, 1945–1953).

the United States. American trade unions endorsed the ERP in public statements that emphasized the importance of "increased production" and "economic integration" in Western Europe.[14] They urged workers to join in the management of the recovery program and had begun, even before the Marshall Plan, to cooperate with public officials in shaping the international aspects of American labor policy.[15] The Labor Department had organized an Office of International Labor Affairs under Phillip Kaiser and a Trade Union Advisory Committee that was collaborating with Kaiser and other officials in the War and State departments to frame overseas labor policy. In addition, the State Department had created the new post of labor attaché, was staffing it with men who had close ties to the American trade unions, and was cooperating with the American Federation of Labor (AFL) to combat communism in the European labor movement.[16]

Despite some resistance to these initiatives, a foundation existed upon which individuals seeking to integrate labor into the Marshall Plan were able to build.[17] Kaiser represented labor's views on the interdepartmental steering committee that studied the recovery program. Officials of both the AFL and the Congress of Industrial Organizations (CIO) served on the Harriman Committee.[18] In addition, Secretary Marshall agreed to appoint qualified labor leaders to key ambassadorial positions when they became available. He also asked the AFL for a list of possible labor appointees to the ECA, an agency, according to Under Secretary Lovett, that was to have "quite an immediate tie-in" with the labor, farm, and industry groups that supplied commodities and services to the administrator.[19]

[14] See, for example, the AFL's declaration on foreign policy quoted in Bruce torep 2070 to Harriman, November 24, 1948, ECA Files, box 45. See also the source cited in note 15.

[15] AFL memorandum to the president, December 19, 1947, Truman papers, OF, folder: 426-L (March 1951–1953). See also the discussion in Chapter 3.

[16] Peter Weiler, "The United States, International Labor, and the Cold War: The Breakup of the World Federation of Trade Unions," *Diplomatic History* 5 (Winter 1981): 1–22. See also Kaiser's letter to Eric Kocher of the American Embassy, Brussels, November 6, 1947, Philip M. Kaiser Papers (Truman Library), box 2, folder: Labor Attachés and State Department Officials – General Correspondence.

[17] For opposition to the trend, see David H. Stowe's memorandum to John R. Steelman, January 20, 1948, Truman Papers, OF, folder: 426-L (March 1951–1953); and Brown memorandum to Smith, November 24, 1948, Clayton-Thorp Office Files, box 15.

[18] Kaiser letter to Kocher, November 6, 1947, Kaiser papers, box 2, folder: Labor Attachés & State Department Officials – General Correspondence; and unsigned "Attitude of Labor towards the ERP," February 2, 1948, RG 59, file: 800.5043/2-248.

[19] Memorandum of Conversation between State Department and AFL officials, April 6, 1948, RG 59, file: 840.50Recovery/4-648. See also Memorandum of Conversation between State Department and AFL officials, February 25, 1948, RG 59, file: 811.5043/2-2548; Lovett letters to President William Green of the AFL, April 14 and 26 and June 17, 1948, Green letter to Lovett, April 20, 1948, Lovett letter to

This list and union participation led to actual appointments. Arlon Lyon of the Railway Labor Executives Association, George Meany of the AFL, and James Carey of the CIO were appointed to the ECA's Public Advisory Board.[20] Bert Jewell of the AFL and Clinton Golden of the CIO became Hoffman's chief labor advisors in Washington.[21] Boris Shishkin of the AFL headed the Labor and Manpower Division in Paris.[22] The Anglo–American Council on Productivity also had labor members, as did the many productivity teams and technical-assistance groups the ECA sent to Europe.[23] In addition, the ECA appointed labor representatives to each of its overseas missions, where they were to supplement the work of the State Department's labor attachés, develop ties between American and European labor organizations, and formulate policy on various "economic, social, technical and other problems affecting the European workers and their trade unions."[24]

The patterns of partnership were not limited to the ECA and private economic groups in the United States. Hoffman and his colleagues also tried to build a transnational network of public–private cooperation in Western Europe, a network that reflected their faith in the capacity of managerial approaches and corporatist collaboration to minimize disruptive social competition and mobilize private interests behind the interrelated goals of economic integration and greater productivity. One branch of this network was connected to the technical-assistance program organized by the ECA at the end of 1948. The program's goal was to stimulate "greater efficiency in [European] industrial production" through the introduction of American production techniques, styles of business organization, and labor–management partnerships. The vehicles for achieving this goal included a variety of technical-assistance projects, engineering schemes, and productivity surveys that were launched in Europe with the aid of American experts, and a host of European labor–management teams that were brought to the United States to study agricultural and industrial production methods. The ECA's industry divisions organized the so-called productivity teams, working closely on the European side with industry, labor, and government

---

Green, April 26, 1948, and Lovett memorandum to Harriman, April 26, 1948, RG 59, file: 840.50Recovery/4-2048. In the last document cited, Lovett sent the AFL's list of ECA candidates to the newly appointed special representative, Averell Harriman.

[20] Information on the labor members of the Public Advisory Board comes from *Biographical Dictionary of American Labor Leaders*.

[21] See Hoffman torep 49 to American Embassy, Paris, July 2, 1948, ECA Files, box 44.

[22] *New York Times*, June 3, 1948, 14.

[23] A discussion of the Council on Productivity and technical-assistance program follows in the text.

[24] Hoffman torep 49 to American Embassy, Paris, July 2, 1948, ECA Files, box 44. See also Hoffman torep 5 to American Embassy, Paris, July 2, 1948, ECA Files, box 44; Harriman repto (representative to) 62 to Hoffman, July 8, 1948, ECA Files, box 5; and Hoffman, "Weekly Report of the Administrator," November 8, 1948, Hoffman papers, box 22, folder: ECA, Miscellaneous 1948–1949.

leaders, and on the American side with such groups as the National Association of Manufacturers, the Chamber of Commerce, and the leading labor unions, farm groups, and trade associations. By the end of 1948, the ECA had allocated approximately $1.5 million for technical assistance. The bulk of this money went to the ECA mission in Greece, where American experts were preparing programs to expand electric-power facilities and increase industrial and agricultural production. At the same time, however, the ECA financed a survey of industrial productivity in France and was laying plans for visiting productivity teams and for a number of technical-assistance projects and production surveys in other participating countries.[25]

The technical-assistance program would continue to grow and would eventually take on the attributes of a cultural crusade on behalf of the " 'American way' " in Western Europe. The technical projects and productivity teams became symbols of the American conviction that Europe could become self-supporting only through a process of economic and cultural reform. The reconstruction of production facilities had to go hand in hand with gains in output per man-hour, and to achieve these gains European managers and workers had to discard archaic habits of work, abandon old traditions of class conflict, and "emulate" the American example. They had to learn, as Hoffman recalled, that the United States was "the land of full shelves and bulging shops made possible by high productivity and good wages" and by a way of life "marked by the primacy of the person in a setting of teamwork."[26]

Similar in nature was the Anglo–American Council on Productivity, a nongovernmental body of British and American industry and trade-union representatives established by Paul Hoffman and Britain's chancellor of the Exchequer, Sir Stafford Cripps. Hoffman sired the idea when he told Sir Oliver Franks, the British ambassador in Washington, that "aid in dollars could be no more than a temporary palliative" unless accompanied by an "increase of [British] productivity." "This was primarily a problem of improving management" and "bringing labour along to see where their true interest lay," both areas in which the introduction of American "know-how" could be of real assistance. A proposition like this had little appeal to an old trade-union leader like Ernest Bevin. He thought the British had "little to learn" from American managers, whose methods of "handling staff" impressed him as particularly "dictatorial and unsuited to European conditions." For a technocrat like Cripps, however, a higher rate of productivity was the only way to increase output and raise living standards at a time when British labor was fully employed. As president of the Board of

---

[25] Foster tel. to Hoffman, November 26, 1948, ECA Files, box 5. See also Hoffman repto 1537 to ECA, November 12, 1948, and Foster repto 1786 to Hoffman, December 3, 1948, ECA Files, box 5; and ECA, *Third Report to Congress* (Washington, DC, 1949), 45–7.

[26] Paul G. Hoffman, *Peace Can Be Won* (Garden City, NY, 1951), 101–4.

Trade and then as chancellor, Cripps had negotiated industry's compliance with government export targets, won labor's support for voluntary wage restraints, and brought both groups together in an Economic Planning Board that advised government on future economic policies. He now hoped that British and American leaders would organize a similar system of corporative collaboration and use it (as he had tried to use the Planning Board and other agencies) to overcome "the conservative outlook both of employers and labour" toward programs aimed at raising Britain's lagging rate of productivity.[27]

With Hoffman thinking along similar lines, a meeting between the two men in July 1948 produced the decision to appoint a twenty-member Council on Productivity composed of British and American labor and management groups. The groups were to investigate capital plant and bottleneck problems in Britain and determine how American labor and management might assist the British "in increasing their productivity." The British group was nominated by the Federation of British Industries and the British Trades Union Congress (TUC), acting through the National Production Advisory Council that had been established during the war. The American group was chosen by Hoffman; the labor representatives in consultation with the ECA's labor advisors and the leading American trade unions; the industry representatives in consultation with Philip Reed of General Electric, who had been one of Hoffman's associates on the BAC and CED.[28]

Reed chaired the American labor–management group that traveled to London at the end of the year for the first meeting of the Anglo–American Council on Productivity. Committees were quickly established to study industry organization, capital-investment trends, and production bottlenecks

---

[27] Franks tel. to FO, July 20, 1948, T232/27/EEC16/8/010; E. A. Berthoud, Assistant Under Secretary of State, Record of a Conversation with the Secretary of State, July 28, 1948, FO 371, 71981, UE5132; and unsigned memorandum of a meeting between Cripps, Hoffman, and other British and American officials in Paris, July 26, 1948, T232/27/EEC16/8/010. See also J. C. R. Dow, *The Management of the British Economy, 1945–1960* (Cambridge, England, 1964), 33; and Sima Lieberman, *The Growth of European Mixed Economies, 1945–1970: A Concise Study of the Economic Evolution of Six Countries* (Cambridge, MA, 1977), 74–5.

[28] Finletter toeca (to ECA) 82 to Marshall, August 5, 1948, ECA Files, box 4. See also the last document cited in note 27, and FO tel. to Franks, July 28, 1948, T232/27/EEC16/8/010; Douglas tel. to Marshall, July 30, 1948, RG 59, file: 103.ECA/7-3048; Douglas tel. to Marshall, July 31, 1948, ECA Files, box 4; Hoffman ecato (ECA to) 104 to American Embassy, London, August 4, 1948, RG 84, London Embassy Records, box 1035, file: 850 Marshall Plan; Harriman repto 308 to Hoffman, August 5, 1948, ECA Files, box 5; Hoffman ecato 179 to Finletter, August 27, 1948, RG 84, London Embassy Records, box 1035, file: 850 Marshall Plan; Finletter toeca 174 to Hoffman, September 3, 1948, ECA Files, box 4; Hoffman ecato 207 to Finletter, September 10, 1948, RG 84, London Embassy Records, box 1035, file: 850 Marshall Plan; and Hoffman torep 1139 to Harriman, September 20, 1948, ECA Files, box 45. See also Hoffman, *Peace Can Be Won*, 101–2.

in Britain. The American members then toured several British plants, where they found the biggest barrier to increased production in the frequently "complacent attitudes" of British labor and management toward scientific production procedures and restrictive business practices. These attitudes they hoped to change. And although the British ruled out action in regard to restrictive practices, the council was able to agree on a program of "industrial education" at all levels of British industry and arrangements under which teams of British managers, technicians, and shop foremen would study production methods in the United States.[29]

The ECA also hoped to extend the American brand of public–private power sharing to the European governments and use it to foster the right kind of economic recovery. In many of the participating countries, of course, trade unions and other private groups already participated through a variety of economic bureaus and planning boards in the formulation of national policies. In Britain, as we have seen, industry and labor representatives collaborated with senior civil servants in the work of the Economic Planning Board. The same collaboration characterized the National Production Advisory Council and the National Joint Advisory Council, both of which operated as clearinghouses for the discussion of issues of general concern to government, industry, and labor. In France, as well, the Monnet Plan organized business and labor in so-called modernization commissions, encouraged them to cooperate with government experts in devising schemes for revitalizing particular industrial sectors, and then coordinated these schemes through a central planning commission that also represented labor, industry, and government. A similar system of economic planning, one founded on corporative forms of collaboration, eventually took shape in Italy and, still later, in western Germany.[30]

In all cases, however, the ECA thought these European systems needed to be reformed if they were to serve as useful instruments of American policy. European leaders needed to imbibe the American faith in the healing power of greater productivity, eliminate restrictive policies, and extend the network of labor–management collaboration from government councils to the shop floor. These were goals of the technical-assistance program and productivity teams that got underway in 1948. As we will see, the Americans also pressured the French into greater efforts to restrain inflation, urged the British to divert national resources from welfare programs to industries

[29] Finletter toeca 355 to Hoffman, November 1, 1948, ECA Files, box 4.
[30] Jean Monnet, *Memoirs*, trans. by Richard Mayne (Garden City, NY, 1978), 236–63; Lieberman, *Growth of European Mixed Economies*, 3–119; Arnold A. Rogow, *The Labour Government and British Industry, 1945–1951* (Oxford, England, 1955); F. Ridley and J. Blondel, *Public Administration in France* (London, 1964), 193–8; John H. McArthur and Bruce R. Scott, *Industrial Planning in France* (Boston, 1969), 73, 79–84; and Richard F. Kuisel, *Capitalism and the State in Modern France: Renovation and Economic Management in the Twentieth Century* (Cambridge, England, 1981), 219–47.

geared to exploit the dollar market, and encouraged the Italians, and later the Germans, to relax efforts to balance budgets and stabilize currencies, develop programs to expand industrial production, and enlarge social services.

Aside from these reforms, the ECA wanted private economic groups to play a more direct advisory role to ERP planners in the participating governments and in the OEEC. Consultation was easily arranged in the case of business, less so in the case of labor. During the interwar years, as Charles Maier has argued, important elements in the European trade-union movement had come to accept the ideology of production and corporatist collaboration espoused by their counterparts in the United States. This development provided a partial basis for their cooperation with government and business in the ERP.[31] The problem was that Communists dominated the European labor movement, which meant that traditional patterns of trade-union solidarity had to be abandoned if "free" labor leaders were going to take an active part in ERP planning. With this goal in mind, policymakers in the State Department and the ECA mounted a concerted effort to break up the Communist-dominated World Federation of Trade Unions (WFTU) and organize a non-Communist labor international that could become a partner in programs to increase production and promote integration.

This effort had the full support of American trade-union leaders, who for all practical purposes acted as labor ambassadors of American recovery policy in Europe. Initially, however, the AFL and the CIO had adopted somewhat different approaches toward their assignments. The AFL's inveterate anticommunism had precluded it from affiliating with the WFTU. It dealt independently with the European trade unions and decided to use the same tactic to mobilize European labor behind the Marshall Plan. In late 1947, the AFL announced plans for a meeting of non-Communist labor leaders to consider the American initiative. By January of the next year, its European representatives were making arrangements for a trade-union conference that would convene the following March. The CIO, for its part, had affiliated with the WFTU and had hoped to preserve labor solidarity by working within that body to rally European workers on behalf of the Marshall Plan. James Carey, who was the CIO's executive secretary and a member of both the Harriman Committee and the Committee for the Marshall Plan, had urged such a course at a meeting of the WFTU's Executive Bureau in late 1947. But action on his motion had been postponed by Louis Saillant, the WFTU's executive secretary, and other labor leaders who were beginning to line up behind the Soviet Union's growing opposition to the Marshall Plan. It was not until February 1948, after Saillant had again delayed action on Carey's motion, that the CIO closed ranks with the AFL

[31] Maier, "The Two Postwar Eras," 327–52.

and the British TUC to sponsor a conference on the Marshall Plan outside
the framework of the WFTU.[32]

Meeting in London in early March, the conference was attended by
American trade-union officials from the AFL, the CIO, and the Railway
Labor Executives Association and by non-Communist labor leaders from
most of the Marshall Plan countries. It was the first step toward the disruption of labor solidarity in Western Europe and the formation of a non-
Communist international devoted to the American goals. Indeed, the conferees promptly endorsed the Marshall Plan and urged organized labor to
collaborate in government programs to administer the ERP and meet national production targets. They also created the European Recovery
Program–Trade Union Advisory Committee (TUAC), instructing it to maintain close contact with the continuing European recovery authority in Paris
and to open negotiations looking toward an official relationship between
the two organizations.[33]

The American trade unions pushed aggressively for an active TUAC propaganda campaign on behalf of the Marshall Plan. They also called for a
strong secretariat, which they hoped to control, and a level of trade-union
representation in the European recovery agencies comparable to that accorded American labor in the ECA. The TUAC should, in their view, become
labor's policymaking authority in matters relating to the ERP. It should
make its authority effective by establishing ties to the participating governments and by moving its headquarters from London to Paris, where it could
work more closely with Harriman's staff and with the permanent European
recovery organization. This became the agenda of the American trade unions
in July when the TUAC reconvened in London. Harriman was on hand to
support their position, as were the ECA's major labor advisors, Bert Jewell,
Clinton Golden, and Boris Shishkin. Jewell spoke with pride of the part
that trade unionists were playing in the administration of the ERP in Washington, and both he and Golden urged the conferees to cooperate in European programs to raise production and unify economies. Harriman made
the same points in his address to the TUAC. He told the conferees that his
door would always be open to European labor leaders, adding that this was
part of a larger policy designed to enlist the support of private groups in
measures to "raise production" and promote "integration." He noted the

[32] Weiler, "The United States, International Labor, and the Cold War," 16–17; John
      P. Windmuller, *American Labor and the International Labor Movement, 1940–1953*
      (Ithaca, NY, 1954), 120–8; Lewis L. Lorwin, *The International Labor Movement:
      History, Policies, Outlook* (New York, 1953), 240–3; and Wexler, *Marshall Plan
      Revisited*, 37–8.
[33] Baruch tel. to American Embassy, London, April 8, 1948, RG 84, London Embassy
      Records, box 1035, folder: 850 Marshall Plan; and Caffery tel. to Marshall, June
      30, 1948, RG 59, file: 840.50Recovery/6-3048; Windmuller, *American Labor*, 130–
      1; Lorwin, *International Labor Movement*, 243; and Weiler, "The United States,
      International Labor, and the Cold War," 18.

"great benefits which came to America through its large area of free trade"
and urged the TUAC to join in efforts to build a similar system in Western
Europe – one based "on greater [economic] unification" and on "a greater
conception of the unity of the people."[34]

Yet there were aspects of the ERP where the interests of American and
European labor did not always coincide. This was particularly the case with
American and British trade-union leaders, whose differences generally paralleled those between their governments. The British were just as anxious
as the Americans to link European labor to the ERP. Bevin made this clear
in his discussions with the French concerning the economic aspects of the
Brussels Pact.[35] At the same time, however, he and others in the Foreign
Office and the Treasury saw no need for a special mechanism of consultation
in London, in part because Bevin maintained close contacts with his old
associates in the trade-union movement, in part because the British TUC
already participated with industry groups in a variety of planning boards
connected with the Ministry of Labour and the Treasury. Nor did they favor
a relationship between the TUAC and the OEEC that conformed to the
organizational imperatives of American rather than British diplomacy. Labor's participation in the ERP should be concentrated at the national level,
they said. The TUAC's relationship with the OEEC should be informal and
should be handled through "*ad hoc*" arrangements that did nothing to
strengthen the Secretariat or enhance the OEEC's authority over matters
pertaining to the internal policies of the participating governments. This
was also the view of Vincent Tewson, the TUC's executive secretary, and
other British labor leaders who were battling the AFL for control of the
TUAC. Tewson agreed with Bevin at a meeting in mid-April that any relationship between the TUAC and the OEEC need not involve the sort of
"elaborate machine[ry]" envisioned by the Americans. The Foreign Office
and the TUC, both men concurred, must "buttress" each other's resolve to
resist "excessive American pressure" to go further on this and other issues
than the British thought desirable.[36]

---

[34] TUC Press Release, July 29, 1948, FO 371, 71807, UR3766. See also Douglas tels.
to Marshall, April 26 and June 14, 1948, RG 84, London Embassy Records, box
1035, file: 850 Marshall Plan; and Samuel Berger, First Secretary, American Embassy,
London, dispatch #1755 to Marshall, August 13, 1948, RG 59, file: 840.50Recovery/
8-1348.

[35] See the record of Bevin's talks with Bidault on March 17 and April 17, 1948, in FO
800/460/EUR/48/16 and /20.

[36] Makins minute of April 13, 1948, and F. K. Roberts, Bevin's Personal Private Secretary, minute of April 14, 1948, FO 371, 71806, UR184. See also the minutes by
H. G. Gee of March 22, 1948, C. T. Crowe of March 30, 1948, P. H. Gore-Booth
of April 2, 1948, Makins of April 3, 1948, and William Strang of April 22, 1948,
FO 371, 71806, UR184; and Roberts minute of June 11, 1948, and Makins minutes
of June 11 and 14, 1948, FO 371, 71806, UR2215.

The alliance between the Foreign Office and the TUC had become apparent as early as the TUAC meeting in late March. TUC officials were not as willing as their counterparts in the AFL to abandon the dream of labor solidarity and take actions that would formally disrupt the WFTU. They wanted the Communists to be responsible for any break and the reason to be a trade-union issue rather than the Marshall Plan. Nor were they anxious to make the sacrifices that the ECA might demand in the name of greater productivity or to abandon their government's line on the larger aspects of recovery policy. They refused to support American-inspired resolutions calling for a European union, a stronger TUAC secretariat, and formal ties to the OEEC, delaying action on these resolutions until the conference accepted compromises that fell between their own and the American positions. The compromises did not elaborate concrete proposals. Although calling for a labor advisory committee to assist the OEEC, they said nothing about the mechanism of consultation or about shifting the TUAC's headquarters from London to Paris. They envisioned instead a decentralized system of labor representation to be achieved by forging new links to Harriman's staff in Paris, to the labor representatives on the ECA's Public Advisory Board, to the ECA's country missions, and to the recovery planners in the participating governments.[37] As Thomas Finletter pointed out, the general thrust of these resolutions dovetailed with the reluctance of British leaders to strengthen the OEEC or "to commit the U.K. to the integration of Europe economically."[38]

Nevertheless, the TUAC's decision to establish closer connections with the ECA and the participating governments represented something of a victory for the Americans, who continued to press their case with unrelenting vigor in the months ahead. The Americans helped to organize another TUAC meeting with a view to reiterating the "important part" that organized labor and other "non-governmental groups" should play in the recovery program. Secretary of State Marshall made plans to address the meeting in order to urge European labor unions to follow the American example by creating cooperative links with their governments and with the OEEC.[39] The State Department, meanwhile, was urging the OEEC to establish an "effective relationship" with the TUAC, while the ECA mission in Italy was working to bring non-Communist trade-union leaders together in a labor advisory

---

[37] Berger dispatch #1755 to Marshall, August 13, 1948, RG 59, file: 840.50Recovery/8-1348; and unsigned memorandum of conversation between Clinton Golden and various State Department officials, August 20, 1948, RG 59, file: 840.5043/8-2048.

[38] Finletter to Harriman, August 2, 1948, enclosed in Harriman's letter to Hoffman of August 18, 1948, RG 286, Acc. 53A405, box 1, folder: Special Representative's Office, 1948.

[39] Harriman repto 1068 to Marshall, October 7, 1948, ECA Files, box 5; and Lovett tel. to Caffery, Paris, October 4, 1948, RG 59, file: 840.50Recovery/9-2848.

committee that would collaborate with American and Italian recovery planners on a variety of ERP projects.[40] By the end of the year, these efforts had begun to succeed. The TUAC had decided to establish links with the International Trade Secretariats. These secretariats represented workers in related industries across the Continent, and the new connection opened broad possibilities for transnational cooperation. Even more important, the OEEC had decided in late December to recognize the TUAC as the official representative of organized labor, a decision that cleared the way for the two bodies to begin laying plans for the appointment of labor advisors who would consult with the OEEC's technical committees in Paris.[41]

The OEEC's decision represented another compromise between the British and American points of view. Initially, the Foreign Office position had stopped short of official recognition, no doubt because of reasons noted earlier, including the fear that a formal relationship might enhance the OEEC's international stature and authority. But the British had been pulled along by the persistent pressure that the Americans generated through the TUAC and by the substantial role accorded American trade unions in the administration of the ECA. The Foreign Office, as Roger Makins explained in a letter to Sir Edmund Hall-Patch, must not "appear to be neglecting European workers or putting them at a comparative disadvantage."[42] By the end of May, the British delegation in Paris had therefore engineered an OEEC resolution welcoming close consultation with the TUAC. Armed with this resolution, Secretary General Robert Marjolin had agreed to frequent meetings between OEEC and TUAC officials and had appointed a manpower counselor who was to cooperate with the TUAC's permanent representative in Paris. These arrangements, although ad hoc and informal, gave the TUAC the substance of what it wanted. By this time, however, American pressure had invested the issue of official recognition with such symbolic importance that even Tewson expected the OEEC to go further. Anything less would be a blow to the non-Communist trade unions and would undermine the TUAC's prestige, discredit its claim to be the legitimate leader of organized labor, and weaken its resolve to support the Marshall Plan over the growing opposition of the WFTU.[43]

[40] Lovett tel. to Caffery, April 9, 1948, RG 59, file: 840.50Recovery/4-548; and W. K. Knight memorandum of conversation, October 1, 1948, 840.50Recovery/10-148.

[41] Caffery tel. to Marshall, September 23, 1948, RG 84, London Embassy Records, box 1035, file: 850 Marshall Plan; Caffery tel. to Marshall, November 24, 1948, RG 59, file: 840.50Recovery/11-2448; Foster repto 1762 to Hoffman, December 2, 1948, ECA Files, box 5; and Foster reptos 2100 and 2131 to Hoffman, December 29 and 31, 1948, ECA Files, box 6.

[42] Makins letter to Hall-Patch, April 30, 1948, FO 371, 71806, UR184.

[43] In addition to the source cited in note 42, see Hall-Patch letter to Marjolin, May 6, 1948, Tewson letter to Marjolin, May 19, 1948, J. V. Robb minute, May 27, 1948, and Hall-Patch tels. to FO, June 2 and 10 (2), 1948, FO 371, 71806, UR1439, UR1711, UR1940, UR2152, and UR2153; and Hall-Patch tel. to FO, June 8, 1948,

The Foreign Office had come to appreciate these considerations as well. Bevin and others continued to oppose an elaborate mechanism of consultation. They still preferred ad hoc arrangements. But in deference to the demands of labor leaders and American policymakers, the British delegation in Paris played a leading role in winning support for the December resolution, which formally recognized the TUAC as the international labor agency with which the OEEC would consult.[44] The resolution appeased the trade unions and satisfied the Americans. As the British had wanted, however, it left the arrangements for consultation more or less on the ad hoc basis established in May and June.

By the end of 1948, then, an Anglo–American compromise had linked the non-Communist trade-union movement to the OEEC. American policymakers and trade unionists had also blended labor into the ECA's administration, had helped to found the TUAC, and had encouraged ties between the European unions, the participating governments, and the ECA country missions. These were important steps toward transnational integration on the labor front and toward the formation of a non-Communist international devoted to the ideology of bureaucratic management and greater productivity. Along with the Anglo–American Council on Productivity, the technical-assistance program, and the productivity teams, these initiatives aimed to re-create in Western Europe a corporative accommodation similar to the one in the United States. An accommodation of this sort was part of the New Deal synthesis as it evolved in the years after the First World War and thus of the larger American design for a European neo-capitalism. Other parts emerged from the ECA's deployment of counterpart funds and its efforts to build supranational institutions.

III

"Production plans," as Harriman put it, were "the heart of the program." In the summer of 1948, ECA planners began shifting their emphasis from relief to the kind of reconstruction Congress expected. By that time, increases in coal production and prospects of a bountiful harvest had made it possible to give greater consideration to capital investment. "[W]e are at a point," Hoffman explained to a meeting of ECA officials in July, "[where] we can plan for a recovery in Western Europe." European leaders, said Bissell,

Roberts minute of June 11, 1948, Marjolin letter to Tewson, June 28, 1948, Evert Kupers and Vincent Tewson letter to Marjolin, August 13, 1948, Marjolin letter to Tewson, August 30, 1948, and Robb minute of October 4, 1948, FO 371, 71807, UR2268, UR3141, UR5091, and UR6306.

44 Robb minute of October 4, 1948, Gee minute of October 5, 1948, Bevin letter to Tewson, October 11, 1948, Hall-Patch tel. to FO, November 25, 1948, Robb minute of November 30, 1948, FO tel. to Hall-Patch, December 8, 1948, Robb minute of December 30, 1948, and Bevin letter to Tewson, December 31, 1948, FO 371, 71807, UR6306, UR6506, UR7948, UR8204, UR7948, and UR6506.

should begin planning for "strategic decisions of true economic importance," the kind of indicative economic planning that could guide their recovery in the right direction, give the OEEC and the ECA a yardstick for measuring progress, and guarantee the gains in productivity that would put an integrated Western Europe on a self-supporting basis. The participating countries, Harriman instructed his mission chiefs, must henceforth "put the maximum of their efforts into expansion of production."[45]

To encourage production, the ECA urged participating governments to place a greater emphasis on capital investment and to shift their American-financed purchases from bulk relief commodities to capital goods.[46] It also proposed to use the control that it shared with participating governments over the local-currency counterpart of American grants, a control that had been looked upon from the start as giving the United States a high degree of leverage. "He who controls the so-called lire fund," said James Clement Dunn, the American ambassador to Italy, "will control the monetary and fiscal, and in fact the entire economic policy of Italy." It might not be wise to "kill the child" by cutting "the pipeline of [American] goods" to uncooperative nations. But the United States could at least exercise its veto over the use of counterpart funds to bring the Europeans into line with its production, trade, and financial objectives.[47]

Although American policymakers would always overrate the significance of this veto, counterpart financing would certainly play a role in their larger policy for reviving production and stimulating growth. One line of this policy called for balancing budgets, adjusting exchange rates, and taking other steps to create a desirable financial environment. A second line tempered these conservative prescriptions with political realism and the new tools of economic liberalism. Aside from urging European leaders to cushion internal adjustments with public-sector spending and income redistribution, Marshall Planners would utilize counterpart funds to supplement capital formation, to offset deflationary impacts on output and employment, and to educate participating governments in American strategies of macroeco-

[45] Harriman repto circular, August 31, 1948, RG 84, London Embassy Records, box 1035, file: 850 Marshall Plan; and "Summary of Conference...," Paris, July 23–24, 1948, RG 286, Acc. 53A405, box 1, folder: Paris Conference, July 22–28. See also Hoffman torep 55 to Harriman, July 2, 1948, ECA Files, box 44.

[46] Hoffman torep 55 to Harriman, July 2, 1948, and Harriman repto 54 to Marshall, July 7, 1948, ECA Files, boxes 44 and 5, respectively; and Harriman circular tels., July 7 and August 31, 1948, RG 84, London Embassy Records, box 1035, file: 850 Marshall Plan.

[47] Dunn tel. to Marshall, December 31, 1947, Records of the Department of the Treasury (Treasury Department, Washington, DC), Acc. 67A1804, box 14, folder: Italy, Aid Program (hereafter cited as Treasury Records, with accession, box, and folder designations); "Summary of Conference...," Paris, July 23–24, 1948, RG 286, Acc. 53A405, box 1, folder: Paris Conference, July 22–28; and Treasury Department Memorandum for the Files, February 9, 1948, Treasury Records, Acc. 66A1039, box 11, folder: Interim Aid to France and Italy.

nomic management. This line of policy, and the political thinking behind it, had begun to emerge in 1947 and 1948, when Keynesians who defended the Marshall Plan in Congress rejected the draconian measures of economic retrenchment recommended by Henry Hazlitt and other advocates of an older economic orthodoxy. The Keynesians thought that financial and monetary adjustments must coincide with, not precede, the revival of production. Their view dovetailed with the policy compromise worked out earlier by free-traders and planners in the State Department and applied by Under Secretary of State Robert A. Lovett, who had warned against a stabilization strategy that relied solely on deflationary fiscal and monetary reforms and thus ran the risk of hampering production and exacerbating political divisions in Western Europe.

The same compromise and political considerations guided the ECA's handling of counterpart funds in the first year of the ERP. These funds were deployed to restrain inflation and to underwrite capital investment.[48] In Britain, for example, counterpart funds were used to reduce the government's short-term public debt.[49] In France, they helped to support the Monnet Plan.[50] In Italy, they were targeted for a variety of agricultural and industrial projects and for a public-works program to absorb part of the large pool of surplus labor.[51] The Italian case provides an example of one type of economic planning, including measures of welfare capitalism, that ECA officials tried to encourage. Italy's rigorous program of monetary stabilization, implemented in late 1947, had gone further than these officials thought desirable. It had stopped inflation but left interest rates high, denied industry the credits it needed to expand, increased unemployment, and precluded social spending. ECA officials therefore urged recovery planners in Rome to relax their concern with inflation and use counterpart funds to

[48] See Harriman repto circular, August 31, 1948, RG 84, London Embassy Records, box 1035, file: 850 Marshall Plan; Hoffman torep A-22 to Harriman, September 14, 1948, Treasury Records, Acc. 66A1039, box 4, folder: Marshall Plan, Local Currency Counterpart, General; and Price, *Marshall Plan and Its Meaning*, 104.

[49] Hoffman ecato 41 to American Embassy, London, July 1, 1948, and Finletter toeca 21 to Marshall and American Embassy, Paris, July 4, 1948, RG 84, London Embassy Records, box 1035, file: 850 Marshall Plan; and Finletter toecas 42 and 65, July 20 and 30, 1948, ECA Files, box 4.

[50] Bruce toecas 354 and 355 to Hoffman, September 13, 1948, RG 286, Acc. 53A177, box 60, folder: FR – Finance; Bruce toeca 358 to Hoffman, September 14, 1948, and memorandum by the Assistant Chief of the Division of Western European Affairs, September 20, 1948, *FRUS, 1948*, 3:649–51, 659–60. See also *FRUS, 1948*, 3:651, footnote 3.

[51] American policy in Italy and Italian–American discussions over the use of counterpart funds can be followed in ECA Aide-Memoires of September 30, 1948, Résumés of Conversations between Alcide de Gasperi and J. D. Zellerbach, October 1 and 12, 1948, Arthur Marget memorandum to Harriman, December 21, 1948, RG 286, Acc. 53A177, box 2, folder: Italy 1951; Harriman repto 1163 to Hoffman, October 14, 1948, and Foster repto 2093 to Hoffman, December 29, 1948, ECA Files, box 5.

underwrite a program of public investment that would tap underutilized capacity, expand industry, reduce unemployment, and meet a dangerous shortage of low-cost housing.[52]

Because inflation still posed the greatest threat to economic stability in other participating countries, controlling it required a measure of fiscal restraint not recommended to the Italians. The problem in these countries was to curb inflation without curtailing production, increasing unemployment, and deepening an already serious social and political crisis. This problem was particularly acute in France, where a rapid expansion of bank credit, mounting budget deficits, and excessive government borrowing had combined with shortages, pent-up demand, and escalating wages to fuel a virulent inflation that was a danger "not alone to [the] French economy but to [the] whole European recovery effort." It hampered the OEEC's efforts to liberalize intra-European trade and to achieve an equitable allocation of ERP aid. It also eroded the value of the franc, curtailed French exports, and made it difficult for the government to proceed with plans to revitalize industry. Political fragmentation and social turmoil left the ruling center parties with little room to maneuver. Rigorous deflation was politically unpalatable and more deficit financing meant additional drafts on the central bank, a course that would aggravate inflation and require parliamentary action at a time when the government was loath to test its mandate.[53]

Under these circumstances, some officials in the ECA and the State Department wondered if General Charles de Gaulle and his *Rassemblement du Peuple Français* might be the best hope for ending the political paralysis in Paris. But most saw de Gaulle as a reactionary nationalist whose economic and political policies would only worsen conditions in France and across the Continent. "He talks about economics as a woman talks about carburetors," explained John D. Hickerson, who headed the State Department's Office of European Affairs. His advisors were "ill-assorted, incompetent, self-seeking, and unstable." Any attempt to support him was likely to benefit the Communists and compromise American policy in Germany. Nor could American officials lay it on the line with the center parties, making it clear that "they have darn well got to produce something workable" or lose American aid. Given the delicate political situation in Paris, tactics of this sort could undermine the government and lead to a victory for de Gaulle or the Communists.[54]

[52] George H. Hildebrand, *Growth and Structure in the Economy of Modern Italy* (Cambridge, MA, 1965), 18–36.

[53] Bruce toeca 358 to Hoffman, September 14, 1948, *FRUS, 1948*, 3:649–51. See also Lieberman, *Growth of European Mixed Economies*, 6; and Warren C. Baum, *The French Economy and the State* (Princeton, NJ, 1958), 43–58.

[54] Hickerson memorandum to Labouisse, October 12, 1948, *FRUS, 1948*, 3:666–7. See also Edward Dickinson and Theodore Geiger of the ECA, memorandum to Bissell, September 8, 1948, RG 286, Acc. 53A405, box 55, folder: Committee – ECA/State Dept. Planning Group; John Hulley of the ECA, memorandum to Geiger, September

The better strategy seemed to be one that relied on American aid and guidance. It was this strategy that the ECA tried to implement when it used counterpart funds to underwrite the Monnet Plan. Doing so relieved the burden of investment on the French budget. It reduced the government's deficit without restricting production and was conditioned on efforts by the French to curb inflation. The ultimate goals were an increase in taxes and a balanced budget, as well as a general overhaul of France's antiquated fiscal system. But since these goals were clearly unattainable in the overheated politics of the French capital, the pragmatic policymakers in the ECA were ready to settle for less significant, but still important, concessions. As they did in other countries, they asked the French to control private credits, restrain wages and prices, reduce government borrowing, and put state-owned enterprise on a self-supporting basis. Through these measures and counterpart financing, they hoped to overcome inflation without crippling production and increasing unemployment, thereby ameliorating the economic and political crisis and encouraging a liberal reconstruction in France.[55]

Of course, the ECA's counterpart policy aimed to do more than restore production and safeguard the political center in France and other participating countries. It also aimed to integrate economies and thus clear a path to greater specialization, more efficient use of resources, and economics of scale. Using counterpart funds to reduce national deficits and stabilize currencies was one way to eliminate monetary barriers to intra-European trade and economic integration. In addition, as we will see later, the ECA utilized these funds to underwrite an OEEC plan for liberalizing trade and payments across the ERP area as a whole. It also tried to discourage counterpart financing for national investment projects that did not contribute to European-wide recovery while giving "special consideration" to those that "involve[d] the participation of several countries."[56] All of these initiatives, together with the technical-assistance program and productivity teams, were parts of the neo-capitalist formulation that had emerged from the New Deal to guide American policy in Western Europe. Adding to this list was the ECA's ongoing struggle to transform the OEEC into a strong, supranational authority.

This struggle further highlighted the faith that American leaders placed

---

21, 1948, RG 286, Acc. 53A405, box 60, folder: AAP Policy Series; Harriman unnumbered repto to Lovett and Hoffman, October 18, 1948, and Harriman repto 1487 to Hoffman, November 8, 1948, ECA Files, box 5; and Memorandum of Conversation by the Secretary of State, November 18, 1948, *FRUS, 1948*, 3:677–82.

[55] In addition to the sources cited in note 50, see Price, *Marshall Plan and Its Meaning*, 104–5; Wexler, *Marshall Plan Revisited*, 101–7; and Monnet, *Memoirs*, 269–70.

[56] Harriman repto 956 to Marshall, September 24, 1948, ECA Files, box 5. See also Hoffman torep A-22 to Harriman, September 14, 1948, Treasury Records, Acc. 66A1039, box 4, folder: Marshall Plan, Local Currency Counterpart, General.

in macroeconomic management and indicative planning on behalf of greater growth and integration. With these goals in mind, the State Department had earlier appealed for the appointment of outstanding representatives to the OEEC. This appeal had encountered stiff opposition from British policymakers who much preferred a more conventional form of intergovernmental cooperation that posed no threat to national interests or sovereignty. Undaunted by their initial lack of success, however, the Marshall Planners soon launched a new campaign to make the fledgling organization into an engine of economic integration. They complained about the "low level" of representation at meetings of the OEEC's Council, doubted that Hall-Patch could provide "dynamic leadership" as chairman of the Executive Committee, and dismissed the Secretariat as a "paper pushing organization."[57] The recovery program, they kept insisting, required the "concerted attention" of the "best brains." But while the United States had chosen a former cabinet officer as its special representative and selected "outstanding" men as ECA mission chiefs, the participating countries had not "shown an equal sense of responsibility." Congress, they warned, would "expect at least this much cooperation from Europe" when it reviewed the recovery program in 1949.[58]

In addition to a higher caliber of national representation, the Americans thought the Executive Committee and the Council should convene at the ministerial level on a regular basis. They would also empower the Secretariat to launch investigations and make recommendations, create a new office of director general, appoint a European of political stature to this post, and authorize him to direct the organization's activities. These reforms would help to circumvent the "tortuously slow" process of decision making by national delegations and enable the OEEC to develop a *European* point of view.[59] A committee of "country representatives," as Harriman explained, could not provide "effective leadership" because national delegations were "inclined to consider first the interests of [their] own country." But a director general of "international political position" could speak for Europe as a whole, "initiate or advocate matters requiring top level consideration," and deal "on a basis of equality with senior government representatives."[60]

Harriman and his staff in Paris pushed the American reforms relentlessly. Charles Bonesteel set them out in a talk with Hall-Patch on May 10, as did

---

[57] Caffery tel. to Marshall from Bonesteel for Harriman, May 6, 1948, *FRUS, 1948*, 3:437; and Geiger memorandum to Bissell, July 17, 1948, RG 286, Acc. 53A405, box 60, folder: AAP Policy Series.

[58] Harriman unnumbered tel. to Marshall, July 17, 1948, RG 59, file: 840.50Recovery/ 7-1748.

[59] Geiger memorandum to Bissell, July 17, 1948, RG 286, Acc. 53A405, box 60, folder: AAP Policy Series. See also Lovett tel. to Harriman, July 22, 1948, *FRUS, 1948*, 3:471-2; and Hoffman torep 996 to Harriman, September 10, 1948, ECA Files, box 45.

[60] Harriman tel. to Marshall and Hoffman, July 31, 1948, *FRUS, 1948*, 3:472-3.

Harriman in a meeting with the chief British delegate on May 12, and with Bevin on May 14. When Paul Hoffman made his first official visit to Paris in late July, he and Harriman urged the same reforms on the other OEEC delegations, stressing in particular how the appointment of a director general would "stir the imagination of the American people." Needed, they reiterated, was an "international figure" who could get the organization moving in the direction of greater integration.[61] The French and the Italians seemed interested and Belgian Prime Minister Paul-Henri Spaak was so enthusiastic that Harriman and others considered him a logical choice for the post of director general. As in the earlier debates, however, the British turned out to be the "principal stumbling block." Harriman found the British delegation "more negative" than the others. Finletter thought that their attitude would do "great damage" to American recovery plans. Spaak concluded that Bevin and Hall-Patch would never "cooperate to make OEEC fully effective."[62] Indeed, thinking in the Foreign Office remained essentially as it had been when the OEEC was formed. The British were against an agency that would override national policies and function as an instrument of American diplomacy. It was "Mr. Harriman himself," as one official minuted, who "would head up the Organisation."[63]

The last remark suggests how the diplomacy of organization was soon transposed into the politics of personality. The issue in this case involved what the British came to call "the Harriman problem."[64] Harriman seemed to epitomize the American tycoon whose enormous personal fortune and success in business fed an appetite for eminence in the public arena. A man of remarkable energy and ambition, with a blunt, sometimes abrasive personal style, he had earlier served as presidential envoy to Great Britain,

---

[61] Hall-Patch letter to Makins, May 10, 1948, FO 371, 71864, UR1663; and Hall-Patch tel. to FO, May 12, 1948, and Bevin tel. to Hall-Patch, May 14, 1948, FO 371, 71863, UR1491 and UR1546.

[62] Harriman unnumbered tel. to Marshall, July 24, 1948, RG 59, file: 840.50Recovery/7-2448; Harriman tel. to Marshall and Hoffman, July 31, 1948, *FRUS, 1948*, 3:472–3; Finletter torep 192 to American Embassy, Paris, September 23, 1948, RG 84, London Embassy Records, box 1036, file: 850 Marshall Plan; Memorandum of Conversation, August 20, 1948, in Harriman letter to Hoffman, August 23, 1948, RG 286, Acc. 53A405, box 1, folder: Special Representative's Office, 1948; Harriman unnumbered tel. to Hoffman and Marshall, August 4, 1948, RG 286, Acc. 53A177, box 87, folder: Personal Tels., June–August 1948; and Harriman unnumbered tel. to American Embassy, London, August 20, 1948, RG 84, London Embassy Records, box 1035, file: 850 Marshall Plan. Although the Americans considered Spaak a desirable choice for director general, they also worried, like the British, that the new job would force him to slight his other international and domestic responsibilities. On this issue, see the documents in *FRUS, 1948*, 3:490–2.

[63] Berthoud memorandum to Bevin, July 31, 1948, FO 371, 71868, UR3953. See also Makins memorandum to Bevin, May 12, 1948, FO 371, 71864, UR1585; Bevin tel. to Hall-Patch, May 14, 1948, FO 371, 71863, UR1546; and FO tel. to Hall-Patch, August 1, 1948, FO 371, 71827, UR3816.

[64] Makins memorandum to Bevin, September 8, 1948, FO 371, 71869, UR5181.

ambassador to the Soviet Union, and secretary of commerce. Although he had resigned the last post to become the ECA's special representative in Europe, Harriman had no intention of being treated as anything less than an official of cabinet rank. He clearly felt slighted when the participating countries appointed heads of delegations – mere "bureaucrats," he called them – who lacked his political and diplomatic stature. Adding to his injury was the fact that some delegations, particularly the British delegation, seemed reluctant to admit the American special representative or members of his staff to meetings of the Executive Committee and the Council. Relations between Harriman and Hall-Patch were especially strained. Harriman thought the British delegate unequal to his responsibilities and held him personally accountable for the OEEC's failure to consult the Americans on major issues of policy. Hall-Patch returned the animosity in spades. "Apparently Harriman thinks himself such a swell that he cannot have any truck with anyone unless they are Ministers." Nobody on the special representative's staff, Hall-Patch added in a letter to Roger Makins, could possibly understand why the foreign ministers of sixteen sovereign states "were not prepared to travel to Paris to have the honour of meeting Mr. Harriman."

The two men had a particularly nasty confrontation in mid-August. "Harriman let fly at me today," Hall-Patch reported to Eric Berthoud in London. He "nurture[d] a considerable grouse that [the ECA was] not being brought sufficiently into the Organisation's work" and "implied it was our fault." Hall-Patch considered the accusation "demonstrably groundless," an ugly by-product of the fact that Harriman's staff contained a "large body of unemployed labour and it is well-known that the devil makes use of such persons." Nor was Hall-Patch the only one annoyed. Nothing irritated Bevin more than what he considered to be Harriman's arrogant meddling in decisions regarding the level of Britain's diplomatic appointments. He made this plain in a talk with Ambassador Douglas in London, using language every bit as blunt as anything in Harriman's diplomatic vocabulary. According to a Foreign Office record, Bevin thought it a "presumption on the part of the United States governmental representatives to deem to interfere with the way we conduct our business in this country." Marshall aid did not give Americans that right. Hall-Patch's appointment in Paris had been approved by the Cabinet and "Mr. Harriman would be well advised to allow us to do our business in our own way and not suggest that any one of our ministers should supersede others."[65]

Although Hall-Patch tried to smooth over relations with the Americans, at least giving the appearance of full consultation, neither he nor his su-

[65] Hall-Patch letter to Makins, May 10, 1948, FO 371, 71864, UR1663; Hall-Patch letter to Berthoud, August 17, 1948, T232/201/EEC7/8/07; and Record of Conversation between the Secretary of State and the U.S. Ambassador, July 21, 1948, FO 800/515/05/48/46.

periors in London were willing to make the structural changes Harriman demanded.[66] They countered with a proposal that called simply for ministerial meetings of the Executive Committee to deal with particular problems on an ad hoc basis. Hall-Patch, of course, chaired the Executive Committee, which meant that he would fix the date, set the agenda, and generally "control the outcome" of every meeting. What the British wanted to avoid was the appointment of a "superman" who had the authority to act independently of participating governments. Their proposal was designed to achieve this goal by outflanking the Americans in Paris.[67]

Indeed, both the British and the Americans closed like pincers on the other delegations. When Hoffman and Harriman urged their proposals on a meeting of French officials, Hall-Patch countered by telling the French that American thinking was "half-baked." When Harriman said he would go to Brussels to lay his scheme before Spaak, Hall-Patch added that Bevin would do the same. When the French and the Belgians showed signs of weakening under heavy American pressure, Bevin and Hall-Patch worked frantically to shore them up. Hall-Patch tried to bring the French into a "common line when dealing with Harriman on this issue." He laid plans for his own meeting with Spaak while Bevin asked the Belgians not to commit themselves until the British had presented their case. At a session in London, he also won Spaak's provisional support for a variant of the original British proposal.[68]

By early September, however, the British were finding it difficult to hold their position against an increasingly clamorous assault. Harriman had launched a strident press campaign in Paris, denouncing the British for failing to cooperate in measures to strengthen the OEEC and unify the European economies. The Foreign Office counterattacked, sending Paul Gore-Booth to help Hall-Patch get "the U.K. point of view" to the Paris press. But as Harriman's campaign spread to Washington, the "mounting tide of American criticism" led policymakers in the Foreign Office to the conclusion that only timely concessions could avert congressional cuts in the next year's ERP appropriation. The problem was how to assuage the Americans without causing difficulties elsewhere. Appointing a director general might appease Harriman's "personal feeling that it is beneath his status

[66] Hall-Patch letter to Harriman, August 18, 1948, T232/201/EEC7/8/07.
[67] Berthoud memorandum to Bevin, July 30, 1948, FO 371, 71867, UR3891; and the brief dated August 7, 1948, attached to Makins memorandum to Bevin of the same date, FO 371, 71868, UR4140.
[68] Hall-Patch tel. to FO, August 1, 1948, FO 371, 71867, UR3871; Hall-Patch tel. to FO, August 1, 1948, FO 371, 71827, UR3816; Gore-Booth minute, August 2, 1948, FO 371, 71868, UR3953; Makins memorandum to Bevin, August 3, 1948, FO 371, 71868, UR3953; FO tel. to Hall-Patch, August 3, 1948, FO 371, 71867, UR3817; Record of Conversation between the Secretary of State and Monsieur Spaak, August 9, 1948, FO 371, 71868, UR4202; and Hall-Patch tel. to FO, August 11, 1948, FO 371, 71868, UR4157.

and dignity to hobnob" with bureaucrats. But it might also alienate Secretary General Marjolin, who had already told Hall-Patch that he would not step aside to "salve Mr. Harriman's vanity." Even worse, the appointment of a high-level political figure could give the OEEC more authority than the British thought desirable and create the impression that they had caved in to American pressure. To avoid these dangers, the Foreign Office decided to capitalize on a suggestion by Stafford Cripps and propose the appointment of an official of "considerable status" who would preside, in Spaak's absence, over regular meetings of the Council. The official would be of "sufficient importance for Mr. Harriman to commune with," but his appointment would not lead to Marjolin's resignation or greatly enhance the OEEC's authority at the expense of national governments.[69]

Bevin put this proposal to Harriman and Hoffman at a meeting in October, only to find them generally unimpressed.[70] The Americans thought that the proposed appointee would be little more than a "session officer." They still wanted a director general. Despite opposition from the British, Harriman won support for a special meeting of the Council to consider this and other organizational changes. The British parried by delaying the meeting and objecting to Harriman's participation. When the Council finally convened, moreover, they would go no further than a decision to establish a special ministerial committee, which became known as the Committee of Nine, to study organizational questions and make recommendations early the next year.[71] This decision, which came in mid-October, effectively postponed the issue and represented a partial victory for the beleaguered British. The Americans had their own reasons to be pleased, however. The Council had appointed Spaak to head up the ministerial committee. Spaak was an advocate of European unification and the Americans were hopeful that under his direction the new group would recognize the need for "dynamic high-level direction of OEEC."[72]

At the same meeting, the Council also approved a new intra-European payments plan and the first annual division of American aid. These were major decisions and in making them the OEEC was beginning to accept important responsibilities. Getting it to do so had been part of the American

[69]   Makins memoranda to Bevin, September 8 and 10, 1948, FO 371, 71869, UR5181 and UR5241; Hall-Patch tel. to FO, August 11, 1948, FO 371, 71868, UR4157; Berthoud memorandum to Makins, September 9, 1948, FO 371, 71869, UR5303; and Makins memorandum to Bevin, September 17, 1948, FO 371, 71870, UR5952.
[70]   Bevin tel. to Hall-Patch, October 14, 1948, FO 800/440/Bel./48/20.
[71]   Harriman letter to Blaisdell, September 27, 1948, RG 286, Acc. 53A177, box 87, folder: Top Secret Correspondence; Kirk tel. to Marshall, October 2, 1948, RG 59, file: 840.50Recovery/10-248; Kirk tel. to Marshall, October 11, 1948, *FRUS, 1948,* 3:490; and Harriman repto 1182 to Hoffman, October 16, 1948, ECA Files, box 5.
[72]   Harriman repto 1182 to Hoffman, October 15, 1948, ECA Files, box 5. See also Lovett tel. to Harriman, October 21, 1948, RG 59, file: 840.50Recovery/10-2148; and Harriman repto 1847 to Hoffman, ECA Files, box 5.

strategy from the start. Aside from the appointment of a director general, the Americans had wanted to keep bilateral negotiations to a minimum, deal collectively with the Europeans through their joint organization, and saddle the OEEC with as many burdens as possible. These were prescriptions for building the new agency into a supranational authority and promoting the "concept of Western Eur[opean] integration."[73] The division of aid for 1948–9 and the new payments plan were the first concrete results of this strategy. Unfortunately, they proved difficult to achieve and did less than expected.

IV

The responsibility for dividing American aid had been an issue since April, when the OEEC asked for American assistance in programming funds for the first full year of the recovery program. The ECA quickly dispatched Charles Bonesteel and a new team of friendly-aid experts to join Henry Labouisse and others who were already working with the OEEC in Paris. It also insisted that the OEEC accept the responsibility for recommending a division of aid and demanded, as the State Department had earlier, that this recommendation be based on a careful screening of individual country requirements and a consolidation of these requirements into a comprehensive plan. Specifically, the OEEC was to draft both a four year master plan and successive annual programs, starting with the one for the fiscal year that began in July 1948. In doing so, it was to review the production targets, investment plans, and import–export requirements of each participating country. These items were to be adjusted to fit a Western European pattern of production and exchange, with aid to each country geared to the contribution it could make to the economic recovery and viability of the group as a whole. The ultimate result of this sort of indicative economic planning, or so the ECA hoped, would be an integrated single market much like the one that helped to account for the remarkable record of economic growth in the United States.[74]

Because this approach assigned the OEEC responsibilities that normally fell "within the province" of sovereign governments, it naturally generated

---

[73] Lovett tel. to Caffery, April 8, 1948, *FRUS, 1948*, 3:414–17. See also Marshall tel. to Caffery, March 22, 1948, and Caffery tels. to Marshall, March 20 and April 28, 1948, *FRUS, 1948*, 3:400–1, 398–9, 404–8.

[74] Caffery tel. to Marshall, April 19, 1948, RG 59, file: 840.50Recovery/4-1948; Lovett tel. to Caffery for Labouisse, April 21, 1948, RG 59, file: 840.50Recovery/4-1948; Caffery tel. to Marshall, April 27, 1948, RG 59, file: 840.50Recovery/4-2748; Marshall tel. to Caffery, May 1, 1948, RG 59, file: 840.50Recovery/5-1448; Lovett tel. to Douglas, April 22, 1948, RG 84, London Embassy Records, box 1035, file: 850 Marshall Plan; and Marshall tel. to Caffery for ECA Mission, May 4, 1948, RG 59, file: 103.ECA/4-2948.

a good deal of nervousness and resistance in Europe.[75] In this area, as in others, the British were anxious to limit the OEEC's authority. Cripps told an ECA official in London that dividing American aid amounted to an "intolerable" burden that the OEEC was ill-equipped to shoulder. In reality, of course, the British were reluctant to have their requirements discussed in a collective forum or subordinated to the needs of Europe as a whole. Like many of the other participants, they wanted the United States to allocate aid, seeing this as allowing greater scope for the sort of bilateral bargaining the ECA hoped to avoid.[76] In meetings during June and July, however, Harriman reminded the Europeans that the principles of mutual self-help and joint responsibility applied to the task of allocating aid. He promised that "close cooperation" between his staff and recovery authorities in Paris would minimize the possibility of subsequent changes in Washington. But he went on to outline procedures that were clearly intended to limit bilateral negotiations, concentrate responsibility in the OEEC, and thereby encourage progress toward economic integration and supranationalism in Western Europe.[77]

Paul Hoffman made the same points during his visit to Paris in late July. In a major address to a ministerial meeting of the Council, which had been hastily convened to receive the new American administrator, Hoffman urged the Europeans to make "collective" use of their resources. They should draft "joint" annual and master programs and include in them proposals for raising production, liberalizing trade, and placing government finances on a sound basis. Any plan for making Europe independent, he argued, could not be "traced on an old design" or "brought about by old ways of doing business," by "old concepts of how a nation's interests are best served," or by "old separatist lines" of economic activity. It required "new patterns of intra-European trade and exchange," "new directions in the use of Europe's resources," and new efforts to adjust national recovery plans to the needs of "Europe as a whole." Failure to realize this, Hoffman warned, could adversely affect American support for the recovery program.[78]

Spurred on by American pressure, the Council had already transmitted

---

[75]   Caffery tel. to Marshall, May 1, 1948, RG 59, file: 840.50Recovery/5-148.
[76]   Cripps quoted in Milward, *Reconstruction of Western Europe*, 181. See also Caffery tel. to Marshall, April 18, 1948, RG 59, file: 840.50Recovery/4-1848; Finletter tel. to Harriman, June 26, 1948, RG 84, London Embassy Records, box 1035, file: 850 Marshall Plan; Harriman repto 24 to American Embassy, London, July 4, 1948, *FRUS, 1948*, 3:464–5; Price, *Marshall Plan and Its Meaning*, 82; and Richard Mayne, *The Recovery of Europe: From Devastation to Unity* (New York, 1970), 118.
[77]   Van Der Beugel, *From Marshall Aid to Atlantic Partnership*, 141–3; and Harriman unnumbered tel. to Hoffman, July 7, 1948, ECA Files, box 5. See also Hall-Patch tel. to FO, July 6, 1948, Records of the British Treasury, Central Economic Planning Division, Record Class T229/191/CP129/64/01 (hereafter cited as T229, with appropriate filing designation).
[78]   Harriman repto 196 to Marshall for ECA, July 25, 1948, ECA Files, box 5.

a directive on the preparation of country programs to member states and had appointed a select Committee of Four to review national submissions, devise a consolidated plan, and propose a division of aid.[79] The committee, known as the "Four Wise Men," began by assuming that consumption would be held to 1947 levels. Programming would cover the total imports of participating countries and a new intra-European payments plan would liberalize trade between members of the group, thereby limiting their imports from the dollar area. Acting on these premises, the committee spent three weeks reviewing country submissions and cross-examining national delegations in Paris. It then withdrew to the seclusion of Chantilly to begin the onerous job of adjusting and coordinating national recovery plans in light of the nearly $5 billion in Marshall Plan loans and grants appropriated for the first fiscal year of the ERP. Throughout the ordeal, the Four Wise Men worked closely with Charles Bonesteel, Lincoln Gordon, and other members of Harriman's staff, most of whom were "favorably impressed" with the committee's "extremely serious" approach and "sincere effort" at the kind of indicative planning that ECA officials saw as one of the keys to the rational development of an integrated European economy.[80]

The Europeans were not nearly so pleased. When the committee finished its work and submitted its report in mid-August, "pandemonium broke loose" in Paris.[81] Several of the participating countries thought their share of ERP aid too small. Some planned an appeal to the Council; others reserved their position pending the outcome of related negotiations for an intra-European payments plan.

These reservations paled when compared to the vigorous objections raised by General Lucius Clay and the American Army. Clay and the army occupation authorities had prepared the bizonal submission, which called for $446 million in direct American aid plus $102 million in the form of drawings on European currencies under the proposed payments plan. The submission envisioned a substantial increase in western Germany's imports and exports, and this seemed to imply an upward revision of the 1947 level-of-industry agreement. Nevertheless, the figure for direct allocation roughly equaled the estimate of bizonal aid that the Truman administration had submitted to Congress during hearings on the Foreign Assistance Act. When the Committee of Four reduced the amount to $364 million, Clay and the Army Department accused it of deliberately shortchanging the Bizone in order to enlarge the share of American aid going to other participating countries. The revised figure violated the wishes of Congress, they warned,

---

[79]   Van Der Beugel, *From Marshall Aid to Atlantic Partnership*, 142, 144–8.
[80]   Harriman repto 349 to Marshall, August 9, 1948, ECA Files, box 5; Van Der Beugel, *From Marshall Aid to Atlantic Partnership*, 147–50; and Lincoln Gordon, "The Organization for European Economic Cooperation," *International Organization* 10 (February 1956): 1–11.
[81]   Quoted in Mayne, *Recovery of Europe*, 119.

and would lead to cuts in the next year's appropriation for the ERP. To protect western Germany, they also urged the ECA to intervene in Paris and get British support for this course.[82]

Hoffman approached the British, but neither he nor Harriman felt comfortable in doing so. They worried that Anglo–American intervention in Paris might "have a bad effect upon the morale and effectiveness of the OEEC as an instrument of European cooperation" and abet British efforts to weaken that body in favor of bilateral dealings in Washington.[83] They undoubtedly had mixed feelings when the British rejected their overture, claiming, ironically, that reopening the division-of-aid debate would undermine the OEEC's integrity and utility.[84] Forced to rely on its own resources, the ECA opened a hectic round of negotiations with OEEC leaders in Paris and with the Army Department in Washington. It was seeking a compromise before the Council formally approved the division of aid and hoping thereby to avoid an American veto that could seriously weaken the OEEC. These negotiations finally succeeded. The OEEC raised the Bizone's direct allocation to $414 million and then offset part of this gain by making Germany a creditor on intra-European account, subject to $80 million in drawings on its currency by other ERP countries.[85] The American intervention aroused some criticism in Europe, where it was seen as detracting from European responsibility and putting the recovery of Germany above that of its victims. But the ECA had contained the damage. Through the exercise of "friendly aid," it had appeased the Army Department, avoided untoward repercussions in Congress, and averted a showdown with the OEEC.

The Council formally approved the revised division of aid at its meeting in late October. In doing so, it completed an exercise in economic planning

---

[82] Harriman unnumbered repto to Marshall for Hoffman, August 21, 1948, ECA Files, box 5; Secretary of the Army Kenneth Royall letter to Marshall, August 23, 1948, enclosing Royall's letter to Hoffman of the same date, RG 59, file: 840.50Recovery/8-2348; Murphy tel. to Marshall for Saltzman and Hickerson, September 4, 1948, RG 59, file: 840.50Recovery/9-448; Murphy letter to Saltzman, September 6, 1948, RG 59, file: 840.50Recovery/9-648; and Milward, *Reconstruction of Western Europe*, 187.

[83] Frank G. Wisner, Deputy Assistant Secretary of State for Occupied Areas, memorandum to the Under Secretary, August 25, 1948, RG 59, file: 840.50Recovery/8-2548. For background on the ECA's approach to the British, see Harriman repto 287 to Hoffman, August 4, 1948, and Hoffman torep 431 to Harriman, August 4, 1948, ECA Files, boxes 5 and 44, respectively. See also Hoffman torep 987 to Harriman and Foster, September 9, 1948, ECA Files, box 45.

[84] Douglas tel. to Marshall, August 26, 1948, RG 59, file: 840.50Recovery/8-2648; and Finletter toeca 152 to Marshall, August 26, 1948, ECA Files, box 4. See also FO tel. to Franks, August 27, 1948, T232/135/EEC3/03/annex1A.

[85] Hoffman torep 825 for Harriman, August 30, 1948, and Harriman repto 706 to Hoffman, September 4, 1948, ECA Files, boxes 44 and 5, respectively; Saltzman letter to Murphy, September 27, 1948, RG 59, file: 840.50Recovery/9-648. See also Campbell, *United States in World Affairs*, 1948-1949, 184–5.

that formed part of an American strategy for designing a new European economic order. So did the simultaneous drive to devise a payments plan capable of removing the impediments to intra-European trade. This had been an American goal since the origin of the Marshall Plan in 1947. Together with the reduction of tariffs and the elimination of import quotas, the liberalization of intra-European payments had been widely perceived as one route to an internal market large enough to optimize output, put the participating countries on a self-supporting basis, and set the stage for a worldwide system based on full convertibility and multilateral trade. It was this kind of thinking that guided American Marshall Planners in the payments negotiations of 1948 and that led, within two years, to the formation of the European Payments Union.

As noted previously, the First Agreement on Multilateral Monetary Compensation had done little to unclog trade channels or promote multilateralism in Europe. This failure was a matter of serious concern to the ECA. If left unchecked, the constriction of intra-European trade would prevent the most efficient use of regional resources, make participating countries dependent on the United States for goods generally available on the Continent, and hamper their efforts to integrate economies and become more productive. "The large intra-European deficits of certain countries," one memorandum elaborated, "have been the chief obstacle to the development of a multilateral system" promising "gains [in] specialization and large-scale production."[86]

One move toward correcting the situation had come in April 1948, when the finance ministers and central bankers of the Brussels Pact powers met to discuss payments problems. Out of this meeting had come the Ansiaux plan, named after Hubert Ansiaux of the National Bank of Belgium, under which creditors on intra-European account would use the local-currency counterpart of their Marshall Plan grants as a basis for new credits to their debtors. Credits would be denominated in the currency of the creditor but backed by dollar grants that the creditor could use to finance imports from the Western Hemisphere. The plan was tailored to the needs of intra-European creditors like the Belgians, who were refusing to extend further credits that could be repaid only in nonconvertible European currencies. It fell through as soon as it became clear that Belgium would receive most of its American aid in the form of loans, rather than grants, that did not generate a local-currency counterpart.

Nor were the Belgians more successful when they tried to achieve the same results through a modified plan. Under this proposal, new intra-European credits would be financed in part by enabling creditors to draw

[86] Emile Despres memorandum to Calvin B. Hoover, September 3, 1948, Charles P. Kindleberger Papers (Truman Library), box 2, folder: General Correspondence. See also Diebold, *Trade and Payments*, 25–7; and Federal Reserve Bank of New York, *Monthly Review* 30 (November 1948): 118–22.

an equivalent amount of dollars from the International Monetary Fund (IMF). Critics in the ECA and the IMF saw serious shortcomings in this proposal. Some of the OEEC countries were not members of the IMF; others were ineligible to draw on its reserves; still others had exhausted their drawings. In addition, the IMF had ruled against special drawings by the ERP countries, partly to conserve its reserves and partly because it assumed that Marshall aid should be sufficient to meet Europe's dollar requirements. Together with the Federal Reserve Board, the Treasury Department, and the other agencies represented on the National Advisory Council (NAC), the ECA also thought that the Europeans must do more to utilize their own resources before turning to the IMF. This thinking reflected the continuing American commitment to the principle of maximum self-help. The Europeans should, according to this view, design a plan that did more to multilateralize intra-European payments, integrate economies, and set the stage for full convertibility with the dollar.[87]

The State Department and the ECA recognized the need to use ERP dollars to sustain intra-European trade, even if the arrangements for 1948 stopped short of full convertibility. They refused to submit concrete proposals of their own or to commit themselves in advance of action by the OEEC. But they had earlier made use of off-shore procurement to facilitate intra-European trade and were now receptive to any permanent scheme that reduced Europe's dependence on the dollar and constituted a "first step" toward a multilateral system of trade and payments. They insisted only that the Europeans accept "full responsibility" for devising such a scheme and keep in mind that "we are more concerned with improvement in trade structure than with working out a payments mechanism."[88]

[87] Douglas tel. to Marshall, April 26, 1948, RG 84, London Embassy Records, box 1029, file: 710 Western Bloc; Kirk tel. to Marshall, May 3, 1948, RG 84, London Embassy Records, box 1029, file: 710 Western Bloc; Caffery tel. to Marshall, May 5, 1948, RG 59, file: 840.50Recovery/5-548; Caffery tel. to Marshall, May 7, 1948, RG 59, file: 840.50Recovery/5-748; W. L. Hebbard, ECA Mission, London, memorandum to Douglas, May 10, 1948, *FRUS, 1948*, 3:439–44; and NAC Staff Committee, Minutes of Meeting, May 11, 1948, and NAC, Minutes of Meeting, June 3, 1948, in General Records of the Department of the Treasury, Records of the National Advisory Council on International Monetary and Financial Policies (National Archives), Record Group 56, NAC Minutes (hereafter cited as RG 56, NAC Minutes). See also Caffery tel. to Marshall, March 4, 1948, Treasury Records, Acc. 66A1039, box 6, folder: ERP Stabilization and Loans, 1948–49; Milward, *Reconstruction of Western Europe*, 267–8; and J. Keith Horsefield, *The International Monetary Fund, 1945–1965: Twenty Years of International Monetary Cooperation*, Vol. 1 (Washington, DC, 1969), 217–22.

[88] Hoffman ecatos 48 and 131 to Harriman, June 3 and 19, 1948, RG 286, Acc. 53A441, box 265, folder: Trade, Facilitation, and Stimulation; and RG 56, NAC Minutes, May 11 and 27, 1948. See also W. A. Tomlinson, Treasury Representative, American Embassy, Paris, memorandum for Marget, June 11, 1948, and George W. Willis, memoranda of ECA–State–Treasury meetings, June 19 and July 7, 1948, Treasury Records, Acc. 66A1039, box 3, folder: Marshall Plan, General Program, II.

By June 1948, the ECA and the NAC had also developed a set of principles that were to steer the Europeans in the right direction. They wanted the participating countries to establish a new clearing mechanism and use it to offset their bilateral credits and debits. The ECA would then cover residual balances in one of two ways. The first would entail the continued use of off-shore procurement, whereby debtors were allocated additional dollars to finance imports from their creditors. The Europeans were urged to consider this method, although policymakers in the ECA thought it would do little to break down bilateral barriers. Instead, the ECA tended to favor a system of conditional dollar grants to intra-European creditors, three of the conditions being that creditors use the local-currency counterpart of these grants to extend new credits to their debtors, that the ECA retain control over the grants, and that creditors and debtors maintain a minimum level of trade. The amount of conditional aid would depend on the volume of trade, and under no circumstances would it cover more than a portion of each creditor's balances.[89]

These two approaches came to be known in the OEEC as the "Marget method" and "Tomlinson method," respectively, borrowing their names from two American financial experts in Paris.[90] A consensus quickly took shape around the Tomlinson method, but there were important differences between the British and the Belgians over how it should be applied. The British, speaking for debtors, argued that creditor countries must finance any reasonable difference between their conditional grants and their surplus on intra-European account. To facilitate new credits, they wanted participating countries to contribute to a European currency fund on which debtors could draw to finance balances that remained after existing bilateral credits had been exhausted. The fund would be administered by the OEEC and contributions would be geared to each country's volume of intra-European trade.[91] An arrangement like this would put the burden of self-help on intra-European creditors, particularly on the Belgians, who wanted their credit liabilities limited to the value of their conditional grants. The OEEC's Com-

[89] Hoffman ecatos 48 and 132 to Harriman, June 3 and 19, 1948, RG 286, Acc. 53A441, box 265, folder: Trade, Facilitation, and Stimulation; Hoffman torep 153 to Harriman, July 14, 1948, ECA Files, box 44; and RG 56, NAC Staff Committee Minutes, May 29, 1948, and NAC Minutes, June 3, 1948. See also Franks tel. to FO, June 17, 1948, T232/135/EEC3/03/annex1A.

[90] The two American financial experts were William M. Tomlinson, a Treasury Department financial expert attached to the American Embassy in Paris, and Arthur Marget, head of the Fiscal and Trade Policy Division at Harriman's headquarters in Paris.

[91] The British proposal had been developed by the London Committee's Subcommittee on Intra-European Trade and Payments. See its report of June 10, 1948, in T232/126/EEC7/8/04(D). See also Berthoud memorandum to Bevin and Makins, June 12, 1948, and Hall-Patch tel. to FO, June 29, 1948, FO 371, 71930, UR2301 and UR2717.

mittee on Payments produced a tentative compromise that essentially endorsed the Belgian position. None of the delegates were enamored of the new proposal. But it seemed likely to have their support until the British Treasury intervened with a veto. This was followed by a reassertion of the British and Belgian positions and a deadlock that would have scuttled the negotiations had it not been for intervention by the ECA.[92]

American experts had been on hand since the opening of the negotiations and had pressed relentlessly for an agreement the ECA could accept. This pressure came to a head during Hoffman's visit to Paris in late July, just as the Committee on Payments had reached a stalemate. In a round of meetings, Hoffman and Richard Bissell urged the OEEC delegations to agree to the principles of a payments scheme and leave the details for discussion later. This seemed particularly good advice because the Committee of Four was about to begin its deliberations on the division of American aid. The committee's work could not proceed very far without prior assurances that some of the payments barriers to intra-European trade would be removed. Under these circumstances, the OEEC countries accepted Hoffman's recommendation.[93] The ECA considered this a "major achievement." "It was not a cure-all," Hoffman told the NAC, but a "first step" toward "real economic cooperation" and multilateralism.[94]

The next step was to incorporate the new principles into a concrete scheme, which the OEEC hoped to have in operation by October. The Committee on Payments promptly set to work. It established a number of subcommittees to estimate bilateral balances between each pair of participating countries over the first year of the recovery program and to design a mechanism for multilateral compensation. By September, it had negotiated the details of a plan that included some, but not all, of the American prescriptions. The plan called for the multilateral offsetting of intra-European

[92] Hall-Patch tels. to FO, July 12 (2), 14, and 15, 1948, and S. D. Waley memorandum to the Minister of State, July 22, 1948, with attached note by the Treasury Department, "European Trade and Payments," July 1948, FO 371, 71931, UR3198, UR3204, UR3294, UR3334, and UR3484; and FO tel. to Franks, July 16, 1948, T232/70/EEC25/13/03/annex1.

[93] Harriman tels. to Marshall, July 12, 17, and 18, 1948, and Caffery tel. to Marshall, July 13, 1948, ECA Files, box 5; Hoffman torep 153 to Harriman, July 14, 1948, ECA Files, box 44; Harriman letter to Marjolin, July 23, 1948, and Administrator's Staff Meeting, Record of Action for August 2, 1948, RG 286, Acc. 53A441, box 264, folder: Intra-European Currency Clearing Proposal; and RG 56, NAC Staff Committee Minutes, July 22 and August 5, 1948. See also McKittrick memorandum to Bissell, with enclosure, July 24, 1948, RG 286, Acc. 53A441, box 264, folder: Intra-European Currency Clearing Proposal.

[94] FO tel. to Dominion Governments, July 26, 1948, T232/135/EEC3/03/annex1A. See also "Résumé of the Intra-European Currency Clearing Proposal," August 9, 1948, RG 286, Acc. 53A441, box 265, folder: Intra-European Payments Plan; RG 56, NAC Minutes, August 17, 1948; Harriman repto 320 to Marshall, August 5, 1948, ECA Files, box 5; and Bruce torep 470 to Harriman, August 7, 1948, ECA Files, box 44.

credits and debits through clearings arranged by the Bank for International Settlements on a monthly basis. As in the First Agreement on Multilateral Monetary Compensation, automatic offsettings would be limited to first-category compensations, that is, those that entailed the cancellation of debits and credits of equal value. Second-category compensations would still require the consent of the parties involved. But the principle of automaticity would be applied to all members of the group, except Portugal and Switzerland, and ERP dollars would be utilized to reduce some of the limitations previously inherent in second-category settlements. A portion of the American aid allocated for the first year of the ERP would go to European creditors as conditional dollar grants equal to part of their residual balances after first-category clearings. Creditors would create a local-currency counterpart of these grants and make it available in the form of "drawing rights" that debtors would use to cover their deficits on current transactions.[95]

At this point, however, agreement began to break down on an old bugaboo, namely Britain's concern for its monetary reserves and ties to the sterling area. The Belgians first raised this concern in late August, when they urged a provision that would permit debtors to transfer their drawing rights from one creditor to another, with a parallel shift in conditional dollar aid. According to the Belgians, who consistently represented the interests of creditors on intra-European account, this provision would introduce a healthy dose of multilateralism into intra-European trade and payments. It would ensure debtor countries the widest possible sources of supply at the lowest possible prices.[96] Not mentioned was the fact that a provision like this would enable the Belgians to earn additional dollars from the British in the form of transferred conditional grants and drawings on Britain's reserves. The problem was that Britain, although a net creditor in intra-European trade, ran a deficit on current account with Belgium. Transferability could add to this deficit by enabling debtors to shift their sterling rights from Britain to Belgium. In addition to the concomitant shift of conditional dollar grants, these transfers could push Belgium's sterling holdings beyond the gold point in the Anglo–Belgian payments agreement and force the British to cover the balance out of their modest gold and dollar reserves. In effect, the Belgian proposal "introduced the dollar sign into Europe," which was exactly what the British wanted to avoid.[97] Nor would the British relent when the ECA endorsed the proposal as a helpful step

[95] C. D. Glendinning, Chief, British Empire and Middle East Division, Treasury Department, letter to Hebbard, August 2, 1948, Treasury Records, Acc. 66A1039, box 3, folder: Marshall Plan, General Program, II; Harriman repto 325 to Marshall, August 6, 1948, ECA Files, box 5; Diebold, *Trade and Payments*, 35–7; and Milward, *Reconstruction of Western Europe*, 271.

[96] Hall-Patch tels. to FO, August 20 and 29, 1948, T232/135/EEC3/03/annex1A.

[97] In addition to the documents cited in note 96, see FO tel. to Hall-Patch, August 30, 1948, T232/135/EEC3/03/annex1A.

toward multilateral trade and economic integration in Western Europe.[98] As Hall-Patch told Harriman in early September, Britain was the "custodian of the reserves of the sterling area." Any "scheme that involves us in a risk of losing gold or dollars cannot be countenanced."[99]

A related problem involved what the documents referred to as the "rest of the sterling area" (RSA), that is, those sterling-area countries that had not been included in the ERP.[100] At issue in this case, as in the case of transferability, was the conflict between Britain's commitment to the sterling area and America's commitment to an integrated Europe. The British were caught between the demands of the OEEC countries for the sterling credits they needed to cover essential imports from the sterling bloc, and the demands of the RSA countries for the dollars they required to finance purchases in the Western Hemisphere. Unable to meet both sets of demands and still protect their reserves, the British had proposed to offset their deficit in trade with the RSA by their surplus on current account with the Colonies. During hearings on the ERP, however, Congress had been led to believe that Britain would use the pool of dollars created by American aid and current-account transactions to finance imports from the Western Hemisphere. Using part of this pool to cover the RSA deficit therefore amounted to an unauthorized diversion of Marshall aid. If allowed, it would also retard Britain's economic recovery, reduce its imports from the ERP countries, and foil plans to build an integrated economic order in Western Europe. As a State Department memorandum pointed out, the determination of British policymakers to "maintain and strengthen" their ties to the sterling area limited their "ability and willingness" to "enter fully into a cooperative European effort" or to assume a more "active and aggressive role in promoting an integrated European economy."[101]

Seen from this point of view, the choice seemed to be between policies that either dismantled the sterling area or sacrificed European unity on the altar of the British Empire. Hall-Patch feared the worst. The Americans, he

[98] Hall-Patch tel. to FO, September 7, 1948, and FO tel. to Hall-Patch, September 8, 1948, FO 371, 71935, UR5036; and Hall-Patch tel. to FO, September 9, 1948, and FO tel. to Hall-Patch, September 11, 1948, FO 371, 71936, UR5083 and UR5102.

[99] Hall-Patch tel. to FO, September 16, 1948, T232/28/EEC16/8/03.

[100] The recovery program covered Ireland, Iceland, and the United Kingdom, as well as Britain's dependent overseas territories. The rest of the sterling area included South Africa, India, Pakistan, Ceylon, Burma, Australia, New Zealand, Southern Rhodesia, and Iraq.

[101] John Lindeman memorandum to Toner, May 24, 1948, with attached memoranda by Havlik and Thorp of May 4 and May 21, respectively, RG 59, file: 840.50Recovery/5-2148. See also Secretary of the Treasury Snyder letter to Lovett, with enclosure, May 14, 1948, and Marshall tel. to American Embassy, London, June 7, 1948, *FRUS, 1948*, 3:1083–8, 1088–9; Franks tel. to FO, July 1, 1948, and FO tel. to Franks, July 10, 1948, FO 371, 72830, UR2861 and UR2892; and Philip S. Brown memorandum for Bissell, September 23, 1948, RG 59, file: 840.50Recovery/10-148.

reported to his superiors in London, thought "we much over-rated the economic value to us of the Commonwealth and the sterling area and that we would probably do much better for ourselves by making up our minds to integrate at once with Europe." It followed from this, he warned, that the ECA would be generous in helping Britain become "the leader of Europe" but would "resist any part of [American] aid being spent on bolstering the structure of the sterling area." Thinking in Washington, however, was more complicated than Hall-Patch appreciated. Although American leaders were convinced that the "sterling area arrangement" impeded Britain's "full cooperation in the European enterprise," they were reluctant to disrupt this arrangement if it meant slowing the pace of recovery in Europe and creating power "vacuums" elsewhere.[102] After all, the sterling area was the world's largest multilateral trading system. Denying its dollar needs could dislocate the economies involved and thrust additional relief and defense burdens on the United States. It could also impede the flow of vital goods from the RSA countries to Europe, a point the Americans understood and one the British never tired of repeating. For this reason, in fact, all of the participating countries had been willing to reduce their share of aid in order to include the whole of Britain's dollar deficit in the OEEC's plans for dividing American assistance and liberalizing intra-European payments.[103]

Indeed, officials on both sides of the Atlantic recognized the need for some method to satisfy both European needs and sterling-area requirements. But given the legislative history of the ERP, this could not be done by direct dollar grants or by offsetting Britain's deficit with the RSA by its surplus with the Colonies. Nor would the British, as the ECA suggested, cover this deficit by drawings on their reserves. The very "sheet anchor" of their policy was the "doctrine of reserve maintenance."[104] "[W]e cannot go into a payments scheme with undefined liabilities to pay gold," concluded a Treasury memorandum. "This is what brought the [Anglo–American] loan agreement

---

[102]   Hall-patch tel. to FO, May 12, 1948, FO 371, 71863, UR1491; and Hector McNeil, Minister of State, memorandum to the Secretary of State, May 14, 1948, FO 371, 71864, UR1631. See also T. L. Rowan, Second Secretary of the Treasury, Record of Conversation with Richard Bissell, July 25, 1948, and unsigned record of a conversation in Paris between Cripps, Hoffman, and other British and American officials, July 26, 1948, T232/27/EEC16/8/010 (#70 and #79).

[103]   FO tel. to Franks, July 10, 1948, Franks tels. to FO, July 12 and 13, 1948, FO tels. to Franks, July 16 and August 20, 1948, T232/70/EEC25/13/03/annex1; R. W. B. Clarke of the Treasury, letter to T. L. Rowan, August 12, 1948, and Treasury Department memorandum, "Sterling Area and E.R.P.," August 20, 1948, T232/68/EEC25/13/03A.

[104]   Treasury memorandum, "Sterling Area," July 3, 1948, T232/126/EEC7/8/04(I). In addition to the documents cited in note 103, see Havlik memorandum to Thorp, May 4, 1948, RG 59, file: 840.50Recovery/5-2148; Finletter toecas 30 and 131 to Marshall, July 10 and August 21, 1948, ECA Files, box 4; and Harriman repto 128 to Marshall, July 16, 1948, ECA Files, box 5.

to such a sorry end [in 1947] and if the Americans insist it will bring European cooperation to the same end."[105]

Averting this danger required a formula that would reconcile Britain's integration into Europe with its leadership of the sterling area, the first step toward which had come with an ECA proposal of late July. Under this proposal, Britain's share of American aid would be reduced by an amount equal to its deficit with the RSA. The United States would make up the difference with a conditional dollar grant of equal value. The conditional grant would be used to cover the dollar requirements of the RSA and the sterling counterpart created would be made available as credits to the Marshall Plan countries in Europe. The proposal amounted to a significant American concession. But in return, the Americans wanted the RSA countries, particularly Australia, to make their own contribution to the ERP. In addition to curtailing nonessential imports from the Western Hemisphere and drawing dollars from the IMF rather than from the Bank of England, they were to fund their accumulated sterling balances in London and extend grants in aid of Britain's recovery.[106] These demands stalled the negotiations until September, when Cripps led a British delegation to Washington for a round of talks on both the RSA problem and the issue of transferability.

By the time the negotiations opened, Australia had made a $32-million grant to Britain and New Zealand was considering a similar gift. Although these gestures fell short of what the ECA expected, they represented an important step and made it possible for the British and American negotiators to resolve the RSA problem along lines suggested by the ECA in late July.[107] The issue of transferability proved a tougher nut to crack, because when Americans said "transferability" British ears heard "convertibility" and British minds conjured up memories of the 1947 sterling debacle. Policymakers in the American Treasury also took that event as their point of departure. Like the British, they viewed the prospect of transferability "soberly and

---

[105]   T. L. Rowan memorandum to the Chancellor of the Exchequer, September 14, 1948, T232/28/EEC16/8/03.

[106]   For the British documentation, see Hall-Patch tel. to FO, July 26, 1948, FO tel. to Franks, July 28, 1948, and Franks tel. to FO, August 26, 1948, T232/70/EEC25/13/03/annex1; and Treasury memorandum, "Sterling Area and E.R.P.," August 20, 1948, T232/68/EEC25/13/03A. For the American documentation, see Hoffman toreps 543 and 744 to Harriman, August 12 and 24, 1948, ECA Files, box 44; Finletter toeca 131 to Marshall, August 21, 1948, ECA Files, box 4; Hoffman torep 1023 to Harriman, September 30, 1948, ECA Files, box 45; Bruce ecato 195 to American Embassy, London, September 3, 1948, RG 84, London Embassy Records, box 1035, file: 850 Marshall Plan; and Brown memorandum to Bissell, September 23, 1948, RG 59, file: 840.50Recovery/10-148. See also RG 56, NAC Staff Committee Minutes, August 5, 1948.

[107]   FO tel. to Franks, August 31, 1948, T232/70/EEC25/13/03/annex1; Rowan memorandum for the Chancellor of the Exchequer, September 14, 1948, with attached brief for the chancellor's talks in Washington, September 14, 1948, T232/28/EEC16/8/03; and Franks tel. to FO, October 3, 1948, FO 371, 71937, UR5987.

somberly." But when it came to recovery policy, as the British ruefully complained, Treasury officials were not the guardians of orthodoxy in the Washington curia. It was the ECA "theologians" who had an "almost exclusive claim to interpret the holy writings" in this area, and for them the "ghost of complete multilateralism [was] still very powerful." The British warned against "throwing away [the] substance for the shadow," noting how the sterling system "constituted a valuable approach towards multi-lateralism" and warning that transferability ran the risk of destroying this system by depleting Britain's gold and dollar reserves.

Not until October were the two sides able to strike a compromise, which the OEEC eventually accepted. Under its terms, debtors would be required to exhaust all possibilities for expending their drawing rights in the country issuing them. Only at that point would transfers be permitted and then only with the consent of the OEEC, an organization in which the rule of una-nimity gave the British what amounted to a veto. These arrangements were balanced against concessions to the ECA's point of view, including a promise that participating countries would work toward a fully automatic system of multilateral compensation and an understanding that unused drawing rights could result in the reduction and transfer of a creditor's conditional aid.[108]

The Anglo–American agreements in Washington enabled the OEEC to approve the intra-European payments plan that the Committee on Payments had drafted the previous August. The Council ratified the plan at its meeting in October, and the first intra-European clearing occurred shortly thereafter. The results fell short of American hopes. It proved difficult to forecast bilateral surpluses and deficits in advance or to compel greater efforts at self-help by debtors who stood to gain from drawing rights on their creditors. Restrictions on the transfer of drawing rights also tended to reinforce es-tablished patterns of bilateral trade, encouraging creditors to export to their debtors and robbing them of the incentive to compete in the dollar area. Despite these flaws, ECA officials regarded the plan as an important ac-complishment. By providing a broader clearing mechanism, they said, it made for better use of existing European resources, reduced Europe's de-pendence on the dollar, and contributed to a modest expansion of intra-European trade. Although far from a "cure-all," as Hoffman had admitted, it was at least a "first-step" down the road to economic integration on the Continent.[109]

[108] Franks tels. to FO, September 22 and 24, 1948, FO 371, 71936 and 71937, UR5532 and UR5637. See also Hall-Patch tel. to FO, September 24, 1948, and Franks tel. to FO, September 30, 1948, FO 371, 71937, UR5640 and UR5917; FO tel. to Dominion Governments, October 7, 1948, T232/135/EEC3/03/annex1A; and Wex-ler, *Marshall Plan Revisited*, 143.
[109] Diebold, *Trade and Payments*, 37, 55–63; and Wexler, *Marshall Plan Revisited*, 142. For candid ECA assessments of the new plan, see Bissell's letter to Geoffrey

Similar problems plagued the OEEC's effort to coordinate national investment and production decisions across the ERP area. These stemmed in part from the reluctance of participating countries to entrust decisions of this sort to a supranational authority, in part from the difficulties entailed in forecasting resource availabilities and other factors over a four-year period. Whatever the source of these difficulties, they were sufficient to wreck the OEEC's attempt to draft the master recovery program the ECA had expected. The ECA had to settle instead for an interim report that frankly revealed the perplexities inherent in long-term economic planning.[110] The economic problems were thus persistent, but still less serious than the political differences over Germany – largely a French concern – and over European integration – largely a British dilemma.

V

At the first session of the London Conference on Germany, which came to an end in June, Allied leaders had agreed in principle to the formation of an International Authority for the Ruhr and had appointed working parties to draw up the terms of a military security board and an Allied occupation statute. The security board would help to guarantee Germany's continued disarmament and demilitarization while the occupation statute would list the powers to be reserved by the Allies after the formation of a West German government. Throughout the negotiations in London, as we have seen, American leaders had remained convinced that Germany's reintegration was the key to reconciling the economic and security imperatives inherent in a German settlement. A good deal of progress had been made in this direction, with more expected when the London Conference resumed in the fall. As in the past, however, everything depended on the cooperation of officials in the French government and the American Army.

Although the London agreements had won a measure of support in Paris, holding this support required the constant attention of the policymakers at

Crowther of the *Economist*, London, September 25, 1948, RG 286, Acc. 53A405, box 60, folder: AAP Policy Series; and Geiger, draft memorandum to Bissell, October 11, 1948, RG 286, Acc. 63A405, box 60, folder: European Payments Union.

[110] Only the Belgians seemed sympathetic with American proposals for the transnational coordination of investment decisions. For American and European policy, see Lovett tel. to Douglas, April 22, 1948, RG 84, London Embassy Records, box 1035, file: 850 Marshall Plan; Caffery tel. to Marshall, May 1, 1948, RG 59, file: 840.50Recovery/5-148; Douglas tel. to Marshall, May 8, 1948, RG 59, file: 840.50Recovery/5-848; Kirk tel. to Marshall, September 4, 1948, RG 59, file: 103.ECA/9-448; Harriman repto 956 to Marshall, September 24, 1948, ECA Files, box 5; and Kirk tel. to Marshall, December 5, 1948, RG 59, file: 840.50Recovery/12-548. On the OEEC and the four-year master plan, see OEEC, *Interim Report on the European Recovery Programme*, 2 vols. (Paris, December 30, 1948); Price, *Marshall Plan and Its Meaning*, 88–92; and Campbell, *United States in World Affairs, 1948–1949*, 175–9.

Foggy Bottom. Germany's requirements had to be balanced against those of France, and this was difficult to accomplish in the face of General Clay's resolute devotion to the German cause. The Bizone's rapid economic progress in the months following the currency reform of June aroused new fears in Paris that American policy placed Germany's recovery above that of France and other participating countries. So did the importuning of American policymakers in the OEEC's division of aid for the first year of the ERP. Clay's estimate of bizonal requirements had seemed to imply an upward revision of the 1947 level-of-industry agreement. Any threat to this agreement was a threat to the Monnet Plan, which also helps to explain why the French raised such a ruckus when the United States took preemptive action on the reparations issue and the Ruhr question.

The reparations imbroglio grew out of the ECA's appointment of an Advisory Committee on Reparations, headed by George Humphrey of the Hanna Company. In taking this action, the ECA had been responding in part to congressional demands for a thorough reassessment of the dismantling and removal of German plants with a view to identifying those that could best contribute to European recovery if left in Germany. But, in part, both the ECA and the State Department were reacting to a report by the technical committee on reparations, which a cabinet-level working group had appointed earlier. The report, issued in July, called for the retention in Germany of more than three hundred plants originally slated for removal as reparations. Policymakers in the State Department opposed this recommendation, claiming that it ignored basic security considerations and would, if adopted, lead to an upward revision of the Bizone's level of industry and to a major controversy with the British and the French. To avoid these difficulties and outmaneuver opponents in the Truman administration, the State Department turned to a time-worn tactic in bureaucratic warfare. It convinced the Cabinet to table the technical report in favor of a new one to be produced by the Humphrey Committee and then won support for a set of instructions that limited the committee's review to those plants that had been marked for retention by the technical group.[111]

The Humphrey Committee thus became the instrument by which the ECA and the State Department hoped to preserve a balance between European and German requirements and avert an ugly row with the Allies. But the British and French had already permitted the technical committee to review the reparations program and had done so on the basis of assurances from the State Department that the results would not significantly alter their dismantling operations. They were in no mood to suspend these operations for yet another review that, in their opinion, would delay work on the list of restricted and prohibited industries, encourage German opposition to the

[111] See the documentation in *FRUS, 1948*, 2:716–17, 721, 726–8, 730–3, 738–43, 774–88, 790–3, 796–8.

reparations program, and wreck Allied efforts to ensure Germany's industrial disarmament. It was not until mid-October that American officials
overcame these objections and the Humphrey Committee began its work.[112]

In late December, however, when the committee presented its preliminary
report, both the British and the French renewed their objections. The report
called for the retention of 167 plants previously scheduled for removal as
reparations. This figure amounted to only half the number of plants identified by the technical group. But it was still substantially larger than the
Allies had expected. If accepted, they argued again, it would hamper their
recovery and leave the Germans with an industrial capacity in excess of
that permitted under the 1947 level-of-industry agreement.[113] The French
were particularly concerned lest an increase in Germany's steel production
jeopardize the Monnet Plan. Their fears became even more pronounced
when the British and American governments published a new plan for reorganizing the Ruhr coal and steel industries.

The most controversial feature of the new plan was a provision granting
the Germans the right to decide the question of future ownership. The
bizonal occupation authorities had considered it essential to reassure the
Germans on this score in order to win their support for programs designed
to maximize the production of Ruhr coal and steel. From the French point
of view, however, a decision of this kind required three-power approval
and would, in any event, prejudice their position on international ownership.
The State Department had wanted to assuage the French by excising the
provision from the reorganization plan and publishing it as a separate declaration of Anglo–American policy. But the British and General Clay had
opposed this course and the provision had been included in the preamble
of the reorganization plan published on November 10, just one day before
Allied leaders reconvened in London to draft a charter for the proposed
Ruhr authority.[114]

Publication of the provision amounted to a "stink bomb" that nearly
scuttled the chances for agreement at the London Conference.[115] The French
denounced the reorganization plan and the work of the Humphrey Committee, claiming that both ignored France's rights and played into the hands
of the Communists and the Gaullists. They also reaffirmed their support
for internationalization of the Ruhr, demanded a voice on the bizonal boards
that were supervising the Ruhr coal and steel industries, and wanted the
functions of these boards transferred to the Ruhr authority in the post-
occupation period. In their view, moreover, these functions should be broadened to include the power to keep Nazi sympathizers from positions of

[112]   *FRUS, 1948,* 2:796–8, 805–7, 811–12, 814–24, 827–9.
[113]   *FRUS, 1948,* 2:834–52.
[114]   *FRUS, 1948,* 2:456–60, 464–5, 492–4, 509–14; and Campbell, *United States in
        World Affairs, 1948–1949,* 468–9.
[115]   Douglas tel. to Marshall, November 11, 1948 *FRUS, 1948,* 2:472.

ownership or management in the Ruhr, prevent excessive concentrations of economic power there, and approve basic investment and production decisions. All of these proposals recapitulated what had been the demands of French policymakers since the inception of the Marshall Plan. If implemented, they would enable the French to shield the Monnet Plan and would make France, rather than Germany, the economic and political hub of the European system.[116]

Neither these demands nor the American responses indicated much progress beyond the gains made at the first session of the London Conference. The American negotiators reiterated their opposition to international ownership of the Ruhr industries, permanent limits on Germany's overall level of production, or provisions that would give the Ruhr authority a "punitive character." Arrangements of this sort could drive the Germans eastward for support against the Western powers or lead to "political unrest" and "work stoppages" in the western zones, either of which would limit Germany's contribution to European recovery and stymie efforts to bring the Germans within the "framework of a stronger economic and political organization of Western Europe." For the American negotiators, such a framework still offered the best solution to the problems of German recovery and European security. They had already included in the London accords of June a provision declaring the promotion of economic integration to be one of the purposes of the Ruhr authority. They now wanted the Allies to reaffirm this purpose and to include in the authority's charter specific provisions pointing toward the integration of a larger European area under the guiding hand of the new agency.[117]

As had been the case in June, however, British and American negotiators were anxious to go as far as possible toward meeting France's requirements. They were already working with the French to organize a military security board and draw up a list of prohibitions and limitations on war-related industries. The British, in addition, were sympathetic with French demands for guarantees against renazification and excessive centralization of the Ruhr. They too favored some supervision of production and investment decisions, and they had their own reasons for wanting to retain limits on German steel production and shipbuilding. Concessions in these areas, they insisted, would meet legitimate French security concerns and prevent the emergence in Paris of an extremist regime that might pull France out of the ERP and the Brussels Pact.[118]

American thinking ran along similar lines. The American negotiators in London were willing to consider permanent arrangements to guard against

---

[116] *FRUS, 1948*, 2:476–9, 482–3, 502–3, 517–22, 530–4, 537–9, 543–4, 547–50, 559–63.

[117] Douglas tel. to Marshall, November 28, 1948, *FRUS, 1948*, 2:530–5. See also related documentation in same volume, pp. 465–71, 492–6, 501–3, 509–14.

[118] *FRUS, 1948*, 2:517–22, 530–4, 538–9.

Germany's remilitarization and rearmament, adapting for this purpose some version of their earlier proposal for a German security treaty. Together with the British, they were also prepared to reserve the question of international ownership for consideration at a final peace conference, give the French a voice on the bizonal coal and steel control groups prior to full trizonal fusion, and maintain Germany's existing level of industry until changes were authorized by three-power agreement or a final peace treaty. At meetings in mid-December, moreover, the Americans agreed in principle to a draft charter for a Ruhr authority under which the new agency would be empowered to prevent excessive concentrations of economic power, guard against a renazification of the Ruhr industries, and exercise certain controls over investment and production decisions during the occupation period.[119]

At the same time, the American negotiators had tried to tailor these concessions to suit their own goals. According to the final agreement, for example, the Germans as well as the French would be assigned a place on the International Authority for the Ruhr, the German vote being cast temporarily by the occupation officials. The United States would also retain a dominant voice in production and allocation decisions during the occupation period and the Ruhr Authority would exercise only those powers specified in the preamble of its charter. These included the power to ensure France's security, but not its economic ambitions, and to lower tariffs and promote an "intimate association" of the European economies. The Americans, in other words, had managed to reconcile France's security needs with their own hopes for European integration and German reintegration, using as the agent of reconciliation the sort of supranational authority Secretary of State Marshall had called for at the Moscow Conference in 1947.[120]

If the Ruhr agreement struck a compromise that French and American leaders could accept, it is just as important to recall that other aspects of the German settlement had yet to be resolved. The French had not given up their demand for postoccupation controls over production and investment decisions in the Ruhr. Trizonal fusion had been postponed, as had the formation of a military security board. Delays in drafting an Allied occupation statute were also making it difficult for the German constituent assembly, meeting in Bonn since September, to frame a Basic Law (constitution) for the new German state. In addition, a final settlement still seemed to require the formation of an integrated Western European order of suf-

---

[119] *FRUS, 1948*, 2:517–22, 530–5, 537–8, 546, 547, 559–67, 569–72, 577–95.

[120] "Communiqué of the London Conference on the Ruhr, December 28, 1948," *FRUS, 1948*, 2:577–81. See also "Draft Agreement for the Establishment of an International Authority for the Ruhr," December 28, 1948, *FRUS, 1948*, 2:581–95. The predominant American position in matters pertaining to allocation, production, and investment decisions had been accepted by the Allies at the London Conference of June and had been reasserted at the insistence of General Clay and the Army Department. See *FRUS, 1948*, 2:498, 503–4, 535–6, 573–6.

ficient size and coherence to contain the Germans as well as the Soviets. American and French leaders had been trying to build this system by means other than the Ruhr Authority – the Americans with their plans to strengthen the OEEC, liberalize intra-European payments, and forge transnational networks of corporative collaboration and power sharing; the French with their scheme for a European customs union and their new proposal, noted later, for a European parliament. British policy raised obstacles to progress on all of these initiatives, however, and is therefore worth discussing in some detail.

The British continued to support a "consolidation of Western Europe," the phrase Bevin had used in his address to the Commons on January 22. But this support now stopped short of a full-fledged customs or economic union. Arrangements of this sort could not be reconciled with the sacred concept of sovereignty, with Britain's ties to the Commonwealth and sterling area, or with the Labour government's economic policies at home. Adding to these objections was a much greater reluctance than before to tie Great Britain to Western Europe at a time when governments there were being buffeted by forces beyond their control. The dramatic events of 1948 – the Communist coup in Czechoslovakia, the Berlin blockade, the ongoing economic crisis, and the repeated eruptions of labor unrest and Communist agitation – were sour reminders of Western Europe's precarious position. Vigorous leadership was essential. But such leadership seemed impossible in countries like France, where the ruling center parties kept faltering under the weight of internecine strife and attacks from the Gaullist Right and Communist Left. At one point in the second half of 1948, a succession of governments in Paris had been followed by a period of two months of political stalemate, with no government at all. Under these circumstances, as Alan Bullock has argued, European political leaders and ordinary people alike rallied to the idea of European unity, seeking in a larger community the strength and security so sorely lacking within the framework of national politics. The same circumstances pushed British policymakers in a different direction. Although Bevin had earlier been willing to link Britain's fate to that of a Western European group, this kind of thinking now receded into the shadows of British diplomacy.[121]

This is not to argue that Bevin would disengage from the Continent. If anything, the events of 1948 had strengthened his conviction that Western Europe needed to be reinforced lest it buckle and break under the weight of Communist subversion and Soviet intimidation. But he was more convinced than ever that neither Great Britain nor Western Europe could save itself unless linked to the United States in a larger North Atlantic community, and was just as certain that the Commonwealth and sterling bloc, not Western Europe, provided the most durable foundation for Britain's eco-

---

[121] Bullock, *Bevin*, 554, 586.

nomic recovery and hope for survival as a great power. This hope formed the major thread of continuity in the fabric of Bevin's thinking. Whether expressed through an Anglo–Western European union or through the Commonwealth connection and the North Atlantic community, the grand design of his diplomacy aimed first at restoring the luster to Britain's faded eminence as a great world power, allied to the United States and other countries, but master of its own fate nonetheless. According to its revised version, however, the British would now play a role somewhat analogous to the one assigned earlier to an Anglo–Western European union. Although Great Britain and Western Europe could not form a "Third Force" between the two great powers, Britain might at least become the pivot in a Western system of overlapping blocs, the sovereign of a middle kingdom that included the sterling area and the Commonwealth, the leader of Western Europe through the Brussels Pact and the OEEC, and the ally of both Western Europe and the United States through the ERP and the North Atlantic Treaty then being negotiated in Washington. These were three of what Bevin called "the four legs of the table," the fourth being a reorganized western Germany.[122]

The grand design, so neatly encapsulated in this homely metaphor, meant that Bevin must take great care in leading Britain into Europe. Such a leap into the dark was fraught with danger. Britain's commitments to the Continent had to be reconciled with its interests elsewhere, including its role as the nexus in a North Atlantic alliance. For this purpose, Bevin now relied on the "empirical" approach invented by his colleagues in the British Treasury, adopting it with the zeal of a convert whose piety exceeds the devotion of those born to the faith. This approach became his guide, and that of the Labour government, in dealing with both the political and economic aspects of Western European integration.

The movement for a European political union began to peak with the Congress of Europe that convened at The Hague in May 1948. Attended by more than seven hundred delegates from thirteen countries, most of whom represented groups long connected with the cause of European unity, the gathering included a number of literary celebrities and an impressive array of prominent political figures, among them twenty former heads of state, the most notable being Winston Churchill. The Congress laid the groundwork for an international organization to promote the unity of Europe, the so-called European Movement. It also declared the time ripe for some merger of national sovereignties and urged the immediate convening of a European assembly of delegates selected by the parliaments of the participating countries. These resolutions had the support of a British delegation, but not of the Labour Party, which had done everything it could to disparage the congress and discourage attendance. The party's position was a mirror of Bevin's conviction that schemes such as those touted at The

---

[122] Record of Bevin–Attlee Conversation, June 19, 1948, FO 800/460/EUR/48/26.

Hague were impractical exercises more likely to weaken than to strengthen Western Europe. Outside of England, however, the Congress had been widely puffed as a portentous event in European history. The gulf between this view and Bevin's was a fair measure of how far British policy lagged behind a tide of public sentiment that other European leaders were less inclined to ignore.[123]

The continental governments were trying to stay ahead of public opinion with new proposals for economic and political integration. In preparation for a meeting of the Consultative Council of the Brussels Pact, the Dutch tabled a resolution urging the appointment of an economic committee to harmonize the policies of the five powers. Similar to the proposal put forward by the Benelux and rejected by the British in March, the Dutch resolution looked to the development of a "common line" on the division of Marshall Plan aid and other questions growing out of the ERP. As earlier, the British debunked this idea and reiterated their preference for ad hoc arrangements that did not overlap with the work being done in Paris.[124] The Dutch resolution nonetheless won support from the French and Belgian delegations when the Consultative Council convened at The Hague on July 19, just one month after the Congress of Europe had adjourned. Belgian Prime Minister Paul-Henri Spaak wanted a permanent committee to coordinate economic and financial policies outside the scope of the OEEC, while French Foreign Minister Georges Bidault issued a dramatic appeal for the unification of Western Europe. Bidault's words echoed those from the other side of the Atlantic. Unification would, he said, "reform and modernize the economic basis of European life by creating a wide market." This would be a step toward long-term viability and toward a peaceful resolution of the German problem and should be taken concurrently with the formation of a European "political assembly" representing the national parliaments of participating states.[125]

Only six months after his celebrated call for a Western union, Bevin, who headed the British delegation at The Hague, was losing the leadership of this cause to greater champions on the Continent. Even the dry records of the meeting suggest his discomfort. He associated himself with the sentiments of his colleagues but then went on to intone the familiar refrains of British policy: Economic coordination should be handled on an ad hoc basis;

---

[123] Vaughan, *Twentieth-Century Europe*, 84–6; and Bullock, *Bevin*, 533–4.

[124] Jebb minute to Berthoud, July 6, 1948, Berthoud minutes of July 7 and 9, 1948, Makins letter to Hall-Patch, July 12, 1948, J. W. Russell minute to Gore-Booth, July 14, 1948, and Makins minute of July 15, 1948, FO 371, 71767, UR3259 and UR3587.

[125] Minutes of the Second Meeting of 20th July 1948 of the Consultative Council Second Plenary Session, The Hague, July 20, 1948, FO 371, 71767, UR3712. See also Minutes of the Second Meeting of the Consultative Council First Plenary Session, July 19, 1948, and Bevin tel. to FO, July 20, 1948, FO 371, 71767, UR3712; and Jebb minute of July 8, 1948, FO 371, 71767, UR3259.

arrangements between the five must not detract from the work being done in Paris; Communists and "fellow travelers" would use a European assembly to propagate their views; proposals for the unification of Europe had to be squared with Britain's commitments elsewhere. "One might follow a missionary with zeal, but missionaries did not always lead to salvation." This was Bevin's verdict, and with it the delegates deferred all issues to a subsequent meeting.[126]

By the time the Consultative Council reconvened in October, the movement for political unification had gained additional momentum. The Foreign Affairs Committee of the French National Assembly had passed a resolution in July urging the government to support plans for a European assembly. Spaak had announced the support of his government on July 29. The French Council of Ministers and the Italian Foreign Office had followed with similar endorsements, and both the French and the Belgians had urged the British to do the same. The Europeans stressed the importance of quick action that would appeal to policymakers in the United States, outbid the Communists in the battle for public opinion, and create a framework for resolving the German problem. Bevin countered with his usual arguments. But even his robust assertions could not conceal how British policymakers had been thrown onto the defensive. They were being roundly criticized for impeding the unification of Europe, which led Bevin to worry that lack of progress on this front and in the negotiations for a European payments plan was beginning to erode the "great spirit" that had been engendered by the Marshall Plan and his own proposal for a Western union.[127]

Bevin decided to steal the lead with a new proposal. Instead of a European assembly elected by parliaments, he called for a council of ministers that would meet annually to consider European issues and make recommendations to participating governments. The proposal amounted to a step down the road being traveled by the Europeans. But the ultimate destination was an ad hoc arrangement that stopped short of merging national sovereignties. British strategy in this case was remarkably similar to that being used to head off American efforts to strengthen the OEEC. It would apply to the political sector the "empirical" approach to integration already applied to the economic sector. Bevin made this clear when he explained his proposal to Prime Minister Attlee:

It would go a long way towards spiking the guns of those who wish to impose a constitution and who criticise H. M. G. for not going fast enough in the direction

[126] See the first two documents cited in note 125. The quotation is from the first document.
[127] Bevin tel. to Cripps, September 29, 1948, FO 371, 71937, UR5970. See also the records of Bevin's talks with French Minister of National Defense Paul Ramadier, September 25, 1948, Paul-Henri Spaak, September 29, 1948, and French Foreign Minister Robert Schuman, October 2, 1948, FO 800/460/EUR/48/35, /10, and /42; and Vaughan, *Twentieth-Century Europe*, 86–8.

of Western Union; while at the same time preserving in effect the full sovereignty of the participating states and in reality basing the whole new system on the so-called "empirical" approach rather than on the alternative basis of the adoption of some formal "constitution."[128]

Bevin pressed this brief with unremitting vigor when the Consultative Council reconvened in Paris on October 25 and 26. Foreign Minister Robert Schuman now spoke for the French and went over the same ground that Bidault had covered three months earlier. Bevin refused to be impressed. He still thought that Britain must not be pulled too deeply into Europe and that nothing should be done to disrupt its ties to the Commonwealth and the sterling bloc.[129] When Schuman proposed a European assembly to be launched by a preparatory committee of delegates nominated by parliaments, Bevin proposed a council of ministers that would keep decisions in the hands of governments. The gap between these positions was substantial. But on Bevin's suggestion the Consultative Council settled on a compromise acceptable to all. The council established a preparatory committee that would consist of representatives appointed by governments and would meet in private, consider both Schuman's proposal and Bevin's alternative, and submit its recommendations for action by the governments involved.[130] This action would come in January. The point to note here is that Bevin had struck a bargain that deferred the issue, defused the criticism of British policy, and gave hope of a settlement in tune with the empirical approach to European unification.

These were exactly the same tactics that Bevin and other British policymakers were using to relieve the pressure for economic integration. In this area, British policy also remained more or less as it had been set by the compromise that Bevin and Cripps hammered out in March 1948. By early September, the London Committee had finished yet another report on the merits of an Anglo–Western European customs union, which Cripps submitted to the Economic Policy Committee with his own memorandum of September 7. Both documents gave short shrift to the long-term strategic advantages of such a union, concentrating instead on the litany of concerns that had preoccupied the economic ministries for over two years. Joining a customs union, the documents warned again, would "come as a great shock to United Kingdom agriculture and to employers and workers in certain sectors of United Kingdom industry, as well as to other members of the British Commonwealth." The government would be unable to shelter key industries against foreign competition, manage the internal migration of labor, achieve a "planned distribution of industry," or implement its policy,

---

[128] Bevin memorandum to Attlee, October 18, 1948, FO 800/460/EUR/48/50. See also the records of Bevin's talks with Spaak and Schuman cited in note 127.

[129] Record of a Meeting of the Consultative Council Held at the Quai d'Orsay 10 A.M. and 3:30 P.M. on October 25, 1948, FO 800/460/EUR/48/53.

[130] Ibid.

laid down in the Agricultural Act of 1947, of "assured markets and guaranteed prices" for agriculture. It would forfeit to a supranational agency a certain amount of its control over foreign trade and exchange rates, and this would make it difficult "to stabilise demand and prices" against "inflationary and deflationary pressures" originating on the Continent. Nor could membership in a European union be reconciled with Britain's interests and commitments elsewhere. Sterling-area arrangements and imperial preferences would have to be "modified" in a way that diminished the contribution the Commonwealth was making to Britain's economic recovery and to the restoration of its international position.[131]

The emphasis continued to be on the empirical approach to European economic integration. An approach like this was actually emerging with the OEEC's plans to liberalize payments and draft a master program to coordinate production across the ERP area. The London Committee had no illusion that "centralized planning," such as that envisioned in the master program, could lead to a rational pattern of production and trade without "painful" internal adjustments in the participating countries. But at least "planning" left more room for governments to regulate the process of integration and thus avert the "disruptive shifts" that would be set in motion by the "automatic" mechanism of a customs union.[132] This conclusion seemed to be validated by commodity studies prepared by British experts in connection with the work of the Customs Union Study Group, which continued to meet periodically in Geneva. The reports, according to one Foreign Office official, raised grave doubts that even substantial safeguards over a protracted period could measurably ameliorate the severe economic dislocations and the "social and political unrest" that would come with Britain's entry into a European customs union.[133] Given these dangers, the British delegation in Geneva had adhered to the position established earlier. It had refused to commit the Labour government to any course of action and had tried, as before, to steer the Study Group into detailed investigations that would delay the day of reckoning for the Labour government.

By late 1948, however, pressure from the Benelux and the French had "manoeuvered" the British into an awkward position. The Benelux delegation was pushing for the immediate formation of a European customs

---

[131] EPC (48) 78, London Committee memorandum, "Implications of a European Customs Union," with cover memorandum by Cripps, September 7, 1948, FO 371, 71854, UR5214. See also Francis Marten's minute of April 14, 1948, Berthoud memorandum to Makins, September 9, 1948, and John Henniker memorandum to Bevin, September 9, 1948, FO 371, 71854, UR5214. Berthoud superintended the Foreign Office's Economic Relations and Intelligence Division, of which Marten and Henniker were members.

[132] See the first source cited in note 131.

[133] See the Foreign Office minute by Marten, September 29, 1948, FO 371, 71851, UR5708. For a summary of the commodity studies, see CU (48) 73 of September 24, 1948, FO 371, 71851, UR5708.

union while the French were proposing a "limited union" to be launched by eliminating tariffs on a small but expanding number of commodities. The British appeared to be "the principal stumbling block," which led them to devise a new strategy for "diverting pressure" and casting themselves in a more favorable light. They proposed to scuttle the Study Group and transfer the bulk of its work to Paris, where the British were in a stronger position than in Geneva and where the OEEC's plans for liberalizing payments and drafting a master recovery program came closer to the empirical approach favored by the Foreign Office and the Treasury. This proposal had the advantage of appearing to be a positive and cooperative gesture, a deception that had failed in Geneva, and of thereby deflecting the pressure for faster progress. As the British delegation subsequently explained, the new strategy avoided "the potentially embarrassing repercussions of the full Customs Union project, e.g. on Commonwealth preference, on the sterling area system, and on U.K. monetary and agricultural policies, without at the same time risking an open breakdown such as might have embroiled us simultaneously with the U.S. and with the W. European countries themselves."[134]

At least part of this strategy had succeeded by the end of 1948. The British had delayed further action on the issue of a customs union and had secured support in the Study Group for measures that transferred much of its work to the OEEC. Success had come largely because the Belgians, the Dutch, and the French were the only enthusiastic supporters of a European union. And even the French, whose proposal for a "limited union" had been "shot down" by the other delegations, were disheartened by all of the problems that hampered progress. These problems had become clearer in the negotiations at Geneva and in the related efforts, by the French, Italians, and Scandinavians, to organize smaller, regional tariff groups. Under these circumstances, most of the participating countries seemed content to scale down the Study Group's work and to concentrate their efforts on the OEEC.[135]

Contrary to expectations, however, the British approach could not shield them against charges of obstructionism or cast their policy in a positive light. It set them at odds with the French, who wanted to anchor their security to a supranational system, and with the Americans, who wanted

[134] CU (48) 80, Report of the UK Delegation to the 3rd meeting of the Economic Committee of the Customs Union Study Group (October 19–23, 1948), November 1, 1948, Henniker minute of November 4, 1948, D. F. MacDermont minute of November 5, 1948, C. M. Anderson minute of November 11, 1948, Instructions to the U. K. Delegation in Geneva, November 29, 1948, and unsigned, undated Instructions to the U.K. Delegation in Geneva, FO 371, 71857, UR7006, UR7615, UR8161, and UR8646.

[135] See the unsigned, undated "General Note" by the U.K. Delegation to the Customs Union Study Group, and the personal report "Customs Union Study Group" by C. M. Anderson, December 7, 1948, FO 371, 71857, UR8647 and UR8661.

to use both free-market forces and supranational coordinators to integrate economies. British and American leaders tangled on almost every issue. The British had opposed American demands for ministerial meetings of the OEEC and for the appointment of a director general. They had also raised objections to the intra-European payments plan, to the OEEC's allocation of American assistance, and to the bilateral aid agreement proposed by the State Department.

Although these differences had been in the making for some time, they exploded like fissures in an earthquake during the second half of 1948. Bevin complained angrily that Britain was being treated like a minor power, lectured on the level of its diplomatic appointments, and threatened with the loss of American aid. He thought his government deserved recognition, not reproach, for doing all that it could in Europe.[136] On the other side of the Atlantic, Hoffman and Harriman were accusing the British of "not entering wholeheartedly into OEEC work." Howard Bruce was denouncing their "opposition to everything we have suggested." Marshall was charging them with "dragging [their] feet" on European economic integration. Clayton was attacking them for "hanging on by their eye-lashes" to the illusion that the United States would help to "preserve the British Empire and their own leadership of it." Douglas was lamenting their preference for social programs instead of productive investment, their "pathological" resentment of America's world leadership, and their "anxiety neurosis" over European unity.[137]

Anglo–American differences were a problem, but not all of the blame could be heaped on the British. American leaders, as some officials admitted, too often adopted a "patronizing" tone in dealing with the British. Despite repeated professions of "equality," they were unable to lift relations "above the pinprick level" and treat the British as "partners in a common enterprise." Nor were they always willing to recognize the contributions that the British had made to the ERP or frankly confront the difficulties that the Commonwealth connection posed to Britain's integration into Europe. This connection helped to maintain stability in areas of the world outside of Europe, or so the Americans admitted. Disrupting it could bring a dangerous "change in [world] power relationships." But to admit this and still call for

[136]   See the record of Bevin's talks with Marshall, October 4, 1948, FO 800/460/EUR/ 48/48. See also Bevin tel. to Cripps, October 31, 1948, FO 800/440/Bel./49/10.

[137]   Marshall tel. to Douglas, August 20, 1948, *FRUS, 1948,* 3:1117; Bruce letter to Harriman, August 17, 1948, RG 286, Acc. 53A405, box 1, folder: Special Representative's Office, 1948; Marshall tel. to Douglas, September 13, 1948, *FRUS, 1948,* 3:1120–1; Clayton memorandum to Lovett, September 17, 1948, RG 59, PPS Records, box 27, folder: Europe, 1947–48; and Douglas tel. to Marshall, August 11, 1948, *FRUS, 1948,* 3:1113–17. See also, Douglas letter to Harriman, May 11, 1948, W. Averell Harriman Papers (W. Averell Harriman Residence, Washington, DC), folder: Finletter, Thomas K.; and Douglas tel. to Marshall, June 11, 1948, *FRUS, 1948,* 3:1089–90.

Britain's integration into Europe amounted to a basic inconsistency that the State Department and the ECA had done little to resolve. These agencies clearly wanted to reconcile what Richard Bissell called the "two orientations" of British diplomacy, a fact that helps to explain why the ECA had been willing to negotiate special arrangements for sterling in the intra-European payments plan. There were other compromises as well and these would accumulate *seriatim* in the months ahead. Yet approaching the problem piecemeal only ensured continuing conflict. A comprehensive formula was necessary and the Americans, unlike the British, had made no effort to devise one that had a chance of being accepted.[138]

VI

Nor had American leaders developed a full picture of what they wanted to accomplish in Europe. By the end of 1948, they had taken great strides in the direction of a European neo-capitalism. They had tried to strengthen the OEEC, launch a new payments plan, and forge transnational networks of corporative collaboration and power sharing, all of which would supposedly help to integrate economies and set the stage for a new era of social peace and material abundance on the Continent. They had also encouraged a political unification of Western Europe and had opened negotiations for a North Atlantic military alliance that would lead, or so they hoped, to the integration of European defense systems. Indeed, American policymakers wanted to build in Europe and elsewhere "a series of regional groups which, through integration in the military, political and economic fields, will strengthen the free world as a whole." But as Douglas and others noted, they had not "sufficiently coordinated" their policies in these fields or defined what they meant by "integration." Was the latter only a means toward multilateral trade and convertible currencies? Or did it entail standard wage and price levels, a common market, monetary authority, and tax structure; and if so, could these be achieved without the political union that some considered "utopian" or the socialist state controls that others thought dangerous?[139]

---

[138] Bliss memorandum to the Ambassador, September 24, 1948, attached to Marshall letter to Douglas, August 15, 1948, RG 59, file: 711.41/8-1648; Department of State Policy Statement, "Great Britain," June 11, 1948, *FRUS, 1948*, 3:1091–1108; Tufts memorandum to Dickinson, August 20, 1948, RG 286, Acc. 53A405, box 55, folder: Committee – ECA/State Dept. Planning Group; and Bissell memorandum, September 22, 1948, *FRUS, 1948*, 3:486–9. See also Labouisse memorandum to Achilles, November 20, 1948, with attached Finletter memorandum, "Points in Respect of British Leadership in European Cooperation," September 29, 1948, RG 59, file: 840.00/11-2048.

[139] Moore memorandum to Kennan et al., October 25, 1948, RG 286, Acc. 53A405, box 33, folder: Program – European Payments Union; Douglas tel. to Marshall, August 31, 1948, *FRUS, 1948*, 3:483–6; and Mills memorandum to Woodward, December 6, 1948, RG 59, file: 840.50Recovery/12-648.

And what were the strategic ramifications of a European union? For American leaders, economic integration had always been a way to reconcile Franco–German differences and build a balance of power in the West sufficient "to contain Soviet power" in the East. By the end of the year, however, Thomas Finletter and others were wondering if this strategy might actually lead Europe "down the road to a new isolationism" or result in a European "Third Force" balanced between the Soviet Union and the United States. Much like the British, Finletter and other American officials wanted to link Western Europe to the United States within the framework of a North Atlantic community. But if this was the goal, then American leaders had to decide what they were "trying to achieve in terms of European unity." They had to harmonize their plans for a North Atlantic community with their program for an integrated Europe, and they had to define the role that Britain would play in both arenas. Until they did, it seemed pointless to charge the British with obstruction or to complain if the Europeans moved ahead on their own.[140]

---

[140] Finletter, "Points in Respect of British Leadership in European Cooperation," September 29, 1948, attached to Labouisse memorandum to Achilles, November 20, 1948, RG 59, file: 840.00/11-2048.

5

Changing course: European integration and the traders triumphant

I

THE FIRST HALF of 1949 saw unmistakable signs of progress toward the strategic and economic goals on the American agenda for Western Europe. Policymakers began to coordinate their economic and military policies and negotiate agreements looking toward the formation of a West German gov ernment. They also extended the transnational pattern of public–private power sharing, further strengthened the OEEC, and helped to revise the intra-European payments plan. In addition, industrial output in the OEEC countries climbed 18 percent above 1938 figures, agricultural production went up, Western Europe's overall volume of trade recovered to prewar levels, and many participating countries made progress in curbing inflation and balancing budgets. These gains came in part because member states were investing approximately one-fifth of their gross national income in new capital goods. Compared to this kind of self-help, as Paul Hoffman admitted to Congress, American assistance was playing a "marginal" role in Western Europe's revitalization. Still, the United States had extended $5 billion in Marshall aid to participating countries and this aid, according to Hoffman, had provided the critical margin on which all other investment depended. It enabled participating countries to cover their deficits in trade with the Western Hemisphere and thus to import the essential commodities that made self-help possible.[1]

Hoffman's remarks came in the midst of a stormy congressional debate over a bill to extend the Economic Cooperation Act for another year. As in 1948, the debate revolved around the cost of the Marshall Plan, the plan's

[1] U.S., Congress, Senate, Committee on Foreign Relations, *Extension of European Recovery, Hearings on S. 833*, 81st Cong., 1st sess., 1949, 417 (hereafter cited as Senate, *Hearings on S. 833*); and ECA, *Fifth Report to Congress* (Washington, DC, 1949), 3–6, 16–27.

impact on the American economy, and the general objectives being pursued. Although Henry Wallace repeated much of the criticism he had leveled against the Marshall Plan a year earlier, the most serious opposition came from the Right. Senator Robert A. Taft again led a coalition of conservatives who sought to reduce the amount of American aid and prohibit support for nationalized industries. The conservatives claimed that Marshall aid (taken together with other commitments) exceeded the limits of American resources and discouraged the Europeans from putting their own house in order. Some argued that further assistance was unnecessary, since European production had surpassed prewar levels. Others wondered how the American taxpayer could be asked to subsidize socialism in Western Europe, particularly in Britain, where Marshall aid presumably defrayed the cost of everything from a "socialized steel industry" to "toupees, hearing aids, false teeth, free babies, and free funerals." Still others worried that "pouring out billions" for such "social experiments" and for "every crackpot theory of the New Deal from leaf raking to pump priming" would "kill the goose that laid the golden egg." It would bankrupt the American treasury, they said, and end in more government control.

The conservatives also feared the revival of European competition. In their view, only the large, highly competitive American corporations and their friends among the great investment banks stood to gain from the Marshall Plan, both in contracts to supply ERP goods to Europe and in the ultimate restoration of a multilateral system of world trade. According to Senator William E. Jenner of Indiana, "the monopolists" were getting the "big end" of the stick, while small firms and their workers were getting the shaft. Senator George W. Malone of Nevada found it astonishing that Democratic Party administrations, which drew such strong support from organized labor, could also follow "the same plans during the last 10 or 12 years as have the very rich, the very top of the manufacturing, producing, and investment groups."[2]

Once again, the majority in Congress defended the Marshall Plan with arguments that reversed the critique mounted by the Right. They argued that American resources were adequate to the task and that Marshall aid was helping to unify Western Europe, contain communism, and pave the way to a multilateral system on which American prosperity depended. The Marshall Plan, they said, was cheaper than the economic and political costs in higher taxes, substantial deficits, and government controls that would result from a massive rearmament program, which the United States would have to shoulder if the Soviet Union and its Communist supporters gained

[2]　U.S., Congress, Senate, Senators Jenner and Malone speaking on S. 833, 81st Cong., 1st sess., March 28 and 24 and April 1, 1949, *Congressional Record* 95:3270, 3100, 3266, 3650. For Wallace's views, see U.S., Congress, House, Committee on Foreign Affairs, *Extension of European Recovery Program, Hearings on H.R. 2362*, 81st Cong., 1st sess., 1949, 581–620 (hereafter cited as House, *Hearings on H.R. 2362*).

control of Western Europe. Although they admitted that some American enterprises might suffer from the revival of European competitors, they also claimed that any losses would be offset "a hundredfold by the advantages to the American export trade as a whole through having a vigorous, healthy western Europe on a basis of higher living standards, higher wage standards, and general expansion of purchasing power." These were the views of Senator Arthur Vandenberg of Michigan, Senator Millard E. Tydings of Maryland, and other defenders of the Marshall Plan. They had the backing of a variety of private interests, most notably of the great investment banks, large multinational corporations, major trade unions, and leading farm associations that had earlier formed what Senator Malone saw as a strange alliance behind the domestic and foreign policies of the New Deal and Fair Deal. As in 1948, these groups joined forces with their collaborators in the Truman administration and in Congress to overwhelm the conservatives and renew support for the recovery program.[3]

American goals remained the same, then, but the first half of 1949 did witness a shift in strategy. Marshall Planners had always assumed that monetary and trade reforms should go hand in hand with programs to restore production and curb inflation. The recovery of prewar production levels and the growing signs of financial stability therefore led inevitably to less emphasis on these initial priorities and greater pressure for the devaluation of currencies, the liberalization of trade, and the formation of a European payments union. This change of course seemed particularly desirable because the recovery of production had done little to correct Western Europe's trade and payments deficit with the dollar area, which actually grew worse in the first half of the new year. This deterioration raised the dreadful prospect that Western Europe would not be self-supporting at the end of the Marshall Plan. Under these circumstances, the devaluation of currencies and the elimination of bilateral payments barriers became the keys not simply to an integrated European economy but also to a multilateral pattern of international trade.

As in the past, British policy seemed to point in a different direction, especially after a second sterling crisis began to develop in the spring of 1949. This crisis was the most glaring example of the so-called dollar gap. But when the Americans tried to close the gap by realigning currencies and integrating economies, the British threatened to shelter their economy in a third international trading system centered in London. Thus, even as the State Department and the ECA made progress on the German front, dis-

---

[3] U.S. Congress, Senate, Senator Vandenberg speaking on S. 833, 81st Cong., 1st sess., March 24, 1949, *Congressional Record* 95:3102. For a sampling of arguments on all sides of the congressional debate, see also in the same source 3099–3102, 3175–89, 3253, 3259, 3262–71, 3355, 3449–57, 3647–50, 3656–62, 3796–3801, 4056–64; Senate, *Hearings on S. 833*, 1–151, 191–9, 415–48, 491–534, 538–40, 543–5; and House, *Hearings on H.R. 2362*, 523–7, 671–93, 709–11, 715.

placing the American Army and winning French support for Germany's continued revival and reintegration, developments in British policy raised new barriers to their plans.

II

One of the goals of the Marshall Plan had always been to forge a Western European bloc of nations of sufficient size and coherence to withstand the dual dangers of Communist subversion and Soviet aggression. Economic integration was central to the achievement of this goal – the only way to reconcile Franco–German differences and weld both countries to a unit of power large enough to generate recovery and contain the Soviets. But economic integration was only one-half of the walnut, to paraphrase Truman's famous aphorism. The Western Europeans also had to organize and arm themselves against potential adversaries and do so in a way that was consistent with the ongoing efforts to unify economies and promote recovery. American policymakers hammered away at this theme at all stages of the North Atlantic Treaty negotiations. At the very start of the negotiations in July 1948, Robert Lovett had warned that the United States would not guarantee " 'a fire-trap' " and that Western Europe must therefore replace old habits of political conflict and economic rivalry with "some form of union based on self-help and mutual aid."[4] John D. Hickerson and George Kennan made the same point, with Kennan arguing that a North Atlantic treaty must not preclude the "real unification of Europe and the development of a European idea."[5] Five months later, as an Allied working party was putting the finishing touches on a draft treaty to be signed in April 1949, Kennan also warned against "a general pre-occupation with military affairs, to the detriment of economic recovery." If rearmament overshadowed recovery, if the North Atlantic Treaty superseded the Marshall Plan, economies would falter, living standards would collapse, and social peace would give way to resumption of the political struggle that had always posed a greater threat than Soviet arms to the security of Western Europe.[6]

Similar thinking guided American policymakers as they began laying plans to reinforce the North Atlantic Treaty with a military-assistance program. In December 1948, the secretaries of state and defense and the administrator of the ECA established the Foreign Assistance Steering Committee with a view to coordinating economic and military-aid programs. Shortly thereafter, the Steering Committee appointed two subsidiary bodies, the Foreign

---

[4] Minutes of the Fourth Meeting of the Washington Exploratory Talks on Security, July 8, 1948, *FRUS, 1948*, 3:163–9.

[5] Minutes of the Fifth Meeting of the Washington Exploratory Talks on Security, July 9, 1948, *FRUS, 1948*, 3:169–82.

[6] PPS/43, "Considerations Affecting the Conclusion of a North Atlantic Security Pact," November 23, 1948, enclosed in Kennan memorandum to Marshall and Lovett, November 24, 1948, *FRUS, 1948*, 3:283–9.

Assistance Correlation Committee in Washington and the United States Correlation Committee on Foreign Assistance Programs in London. The latter was chaired by Ambassador Lewis Douglas and included among its members the American representatives on various agencies of the Western European Union that had been established under the Brussels Pact. One key member was Averell Harriman, the ECA's special representative in Europe, who represented the United States on the Western Union's Financial and Economic Committee and at meetings of the union's finance ministers.[7] The assumption was that coordinating arrangements of this nature would help to tailor the rearmament program to the goals of the Marshall Plan. The same assumption led American policymakers to demand that rearmament follow the recovery model, particularly in regard to such ideas as collective action, coordination and standardization of production and supply, and development of a common strategic concept. In this way, rearmament would contribute to the unification of Western Europe and at the same time spur recovery by boosting European confidence in a secure future.[8]

This strategy could work, as Kennan had argued earlier, only if military requirements did not overshadow the needs of recovery. European economies were "stretched to the limit," he and other Americans kept explaining. Substantial increases in military production would divert manpower, raw materials, and investment capital from the recovery program, generate inflation, and wreck plans to expand exports and raise living standards. European leaders viewed the matter in much the same light. The common assumptions seemed to be that additional military production had to be kept within the bounds of current recovery programs and that any shortfall in European resources would have to be offset by American aid above normal ECA allocations.[9] Accordingly, the agreement that was finally worked out called for a limited program of incremental defense production by the Western Union countries to be undertaken in accordance with the

---

[7] Lawrence S. Kaplan, *A Community of Interests: NATO and the Military Assistance Program, 1948–1951* (Washington, DC, 1980), 23, 29; Richard P. Stebbins, *The United States in World Affairs, 1949* (New York, 1950), 142; Harriman tel. to Marshall, January 9, 1949, and Lovett tel. to Caffery, January 10, 1949, RG 59, file: 840.00/1-949; Acheson tel. to Douglas, February 14, 1949, RG 59, file: 840.00/2-949; Acheson tel. to Douglas, February 21, 1949, RG 59, file: 840.00/2-1549; Douglas tel. to Acheson, February 22, 1949, and Acheson tel. to Douglas, March 3, 1949, RG 59, file: 840.00/2-2249; and Acheson letter to the Secretary of the Army, March 8, 1949, RG 59, file: 840.50Recovery/3-849.

[8] Stebbins, *United States in World Affairs, 1949*, 135; and Kaplan, *Community of Interests*, 10, 11, 16–18, 20–2.

[9] Holmes tel. to Acheson, January 29, 1949, RG 59, file: 840.00/1-2949. See also Hoffman torep 2750 to Harriman, January 8, 1949, and Caffery tel. to Acheson, January 22, 1949, *FRUS, 1949*, 4:367–8, 626–30; Holmes tel. to Acheson, January 22, 1949, RG 59, file: 840.00/1-2249; Douglas tel. to Acheson, February 24, 1949, RG 59, file: 840.00/2-2449; and Douglas tel to Acheson, March 2, 1949, RG 59, file: 840.00/3-249. See also Kaplan, *Community of Interests*, 25–6.

American principles of mutual aid, coordinated planning, and standardized production. The Europeans also accepted the idea of a common strategic concept and agreed to finance defense production from noninflationary sources. In return, the Americans pledged a military-aid program under which the Europeans would receive equipment and supplies as well as financial compensation to offset the impact of increased military production on civilian economies.[10]

These were the terms agreed to in March 1949 and subsequently incorporated into the military-assistance program that President Truman submitted to Congress following ratification of the North Atlantic Treaty. Through their implementation (as the Senate Foreign Relations Committee said of the treaty), the United States sought to create "a favorable climate for further steps toward progressively closer [Western] European integration" and thus toward a viable balance of power on the Continent. To this extent, the goals of American diplomacy remained as they had been since the start of the Marshall Plan. Nor did the new initiatives spell a fundamental change in priorities or tactics. Officials in Congress and in the Truman administration placed greater emphasis than before on organizing Western Europe's defenses, an emphasis provoked by the escalation of East–West tensions that accompanied the Czechoslovakian crisis and the Berlin blockade. But they continued to give the highest priority to economic recovery and to rely primarily on economic rather than military tools to achieve their objectives. In truth, they assumed that American resources were not sufficient to absorb a massive military, as well as economic, aid program, that mere assurances of armed intervention would deter Soviet aggression, and that such pledges might even make it possible to cut defense expenditures and achieve Truman's goal of a balanced budget.[11]

At the same time, recovery planners and military leaders in Washington were settling some of the bureaucratic and policy disputes that had made American diplomacy toward Germany so refractory. Western Europe's recovery and security hung on a resolution of the German problem. And in solving the problem, as in coordinating recovery and rearmament policies, economic and military imperatives appeared to dictate a strategy aimed at integration. There was no thought yet of rearming Germany and making it a member of the North Atlantic pact. But reintegrating the Allied occupation zones into a unified Western Europe would at least forestall a trend toward

[10] Kaplan, *Community of Interests*, 26, 32, Caffery dispatch #229 to Acheson, March 4, 1949, RG 59, file: 840.00/3-449; Acheson tel. to Douglas, March 12, 1949, RG 59, file: 840.00/3-1149; and Katz repto 3407 to Hoffman, March 31, 1949, ECA Files, box 6.

[11] Stebbins, *United States in World Affairs, 1949*, 111, 79–80; and Gaddis, "The United States and the Question of a Sphere of Influence in Europe," 75. For a fuller discussion of how the idea of European unity impacted on the North Atlantic Treaty negotiations, see also Lawrence S. Kaplan, *The United States and NATO: The Formative Years* (Lexington, KY, 1984), 65–120.

neutralism in the former Reich, avert a dangerous Soviet–German rapprochement, and make it possible for the Western powers to utilize Germany's resources without again becoming its victims. Seen in this light, Germany's reintegration was not simply the best way to build a Western European market large enough to generate abundance. It was also the key to a workable balance of power among the Western states.

Creating this balance still depended on the degree to which Germany's revival could be made acceptable to the French, which in turn depended on Britain's integration into Europe and the Army Department's cooperation in a policy that reconciled French and German requirements. This was the view from Foggy Bottom, with only Kennan and a handful of dissenters noting the serious problems that might result from the de facto division of Germany and Europe into rival blocs. For others, the most pressing difficulties lay elsewhere. They had to do with ongoing efforts to shove the British into Europe and to overcome opposition in the French government and the American Army. On this last front, there were substantial if hardwon gains in the first half of 1949.

By the end of 1948, the Allies had agreed in principle to establish an International Authority for the Ruhr, which was to allocate coal, coke, and steel between exports and German consumption and work with other Allied agencies, especially the proposed Military Security Board, to ensure Germany's disarmament and demilitarization. Allied negotiators reached agreement in January on a set of instructions that would guide the Military Security Board, but neither the Security Board nor the Ruhr Authority had become operational. Both agencies awaited formal approval by the Allied governments, which had yet to hammer out accords on such other issues as the Basic Law (constitution) of the proposed German state, the powers to be reserved under the Occupation Statute, the prohibitions and restrictions to be retained on German industry, and the capital equipment and plant facilities to be removed as reparations.

The Allies divided on all of these issues – the British and the French against the Americans on the reparation question; the Americans and the British against the French on virtually every other item. Franco–American differences were particularly sharp and demonstrated again how difficult it was to arrange a German settlement that harmonized ostensibly inconsistent security (and economic) imperatives. As they had since 1945, the French were trying to control Germany's productive capacity, particularly the capacity of the Ruhr coal and steel industries, in order to limit its potential for rearmament and protect the steel-production targets in the Monnet Plan. Their program called for controls over production and investment in the Ruhr, guarantees regarding ownership and management of the Ruhr industries in the postoccupation period, and some mechanism to prevent Germany's rearmament after the Military Security Board and other Allied agencies disbanded. In addition, the French were demanding an extensive

list of prohibitions and restrictions on German industry and raising strenuous objections to the recommendation of the Humphrey Committee, issued
in January 1949, that Germany retain 167 plants previously slated for
removal as reparations. In all of these respects, French demands collided
with American policy.[12]

The first months of 1949 saw only incremental progress on these issues.
The French, with strong backing from the British, wanted to link the reparations question to the prohibitions and restrictions on German industry,
obviously hoping for American concessions they could not get if the subjects
were treated separately. The proposal sent General Clay into a fit of opposition. The State Department, pulled in one direction by the Allies and
in another by the Army Department, finally agreed to discuss the issues
simultaneously, but only on terms that precluded substantive concessions.
Both sides mustered the usual arguments. The British and the French took
the high ground of national security, warning of a new German menace if
programs of industrial disarmament were curbed. The Americans accused
the Allies of being more concerned with their economic interests than with
their security. They stressed the congressional pressures to put western Germany on a self-supporting basis, the importance of developing its resources
for the benefit of Western Europe as a whole, and the need to assuage
German nationalism. The issues remained as contentious as ever. But in this
case, the familiar pattern of negotiation resembled nothing more than the
ritual of accommodation between lovers whose squabbles are prelude to an
embrace. After weeks of argument, the negotiators settled the dispute over
reparations and dismantling by subtracting a small number of important
plants from the Humphrey Committee's list of those to be retained in Germany. So far as prohibitions and restrictions were concerned, they struck
a compromise that satisfied the British and French respectively by restricting
German shipbuilding and maintaining the current limit on steel production
in the Ruhr.[13]

Government approval of these arrangements, like those pertaining to the
Military Security Board and the Ruhr Authority, depended on the successful
conclusion of negotiations regarding trizonal fusion and a German Occupation Statute. In these negotiations, the issues were far more intractable.
Trizonal fusion was being delayed by disputes over an American demand
for a predominant voice in matters relating to Germany's foreign trade and
over the voting procedure in cases involving the exercise of powers reserved
to the Allies under the Occupation Statute. Although a draft statute had

---

[12]   For a summary of these issues, see Wayne G. Jackson, Special Assistant to the Director
       of the Office of European Affairs, memorandum to John D. Hickerson, Director of
       the Office, January 6, 1949, *FRUS, 1949*, 3:73–82.
[13]   Campbell, *United States in World Affairs, 1948–1949*, 479–82; *FRUS, 1949*, 3:546–
       94; Department of State, *Bulletin* 20 (April 24, 1949): 524–31; and Bullock, *Bevin*,
       662–4.

been prepared, the give-and-take of the negotiating process had also produced what the Americans saw as a long, complicated, and "iniquitous document" that reserved far too much authority for the Allies and thus ran the risk of alienating the Germans and giving the French new opportunities to restrict Germany's recovery.[14]

In Washington, meanwhile, disputes and delays on these and the other issues had revived the old controversy over the best approach to the German problem. Clay and his superiors in the Army Department complained of "foot dragging tactics" by the French and the British and of a lack of support from the State Department, where officials were supposedly preoccupied with the NATO negotiations and generally ignorant of the problems the Army Department faced in Germany. The State Department, they protested, was too inclined to approach issues on a piecemeal basis and too anxious to make concessions that would hamper recovery in Germany and erode the American position there. They wanted to adopt a "package" approach. They would demand concessions to all of "our plans in Germany" and withhold ECA assistance and support for the Ruhr Authority and the North Atlantic Treaty until concessions were forthcoming.[15]

For the State Department and the ECA, this was just the sort of high-handed strategy that had so far failed. Averell Harriman thought it ridiculous to expect French concessions on all issues. Kennan accused the Army Department of being "too rigid" in negotiating with the Allies. Clay had failed "to make use of the accepted give and take" of the negotiating process, had refused to balance Germany's needs against those of France and the other ERP countries, and had attempted to solve the German problem on a strictly "nationalist basis." "There is no solution of the German problem in terms of Germany," Kennan explained in words similar to those that had echoed through the State Department since the inception of the Marshall Plan; "there is only a solution in terms of Europe." Secretary of State Dean Acheson, who had succeeded Marshall in January, made essentially the same argument, stressing in particular the need to hammer out an intergovernmental agreement on German policy before adopting a more aggressive posture toward the Allies.[16] Still at issue was the difference between the Army Department's emphasis on Germany's recovery and the State De-

[14] Jacob D. Beam, Acting Special Assistant to the Office of German and Austrian Affairs, memorandum to Robert D. Murphy, Acting Director of the Office, March 29, 1949, *FRUS, 1949*, 3:138–40. See also undated State Department paper, and Murphy paper, March 30, 1949, *FRUS, 1949*, 3:131–6.
[15] Geoffrey W. Lewis, Office of Occupied Areas, memorandum to Charles E. Saltzman and Walter Wilds, State Department, January 28, 1949, and Record of Teletype Conference between Washington and Berlin, March 17, 1949, *FRUS, 1949*, 3:87–9, 105–13. See also Clay tel. to Army Department, January 23, 1949, *FRUS, 1949*, 3:84–7.
[16] Lewis memorandum to Saltzman and Wilds, January 28, 1949, and Kennan paper, March 8, 1949, *FRUS, 1949*, 3:87–9, 96–102.

partment's support for an approach that would solve the German problem within the context of a larger reorganization of Western Europe.

With a view to resolving this difference, the National Security Council (NSC) appointed a special subcommittee to formulate a comprehensive statement of American policy. As established, the new agency and its steering group were chaired by State Department representatives, who also produced the original drafts of the policy statement.[17] These arrangements more or less ensured that the State Department's views, rather than those of the Army Department, would define the shape of American policy. Indeed, the resulting position papers as well as the final NSC document submitted to the president at the end of March, stressed the importance of reintegrating Germany into a "strong common structure of free Europeanism." A "segregated" Germany, it was argued, might again dominate the Continent economically, "provide a fertile field for the rebirth of aggressive German nationalism," enable the Germans "to play off West against East," or lead to a dangerous Soviet–German rapprochement. It could produce circumstances under which the sort of paper guarantees demanded by the French, guarantees regarding Germany's disarmament and demilitarization, would only create a "delusive sense of security." But an approach that reintegrated a unified western Germany into the framework of a "general European union" would reconcile the competing economic and security imperatives inherent in a German settlement. It would ensure that Germany's resources were used to Western ends and peaceful purposes and that democratic politics would take root and grow in the former Reich. This was the route to economic recovery and to a balance of power that could contain the Soviet Union. Taking it, however, required a simplified occupation statute, a termination of military rule, and other measures to induce the Germans into voluntary association with the West.[18]

The NSC document, which President Truman approved, finally resolved the old tension between the Army and State Department approaches to European recovery and security. A major triumph for the State Department and the ECA, it guided American leaders in their negotiations with the British and French at the Washington Foreign Ministers Conference of late March and early April 1949. The ministers had convened for the formal signing of the North Atlantic Treaty, but Acheson had also made arrangements for a wide-ranging discussion of the German problem. The idea was to reach an agreement that would remove Germany as a serious source of

[17]   Lewis memorandum to Saltzman and Wilds, January 28, 1949, *FRUS, 1949,* 3:87–9.

[18]   Murphy paper, March 23, 1949, *FRUS, 1949,* 3:118–27. See also Kennan paper, February 7, 1949, Beam paper, February 24, 1949, Kennan paper, March 8, 1949, Beam memorandum to Murphy, March 29, 1949, Murphy paper, March 30, 1949, and Acheson memorandum to Truman, with accompanying State Department paper, March 31, 1949, *FRUS, 1949,* 3:90–3, 94–6, 96–102, 138–40, 140–2, 142–56.

contention among the Western powers before talks with the Russians over the Berlin blockade began. Acheson opened the conference with a proposal under which the new German government, rather than the Allied occupation authorities, would assume the responsibility for managing Germany's affairs. The Allies would reserve certain powers in areas specified in the London accords of June 1948, and these powers would be enumerated in a simplified occupation statute. But in these and other areas, the Allied role would be one of passive supervision and would be performed by civilian rather than military officials. The British and French endorsed this proposal, as well as other arrangements that resolved in America's favor some of the earlier differences over trizonal fusion and voting procedures when exercising reserved powers.[19] Agreement had come easier than expected. The French were beginning to show signs of softening their policy toward Germany in favor of a strategy of rapprochement. In addition, the British and the French were eager to win American approval of the agreements pertaining to the Ruhr Authority, the Military Security Board, and the restrictions on German industry, and particularly anxious to "perfect 3-power" agreement on these matters prior to "4-power discussions" on the Berlin crisis.[20]

The Washington Conference completed the work that Marshall Planners had begun in London a year earlier. It ended the conflict between the Army and State departments. General Clay and the other military governors would now give way to an Allied High Commission of civilian officials. The conference also brought the French into closer accord with American efforts to resolve the German problem within the context of a larger Western European settlement. As such, it set the stage for full trizonal fusion, for the formation of the German Federal Republic, and for West Germany's subsequent accession to the ERP and the OEEC. Together with the failure of the four-power talks on the Berlin crisis, it formalized the division of Germany and began the process whereby the Federal Republic would be brought, in the language of the Washington agreements, "within the framework of a European association."[21]

These gains would come only after policymakers in Washington had hurdled barriers raised at the last minute by General Clay, whose well-deserved reputation for being an obstreperous and irascible negotiator remained intact during the final months of military government. Something of an autocrat, with a dedication to task greater than that of his opponents, Clay saw himself as godfather to the new German state and was determined

---

[19] For the discussions in Washington and the agreements reached, see *FRUS, 1949*, 3:156–86; and Acheson, *Present at the Creation*, 286–90.

[20] Schuman cited in Bullock, *Bevin*, 668.

[21] The quotation is from "Message to the Bonn Parliamentary Council from the Foreign Ministers of the US, UK, and France," [Washington, April 8, 1949], *FRUS, 1949*, 3:186.

to shape it according to ideological prejudices that did not always square with those of the Marshall Planners or with practical realities as defined in Washington. He had little sympathy with the German trade unions or with the Social Democrats who had been pressing for a Basic Law that would concentrate more power in the hands of a central government than either Clay or the Christian Democrats thought desirable. In the parliamentary assembly that had convened in Bonn the previous September, the two German parties had finally struck a compromise on this issue. The Allied Foreign Ministers meeting in April had been willing to accept this compromise, with limited revisions, and had issued a directive along these lines to the military governors. But Clay and his French counterpart set the directive aside. They demanded fundamental revisions that would place more authority in the Lander and work to the political disadvantage of the German Socialists. These demands threatened to destroy the delicate balance in the Bonn assembly and drive the Socialists into open opposition to the Basic Law. Yet it was not until Acheson threatened to remove the negotiations from Clay's hands that the general reversed course and settled for modest changes in the Basic Law, which was then adopted by the Bonn assembly and approved by the military government in the first half of May.[22]

Nor was Clay's obstructionism on this issue the only source of complaint. The Germans, their nationalism aroused by the struggle in Bonn, also resented the powers that the Allies reserved under the Occupation Statute. The statute was a constant reminder of the limits on their sovereignty, as was the scaled-down version of the reparations program and the reduced list of prohibitions and restrictions on German industry. Other critics lamented Clay's decisions to relax the decartelization program in Germany, contain socialist experiments, and place the Ruhr industries under a German management that included some business leaders with former ties to the Nazis.[23] Still others, particularly trade unionists on both sides of the Atlantic, complained bitterly about the wage–price differential in German industry, the delays in returning union property confiscated by the Nazis, the lack of labor representation on Clay's staff and various bizonal agencies, and the

[22] Campbell, *United States in World Affairs, 1948–1949*, 482–93; Bullock, *Bevin*, 668–9, 690–1; and John H. Backer, *Winds of History: The German Years of Lucius DuBignon Clay* (New York, 1983), 273–6.

[23] See the columns by Thomas L. Stokes in the *Washington Star*, January 26, 1949, and by Joseph Alsop in the *Washington Post*, February 23, 1949, in the Blaisdell Papers, box 8, folder: Ruhr Material, 1946–1949. See also Cleon Swayzee, Director of the State Department's Division of International Labor and Social Affairs, memorandum to Edwin M. Martin, Director of the State Department's Office of European Regional Affairs, December 24, 1948, RG 59, file: 862.5043/1-1449; Murphy dispatch #203 to Acheson, February 17, 1949, RG 59, file: 862.5043/2-1749; Matthew Woll of the AFL, letter to Acheson, February 23, 1949, with enclosed letters from Woll to Clay, January 5 and February 14, 1949, RG 59, file: 862.5043/2-2349; memorandum of conversation between Acheson and various officials of the AFL and the State Department, March 9, 1949, with attached AFL memorandum to Acheson, March 9, 1949, RG 59, file: 811.5043/3-949.

general's strong opposition to codetermination and all-German trade unions.

In the second half of 1949 (as Chapter 6 will show), complaints of this sort would lead American policymakers to urge a further reduction of Allied occupation controls, hoping thereby to stem the tide of German nationalism and tie the Germans more closely to the Western alliance. At the same time, trade-union complaints would subside because the American High Commissioner was far more disposed than Clay to extend to Germany the kind of corporative collaboration that had become a major feature of the recovery program elsewhere. Plans would be laid to form a West German trade-union federation modeled after the major American labor organizations, to bring the new federation into a non-Communist labor international, and to link both groups to the transnational system of public–private cooperation that had begun to emerge earlier.[24]

Through these and related steps, American leaders sought to transform labor–management conflicts in Germany and elsewhere into administrative politics and bureaucratic bargaining. The Americans would do so by re-creating in Western Europe the kind of power-sharing arrangements that government, business, and labor had fashioned in the United States. Arrangements of this sort formed one element of the New Deal synthesis for a European neo-capitalism, others being the reform of European finances, the export of American technical "know-how," the elimination of trade and payments barriers, and the formation of supranational institutions. The politics and diplomacy of productivity revolved around American initiatives in these areas, as well as those on the labor front.

III

As noted earlier, American policymakers and trade-union leaders had thought it necessary to reform and reorganize the European labor movement in order to achieve the goals of the Marshall Plan. Non-Communist labor organizations had to retire from the World Federation of Trade Unions (WFTU) and form a new international that would collaborate in government programs to integrate economies, restore production, and ensure social peace. The American Federation of Labor (AFL) had been working toward these ends for some time, and the majority of the unions represented at the 1948 convention of the Congress of Industrial Organizations (CIO) had also thrown their support behind a resolution to withdraw from the WFTU. The resolution had been opposed by a minority of left-wing unions that had tangled with the majority in earlier debates over the Marshall Plan and Henry Wallace's presidential bid. The majority's support for the resolution

[24] In addition to the last four citations in note 23, see Swayzee memorandum to Acheson, March 8, 1949, RG 59, file: 800.5043/3-1449; U.S. High Commissioner for Germany, *First Quarterly Report on Germany* (Washington, DC, March 1950), 29–30; and Backer, *Winds of History*, 256–60.

of late 1948 presaged its subsequent decision to expel the Communist-dominated unions from the CIO.[25]

Armed with the majority resolution, a CIO delegation traveled to London in early January to coordinate strategy with the British Trade Unions Congress (TUC), which had passed a similar resolution at the meeting of its General Council in October. This set the stage for a showdown with Louis Saillant and the Communist labor leaders when the WFTU's Executive Bureau convened in Paris on January 17, 1949. What followed resembled a riot. With CIO support, the TUC urged the WFTU to suspend activities for one year or until the Communist parties of Europe stopped dictating trade-union policies. In the debate that ensued, James Carey of the CIO made a rousing speech, attacking the Communist trade unions for their failure to support the Marshall Plan and accusing them of putting the interests of the Politburo above those of the working class. Shouting erupted from all sides. The British and American representatives repulsed an effort by the Communists to defer action, demanded a vote on the TUC resolution, and walked out of the meeting when their demands were ignored.[26]

Shortly thereafter, representatives of the CIO and the TUC met with Irving Brown of the AFL at another session of the Trade Union Advisory Committee (TUAC) in Bern. They organized a secret "liaison committee" that was to open discussions with the national trade unions and the international trade secretariats on the formation of a non-Communist international.[27] The new committee had a rough row to hoe. Its work was slowed by internecine rivalries and personal jealousies, particularly by the AFL's resentment over TUC control of key posts in the TUAC and by its reluctance to concede the CIO an equal status in the new international. Policymakers in the State Department followed these quarrels with considerable impatience. Nevertheless, they refused to play favorites and rejected a CIO appeal for presidential mediation.

The ECA took a different tack. Under cover of the technical-assistance program, it brought a group of TUC officials to the United States, where they spent most of their time mending fences with the American unions and trying to persuade the AFL and the CIO to push ahead with plans for a non-Communist federation. The TUC's mediation, together no doubt with the CIO's decision to purge its left-wing affiliates, laid the groundwork for

[25] Windmuller, *American Labor and the International Labor Movement*, 144–6.
[26] Caffery tel. to Marshall, January 12, 1949, RG 59, file: 800.5043/1-1249; Holmes tel. to Marshall, January 13, 1949, RG 59, file: 800.5043/1-1349; Windmuller, *American Labor and the International Labor Movement*, 146–8; and Lorwin, *International Labor Movement*, 260.
[27] Foster repto 2378 to Hoffman, January 21, 1949, ECA Files, box 6; Higgs, Bern, tel. to Acheson, January 23, 1949, RG 59, file: 800.5043/1-2349; and Higgs tel. to Marshall, January 24, 1949, RG 59, file: 800.5043/1-2449.

an AFL–CIO agreement fixing the conditions under which both groups would participate in the proposed federation. All sides subsequently closed ranks at another conference of Western trade unions, which met in Geneva on June 25–26. It was at this conference that arrangements were made to draft the constitution of what would become, in late 1949, the International Confederation of Free Trade Unions.[28]

American policymakers were pleased by these developments. They looked forward to bringing the new international into the networks of public–private cooperation that revolved around the State Department and the ECA.[29] Indeed, even while encouraging the American trade unions in their campaign to disrupt the WFTU, the State Department had continued to meet regularly with labor leaders on a variety of other matters. Its Division of International Labor and Social Affairs acted as liaison between the trade unions and the secretary of state's office. Acheson, in response to requests from the AFL, was thinking of upgrading this relationship as part of the general reorganization of the State Department in 1949. At the same time, he and other policymakers were supporting labor's representation at international conferences and on such UN agencies as the Economic and Social Council and the World Health Organization.[30]

For the ECA as well, the earlier pattern of public–private power sharing continued. "The trade unions of America," Hoffman repeated in 1949, had "a status of full partnership in ECA not only from the standpoint of operations but from the standpoint of making policy."[31] To lend credibility to this declaration, he and Harriman appointed trade-union officials as ECA mission chiefs in Norway and Sweden.[32] They also worked closely with the State Department and the American and European trade unions to organize

[28] Douglas tel. to Acheson, March 4, 1949, RG 59, file: 841.00(W)/3-449; Swayzee memorandum to Acheson, March 8, 1949, RG 59, file: 800.5043/3 1449; Acheson circular airgram, March 23, 1949, RG 59, file: 800.5043/3-2349; Brown memorandum to the Under Secretary of State, April 4, 1949, RG 59, file: 811.5043/5-349; Acheson airgram to the American Embassy, Montevideo, May 13, 1949, RG 59, file: 800.5043/2-1649; Windmuller, *American Labor and the International Labor Movement*, 151–7; and Lorwin, *International Labor Movement*, 262–6.

[29] Swayzee memorandum, March 9, 1949, Dean G. Acheson Papers (Truman Library), box 64, folder: Memoranda of Conversations; and Acheson circular airgram, March 23, 1949, RG 59, file: 800.5043/3-2349. See also Weiler, "The United States, International Labor, and the Cold War," 20–1.

[30] Swayzee memorandum to Acheson, March 8, 1949, RG 59, file: 800.5043/3-1449; Swayzee memorandum, March 9, 1949, Acheson Papers, box 64, folder: Memoranda of Conversations; Woll letter to Acheson, March 14, 1949, Acheson letter to Woll, April 4, 1949, and Swayzee Memorandum of Conversation, March 14, 1949, RG 59, file: 800.5043/3-1449.

[31] Hoffman torep 3210 to Harriman, February 8, 1949, ECA Files, box 46.

[32] Harriman letter to Hoffman, February 23, 1949, and Hoffman letter to Harriman, March 2, 1949, RG 286, Acc. 53A405, box 1, folder: Special Representative's Office, 1949; and Hoffman torep 4451 to Harriman, April 9, 1949, ECA Files, box 47.

American tours for non-Communist labor leaders from the participating countries. In mid-March, for example, a delegation of twelve Swedish labor leaders visited the United States, where they toured various industrial facilities, met with their counterparts in the AFL, CIO, and Railway Brotherhoods, and conferred with government officials in the ECA and the Labor Department.[33]

On this and other tours, arranged under the ECA's technical-assistance program, the hosts always took pains to impress the visitors with the close ties between government and labor in the United States and with the gains in productivity, living standards, and labor peace to be derived from cooperative labor–management relations. One delegation of key Italian labor leaders spent several days touring the plant facilities and talking to the workers of the Crown Zellerbach Corporation, a large paper manufacturer that had been selected by the National Planning Association as an outstanding example of labor–management harmony in the United States. Its president, James Zellerbach, headed the ECA mission in Italy and made arrangements for the tour.[34]

The same bill of fare was served to visiting labor–management teams organized, with ECA assistance, by the Anglo–American Council on Productivity. The council held its second session in New York in early 1949, with labor and management representatives from both countries on hand. This session was followed by the first team visit of eight managers and eight trade-union leaders from the British steel-foundry industry. Like other productivity teams, the group spent approximately six weeks in the United States, met with government, management, and labor officials, and listened to one American trade unionist tell how the "cooperation of management and labor" had resulted in greater productivity and "rising standards of living" for American workers.[35] Similar teams from Denmark and Norway also toured farm and industry facilities and talked with public and private leaders, learning about the the cooperative links between the American government and private economic groups and receiving instruction in American labor-training techniques, American methods of arbitrating labor–management disputes, and what Hoffman called the American "miracle of mass production." The blessings of "American know-how, wage earners' freedom and property available to all" would come "to pass in Europe,"

---

[33]   Hoffman toreps 3876 and 3899 to Harriman, March 16 and 17, 1949, ECA Files, box 47; and Assistant Secretary of State George V. Allen letter to Ambassador H. Freeman Matthews, Stockholm, March 23, 1949, RG 59, file: 840.50Recovery/3-249.

[34]   Hoffman torep 4245 to Harriman, April 1, 1949, ECA Files, box 47.

[35]   Hoffman torep 3825 to Harriman, March 15, 1949, ECA Files, box 46. See also Hoffman torep 5362 to Harriman, May 19, 1949, ECA Files, box 48; and ECA, *Fifth Report to Congress*, 47.

the ECA promised, once the Europeans began adopting American ideas for "worker and employer teamwork" and for "more efficient production."[36]

Public–private cooperation also remained evident in other aspects of the recovery program. ECA officials worked with industry counterparts on the Humphrey Committee during the last days of its study of German reparations.[37] They turned to private bankers on the ECA's Advisory Committee on Fiscal and Monetary Problems when drafting a proposal to revise the European payments plan. They continued to rely on the Council on Foreign Relations for studies of American aid policy and on such groups as the Business Advisory Council when recruiting private experts.[38] Needless to say, they were also pleased when the TUAC finally began meeting with the OEEC's technical staff and when the European agency recognized the International Federation of Agricultural Producers as its private advisory body on agricultural policies.[39]

Each initiative reinforced the ECA's attempt to build a transnational system of corporative collaboration, not simply to marshal support for the ERP, integrate economies, or bring social peace to Western Europe, but also to build a public–private partnership on behalf of greater productivity. This last goal inspired the ECA's technical-assistance program, of which the productivity teams were a part. By June 1949, the ECA had expended nearly $2.5 million on a variety of technical-assistance projects in Denmark, Greece, Ireland, Italy, the Netherlands, Norway, the United Kingdom, and the overseas territories of the participating countries. The projects included a study of methods to control malaria in British East and West Africa, a program of veterinary research in the United Kingdom, and a host of plans to improve public administration in Italy, Greece, and other participating

---

[36] Hoffman toreps 3288 and 3130 to Harriman, February 14 and March 10, 1949, ECA Files, box 46. See also Hoffman toreps 2734, 3279, 3338, and 3374 to Harriman, January 7 and February 12, 16, and 17, 1949, ECA Files, box 46.

[37] ECA, *Fourth Report to Congress* (Washington, DC, 1949), 57–8.

[38] For the role of the Advisory Committee on Fiscal and Monetary Problems, see the minutes of its meetings on January 17 and April 22, 1949, RG 286, Acc. 53A405, box 33, folder: Outside Organizations – Advisory Council on Fiscal and Monetary Problems. For the work of the Council on Foreign Relations during this period, see the material in the William L. Clayton Papers (Truman Library), box 73, folder: Council on Foreign Relations. On recruitment, see Foster repto 2625 to Hoffman, February 9, 1949, ECA Files, box 6.

[39] Foster repto 3335 to Hoffman, March 26, 1949, Caffery repto 3652 to Hoffman, for Golden and Jewell, April 13, 1949, and Harriman repto 4335 to Hoffman, May 21, 1949, ECA Files, box 6; and Harriman reptos 4432, 4905, and 5059 to Hoffman, May 29, June 25, and July 5, 1949, ECA Files, box 7. The TUAC was not fully satisfied with the arrangements for regular meetings with the OEEC's technical staff. The meetings were generally confined to aspects of the recovery program affecting labor, and the TUAC also wanted observer status on the OECC's key horizontal and vertical committees.

countries. Approximately one hundred fifty American "experts" had been assigned to work on these and other projects abroad, with half as many European specialists involved in technical studies in the United States. The purpose in all cases was to "bring about lasting improvements in the level of productivity and efficiency and help reduce costs in some of the key areas of the European economies."[40]

Creating a climate conducive to greater growth and higher rates of productivity also remained the central objective of the ECA's counterpart policy. By June 1949, counterpart deposits in all of the participating countries totaled $2.683 billion. Approximately $2.140 billion of this amount had been approved for specific programs, the great bulk for investment projects to expand production in such key sectors as coal mining, public utilities, railroads, and agriculture, the rest for programs of fiscal and monetary stabilization. In the United Kingdom, where the redirection of production into export had created domestic shortages and pressure on prices, the ECA was still helping to curb inflation by using virtually all of the sterling fund to retire the Bank of England's short-term public debt. In the Netherlands, part of the counterpart fund went to restrain inflationary pressures, the remainder to underwrite a program of land reclamation and redistribution and to provide low-cost housing for industrial workers. In Italy, counterpart funds already earmarked for specific purposes were withheld in an effort to force the Italian government to relax its deflationary policies and work out a national investment budget that would boost production and alleviate unemployment.[41]

The Italian and Dutch cases, like that of France, provided good examples of the liberal reformism and Keynesian strategies that typified so much of the ECA's counterpart policy. In France, over $1 billion in counterpart funds had been released. Most of the funds went to support the Monnet Plan for industrial expansion and modernization, the balance to redeem short-term bills held by foreign central banks. The whole program aimed to increase production while controlling inflation, this by relieving the burden of investment on the French budget and enabling the government to avoid additional drafts on the Bank of France. We have seen how Keynesians in the ECA had inaugurated this strategy at the end of 1948 and had coupled it with pressure on the French government for a program of fiscal and monetary reform. They did not relax this pressure when the French economy began to deflate in the spring of 1949. They escalated counterpart releases to counteract deflationary pressures and stimulate the economy, with half of all releases to date coming in the second quarter of the new year. But they also kept the French government on a short leash and continued to link their aid with demands for an effective program of fiscal

[40] ECA, *Fifth Report to Congress*, 46–8.
[41] ECA, *Fifth Report to Congress*, 40–5; and Milward, *Reconstruction of Western Europe*, 197–8.

and monetary management. Although the French Treasury, its tax revenues declining, wanted an automatic program of counterpart releases for
the remainder of 1949, the ECA would authorize releases only on a
month-by-month basis, and then only if the French pushed ahead with
budgetary and tax reforms and took steps to expand exports and increase
reserves.[42]

Although these initiatives aimed to create an environment in which greater
productivity would put Western Europe on a self-supporting basis, it would
be wrong to conclude that they constituted the major thrust of American
recovery policy in the first half of 1949. The ECA targeted only a modest
amount of funds for the technical-assistance program, including the so-
called productivity teams, in fiscal year 1949–50, and only a "negligible
portion" of the commodities it shipped to Europe consisted of the capital
goods that would "increase the productivity of the European farm or fac-
tory." Nor had it enjoyed much success in conditioning American aid on
the setting and achievement of national production goals or in compelling
participating countries to coordinate investment and production decisions
"on a sound economic basis." "Everybody talk[ed] about productivity but
nobody [did] much about it." Despite its statements that productivity was
"the way to European recovery," the ECA had "paid surprisingly little
attention" to the "practical measures" for optimizing output.[43]

These were the conclusions reached in the Office of the Special Representative by an informal group of economic experts known as the "Snack
Bar Policy Board." The experts mistakenly interpreted the evidence as in-
dicating a retreat from productivity, when it pointed instead to a greater
emphasis on fixing realistic exchange rates, liberalizing trade, and organizing
a European clearing union – all of which had been central elements in the
free-traders' approach to economic growth and integration since the start
of the recovery program. Nor did this shift portend any slackening of the
ECA's commitment to supranational institutions of economic coordination
and control. American policy continued to blend the planners' and traders'

[42] Bruce toeca 744 to Acheson, March 16, 1949, Reed toecas 932 and 943 to Acheson,
May 20 and 25, 1949, RG 286, Acc. 53A177, box 60, folder: France, Finance,
Economic, and Financial Reports; Bruce toeca 794 to Hoffman, April 4, 1949, Hoffman ecatos 606 and 632 to ECA Mission, Paris, April 6 and 22, 1949, ECA Mission,
Paris, toecas 949 and 1051 to Hoffman, May 23 and June 30, 1949, *FRUS, 1949*,
4:637–41, 643–5, 647–8; Bruce toecas 794, 796, 813, and 821 to Hoffman, April
4, 5, 7, and 8, 1949, and Miller memorandum, "Policy with Regard to French
Counterpart Release," April 13, 1949, Treasury Records, Acc. 67A1804, box 4,
folder: France, Aid Program, Vol. I. See also ECA, *Fifth Report to Congress*, 41–2.
[43] The Snack Bar Policy Board, "Productivity   The 'Ninth Principle,' " June 13, 1949,
Everett H. Bellows Papers (Truman Library), box 1, folder: Material on Productivity
Program. According to this document, the "Board" was an "informal discussion
group which originated at the Snack Bar at the Talleyrand Hotel in the summer of
1949." Its members included Shaw Livermore, Robert Oshins, Taylor Ostrander, Sol
Ozer, and Henry Reuss.

approaches, seeking through a stronger OEEC to coordinate national policies so that free-market forces could integrate economies and generate
growth. Involved instead was an American realization that only faster progress in the direction mapped out in the traders' approach could do what
the recovery of prewar production had failed to accomplish: correct the so-
called dollar gap and bring the participating countries into a one-world
system of multilateral trade and convertible currencies.

What worried the Americans most in 1949 was Western Europe's worsening trade and payments deficit with the United States and the rest of the
dollar area. Although its overall volume of trade had recovered to prewar
levels, exports to the dollar area had begun to decline, in part because of
the economic recession that began in the United States but also (as the
Economic Commission for Europe pointed out) because of the resistance
to coordinated planning and the lingering desire for national self-sufficiency.
Too many Marshall Plan countries were still pursuing policies that prevented
the specialization, the economies of scale, and the increases in labor productivity required to drive down prices and balance accounts with the dollar
area. Without corrective measures, as the OEEC's interim report made clear,
Western Europe's dollar gap would remain at a staggering $3 billion when
the Marshall Plan came to an end in 1952.[44]

The problem was how to reduce the dollar gap before the Marshall Plan
expired, and it was this problem that reignited an old controversy in Anglo–
American relations. The general direction of British policy had been clear
for some time. At the inception of the Marshall Plan and during the payments
debates of 1948, the British had urged the OEEC countries to conserve
dollars by curbing imports from the Western Hemisphere and redirecting
trade to the sterling bloc and other soft-currency markets. Their own trade
policy had relied on a variety of quotas, exchange controls, and other devices
to restrict dollar imports and safeguard reserves. With the onset of the
American recession and the concomitant decline in dollar sales, these measures had been reinforced with bilateral commercial agreements that shifted
even more British purchases to nondollar markets. At the same time, the
British renewed efforts to persuade other participating countries to adopt
a similar strategy. This push came in February, when the OEEC's Council
proclaimed 1949 the "year of financial and monetary stabilization" and
urged a broad plan to expand exports, limit nonessential dollar imports,
coordinate national monetary and financial policies, and revise existing
payments arrangements. In discussions over the next weeks, the British
emphasized the restrictive features of this program, calling, in Harriman's

[44] ECA, *Fifth Report to Congress*, 4–10; United Nations, Economic Commission for
Europe, *Economic Survey of Europe in 1948* (Geneva, 1949), especially 211–28;
OEEC, *Interim Report*, Vol. 1; and Summary of Discussions, Conference of Chiefs
of ECA Special Missions, Paris, April 11–12, 1949, RG 286, Acc. 53A405, box 1,
folder: Special Representative's Office, 1948.

words, for "a drastic nonselective reduction of dollar imports" and for the "development, more or less regardless of cost factors, of new sources of supply in nondollar areas of goods normally imported from [the] dollar area."[45]

American leaders admitted that Western Europe had to restrain consumption and restrict dollar imports. But in their view, these restrictions should be selective and should be coupled with a policy that stressed the development of dollar-earning exports in both the participating countries and their overseas territories. A "relentless and undiscriminating" reduction of dollar imports or any attempt to replace these imports with "home-subsidized or protected production" or with "high-cost non-European" imports on the basis of bilateral and preferential trading arrangements would only freeze Europe's cost and price structure at existing high levels. Living standards would decline, unemployment would increase, and participating countries would be unable to compete in a fully multilateral system of world trade.[46] For officials on the new Policy Board at Harriman's headquarters in Paris, these dreary details pointed to the direction that the OEEC must take. It was time, they said, to emphasize the more "creative aspects" of the recovery program and to take steps to enhance productivity, reduce costs, and make European exports competitive.[47]

Harriman made the same points in meetings with OEEC officials on March 7 and 8. He warned that the British strategy would raise rather than lower European costs and prices, make it difficult for the participating countries to achieve a viable payments position, and ruin the chances for continued congressional support of the Marshall Plan. He thought it better to stress the "dynamic, expansive possibilities," which meant concentrating on measures that would optimize European productivity and contribute to the growth of world trade. These arguments were apparently persuasive, at least to the OEEC as a whole. In a Plan of Action for 1949, it elaborated the Council's earlier proclamation in a way that seemed to validate the American, not the British, approach to the dollar gap. The plan stressed the importance of increasing productivity, developing dollar-earning exports, fixing realistic exchange rates, and multilateralizing trade and payments.[48]

In line with these recommendations, American officials launched a number of new initiatives to increase European sales in the Western Hemisphere. They initiated a study of European export opportunities, used technical-

---

[45] Harriman repto 2983 to Hoffman, March 8, 1949, ECA Files, box 6; and Harriman repto 3068 to Hoffman, March 12, 1949, *FRUS, 1949*, 4:374–7.

[46] Katz repto circular 163 to ECA, Washington, April 2, 1949, ECA Files, box 8.

[47] Foster letter to Hoffman, March 5, 1949, RG 286, Acc. 53A405, box 1, folder: Special Representative's Office, 1949. See also Harriman repto 2915 to Hoffman, March 4, 1949, *FRUS, 1949*, 4:373–4.

[48] Harriman repto 3068 to Hoffman, March 12, 1949, *FRUS, 1949*, 4:374–7. See also Harriman repto 2983 to Hoffman, March 8, 1949, ECA Files, box 6; and Labouisse memorandum to Acheson, March 29, 1949, *FRUS, 1949*, 4:380–1.

assistance funds to pinpoint American consumer preferences for European producers, investigated the prospects for simplifying American customs procedures, and instructed the ECA's local missions to report on steps by the participating countries to eliminate barriers to trade expansion.[49] They also urged participating countries to study ways of developing the dollar-earning potential of their overseas holdings, began using counterpart and technical-assistance funds to finance limited investment projects and technical surveys in these areas, and continued their earlier program of stockpiling strategic materials from the colonial territories. These last initiatives dovetailed with President Truman's Point Four proposal of January 1949 and aimed, among other things, at developing a triangular pattern of trade that would provide the European countries with dollars and the United States with strategic raw materials.[50]

In addition, American leaders wanted to drive down European prices by readjusting exchange rates. As Richard Bissell explained in a telegram to Harriman, American recovery policy had thus far concentrated on reviving production, improving consumption, and curbing inflation. Having made progress toward these goals, the United States was in a position to consider a "broad revaluation of European currencies." Devaluation would bring European prices more nearly in line with those in the Western Hemisphere, "remove the necessity of discriminatory practices toward the U.S.," and permit "price incentives" rather than government controls to redirect European investment into industries geared to exploiting the dollar market.[51] Accordingly, the ECA inaugurated a major review of European exchange rates while similar but separate studies went forward in the State Department, the Treasury Department, and the National Advisory Council.[52] In the International Monetary Fund (IMF), the U.S. executive director also overcame British opposition and won support for a resolution authorizing

[49] Raymond Vernon, State Department, "Trade Policies of the ECA Program," April 13, 1949, RG 59, file: 840.50Recovery/4-749; Katz reptos 3801 and 3808 to Hoffman, April 22, 1949, and Foster repto circular 184 to Hoffman, April 27, 1949, ECA Files, box 6; J. D. Coppock, International Trade Policy Division, State Department, Memorandum of Conversation, May 4, 1949, and Winthrop G. Brown, Director, International Trade Policy Division, memorandum to Wayne C. Taylor of ECA, May 4, 1949, RG 59, file: 840.50Recovery/5-449; and editorial note, *FRUS, 1949*, 4:421.

[50] ECA, *Fifth Report to Congress*, 48, 53, 57-8; Foster repto unnumbered to Hoffman, March 19, 1949, ECA Files, box 6; and Harriman repto 4781 to Hoffman, June 17, 1949, ECA Files, box 7.

[51] Bissell torep 3983 to Harriman, March 17, 1949, *FRUS, 1949*, 4:377-80.

[52] Hoffman torep 3548 to Harriman, February 28, 1949, ECA Files, box 46. See also Katz repto 3391 to Hoffman, March 30, 1949, ECA Files, box 6; Summary of Discussions, Conference of Chiefs of ECA Special Missions, Paris, April 11-12, 1949, RG 286, Acc. 53A405, box 1, folder: Special Representative's Office, 1948; and Alex M. Rosen, State Department, "Meeting of ECA Finance Officers in Paris, April 4-6, 1949," April 19, 1949, RG 59, file: 840.50Recovery/4-1949.

the IMF to conduct its own investigation and instructing its managing director, Camile Gutt of Belgium, to begin discussions with the Western European countries involved.[53]

In spite of these initiatives, the Americans never considered devaluation as anything more than a palliative. Technical assistance, labor–management collaboration, and other programs to increase productivity promised a more durable solution, but only if implemented within the framework of an integrated Western European system that included a revived western Germany. Such a broadly based system would eliminate the structural deficiencies that were the root cause of Europe's dollar problem. To create this system, American policymakers continued to urge the Europeans to develop central institutions of coordination and control. Their increasing reliance on the traders' approach also prompted calls for the reduction of tariffs, the elimination of bilateral payments barriers, and the formation of a more effective clearing union. The State Department, for example, lent support to ratification of the Franco–Italian tariff union and to negotiations looking toward full economic union between the Benelux countries. The ECA urged the participating countries as a group to strengthen the OEEC and revise the 1948 payments plan.[54] These proposals continued to encounter stiff opposition in London, however. So did the American pressure for devaluation. Both developments made the Anglo–American controversy more explosive and compromise more difficult.

IV

The Labour government's response to the new American moves can be understood only in the context of its overall policy, which was now firmly fixed and irreversible. In the Labour Party and in other quarters, advocates of a "third force" still envisioned an Anglo–Western European union under vigorous British leadership and independent of both the United States and the Soviet Union. The idea appealed irresistibly to those who hankered after a witch's brew that would infuse new life into a flagging Empire. But a

[53] J. Burke Knapp memorandum to Thorp, April 4, 1949, with attached memorandum by Frank Southard, Under Secretary of the Treasury and U.S. Executive Director, IMF, to Secretary of the Treasury Snyder and Assistant Secretary Martin, March 31, 1949, RG 59, file: 840.50Recovery/4-449; Acheson tel. to Douglas, April 7, 1949, RG 59, file: 840.50Recovery/4-2449; Acheson tel. to Certain Diplomatic Offices, April 12, 1949, *FRUS, 1949*, 4:382-3; and Finletter torep 808 to Harriman, April 13, 1949, Harriman Papers, folder: United Kingdom.

[54] Hoffman torep 6056 to Harriman from Bissell, June 23, 1949, ECA Files, box 48; Acheson tel. to Caffery, February 3, 1949, RG 59, file: 651.6531/2-349; Caffery tels. (2) to Acheson, February 9, 1949, RG 59, file: 651.6531/2-949; State Department memorandum to the Italian Embassy, Washington, February 3, 1949, RG 59, file: 651.652/2-349; Acheson circular tel., February 11, 1949, RG 59, file: 651.652/2-1149; and Caffery tel. to Acheson, March 26, 1949, RG 59, file: 651.652/3-2649.

concoction like this was years in the making and the recipe included large doses of European self-help not easily administered. A good doctor relied on more practical potions, or so Bevin believed. Although Bevin still talked wistfully of an independent Anglo–Western European group, he no longer considered this prescription an antidote to Britain's ailments. Nor did he see it as a formula for reinvigorating the British Empire. Because Britain could not depend on Western Europe or survive without American aid, he thought the only reliable remedy was to be found in a North Atlantic association that included the United States as well as the Commonwealth and Western Europe. But if the old plan for a middle kingdom was discarded, elements of the original design survived in Bevin's conception of Great Britain (and the Commonwealth, of course) as the pivotal power in the North Atlantic system. It was within this framework that Bevin now hoped to realize his grand ambition: the restoration of the British Empire as a major force in world affairs.

Britain's policy toward Western European integration had to be cast in a North Atlantic framework. This was the conclusion coming from Bevin, Cripps, Attlee, and other members of the cabinet-level Economic Policy Committee, from Sir Edmund Hall-Patch in Paris, and from a Foreign Office committee working under the direction of Permanent Under Secretary of State Sir William Strang. According to those involved, the British could not expect to safeguard their security, let alone recapture their position in the world arena, without the active support of the United States, which would not be forthcoming if Britain's "economic structure had been hopelessly impaired" in an unsuccessful effort to integrate the European economies. The British must never "lose sight of the fact that, if war comes, the co-operation of the U.S.A. is decisive to the security of this country." Nor must they sacrifice the "things necessary to [their] own survival" or forget that the Commonwealth countries had "supported us with blood and treasure in more than generous measure in two world wars in this century." The Western Europeans were less reliable allies. They pursued "entirely selfish policies" and would not be "of any succour to us ... in time of real difficulty." Although Britain might take the lead in an "unremitting effort" to rekindle a spirit of independence in Western Europe, "all this effort would be in vain if by making it we estrange the Commonwealth." "Do not put all your eggs in the European basket," Hall-Patch warned. "It is a pretty shoddy contraption and there are no signs yet that the essential repairs are going to be made."[55]

It would be a mistake to conclude from the preceding that British leaders wanted to withdraw from Western Europe. They had "vital interests" there,

---

[55] EPC (49) 6, Bevin and Cripps memorandum, "Our Policy to O.E.E.C. and our Proposals for its Structure," January 25, 1949, PREM 8/980; and Hall-Patch letters to Berthoud, April 4 and 16, 1949, FO 371, 77999, UR3483 and UR4063. See also EPC (49) 5th Meeting, January 26, 1949, PREM 8/980.

as Bevin and Cripps noted, and wanted to give political direction to the area and go as far as practical to coordinate their economic policies with those of the OEEC countries. But they refused to give a lead in Europe at the expense of Britain's sovereignty, its ties to the United States, or its commitments to the Commonwealth. These were the legs of the table that Bevin had described, and the British could not lean too heavily on the European leg; because if they did and Western Europe collapsed, "it would be hard for us then to recover our position vis-à-vis the rest of the world" or to count on "continued United States military, political and economic support." "[W]e must do nothing to damage irretrievably the economic structure of our own country" or to make it a less "viable unit apart from the rest of Western Europe." Economic union was out of the question, as was a customs union or any arrangement that deprived the Labour government of its ability to regulate the pace of Britain's integration into Europe. Progress down this road had to be on a step-by-step, project-by-project basis. This was the empirical approach. It meant that each venture in collaboration had to be "referred back to the United Kingdom government and ... considered on its merits."[56]

The Economic Policy Committee reached these conclusions in late January. Hall-Patch added his warning in mid-April, and the Permanent Under Secretary's Committee pulled the major themes together in a paper of early May entitled "A Third World Power or Western Consolidation?" The question was rhetorical. The paper dismissed as impractical various proposals for a third force "co-equal with, and independent of, the United States and the Soviet Union" and consisting either of the Commonwealth, or of the United Kingdom, Western Europe, and their overseas territories, or of a combination of these two groups. The Commonwealth countries did not constitute a coherent economic, political, or strategic unit. Nor could their defense requirements or need for investment capital be met without American support. "The attraction exerted by pound sterling and the Royal Navy," the report explained, "is now less strong than that of the dollar and the atom bomb." Under these circumstances, any "attempt to turn the Commonwealth into a Third World Power would only confront its members with a direct choice between London and Washington, and though sentiment might point in one way interest would certainly lead the other."

Nor would the prospects be better in an Anglo–Western European union, even one that included western Germany or, for that matter, all of Germany. Western Europe was "patently dependent on American aid" for its recovery and thereafter on a substantial exchange of goods and services with the United States and the Commonwealth, as well as with the Eastern European countries. Besides, the centrifugal forces of nationalism would reassert themselves as recovery progressed, precluding political unification. Even if

[56] See the first and last documents cited in note 55.

achieved, a unified Western Europe would be unable to match the scale of Soviet power without remilitarizing Germany and sacrificing recovery to a massive rearmament, options that raised dangers every bit as serious as the threat of Soviet aggression.

The objections to either of these groups considered individually applied with equal force when the groups were combined, leading the Permanent Under Secretary's Committee to the "inescapable" conclusion that only a "Western Consolidation" that included the United States could contain the Soviets and serve the "interest of Commonwealth solidarity and of European unity." But "unity" did not mean "union." It would "be wise not to place undue reliance on [European economic integration] at the expense of our relations with the Commonwealth and the United States," the report argued, "[because] if we went too far along this road [we might] find Europe overrun and our own segment of the economy unable to function on its own." Nor did Western consolidation mean the end of the United Kingdom as a great world power. On the contrary, it was the only way for the United Kingdom to recapture its lost position. Although the United States would be the most powerful nation in the group (albeit easier to deal with, more amenable to British influence, and less reckless than some of the Western European states), the United Kingdom would retain the allegiance of the Commonwealth, play a leading role on the Continent, and thereby act as a balance wheel in the "Western system." Over time, the "elements of dependence" in the current situation would give way to those of "interdependence" and the United Kingdom would emerge as an equal partner with the United States in an economic and security system that served the interests of both countries.[57]

The committee's report summarized the main lines of Bevin's grand design and how it applied to Western Europe. The British would cooperate in that region's recovery and defense. It was in their interest to do so. But they would also adhere to the empirical approach, evaluate each step in the process of integration, and by no means surrender Britain's right to place its own interests first. The British would apply this approach in the debates over the political unification of Western Europe, the reorganization of the OEEC, and the revision of the intra-European payments plan. In each case, they would find themselves increasingly isolated from their associates on the Continent and at odds with their colleagues in the United States.

As noted in the last chapter, Bevin had reluctantly agreed to some kind of European political organization at the October 1948 meeting of the Consultative Council of the Brussels Pact powers. Two very different organizations had been suggested: French Foreign Minister Robert Schuman's project for a European assembly elected by parliaments and Bevin's proposal for a council

---

[57] PUSC (22) Final Approved, Permanent Under-Secretary's Committee, "A Third World Power or Western Consolidation?," May 9, 1949, PREM 8/1204.

of ministers that would keep decisions in the hands of governments. No resolution of these differences had been possible. The Consultative Council had turned the whole matter over to a preparatory committee, which was to study the issues and make recommendations later that year.

Bevin reviewed his thinking in a meeting of the Cabinet just three weeks before the preparatory committee began its work. He told his colleagues that progress toward European union should be "gradual" and that "enduring results" were not likely "to be achieved by the adoption of grandiose paper constitutions" of the sort being proposed by Schuman and the European federalists. But a "purely negative attitude" would also court disaster. The Americans might reduce their support for the ERP. The French might lose confidence in the capacity of the Western states to shape a secure future. To avoid these dangers, Bevin thought it best to continue the strategy he had adopted at the recent meeting of the Consultative Council. The Cabinet agreed and instructed the British delegation to the preparatory committee to oppose an "elaborate federal constitution" and stand by Bevin's proposal for a European committee of ministers. The idea was to placate the Americans and preempt the French while at the same time preserving "the full sovereignty of the participating States and also the principle of the empirical approach to which [the foreign secretary] attached so much importance."[58]

Given these instructions, there was no reason to believe that the preparatory committee could succeed where the ministers had failed. The lack of enthusiasm apparent in the Cabinet's instructions was as evident in the composition of the British delegation, only one member of which, Hugh Dalton, enjoyed ministerial standing. The contrast between the British group and the strong French delegation was a fair measure of the importance each side attached to a federated Europe. It also foretold the outcome of the deliberations that began in late November. The British delegation repeated Bevin's plan for a council of ministers and turned a deaf ear when the French tabled another proposal for a European assembly to consist of the OEEC countries and western Germany. Building on a recommendation coming from the European Movement, the majority of the delegations then suggested a European institution having two parts: a parliamentary assembly and a committee of ministers. The idea seemed appealing and some members of the British delegation showed signs of weakening until Bevin, the Cabinet behind him, intervened with the usual objections. Thereafter, the majority issued a report calling for a bicameral body, the British reserved their position, and the preparatory committee adjourned for the Christmas holidays.[59]

During the adjournment, the Foreign Office worked frantically to devise

[58] CP (48) 249, Bevin memorandum, "North Atlantic Treaty and Western Union," November 2, 1948, CAB 129/30; and CM (48) 68th Conclusion, November 4, 1948, CAB 128/13.

[59] Vaughan, *Twentieth-Century Europe*, 88; and Bullock, *Bevin*, 641–2.

a formula that would give the Europeans what they wanted but still fit in with the grand design of Bevin's policy. Bevin held no brief against a European union that assuaged the French, tied the Germans to Western Europe, and provided a framework for economic and political collaboration when the Marshall Plan ended. But it would not do to "put the roof on before we have built the building," as he had told the Commons earlier.[60] Construction had to proceed by "trial and error," not according to a rigid blueprint, and the final edifice had to include a room for the Commonwealth and a North Atlantic corridor to accommodate Britain's role as the balance wheel in a Western consolidation. Although these specifications had thus far precluded a European assembly, Bevin was now prepared to combine Schuman's plan with his own proposal – so long as the final design adhered to "the principle of the empirical approach." Safeguarding this principle was the only way to keep Britain from being pushed pell-mell into the wrong kind of union, and the best way to do this was by applying to the European assembly the sort of government control already captured in Bevin's proposal for a council of ministers. National delegations would be appointed by governments, not elected by parliaments, and would vote as a bloc. Even then, the assembly would be little more than a forum for deliberating proposals initiated and decided in the ministerial council, where each government would have a veto.[61]

This was the scheme put forward by Bevin in talks with Schuman on January 13–14, by the British delegation in the preparatory committee when it reconvened on January 18, and by Bevin again in the next session of the Consultative Council, on January 27–28. The Europeans were scarcely enthusiastic. They preferred an assembly elected by parliaments and with the freedom to set its own agenda. Nevertheless, both sides inched their way to a compromise that envisioned a Council of Europe consisting of a Consultative Assembly and a Committee of Ministers. Each participating state would determine the method of selecting its delegation to the Consultative Assembly and delegates would have limited freedom to discuss issues and make recommendations to the Committee of Ministers, where real power would reside. On January 28, the Consultative Council agreed in principle to an arrangement like this. Its Permanent Commission filled in the details later, and, in May, ten European nations signed the Statute of the Council of Europe.[62]

Secretary of State Acheson promptly hailed the Council of Europe as an important step "toward the political integration of the free nations of Eu-

---

[60]   Bevin cited in Young, *Britain, France, and the Unity of Europe*, 112.
[61]   Young, *Britain, France, and the Unity of Europe*, 113–15. Bevin's remark is quoted from page 113. See also CM (49) 2nd Conclusion, January 12, 1949, CAB 128/15.
[62]   Young, *Britain, France, and the Unity of Europe*, 115; Bullock, *Bevin*, 658–9; and Vaughan, *Twentieth-Century Europe*, 88.

rope."[63] Britain's participation in the Assembly seemed particularly important; it amounted to a concession that Bevin had refused to make earlier. But too much can be made of Acheson's enthusiasm and Bevin's concession. The statute, after all, left the principle of government control intact. The Assembly was a consultative body only, was subject to the control of ministers, each exercising a veto, and was precluded by the statute from discussing economic and defense issues that fell within the jurisdiction of the OEEC, the Brussels Pact, or the North Atlantic Treaty. Given these stipulations, or so the British assumed, the Council would function as another vehicle of intergovernmental collaboration, not as an agency of integration. The empirical approach would be protected and the British would be in a position to put the brake on any development that might draw them too deeply into Europe. Policy objectives and organizational strategies still ran along parallel tracks, just as they did in Bevin's response to the American proposals for a stronger OEEC.

At the end of 1948, it will be recalled, the OEEC had established a special Committee of Nine under Paul-Henri Spaak to investigate the prospects for strengthening the organization. In doing so, it was responding to American pressure for structural changes. The changes the Americans had in mind included a stronger Secretariat, more frequent ministerial meetings of the OEEC Council, and appointment of an "outstanding personality" to a new post of director general. In ensuing discussions, Spaak endorsed the American demand for a prominent European "political personality" to direct the organization.[64] Support also came from French Foreign Minister Schuman, who told Ambassador Harriman in January that the OEEC must be strengthened through greater "direction at [the] political level."[65]

The British, on the other hand, were still hesitant to make the European authority independent of national governments or to entrust its direction to a single political figure, particularly to Spaak or any other advocate of economic integration and supranationalism. They were ready to accept a greater degree of "political direction." But under their plan, this direction would be achieved through more conventional forms of intergovernmental cooperation. They proposed a high-level committee of national ministers chaired by Spaak as president of the OEEC Council and including ministerial officials from Britain, France, Italy, and one of the Scandinavian countries.[66] The committee would meet quarterly in Paris, facilitate and review the work

[63] Acheson cited in Stebbins, *United States in World Affairs, 1949*, 111.
[64] Kirk tel. to Marshall, January 5, 1949, RG 59, file: 840.50Recovery/1-549.
[65] Harriman repto 2228 to Hoffman, January 10, 1949, ECA Files, box 6.
[66] Harriman repto 2210 to Hoffman, January 9, 1949, *FRUS, 1949*, 4:369–70; Harriman repto 2285 to Hoffman, January 14, 1949, ECA Files, box 6; and Finletter Memorandum of Conversation with Sir Stafford Cripps, January 6, 1949, Harriman Papers, folder: Finletter, Thomas K.

of the European organization, and advertise its activities. But it would function essentially as a consultative body. It would not diminish the supreme authority of the Council, and all of its recommendations would pass through that body and the OEEC's Executive Committee for approval by national delegations acting on behalf of their governments. As Bevin and Cripps made clear, the proposal would promote Anglo–European cooperation without sacrificing Britain's sovereignty or linking its fate too closely to more vulnerable countries on the Continent.[67]

At a meeting in late January, the Consultative Council of the Brussels Pact instructed Spaak to embody the British proposal in a resolution to be considered by the Committee of Nine. The British and French then tried to rally support for the plan in the OEEC.[68] By early February, however, opposition had begun to crystallize among the smaller countries. These countries were worried that a ministerial group would limit the authority of the Executive Committee, on which they were represented, and enable the great powers to dominate the OEEC. At the same time, Harriman was warning that Congress expected "greater leadership" from the OEEC and Spaak, who was always in tune with American policy, was circulating a draft resolution that exceeded his instructions from the Consultative Council.[69] Spaak's resolution would enhance the functions of the Secretariat and give the committee of ministers considerable discretionary authority. A committee of five ministers chaired by the president of the Council would direct the Secretariat, convene sessions of the Council and the Executive Committee, execute the decisions of both bodies, and generally manage the work of the organization when they were not in session.[70]

Spaak came armed with his resolution to the Committee of Nine when it convened in Paris on February 16, only to find himself outmaneuvered by Cripps, who represented the British government. Cripps tabled the same proposal the British had suggested earlier. Even before the meeting, however, he and Bevin had devised a compromise that would give them what they wanted while at the same time appeasing the smaller powers and isolating Spaak. Having stopped Spaak with the original proposal, Cripps fell back on this compromise and won support for it from the Committee of Nine. According to the compromise, which the Council later approved, Spaak or his successor as chairman of the Council would be empowered to convene a Consultative Group consisting of ministers from the countries represented on the Executive Committee. The Consultative Group would have no au-

[67] See the first document cited in note 55.

[68] Foster repto 2537 to Hoffman, February 3, 1949, ECA Files, box 6; and British Embassy, Rome, Aide-Mémoire, February 3, 1949, FO 371, 77970, UR13349.

[69] Harriman repto 2708 to Hoffman, February 15, 1949, ECA Files, box 6; and T. L. Rowan memorandum to Cripps, February 10, 1949, FO 371, 77970, UR1420. See also Harriman repto 2210 to Hoffman, January 9, 1949, *FRUS*, 1949, 4:369–70.

[70] Hall-Patch tels. (2) to FO, February 10, 1949, and Foreign Service Officer John Henniker memorandum, "Ministerial Committee of Five," February 10, 1949, FO 371, 77970, UR1317, UR1294, and UR1678.

thority to make decisions on its own, thereby protecting the integrity of the Council and the Executive Committee and preserving the emphasis on intergovernmental cooperation. But it could meet regularly at the request of its chairman, review the activities of the organization, discuss "high-level" business, and work closely with the Secretariat in preparing agenda for sessions of the Council and the Executive Committee. In addition, the resolution authorized the Council to convene at the ministerial level frequently (and no less than four times a year) and endorsed a recommendation from the secretary general to enlarge the staff and functions of the Secretariat.[71]

The resolution fell short of what the ECA had wanted – that is, a real executive with supranational authority. Nonetheless, American leaders were pleased with the results so far and hopeful that additional steps would follow. Bissell thought it especially important that the OEEC act quickly to appoint "highly competent people" to the enlarged staff of the Secretariat and thus help to make the OEEC a "nucleus for greater European unity in [the] economic field." The "future of European economic unity," he cabled Harriman, "depends in part upon [the] creation through OEEC of [a] competent and disinterested staff of international civil servants."[72] Harriman gave similar advice to the first meeting of the Consultative Group. He wanted the group to "direct [the] activities of OEEC" and the Secretariat to be "strengthened" by the appointment of additional "experts" who would prepare work for the organization's committees.[73] In addition, Harriman suggested that he or his agent participate in meetings of the Consultative Group. This participation would accord with his status as the American special representative and enable his office to play an appropriate role in directing the work of the European organization. Spaak was sympathetic, as usual. He told the British ambassador in Brussels that it would be a mistake to treat the Americans as "bankers in the background." Harriman was "extremely sensitive" to this kind of treatment, he said, and holding to the original arrangement, whereby Harriman would attend meetings only at the explicit invitation of the Consultative Group, "would be an invidious and inevitable cause of offense."[74]

The British, predictably, saw in Harriman's participation something akin to a Trojan horse. His presence would immeasurably complicate their efforts to dominate the OEEC. It would make it difficult to control the smaller participating countries in the organization or to parry American attempts to equip the European agency with supranational powers. Hall-Patch put

[71] In addition to Henniker's memorandum cited in note 70, see Henniker's memoranda of February 12 and 16, 1949, FO 371, 77970, UR1450 and UR1698; and Foster repto 2643 to Hoffman, February 10, 1949, and Harriman reptos 2709, 2748, and 2659 to Hoffman, February 15, 17, and 18, 1949, ECA Files, box 6.
[72] Hoffman torep 3420 to Harriman from Bissell, February 18, 1949, ECA Files, box 46.
[73] Harriman repto 2784 to Hoffman, February 21, 1949, ECA Files, box 6.
[74] Sir George Rendel, British Ambassador to Belgium, tel. to FO, February 28, 1949, T232/201/EEC7/8/07.

this position in constitutional terms, claiming that the Americans had not signed the OEEC convention and therefore could not participate in the organization's work. Bevin and Cripps agreed, and when the Consultative Group reconvened on March 4, Cripps defeated Spaak's proposal in favor of an arrangement whereby the special representative would attend only one meeting of the group each session. In addition, Harriman would attend at the invitation of the group, not at his own initiative, and as an observer, not as an active participant.[75]

The British regretted going even this far when the Consultative Group met again on March 8. Harriman was invited but was admitted only after the group had concluded the substantive part of its business. Furious at this treatment, he unburdened himself in a long harangue, lamenting his exclusion from previous meetings and complaining that he was not being treated as a "partner" in the OEEC's work. Hall-Patch described the scene in a telegram to the Foreign Office. Harriman's manner, he reported,

> was sour and ungracious; he was uncompromising in his utterances and did not use his words very wisely. The whole performance was in the worst possible taste and made a bad impression on those present... his whole attitude showed clearly that the decision which excluded him from the earlier discussions had been a wise one. The attempt to build up a European organisation for co-operation would be frustrated if Harriman or any other representative of his were present for all the discussions. As might be supposed, we found afterwards that the reaction of all members of the Consultative Group was the same and, in condemning this as a deplorable exhibition, the rule of unanimity was not broken.[76]

With this meeting, the "Harriman problem" resurfaced as a factor in Anglo–American diplomacy, although we must not lose sight of the fact that this problem was merely a symbol of the far more important battle for control of the European organization. Bevin discussed the issues involved with Ambassador Douglas in London, as did Sir Oliver Franks with Acheson and Hoffman in Washington. According to the official line, the Americans could not expect to participate in the deliberations of a body to which they did not belong. Their presence would inhibit frank discussion, prevent the British from giving a positive lead in Europe, and wreck the Consultative Group. Reinforcing these arguments was the contention that American intervention would feed "isolationist" sentiment in Britain and Communist propaganda in Western Europe. Unofficially, the British were equally concerned about the formation of an American bloc in the OEEC, where it would be "only natural that some of our weaker brethren should play to the American gallery if an American representative is always there."[77]

[75]   Hall-Patch tels. to FO, March 1 and 4, 1949, and FO tel. to Rendel, March 1, 1949, T232/201/EEC7/8/07.
[76]   Hall-Patch tel. to FO, March 8, 1949, T232/201/EEC7/8/07.
[77]   FO tel. to Franks, March 10, 1949, T232/201/EEC7/8/07. See also Bevin draft dis-

Below the surface of these arguments was a well of personal animosity between Harriman and those who would thwart his ambition. Harriman's "absurd touchiness," according to Hall-Patch, made the issue of American representation "difficult to handle" precisely because the special representative insisted "on treating on a personal basis things which have nothing to do with personalities."[78] The British formed the opinion that Harriman was acting out of personal pique and without instructions from the State Department or the ECA.[79] He was "exceedingly bitter about his exclusion from the Consultative Group" and was going around Paris "speaking very openly on the subject of his 'humiliation,'" attributing it to Cripps and complaining that "this was not the way to treat 'one of the best friends England ever had.'" Recounting Robert Marjolin's views in words that surely expressed his own opinion, Hall-Patch reported to the Foreign Office that had Harriman "been a normally balanced man he would have accepted his humiliation and would not have let it influence his intellectual judgment." But instead he was busy attacking every proposal the British put forward and then "thinking up reasons for disliking them."[80]

Neither Marjolin, nor Hall-Patch, nor policymakers in London would compromise just to salve Harriman's wounded ego. The official British position throughout was that the OEEC must remain a European organization: American representatives should participate by invitation only and should be confined to the role of observers. But Marjolin was fearful lest Harriman become so "personally soured" as to "menace" the OEEC by organizing an "unholy Alliance" of countries that were "counting on the continuation of American aid beyond 1952." To prevent this and forestall American pressure for official representation in either the Consultative Group or the Executive Committee, the British were ready to accept an arrangement whereby the Executive Committee would constitute itself as an informal working party for occasional meetings with Harriman or his representative. Hall-Patch thought this arrangement would work so long as the most important business was conducted in official sessions closed to the Americans.[81]

Hall-Patch made an appointment to explain the new proposal to Harriman on March 16, only then to undergo another round of the rude treatment

patch to the British Embassy, Washington, March 10, 1949, attached to Rowan memorandum to Cripps, March 10, 1949, Hall-Patch letter to Berthoud, March 16, 1949, and Franks tel. to FO, March 17, 1949, T232/201/EEC7/8/07.

[78] Hall-Patch letter to Makins, March 31, 1949, T232/201/EEC7/8/07.

[79] Franks tel. to FO, March 17, 1949, FO tel. to Hall-Patch, March 18, 1949, and Rowan memorandum to Bridges, March 22, 1949, T232/201/EEC7/8/07.

[80] J. E. Coulson of the United Kingdom Delegation to the OEEC, minute, March 16, 1949, and Hall-Patch letter to Makins, March 31, 1949, T232/201/EEC7/8/07. See also Rowan memorandum to Bridges, March 22, 1949, T232/201/EEC7/8/07.

[81] Coulson minute, March 16, 1949, T232/201/EEC7/8/07. See also FO tel. to Hall-Patch, March 18, 1949, and Rowan memorandum to Bridges, March 22, 1949, T232/201/EEC7/8/07.

that characterized relations between the two men. On "ringing up" to confirm his appointment, Hall-Patch learned that "our Averell was deporting himself on some sunny ski-ing slope in Switzerland." His only comment was " 'lucky man.' " Actually, Hall-Patch was the lucky one, because he found it much easier to deal with Harriman's deputy, William Foster. Both Hall-Patch and Foster repeated the usual arguments, of course: Hall-Patch contending that American participation was a privilege not a right, Foster insisting that Harriman be consulted at every turn. But thereafter the two men agreed to an arrangement whereby Harriman would meet informally with the Executive Committee for wide-ranging but off-the-record talks. The group met for the first time on April 9 and on a weekly basis thereafter, with Harriman or one of his lieutenants representing the ECA. Harriman seemed to be pleased with the arrangement, temporarily at least. Hall-Patch though it diverted "some of E.C.A.'s enthusiasm for taking too positive a part, in and out of season, in sides of the Organisation's work where the Americans were not always welcome."[82]

Hall-Patch had spoken too soon. Within a few weeks, Harriman would be meeting regularly with the Consultative Group, from which he had once been barred, in order to hammer out the terms of a new intra-European payments plan. The debates on this subject brought Anglo–American relations to their lowest point since the inception of the Marshall Plan. The Americans wanted a payments agreement that would allow normal market forces to integrate economies and clear the path to Western Europe's participation in a multilateral system. The British were reluctant to open their economy to competitive pressures or risk their leadership of the sterling area. Negotiations over the new intra-European payments plan, like those over the OEEC, thus brought to the fore old differences over the nature of the European and world economies, differences that were further underscored by the American support for devaluation and the concomitant pressure on the British pound.

V

The 1948 payments plan had failed to break the network of bilateral trading arrangements in Europe, promote a rational integration of the European economies, or stimulate European exports to the dollar area. Debtors had lacked the incentive to increase exports so long as their bilateral deficits earned them indirect dollars in the form of ECA-financed drawing rights. Creditors had either settled for guaranteed sales to their debtors or restricted exports in order to limit the latter's claim to larger drawing rights in the

---

[82] Hall-Patch minute, March 16, 1949, T232/201/EEC7/8/07; and Hall-Patch memorandum, "Informal Meetings between O.S.R. and the Heads of Delegations of the Executive Committee of the O.E.E.C.," May 16, 1949, FO 371, 78033, UR5132. See also Hall-Patch letter to Berthoud, March 16, 1949, T232/201/EEC7/8/07.

future. Although the plan had stimulated trade, it had also subsidized in-efficient producers and high-priced sales, permitted government controls instead of the price mechanism to determine the distribution of resources, and encouraged participating countries to earn dollars through the operation of the payments system rather than through exports to the Western Hemisphere.

These shortcomings had to be corrected if European–American accounts were going to be balanced and the path cleared to a worldwide system based on full convertibility and nondiscrimination. No one in the ECA expected the participating countries to achieve viability by the end of the ERP period. The idea was to limit Western Europe's dollar deficit as much as possible and to do so in a way that was consistent with the long-term goal of multilateral trade. Otherwise, as Harriman told a meeting of ECA officials in April, the United States "would be faced with a diminishing European trade which would require a very definite adjustment in the economic and political situation in the States." European producers had to reduce their prices in order to increase sales in the dollar markets, and the way to drive down prices was to push ahead with the traders' approach to European integration. Trade barriers and bilateral payments agreements had to give way to multilateralism and convertibility, thereby creating a free-trade area in which greater competition and economies of scale would enhance pro-ductivity and set Western Europe on the road to viability. "As far as prac-ticable," in Harriman's words, "the Europeans should be made to consider Europe as an economic union."[83]

With these conclusions as their guide, ECA policymakers urged revisions in the 1948 payments agreement that would make for freer trade in Europe, greater "competition within [the] participating country area," and more European exports to the dollar market.[84] One proposal would make drawing rights convertible into dollars, bringing European producers into direct com-petition with American exporters and forcing these producers to reduce costs and lower prices. But because this proposal was stronger "medicine" than the Europeans could take without further doses of American aid,

---

[83] "Summary of Discussions, Conference of Chiefs of ECA Special Missions, Paris, April 11–12, 1949," RG 286, Acc. 53A405, box 1, folder: Special Representative's File. See also Theodore Geiger of ECA, "General Conclusions on ERP Monetary Policy," March 26, 1949, and James A. McCullough of ECA, undated, "Notes on Fiscal and Trade Policy Consultative Meetings, March 25 and 28, 1949," both attached to McCullough memorandum to Bissell, March 31, 1949, RG 286, Acc. 53A405, box 60, folder: European Payments Union: unsigned, undated [May 1949] ECA mem-orandum, "Trade Policy for ECA," Harriman Papers, folder: European Payments Union; and Arthur Smithies, "U.S.–U.K. Economic Relations," attached to Smithies memorandum to Bissell, May 31, 1949, and ECA Policy Group, undated "Annotated Outline of Purpose and Scope of ECA–UK Talks," June 22, 1949, RG 286, Acc. 53A405, box 60, folder: Anglo–American Relations.

[84] Bruce torep 3775 to Harriman, March 12, 1949, ECA Files, box 46.

Hoffman and other ECA officials in Washington decided to use convertibility "primarily as a bargaining device to obtain [the] less ambitious objective of transferability."[85] Their strategy would make drawing rights, and the conditional dollar grants that supported them, automatically transferable among the OEEC countries. This strategy would help to multilateralize intra-European trade. It would also introduce an element of dollar competition by encouraging participating countries to earn additional dollars, in the form of transferred conditional grants, from each other. Debtors would be given the incentive to shop for imports in all markets and creditors the incentive to reduce prices and become more aggressive in their export policies.[86]

Richard Bissell explained this line of thinking to a meeting of European leaders in Paris on April 14; a week later, Harriman's office formally presented the American proposal to the OEEC's Committee on Payments. The proposal called for the "maximum practical" transferability of drawing rights and conditional dollar grants and for the substantial convertibility of these rights into dollars at the discretion of debtors.[87] As a British memorandum explained, the Americans were concerned about Western Europe's continued inability to penetrate markets in the Western Hemisphere. If left uncorrected, this situation would lead to a permanent dollar gap and the formation of "two economic worlds," a dollar area and a soft-currency trading bloc ringed with barriers against low-cost American exports. The OEEC countries would be trapped in an inefficient pattern of high-cost trade with each other. European–American accounts would be balanced eventually, but at a low level of exchange. To avoid these dangers, the Americans thought it necessary to introduce a degree of multilateralism into intra-European trade, which was exactly what their proposal intended to accomplish.[88]

The proposal, however, could have consequences wholly unintended by

[85] Hoffman torep 4763 to Harriman, April 23, 1949, ECA Files, box 47; and Hoffman torep 4720 to Harriman, April 21, 1949, *FRUS, 1949*, 4:383–5. See also Hoffman torep 4696 to Harriman, April 20, 1949, ECA Files, box 47.

[86] In addition to the sources cited in note 85, see Bruce torep 3775 to Harriman, March 12, 1949, ECA Files, box 46; and Hubert F. Havlik, Chief, Payments Section, OSR, "Possible Basis for ECA Position on Revision of Payments Scheme," April 11, 1949, and Havlik and Kingman Brewster of OSR, "ECA Objectives and Principles in Revision of Payments Agreement," April 13, 1949, RG 286, Acc. 53A177, box 112, folder: Inter-European.

[87] For the quotation, see *FRUS, 1949*, 4:383, footnote 1. See also unsigned "Notes of Meeting on April 14, 1949 in Mr. Katz's Office," RG 286, Acc. 53A177, box 112, folder: EPU; unsigned "Notes of Meeting on April 14, 1949 at 5 P.M. at OEEC," RG 286, Acc. 53A177, box 112, folder: Inter-European; and Katz repto circular 180 to Hoffman, April 22, 1949, ECA Files, box 8. See also Hall-Patch tel. to FO, April 16, 1949, FO 371, 77929, UR3741.

[88] Under Secretary of the Treasury Denis Rickett memorandum, "Intra-European Payments Scheme for 1949/50," T232/133/EEC3/03E.

American leaders. By transforming drawing rights into potential dollar liabilities, it might lead creditors to protect their reserves by demanding a larger share of ERP allocations or by restricting imports and thus creating deficits that debtors would have to cover by expending their drawing rights within the country issuing them. The first course would paralyze the OEEC's division-of-aid and programming activities, with disastrous effects on the recovery plans of participating countries. The second would lead to a general contraction of intra-European trade as participating governments fastened the same restrictions on imports from each other as they placed on imports from the United States.

The OEEC countries pointed out these possibilities when the Committee on Payments began debating the American proposal. As in the past, the Belgians and the British demanded special consideration. Belgium's surplus on intra-European account was double its deficit in trade with the Western Hemisphere, which meant that Belgium could cover only half of the surplus even if it granted drawing rights equal to all of its dollar aid. The Belgians were as reluctant as ever to finance any part of the difference through new credits, as the ECA expected. They demanded a share of ERP aid, in the form of direct allocations, conditional grants, and transferred drawing rights, equal to the whole of their European surplus. They also wanted part of this share as "free dollars" that could be added to their reserves or used in other ways currently prohibited by ECA rules governing the expenditure of Marshall Plan funds. The British, for their part, objected to the principle of transferability. In operation, this principle could cost them conditional aid or lead to direct gold and dollar payments to Belgium and Switzerland (Britain's major European creditors), should either country accumulate sterling rights above the gold point in their payments agreements with the British Treasury. Much the same would happen if drawing rights were directly convertible into dollars, which explains why the British opposed this feature of the American proposal as well. The United States, they insisted, had to decide whether it wanted to expand intra-European trade or promote multilateralism on a nondiscriminatory basis. It could not do both. If nondiscrimination became the goal, Britain would have to impose the same restrictions on imports from all participating countries as it imposed on those from its creditors.[89]

[89] Havlik Memorandum of Conversation with Ansiaux, Chairman, OEEC Payments Committee, May 4, 1949, RG 286, Acc. 53A177, box 112, folder: Inter-European. See also Katz repto 3810 to Hoffman, April 22, 1949, ECA Files, box 6; Hoffman torep 4763 to Harriman, April 23, 1949, ECA Files, box 47; Havlik Memorandum of Conversation with Ansiaux, April 28, 1949, and Mr. Levy-Hawes, OSR, Payments Section, Memorandum of Conversation, April 29, 1949, RG 286, Acc. 53A177, box 112, folder: Inter-European; Foster repto 3920 to Hoffman, April 29, 1949, *FRUS, 1949*, 4:385–7; and Foster repto 3953 to Hoffman, April 30, 1949, ECA Files, box 8. See also Hall-Patch tels. (2) to FO, May 19, 1949, T232/211/EEC3/010A. As the

Involved here was the familiar dispute between the British, who wanted generous terms for debtors, and the Belgians, who were committed to an economic orthodoxy that benefitted creditors and had strong support in the American Treasury. The ECA tried to mediate between these two positions. In mid-May, for example, Harriman proposed as the basis of a compromise a mixed system of bilateral and multilateral drawing rights. Twenty-five percent of all drawing rights would be bilateral, would be negotiated according to the procedures worked out in the 1948 payments plan, and would be nontransferable. The remainder would be assigned to debtors for use in any participating country, would be transferable, and would be backed (on a dollar-for-dollar basis) by conditional grants from an unallocated pool of ECA funds. A technical subcommittee of the Committee on Payments issued a majority report on May 24 that generally endorsed the ECA's revised proposal. But both the ECA proposal and the subcommittee report still envisioned the transfer of conditional grants and the convertibility into dollars of at least half of all multilateral rights. The British refused to accept these provisions. The Americans were unable to budge them and the Committee on Payments was forced to adjourn without agreement.[90]

Thereafter, negotiations went forward in the Consultative Group of Ministers and in a special Group of Four composed of Harriman and the finance ministers of Britain, France, and Belgium. The British now suggested that Belgium's surplus be financed through off-shore purchases (thereby excluding Belgium from the payments scheme) or through some combination of conditional dollar grants, minimum British gold payments, and irredeemable Belgium credits.[91] The Belgians rejected the first proposal as effectively removing them from the "European family."[92] Nor would they negotiate

American documents point out, the French were also concerned lest the ECA's proposal result in new intra-European trade restrictions and wreck their export program.

[90] Foster reptos 3915 and 4105 to Hoffman, April 29 and May 10, 1949, Katz repto 4188 to Hoffman, May 13, 1949, and Harriman repto 4258 to Hoffman, May 17, 1949, ECA Files, box 6; Harriman repto circulars 200, 206, 213, and 218 to Hoffman, May 7 and 17 and June 1 and 4, 1949, ECA Files, box 8; Havlik Memoranda of Conversations with Ansiaux, April 28 and May 4, 1949, Levy-Hawes memorandum, May 12, 1949, Havlik memorandum to Tasca, May 26, 1949, and Havlik memorandum to Harriman, June (?), 1949, RG 286, Acc. 53A177, box 112, folder: Inter-European; Hoffman torep 5369 to Harriman, May 19, 1949, ECA Files, box 48; Hoffman torep 5418 to Harriman, May 23, 1949, *FRUS, 1949*, 4:395–7; and ECA Observer's Statement, May 25, 1949, RG 286, Acc. 53A177, box 112, folder: EPU. See also Hall-Patch tels. to FO, May 24, 25 (2), and 26, 1949, T232/211/EEC3/010A.

[91] T. L. Rowan and Sir Edwin Plowden, Chief Planning Officer, Treasury, memorandum to Cripps, May 17, 1949, Cripps draft memorandum, May 17, 1949, and Treasury draft tel., May 26, 1949, T232/211/EEC3/010A; FO tel. to Hall-Patch, May 27, 1949, T232/212/EEC3/010B; and Hall-Patch tels. (2) to FO, June 5, 1949, T232/213/EEC3/010C.

[92] Treasury draft tel., May 26, 1949, T232/211/EEC3/010A; and unsigned "Notes on Conversation with Mr. Ansiaux, May 28, 1949," Treasury Records, Acc. 68A2809, box 27, folder: EUR/o/71 – Secretary Snyder's European Trip, 1949.

irredeemable credits, which amounted to "gifts," or continue to accumulate dollar grants unless free to use at least part of the proceeds as they saw fit.[93] According to their latest proposal, Belgium would extend long-term credits to its major debtors, including credits equal to half of its surplus in trade with Britain. But it would do so only if the British covered the balance through gold payments to the Belgian Treasury, if all participating countries accepted the majority report of May 24, and if Belgium's share of ERP aid equaled the balance of its surplus in intra-European trade.[94]

American leaders had previously opposed aid in excess of a participating country's deficit with the Western Hemisphere, which was what the Belgians had in mind. But they were now willing to accept some variation of this plan – including the provision of "free dollars" – as the best way to finance Belgium's intra-European surplus and limit Britain's dollar liability. In their view, however, the Belgians had to settle for dollar aid in an amount less than their surplus, making up the difference with new credits out of their own resources. In addition, all of the other participating countries had to accept the majority report of May 24, make multilateral drawing rights and conditional grants transferable, and permit debtors to convert a portion of these into dollars.[95] On these key points, the American position remained firm, as did the British opposition. Although the British would agree to make drawing rights transferable – a concession on their part – they still insisted that convertibility or the transfer of conditional grants would cost them dollars they could not afford.[96]

Indeed, by this time the negotiations were being complicated by the serious drain on Britain's reserves that had begun in April. For the British, the drain was largely a by-product of the American recession and the speculation against sterling caused by the IMF investigation and the widespread rumors of mounting pressure for British devaluation. For the Americans, the real sources of the problem lay in the low productivity and high prices that robbed British exporters of the incentive to compete for markets in the dollar area. Whatever the causes, both sides could agree that the drain was

[93] Hall-Patch tel. to FO, June 5, 1949, T232/213/EEC3/010C. In addition to the last document cited in note 92, see Hall-Patch tel. to FO, June 6, 1949, T232/213/EEC3/010C.

[94] "Belgian Proposal," June 4, 1949, RG 286, Acc. 53A177, box 112, folder: Inter-European. See also Harriman repto 4593 to Hoffman, June 8, 1949, ECA Files, box 7; and Hall-Patch tels. to FO, June 6 and 9, 1949, T232/213/EEC3/010C.

[95] Harriman reptos unnumbered and 4791 to Hoffman, June 11 and 15, 1949, ECA Files, box 7; Hoffman toreps 5860, 5861, and 5990 to Harriman, June 15 (2) and 20, 1949, ECA Files, box 48; Hall-Patch tel. to FO, June 3, 1949, T232/212/EEC3/010B; and Hall-Patch tels. to FO, June 5, 8, and 9 (2), 1949, T232/213/EEC3/010C.

[96] Havlik memorandum to James L. Houghteling, Program Review Division, OSR, June 23, 1949, RG 286, Acc. 53A177, box 112, folder: Inter-European; Harriman repto 4882 to Hoffman, June 24, 1949, ECA Files, box 7; and Hall-Patch tel. to FO, June 5, 1949, and FO tel. to Hall-Patch, June 11, 1949, T232/213/EEC3/010C.

rapidly reaching crisis proportions. By mid-June, Britain's reserves had fallen well below the $2 billion considered necessary to protect the value of pound sterling and were still falling at a rate of between $100 million and $150 million a month.[97]

Under these circumstances, Cripps, Bevin, and other British policymakers were even more determined to prevent changes in the payments plan that might cost them dollars and lead to devaluation. They told Harriman that loose talk of devaluation in Washington was fueling speculation against sterling and making it difficult to negotiate a payments plan. Cripps was convinced that American pressure on the payments front was part of a larger campaign to devalue the pound, something he opposed. Any benefits from devaluation would be short-lived, he and others insisted, and would be offset by higher prices on British imports and by the need for compensatory wage increases and additional outlays for social services. They also warned that devaluation would undermine Britain's ability to support the Brussels Pact and the North Atlantic Treaty. It would trigger competitive depreciations in Western Europe as well and would reverse the gains that had been made in economic stability and political peace.[98]

At least some American leaders shared these concerns. They worried that devaluation would increase the cost of dollar imports for the OEEC countries and in this way retard European recovery and prolong the recession in the United States. Devaluation might also relieve the pressure for the internal reforms, including the elimination of restrictive business and trade-union practices and the diversion of resources from social programs to productive investment, that alone could boost productivity and bring British and European prices into line with those of the Western Hemisphere. Ambassador Douglas and his staff reached these conclusions, although they also thought that British policymakers were as reluctant to engineer internal reforms as they were to devalue the pound. Their greatest fear was that American pressure would lead the Labour government to protect its reserves by forging an "autarchic" trade and payments area "centered on London and using sterling as its basic currency."[99]

[97]   Unsigned memorandum, "Sterling," [June 1949], and Holmes tel. to Harriman and Douglas, June 13, 1949, RG 59, file: 841.51/6-2149; Douglas tel. to Harriman, June 22, 1949, Harriman Papers, folder: United Kingdom; Douglas tel. to Acheson, June 28, 1949, RG 59, file: 841.5151/6-2849; and Douglas tels. to Acheson, June 16 and 22, 1949, and Thorp memorandum to Acheson, June 27, 1949, *FRUS, 1949*, 4:784–90, 793–6.

[98]   Holmes tel. to Douglas and Harriman, June 13, 1949, RG 59, file; 841.51/6-2149; Douglas tel. to Acheson, June 23, 1949, RG 59, file: 841.5151/6-2349; unsigned "Notes on Conversation with Mr. Ansiaux, May 28, 1949," Treasury Records, Acc. 68A2809, box 27, folder: EUR/o/71 – Secretary Snyder's European Trip, 1949; and Hall-Patch letters to Gore-Booth, May 28 and 31, 1949, T232/57/EEC14/8/04.

[99]   Douglas tel. to Acheson, June 22, 1949, *FRUS, 1949*, 4:787–90. See also Douglas tels. to Acheson, May 18 and June 16, 1949, and Harriman tel. to Acheson, June

This fear became the prism through which American officials viewed a major British proposal for the liberalization of intra-European trade. Although planning for this proposal had begun earlier, the records leave little doubt that British leaders intended their initiative to preempt American pressure in the payments negotiations. The British wanted the ECA to choose between its commitment to the principles of transferability and convertibility and its commitment to the liberalization and expansion of intra-European trade. For American policymakers, the two were linked; for the British, making drawing rights convertible and conditional aid transferable would lead to a new wave of restrictionism. Expanding trade on a multilateral basis was best achieved by removing quantitative restrictions on imports, which is what the British now proposed to do if the ECA abandoned its demands for convertibility and transferability.

The records also call into question the sweep and sincerity of the British proposal. Cripps told the Economic Policy Committee and the Cabinet, when they approved the proposal at meetings in late May, that reducing import quotas would eliminate bilateral rigidities and encourage European producers to lower costs and become more efficient. These gains, he said, would benefit consumers and make European goods more marketable in the dollar area. But the proposal would remove quotas on private trade only, not on the substantial volume of imports purchased on government account. Barely $32 million in new goods would be admitted into the United Kingdom, and even this amount might be reduced by manipulating exchange controls and raising tariffs. In addition, quotas would be retained on imports from Belgium and Switzerland, Britain's major creditors on the Continent. The exclusion of these countries and the elimination of provisions for currency convertibility and transferability would reduce the risk to Britain's reserves. These were two of the three conditions attached to the British proposal, the third being an American decision to waive Article 9 of the Anglo–American loan agreement. Article 9 permitted the British to discriminate against American imports only in cases where discrimination benefitted "war-shattered" economies. If left standing, it would force the British to exclude the sterling Dominions from the advantages of the trade-liberalization proposal. The British would have to discriminate in favor of the OEEC countries against the Dominions (as well as against the United States), and this action would disrupt the sterling bloc. Once again, Britain's interests in Europe had to be reconciled with its commitments to the sterling area.[100]

25, 1949, *FRUS, 1949*, 4:391–4, 784–6, 792–3; and unsigned memorandum, "Sterling," [June 1949], RG 59, file: 841.51/6-2149.

[100] Rowan and Plowden memorandum to Cripps, May 17, 1949, Cripps draft memorandum, May 17, 1949, and FO tel. to Franks, May 26, 1949, T232/211/EEC3/010A; S. E. G. Luke memorandum to Attlee, May 25, 1949, EPC (49) 19th Meeting, May 26, 1949, CP (49) 124, Cripps memorandum, May 28, 1949, and CM (49) 39th Conclusion, May 30, 1949, PREM 8/971; and Cripps note

By late June, the British proposal had taken on the air of an ultimatum. The British would accept full transferability of drawing rights and remove quantitative restrictions on private imports. But they would do so only if transferability did not involve conditional grants or convertibility into dollars; if quotas were retained on imports from their creditors; if the other OEEC countries loosened their restrictions on imports from the sterling area; if Switzerland remained outside the new payments scheme; and if Belgium was included on terms that severely limited its claims on Britain's reserves.[101] Despite these conditions, the British presented their proposal as going "a long way towards . . . complete multilateralism." In the short term, they admitted, it meant suspending Article 9 and extending the pattern of discrimination against American goods. But by linking Western Europe and the sterling bloc, it would also create a soft-currency trading area large enough to enhance productivity, reduce costs, and set the stage for an eventual return to full convertibility and nondiscriminatory trade. The only alternative, the British warned, was a "greater degree of bilateralism than at present."[102]

These arguments were geared to fit a line of thinking emerging in the minds of both European and American leaders. The French and Belgians were talking of the increases in productivity and of the greater exports that would come from forming a European free market.[103] The Americans were discussing the potential benefits of a large soft-currency trading area that included the OEEC countries and as much of the nondollar world as possible. In theory at least, an arrangement of this sort would bring "gains in productivity from geographical specialization, from production specialization and the economies of scale, and from an intensification of competition" between the participating countries – gains so great that it would be possible to permit "the group as a whole, for a limited period of time, to insulate itself" from full competition with the dollar area.[104]

of discussion with Harriman and Finletter, May 17, 1949, FO 371, 78033, UR5417. See also Rickett minute, April 27, 1949, T232/133/EEC3/03E.

[101]   Harriman repto 4434 to Hoffman, May 28, 1949, ECA Files, box 7; Hoffman torep 5590 to Harriman, June 1, 1949, ECA Files, box 48; Havlik, "Comments on British and French Counter-proposals," June 2, 1949, RG 286, Acc. 53A177, box 112, folder: Inter-European; Harriman repto 4824 to Hoffman, June 21, 1949, Harriman Papers, folder: United Kingdom; Douglas tel. to Acheson, June 23, 1949, RG 59, file: 841.5151/6-2349; and Thorp memorandum to Acheson, June 27, 1949, *FRUS, 1949*, 4:793–6. See also FO tels. to Hall-Patch, June 11 and 14, 1949, T232/213/EEC3/010C; and FO tel. to Franks, June 17, 1949, and Franks tel. to FO, June 19, 1949, FO 371, 78075, UR6257 and UR6259.

[102]   FO tel. to Franks, May 26, 1949, T232/211/EEC3/010A; and Draft Memorandum of Conversation, June 9, 1949, *FRUS, 1949*, 4:781–4.

[103]   Horace G. Reed, ECA Mission, Paris, toeca 880 to Acheson, May 3, 1949, RG 286, Acc. 53A177, box 87, folder: Eyes Only – Pers., Chrono. – May to Dec. 1949; and Havlik, Memorandum of Conversation with Ansiaux, April 28, 1949, RG 286, Acc. 53A177, box 112, folder: Inter-European.

[104]   See Theodore Geiger memorandum, March 26, and "Notes on Fiscal and Trade

But these gains would come only if the trading area were organized on the right basis. The area would have to permit maximum freedom of trade and payments between the countries involved and entail at least some competition with the dollar. The British proposal did not measure up to these specifications. It left room for bilateral bargaining with the Belgians and limited the pressure on prices by rejecting convertibility and shifts of conditional aid. Nor did it say anything about devaluing European currencies or eliminating the jungle of crossrates and exchange controls that American leaders were coming to see as one of the major barriers to the free flow of money and goods. Without these features, or so American policymakers feared, the British proposal would lead to a "preferential trading and payments system" tied to sterling, sheltered from effective price competition, and unable, even in the long run, to withstand the pressure of full convertibility.[105]

American and British leaders were thus at loggerheads when the Group of Four reconvened on June 23 for another round of debate in the payments negotiations. Cripps represented the British and repeated the usual arguments against convertibility and the transfer of conditional grants. Under no circumstances would the Labour government agree to a scheme that ran the risk of draining its gold and dollar reserves and breaking the sterling bloc. In a conversation with Harriman on June 22, Hall Patch also "spoke with some heat about the dangers and risks to the whole sterling area which the attitude of E.C.A. was forcing upon us." Three days later, the Foreign Office reminded its overseas missions of the "special responsibilities" that the United Kingdom had "to the sterling area and to that still wider area which carries on a part of its trade in sterling. We are the custodians of the central reserves of the largest multilateral trading area in the world," it explained, "...and we cannot afford to take any risks which are not absolutely necessary." The British had taken a risk like this in 1947, with disastrous results, and they were not about to repeat this mistake, or that of 1931, when another convertibility crisis had brought down the second Labour government.[106]

Policy Consultative Meetings, March 25 and 28," both attached to James A. McCullough memorandum to Bissell, March 31, 1949, RG 286, Acc. 53A405, box 60, folder: European Payments Union; and undated memorandum from ECA Planning Group to Bissell, with attached "Annotated Outline of Purpose and Scope of ECA–UK Talks," by John Hully and H. Van B. Cleveland, June 22, 1949, RG 286, Acc. 53A405, box 60, folder: Anglo–American Relations.

[105]   In addition to the sources in note 104, see Hoffman torep 5590 to Harriman, June 1, 1949, ECA Files, box 48; Havlik, "Comments on British and French Counterproposals," June 2, 1949, RG 286, Acc. 53A177, box 112, folder: Inter-European; and Hoffman torep 5952 to Harriman, June 17, 1949, ECA Files, box 48. See also Harriman tel. to Acheson, June 25, 1949, *FRUS, 1949*, 4:792–3. See also Hall-Patch tel. to FO, June 22, 1949, T232/214/EEC3/010D.

[106]   Hall-Patch tel. to FO, June 22, 1949, T232/214/EEC3/010D; FO circular tel., June 24, 1949, T232/215/EEC3/010E; and Bullock, *Bevin*, 706. See also the documents cited in note 107.

Cripps recalled the 1947 debacle in his meeting with the Group of Four on June 23, coupling this with a reminder of the benefits that would come from reducing import quotas within a soft-currency trading area that included the sterling Dominions as well as the OEEC countries. The British were willing to take this course so long as the ECA did not "introduce the dollar sign" into the European payments system. This meant that Britain's creditors, particularly the Belgians, had to renounce convertibility and the transfer of conditional aid and finance their trade surplus through a combination of ECA grants and essentially irredeemable credits. The last condition would require Belgium to shoulder the burden of Britain's deficit by accumulating an unlimited amount of unusable sterling. This situation was unacceptable to Spaak, as it was to Harriman and French Minister of Finance Maurice Petsche. All three men were willing to make some concessions. Petsche suggested that only 40 percent of all drawing rights (and conditional aid) be made transferable; Harriman agreed to 50 percent; Spaak pledged additional Belgian credits, and both he and Harriman abandoned convertibility. But they still insisted on the transfer of conditional aid, even if this entailed a further drain on Britain's reserves. Belgium and other creditors, they said, could not afford to accumulate an unlimited amount of blocked sterling. They would protect themselves from this eventuality by erecting a network of exchange controls that hampered trade expansion, discouraged competition, and prevented integration. The result would be the same if Britain's terms were accepted: a permanent high-cost trading area tied to sterling and protected against dollar competition by a wall of restrictionism. European viability would remain an elusive goal, as would the dream of a worldwide system based on full convertibility and multilateralism.[107]

The deadlock seemed to portend a major crisis in Anglo–American relations and a breakdown of the ERP. The evidence suggests that all sides viewed the impasse in these terms. British and American policymakers felt backed into a corner; the British by the pressure on their reserves, the Americans by the need to show progress toward economic integration and multilateralism in Europe. Officials on both sides of the Atlantic thought that the impasse ran the risk of eroding public and legislative support for the Marshall Plan and the Atlantic pact, wrecking plans to build a Western European bloc, and encouraging the Soviets. The British used these arguments in a last-ditch effort to wean the Belgians and the French away from the ECA's proposal. In addition, they warned that transferring conditional dollar grants would bring the American recession into Europe. As Hall-Patch told a French colleague in Paris, the chances of expanding intra-European trade and thus of "checking the effects of the American recession" would be negligible if transferability forced Britain and other participating countries into a wave of restrictionism. These arguments had an impact on the Belgians and

---

[107] EPC (49) 67, "Meeting of Ministerial Group of Four," June 24, 1949, PREM 8/971. See also Rendel tel. to FO, June 23, 1949, T232/214/EEC/010D.

the French. Both countries submitted new proposals that went a considerable distance toward eliminating the threat to Britain's reserves. But if this suggests a British-inspired bloc against the United States, the fact is that policymakers in London were also moving toward a compromise.[108]

By the end of June, the British had prepared a plan to reduce dollar imports by a staggering 25 percent, a reduction amounting to $600 million over the next year. This reduction was part of a broader program for alleviating the pressure on pound sterling that also included similar reductions by the sterling-area countries, a larger share of ERP aid, American and Canadian initiatives to support sterling, and waiver of Article 9. The last step was still necessary to permit the United Kingdom and other soft-currency countries to raise restrictions against American goods, reduce quotas on imports from each other, and thereby expand trade without losing dollars.[109]

All of these initiatives required American cooperation, which Cripps hoped to secure by accepting a compromise payments plan drawn along lines suggested in the latest Belgian and French proposals. As approved by the Economic Policy Committee at a meeting on June 28, this compromise would entail the transfer of conditional aid and hence gold and dollar payments to Belgium. But it would keep these payments to a minimum and would bring "political advantages out of all proportion to the cost involved."[110] The advantages anticipated included an Anglo–American understanding regarding the relationship between the sterling bloc and the dollar area. With this in mind, plans had been made for discussions with Secretary of the Treasury John W. Snyder and a group of American and Canadian financial officials who would visit London in July. The hope was for discussions that would enable the British to put the sterling crisis in a larger political context, warn of the dangers to the North Atlantic alliance if they were forced into a " 'Schachtian' managed autarky," and thus win American support for measures that would underwrite the reserves of the sterling area. This support would help to reconcile Britain's commitment to the sterling area with America's plans for a multilateral world, prevent a division of the globe into rival sterling, dollar, and ruble blocs, and preserve what Bevin called "the united front of the Western Powers."[111]

[108] Hall-Patch tel. to FO, June 26, 1949, PREM 8/971. See also Hall-Patch tel. to FO, June 22, 1949, T232/214/EEC3/010D; Hall-Patch tel. to FO, June 25, 1949, and Rendel tel. to FO, June 25, 1949, T232/215/EEC3/010E; and Douglas tel. to Harriman, June 27, 1949, Harriman Papers, folder: Snyder Trip, July 1949.

[109] Henniker minute to Bevin, June 23, 1949, FO 371, 78083, UR6981; and EPC (49) 66, "The Dollar Situation," June 22, 1949, and EPC (49) 22nd Meeting, June 24, 1949, PREM 8/412 (pts. 1–3).

[110] EPC (49) 23rd Meeting, June 27, 1949, T232/215/EEC3/010E. See also the report of the London Committee's Subcommittee on Intra-European Trade and Payments, June (?), 1949, T232/215/EEC3/010E.

[111] Gore-Booth memorandum to Bevin, June 30, 1949, FO 371, 78083, UR6963; and FO tel. to Hall-Patch, June 29, 1949, FO 800/460/EUR/49/17. See also EPC (49)

The threat of a larger crisis in the Western alliance also pushed the Americans toward concessions in the payments negotiations. This effect became clear when the National Advisory Council (NAC) agreed to temporary British restrictions on dollar imports and welcomed the British proposal for liberalizing intra-European trade. This proposal, according to the NAC, could mean a further step toward "economic integration." The NAC reserved judgment on whether trade liberalization should be extended to the sterling Dominions, thereby forming a large soft-currency trading area as the British had suggested. But it was willing to consider this course as part of a larger program that also included the devaluation of European currencies and other measures designed to "restore multilateral trade on a world basis and global convertibility of currencies."[112] These decisions, taken in meetings on June 28 and 30, essentially confirmed an agreement reached earlier by Secretary of State Dean Acheson, Secretary of the Treasury John Snyder, and ECA Administrator Paul Hoffman. Drawn up by the State Department and communicated to Ambassador Douglas on June 27, the agreement would waive Article 9, acquiesce in "drastic, and inevitably discriminatory, British import restrictions," and accept the British proposals for a "wide non-dollar trading area (including proposals as to payments arrangements)" – provided the British devalued their currency and took further steps to make the soft-currency area a "self-liquidating" expedient.[113]

The issue of devaluation would remain a serious sticking point in Anglo–American relations. It would be the subject of negotiations that began with Snyder's visit to London and dragged on through the following September. But our concern here is with the payments negotiations, and in this area the Americans had made a critical concession by modifying the ECA's original position. The modification they had in mind turned out to be more or less identical to the compromise plan that the Belgians and the French had proposed and the British approved on June 28. In the earlier negotiations, Hoffman and Harriman had been threatening to act unilaterally unless the British accepted their proposal for substantial transfers of conditional aid.[114]

72, "The Dollar Situation," June 22, 1949, and EPC (49) 24th Meeting, July 1, 1949, PREM 8/412 (pts. 1–3).

[112]   The NAC action of June 30 is summarized in Acheson tel. to Douglas, June 30, 1949, *FRUS, 1949*, 4:797–9. See also RG 56, NAC Minutes, June 28 and 30, 1949; and NAC Staff Committee, Memoranda to the NAC (NAC documents 850 and 851), June 29, 1949, RG 59, file: 840.50/6-2949.

[113]   Thorp memorandum to Acheson, June 27, 1949, *FRUS, 1949*, 4:793–6. See also Acheson tel. to Douglas, June 27, 1949, *FRUS, 1949*, 4:796–7. For more on thinking in the State Department, see Webb tel. to Douglas, May 28, 1949, *FRUS, 1949*, 4:397–9.

[114]   Hoffman torep 5967 to Harriman, June 18, 1949, ECA Files, box 48; Bonesteel repto 4851 to Hoffman, June 22, 1949, ECA Files, box 7; and Hoffman torep 6081 to Harriman, June 23, 1949, ECA Files, box 48.

But in addition to dropping their demand for convertibility, in order "to ease [the] UK position," they now decided to limit drastically the percentage of drawing rights and conditional dollar grants that could be transferred at the option of debtors.[115]

This confluence of the American and British positions finally cleared the way for an OEEC agreement on the principles of a new payments plan. Under the agreement, approved by the Council on July 1, only 25 percent of all drawing rights and conditional aid would be transferable and none would be convertible into dollars. Belgium's surplus would be financed partly by ERP dollars, including conditional grants, and partly by additional Belgian credits. To limit the gold and dollar demands on the British Treasury, the ECA promised to increase Belgium's share of ERP aid, the French pledged to expend their sterling rights in the sterling area, and the Belgians agreed to accept sterling transfers equal to no more than $40 million. This figure was roughly $15 million more than the British wanted. But it represented their maximum dollar liability under the payments scheme and was $15 million less than they had paid to the Belgian Treasury under the 1948 plan. Slight wonder that the Economic Policy Committee recorded its hearty "appreciation" for the role that Cripps had played in "securing a satisfactory agreement."[116]

VI

In their subsequent statements, ECA officials touted the agreement as another victory for their policy goals in Europe. Making drawing rights transferable would supposedly eliminate bilateral rigidities, integrate economies, and expand trade. Shifting conditional grants would foster competition and greater competition would drive down prices and help redirect European exports to the dollar area.[117] This rosy assessment underestimated the losses and inflated the gains on the American ledger. The Americans had dropped the demand for convertibility and had allowed the Belgians to accumulate

[115] Harriman repto circular 232 to ECA Missions in Europe, June 25, 1949, *FRUS*, 1949, 4:403–5. See also Harriman repto unnumbered, June 26, 1949, ECA Files, box 7; and Brewster, "Summary of Proposals and Issues Raised at Meeting of Experts Evening of June 29th, 1949," RG 286, Acc. 53A177, box 112, folder: Inter-European.

[116] EPC (49) 24th Meeting, July 1, 1949, PREM 8/971. See also Hall-Patch tel. to FO, June 29, 1949, T232/215/EEC3/010E; Commonwealth Relations Office circular tel., July 1, 1949, and Hall-Patch tels. (2) to FO, July 1, 1949, T232/216/EEC3/010F. For American documentation, see Harriman repto circular 239 to ECA Missions, July 1, 1949, *FRUS*, 1949, 4:405–7; Harriman repto 5038 to Hoffman, July 2, 1949, ECA Files, box 7; and Harriman repto 5003 to Hoffman, July 1, 1949, Harriman Papers, folder: O.E.E.C.

[117] Harriman repto circular 240 to Hoffman, July 4, 1949, ECA Files, box 8; and Hoffman toreps 6280 and 6258 to Harriman, July 7, 1949, ECA Files, box 48.

dollars in excess of the latter's deficit with the Western Hemisphere. Nor could the final agreement do much to end bilateralism or to encourage European producers to forsake their high-priced sales on the Continent for greater exports to the dollar area: Only 10 percent of intra-European trade would be financed with drawing rights and only 25 percent of these rights would be transferable.[118]

The agreement clearly signaled a shift in American policy, and this shift would become more pronounced in the months to come. The Americans would press ahead with their efforts to forge national and transnational networks of private cooperation and public–private power sharing, to build central institutions of economic coordination and control, and to export American production skills, technical know-how, and Keynesian strategies of fiscal and monetary management. These would remain important lines of policy in their New Deal design for a revitalized European neo-capitalism. But in the ECA's view, the recovery of prewar production levels, the growing signs of financial stability, and the worsening dollar gap had altered the European economic landscape and made new recovery strategies necessary. The realignment of currencies and the elimination of trade and payments barriers had now become central to an economic integration that would enhance productivity and set the stage for a fully multilateral system of world trade.

No one could predict whether such measures would be enough to offset the economic impact of rearmament or win France's continued support for Germany's revival and reintegration, both of which were vital to sustaining the recovery program and containing the Soviet Union. Nor was it at all clear that British policymakers would put their fate in the hands of a merciless market (as was implicit in the turn to the free-trader's approach), or subordinate their sovereignty to a supranational authority. Most of the evidence pointed to irreconcilable differences between the Americans and the British. The Americans thought in terms of central institutions with the power to coordinate national policies so that normal market incentives could operate across the ERP area as a whole. The British envisioned more conventional agencies of intergovernmental collaboration. The Americans wanted to harness free-market forces to the cause of economic integration and multilateralism. The British wanted to bottle them up in a socialist empiricism that sheltered their economy, kept them at arms-length from the Continent, and safeguarded their reserve position and ties to the Commonwealth.

On a resolution of these differences hung the success or failure of the American design for a European neo-capitalism. The compromise on a new payments plan had done little to effect this resolution. Nor could it do much

[118] J. H. W. [John H. Williams], "The Revision of the Intra-European Payments Plan," *Foreign Affairs* 28 (October 1949): 153–5.

to end the sterling crisis, which now loomed as a symbol of how the worsening dollar gap imperiled the entire recovery program. Indeed, both British and American leaders had looked upon the compromise as mere prelude to a larger Anglo–American settlement that would realign the dollar and sterling areas, prevent a division of the Western world into rival currency blocs, and provide the basis for continued progress toward European viability and multilateralism. Both sides had laid down terms for this settlement. It remained to be seen if these terms could be harmonized through the negotiations that would begin with Snyder's visit to London in July.

6

Two worlds or three: the sterling crisis, the dollar gap, and the integration of Western Europe

IN THE SECOND HALF of 1949, the specter of the dollar gap hung over the Marshall Plan like Banquo's ghost over the feast. Unless corrected, the dollar gap would foreclose the American plan for a multilateral world based on nondiscrimination and full convertibility. The termination of Marshall aid in 1952 would drive participating countries deeper into the arms of an economic autarky. Gains in production and financial stability would be reversed, living standards would decline, and redistributive battles would resume. Once again the door would be thrown open to Communist parties in France and Italy. It would be more difficult to solve the German problem and forge a balance of power in the West sufficient to contain the Soviet bloc in the East. Progress in these directions had already been complicated by the resurgence of German nationalism and the successful Soviet test of an atomic device. Nor were these the only complications. The collapse of the Nationalist government in China and the spread of Communist insurgencies in Southeast Asia added a global dimension to the dollar famine. They pointed up the need for remedies that would bring economic progress and political stability not only to Europe but also to the sterling area and the overseas territories of other participating countries.

As in the past, American and British leaders disagreed regarding the best remedies to be applied. The Americans continued to prescribe the realignment of currencies, the elimination of trade barriers, and the coordination of national policies. These and other elements of the New Deal synthesis, if applied to Western Europe, would forge an integrated order similar to the vigorous neo-capitalist economy that had grown up in the United States. In addition to linking Germany to the anti-Soviet cause, they would generate the economic growth needed to stabilize European politics and solve the global shortage of dollars. Policymakers in London, however, still found these American formulas distasteful. They were reluctant to devalue the pound so long as this or related measures ran the risk of breaking their economic plans on the shoals of an unfettered market. Nor would they join the movement for European integration or take any steps that might compromise their ties to the Commonwealth and darken their vision of Britain as the balance wheel in a Western consolidation.

These differences came to a boil when Secretary of the Treasury John Snyder journeyed to London in July for trilateral financial talks with the British and Canadians. The talks drew a sharp contrast between the British and American views of the dollar problem, revived old fears of a separate sterling bloc, and triggered a search for new solutions in London and Washington. The results of this search added up to greater flexibility and major changes on both sides. These changes then cleared the way for a resumption of the financial talks in September and for a brief moment of Anglo–American cooperation at an OEEC meeting in late October. As we will see, however, they also led to a stormy debate in Washington, to bitter recriminations in Paris, and to disillusionment on both sides of the Atlantic when Anglo–American relations erupted in new controversy at the end of the year.

II

Sir Stafford Cripps took charge of British planning for the talks and incorporated the results in an important memorandum to the Economic Policy Committee. The memorandum, dated July 4, was a major statement of British policy. In a section entitled "The Choice Before Us," the chancellor outlined three alternative policies for dealing with the drain on Britain's reserves. The first, or "two-world policy," would amalgamate the Commonwealth and Western Europe into a soft-currency bloc tied to sterling and sheltered by a wall of restrictions against dollar competition and swings in the American business cycle. Similar to the middle kingdom envisioned earlier, the amalgamation would divide the globe into three currency regimes, the "free world" into two. But Cripps harbored little optimism for this policy. It would drive Canada and other Dominions from the Commonwealth and spell the end of Great Britain as a world power. It would also "cut across the essential political and strategic requirements of the country as represented by the North Atlantic Pact, Western Union and Commonwealth solidarity." And by reducing the volume and raising the cost of food and raw-material imports, it would lead to higher prices, lower living standards, and greater unemployment at home. But if a two-world policy was out of the question, neither could the British enter immediately into a one-world system based on full convertibility and multilateralism. Although multilateralism was the ultimate goal, the British economy was weak and exposing it to the full fury of an unregulated market would also bring higher unemployment, drastic cuts in social expenditures, and other short-term dislocations. This was Cripps's dreary appreciation. It made the second alternative no more appealing than the first to a government that was committed by ideology and platform to economic planning and the welfare state.

If Britain could not close the dollar gap by entering immediately into a multilateral system or by lowering a sterling curtain around the Empire, then the only alternative was what Cripps called a "constructive compromise" with the United States. By this he meant a policy that reconciled America's commitment to multilateralism and private-enterprise capitalism with Labour's adherence to Commonwealth solidarity and "Party policies." Cripps was not looking down a one-way street; the British would make their own contribution in exchange for an American bailout. They would hold the line on government expenditures, improve productivity, and re-direct exports to the dollar area. They would even consider some measure of convertibility with the dollar, but only as part of a comprehensive set-tlement to which the American contribution would be substantial. Over the long term, the Americans would have to iron out the business cycle and sustain a high level of demand for imports. They would have to lower tariffs, continue aid programs, stimulate private investment in the sterling area, and help the British replenish their reserves and reduce the sterling balances in London. In addition, Cripps envisioned an American potpourri of short-term measures to relieve the pressure on pound sterling. These measures included intensification of the American stockpiling program and other steps to increase dollar purchases in the sterling area; flexible administration of American customs procedures; waiver of Article 9 of the Anglo–American loan agreement; support for World Bank and IMF loans to India and other sterling-area countries; international commodity agreements to prop up the price of sterling-area exports; and revision of the Foreign Assistance Act to facilitate Britain's off-shore purchase of Canadian wheat and to permit British rather than American vessels to carry a higher percentage of ERP goods to Europe.

This was a tall order, but Cripps was sanguine about the prospects of American support, if only because the alternatives were so bleak. If the British were forced into autarky, the American economy would suffer and it would be difficult for the Allies to maintain a united front against the Soviet Union. These dangers were inducements to American action, as was the apparent movement of American economic doctrine in a direction al-ready charted by the Labour Party. Since the inception of the New Deal, according to Cripps, the United States had "advanced steadily towards the welfare State, gone a considerable way in the redistribution of wealth, put into force stabilisation policies on prices and at times on quantity for all the major agricultural industries, and developed Social Services." Truman's re-election had "reaffirmed the preference of the American people for the social and economic policies of the New Deal." The next step was to extend these policies to the international economy. Indeed, Cripps envisioned a New Deal for the Western world, to be achieved by internationalizing the American market, stabilizing commodity prices, and redistributing American wealth on a global scale. Policies like these would remodel the New Deal in the image of British socialism. But Cripps might argue that the Marshall Plan pointed in this direction anyway, what with its transfer of American wealth to Western Europe and its commitment to a stabilization strategy that blended free-market maxims with economic planning and coordination.[1]

Others could be forgiven if they did not share the chancellor's optimism, as became clear when the Economic Policy Committee reviewed his paper on July 7. Everyone conceded that the New Deal had transformed the United States into a mixed economy. But the American synthesis still gave far greater weight than British socialism to the "automatic" regulators of the market. Even Cripps admitted this much, while others wondered if a "constructive compromise" could bridge the gap between the systems. They were especially suspicious of currency convertibility and other free-trade strategies, which, if adopted, would make it difficult to shield the British economy from the vagaries of an unregulated market and swings in the American business cycle. Because of these concerns, the Economic Policy Committee wanted the chancellor's paper to serve as a "guide" only when the British negotiators met with Secretary Snyder and his American and Canadian associates. Following Cripps's advice, the negotiators were to introduce devaluation and convertibility at the last stages of the talks and make no commitments without prior American concessions.[2]

These instructions underscored the difference between the British approach to the dollar gap and the approaches favored by the United States and Western Europe. The National Advisory Council (NAC) action of late June and other pronouncements had called for adjustments to the British, not the American, economy and had made devaluation the sine qua non of further progress toward European integration and equilibrium between the dollar and nondollar worlds. Snyder discovered similar differences between the British and their OEEC associates when he toured the Continent on the eve of the financial talks in London. He found the Belgians, French, and Italians greatly exercised over the existing snarl of trade and payments restrictions. They were ready, Snyder thought, to reduce restrictions and adjust exchange rates, seeing these as steps toward an economic integration that would raise productivity and close the dollar gap. There was even talk of a "nuclear" approach that would begin with the elimination of exchange and trade controls between France, Italy, and the Benelux countries. But the nuclear approach would mean breaking the crossrates that supported the dollar value of sterling on continental exchanges, something the French would do only with American support and only if the British refused to

[1] EPC (49) 73, Cripps, "The Dollar Situation: Forthcoming Discussion with U.S.A. and Canada," July 4, 1949, PREM 8/1412 pt. II.

[2] EPC (49) 27th Meeting, July 7, 1949, PREM 8/1412 pt. II.

devalue. Devaluation of the pound, the French told Snyder, was the key to trade and monetary integration in a larger area and thus to European viability with the Western Hemisphere.[3]

Yet the British would not take the initiative in this direction without some indication that officials in Washington would follow policies at home and abroad that were consistent with Britain's commitment to the welfare state and America's position as an international creditor. This is what Snyder learned when he arrived in London on July 8 for talks with Bevin, Cripps, and a group of Canadian financial officials. Snyder and his colleagues, Ambassadors Lewis Douglas and Averell Harriman, wanted to avoid any hint of dictating to the British. Resorting to threats could embarrass the Labour government and enable British leaders to blame the United States for their problems. But the Americans also wanted an explanation of the current crisis, stressing in their own analysis how the high cost and low productivity of British industry and the diversion of resources to social programs had hampered Britain's efforts to move toward the goal of full convertibility.[4] The British were not disposed to define the crisis in the same terms or to accept the solutions implied in the American brief. They readily admitted that Britain's cost and price structure was too high, but only in selected industries, and they would consider devaluation and other remedial action only as parts of an overall solution to which the United States made the greatest contribution. Indeed, Bevin, Cripps, and the other British negotiators resolutely refused to be put on the defensive. Although multilateralism was their goal, they also cited the New Deal's commitment to "full employment" and asked the Americans to reconcile the two objectives. Deflation, devaluation, and cuts in social expenditures, they said, would work against this commitment. Nor would they address the roots of the

[3] Unsigned, "Summary of Conversation on July 5 between Mr. John Snyder, Mr. McChesney Martin, and Mr. Maurice Petsche," July 5, 1949, Bruce tel. to Acheson, July 6, 1949, and "Files of Official Conversations of Secretary Snyder during His Visit to Paris in July 1949," attached to Tomlinson memorandum to Harriman, August 4, 1949, Harriman Papers, folder: Snyder Trip, July 1949; unsigned Memorandum of Conversation with French financial officials, July 21, 1949, Tomlinson letter to George H. Willis, Director, Office of International Finance, Treasury Department, July 30, 1949, enclosing "Summary of Conversations Held on July 6 and 7 between French and American Experts," Treasury Records, Acc. 68A2809, box 27, folder: EUR/o/71 – Secretary Snyder's European Trip, 1949. See also the report on Snyder's European trip in the Snyder Papers, box 32, folder: Trip File – Europe, July 2–24, memoranda.

[4] On the background of the British talks and American strategy, see Bruce tel. to Acheson, July 6, 1949, Harriman Papers, folder: Snyder Trip, July 1949; Bruce tel. to Acheson, July 7, 1949, Acheson tel. to Douglas, July 7, 1949, and Douglas tels. (2) to Acheson, July 8, 1949, RG 59, file: 841.5151/7-649; and L. D. B. [Lucius D. Battle], Acheson's private secretary, memorandum of telephone conversation between Hoffman and Acheson, July 7, 1949, Acheson Papers, box 64, folder: Memoranda of Conversations. See also the documents in notes 5 and 6 for an elaboration of the American arguments.

sterling crisis, which the British referred to as a dollar crisis brought on by the worldwide shortage of American currency and aggravated by the recent American recession.

This line of analysis enabled the British to stress what they saw as the unfair terms of trade between the dollar and nondollar worlds. It highlighted the impact on European trade of high American tariffs and swings in the American business cycle, and it had the advantage of placing the burden of corrective action on American shoulders. Bevin and Cripps ticked off the list of American "first aid measures" noted in Cripps's paper of July 4 and then made it clear that long-term equilibrium required even more sweeping adjustments by the United States. In addition to lowering tariffs and continuing aid programs, the American government had to stimulate private investment abroad, sustain a high demand for imports, and negotiate international commodity agreements to stabilize the price of raw materials exported from the sterling area. The only alternative, Bevin warned, entailed autarkic policies that would insulate the British economy from American recessions and unfair competition – even at the cost of dividing the world into separate ruble, dollar, and sterling blocs.[5]

Bevin intended his warning as a bargaining ploy, not as a prophecy of British policy. The British did not consider a third-currency bloc to be a viable alternative, and it had been ruled out in Cripps's paper of July 4. Their goal was a one-world system. But their strategy was to win American concessions before announcing their own, and the concessions they had in mind made Secretary Snyder very nervous. Snyder's reports to Washington sounded an alarm. The British, he warned, wanted to adjust the dollar world to their pattern of internal planning. Through guaranteed access to the American market and government intervention to bolster prices, they sought to "insure stability on a *status quo* basis" and prevent "the kind of flexibility required to shake out high costs and restrictive elements." The British claimed to be "striving toward multilateral non-discriminatory trade and convertibility," he reported. In reality, however, these objectives were "subservient" to "maintaining stability and thus protecting rigidities" in

---

[5] Undated "Record of Discussions Held by United Kingdom Ministers with Mr. Snyder and Mr. Abbott on 8th, 9th, and 10th July, 1949," T232/90/EEC31/06B; Makins minutes, July 8, 9 (with attached note by Makins of same date), and 11, 1949, FO 371, 75580, UE4291, UE4292, UE4328, and UE4377. For American reports, see Douglas tels. to Acheson, July 4, 7, and 8, 1949, RG 59, file: 841.5151/9-149; Snyder tels. to Acheson, July 9 and 10, 1949, *FRUS, 1949*, 4:799–801, 801–2; unsigned Treasury report, "Tripartite Financial Discussions with the United Kingdom and Canada," August 22, 1949, Treasury Records, Acc. 68A2809, box 27, folder: EUR/o/71 – Secretary Snyder's European Trip, 1949; Snyder's undated memorandum to President Truman, "Summary and Conclusions of the European Trip," Snyder Papers, box 33, folder: Trip File – Europe, July 2–24, memoranda from Foley; and the report on Snyder's trip in the Snyder Papers, box 32, folder: Trip File – Europe, July 2–24, memoranda.

"the sterling area as a whole." After three days of discussion, Snyder, Cripps, and Bevin could get no farther than an agreement to continue the trilateral talks in Washington the following September. The Americans were thoroughly discouraged, and none more so than Snyder, who was appalled by the Labour government's drift toward "international state planning." Snyder wore his faith in free enterprise like a chastity belt. He would not be seduced by appeals to the New Deal and "got out of the country as fast as possible."[6]

The collapse of the London talks raised new fears that British autarky would ruin the chances for economic recovery and integration in Western Europe and for a fully multilateral system of world trade. These fears multiplied in late July, when the British handed the OEEC a supplemental request for aid based on their revised dollar deficit for 1949–50. The OEEC was just beginning the arduous task of dividing American aid for the next program year, and allocations were to be based (as in the past) on each country's deficit with the Western Hemisphere. The British now anticipated a deficit of $1.585 billion, a sum nearly $500 million greater than the estimate they had submitted several weeks earlier. If accepted, the new request would entitle them to roughly 40 percent of the American aid projected for 1949–50 and mean substantial reductions in the shares allocated to other countries. The news came as a "great shock to the other delegations" in Paris, who left immediately to consult their governments. As even the Foreign Office admitted, it was hard to escape the conclusion that Britain was solving its dollar problem by "putting the squeeze on Europe."[7]

The British submission threw the OEEC into turmoil. Most of the delegates thought that time did not allow for detailed screening of Britain's requirements and that such an approach would not address the sources of the sterling crisis anyway. At the ECA's insistence, they nevertheless resumed the division-of-aid exercise, only to produce a recommendation that all but one of the participating countries rejected. This development forced the

[6] Snyder tels. to Acheson, July 9 and 10, 1949, *FRUS, 1949*, 4:799–801, 801–2; and Acheson, *Present at the Creation*, 322.

[7] Hall-Patch tel. to FO, July 24, 1949; and Berthoud minute to Bevin, July 15, 1949, FO 371, 78015, UR7772. See also Treasury memorandum to Cripps, July 15, 1949, FO 371, 78015, UR7568; Katz repto 5378 to Hoffman, July 26, 1949, ECA Records, box 7; Hugh Millard, U.S. Charge at Brussels, tel. to Acheson, July 29, 1949, RG 59, file: 840.50Recovery/7-2949; Philip W. Bonsal, Political Advisor to Harriman, repto circular 266 to Hoffman, August 1, 1949, ECA Files, box 8; Hoffman ecato 1236 to ECA, London, August 5, 1949, ECA Files, box 42; and Katz reptos 5434 and 5468 to Hoffman, July 28 and 29, 1949, and Hoffman torep 6935 to Harriman, August 5, 1949, *FRUS, 1949*, 4:408–9, 409–11, 415–18. An undated copy of the British supplemental request is enclosed in Brad Patterson, Secretary to the Working Group, memorandum to the Working Group on Britain, August 22, 1949, Department of State Records, Record Group 43, Records of International Conferences, Commissions, and Expositions, box 1, folder: D–2 Series, WGB (hereafter cited as RG 43, with box and folder designation).

Council to refer the matter to a special committee consisting of the secretary general, Robert Marjolin, and the head of the Belgian delegation, Baron Snoy. The Snoy–Marjolin report reduced Britain's allocation to $962 million, a sum the Labour government accepted, and on this basis the Council and the ECA were able to complete the division of aid for 1949–50.[8] Nevertheless, the entire exercise had revealed again how difficult it was to reconcile national ambitions with European needs. It left all sides feeling that current formulas had failed to solve the dollar gap and accelerated the search for new solutions that had begun with Snyder's European tour in early July.

One solution would change the basis on which American aid was allocated. Dividing aid according to anticipated deficits with the Western Hemisphere had led participating countries to exaggerate their needs in order to increase their shares of American support. It had done nothing to encourage them to narrow the dollar gap; narrowing the gap would reduce their slice of the ERP pie. These were the conclusions reached in Paris, where the OEEC followed a British lead and decided to fix permanently the division of aid on the basis of national allocations for 1949–50. This decision ended the annual division-of-aid exercise and removed the incentive for participating countries to increase their dollar deficits. The ECA accepted the decision, but took it two steps further. It set a larger portion of its aid aside for special projects, thereby reducing the amount available for national allocations, and then began gearing these allocations to each country's performance in closing the dollar gap and achieving the other goals of the ERP.[9]

Beyond these adjustments, Marjolin and his allies in the Secretariat were urging a sweeping study of the dollar gap with a view to a major reorientation of the ERP. Their thinking stressed the significance of the American recession and the need for solutions that would place the burden of equilibrium on the United States. Noting that inflation had been contained and production restored in most of the participating countries, they claimed that Western Europe had put its own house in order and that viability now depended on a "high and stable level of [economic] activity in the United States, with national income steadily increasing and trade barriers being gradually reduced."[10] This kind of thinking was one incentive to a com-

---

[8] Milward, *Reconstruction of Western Europe*, 205–6; Price, *Marshall Plan and Its Meaning*, 128; and Van Der Beugel, *From Marshall Aid to Atlantic Partnership*, 163–4.

[9] Milward, *Reconstruction of Western Europe*, 206–7; Price, *Marshall Plan and Its Meaning*, 114–15; and Van Der Beugel, *From Marshall Aid to Atlantic Partnership*, 164. See also Berthoud minute to Strang, October 11, 1949, with attached undated paper, "Future of ERP" [by R. W. B. Clarke of the Treasury], FO 371, 78133, UR10311.

[10] See the memorandum by the staff of the Secretariat, "The Next Steps" [July 5, 1949], T232/116/EEC17/19/04. See also Eric Roll of the British delegation to the OEEC, "Record of Conversation," July 12, 1949, T232/90/EEC31/06B. Given the thrust of the Secretariat's proposed study, it should not be surprising to learn that it apparently

prehensive review of the Marshall Plan, the other being the American–British–Canadian financial talks scheduled to resume in September. As Hall-Patch told Harriman on July 18, the trilateral talks raised concern in Paris that Europe was being left out in the cold. The other delegations wanted to launch their own study of the dollar famine, incorporate the results in a revised long-term program, and then "rush off to Washington to put the 'European case.' " Their attitude, he reported, "was that if the U.K. proposed to have talks in Washington in September, then why not everybody else?"[11]

Although British policymakers also believed that "U.S. internal policy" had to be "talked about," it should come as no surprise to learn that they did their best to sidetrack the Secretariat's initiative. They did not want an "over-enthusiastic eruption" in Paris at a time when they were "going for [their own] deal with the U.S.A." It would be best if the OEEC were "to disappear," explained R. W. B. Clarke of the Treasury. "The 'one world' deal has to be a U.S.–U.K. deal," and now that "we are beginning to get back to proper lines of discussion with the Americans, Paris is really redundant." The OEEC could not be deterred, however, and the British were forced to revise their tactics. Their goals now were to keep the Europeans "off the grass" until the trilateral talks were over and to direct the OEEC's work into lines that reinforced the British case in Washington. "The correct order of discussion" should be, as Hall-Patch told Harriman, "the Anglo–American–Canadian talks first, then European–American talks" in which the British also would take the lead. The first round of talks would resolve the "acute sterling–dollar difficulties," for which the OEEC had "no responsibility," and enable the British to play their "full part" in the larger discussions. Operating from his position as chairman of the Executive Committee, Hall-Patch had no trouble steering the OEEC in the preferred direction. Marjolin was assigned the task of preparing a report that would not be due until mid-October, one month after the trilateral talks in Washington. When the energetic secretary finished a draft at the end of July, in time, he thought, for a final report by September, Hall-Patch said no and held to the original schedule. He did so even though the draft focused on the structural sources of disequilibrium and the American responsibility for correcting them, a focus that proved to at least some British leaders that the OEEC could "act in a helpful way" at the appropriate time.[12]

was suggested by the British members of Marjolin's staff, who appear to have acted without the approval of the British government.

11 Hall-Patch, "Note on an Interview with Mr. Harriman," July 18, 1949, Records of the British Treasury, Economic Advisory Section, Record Class T230/153/EAS27/86/01A(#10) (hereafter cited as T230, with appropriate filing designation).

12 Clarke memorandum to Leslie Rowan, July 13, 1949, T232/116/EEC17/19/04; Roll, "Record of Conversation," July 12, 1949, T232/90/EEC31/06B; undated memorandum enclosed in Rowan letter to Hall-Patch, August 3, 1949, T232/111/EEC17/012; Hall-Patch, "Note of an Interview with Mr. Harriman," July 18, 1949, T230/153/

With the Secretariat's report put off until October, the search for solutions to the dollar gap shifted from Paris to London and Washington. Policy-makers in both capitals were hard at work on the problem, which remained essentially a problem of reconciling Britain's commitments to the Commonwealth and the welfare state with America's plans for European integration and multilateralism. Snyder's visit to London in July had yielded no hope of a reconciliation. In the weeks that followed, however, the serious economic and political implications of continued stalemate had induced officials on both sides to lay the groundwork for a compromise that would come when the financial talks resumed in Washington.

III

In London, as we have seen, the Cabinet had ordered a 25 percent cut in dollar imports and the Commonwealth countries had done the same. Deflation had been ruled out and the Americans were told of this. Nor was there much support for devaluation of pound sterling. Although Cripps had held out this prospect in talks with Snyder, neither he nor others saw devaluation as more than a bargaining lever, a "card to hold and not to play" except as part of a comprehensive settlement to which the Americans would make the first and largest contribution. The nature of this settlement would be the subject of trilateral talks in September. Cripps would join Bevin to lead the British delegation, and the question in midsummer was whether they, or Britain's reserves, could last that long. Both men had been taxed to the limit. Bevin was worn out and suffering frequent attacks of angina. Cripps was no better. Unable to eat or sleep comfortably, his resources drained by the long battle to save sterling and by the exhaustion of palatable remedies, he left London for five weeks of rest in a Swiss clinic.[13]

There were no signs in the chancellor's absence that the initial program of import cuts was doing much to stabilize sterling. Reserves continued to fall at a rate that would drain the Bank of England in less than a year.[14] The Cabinet decided to approach the Americans on a preliminary basis, partly to prepare the ground for the Washington talks but also to seek short-term support for the flagging pound. Sir Oliver Franks, the British ambassador in Washington, mounted an offensive on issues ranging from the

EAS27/86/01A(#10); and Rowan minute to Sir Edward Bridges, July 27, 1949, T232/116/EEC17/19/04. See also Berthoud minute to Bevin, July 15, 1949, and Treasury memorandum to Cripps, July 15, 1949, FO 371, 78015, UR7568; UK del., "Note of a Discussion on July 18, 1949," July 20, 1949, T230/153/EAS27/86/01A(#6); and Roll, "Record of Conversation," July 21, 1949, T232/91/EEC31/06C.

13   Sir Norman Brook, Cabinet Permanent Secretary, "Summary of Main Points Covered in Ministerial Discussions since 12th July, 1949," August 17, 1949, PREM 8/1178 pt. I; Bullock, *Bevin*, 727; and Colin Cooke, *The Life of Richard Stafford Cripps* (London, 1957), 389.

14   CP (49) 158, Attlee, "The Dollar Situation," July 21, 1949, PREM 8/1178 pt. I.

strategic stockpiling of sterling-area raw materials to India's application for loans from the World Bank and the IMF. British policymakers in Paris asked their American counterparts about the off-shore procurement of Canadian wheat and the same issue would be put to Hoffman and other American officials when they arrived in Europe at the end of the summer. None of these initiatives would succeed, however. The Americans were unwilling to discuss issues on a piecemeal basis or to support a currency that was overvalued.[15]

In early August, these setbacks combined with others to change the Labour government's approach to the sterling crisis and the upcoming talks in Washington. By that time, it seemed as though the government was being undone by its own success. National production had jumped 6 percent over the previous year and had far outstripped prewar levels. Productivity was increasing at an annual rate of 4.5 percent, capital investment was high, and unemployment had virtually disappeared. But good news was the handmaiden of bad fortune. The full utilization of resources generated inflationary pressures. Prices, which climbed a modest 3 percent in the previous twelve months, jumped 2 percent in May 1949. Wages were up 3 percent and trade unions were campaigning for another round of hikes. Adding fuel to the fire were the enormous expenditures at all levels of government. The taxes to support these expenditures absorbed about 39 percent of national income, and were a disincentive to workers and investors alike. Data like these filled the arsenal of criticism on which Lewis Douglas and other Americans drew when explaining the sterling crisis to their British clients. But the data in this case came from Lord President of the Council Herbert Morrison, who also urged the Cabinet in late July to hold the line on government expenditures and devise new programs to redirect exports to the dollar area.[16]

Morrison's proclamation broke the dam. It led directly to a Cabinet review of public expenditures and then to an important directive from 10 Downing Street. The directive mandated a 5-percent reduction in the rate of public spending and a full-scale study of the government's investment program.[17]

---

[15] UK del., "Note of a Discussion on July 18th," July 20, 1949, T230/153/EAS27/86/01A(#6); CM (49) 51st Conclusion, July 29, 1949, CAB 128/16; and Brook, "Summary of Main Points Covered in Ministerial Discussion since 12th July 1949," August 17, 1949, PREM 8/1178 pt. I.

[16] CP (49) 159, Morrison memorandum, "The Economic Situation," July 21, 1949, PREM 8/1178 pt. I. See also CM (49) 50th Conclusion, July 28, 1949, CAB 128/16; and Robert L. Hall, Director, Economic Section, Cabinet Office, minute to Brook and Attlee, July 22, 1949, and CM (49) 48th Conclusion, July 25, 1949, PREM 8/1178 pt. I. For an example of Douglas's views, see Hector McNeil, Minister of State, Record of Conversation [with Douglas], August 11, 1949, T232/91/EEC31/06C.

[17] CM (49) 51st Conclusion, July 29, 1949, CAB 128/16; and Brook, "Summary of Main Points Covered in Ministerial Discussions since 12th July, 1949," August 17, 1949, PREM 8/1178 pt. I.

Officials in the Treasury who were wedded to "liberal" economic doctrine also seized on the currency crisis to urge devaluation as the first step in a larger program that would cut social expenditures, dismantle economic controls, and bring Great Britain into a multilateral system of world trade. With Cripps still recuperating in Switzerland, top policymakers were in no position to act on this recommendation. But in their case, too, the deteriorating economic situation and the lack of American support had led most to the conclusion that devaluation was a "necessary step." Attlee conveyed the news to the ailing chancellor in a letter of August 5, telling him that devaluation would prevent the depletion of reserves and preserve the government's freedom to maneuver. Only the timing of an announcement remained for debate, and this issue was settled in a grueling meeting of ministers at Chequers on August 19. Cripps was the last holdout. He had returned to London for the meeting a week earlier than planned and it took three hours for Attlee and the others to persuade him. The announcement was set provisionally for September 18.[18]

In addition to safeguarding reserves and harnessing inflation, these measures aimed to improve Britain's position in the trilateral negotiations. Acheson had warned the British against coming to Washington hat-in-hand with no program of their own. Ambassador Franks and others had taken this warning to heart and had persuaded the Cabinet that measures of self-help would greatly improve the prospects of American assistance. This advice applied with particular force to devaluation. As Attlee explained to Cripps in his letter of August 5, "we should not gain, but lose, with the Americans if we appear to be trading an offer of devaluation for concessions on their part." All of Attlee's advisors agreed that this strategy, of which Cripps had been the architect, must now be abandoned. It was preferable to act under "our own volition and not under American pressure," the prime minister concluded, and more likely that such a course would bring reciprocal concessions from the United States.[19]

This conclusion was to guide Bevin and Cripps when the trilateral talks resumed in Washington. According to a brief prepared in the Treasury, they

---

[18] Attlee letter to Cripps, August 5, 1949, PREM 8/1178 pt. I. See also "Note on a Meeting of Ministers Held at Chequers," August 19, 1949, CAB 128/21, and the last source cited in note 17. Cripps had become more enthusiastic by the time devaluation was discussed and approved by the whole Cabinet. See CM (49) 53rd Conclusion, August 29, 1949, CAB 128/16. For the evolution of British policy on devaluation and the disputes inside the Labour government, see Philip M. Williams, ed., *The Diary of Hugh Gaitskell, 1945–1956* (London, 1983), 126–33 (hereafter cited as *Gaitskell Diary*); and Williams, *Hugh Gaitskell: A Political Biography* (London, 1979), 197–203.

[19] Attlee letter to Cripps, August 5, 1949, PREM 8/1178 pt. I. See also Franks tel. to FO, August 11, 1949, FO 800/516/US/49/42; and Hall minute to Brook and Attlee, July 22, 1949, and Brook, "Summary of Main Points Covered in Ministerial Discussions since 12th July 1949," PREM 8/1178 pt. I.

were to seek Anglo–American agreement to a program that would bring the dollar and nondollar (sterling) areas into balance. The negotiators were to deny that social expenditures had contributed to the sterling crisis or that inflationary pressures were driving the Labour government to shelter sterling within a high-cost, soft-currency trading bloc. They were to emphasize instead the government's commitment to a one-world system and the contribution it was making to the attainment of that goal, including the new measures to curb inflation, increase productivity, and redirect exports. The brief did not mention the decision to devalue. But this decision was part of the British contribution too, and the Americans would be so informed at the outset of the talks. At the same time, the brief went on to spell out what the Americans might do to promote equilibrium. Aside from maintaining a stable demand for imports, the Americans were to consider the whole range of short- and long-term measures that Cripps had enumerated in his earlier discussions with Snyder. The hope was for immediate, short-term assistance that would buy time for a continuing Anglo–American organization to hammer out a permanent solution to the dollar gap.[20]

Although the Treasury's brief focused on the economic dimensions of the sterling crisis, British policymakers were acutely aware that economic questions could not be divorced from the larger strategic and political context. This context had been elaborated in the paper produced by the Permanent Under Secretary's Committee, "A Third World Power or Western Consolidation?" The paper's conclusions were then reaffirmed in several meetings of the Cabinet and in a minute of August 26 by Under Secretary of State Roger Makins. In words that called up Bevin's grand design, the under secretary noted Great Britain's position as "the nodal point of three systems, the Commonwealth, Western Europe and the Atlantic Community." This position was the key to its security, leadership in Europe, and status as a world power. Maintaining it, however, depended on the close collaboration and support of the United States. The willingness of policymakers in Washington to hold "exclusive talks" with the British gave hope of such support, suggesting, according to Makins, that American leaders now considered Britain as their "principal partner in world affairs" and thus "as a great deal more than a European power."

Yet Makins did not doubt that the Washington talks marked a "turning point in the world position" of Great Britain. Success would confirm Bevin's grand design; failure would force the British to choose between self-sufficiency and "throwing in [their] lot with Europe." Both alternatives raised the most alarming prospects. The British would be isolated in a European union, unable to assert leadership and outnumbered by conservative governments committed to free-market economies. Nor would they

---

[20] CP (49) 185, Cripps, "The Economic Situation – Washington Talks," August 29, 1949, PREM 8/1178 pt. I. See also CM (49) 53rd Conclusion, August 29, 1949, CAB 128/16.

fare better in a self-contained sterling bloc. The burden of self-sufficiency, especially in the area of defense, would impose "an intolerable strain" on the resources and cohesion of the Commonwealth. The Anglo–Canadian relationship would be disrupted; India and Pakistan would be "cut adrift economically"; and Britain would be forced to turn for resources and markets to the ruble bloc – with all of the "political consequences which would follow from this." Indeed, the "political and strategic" basis of the government's foreign policy would be threatened by a collapse of the Washington talks, which represented Britain's "last chance" to "maintain [its] relationship with America" and thus its position as the balance wheel in a Western consolidation.[21]

If their policy objectives stayed the same, the British had nonetheless discarded Cripps's original negotiating strategy. They had decided instead to take the initiative without waiting for American concessions. Although the pressure on sterling and the desire to safeguard social programs had left them with few alternatives, British leaders had also come to believe that only initiatives on their part would bring American support for the grand design that guided their diplomacy. Nor was this conviction without foundation. American policymakers remained committed to their own design, of course. But they were also more willing than before to make adjustments in light of the dollar gap, to reconcile their goals in Europe with those in other areas of the world, and to achieve these goals by assigning the British a special position.

While the British were formulating strategy in London, policymakers in Washington organized an interdepartmental group to prepare an agenda for the trilateral talks. As part of the preparation, the Central Intelligence Agency reported on the security implications of the sterling crisis. The National Security Council was asked to investigate these implications as well and the Defense Department began looking into the potential ramifications of a retrenchment in Britain's military commitments. Most thought the problem was more than a military one. The Policy Planning Staff concluded that security studies were pointless until more was known about how the British would handle the crisis. The State Department drew up an agenda that concentrated on economic rather than security issues.[22] Yet there was

---

[21] Makins, "Anglo–American–Canadian Talks: General Considerations," August 26, 1949, FO 371, 75594, UE6686. See also Makins minute to Bevin, August 26, 1949, FO 371, 75594, UE6686.

[22] On arrangements for the trilateral talks and policy planning in Washington, see J. Burke Knapp, memorandum to Acheson, July 20, 1949 RG 59, file: 841.51/7-2049; F. R. Hoyer-Millar, British Minister to the United States, letter to Acheson, July 22, 1949, Acheson tel. to Douglas, July 29, 1949, and Acheson letter to Canadian Ambassador Hume Wrong, August 2, 1949, RG 59, file: 841.5151/7-2249; Hoffman torep 6952 and Foster torep 7136 to Harriman, August 8 and 17, 1949, ECA Files, box 49; John H. Ohly, Special Assistant to the Secretary of Defense, memorandum for the Under Secretary of State, September 1, 1949, RG 59, file: 841.51/9-149; PPS

no doubt in Washington that Britain could help to "protect our world position" only if the Labour government avoided an economic collapse at home and retrogressive policies that "seal[ed] off the sterling area from the dollar world."[23]

To avert such calamities, American officials thought the British needed to take a variety of corrective actions. According to policymakers in the State Department, the British had to devalue the pound, fund outstanding sterling balances, and redirect exports. They should also curtail their expensive social programs, which had resulted in a " 'suppressed inflation,' " a "prolonged period of 'over-employment' and a pervasive feather-bedding for all productive elements" in British society. British industry had operated at a high level of production, according to this line of analysis, only because "protected domestic demand" made it unnecessary to cut costs and divert goods to the dollar area. Because of secure employment, food subsidies, and social services, workers had lost the incentive to "exert maximum effort" and initiative elsewhere had been crippled by "stifling levels of taxation." Correcting all of these abuses would be desirable. But at the very least, the Labour government must devalue the pound and corral inflation. These initiatives would enable the British to expand exports and would remove the incentive to protect their position by building a high-cost, soft-currency trading bloc.[24]

Devaluation was the common denominator in American thinking. In a

meetings #132 and #137 of September 2 and 12, 1949, RG 59, PPS Records, box 32, folder: Minutes of Meetings 1949; and William Bray, Office of the Coordinator for Foreign Aid and Assistance, State Department, memorandum to the Coordinator, Henry R. Labouisse, Jr., September 3, 1949, *FRUS, 1949,* 4:830–2.

[23]   Chief, Division of British Commonwealth Affairs, State Department, note to the Assistant Secretary of State for European Affairs, August 9, 1949, *FRUS, 1949,* 4:805–6. See also Nitze memorandum to Webb, August 15, 1949, RG 59, file: 711.41/8-1549; Paper Prepared in the United States Embassy in the United Kingdom, August 18, 1949, *FRUS, 1949,* 4:806–20; PPS/61, "Policy Relating to the Financial Crisis of the United Kingdom and the Sterling Area," August 31, 1949, RG 59, PPS Records, box 3, *Reports and Recommendations, 1949,* Vol. 3; and Kennan, *Memoirs,* 484–8.

[24]   Thorp memorandum to Webb, August 15, 1949, RG 59, file: 841.51/8-1549. See also Nitze memorandum to Webb, August 15, 1949, RG 59, file: 711.41/8-1549; Thorp memorandum to Webb, August 15, 1949, RG 43, box 1, folder: D-2 Series, WGB; unsigned memorandum by the American Embassy, London, "The UK's Domestic Policies and the Sterling Area Crisis," August 24, 1949, RG 59, file: 841.5151/8-2449; "U.K. Government Social and Labor Policies: Impact on External Position," British Commonwealth Working Group, Paper No. 17, August 9, 1949, attached to Patterson memorandum (D-6/15) to the Working Group on Britain, August 12, 1949, RG 43, box 2, folder: D-5 Series, WGB: Trade and Commercial Policy Working Group and Sub-groups; and Steering Committee Paper No. 5, "United States Position on the Level of Productivity in the United Kingdom," August 25, 1949, RG 43, box 311, folder: Tripartite Economic Discussions, Miscellaneous.

paper of August 3, the ECA called for a "maximum" liberalization of trade in the nondollar area and a general restructuring of European exchange rates. The former would create an internal market large enough to increase productivity and enhance "Western Europe's competitive position in the world economy." The latter would "improve the dollar position" of the participating countries and lessen their need to discriminate against American trade, a discrimination that ECA officials could accept only as the temporary by-product of a successful program to integrate economies.[25] Five days later, the NAC reached the same conclusions in a statement that reaffirmed its action of late June.[26] And shortly thereafter, Assistant Secretary of the Treasury Frank Southard took the American case to the IMF. Over British opposition, he initiated a special IMF study of the worsening dollar gap and prepared a draft report that urged an immediate realignment of European currencies. The report won the study committee's approval and was almost certain to have the support of the IMF's Board of Directors when it convened in September.[27] This prospect and the pressure it would put on sterling, as Southard and others must have known, made it virtually impossible for the British to avoid devaluation.

Although American policymakers would put the burden of corrective action on the British, the serious economic and political implications inherent in the sterling crisis also led to the conclusion that measures of self-help must be combined with additional assistance from the United States. Some officials thought the British would "do almost anything we ask them." Others, particularly in the Treasury, were reluctant to take steps that might compromise the principles of multilateralism or relax the pressure for internal reform in Britain. But most urged self-restraint and moderation. They warned that dictating to the British would lead to ideological acrimony. It would be perceived as interference in Britain's internal affairs and as an effort to discredit the Labour government, and it could result in an anti-American backlash during the British elections in 1950. In light of these dangers, the State Department thought it best to adopt a helpful posture that would enable the British to make the necessary adjustments. The United States should combine measures of immediate assistance, such as those

---

[25] Hoffman torep 6847 to Katz, from Bissell, August 3, 1949, *FRUS, 1949,* 4:412–15.

[26] NAC documents #866 and #867 of August 11 and 24, 1949, in RG 43, box 311, folder: Tripartite Economic Discussions, Miscellaneous. See also the undated NAC paper in *FRUS, 1949,* 4:419–21.

[27] This part of the story can be followed in Southard's memoranda to Snyder and Assistant Secretary of the Treasury Martin, September 5, 8, and 12, 1949, Snyder Papers, box 20, Alphabetical File, folder: International Monetary Fund. As these documents point out, Snyder subsequently agreed to delay action by the IMF's Board of Directors until mid-September. It seems likely that he did so, however, only after British officials in Washington for the financial talks had informed him of their decision to devalue.

proposed by Cripps, with a long-term plan that might include some form of economic union with Great Britain and Canada.[28]

Opinion in the ECA ran along similar lines. Keynesians in that agency had been thinking about an "incentive" fund to ease the "internal strain" that would accompany currency devaluation and trade liberalization.[29] They established a $150-million reserve for this purpose in late August, marking the first time that ERP aid would go, solely on the basis of merit, to countries that were making the sacrifices necessary to lower costs, optimize output, and integrate economies.[30] In addition, both the ECA and the State Department began to reformulate current programs in order to deal with the sterling crisis. Codified in a "Work Program for Western European Economic Integration," this reformulation would lead in the fall to a general assault on the dollar gap.[31]

One line of attack would steer a higher percentage of counterpart funds into "critical sectors" where industries were geared to the dollar market and enjoyed a "comparative advantage" without government subsidies, protective tariffs, or restrictive arrangements. This approach would "minimize the use of counterpart funds for purely financial purposes" and "maximize their use for investment purposes."[32] Although conservative officials in the

[28]   Joseph C. Satterthwaite, Director, Office of Near Eastern and African Affairs, memorandum to Perkins, August 9, 1949, and Paper Prepared in the United States Embassy in the United Kingdom, August 18, 1949, *FRUS, 1949*, 4:805–6, 806–20; Douglas letter to Acheson, August 15, 1949, Acheson Papers, box 64, folder: Memoranda of Conversations; Memorandum for the File, Under Secretary's Meeting of August 17, 1949, RG 59, file: 841.5151/8-1749; Nitze, "Measures Required to Achieve Long-Term Objectives," attached to Carlisle H. Humelsine memorandum to the members of the Under Secretary's meeting, August 19, 1949, RG 59, file: 841.5151/8-1949; and PPS/61 of August 31, 1949, RG 59, PPS Records, box 3, *Reports and Recommendations, 1949*, Vol. 3.

[29]   Hoffman torep 4395 to Harriman, April 7, 1949, ECA Files, box 47; and Hoffman torep 5258 to Harriman, May 17, 1949, ECA Files, box 48.

[30]   Harriman repto 5953 to Hoffman, August 25, 1949, ECA Files, box 7; Katz repto circular 302 to ECA, Washington, August 31, 1949, ECA Files, box 8; George B. Bingham, ECA Mission Chief, Paris, toeca 1188 to Hoffman, September 2, 1949, RG 286, Acc. 53A177, box 87, folder: Eyes Only, Personal Correspondence, Sept.– Oct. 1949; Hoffman ecato 840 to OSR, Paris, September 3, 1949, RG 286, Acc. 53A177, box 96, folder: Reserve; Foster torep 7731 to Harriman, September 13, 1949, ECA Files, box 49; and Harriman repto 6844 to Hoffman, October 12, 1949, ECA Files, box 8.

[31]   Harriman repto circular 382 to ECA Missions in Europe, November 10, 1949, *FRUS, 1949*, 4:445–7; "Confidential Rough Draft: Outline of Work Program on Western European Economic Integration," attached to Nitze memorandum to Webb, November 16, 1949, RG 59, PPS Records, box 27, folder: Europe 1949; Katz letter to Foster, November 23, 1949, RG 286, Acc. 53A405, box 1, folder: Special Representative's Office, 1949; and Acheson tel. to American Embassy, Paris, December 6, 1949, RG 59, file: 840.50Recovery/12-649.

[32]   Harriman repto circular 351 to Hoffman, October 11, 1949, Harriman repto 6870 to Hoffman, October 14, 1949, Harriman repto circular 404 to Hoffman, November

Treasury thought the plan would unleash inflationary pressures, Keynesians in the ECA said these pressures could be restrained by appropriate tax policies and by using budget surpluses to retire debts. These policies would make it possible to channel counterpart funds into critical sectors across the ERP area, resulting in an integrated European economy in which freer trade and greater specialization worked to raise productivity and close the dollar gap.[33]

Another line of action envisioned dollar-earning and dollar-saving investment projects in the dependent overseas territories of the participating countries.[34] Designed to supplement the Point Four program, projects of this sort would help to close Western Europe's dollar deficit and lay the economic foundation for political stability in strategically important areas of the underdeveloped world. The ECA set aside counterpart funds as well as $20 million from its reserve fund to finance these projects. In addition, Paul Hoffman and other ECA officials extended the system of corporative collaboration and used it to stimulate private investment in the underdeveloped regions. They created a private Advisory Committee on Overseas Territories, chaired by Dr. Isaiah Bowman, along with a subsidiary investment panel headed by former under secretary of state William L. Clayton and E. G. Callado of the Standard Oil Company of New Jersey.[35] They also

29, 1949, Harriman repto 8048 to Hoffman, December 20, 1949, and Bonsal, Paris, repto 8195 to Hoffman, December 28, 1949, ECA Files, box 8; Hoffman torep 8476 to Harriman, October 12, 1949, Foster torep 8489 to Harriman, October 12, 1949, and Hoffman torep 9244 to Harriman, November 10, 1949, ECA Files, box 50; and Harriman repto D-31 to Hoffman, December 2, 1949, RG 286, Acc. 53A405, box 50, folder: Finance – Investments.

33   For thinking in the ECA, see in addition to the sources cited in note 32, Foster torep 8489 to Harriman, October 12, 1949, and Hoffman torep 9244 to Harriman, November 10, 1949, RG 286, Acc. 53A405, box 50, folder: Finance – Investments. For thinking in the Treasury Department, see the unsigned, undated memorandum "ECA Local Currency Counterpart: NAC Policy and Procedure," Treasury Records, Acc. 66A1039, box 4, folder: Marshall Plan – Local Currency Counterpart, General. The principal author of this memorandum was Victor Abramson of the Treasury's Office of International Finance. For the views of Abramson, Hebbard, and other Treasury officials on the ECA's new counterpart and investment policy, see Hebbard memorandum to W. John Keeney, ECA Mission Chief, London, October 17, 1949, Abramson letter to James E. Wood, Treasury representative in Brussels, October 26, 1949, Abramson letter to Andrew Kamarck, Treasury representative in Rome, October 28, 1949, Kamarck letter to Abramson, November 8, 1949, Wood letter to Abramson, November 10, 1949, William M. Tomlinson, Treasury representative in Paris, letter to Abramson, November 15, 1949, and Charles R. Hurley, assistant Treasury representative in London, letter to Abramson, December 8, 1949, Treasury Records, Acc. 66A1039, box 4, bolder: Marshall Plan – Local Currency Counterpart, General.

34   Hoffman torep 6500 to Harriman, July 19, 1949, ECA Files, box 48.

35   Foster torep 8489 to Harriman, October 12, 1949, ECA Files, box 50; Hamlin Robinson, State Department Investment and Economic Development Staff, memorandum to Labouisse, November 22, 1949, RG 59, file: 840.50Recovery/11-2249; Harriman repto 7759 to Hoffman, December 6, 1949, ECA Files, box 8; and Record

worked with the President's Advisory Committee on Financing Foreign Trade, led by Winthrop Aldrich of the Chase National Bank, to establish three investment groups that would cooperate with similar European groups to identify development projects for American investors.[36]

The same sort of cooperation and public–private power sharing marked other parts of the ECA's campaign to narrow the dollar gap. President Truman and Paul Hoffman joined with Clarence Frances of the General Foods Corporation to organize a dollar board that would collaborate with similar boards in Britain and France. Their job was to increase European sales in the Western Hemisphere, beginning with a market analysis financed out of the ECA's technical assistance funds.[37] At the same time, the ECA (and the OEEC) formed new ties to the International Federation of Agricultural Producers and to farm organizations in the participating countries, seeking through them to encourage European farmers to adopt American production techniques, integrate economies, and redirect exports to the dollar area.[38]

Similar goals informed the ECA's ongoing effort to establish labor advisory committees (France being the latest to take this step) and production councils composed of government, labor, and management representatives.[39] The councils were to be modeled on the Anglo–American Council

of Action, Investment Panel – Advisory Committee on Overseas Territories, October 25, 1949, and Record of Action, Advisory Committee on Overseas Territories, November 7, 1949, RG 286, Acc. 53A405, box 33, folder: Outside Orgs. – AC Overseas Territories.

[36] For this part of the story, including some of the recommendations coming from the groups involved, see Record of Action, Investment Panel – Advisory Committee on Overseas Territories, October 25, 1949, RG 286, Acc. 53A405, box 33, folder: Outside Orgs. – AC Overseas Territories; Minutes of Joint Meeting of NAC and Committee for Financing Foreign Trade, June 7, 1949, Minutes of Meeting of Committee for Financing Foreign Trade, June 7, 1949, Record of Action, Investment Panel – Advisory Committee on Overseas Territories, July 27, 1949, Harland Cleveland memorandum to Bissell, November 30, 1949, and Cleveland memorandum to Hoffman, December 8, 1949, RG 286, Acc. 53A405, box 50, folder: Finance – Investments (Aldrich Committee); Cleveland memorandum to Foster and Bissell, November 10, 1949, John D. Sumner Papers (Truman Library), box 8, folder: Economic Cooperation Adm., General ERP and Marshall Plan; Aldrich, "Report on the Establishment of the Committees of Banking Institutions in France and Belgium to Facilitate the Implementation of the Point IV Program," attached to Cleveland memorandum to Foster, November 22, 1949, Cleveland letter to Bingham, December 7, 1949, RG 286, Acc. 53A405, box 50, folder: Finance – Investments (Aldrich Committee).

[37] On the activities of the British and American dollar boards, see the information in RG 286, Acc. 53A405, box 1, folder: British Dollar Exports Board. On the French board, see Bingham toeca 1294 to Hoffman, October 22, 1949, Treasury Records, Acc. 67A1804, box 4, folder: France, Aid Program, Vol. II.

[38] Harriman repto 7113 to Hoffman, October 28, 1949, ECA Files, box 8.

[39] Harriman repto 7073 to Hoffman, October 27, 1949, and Bonsal repto 8221 to Hoffman, December 29, 1949, ECA Files, box 8; and ECA, *Seventh Report to Congress* (Washington, DC, 1950), 53.

on Productivity, which continued with the ECA to sponsor scores of productivity missions to the United States. By the end of 1949, the Council on Productivity had authorized fourteen such missions, the ECA another hundred. Most were labor–management teams. According to the ECA, they came to observe the American method of mass production, the American pattern of labor–management cooperation on behalf of "higher productivity," and "the resulting high standards of living of American life."[40]

The productivity teams, dollar boards, investment groups, and advisory panels attest to the broad front on which the American leaders operated in the second half of 1949. They were part of a major offensive designed to head off a dangerous division of the "free world" into rival economic blocs. As in the past, most of these initiatives squared with the larger American design for a neo-capitalist order in Western Europe. One result would be the creation of an integrated system with the strength and coherence needed to transform Western Europe from a costly dependent into a valuable partner in the postwar world. If anything, the worsening dollar gap had brought the need for such a system into bold relief, as had the growing disenchantment of the Germans and the escalation of Cold War tensions. But these same developments, along with others, also forced some officials in Washington to wonder if this system could be created as originally conceived. These officials began to reassess the role that Britain would play in Europe, a reassessment that led first to compromise at the trilateral talks in September and then to a major reformulation of American policy in late 1949.

The reassessment began in George Kennan's Policy Planning Staff. A sensitive, articulate man, never at ease with himself or his world, Kennan was prone to psychological as well as geopolitical views of global events and able to express these views with a nimbleness that has made him an eminently quotable source to generations of historians. He had an inveterate dislike of Soviet communism and a deep appreciation of the Germans, both of which inspired his vision of separate North Atlantic and European unions. Kennan had articulated his conception of a North Atlantic union at the outset of the Marshall Plan, speaking of England's "body politic" as "seriously sick" and unable to face the future except through some form of association with Canada and the United States.[41] It was also then that Kennan began to formulate his thinking on the future of Europe. At that point, as we have seen, he had spurned the hopes of junior officials who thought the Marshall Plan might prepare the ground for the unification of Europe as a whole. He accepted the division of the Continent as inevitable and looked to economic integration in Western Europe as an instrument of the containment doctrine he had fathered.

[40] Foster ecato 1838 to American Embassy, London, December 29, 1949, ECA Files, box 42; and ECA, *Seventh Report to Congress*, 51–2.
[41] Kennan, "Situation with Respect to European Recovery Program," September 4, 1949, *FRUS 1949*, 3:397–405.

This had remained Kennan's position until 1948, when the North Atlantic Treaty negotiations and other developments led him to take up arguments anticipated by his junior colleagues a year earlier. He now complained that the North Atlantic alliance would freeze the division of the Continent into hostile blocs, lead to irredentist claims, and perpetuate Western Europe's dependence on the United States. He proposed to avoid these dangers through a Soviet–American agreement that would make a united Germany the basis of a neutral zone from which the superpowers could withdraw. This proposal found little support in the State Department. On the contrary, its rejection set the stage for Kennan's progressive isolation from his colleagues, his retreat to private life in 1950, and his contribution to the "disengagement" debate of the next decade. Kennan's story has been told elsewhere, however. It need not detain us here, except insofar as he helped to reformulate the American approach to European integration.[42]

In April 1949, Gladwyn Jebb, Kennan's counterpart in the Foreign Office, had made arrangements to meet with Kennan in England the following July to discuss the question of European unification. At Jebb's suggestion, the discussion was to be off the record and was to focus on such issues as the British and German roles in a European union and the prospects of such a union emerging as an independent third force in world affairs. In preparation for these talks, Kennan and his colleagues on the Policy Planning Staff held a series of remarkable seminars with representatives of other government agencies and with a number of outside consultants. The latter included the political scientists Arnold Wolfers and Hans J. Morgenthau, the Protestant theologian Reinhold Niebuhr, and the physicist J. Robert Oppenheimer, who had directed the Los Alamos laboratory that devised the first atomic bomb. Oppenheimer was then head of the Institute for Advanced Study at Princeton University. Niebuhr, Morgenthau, and Wolfers, along with Kennan, would later emerge as leaders of a flourishing school of "realist" scholars. Together, in May and June of 1949, all of these men helped to launch the State Department's first full-blown effort to hammer out a policy on European unification.[43]

Among those involved in the seminars, there was general agreement that Britain and other ERP countries should take all measures short of merging sovereignty to reinforce their association. They should strengthen their po-

[42] Kennan has told his own story. See his *Memoirs*, especially 342–87, 417–96. For an excellent short summary of Kennan's views, see also Gaddis, "The United States and the Question of a Sphere of Influence in Europe," especially 76–7.
[43] Kennan memorandum to Acheson, Webb, Bohlen, Jessup, and Rusk, April 14, 1949, with attached letter from Jebb to Kennan, April 7, 1949, RG 59, file: 841.51/4-1449; memorandum of conversation between Kennan and F. R. Hoyer-Millar, April 28, 1949, RG 59, file: 841.51/4-2849; Kennan letter to Hoyer-Millar, April 28, 1949, RG 59, file: 841.51/4-2849; and minutes of the 69th, 78th, and 79th meetings of the Policy Planning Staff, April 27 and May 17 and 18, 1949, RG 59, PPS Records, box 32, folder: Minutes of Meetings, 1949.

litical ties through the OEEC and the Council of Europe, bring western Germany into all parts of the associative structure, and clear a path to economic "integration" by making currencies convertible and liberalizing trade. Yet even if such a structure could be developed fully, some worried that it might not be strong enough to contain German nationalism and Soviet expansion. This was the problem, because if it was not strong enough, there was little prospect of creating something stronger. The British would never make the sacrifices of sovereignty required for a full-fledged union, and without the British a merger of European sovereignties would be too feeble to control the Germans.

Of all the participants, only Kennan seemed concerned about the future of Eastern Europe or ready to contemplate a strictly continental union under German leadership. In the seminars and in a preliminary draft of staff document No. 55 (PPS/55), he argued against a union that did not leave room for the Soviet satellites. Only an all-European union, even one that emerged as an unaligned "third force," would be large enough to control the Germans and permit the superpowers to "disengage" from the Continent. It should be founded on a rapprochement between France and Germany and should have Britain's help in the form of military guarantees and economic collaboration. Beyond this, however, Kennan would "abstract" the British from the Continent, bringing them instead into a North Atlantic group that included the United States, Canada, and some of the other Commonwealth countries. An arrangement like this might reduce Britain to little more than an "education and travel center." ("You wouldn't eliminate the grouse shooting," worried one of the consultants. No, said Kennan, "That's part of education.") But it would clear the way for a tighter continental association than was possible with British participation. It would also help to solve the sterling–dollar problem, forge a wider system of multilateral trade, and protect Britain's strategically important commitments to the Commonwealth and the sterling bloc.[44]

---

[44] PPS, Minutes of 81st Meeting, May 20, 1949, RG 59, PPS Records, box 32, folder: Minutes of Meetings, 1949; and PPS, Minutes of 101st Meeting, June 14, 1949, RG 59, PPS Records, box 27, folder: Europe 1949. See also PPS, Minutes of the 84th, 87th, 97th, 99th, 100th, 101st, and 102nd Meetings, May 25 and 27 and June 8, 13 (two meetings), and 14 (two meetings), RG 59, PPS Records, box 27, folder: Europe 1949; Introduction to the 93rd Meeting of the PPS, June 6, 1949, RG 59, PPS Records, box 27, folder: Europe 1949; Frank Altschul letter to Kennan, June 9, 1949, Morgenthau letter to Kennan, June 10, 1949, Niebuhr letter to Kennan, June 18, 1949, Gordon Merriam of the PPS, memorandum to Carlton Savage of the PPS, June 20, 1949, Ware Adams of the PPS, "European Unity," June 20, 1949, Dorothy Fosdick of the PPS, "Brief Summary of Trend of Discussions with Consultants on European Union and Related Matters," June 22, 1949, and Savage, "Principles Developed during Discussions on European Integration," June 22, 1949, RG 59, PPS Records, box 27, folder: Europe 1949; Policy Planning Staff Paper 55, July 7, 1949, RG 59, PPS Records, box 3, *Reports and Recommendations, 1949*, Vol. 3; and Kennan, *Memoirs*, 476–81.

Although a "fundamental policy decision" was not forthcoming, Acheson authorized Kennan to use the preliminary draft of PPS/55 as a basis for his unofficial talks with Jebb and other British and French leaders.[45] In the discussions themselves, the French were virulently opposed to separate continental and North Atlantic groupings while the British were unwilling to base current policy on future prospects in Eastern Europe.[46] But both the British and the Canadians favored closer association with the United States than with Western Europe, a proposition to which Kennan was now firmly committed. In a brief report on his talks and in a meeting with Acheson and Snyder, Kennan argued again that Britain must not be tied to the Continent in a way that weakened its strategically important commitments to the sterling area, particularly at a time when political conditions in Asia were far from stable. Given these conditions, he concluded, the United States should adopt a helpful posture in dealing with the sterling crisis at the upcoming talks in Washington.[47]

By the time of the trilateral talks, Kennan had also conveyed his thinking to Sir Derick Hoyer-Millar of the British Embassy in Washington.[48] The British had the benefit of additional information published in the *Wall Street Journal* and in a series of articles by Joseph and Stewart Alsop. One of these articles gave Kennan the credit for a recent presidential address to the American Legion, in which Truman referred to the sterling crisis as an Anglo–American problem and promised cooperation in its solution. The Alsops then went on to outline the State Department's plan for separate "economic, political, and strategic groupings" in the North Atlantic and Western Europe. This "dual concept" supposedly derived from certain conclusions reached by "most of the chief policy-makers in the Government," which the columnists elaborated as if they had read Kennan's draft of PPS/55.[49] None of this added up to official approval of Kennan's thinking. But

---

[45] Summary of Daily Meeting with the Secretary, July 1, 1949, RG 59, Records of the Office of the Executive Secretariat, Summaries of Secretary's Daily Meetings, 1949–1952, box 1 (hereafter cited as RG 59, Secretary's Daily Meetings, with box number).

[46] Kennan, *Memoirs*, 482.

[47] Kennan memorandum to Webb and Acheson, August 22, 1949, RG 59, PPS Records, box 27, folder: Europe 1949. Surprisingly, this is the only document available on the Kennan–Jebb talks. Jebb does not mention the talks in his memoirs. Nor could I find information regarding the talks in the records of the British Foreign Office. In his memoirs, Kennan focuses only on those aspects of the talks dealing with the future of Eastern Europe and the relationship of this region to a Western European union. For Kennan's meeting with Acheson and Snyder after his return from England, see his *Memoirs*, 485–6.

[48] Denis Allen of the British Embassy, Washington, letter to Michael R. Wright of the Foreign Office, September 2, 1949, FO 371, 75587, UE5640.

[49] Alsops, "Boldness at Last," *Washington Post*, September 2, 1949, 21. See also Roy Cromley, "Merger with U.K.?" *Wall Street Journal*, August 16, 1949, 1; Truman's address to the American Legion, August 29, 1949, U.S., *Public Papers of the Pres-*

it told the British something about the drift of policy in Washington. Taken together with other developments, it also helps to explain the outcome of the trilateral talks and much of the European reaction that followed.

IV

The trilateral talks confront us with something of a problem. We have the benefit of official records for the technical discussions that began in late August. But technical experts neither dealt with the larger dimensions of Anglo–American diplomacy nor made important decisions. These aspects of the conference were reserved for ministers whose meetings were conducted off the record. The historian is thus reduced to describing all too briefly one of the most important meetings of 1949, to speculating on matters of great significance, and to drawing conclusions on the basis of a paltry stock of records that are not altogether reliable. One thing is clear, however. To draw the right conclusions, we must place the trilateral talks in the context of the preparations that preceded them.

At least some British and American officials had comparable views on the strategic and political interests at stake and how they might be guaranteed. British policymakers had by this time forged a consensus. They would not take their country into Europe "beyond the point of no return."[50] They defined their security and their aspirations in terms of the Commonwealth's solidarity and Britain's position as the hub in a North Atlantic system of overlapping blocs. Not all American officials shared this view. But Kennan and others had come to the conclusion that Britain's leadership of the sterling bloc deserved American support. The State Department and the ECA could not pledge to manage the American economy with a view to the needs of British producers. Nor could they support the overvalued pound or prop up the prices of sterling-area raw materials. But they were refocusing their work on the problem of the dollar gap. They were anxious to act on many of the short-term measures proposed by the British, and they would do what they could to adjust tariffs, end shipping subsidies, and stimulate investment abroad. It would take time to achieve results in these areas. There was no guarantee that Congress would go along and there was also the problem of dealing with the Treasury, where officials were far less willing to strike a flexible posture in negotiating with the British.

The differences between the State and Treasury departments were built into the structure of the American delegation to the trilateral talks. Snyder headed the American team; Acheson was second in command; and each

idents: *Harry S Truman, 1949* (Washington, DC, 1964), 446–51; and Kennan, *Memoirs*, 486.
[50] The quote is from an unsigned "Note on Integration," December 29, 1949, T232/196/EEC7/1/08.

approached the conference from a different point of view. Snyder was a fiscal conservative and very sensitive to elements on Capitol Hill who thought the British were looking for another handout to support their extravagant social programs. He told a press conference on the eve of the talks that the sterling crisis was a British problem for which the United States had no solution of its own. Acheson viewed things in a different light. His philosophy combined a belated respect for the New Deal with a patrician disdain for congressional opinion, a commitment to balance-of-power diplomacy, and a deep respect for the community of British and American culture – so much so that critics would later denounce him, in Joseph McCarthy's unforgettable epithet, as a "pompous diplomat in striped pants with a phony British accent." In truth, Acheson did think of himself as an Anglo–American. He recounted with obvious pride how his parents had celebrated the queen's birthday by hoisting the Union Jack and raising a toast in Her Majesty's name. He had also developed a special admiration for British diplomacy in the Victorian period, when, to his way of thinking, the power of the British navy and the overseas investments of the great London banks had contributed to a long period of international stability.[51]

Acheson thought the time had come for Britain and the United States to share this responsibility. He believed that British and American interests were largely identical and that a reinforcing relationship was therefore desirable. He brought this conviction to bear on the sterling crisis, describing it in his memoirs as an Anglo–American crisis that "could be managed only under our leadership and with British association."[52] Cultural and geopolitical considerations thus were wedded in Acheson's approach to the Anglo–American dialogue in Washington, which he compared to a marital tête-à-tête on a delicate topic. "It was like the rare, inevitable but difficult evenings when husband and wife had to go into their mutual way of life," as the British ambassador reported him saying. It "was all too dreadful for anything" but nonetheless "had very occasionally to be done."[53]

Even though the State Department took a back seat to the Treasury on the American delegation, Acheson's view seemed to govern the outcome of the trilateral talks. The difficult moments came shortly after the ministers crowded into a small conference room in the new State Department building. The first session on September 7 was "a complete waste of time" in which early expectations were quickly deflated.[54] The Americans would not raise the price of gold to increase the dollar value of European reserves. Nor

[51]   McCarthy quoted in David S. McLellan, *Dean Acheson: The State Department Years* (New York, 1976), 225. See also McLellan, *Acheson*, 30–1, 50–1; Charles L. Mee, Jr., *The Marshall Plan: The Launching of the Pax Americana* (New York, 1984), 22–3; and Acheson, *Present at the Creation*, 322.
[52]   Acheson, *Present at the Creation*, 323.
[53]   Franks tel. to FO, for Strang, August 11, 1949, FO 800/516/US/49/42.
[54]   Acheson, *Present at the Creation*, 324.

would they agree to balance-of-payments loans by the World Bank, permit the IMF to cover the foreign-exchange requirements of the sterling-area countries, or negotiate international commodity agreements to fix the price of sterling-area raw materials. There was also a barbed exchange between Hoffman and Bevin regarding Britain's expenditures on the welfare state. Hoffman's faith in the power of productivity had endeared him to Cripps, but not to Bevin, who seems to have considered the administrator to be more of a salesman than a prophet. Hoffman thought that social programs should be reduced and resources channeled into production for export. Bevin said he would urge British workers to sacrifice for the export trade when Congress lowered the American tariff. Nor did Bevin and other British delegates respond favorably when Richard Bissell urged restoration of the price mechanism as the best way to solve the sterling crisis. Equilibrium in the balance of payments, said Sir Henry Wilson-Smith, was a prerequisite to full convertibility.

After this brief storm, the air cleared and the negotiations began to bear fruit. Cripps and Bevin announced their plan to devalue the pound, cut costs, control inflation, and redirect exports. Franks cabled London that this program of self-help "was very well received." As the British had anticipated, it broke the dike of American resistance and released a flood of reciprocal concessions. The Americans were ready to expand the list of British imports eligible for ECA financing, review their stockpiling program with a view to stepping up purchases from the sterling area, permit a higher volume of rubber and tin imports, simplify customs procedures, and negotiate tariff reductions under the Reciprocal Trade Agreements Act. They were also willing to encourage private investment in the sterling area, urge the World Bank to underwrite development projects there, and establish a continuing tripartite organization to investigate ways of handling the accumulated sterling balances in London and of reducing Britain's dollar expenditures on shipping and oil transactions.[55]

55 Franks tel. to FO, for Strang, September 7, 1949, FO 371, 75587, UE5674. See also Acheson, *Present at the Creation*, 324–5; Thorp Memorandum, "U.S. Steps to Aid Sterling Area – Status Report," September 6, 1949, RG 43, box 311, folder: Tripartite Economic Discussions, Miscellaneous; Report of the Working Group on Overseas Investment, September 10, 1949, RG 43, box 311, folder: Com/Top D-1; Report of the Working Group on Commodities and Stockpiling, September 10, 1949, RG 43, box 311, folder: Com/Top D-2; Report of the Working Group on ECA Eligibility, September 10, 1949, RG 43, box 311, folder: Com/Top D-3; Report of the Committee on Customs Procedures, September 12, 1949, RG 43, box 311, folder: Com/Top D-4; Minutes of the 3rd and 4th meetings of the Combined Official Committee, September 12, 1949, RG 43, box 311, folder: Tripartite Economic Discussions, Miscellaneous; Minutes of NAC meeting #134 of August 11, 1949, and NAC Documents #866 of August 11, 1949, #867 of August 10, 1949, and #868 (revised draft) of August 22, 1949, RG 56, NAC Minutes. See also the communiqué issued at the end of the Washington talks in *FRUS, 1949*, 4:833–9. For British records of the trilateral talks, see Franks tel. to FO for Strang and Edward Bridges, September 19, 1949, FO

The formation of a tripartite organization was widely regarded as one of the three most important developments coming out of the Washington Conference, the other two being the British decision to devalue and the American decision to waive Article 9 of the Anglo–American loan agreement. Waiving Article 9 would permit the British to include the sterling Dominions in their proposal to liberalize intra-European trade. That proposal looked to a large, soft-currency trading area based on discrimination against the dollar. American officials were willing to tolerate such a development, in part because the ECA thought it likely to integrate markets and bring the economic gains that would make Western Europe self-supporting. But the British also made American approval easier, first by promising to consider a greater degree of transferability in intra-European payments and then by extending the benefits of trade liberalization to countries outside the sterling group and the ERP area. These stipulations limited the need for discrimination against the dollar. They also gave some assurance that the soft-currency area would be a temporary expedient rather than a permanent currency bloc.[56]

The Labour government's decision to devalue the pound by a whopping 30 percent provided a similar assurance. Cripps announced the decision on September 18, just six days after the Washington talks had adjourned. The announcement immediately triggered a major depreciation and realignment of European currencies, which helped to reduce export prices and remove one of the impediments to a further liberalization of intra-European trade. It was "a bold and imaginative measure of far-reaching importance," Hoffman said of the British decision, a definite step toward "a single [European] market" and a worldwide system of multilateral trade.[57]

Hoffman's euphoria was an indication of how policymakers in Washington viewed the results of the trilateral talks. Both the State Department and the ECA considered the conference a great success. There were even

800/516/US/49/49; CP (49) 191, Cripps, "The Washington Discussions, 7th–12th September, 1949," September 20, 1949, PREM 8/1178 pt. I; and unsigned "Top Secret" report, September 29, 1949, T232/100/EEC31/011.

[56] Acheson is not always a reliable reporter, as seen by his insistence (*Present at the Creation*, 324) that American negotiators refused to waive Article 9. Although the article was not canceled, the Americans agreed to waive it temporarily. Secretary Snyder undertook to win approval for this course from top congressional leaders and had accomplished this job by early October. This part of the story can be followed in the British documents. See especially Franks tel. to FO, September 14, 1949, FO 371, 75587, UE5836; Franks tel. to FO, September 21, 1949, FO 371, 78087, UR9630; and Franks tels. to FO, September 26, 28, and 29, 1949, FO 371, 78118, UR9787, UR9810, and UR9847.

[57] Hoffman press statement of September 19, 1949, Hoffman Papers, box 25, folder: Economic Cooperation Administration – Speeches and Statements, 1948–1949. The text of Cripps's announcement is in *New York Times*, September 19, 1949, 6. By September 22, eighteen members of the IMF had depreciated their currencies. See the press statement by Camille Gutt of the IMF, September 22, 1949, in the Truman Papers, OF, folder: 85-E – United Nations Monetary and Financial Conference.

signs that some officials thought the outcome represented a major reshaping of American policy. One day after the talks, for example, George Kennan and Under Secretary of State James Webb presented a summary of the conference to the Combined Policy Committee on Atomic Energy. Webb gave as one of the "most important conclusions" the "mutual conviction that the three countries were partners in the economic crisis." Part of the American contribution to the partnership, he said, would be to shoulder a portion of Great Britain's "economic commitments in the Far East, particularly India." Kennan then elaborated the "current Departmental thinking." He told the committee that "it would be better if the United Kingdom were not too closely tied politically and economically to Western Europe." Britain should be aligned instead "with the United States and Canada." This alignment would take account of her strategic commitments to the sterling area and speed progress toward integration in Western Europe.[58]

Commentators in the Foreign Office interpreted the results in a similar light. In a series of minutes, E. A. Berthoud and others noted how the talks had validated the thesis that Great Britain was "of the highest importance to the United States, in other words, that the United States and the United Kingdom are interdependent." American leaders had been willing to establish a trilateral organization "outside the O.E.E.C. context" and to help Great Britain "beyond the scale of their general help to the O.E.E.C." These developments seemed to indicate a trend in American thinking away from Anglo–European integration toward "Anglo–American collaboration." This trend could not "but weaken the O.E.E.C." while reinforcing the Labour government's decision "not to get further entangled in Europe." After all, Berthoud concluded, the Americans clearly had no wish to see Britain "go too far in this direction."[59]

Dwelling for a moment on these British and American commentaries helps to place the European reaction to the trilateral talks in the right perspective. The Europeans had not been invited to the Washington Conference or fully consulted in advance of British devaluation. These developments were grounds for suspecting that an Anglo–American condominium was in the making and that British leaders, having formed new ties with the United States, were seeking national advantage at the expense of real economic cooperation with the Continent. Officials in the OEEC, who were already concerned about the paralysis that had gripped their organization in the wake of the sterling crisis, now feared a weakening of American support for Britain's integration into Europe. One angry European told his American counterpart at the United Nations that the "OEEC is dead. You have killed

---

[58] Minutes of the Meeting of the American Members of the Combined Policy Committee, Washington, September 13, 1949, *FRUS, 1949*, 1: 520–6.

[59] See the minutes by Michael Wright, September 16, 1949, Berthoud, September 13, 1949, and C. J. Child, September 14, 1949, FO 371, 75587, UE5640; and Berthoud minute to Makins, October 12, 1949, FO 371, 75594, UE6561.

it by your tri-partite financial talks in Washington." The decision to form a continuing trilateral organization lent credibility to this charge, as did press reports that American policy envisioned separate North Atlantic and Western European groupings.[60] In Europe, noted one American official, the outcome of the Washington talks looked "almost like the Anglo–German Naval Treaty of 1935, or other episodes of a similar character, which have the capacity to shake confidence and alter policy in a fundamental way."[61]

The French were particularly disillusioned by the outcome of the trilateral talks. Although Bevin and Schuman had vowed to keep each other posted on developments growing out of the sterling crisis, Bevin had allowed their consultation to lapse on the eve of the Washington meeting. Schuman had been further disappointed by the subsequent exclusion of France from the talks.[62] As it turned out, he and other European ministers were in the American capital on unrelated business at the time of the trilateral meeting and were briefed by the British and American delegations. But they were not told of Britain's decision to devalue. To avoid a last-minute run on their reserves, the British had kept the decision, code-named "Rose," a closely guarded secret. Under Secretary of State Makins conveyed the news to French Minister of Finance Maurice Petsche just thirty-six hours before it was announced to the public. Petsche considered it *"une decision brutale."* Other French officials reacted with "complete consternation"; one became "somewhat hysterical." On September 20, the French ambassador in London told Permanent Under Secretary William Strang that Schuman had been "badly treated." The British and the Americans had shown no confidence in Schuman's "powers to keep a secret."[63]

---

[60] G. Hayden Raynor, U.S. delegation to the UN, memorandum, September 24, 1949, *FRUS, 1949*, 4:425. On the European reaction, see Bruce tel. and dispatch to Acheson, both of September 11, 1949, RG 59, file: 840.00/9-1149; Julius C. Holmes, Counsel, U.S. Embassy, London, tel. to Acheson, September 22, 1949, RG 59, file: 841.5151/9-2249; Millard tel. to Acheson, September 22, 1949, RG 59, file 855.5151/9-2249; Millard airgram to Acheson, September 23, 1949, RG 59, file: 855.00(W)/9-2349; Charles H. Bonesteel, Special Assistant to Harriman, Paris, tel. to Army Department, September 24, 1949, RG 59, file: 851.00(W)/9-2449; Millard tel. to Acheson, September 27, 1949, RG 59, file: 841.5151/9-2749; Dunn tel. to Acheson, October 1, 1949, RG 59, file: 841.5151/10-149; and Holmes tel. to Acheson, September 23, 1949, *FRUS, 1949*, 4:841–3. For press reports, see especially the article "Boldness at Last," by Joseph and Stewart Alsop, and the article "Whither Britain?" by Walter Lippmann, *Washington Post*, September 26, 1949.

[61] Eugene Rostow, Special Aid to Gunar Myrdal, Executive Secretary of the Economic Commission to Europe, letter to Acheson, October 12, 1949, RG 59, file: 841.51/10-1949. Attached to this letter is a memorandum from Rostow to Myrdal of October 12, 1949. The memorandum is printed in *FRUS, 1949*, 4:848–9. It gives more information on the European reaction to the Washington talks and British devaluation.

[62] Unsigned record of a conversation between Bevin and Schuman, July 23, 1949, FO 800/516/US/49/41; and Strang letter to Sir Oliver Harvey, British Ambassador to France, September 2, 1949, FO 371, 75587, UE5800.

No doubt the French were dismayed by the size of the British devaluation, which they thought would "deal a heavy blow to the French economy."[64] But the real reasons for their bitter reaction are to be found elsewhere. Like many of their OEEC colleagues, the French were more concerned about Britain's "desolidarization" from the Continent and the formation of an "Anglo–Saxon bloc." This course would amount to a "complete break with [the] principles of OEEC, Western Union and [the] Council of Europe," the very principles, according to the French, upon which their support for European integration and German reintegration depended. Apparently they were to be left alone with the Germans on the Continent. In their view, the possibility even existed that Anglo–American leaders envisaged a Western European union under German domination. They pointed out, for example, that American officials were supporting a substantial devaluation of the German mark and tolerating Germany's practice of charging higher prices for its exported coal than for coal sold in the German market, both of which were pro-German policies "unfair" to France.[65]

Adding fuel to the fiery French reaction was the havoc wrought by Britain's devaluation on plans for a regional union of France, Italy, and the Benelux countries. The story of this proposed union, known variously as Fritalux, Finebel, Benefit, or Little Europe, has been told so well by Alan Milward that only a brief account is needed here. The point to bear in mind is that French planning for a regional union had begun after the last round of the London Conference on Germany and had been sustained by Great Britain's long opposition to devaluation. These developments had seemed to point to the revival of western Germany and its reintegration into a Western European system from which Britain would remain apart. This prospect had alarmed the French, who promptly devised a variant of their earlier plan for a European customs union: a regional economic union that would be strong enough either to absorb western Germany or to contain it.

The latest round in the Fritalux negotiations had come in the middle of the trilateral talks, when Petsche handed his Italian and Benelux colleagues in Washington a proposal calling for free rates of exchange between the five countries, the complete removal of quantitative import restrictions, and the free movement of capital. Some Foreign Office officials saw nothing "sinister" in this. Others saw a French-inspired conspiracy to lock Britain out of Europe. The latter were not disappointed when British devaluation

[63] Franks tel. to FO, from Makins to Cripps, September 16, 1949, FO 800/465/Fr/49/14; and Strang minute, September 20, 1949, FO 371, 75591, UE6048. See also Franks tel. to FO, September 17, 1949, T232/111/EEC17/012; and State Department, Memorandum of Conversation, September 15, 1949, *FRUS, 1949*, 4:654–61.

[64] Strang minute, September 20, 1949, FO 371, 75591, UE6048.

[65] Bruce tel. to Acheson, September 23, 1949, *FRUS, 1949*, 4:663–5. See also Bruce tel. to Acheson, September 22, 1949, *FRUS, 1949*, 4:661–3.

knocked the Fritalux talks into a cocked hat, forcing the five countries to suspend negotiations in order to assess the impact of devaluation on their own currencies. If this was good news to the British, however, it added weight to the French conviction that policymakers in London put their own interests above those of Western Europe. Above all else, this conviction accounted for the overheated French reaction to the Washington talks and to the subsequent devaluation of the pound.[66]

Officials in the State Department were stung by the fury of the French reaction. "Where did we go wrong?" Acheson asked. "What did we miscalculate or overlook?" He and others tried to assuage the French by denying any thought of a special Anglo–American partnership or of a retreat from their support for European unification. It was all a misunderstanding, they said, for which Acheson accepted full responsibility.[67] But these assurances were of little comfort to the policymakers in Paris. They too had read the Alsops' article. They had heard the president's speech to the American Legion. They had listened to the views that Kennan expounded during his summer trip to Europe. Like the formation of a trilateral organization in Washington, these were signs of a new direction in American policy, and they could not be wiped from the French mind with belated assurances from the State Department.

Besides, the French were concerned about more than an Anglo–American partnership. They worried that American policy now placed the burden of Germany's reintegration on them. Nor were their fears without foundation. In the month between the trilateral talks in Washington and a major OEEC meeting in Paris, the British consolidated their thinking on European integration and the Americans moved toward the position anticipated in Kennan's earlier work. By November, it looked very much like Britain and the United States had struck a partnership that resolved their differences at France's expense.

V

On October 11, Kennan and the Policy Planning Staff produced the working draft of a long-overdue conclusion to PPS/55. The draft urged continued support for the United Nations, the North Atlantic Treaty, the Council of Europe, and the OEEC, which together constituted the institutional frame-

---

[66] FO Tel. to Franks, September 21, 1949, FO 371, 78111, UR9528. See also Franks tels. to FO, September 17 (2) and 20, 1949, and Hall-Patch tel. to FO, September 24, 1949, FO 371, 78111, UR9528, UR9546, UR9623, and UR9711; and Milward, *Reconstruction of Western Europe*, 294, 301–2, 306.

[67] Acheson Memorandum, October 19, 1949, *FRUS, 1949*, 4:847–9. See also Webb tel. to Acheson, September 24, 1949, *FRUS, 1949*, 4:665–6; *FRUS, 1949*, 4:666, footnote 3; and Acheson tel. to Webb and Assistant Secretary of State Dean Rusk, September 26, 1949, Acheson Papers, box 64, folder: Memoranda of Conversations.

work for collaboration between the countries involved. Within this framework, however, it envisioned closer ties between particular groups of countries. It looked ahead to a close association between the United States, the United Kingdom, and some of the Commonwealth countries, and to a greater degree of unity between the countries of Western Europe. The French should engineer a rapprochement with the Germans, it said, thereby laying the foundation of a continental group able to contain the Soviets. The United States and Great Britain would help by providing military guarantees under the North Atlantic Treaty and by strengthening their ties to the OEEC and the Council of Europe. But in no event should this assistance prevent either country from meeting its responsibilities in other areas of the world.[68]

These conclusions differed little from those in PPS/55; nor did they lead to a quick consensus in the State Department. In meetings with the Policy Planning Staff and in a flurry of memoranda, officials in other wings of the State Department blasted Kennan's central assumptions. They argued that Germany would dominate a strictly continental group and that this prospect would discourage the French from seeking a solution to the German problem. The general result, they said, would be a dangerous recrudescence of economic autarky and political rivalry. Although Kennan seemed resigned to a "third force in Europe which might ultimately be dominated one way or another by the Germans," his critics were not. They wanted to push the British further into Europe and thought this could be done without raising the "$64 question" of sovereignty. The United States should be seeking restrictions on the exercise of sovereign power rather than an immediate merger of national sovereignties. It should hack "away at sovereignty in limited areas," as Willard Thorp put it, by building "central institutions" of economic coordination and control.[69]

The Policy Planning Staff made some revisions in light of these criticisms, whereupon Acheson blended the results with his own views in a long telegram to Assistant Secretary of State George Perkins, who was in Paris for a meeting of the American ambassadors in Europe.[70] Economic integration,

[68] Working draft of October 11, 1949, RG 59, PPS Records, box 27, folder: Europe 1949.

[69] Thorp memorandum to PPS, October 14, 1949, RG 59, PPS Records, box 27, folder: Europe 1949; and PPS, Minutes of the 151st Meeting, October 17, 1949, RG 59, PPS Records, box 32, folder: Minutes of Meetings 1949. See also PPS, Minutes of the 148th Meeting, October 11, 1949, RG 59, PPS Records, box 32, folder: Minutes of Meetings 1949; and Llewellyn E. Thompson memorandum to PPS, October 12, 1949, PPS, Minutes of the 149th Meeting, October 12, 1949, Henry A. Byroade, Director, Office of German and Austrian Affairs, memorandum to PPS, October 13, 1949, Hickerson memorandum to PPS, October 15, 1949, and PPS, Minutes of the 152nd Meeting, October 18, 1949, RG 59, PPS Records, box 27, folder: Europe 1949.

[70] The revised draft conclusion, dated October 13, 1949, is in RG 59, PPS Records, box 27, folder: Europe 1949.

Acheson wrote, was the only way to reverse "nationalist trends on the continent" and harness Germany's resources "to the security and welfare of Western Europe as a whole." European leaders should therefore move ahead with plans to liberalize trade. They should build "supranational institutions" and be assured of British support for their initiatives. But this support must stop short of merging Britain's sovereignty with that of a continental group. The real "key to progress," Acheson insisted, lay in "French hands." Even with the closest possible ties between the United States, the United Kingdom, and the Continent, "France and France alone" could "take the decisive leadership in integrating Western Germany into Western Europe."[71]

It was the last aspect of Acheson's telegram that produced strenuous objections from the American ambassadors in Paris. Perkins noted how the thinking behind it was based not only on "purely European" considerations but also on those having to do with "Great Britain's world position" and the "deep conviction," particularly in the Pentagon, "that the US needed Great Britain above everything else." The ambassadors were not impressed. They acknowledged the factors keeping Britain out of Europe, its commitments to the Commonwealth and the welfare state being the most salient. But they also thought that Britain's empire was collapsing and that this development, which was every bit as important as the rise of Soviet power, made it easier for the British to integrate into Europe. The ambassadors were particularly critical of the notion that France by itself could take the lead in bringing western Germany into an integrated Europe. David K. E. Bruce, who had replaced Caffery as the American ambassador to France, thought that the interdependence of the British and European economies made the goal of integration unattainable "without the full participation of the U.K." Others warned that economic and security concerns would prevent France from giving a lead unless assured of Britain's partnership. Still others added weight to this warning by reminding Perkins that the real choice lay between Germany's reintegration into a Western system or its alignment with the Soviet bloc. Given these dangers, the ambassadors argued, it was time to present the Labour government with "a 'must' program," to say no to British demands, and to quit being so "tender with Britain." Unless the United States acted more firmly, Bruce concluded, "the participating countries of the Marshall Plan are going to see their golden goose killed by the principal participant in the Plan's benefits."[72]

The great integration debate continued in a rancorous exchange of letters

[71] Acheson tel. to Perkins, October 19, 1949, *FRUS, 1949*, 4:469–72.
[72] Summary Record of a Meeting of United States Ambassadors at Paris, October 21–22, 1949, *FRUS, 1949*, 4:472–96. See also Bruce tel. to Acheson, Webb, and Hoffman, from Perkins, October 22, 1949, *FRUS, 1949*, 4:342–4; and Perkins memorandum to Acheson, November 7, 1949, Truman Papers, PSF, folder: Subject File – Conferences, Paris Conf., Oct.–Nov. 1949.

between Charles Bohlen, the American minister in France, and the somewhat beleaguered George Kennan in Washington. Kennan defended PPS/55; Bohlen attacked it as giving the wrong signals to Europe, encouraging Britain's desolidarization from the Continent, and scuttling the chances for Germany's reintegration. Kennan saw all problems leading back to Paris and dismissed French security concerns as the result of "neurosis"; Bohlen traced the same difficulties to London and viewed French alarm as being based on "cold-blooded" realism. For Kennan, imperial commitments prevented the British from integrating into Europe; for Bohlen, these commitments were founded on the misguided "fiction" that Britain could still act as both a European and a world power.[73]

Policymakers on both sides of this debate saw integration as the goal to be pursued. All said that success depended on a Franco–German rapprochement. All wanted the French to bend every effort to accommodate their ancient enemy. All thought the British should go as far as possible toward active collaboration with the continental group. Nonetheless, Acheson's telegram had signaled the State Department's willingness to recognize the principle of British exceptionalism. Acheson and other top policymakers would now exempt Great Britain from their plans for an integrated Western Europe.

A similar revision of policy was underway in the ECA. In late September and early October, ECA officials held a series of meetings on the subject of European unification, out of which came important policy papers by Lincoln Gordon of Harriman's staff in Paris and Richard Bissell, Theodore Geiger, and Harold Van B. Cleveland of ECA headquarters in Washington. According to these papers, the pressure in Congress for European unification, the currency devaluations of late September, and the achievement of initial production and financial goals required the ECA to abandon its original "salvage function" and concentrate on unifying Europe. As in 1947 and 1948, policymakers assumed that Western Europe could not become self-supporting without first eliminating "the stifling effects on the process of economic growth, on competition and on the spirit of enterprise" inherent in "the tight compartmentalization" of national economies. Needed was one or more "free trade areas" in which "mass production for mass consumption and intensive internal competition can restore the dynamic of enterprise and economic growth." The ultimate goal was a full-scale Eu-

---

[73] Bohlen letter to Kennan, October 29, 1949, RG 59, Records of Charles E. Bohlen, 1942–1952, box 3, folder: A–K Correspondence – Bohlen 1949–July 1951 (hereafter cited as Bohlen Records, with appropriate box and folder designation). See also Bohlen letter to Kennan, October 6, 1949, and Kennan letter to Bohlen, October 12, 1949, RG 59, Bohlen Records, box 3, folder: A–K Correspondence – Bohlen 1949–July 1951. For more on Bohlen's views, see his undated memorandum, "U.S. Policy and Western European Integration," prepared for Ambassador Bruce on the eve of the ambassadors' meeting in Paris, in Harriman Papers, folder: Ambassadors' Meeting – 1st Mtg., Paris, Oct. 21–22, 1949.

ropean union. But because this union could not be accomplished immediately, the short-term objective was enough pooling of sovereignties to create an integrated economy relatively free of currency restrictions and quantitative import quotas. Such an economy would make it possible to base investment decisions on the "broader market prospects and the enormously increased possibilities of specialization created in a large and diverse geographical area." The results, over a period of ten to twenty-five years, would "transform the economic face of Europe, European productivity, and European living standards."

These familiar prescriptions, however, no longer applied in equal doses to Britain and the Continent. The ECA wanted the continental countries to move rapidly toward new "supranational institutions" that would manage the "day-to-day coordination of national economic policies." These institutions might include a central reserve and dollar pool, a monetary authority to coordinate central bank policies, and a trade commission to prevent restrictive public and private trade arrangements. Envisioned here was a New Deal for Europe, a program, in other words, that would redesign Europe in the image of American neo-capitalism. The ECA urged the continental countries to commit themselves to this goal by early 1950. They should establish appropriate regional authorities over the next twelve months and eliminate all trade and payments barriers during the remaining ERP period. The British, however, would have to stay out of the European association even while going as far as possible to harmonize their policies with those of the continental group.[74]

Thinking in the ECA and the State Department thus ran in similar directions, diverging only when it came to such tactical matters as the pace of integration and the degree of European or American initiative involved. These differences became apparent in interagency discussions leading up to a major address that Hoffman would give to the OEEC. The ECA prepared the original drafts of the speech, which reflected the demands outlined by Bissell, Gordon, Geiger, and Cleveland. The emphasis was on European

---

[74] Lincoln Gordon, Director, OSR Program Division, memorandum for Harriman and Katz, October 11, 1949, RG 59, Bohlen Records, box 6, folder: European Integration; and Geiger, Cleveland, and Bissell, "The Economic Integration of Western Europe," October 15, 1949, Harriman Papers, folder: Policy – General. The latter document is a revised version of two earlier and slightly different drafts, both with the same title, both written by Geiger and Cleveland, and both dated October 13, 1949. One of these earlier drafts can be found in RG 59, PPS Records, box 27, folder: Europe 1949. The other is located in RG 286, Acc. 53A405, box 33, folder: Program – European Payments Union. Similar thinking can also be found in an untitled memorandum by Geiger, September 1, 1949, and in a memorandum from the ECA's Policy Group to Bissell, July 12, 1949, both in RG 286, Acc. 53A405, box 60, folder: European Union. See also Hoffman torep 6866 to American Embassy, Paris, August 4, 1949, ECA Files, box 49; and Hoffman torep 8349 to Harriman, October 6, 1949, *FRUS, 1949*, 4:426–9.

unification, on supranational institutions, and on a timetable for action. Policymakers in the State Department preferred the word "integration" to "unification," claiming that the former was less "specific" and would give the Truman administration more "flexibility" in dealing with participating countries and with Congress. They also objected to any American "blueprint" for specific regional authorities or to any public expression of a timetable for progress. They were "quite concerned" about pushing for prompt action in areas that involved questions of sovereignty and anxious to preserve the appearance of European initiative. After all, if the Americans announced timetables and blueprints and the Europeans failed to act on them, the failure might be attributed to American policy or provoke congressional cuts in Marshall aid.[75]

It is important to understand that the State Department did not object in principle to the ECA's emphasis on supranationalism. Both agencies continued to blend the planners' and traders' approaches that had emerged at the start of the Marshall Plan. Acheson's telegram to the ambassadors in Paris had called for the merger of national sovereignties and for the liberalization of intra-European trade and payments. He and others were simply reluctant to incorporate detailed blueprints in a public pronouncement. In deference to their concerns, the ECA excised from the speech any reference to a timetable for progress or to a European reserve board and trade commission. Thereafter, both Acheson and Truman approved the speech, which the ECA then began to trumpet as a major statement on a par with the address that George Marshall had delivered at Harvard University two and a half years earlier.[76]

All of the fanfare created an air of anxious expectation in Paris. By the time Hoffman rose to address the OEEC's Council on October 31 – "burning with missionary zeal," according to the British – Marjolin and others were wondering if the Americans were once again going to set standards higher than the Europeans could meet.[77] Indeed, Hoffman's standard was nothing less than the total reorganization of Western Europe in an American

---

[75] C. Tyler Wood torep 8918 to Hoffman and Harriman, Paris, October 29, 1949, ECA Files, box 50; Webb, Memorandum of Conversation between Snyder, Acheson, Hoffman, Foster, and Webb (October 25, 1949), November 3, 1949, Acheson Papers, box 67, folder: Memoranda of Conversations; and Acheson tel. to Perkins, October 19, 1949, *FRUS*, *1949*, 4:469–72. See also PPS, Minutes of the 152nd Meeting, October 18, 1949, RG 59, PPS Records, box 27, folder: Europe 1949.

[76] Hall-Patch tel. to FO, October 25, 1949, T232/150/EEC78/11/08A; and Franks tel. to FO, October 28, 1949, and Hall-Patch tel. to FO, October 30, 1949, FO 371, 78021, UR10861 and UR10902.

[77] Hall-Patch tel. to FO, October 30, 1949, FO 371, 78021, UR10902. Richard Bissell had arrived in Paris several days before Hoffman and had conveyed the contents of Hoffman's speech to Hall-Patch, Marjolin, and others. See Hall-Patch tels. (2) to FO, October 25, 1949, T232/150/EEC78/11/08A. According to the second of these telegrams (#1196), Bissell had prepared the original draft of Hoffman's speech.

mold. The time had come, Hoffman told the Council, for

an integration of the Western European economy. The substance of such integration would be the formation of a single large market within which quantitative restrictions on the movement of goods, monetary barriers to the flow of payments, and eventually all tariffs are permanently swept away. The fact that we have in the United States a single market of 150 million consumers has been indispensable to the strength and efficiency of our economy. The creation of a permanent, freely trading area comprising 270 million consumers in Western Europe, would have a multitude of helpful consequences. It would accelerate the development of large-scale, low-cost production industries. It would make the effective use of all resources easier, the stifling of healthy competition more difficult. Obviously, such a step would not change the physical structure of European industry or vastly increase productivity overnight. But the massive change in the economic environment would, I am convinced, set in motion a rapid growth in productivity. This would make it possible for Europe to improve its competitive position in the world and thus more nearly satisfy the expectations and needs of its people.

The alternative to such a course was to leave Europe in a "precarious balance with the dollar area" after the end of Marshall aid. In that event, Hoffman warned, monetary resources would shrink and participating countries would react by restricting imports and targeting exports. There would be increasing costs, "bilateral barter," and a general resurgence of the "vicious cycle of economic nationalism." Taking this route would "spell disaster for nations and poverty for people," which was why Hoffman considered integration "not just an idea" but a "practical necessity." To achieve it, he said, the Europeans must liberalize trade, make currencies transferable, and coordinate national economic policies, either by adapting existing organizations or by devising "new central institutions." He did not mention the ECA's hopes for a central bank and trade commission. Nor did he lay out a timetable for progress. But he did insist that participating countries come up with a collective plan by early 1950.[78]

Although sometimes interpreted as a watershed in the history of the Marshall Plan, Hoffman's address added little to what he had told the Council in his maiden speech of July 1948. What had changed was the larger economic and political context in which American policy operated. The persistence of the dollar gap had compelled the ECA to become more concerned with Europe's long-term viability and had led in early 1949 to a greater emphasis on liberalizing intra-European trade. The ECA's papers were also rife with references to the importance of maintaining "political stability and military security" in Western Europe and to the Soviet Union's

[78] Hoffman's speech is quoted from Harriman repto circular 367 to ECA, Washington, October 30, 1949, ECA Files, box 8.

"possession of [an] atomic bomb."[79] In the background, as well, was the deteriorating situation in China, the spread of revolutionary insurgencies in Southeast Asia, and the growth of nationalism in Western Europe, particularly western Germany. Acheson, Kennan, Perkins, and other participants in the great integration debate had referred to the threatening forces of nationalism and to the Pentagon's concern with the global situation. Out of such concerns had come a heightened appreciation of Britain's "world position" and a concomitant decision to exempt the British from the process of European integration. But out of them, too, had come a deeper conviction that faster progress toward Western European integration was the only way to correct the dollar gap, solve the German problem, and create a stable correlation of forces on the Continent.

The tactical revisions in American policy suited the British very well. In the interval between the trilateral talks and the OEEC meeting, London had been abuzz with rumors of what Hoffman might announce in his speech to the Council. The British had reason to believe that he would follow the line set in the Washington talks. But no one could tell for sure, especially because the Americans had launched a new campaign to strengthen the OEEC. Adding to the anticipation was the news that Hoffman's speech in Paris would coincide with a meeting in Strasbourg of the Committee of Ministers of the Council of Europe, in which there was a mounting clamor for European federation.

In these circumstances, the British codified their policy toward Western Europe in two papers approved by the Cabinet on October 27. The papers explicitly rejected supranationalism in favor of the principle known generally as the "point of no return." This principle held that Britain could not be drawn into Europe beyond the point where it could extricate itself safely or at the expense of its economic well-being, its commitments to the Commonwealth, and its position as the pivot in a North Atlantic system of overlapping blocs. But the significance of the papers is not to be found in this recapitulation of past policy. It is to be found in the assumption that British diplomacy now had support in Washington. Both papers referred explicitly to the Anglo–American understanding that had emerged from the trilateral talks.[80]

Reinvigorated by this understanding, the British were ready to state their policy with a boldness that betrayed a new sense of confidence. Bevin took the lead when he wrote to Acheson on October 25 that British policymakers

[79] The quotes are from a paper by Richard Bissell, as cited in Milward, *Reconstruction of Western Europe*, 284.

[80] CM (49) 62nd Conclusion, October 27, 1949, CAB 128/16. See also CP (49) 204, Bevin, "Council of Europe," October 24, 1949, and CP (49) 203, Bevin and Cripps, "Proposals for the Economic Unification of Europe," October 25, 1949, CAB 129/37 pt. I.

would do everything possible to support Western European union. But above all, they "must have regard to the position of the United Kingdom as a power with world-wide responsibilities," specifically to its responsibilities "as a leading member of the British Commonwealth and sterling area," to its duties as a partner in the North Atlantic Treaty and the Brussels Pact, and to its "obligations" under the Washington agreements of September. Reconciling all of these responsibilities, he said, necessarily precluded Britain's full-fledged integration into Western Europe.[81] Hall-Patch delivered a similar message to Henry Tasca of the ECA. Makins did the same in a conversation with George Perkins, as did Cripps in a talk with Ambassador Harriman.[82] On November 1, moreover, Cripps loudly proclaimed British policy to the OEEC in an address every bit as important as the famous integration speech Hoffman had delivered the day before. He reminded his audience that Great Britain was the "centre of the largest multilateral trading area in the world, for which [it] acted as banker," but then went on to say that British leaders were anxious to reconcile their responsibilities in this area with "support for the development of unity in Europe." Although they could not integrate into Europe, said Cripps, they would consider "sympathetically" any regional scheme consistent with Britain's "other responsibilities."[83]

If the British had doubts about how their policy would be received in Washington, the Americans seemed anxious to dispel them. In his response to Bevin's note of October 25, Acheson had pressed the British to give a positive lead in Europe. But he had also ruled out Anglo–Western European unification.[84] Hoffman had told Cripps in a private conversation that he "conceive[d] of integration on a regional basis" and was "not expecting the United Kingdom to come in."[85] Harriman had made the same points in a subsequent talk with Berthoud.[86] In addition, Hoffman had seen Cripps's address in advance, had been "thrilled" by its contents, and had later taken pains to defend Britain's special position in meetings with the Europeans and in off-the-record briefings for journalists.[87] While they were together

[81] FO tel. to Franks, from Bevin, October 25, 1949, T232/150/EEC78/11/08A.
[82] Hall-Patch tel. to FO, October 26, 1949, FO 371, 78020, UR10772; Makins, Record of Conversation [with Perkins], October 26, 1949, T232/EEC78/11/08A; and Hall-Patch, "Note of Discussion between Chancellor of Exchequer and Mr. Harriman and Mr. Katz on October 28, 1949," October 29, 1949, T232/126/EEC7/8/04(J).
[83] Cripps's speech is cited from Hall-Patch tel. to FO, November 1, 1949, FO 371, 78022, UR11020.
[84] Acheson tel. to Douglas, October 28, 1949, *FRUS, 1949*, 4:348–9; and FO tel. to Hall-Patch, from Bevin for Cripps, October 31, 1949, FO 371, 78021, UR10935.
[85] Hall-Patch tel. to FO, October 30, 1949, FO 371, 78021, UR10902.
[86] Berthoud, "Record of a Conversation with Mr. Harriman in Paris on November 5th, 1949," November 5, 1949, FO 371, 78099, UR11395.
[87] Hall-Patch tel. to FO, November 1, 1949, FO 371, 78022, UR11019. See also

in Paris, moreover, Hoffman and Cripps had come up with a "Plan of Action" that would meet the demands enumerated in the administrator's speech. Approved by the Council on November 2, 1949, the plan called for "a single large market in Europe." It committed the participating countries to devise by early 1950 a definite program to eliminate quantitative restrictions, make currencies transferable, and develop new "central institutions as may be appropriate."[88]

Anglo–American collaboration had been particularly evident in the area of trade liberalization, where both Cripps and Hoffman thought the OEEC was moving too slowly to eliminate import restrictions. An OEEC decision of July had ordered participating countries to submit "free lists" of the commodities from which quotas would be removed.[89] The British were anxious to take the lead in this area and were able to do so after the Washington conferees agreed to waive Article 9 of the Anglo–American loan agreement. The Americans had high hopes as well. In their view, the elimination of import quotas would remove one of the most "pernicious and serious obstacle[s]" to a "single market area in Europe" and thus to a "progressive improvement [in] productivity without which dollar viability [was] impossible." The Americans had pressed relentlessly for the most liberal lists possible, had warned that Congress expected nothing less, and had promised to use their "incentive" fund to ease the internal dislocations that might result from greater competition.[90]

When the lists were published in October, however, it was clear that American promises had not put the wind in European sails. Most of the lists exempted whole categories of commodities. None included imports purchased on government account. The Italians would eliminate quotas only as new tariffs came into operation. The French said that German competition made substantial removals impossible. Taken together, the lists freed only about 30 percent of the total trade between participating countries, and almost all of this consisted of raw materials or finished products that did not compete with domestic production. The British had exempted

E. M. W. Atkinson minute, November 2, 1949, and Franks tel. to FO, November 8, 1949, FO 371, 78022, UR11123 and UR11259.

[88] Hall-Patch tel. to FO, November 1, 1949, FO 371, 78022, UR11019; and text of OEEC Council decision of November 2, 1949, RG 286, Acc. 53A405, box 33, folder: Outside Orgs. – O.E.E.C.

[89] Harriman repto 5165 to Hoffman, July 12, 1949, ECA Files, box 7; Katz repto circulars 275, 278, 279, 281, and 284 to ECA, Washington, August 4, 5, 6, 8, and 9, 1949, and Bonsal repto circular 309 to ECA, Washington, September 7, 1949, ECA Files, box 8.

[90] Katz repto circular 278 to ECA, Washington, August 5, 1949, and Harriman repto circular 305 to ECA, Washington, September 3, 1949, ECA Files, box 8. See also Hoffman torep 8172 to Harriman, September 29, 1949, ECA Files, box 50; and Harriman repto circular 361 to Hoffman, October 22, 1949, ECA Files, box 8.

imports from Belgium, Switzerland, and West Germany, countries with which they ran a deficit. But despite these exemptions and the one for government imports, their list was by far the most generous.[91]

This was why Cripps could join Hoffman in demanding faster progress. Harriman repeated this demand in a meeting of the Consultative Group, as did Hoffman in his famous integration speech. Given these pressures, it was not surprising that the OEEC's Plan of Action called for the elimination of import quotas on 50 percent of all private trade by the beginning of 1950.[92] American and British leaders had worked hand in hand to back a plan that seemed to accommodate Britain's position as a world power. It was "comforting to know," Hall-Patch wrote of the plan, "that the part which appears to have been reserved for the United Kingdom is consistent with the policy recently approved by Ministers."[93]

Armed with this assurance, another team of British negotiators tackled the political side of the European agenda when the Committee of Ministers of the Council of Europe convened in Strasbourg on November 3. The Council's Consultative Assembly had held its first meeting the previous August. Coming under the influence of ardent federalists, it had voted for "a European political authority" and had passed resolutions calling for greater independence of the ministerial committee, the elimination of trade barriers, the formation of a clearing union, and the coordination of national economic policies.[94] The outcome had reinforced Bevin's prejudice against the Assembly, which he tended to view as a forum for crackpots whose utopian dreams did not square at all with the grand design of his diplomacy. He said as much in the Foreign Office paper that the Cabinet approved on October 27. This paper then became his brief when the Committee of Ministers convened in early November. Bevin threw his weight behind a motion to make the new West German government an associate member of the Council, hoping thereby to link the Germans to the Western European system. But he got his back up when it came to granting the Assembly more autonomy. He had its economic recommendations referred to the OEEC

[91]   Harriman reptos 6986, 7070, and 7130 to Hoffman, October 21, 26, and 29, 1949, and Harriman repto circular 369 to Hoffman, November 2, 1949, ECA Files, box 8.

[92]   Harriman reptos 7132, 7133, and 7190 to Hoffman, October 30 and November 2, 1949, ECA Files, box 8; and Hall-Patch tels. (2) to FO, October 30, 1949, FO 371, 78121, UR10922 and UR10929.

[93]   Hall-Patch tel. to FO, October 30, 1949, FO 371, 78021, UR10902.

[94]   American observers reported extensively on the first session of the Council of Europe. William Koren, Jr., tel. 46 to Acheson, September 6, 1949, RG 59, file: 840.00/9-649. See also Koren tels. to Acheson, August 25, 28, and 30 and September 4 and 6 (2), 1949, Frances E. Willis, First Secretary, American Embassy, Paris, dispatch #1423 to Acheson, September 2, 1949, and Koren memorandum in Bruce dispatch #820 to Acheson, September 14, 1949, in RG 59, file: 840.00/8-2549, /8-2849, /8-3049, /9-449, /9-649, /9-249, and /9-1449; and Vaughan, *Twentieth-Century Europe*, 90.

and held the Council as a whole to its original mandate, which reserved all powers to the Committee of Ministers. Both decisions safeguarded the empirical approach as well as Bevin's vision of the Council as an intergovernmental forum, not a supranational authority.[95]

The week between October 31 and November 5 – between the Paris and Strasbourg meetings – thus witnessed a vigorous reassertion of Britain's policy toward Europe. From the British point of view, moreover, this policy now had support in Washington. The ECA and the State Department seemed ready to exempt Great Britain from their plans for European unification and to uphold its world position against the strictly continental concerns of the other OEEC countries. As seen from London, a special Anglo–American relationship had taken root at the Washington Conference of September, had been nurtured in the weeks that followed, and had blossomed at the OEEC meeting of late October.

The bloom was off the rose by mid-November, however, withered by reports in London that Acheson considered Bevin's pronouncements too negative and that Hoffman was disappointed by developments that followed the meeting in Paris.[96] The Americans, as it turned out, had interpreted the Washington talks in a different light. They had acknowledged the principle of British exceptionalism; but in return they had expected the British to cultivate the ground for a unified Europe. When the British refused to do so, the heady atmosphere of Anglo–American relations was dispelled, just weeks after the Washington Conference had seemed to strike the terms of a special partnership.

VI

One source of tension involved the different American and British assessments of a strictly continental union. The ECA's policy went in two compatible directions: toward trade and payments liberalization across the ERP area as a whole and toward the formation of one or two tight economic groups that would later grow by accession and amalgamation. In the summer and early fall of 1949, it gave priority to the Fritalux association, which would begin with France, Italy, and the Benelux and then expand to include Austria, West Germany, and some of the other continental countries. Harriman had lent support to the Fritalux negotiations in the spring; Snyder during his European visit in July; Hoffman in talks with the Belgians, French, and Italians in September. In addition, Hoffman referred explicitly to the value of regional groupings in his speech to the OEEC. He told European leaders that the ECA would use up to half of its incentive fund to support

[95] Bullock, *Bevin*, 735; Vaughan, *Twentieth-Century Europe*, 90; Young, *Britain, France, and the Unity of Europe*, 115–16.
[96] See, for example, Hall-Patch letter to Strang, November 8, 1949, FO 371, 78024, UR11642.

the Fritalux project. At the same time, he and other ECA officials urged the British to throw their weight behind the project as the first step toward "wider unity" in Western Europe. Hoffman, Bissell, and William C. Foster paid a special visit to the British Embassy in Washington to impress upon Ambassador Franks the importance of a "common line" on the Fritalux negotiations. Hoffman reissued this appeal when he met with Cripps in Paris, as did Harriman in a talk with the chancellor in early November. There was no hint that Britain should join the continental group, a source of some solace to officials in London. The Americans also went out of their way to urge the Fritalux countries to maintain the sterling–dollar crossrates, remove quantitative import restrictions on a nondiscriminatory basis, and accept fixed rather than floating exchange rates. These were all issues of concern to the British, and the Americans clearly intended their concessions to elicit strong support for the Fritalux project in London.[97]

Yet these gestures were not sufficient to assuage the British. The Treasury had come to the conclusion earlier that British exports would be at a comparative disadvantage in competition with those of an efficient continental unit, while the Foreign Office had worried that a powerful European bloc would fall beyond the pale of Britain's influence. These concerns had emerged in the original debates over the merits of a European customs union and had then resurfaced, in slightly altered form, during the Fritalux negotiations. Despite American assurances, the British continued to worry that Fritalux would discriminate against their exports or throw a wrench into the OEEC's program to liberalize trade among the participating countries as a group. They much preferred this larger program, which was easier to control and involved fewer risks of discrimination against their trade. In addition, Fritalux raised the thorny political question of what to do with the Germans. Including them could revive the specter of a "German dominated bloc" that rivaled Britain's influence on the Continent; keeping them out could drive them eastward for economic support and markets unavailable in the West. "It is impossible not to dislike the implications of Fritalux," wrote Hall-Patch in a cable that summarized British thinking. "Not only does it raise awkward political problems, such as the role of Germany, but there is the clear danger that these arrangements may be converted into a protective mechanism."[98]

97   Berthoud, "Record of Conversation with Mr. Harriman in Paris on November 5th, 1949," November 5, 1949, FO 371, 78099, UR11395; and Franks tel. to FO, October 6, 1949, FO 371, 78111, UR10088. See also Franks tels. to FO, September 17 and October 5, 1949, FO 371, 78111, UR9528 and UR10044; Hall-Patch tel. to FO, October 26, 1949, FO 371, 78020, UR10772; and Hall-Patch tel. to FO, October 30, 1949, FO 371, 78021, UR10902; Hoffman torep 7997 to Harriman, September 23, 1949, ECA Files, box 49; and Hoffman torep 8214 to Harriman, September 30, 1949, Hoffman torep 8219 to Harriman from Bissell, October 1, 1949, and Hoffman torep 8350 to Katz, October 6, 1949, ECA Files, box 50.
98   Berthoud, "Record of Conversation with Mr. Harriman in Paris on November 5th,

Neither Hall-Patch nor other British officials favored open opposition to the Fritalux negotiations. Such opposition might stir a wave of "public recriminations" in the United States and Western Europe.[99] But neither would they use their influence to support the project or intercede when the negotiations began to falter. They preferred to see the project collapse under its own weight and to help its demise by throwing their influence behind the OEEC's program to eliminate half of the quantitative restrictions on intra-European trade. The last course had the double advantage of appearing to be supportive of the ECA's goals while at the same time removing at least part of the incentive for a regional grouping.

On the surface, at least, the course of events satisfied British hopes completely: By the end of 1949, Fritalux had been put in "cold storage."[100] The negotiators had stumbled over obstacles of their own making and even the ECA had withdrawn its support. In November, the French had submitted a new proposal that looked to the gradual elimination of import quotas (but not tariffs) on trade between the five countries and to an automatic system of exchange-rate adjustment, the negotiation of interindustry agreements, and the creation of collective authorities to coordinate national policies. Although the proposal left room for Germany's accession to the group, it was clearly intended by the French to regulate economic development in the former Reich and to shield themselves against an invasion of German imports. But the Dutch would participate only if the Germans were included from the start, if exchange controls remained intact, and if tariffs were equalized and quotas removed at a faster rate than the French envisioned. In addition, the Italians wanted provisions for the free movement of surplus labor, the Belgians objected to interindustry agreements, and neither the Belgians nor the Dutch were keen on the sort of *dirigiste* regime conceived by the French. This last point was also the heart of the problem for the Americans. They described the French plan as "cautious and protectionist," a scheme by which tariffs, cartel agreements, and administrative coordinators would become the "second line of defense" against the Germans once import quotas and exchange controls were removed. The Europeans, according to Hoffman, must think "not in terms of dividing markets, but [of] expanding markets." Only a "broader competitive market," the State Department added, would permit the gains in specialization, efficiency, and productivity needed to raise living standards and close the dollar gap.[101]

1949," November 5, 1949, FO 371, 78099, UR11395; and Hall-Patch tel. to FO, December 13, 1949, FO 371, 78113, UR12489. See also Hall-Patch tel. to FO, September 24, 1949, FO 371, 78111, UR9711; and E. A. Cohen of the British Treasury, letter to Leslie Rowan, October 3, 1949, T232/150/EEC78/11/08A.

99   Hall-Patch tel. to FO, December 13, 1949, FO 371, 78113, UR12489.

100   Hall-Patch tel. to FO, December 13, 1949, FO 371, 78113, UR12535.

101   Katz repto 7581 to Hoffman, November 25, 1949, ECA Files, box 8; Hoffman torep 8141 to Harriman, September 28, 1949, ECA Files, box 50; Hoffman torep 9911 to Harriman, December 8, 1949, ECA Files, box 51; and Statement Issued by

Although the change of heart in Washington at first seemed to vindicate Britain's unstated hostility to Fritalux, it had not come without damage to Anglo–American relations. The British had miscalculated the degree of American interest in the Fritalux project during the early stages of the negotiations. There were reports from Washington that the State Department lacked enthusiasm, the Treasury Department was indifferent, and the ECA was shopping for a cheap garment to wear when it asked Congress to appropriate funds for the next year of the ERP.[102] Nothing could have been further from the truth. Hoffman had spoken "passionately" of his hope that Fritalux would lead to integration across a wider area. This course would restore "dynamism and expansion" to European production while ensuring that "Western Germany could find a home and a solution and have no opportunity behind a wall of quotas and tariffs to build a war machine." Given these stakes, Bissell had warned Ambassador Franks of untoward consequences if Britain and the United States "diverged" on the Fritalux question so shortly after the Washington Conference. Hoffman had made the same point in talks with the ambassador, had become "profoundly disturbed and depressed" when the Fritalux negotiations began to falter, and had strongly implied that the British were somehow responsible. The Labour government, he told Franks in a long conversation on November 11, had failed to give "full support" to the ECA's plan for "the building of regional groups within Western Europe."[103]

In his talk with Franks, Hoffman identified a related area where British and American policies were diverging. This involved the ECA's ongoing effort to strengthen the OEEC. As we have seen, the American design for an integrated Europe had always dictated an organizational strategy that

the Department of State, December 1, 1949, *FRUS, 1949,* 4:454–5. See also Katz repto circular 324 to Hoffman, September 24, 1949, ECA Files, box 8; Webb circular airgram to Certain Diplomatic Offices, October 6, 1949, RG 59, file: 640.002/10-649; Harriman repto circular 357 to Hoffman, October 15, 1949, ECA Files, box 8; Hoffman ecato 965 to Bingham, November 9, 1949, *FRUS, 1949,* 4:443–5; Foster ecato 1646 to American Embassy, London, November 18, 1949, ECA Files, box 42; Harriman repto 7686 to Hoffman, December 1, 1949, ECA Files, box 8; Martin, Memorandum of Conversation, December 5, 1949, RG 59, PPS Records, box 27, folder: Europe 1949; Hoffman torep 9906 to Harriman, December 8, 1949, ECA Files, box 51; and Milward, *Reconstruction of Western Europe,* 310–14. See also Frances Lynch, "French Reconstruction in a European Context," and Richard T. Griffiths and Frances Lynch, "The Fritalux/Finebel Negotiations, 1949–1950," European University Working Papers Nos. 86 and 84/117 (1984).

[102] Under Secretary of the Treasury Allan Christelow letter to Under Secretary of the Treasury E. W. Playfair, October 18, 1949, FO 371, 78112, UR10776; and Franks tel. to FO, October 28, 1949, FO 371, 78021, UR10861.

[103] Hall-Patch tel. to FO, October 30, 1949, FO 371, 78021, UR10902; Franks tel. to FO, November 11, 1949, FO 371, 78023, UR11383; and Franks tel. to FO, October 5, 1949, FO 371, 78111, UR10044. See also Franks tel. to FO, October 6, 1949, FO 371, 78111, UR10088.

centralized authority in a corporate body with a European identity. This design did not belie the faith that American leaders placed in the integrating powers of the market. On the contrary, it revealed their conviction that economic integration could be achieved only between countries with roughly congruent monetary and fiscal policies. Bringing this congruence about required centralized coordination. "We believe," as Foster explained, "that if the elimination of QRs [quantitative restrictions] is to be permanent there must be really effective machinery for direct co-ordination of national policies by agreement or by some international control over actions of governments and central banks."[104] Just as important was the parallel conviction that some measure of supranationalism would be needed to harness Germany's resources to the cause of recovery and security in Western Europe. For policymakers in Washington, then, economic and security imperatives ran along a path that led to central institutions of economic coordination and control. For those in London, the same imperatives followed a course in the opposite direction.

These differences, so apparent from the start, reemerged in the second half of 1949, when the ECA and the State Department renewed their campaign to reorganize the OEEC. Even before the Washington Conference, both agencies had called again for the creation of a new post of director general and for the appointment to that position "of a leader with sufficient authority, stature and international prestige to influence member governments toward greater European cooperation." The leader they had in mind was Paul-Henri Spaak, who seemed imminently available after a cabinet change relieved him of his duties as prime minister of Belgium and president of the OEEC's Council. The French and the Belgians seemed to support the American proposal. But the British position had not changed since the issue was mooted several months earlier.[105] As Harriman pointed out, "the reasons why we wanted Spaak were the very reasons why the British were opposing him, namely, the making of OEEC [into] an effective organization freed from the present British curb-rein."[106]

Harriman and other Americans in Europe wanted the State Department and the ECA to compel the British to cooperate.[107] Truman himself felt "quite strongly" that the United States should "press this matter and do

[104] Foster quoted from Milward, *Reconstruction of Western Europe*, 313.

[105] Perkins memorandum to Acheson, September 9, 1949, *FRUS, 1949*, 4:421–3. See also Douglas MacArthur, State Department Division of Western European Affairs, Memorandum of Conversation, September 15, 1949, RG 43, box 312, folder: Memos of Conversations, Foreign Ministers and Secretary of State, September 1949; and Harriman repto 6563 to Hoffman, September 27, 1949, RG 59, file: 103.ECA/9-3049.

[106] Harriman repto 6817 to Acheson, October 12, 1949, Harriman Papers, folder: OEEC.

[107] Ibid.; and Bruce tel. to Acheson, October 22, 1949, RG 59, file: 840.00/10-2249.

everything possible to make OEEC fully effective."[108] In mid-October, Acheson sent Bevin a personal note pointing out that Spaak's appointment would strengthen the OEEC and dispel the growing conviction that the organization had failed "to function with full effectiveness as an instrument of cooperation."[109] In talks with Bevin, Ambassador Douglas also warned that Congress might curtail its support for the third year of the Marshall Plan unless further "progress toward economic integration" was forthcoming. Spaak's appointment, he said, would be a "symbol" of such progress.[110]

Despite American blandishments, the organizational imperatives in British diplomacy dictated a different course. In his response to Acheson's personal appeal, Bevin said only that Spaak's services were still needed in Belgium and that his lack of ministerial stature made his appointment as director general inappropriate.[111] According to Ambassador at Large Philip C. Jessup, however, the British were worried that Spaak would try, in Cripps's words, to " 'overlord' " the economic policies and foreign affairs of the participating countries.[112] Indeed, equipping the OEEC with supranational authority hardly squared with the grand design that guided British diplomacy, as Bevin himself made clear in his talks with Ambassador Douglas. Great Britain, he said, was "a world Power as opposed to a purely European Power." The British had "obligations in the Far East, to the Commonwealth, and under the Atlantic Pact" and thus "could not tolerate being treated as if we were only a part of Europe." Neither could they "enter into obligations in Europe in a form which would not allow us to extricate ourselves if Europe showed signs of following policies prejudicial to our interests or to our position as a world Power."[113] So long as Britain remained in the OEEC, the European agency would have to function as a vehicle of intergovernmental collaboration in which all decisions "were discussed in detail beforehand and approved by all member countries."[114]

Harriman, Hoffman, and Acheson were frankly exasperated by the British

[108]	Webb memorandum, "Meeting with the President, Saturday, October 1, 1949," October 1, 1949, RG 59, file: 840.50/10-149.
[109]	Acheson tel. to Douglas, London, October 14, 1949, *FRUS, 1949*, 4:429–30.
[110]	Douglas tels. to Acheson, October 18 and 26, 1949, *FRUS, 1949*, 4:430–1, 435–7.
[111]	Douglas tel. to Acheson, October 26, 1949, RG 59, file: 840.00/10-2649. See also Harriman repto 6563 to Hoffman and Acheson, September 27, 1949, Harriman Papers, folder: OEEC.
[112]	Ambassador Warren R. Austin tel. to Acheson, from Jessup, September 30, 1949, RG 59, file: 840.50Recovery/9-3049.
[113]	Bevin dispatch to Hall-Patch, October 26, 1949, FO 371, 78134, UR10815. For the American records, see Douglas tels. to Acheson, October 18 and 26, 1949, *FRUS, 1949*, 4:430–1, 435–7. Bevin made the same points in a conversation with the French ambassador. See his dispatch to Hall-Patch, October 15, 1949, FO 371, 78133, UR10409.
[114]	Hall-Patch tel. to FO, October 6, 1949, FO 371, 78099, UR10084. See also the

attitude. After the Washington Conference, they were ready to admit that Britain could not "mesh its economy as fully into that of the continent as we believe it essential that the continentals do among themselves." But they fully expected the British, once endowed with this exemption, to champion the cause of integration and to collaborate with any group that emerged. Britain must abandon its practice of "standing off too much from the continent," because none of the continental countries, least of all France, would take the lead without assistance from London. As Acheson explained to Bevin in a subsequent communication, there was a "growing conviction" in Washington that greater progress toward European economic integration was "essential" and that such progress was impossible "without the strong support and, to the greatest extent possible, participation of the UK, backed by the rest of the Commonwealth."[115]

Hoffman made some of the same points a week later, when he arrived in Paris to deliver his integration speech to the OEEC. By that time, of course, ECA planning envisioned the formation of tight regional groupings capped by a supranational monetary authority and trade commission. It was up to the OEEC to move in this direction, and to do so the organization needed to be strengthened by the appointment of a strong director general. In meetings with Bevin and Cripps, Hoffman repeated the familiar arguments about impressing Congress and giving political direction to the OEEC countries, leaving the impression that Spaak's appointment was "second only in dramatic importance to the theme of European integration."[116] Bevin and Cripps plodded through the usual list of British reservations, but it was Hall-Patch who cut to the core of their objections when he cabled the Foreign Office that

the potential danger of this proposal is that policy-making will tend to move away from the delegations to the Chairman of the Council acting in concert with Harriman. Once Spaak is independent Chairman, Harriman will be increasingly reluctant to deal with any lesser lights in Paris. Hitherto, policy has been made by consultation between delegations acting on instructions from their Governments and then bringing their concerted opinion to bear on Harriman. Under the new dispensation, Harriman will tend to reach decisions 'on the political level' with Spaak, which both

minute by D. Aien, October 10, 1949, Berthoud minute to Strang, October 11, 1949, and Cripps's minute of October 14, 1949, FO 371, 78099, UR10405 and UR10719.

[115] Foster torep 8841 to Harriman, Katz, and Bissell, October 27, 1949, RG 286, Acc. 53A177, box 87, folder: Eyes Only, Personal Correspondence, Sept.–Oct. 1949; and Acheson tel. to Douglas, October 28, 1949, *FRUS, 1949*, 4:348–9.

[116] Hall-Patch tel. to FO, October 30, 1949, FO 371, 78099, UR10909. See also unsigned "Record of Conversation at H.M. Embassy, Paris, on 2nd November," November 4, 1949, FO 371, 78134, UR11296. Harriman was present at these meetings and had made the same points in an earlier conversation with Cripps. See Hall-Patch letter to Makins, October 29, 1949, with attached note of discussion between Cripps, Harriman, and Katz on October 28, 1949, FO 371, 78036, UR10981.

will seek inevitably to impose on delegations. It would be a totally different set-up ...not without dangerous possibilities.[117]

In deference to American opinion, Bevin reluctantly agreed to air Hoffman's proposal before a meeting of OEEC ministers. What happened after that depends on the documents consulted. According to the British documents, Bevin had undertaken to present the case for Spaak's appointment on behalf of the Americans, which he did at an informal meeting in the Quai d'Orsay on November 4. The British report shows Bevin surrendering the chair to Paul Van Zeeland of Belgium and then giving an impartial account of the American and British positions to a group of ministers who were frankly unenthusiastic about Spaak's appointment. According to the American records, however, Bevin had promised that Hoffman and Harriman could present their own brief, only then to summon the ministers after Hoffman had left Paris, exclude Harriman from the meeting, and present the issue with such a bias that none of the ministers were disposed to act.[118]

The Americans clearly felt "put out" by what had happened. Harriman complained again of being locked out of ministerial meetings. He took the matter up in a difficult interview with Bevin, as he had done earlier in a conversation with Berthoud that also ranged over the Fritalux negotiations and Germany's reintegration into Western Europe. Hoffman made the same connections in his talk with Ambassador Franks on November 11, when he implied that Britain had not done enough to strengthen the OEEC, support Fritalux, or otherwise create an integrated European framework that could control the Germans and reassure the French.[119]

The documents leave no doubt that differences over the Fritalux project and the OEEC had soured relations between the two countries, barely two months after the Washington Conference had ended in sweet predictions of an Anglo–American partnership. But as Hoffman's remark points out, the depths of disillusionment in Washington cannot be fathomed without

[117] Hall-Patch tel. to FO, for Makins, October 31, 1949, FO 371, 78099, UR10930.
[118] For the British records, see unsigned "Record of Conversation at H.M. Embassy, Paris, on 2nd November," November 4, 1949, and Sir Oliver Harvey, British Ambassador to Paris, tel. to FO, November 3, 1949, FO 371, 78134, UR11296 and UR11324; and Berthoud, "Record of an Informal Meeting of the 12 Members of the Committee of Ministers of the Council of Europe Held at the Quai d'Orsay, Friday November 4th," November 4, 1949, FO 371, 78099, UR11395. For an American account, see Harriman tel. to Acheson, November 6, 1949, *FRUS, 1949*, 4:440–3.
[119] Harvey tel. to FO, from Bevin, November 8, 1949, FO 371, 78099, UR11217. See also Berthoud minute to Bevin, November 4, 1949, FO 371, 78100, UR12840; and Berthoud, "Record of Conversation with Mr. Harriman," November 5, 1949, Berthoud minute, November 6, 1949, and Makins minute, November 8, 1949, FO 371, 78099, UR11395 and UR11410.

reference to the German problem. All three issues were connected by the American conviction that solving this problem depended on bringing Germany within an integrated European framework. Germany's reintegration had been a central theme in Kennan's work, in the ECA position papers, and in the great integration debate that rang through the State Department in the fall of 1949. One of the "major preoccupations" of policymakers in the State Department, reported the British Embassy at the height of the battle over Spaak's appointment, was to see "that Western Germany was brought and kept within the Western fold." In their eyes, as Franks had noted earlier, Britain was "not giving a strong enough lead" in this direction.[120]

The German issue loomed especially large because of the outburst of nationalism and agitation against the dismantling program that had accompanied the German election campaign of August. Chancellor Konrad Adenauer, who headed the new German government, urged the Allies to halt dismantling and curb other restrictions on German industry, stressing in his pleas the adverse consequences of these policies on Germany's recovery and their tendency to feed Soviet propaganda, strengthen extremist sentiment, and undermine his government. Under these circumstances, Hoffman, Acheson, U.S. High Commissioner John J. McCloy, and other American officials thought that timely concessions were needed if the Federal Republic was going to be brought into the Western community. The only alternative, according to the State Department, was a new Rapallo Pact or a neutral Germany that played West against East to the detriment of European recovery and security. Acheson spoke in these terms when he discussed the reparations problem with Bevin and Schuman in September and October, only to learn that both men wanted to hold the line against further concessions.[121]

By November, the situation had changed and at least some progress was possible. Impressed with the spreading opposition to dismantling in West Germany (and in his own party), Bevin was ready to scrap the program in return for German concessions on other issues. At the same time, a reshuffling of the government in Paris left Schuman in a stronger position to push his own plans for a rapprochement with the Germans. Both men now agreed to join Acheson at a Foreign Ministers meeting in Paris, out of which came a new directive that the Allied High Commission then used to negotiate the Petersberg Protocol with the Federal Republic. Signed later in November, the protocol further curtailed the dismantling of plants that were unrelated to war production and relaxed other restrictions on German industry. The

---

[120] Rowan letter to E. A. Hitchman of the British Treasury, November 15, 1949, T232/196/EEC7/1/08; and Franks tel. to FO, November 9, 1949, T232/150EEC/78/11/08A.

[121] This part of the story can be followed in *FRUS, 1949*, 3:290–4, 295–304, 594–5, 597–9, 599–603, 608–9, 614–18.

Federal Republic promised in return to join the Ruhr Authority, prohibit cartelistic business practices, cooperate with the Military Security Board, and conduct its political affairs according to democratic principles.[122] To appease French opinion, the protocol had not raised the level of German steel production. In addition, McCloy had agreed to study the dual pricing of German coal and to limit the Germans to a 20-percent devaluation of the mark.[123]

Although the Petersberg Protocol was an important achievement, clearing the impediments to Germany's recovery amounted to only half of the American program. Acheson also thought it important to reassimilate Germany into an integrated Western European system. Early in November, amid all of the controversy over Spaak's appointment, he had added the issue of European integration to the agenda of the Paris meeting. The British Embassy in Washington warned of "inspired" press reports that Acheson would raise the issue with reference to "Germany's place in Western Europe." There was a strong feeling in Washington, Ambassador Franks reported, "that even though the United Kingdom cannot be more than an associate member or perhaps a benevolent spectator, it ought to make every effort to show the other Western European Governments how best to achieve closer economic co-ordination among themselves." The Americans saw economic integration as the "salvation" of Western Europe, said Franks, if only because the German problem was insoluble except in this context. But they also understood that French policymakers were apprehensive lest they be left alone to face the Germans in an integrated Europe. For this reason, the Americans thought that progress toward European integration and German reintegration depended on a strong British lead. It was "Germany's rather than the United Kingdom's closer integration into Europe," Franks concluded, that was "now chiefly preoccupying the State Department."[124]

This was exactly the point that Acheson made when the subject came up at the Foreign Ministers meeting in Paris. He told his associates, in Bevin's words, "that unless Germany became part of a Western European whole he saw no possibility of her developing on other than nationalistic lines." Bevin was the target of this remark, and if there were any doubts, Schuman quickly dispelled them. Schuman had earlier told Bevin of the swell of attacks against British obstructionism in the French press and across Western Europe, to which he now added his opinion that "Europe was inconceivable without Great Britain." France would make a contribution "in the form of a Franco–German reconciliation." But Britain had to contribute as well, and this contribution should take the form of a "synthesis" that reconciled

---

[122] See the documents in *FRUS, 1949*, 3:618–21, 621–5, 305–6, 306–8, 343–8, 632–3, 634–5, 635–8.

[123] This story can be followed in *FRUS, 1949*, 3:448–77.

[124] Franks tels. to FO, November 5 and 9, 1949, T232/150/EEC78/11/08A. See also FO tel. to Franks, November 8, 1949, T232/150/EEC78/11/08A.

its obligations to Western Europe with its commitments elsewhere. As in earlier debates on the same subject, Bevin found himself on the defensive, a posture that brought out the best and the worst in him. Reeling like a boxer under heavy blows, he began with a pugnacious defense of Britain's contributions and ended by crying foul. The attacks against Great Britain were unfair, he said. Continued criticism would alienate the British electorate and disrupt the Western alliance. Acheson remained unperturbed – and undeterred. Although he did not mean to minimize the contributions of Great Britain, least of all those of its foreign secretary, he nonetheless felt bound to point out that "we were in the grips of so strong a tide that we must redouble our efforts." He was speaking of the British effort, as he was when he told the ministers that their slogan should be " 'once more unto the breach' "[125]

Bevin had regained his form when he and Acheson met for another bout the following day. Never at home in a corner, he liked to seize the initiative from the start, as he had done when telling Ambassador Harriman earlier how tiresome it was to act as a one-man "clearing house" for ambiguous European plans dreamed up in Washington. This was the same tactic Bevin used in his rematch with Acheson. When Acheson brought up the subject of integration in connection with Spaak's appointment as director general, Bevin demanded to know what the Americans meant by "integration" and what they thought the "superman" should do. Acheson defined integration as a process, mentioning the "free movement of goods, of labour, and of funds." But on the duties of a director general he could offer nothing but a promise to communicate his views at a later date. Bevin insisted that Acheson communicate directly with all of the participating governments, "rather than through me," and with this démarche the meeting adjourned.[126]

Acheson's proposal, sent to London on November 16, urged the appointment of an "outstanding European public personality" to the post of director general. The appointee would have "international status" and would formulate issues for discussion, work with participating governments to implement agreed policies, and represent the OEEC to world opinion.[127] Although the job description looked more appropriate to a salesman than to a director general, the key was to be found in the words "international status," which expressed the familiar American vision of a truly *European* authority independent of participating governments. Hall-Patch thought it best to give some ground to American dreams, agree to the new position, and then see that it went to a British minister. But Bevin understood that appointing a figure of international status meant endowing the OEEC with

[125] Harvey tel. to FO, from Bevin, November 11, 1949, FO 371, 78023, UR11397.
[126] Makins minute, November 8, 1949, FO 371, 78099, UR11410; and FO tel. to Franks, November 12, 1949, FO 371, 78134, UR11438. See also McCloy tel. to State Department, November 12, 1949, *FRUS, 1949*, 4:447–8.
[127] Acheson tel. to Douglas, November 16, 1949, *FRUS, 1949*, 4:448–50.

supranational power. It meant bringing Britain into Europe at the expense of its world position. Bevin told Douglas that Britain would not take the lead on behalf of the American proposal. Neither would it object if other countries were amenable and if the proposal involved no change in the OEEC's constitution. The last stipulation effectively ruled out a director general of international status, a position that Attlee reaffirmed when Douglas carried the American brief to 10 Downing Street on December 1. Douglas said that Acheson's proposition would fall to the ground without positive British support. Attlee replied that Van Zeeland of Belgium had prepared a similar proposal, that both proposals should be laid before the Consultative Group, and that Britain would remain a neutral bystander.[128]

Attlee and Bevin had made it clear that Britain would write its own role rather than play the part assigned in an American script. Cripps was no different when he took center stage at the meeting of the Consultative Group on December 20. Harriman had been working behind the scenes to circulate the American proposal and coordinate signals with Van Zeeland. But when he arrived for the meeting, he was shocked to learn that Cripps had convened the body earlier and had won its support for a resolution that "completely emasculate[d]" Acheson's proposal. This was too much for the ambassador, who recovered from his "bewilderment" fast enough to rebuke the ministers with a stern lecture. He queried Cripps about his government's promise to play a neutral role, went on to restate the American position, and finished with an ultimatum. Unless concessions were forthcoming, he said, the United States would be " 'obliged to review its attitude toward [the] plan.' " This latest intervention " 'à la Harriman,' " sent the meeting into a brief convulsion, following which the ministers made some gestures to American opinion. There was no compromise of principle. The ministers refused to alter the convention or appoint an "international official." But they agreed provisionally to appoint a special "envoy" as "dynamic liaison" to the United States, other international organizations, and nonmember governments. The envoy would act in an advisory capacity only, would take his instructions from the Council and the Consultative Group, and would not control the Secretariat. Nor would he be able to hold another office, either in his own country or in an international organization. This provision effectively excluded Spaak, who was still a member of the Belgian parliament and president of the Council of Europe's Consultative Assembly.[129] In truth,

[128] Douglas tel. to Acheson, November 23, 1949, *FRUS, 1949,* 4:451–3; Douglas tel. to Acheson, December 1, 1949, RG 59, file: 840.50Recovery/12-149; Hall-Patch letter to Strang, November 21, 1949, Bevin dispatch to Franks, November 23, 1949, and FO tel. to Franks, December 2, 1949, FO 371, 78135, UR11887, UR11886, and UR12183; and Berthoud minute to Strang and Attlee, December 1, 1949, PREM 8/982.

[129] Katz repto 8075 to Hoffman, December 21, 1949, *FRUS, 1949,* 4:464–7; Hall-Patch tel. to FO, December 20, 1949, FO 371, 78100, UR12816; and Hall-Patch letter to Makins, December 23, 1949, FO 371, 78315, UR13040. See also Hall-

as Acheson pointed out, it did not provide an "acceptable basis for Spaak or any other strong European personality to consider taking [the] position."[130]

Stymied on this front, the Americans also found little support for their definition of integration. Acheson had defined integration as a process that included the free movement of goods, capital, and labor. This process entailed the removal of import quotas, the use of tariffs "as a cushion and not as a quantitative restriction," and the convertibility of European currencies. Initiatives of this sort had made up the traders' part of the American policy synthesis since the beginning of the Marshall Plan. In operation, as Berthoud rightly noted, they aimed to re-create in Western Europe the kind of "large free market" that "exists in America" and, with it, "the American conception of life" based "on free competition and the advantages of mass production." According to Berthoud, moreover, this part of the American program was "quite consistent with our objective of returning to a multilateral trade and payments world" and certainly less ambitious than the resolutions passed by the European Assembly in August.[131]

Others were not so sure. Although Cripps had taken the lead in cutting quantitative import restrictions in October, he and other British officials had become more cautious by December, when the ECA submitted a sweeping new proposal for the elimination of import quotas and the formation of an intra-European payments union. The proposed payments union would rely on both free-market mechanisms and administrative devices to integrate economies, specifically on the full transferability of currencies and on an executive board with considerable autonomy of participating governments. It would be negotiated in the months ahead, with results that are reported in the next chapter, the point to note being that American ambitions were outreaching what Britain and the other participating countries thought possible. The French and the Italians worried that unleashing competitive forces too quickly would destabilize their economies and lead to untoward social and political repercussions. Cripps agreed. He told the Europeans that trade liberalization had gone far enough, and the Americans that their proposal amounted to a "fifty-year programme." In addition, the British were far from happy with the idea of a semiautonomous executive board, which raised anew the specter of supranationalism so recently laid to rest in the debate over the appointment of a director general.[132]

Patch tel. to FO, December 20, 1949, FO 371, 78100, UR12815; and Katz repto circular 428 to Hoffman, December 22, 1949, ECA Files, box 8.
[130] Acheson tel. to Bruce, December 23, 1949, *FRUS, 1949*, 4:468.
[131] Hall-Patch letter to Makins, November 12, 1949, and Berthoud letter to Gore-Booth, November 17, 1949, FO 371, 78024, UR11817 and UR11584. See also FO tel. to Franks, November 12, 1949, FO 371, 78134, UR11438; Berthoud minute to Makins, November 17, 1949, FO 371, 78024, UR11817; and Berthoud minute to Jebb, November 26, 1949, FO 371, 78025, UR12242.
[132] Cripps quoted in Milward, *Reconstruction of Western Europe*, 304. See also Hall-

VII

British and American policymakers would enter the new year still at log-gerheads over some of the same issues that had divided them during Snyder's visit to London six months earlier. Much had been accomplished, to be sure. The trade-liberalization program had been launched, the sterling crisis managed, the dollar gap addressed, and the Petersberg Protocol signed. Perhaps most important, the ECA and the State Department had accepted the principle of British exceptionalism. But they had done so to expedite progress toward European integration and were sorely disappointed when the British refused to give a lead in that direction. Particularly disturbing were the indications of Britain's opposition to a continental union that might come under Germany's leadership. Although the Americans saw in such a union a way to control the Germans and deter the Soviets, the British appeared to be applying to Western Europe a variant of their traditional policy toward the Continent as a whole, whereby the balance of power was maintained against any state that threatened to dominate. American poli-cymakers interpreted the collapse of Fritalux in such a light, a development that led to great disappointment in Washington and to new tensions in the Anglo–American relationship.

In truth, not all of the new tensions could be blamed on the British. Britain had its own design, part of which struck a sympathetic chord in Washington. American policymakers, Kennan notwithstanding, did not envision an At-lantic union any more than did the British, who jealously guarded their right to nourish internal economic plans and social programs without ex-ternal intrusions. But both sides had come to the conclusion that shoring up Britain's position around the world would serve the larger interests of the Western alliance. It was this conclusion that led American policymakers to accept the principle of British exceptionalism and thrust the burden of Germany's reintegration onto France. What the Americans failed to under-stand was that Britain could not retain its freedom elsewhere if forced to liberalize trade at the cost of its reserves or if required to square its policies with those of a continental group. If progress was going to be made, the Americans had to underwrite the reserves of the sterling area and give Great Britain a special position in their plans for a European payments union. For their part, the British had to leap "once more unto the breach." They had to tolerate the trend toward a "nuclear" Europe, because there were clear signs that France was moving toward this goal and accepting it was the price Britain would have to pay for its commitment to the Empire and its position as the "nodal point of three systems."

Patch tels. (2) to FO, December 10, 1949, T232/150/EEC78/11/08A; Berthoud minute to Broad, December 22, 1949, FO 371, 78113, UR12943; and Hall-Patch letter to Makins, December 23, 1949, FO 371, 78135, UR13040.

7

Between union and unity: European integration and the sterling–dollar dualism

I

BECAUSE 1950 was a watershed in the history of the Marshall Plan, a year that marked the plan's greatest triumph in the European Payments Union and its denouement in the wake of the Korean War, it is important to begin this chapter covering the first half of the new year with an introduction that also reviews the major themes of the narrative so far. As we have seen, much of American recovery policy was dominated by a corporative view that compressed the lessons supposedly learned from both ends of American history. American Marshall Planners aimed to bring to pass in Western Europe "the miracle wrought by the Founding Fathers" and the New Dealers in their own country.[1] They wanted to replace the old European system of separate sovereignties and redistributive politics with a unified and productive order similar to the one that had evolved in the United States under the Constitution of 1787 and the corporative neo-capitalism of the twentieth century. They were committed by political philosophy and economic doctrine to a policy that combined the principle of federalism with the New Deal synthesis. The first entailed at least some merger of economic sovereignties. The second blended an older faith in the rationalizing power of the market with a modern belief in economic planning and bureaucratic management.

So far as European recovery was concerned, American ideals translated into practical plans for liberalizing trade and payments, building central institutions of coordination and control, and devising public–private partnerships for greater growth and efficiency. In the American dream, these and related initiatives would lead neither to the laissez-faire capitalism of a bygone day nor to the paternalistic statism of an Orwellian nightmare. They would lead instead to an organic economic and political order in which class conflict gave way to class collaboration, national rivalry to

[1] Unidentified source cited in Bullock, *Bevin*, 76.

rapprochement, economic autarky to economic regionalism and, then, to a multilateral system of world trade. Nor did these potential benefits exhaust the list. The same initiatives, and those having to do with the North Atlantic Treaty, would also create a unit of power strong enough to control the Germans and contain the Soviets. The idea of integration continued to link these security objectives to economic goals. It was the interlocking concept in the American plan for Western Europe, the key to a large single market, a workable balance of power among the Western states, and a favorable correlation of forces on the Continent.

Because the New Deal policy synthesis cut across older economic orthodoxies and more conventional conceptions of national interest, it had always raised a formidable array of obstacles on both sides of the Atlantic. One of these lay in the stubborn devotion of the Belgians to the free-trade precepts of classical economic doctrine. This doctrine suited Belgium's position as a major creditor on intra-European account and had strong support in the American Treasury, where policymakers were increasingly critical of the ECA's attempt to balance stable employment and regional coordination against their own commitment to multilateral trade and convertible currencies. Another barrier was found in the lingering determination of the French to guide Germany's recovery into channels that protected their economic and security ambitions. French plans for a *dirigiste* regime could not be squared with the New Deal synthesis that guided American Marshall Planners, who also worried that curbing Germany's development would leave Western Europe economically and militarily weak, forever dependent on American aid and protection, and forever vulnerable to Soviet aggression, to resurgent German nationalism, or to a replay of Rapallo.

The Americans had hoped to ease French security concerns by creating a Western European system balanced between British and German power. But progress in this direction had been stalled by the British, who were reluctant to support policies that would draw them too deeply into Europe or expose their economy to the competitive pressures of an unfettered market. Although American leaders had conceded the principle of British exceptionalism, the bitter battles of late 1949 would be followed in the new year by controversies over the ECA's plan for a European clearing union. Like the Belgians, moreover, the British could count on some support in Washington, where strategic and military considerations were driving the State Department toward an Anglo–American partnership that recognized Britain's commitments in areas of the world deemed vital to the Western alliance.

Considerations of this sort would prompt new efforts to reconcile Britain's role in Western Europe with its leadership of the Commonwealth and sterling area. In the first half of 1950, policymakers in London and Washington would finally hammer out a compromise that brought the British into a European payments union on terms that underwrote the international position of pound sterling. The compromise removed some of the impediments to Western European integration. But it also acknowledged Britain's claim to a unique place among the ERP countries, thereby taking British and American policymakers farther down the road mapped out in the great integration debate and the trilateral talks of 1949. Together with the failure of Allied leaders to organize a framework for coordinating national policies, it pointed up the dualism in Anglo–American diplomacy that compelled the French to bear the burden of Germany's reintegration. The result was a continental system that excluded Great Britain.

II

In late 1949, as noted in the last chapter, the ECA had drawn up an intra-European payments plan that aimed to make European currencies fully transferable on current-account transactions. Its larger goal was to eliminate bilateral barriers to the expansion of trade between the OEEC countries and to the creation of an integrated market that Paul Hoffman and others saw as one of the secrets to European economic growth and viability. Indeed, the ECA linked its plan to intra-European trade reform, specifically to the rapid reduction of quantitative import restrictions and the multilateraliza- tion of any restrictions that remained. These restrictions had grown out of the disequilibrium in intra-European payments, which the ECA would cor- rect through a payments scheme that combined the planners' and traders' approaches and used both to drive participating countries to balance ac- counts on current transactions.

The ECA's plan envisioned the fully automatic and multilateral offsetting of credits and debits among participating countries, leaving each country in net surplus or deficit to the group as a whole. Offsetting arrangements would include the sterling area as well as the ERP countries, would be administered through a new clearing union, and would be based on a com- mon unit of account for calculating the surplus or deficit position of member states. The ECA would use conditional dollar grants to cover "structural deficits and surpluses" that could not be financed through the payments system. But it would also build into the system automatic and administrative mechanisms "to induce both debtors and creditors to move towards equi- librium" in ordinary settlements. The automatic mechanism would involve an obligation on creditors and debtors respectively to cover a portion of their surpluses or deficits through new credits or gold and dollar payments to the clearing union. The principal administrative mechanism would com- prise continuous consultation among member states, mutual review of in- ternal policies, and collective recommendations for maintaining equilibrium by adjusting these policies or revising exchange rates.[2]

[2] Harriman repto 7841 to Hoffman, December 9, 1949, ECA Files, box 8. See also

Consultation would be institutionalized in a managing board operating within the framework of the OEEC but empowered to launch investigations and take action by *majority* rather than unanimous vote. The board would not be a truly supranational authority. But neither would it be another of those "OEEC-type committees" that made decisive and effective action impossible. For policymakers in the ECA, the board represented a compromise between these organizational strategies, one that would circumvent the question of sovereignty while limiting the exercise of national power through what amounted to government vetoes. In addition, there would be an ECA representative on the board, who would be backed up by ECA control over the use of conditional funds contributed to the union. These provisions and those regarding the voting formula would give the board considerable independence of participating governments and substantial influence over national policies. Over time, or so the ECA hoped, they might transform the board into a supranational instrument of economic coordination and control.[3]

The new year opened with what appeared to be a happy note of consensus on the ECA's proposal. The OEEC had appointed a working group that was considering a plan, drafted by Hubert Ansiaux of Belgium, similar to what the ECA had in mind.[4] American policymakers had seen the Ansiaux draft, which included provisions for multilateral offsetting, administrative coordination, and automatic incentives. They urged greater emphasis on these points in the final plan, particularly on the managing board's authority to coordinate national policies, and by mid-January the financial experts had finished a second draft, which ECA officials considered "excellent." Averell Harriman also reported "general agreement" among members of the working group and good prospects for OEEC approval at a "very early date."[5] Hoffman made the same forecast, telling a congressional committee

Hoffman torep 8769 to Harriman, October 25, 1949, and Foster torep 9606 to Harriman, November 26, 1949, ECA Files, box 50: Hoffman torep 9788 to Harriman, December 3, 1949, ECA Files, box 51; Harriman repto 7717 to Hoffman, December 3, 1949, and Harriman repto circulars 416 and 421 to Hoffman, December 12 and 14, 1949, ECA Files, box 8; and Bissell letter to Nitze, December 15, 1949, RG 59, PPS Records, box 27, folder: Europe 1949.

3 Hoffman torep 8769 to Harriman, October 25, 1949, and Foster torep 9606 to Harriman, November 26, 1949, ECA Files, box 50; Harriman repto 7717 to Hoffman, December 3, 1949, ECA Files, box 8; and Hoffman torep 9824 to Harriman, December 5, 1949, ECA Files, box 51.

4 For the Ansiaux plan, see Philip Bonsal, Political Adviser to Harriman, repto 8248 to Hoffman from Tasca for Katz, December 30, 1949, ECA Files, box 8. On the initial meetings of the OEEC's working group, see Bonsal reptos 8202, 8230, and 8242 to Hoffman from Tasca for Katz and Gordon, December 28, 29, and 30, 1949, ECA Files, box 8.

5 Hoffman torep 566 to Harriman, January 19, 1950, ECA Files, box 63; and Harriman repto circular 14, January 17, 1950, ECA Files, box 20. See also Hoffman torep 36

that a payments union would be operating within ninety days.[6] What followed, however, proved nothing if not the old adage that even the best laid plans often go awry. Despite the early signs of quick progress and consensus all around, the ECA soon found itself locked in a desperate battle to defend its views against critics on both sides of the ocean.

Officials in other departments of the Truman administration worried that a regional currency union, particularly one with American membership, would contravene prior commitments to the IMF. It would render the IMF little more than a "rubber stamp," they said, and involve a wholesale retreat from the international approach to equilibrium spelled out in the IMF charter and in the General Agreement on Tariffs and Trade. Assistant Secretary of the Treasury Frank Southard, who also acted as American executive director of the IMF, was especially reluctant to create a regional payments union with a managing board strong enough to rival the prestige of the IMF or challenge its authority in matters pertaining to the internal policies of member states. In addition, he and others in the Agriculture, Commerce, and Treasury departments were not convinced that a special regional arrangement was as necessary as it might have been prior to the devaluations of late 1949, which had done a good deal to improve Western Europe's balance of payments with the dollar area. On the contrary, they worried that a regional union might reverse these gains. It might encourage the ERP countries to export to one another rather than to the Western Hemisphere, they said. It might even lead to the formation of a permanent soft-currency trading bloc, with results that would integrate Western Europe at the expense of viability between the dollar and nondollar areas.

These fears were a partial reflection of the lingering and well-founded suspicion that British leaders would be reluctant to abandon bilateral controls for the automatic and multilateral mechanism of a payments union. Special arrangements might be necessary to protect Britain's leadership of the sterling area and its commitment to the welfare state, arrangements that could well result in the sort of soft-currency bloc a European union was designed to prevent. Given these suspicions, some American officials preferred a "nuclear" approach that would involve a smaller, more homogeneous group of continental countries, by which they meant a group more committed than Britain to free-market economies. At the very least, they thought that the proposed union must provide for full transferability and substantial gold settlements in order to force participating countries toward a multilateral system of world trade and payments.[7]

to Harriman, January 3, 1950, ECA Files, box 63; and Harriman repto circulars 6 and 13 to Hoffman, January 7 and 17, 1950, ECA Files, box 20.

[6] Hoffman's remark is reported in *New York Times*, January 14, 1950, 1.

[7] Irving S. Friedman, Treasury Department, memorandum to A. N. Overby, Deputy Managing Director, IMF, November 2, 1949, and Overby letter to Snyder, with

These differences came to a head during a stormy meeting of the National Advisory Council (NAC) on January 23. The NAC agreed to support a European payments union, but only if the union's operations did not conflict with the commitment to nondiscrimination spelled out in other agreements or prevent any participating country or group of countries "from moving as rapidly as possible toward full currency convertibility and closer integration, independently of the rate of progress evidenced by the other members of the clearing union." In addition, the payments union was to maintain close working relations with the IMF. It was to defer to the IMF's primary jurisdiction in matters relating to exchange rates and internal financial policies and was to have no American representation on its managing board, lest this involve the United States in a "conflict of recommendations" between the board and the Fund.[8] These last reservations struck directly at the planners' approach, which formed one of the central elements in the ECA's equation for a European neo-capitalism. They would reduce the ECA's ability to influence the managing board and the board's effectiveness as an agency of economic coordination and control.

While these disputes were being ironed out in Washington, the Europeans were raising their own objections to the ECA's proposal. Under the OEEC's Plan of Action of November, the participating countries were committed to integrating economies by reducing import quotas, multilateralizing payments, and building central institutions. But most were unwilling to move as rapidly in this direction as the ECA expected, in large part because unleashing competitive pressures and coordinating national policies could interfere with the economic and political agendas they were pursuing at home. As Imanuel Wexler has pointed out, for example, the elimination of import quotas within the framework of an automatic and multilateral payments mechanism would worsen the payments position and drain the reserves of participating countries that tolerated a certain level of inflation as a prop to full employment. It would force these countries and those that emerged as net debtors on intra-European account to defend the balance of payments by deflating economies. In some cases, it would mean importing

enclosed memoranda by Friedman, December 29, 1949, Snyder Papers, box 20, folder: Alphabetical File, International Monetary Fund; Hoffman torep 263 to Harriman, January 10, 1950, ECA Files, box 63; G. H. Willis of the Treasury Department, letter to Henry Tasca, January 11, 1950, Treasury Records, Acc. 66A1039, box 3, folder: Marshall Plan Correspondence (Official); Southard memorandum to Snyder, January 16, 1950, Snyder Papers, box 11, folder: ECA and International Trade Organization, 1950; NAC, Minutes of 146th Meeting, January 19, 1950, RG 56, NAC Minutes; and Milward, *Reconstruction of Western Europe*, 322–4.

8   Acheson tel. to Douglas, January 27, 1950, *FRUS, 1950*, 3:623–4. See also NAC, Minutes of 147th Meeting, January 23, 1950, RG 56, NAC Minutes; and Arthur W. Marget, Federal Reserve Board of Governors, letter to Katz, January 24, 1950, Milton Katz Papers (Truman Library), box 18, folder: Personal Correspondence – M.

unemployment from trading partners that pursued excessively deflationary policies.[9]

Of all the participating countries, only Belgium stood squarely to the right of the ECA. The Belgians were major creditors on intra-European account and primarily responsible for the so-called Ansiaux plan drafted by the OEEC working group. Despite the similarities between this plan and the ECA's initial proposal, the two were fully parallel only in their support for a strong managing board with "wide powers" to influence the internal policies of member states. Otherwise, the Belgian position came closer to the economic orthodoxy championed by policymakers in the Treasury Department and their allies in the IMF. This was particularly true when it came to settling intra-European imbalances. Here the Belgians followed "the gold standard approach." They demanded terms "hard" enough to eradicate the inflationary pressures that led some participating countries to restrict intra-European trade and discriminate against the dollar, with results, they said, that perpetuated the division of the nonruble world into hard- and soft-currency blocs. This division was no less a concern to policymakers in the ECA. But where they would have creditors and debtors share the responsibility for balancing accounts, the Belgians would follow a beggar-thy-neighbor policy that put the burden of equilibrium on the backs of their debtors. They saw the payments scheme as a way to expand their intra-European surplus and earn from their trading partners the dollars to finance Belgium's deficit with the Western Hemisphere and its program of industrial modernization. For these reasons, they wanted outstanding debts funded immediately and bilateral agreements replaced with an automatic system in which import quotas would be eliminated in rapid order, credit margins would be held to a minimum, and debtors would settle in gold once these margins were exhausted.[10]

The other participating countries favored terms that were more lenient on debtors, respected national autonomies, or left room for bilateral bargaining. Like the Belgians, the Italians wanted credit margins kept to a minimum and gold payments started as soon as possible. But they also wanted the payments union to supplement, not replace, bilateral credit agreements and would deny its managing board the power to regulate national policies, particularly their own policies, which were decidedly deflationary. The Scandinavians were reluctant to eliminate quantitative import

[9] Wexler, *Marshall Plan Revisited*, 165–6.

[10] L. F. Crick, UK Treasury and Supply Delegation, Washington, letter to George Bolton of the Bank of England, February 10, 1950, T230/157/EAS81/01C. The Belgian position is summarized in Hugh Ellis-Rees letter to Berthoud, January 24, 1950, FO 371, 87083, UR323. See also unsigned memorandum, "European Payments Union," February 13, 1950, T232/172/EEC17/8/02; and Hall-Patch letter to E. A. Hitchman, Third Secretary of the Treasury, February 14, 1950, T230/157/EAS81/01C.

restrictions because doing so would aggravate their deficits or force them to balance accounts at the expense of full employment. The French took a similar position. They had shelved the Fritalux plan, at least temporarily, in favor of a scheme under which all participating countries would immediately eliminate quotas on 60 percent of their imports, whereupon the OEEC would arrange an additional 15 percent reduction by the end of the year. The French proposal looked generous. But the idea behind it was to preempt an ECA program that would eliminate all restrictions by mid-1951. To policymakers in Paris, this program would open the floodgates to German competition, cause "acute internal difficulties," and "lead to the fall of the French government." France would avoid these dangers by capping trade liberalization at 75 percent of imports on private account and conditioning even this much progress on concessions by the other OEEC countries. Britain and Germany would have to end their dual pricing of coal, which charged France a higher price than that paid by domestic consumers, and all of the participating countries would have to make arrangements for liberalizing government imports, coordinating national policies, and framing a common list of commodities on which all quotas would be removed.[11]

If these conditions and reservations were not enough to puncture the ECA's balloon, there was also the unmitigated opposition of the British. The Labour government had eliminated quantitative restrictions on over 60 percent of Britain's imports from the OEEC countries as a group. This was a higher overall percentage than that achieved by any other government, and the British wanted to hold the line against further reductions until their trading partners caught up with them. In truth, they could go further only by removing quotas on imports from their creditors, especially the Belgians and the Swiss, and they would not do this without guarantees against the loss of gold and dollars. Nor would they agree to a common list of liberalized commodities or to the elimination of dual-pricing policies, the reduction of quotas on government imports, and the coordination of national economies. Such measures would violate their whole approach to economic management, which aimed to sustain employment through mildly inflationary policies and then to contain inflation through government controls. To abandon these controls meant importing nonessential commodities and deflationary pressures from abroad, a course that would undercut employment, imperil reserves, and slow progress toward viability with the dollar area.[12]

---

[11] In addition to the source cited in note 10, see Hall-Patch letter to Berthoud, January 7, 1950, FO 371, 86973, UR1014; Hall-Patch tel. to FO, January 17, 1950, FO 371, 87083, UR323; and Wexler, *Marshall Plan Revisited*, 165.

[12] Hitchman memorandum to William Armstrong, Principal Private Secretary to the Chancellor, January 4, 1950, with attached draft telegram, Hitchman memorandum to Cripps, January 4, 1950, FO tels. (2) to Hall-Patch, January 4, 1950, UK del., Paris, Record of a Meeting of the Central Group on 5th January 1950, January 6, 1950, and unsigned draft paper for consideration by the President of the Board of Trade, January 11, 1950, T232/184/EEC6/89B; FO tels. to Hall-Patch, January 18

The British took a similar position when it came to the payments union, refusing to support a managing board with supranational powers and consistently defending the interests of debtors over those of creditors. They thought that participating countries should discriminate against persistent creditors and that debtors should enjoy the widest credit margins possible. Indeed, they effectively rejected the idea of partial gold and dollar settlements, which they said would penalize debtors for liberalizing trade and for the unreasonably deflationary policies pursued by other countries. The British also reserved the right to reimpose quantitative import restrictions, if need be on an unilateral and discriminatory basis, in order to protect their reserves and full-employment programs. For the same reasons, they wanted the proposed clearing union to function as a "lender-of-last resort," not as "a super state." It should supplement, not supersede, the existing network of bilateral payments agreements, or so the British argued, because abrogating these agreements would enable the continental countries to exchange their accumulated sterling balances (valued at approximately $1.2 billion) for the clearing union's common unit of account. Aside from draining the British Treasury of gold and dollars, this scheme would substitute the common unit for pound sterling as Western Europe's major reserve and trading currency.[13]

Once again, America's plans for an integrated Western Europe and a multilateral system of world trade ran afoul of Britain's commitments to the sterling area and the welfare state. As Hoffman and others complained, the British were as reluctant as ever to "open their closely controlled and planned economy" to the influence of automatic market forces or supranational authorities. They would not abandon the bilateral agreements that permitted them to control the trade of other countries, husband the reserves of the sterling area, and protect the position of pound sterling as an international currency.[14] Nor would it be easy to break their opposition, if only because it dovetailed at key points with the position of other participating countries.

Anglo–American differences came to a head when the OEEC's Consultative Group and Council met in late January. Hoffman decided to attend

(2) and 21 (2), 1950, T232/185/EEC6/09C; and Berthoud memorandum to Under Secretary of State Christopher Mayhew, January 20, 1959, FO 371, 87072, UR322.

[13] Crick letter to Bolton, February 10, 1950, T230/157/EAS81/01C. See also Harriman repto circulars 16 and 18 to Hoffman, January 24 and 26, 1950, ECA Files, box 20; Harriman repto 530 to Hoffman, January 28, 1950, ECA Files, box 17; unsigned memorandum, "European Payments Union," February 13, 1950, T232/172/EEC17/8/02; and Hall-Patch letter to Hitchman, February 14, 1950, T230/157/EAS81/01C.

[14] Acheson Memorandum of Conversation, March 1, 1950, *FRUS, 1950*, 3:634–8. See also Harriman repto 530 to Hoffman, January 28, 1950, ECA Files, box 17; unsigned, undated draft of ECA cable to Harriman, and Hulley draft memorandum, "Solution of British Objections to Clearing Union Proposal," January 30, 1950, RG 286, Acc. 53A405, box 60, folder: European Union.

the meetings and seek agreement in principle to reduce import quotas, eliminate dual-pricing policies, and organize a payments union. He made this decision over the opposition of Ambassador Franks and other British policymakers, who thought it best for the Europeans to meet without American interference. They were convinced that Hoffman's demands would lead to British opposition, which in turn would open the Labour government to charges of obstructing European integration and play into the hands of the Tories in the elections scheduled for February 24. Richard Bissell did nothing to alleviate these fears when he announced the ECA's recent decision to gear a substantial portion of its aid, perhaps as much as 25 percent, to the performance of participating countries in liberalizing trade and taking other steps to integrate economies. The decision infuriated Stafford Cripps, who thought it amounted to a "dollar dictatorship," a "crass interference" in the internal affairs of participating states, and a "gift to Communist propaganda." He threatened to speak against the American decision, even though this might inject the issue into the British elections and damage Anglo–American relations.[15]

By the time the Consultative Group and Council convened in Paris, neither side was disposed to compromise. Hoffman made it clear that he could no longer sell the ERP to Congress merely "on the improvement of production in Europe." Something more was needed, and what he and Congress had in mind "was a single European market" to be achieved by reducing trade barriers, multilateralizing payments, and coordinating national economies. The OEEC had enumerated these goals in its Plan of Action of November, which Hoffman had taken as a promise of concrete progress. He told the Europeans that failure to honor this promise would jeopardize additional funding for the ERP, especially in light of an anticipated budget deficit in the neighborhood of $5 billion.[16]

Although Hoffman had some support from the other OEEC delegations, the British resolutely defended the ground they had staked out earlier. The Italians wanted to prohibit dual pricing and draw up a timetable for the rapid elimination of import quotas. The Dutch took a similar position, as did the Belgians, who also defended the Ansiaux plan for a European payments union. The French called again for the removal of quotas on 75 percent of private imports and for the coordination of national economies, the development of a common list, and the reduction of quantitative re-

---

[15]   FO tel. to Franks, January 21, 1950, FO 371, 86969, UR103. See also Franks tel. to FO, January 19, 1950, FO 371, 86969, UR103.

[16]   Makins Record of Conversation of January 25, 1950, January 26, 1950, FO 371 86970, UR104. See also unsigned Note of Discussion, January 26, 1950, T232/185/ EEC6/09C; Harriman repto 530 to ECA, Washington, January 28, 1950, Harriman Papers, folder: O.E.E.C.; UK del., Record of Fourth Meeting of the Consultative Group on January 27, 1950, January 30, 1950, FO 371, 87073, UR322/23; and Harriman repto circular 30 to Hoffman, February 4, 1950, ECA Files, box 20.

strictions on government trade. In their view, action in these areas would help to create a large common market in Western Europe. But the British said the goal was viability, not integration. They would go no further in liberalizing trade without a payments scheme that protected their bilateral agreements and made provisions for the accumulated sterling balances on the Continent.[17] Nor would they open their economy to external pressures, either by endowing a payments union with supranational power or by accepting the recommendations put forward by the French and the Belgians. The Labour government, as Cripps told his colleagues in Paris, would not reshape its "planned economy" to fit the free economies of the Continent.[18]

After a week of meetings, the OEEC countries could get no further than a promise to organize a payments union and eliminate quantitative restrictions on 60 percent of their private imports by mid-1950, 75 percent by the end of the year. Both promises were hedged with numerous reservations, not the least of which was the need to harmonize the European clearing union with the monetary arrangements of the sterling area.[19] Hoffman was keenly disappointed. The results hardly measured up to the concrete goals enumerated in his integration speech and in the OEEC's Plan of Action. He warned again that a "suitable payments union" was the sine qua non of additional aid.[20] The British were not impressed. Although Hoffman's warning hung like the sword of Damocles over the heads of the negotiators in Paris, Cripps made it plain that little could be expected until after the British elections in late February.[21]

Many of the continental countries blamed the United States for the lack of progress in Paris. They believed that divisions between the ECA and the Treasury Department, rumors of which were current in Europe, had pre-

---

[17]   In addition to the British sources cited in note 16, see UK del., Record of the Second Meeting of the Consultative Group on January 26, 1950, FO 371, 87073, UR322; Harriman reptos 530 and 616 to ECA, Washington, January 28 and February 2, 1950, ECA Files, box 17; and Harriman repto circular 30 to ECA, Washington, February 4, 1950, ECA Files, box 20.

[18]   UK del., Record of Second Meeting of the Consultative Group on January 26, 1950, FO 371, 87073, UR322. See also UK del., Record of Fourth Meeting of the Consultative Group on January 27, 1950, January 30, 1950, FO 371, 87073, UR322/23.

[19]   OEEC, *Report to the Economic Co-operation Administration on the Second Annual Programme, July 1, 1949–June 30, 1950* (Paris, 1950), 232. See also Hall-Patch tel. to FO, February 1, 1950, FO 371, 87073, UR322; and Harriman repto 642 to Hoffman, February 3, 1950, ECA Files, box 17.

[20]   Harriman repto 530 to Hoffman, January 28, 1950, Harriman Papers, folder: O.E.E.C. See also Harriman repto circular 30 to Hoffman, February 4, 1950, ECA Files, box 20. Hoffman also expressed his disappointment in a press conference shortly after his return from Paris. See Hoffman torep 1053 to Harriman, February 3, 1950, ECA Files, box 63.

[21]   See, for example, Holmes tel. to Acheson, January 30, 1950, *FRUS, 1950*, 3:624–5.

vented Hoffman from adopting a more flexible attitude in the Paris negotiations. They also worried that failure to reach agreement would weaken
the OEEC and wreck the chances for European integration.[22] To avert such
disasters, the Belgians, French, and Dutch were thinking of reviving the
Fritalux negotiations. And urging them on was a group of American policymakers led by Hoffman, who encouraged the continental countries to "proceed with [an] open ended arrangement" that embodied the goals set out
in their Plan of Action, left room for the British, and included the Germans.[23]

The last stipulation squared with the American plan to bring West Germany within the framework of an integrated Western Europe. For policymakers in the State Department, further progress in this direction meant
making the Federal Republic a member of the Council of Europe, as well
as the payments union, and taking additional steps to revive its economy
and foreign trade.[24] There were good signs of German support for this
course, which offered the alluring prospect of eliminating the attenuated
system of Allied occupation controls and giving the Federal Republic equal
status in the Western community of nations. Chancellor Konrad Adenauer
had become a leading advocate of European economic union and Franco–
German rapprochement. His government had taken steps to eliminate quantitative restrictions on imports from the other OEEC countries and had also
reduced the differential between the internal and external price of German
coal.[25]

The difficulties, as always, were to be found in France's determination to
control the Germans and Britain's reluctance to integrate into Europe.
French policies that would detach the Saar from Germany, admit it as an
independent member of the Council of Europe, and lease its coal mines to
French companies sparked vigorous opposition in Bonn and stalled the

[22] The American Charge in Ireland tel. to Acheson, February 7, 1950, *FRUS, 1950*,
       3:626–7; Harriman repto 744 to Hoffman, February 9, 1950, ECA Files, box 17;
       and Harriman repto 861 to Acheson, February 14, 1950, RG 286, Acc. 53A177,
       box 88, folder: Eyes Only, Personal Correspondence, Jan.–Feb. 1950.
[23] Harriman repto 530 to Hoffman, January 28, 1950, ECA Files, box 17. See also
       Harriman reptos 254 and 616 to Hoffman, January 14 and February 2, 1950, ECA
       Files, box 17; Harriman repto circular 30 to Hoffman, February 4, 1950, ECA Files,
       box 20; Berthoud memorandum to Bevin, February 6, 1950, FO 371, 87084, UR323;
       Harriman repto 119 to the American Embassy in the United Kingdom, February 7,
       1950, *FRUS, 1950*, 3:625–6; Foster torep 1150 to Harriman and Katz, February 7,
       1950, ECA Files, box 63; J. E. Chadwick of the Foreign Office, memorandum to
       Bevin, February 13, 1950, FO 371, 87804, UR323; and Foreign Office Record of a
       Conversation, February 14, 1950, FO 800/460/Eur/50/7.
[24] Memorandum of Conversation by John W. Auchincloss of the State Department's
       Bureau of German Affairs, February 9, 1950, *FRUS, 1950*, 4:591–6.
[25] McCloy torep 17 to Harriman, January 5, 1950, RG 286, Acc. 53A177, box 88,
       folder: Eyes Only, Personal Correspondence, Jan.–Feb. 1950; and Richard P. Steb-
       bins, *The United States in World Affairs, 1950* (New York, 1951), 118.

Federal Republic's accession to the Council of Europe.[26] Nor would the French bring West Germany into the Fritalux negotiations, as the Dutch were insisting, without substantial dollar assistance to cover its deficit in intra-European trade. The ECA thought this deficit would disappear once the participating countries began extending to the Germans the same trade concessions that Bonn had extended to them. In Paris, however, the goal was an integrated Western Europe dominated by France, not Germany. For this reason, the French wanted to retain certain restrictions on German competition and balance Germany's membership against the countervailing power of Great Britain. The Italians felt the same way, telling Bevin at one point that Britain must play a greater role in Western Europe "because of the menace of Germany."[27]

Yet the British would neither integrate into Europe nor support a strictly continental group that included West Germany. Their official position remained the same: They held no brief against Fritalux or any regional group that did not discriminate against British trade. Unofficially, however, they assumed that a measure of discrimination would be involved; French Minister of Finance Maurice Petsche admitted as much in an exchange of letters with Cripps. Even more alarming was the possibility that Fritalux would divide Western Europe into rival economic blocs, with France and her partners arrayed against the United Kingdom and the Scandinavian countries. This arrangement would enable the Germans "to play one Power or group of Powers off against another." Still worse, as Bevin told the French, it would split the North Atlantic alliance and work to the advantage of the Soviet Union. Cripps asked Hoffman not to "hustle us unduly." He and Bevin wanted to discuss all aspects of the German problem with the Americans. They also wanted more time to draft an intra-European payments proposal that would "harmonize their position in Europe with their position as centre of the sterling area," thereby bringing "Germany into the fold" and keeping "Europe united." With these goals in mind, Bevin made arrangements for another foreign ministers conference in London and persuaded the Fritalux countries to postpone their negotiations pending the outcome of this conference and receipt of the new British proposal.[28]

[26] Stebbins, *United States in World Affairs, 1950*, 115–17. The Saar question can be followed in *FRUS, 1950*, 4:927–39.
[27] Unsigned Record of Conversation, February 3, 1950, FO 371, 87084, UR323. See also Harriman reptos 254 and 733 to Hoffman, January 14 and February 8, 1950, ECA Files, box 17; Harriman Memorandum of Conversation with M. Van Zeeland, February 10, 1950, Harriman Papers, folder: Memoranda of Conversations; Foreign Office Record of Conversation, February 14, 1950, FO 800/46/Eur/50/7; Berthoud memorandum to Philip Broad of the Foreign Office, February 14, 1950, and Broad memorandum, February 14, 1950, FO 371, 87084, UR323; and Acheson Memorandum of Conversation, March 1, 1950, *FRUS, 1950*, 3:634–8.
[28] Foreign Office Record of Conversation between Bevin and Schuman, March 7, 1950,

Actually, neither the Europeans nor the Americans wanted to proceed without British support and cooperation. Both were aware that a continental union would raise "serious political complications" concerning Germany. Both assumed that British concessions would get the stalled negotiations moving again. Both used the threat of a strictly continental group to extract such concessions. The French warned that the Fritalux negotiators could not be idled indefinitely. The warning, or so the British suspected, aimed to force Britain down a narrow road that led inexorably to concessions and from which it could exit only by accepting responsibility for wrecking the Fritalux talks or the larger negotiations for a European payments union. The French strategy had parallels elsewhere. Dirk Stikker of the Netherlands told Harriman that Fritalux should be " 'kept on ice' " as a " 'stimulant' " to the British; Acheson and Hoffman warned that Britain's obstructionism would lead straight to a continental union that included West Germany.[29]

The British could play this game as well as any of their partners. They told the French that proceeding with Fritalux would impair Anglo–French collaboration on the Continent. They also mapped out a plan to bring the United Kingdom and the Scandinavian countries together in the so-called Uniscan group, thereby giving credibility to their claim that regional economic blocs would divide Western Europe.[30] In February, moreover, the British proposed to modify the Anglo–German trade agreement along lines that would make it difficult for the Federal Republic to participate in Fri-

FO 800/440/Bel/50/2; Cripps letter to Hoffman, March 7, 1950, Hoffman Papers, box 26; and Foreign Office Record of Conversation between Bevin and Harriman, March 8, 1950, FO 800/517/US/50/7. See also Unsigned Record of Conversation, February 3, 1950, and Bevin letter to Hall-Patch, February 8, 1950, with enclosed message from Cripps to French Finance Minister Maurice Petsche, February 3, 1950, FO 371, 87084, UR323; Bevin letter to Acheson, February 11, 1950, *FRUS, 1950,* 3:627–9; Foreign Office Record of Conversation, February 14, 1950, FO 800/460/ Eur/50/7; Bevin letter to Ellis-Rees, February 14, 1950, with enclosed message from Petsche to Cripps, February 13, 1950, FO 371, 87084, UR323; and Harriman Memorandum of Conversation with Dirk Stikker of the Netherlands, February 15, 1950, RG 286, Acc. 53A177, box 88 folder: Eyes Only, Personal Correspondence, Jan.– Aug. 1950.

[29] Holmes tel. to Acheson, February 16, 1950, *FRUS, 1950,* 3:630–1; and Harriman Memorandum of Conversation with Stikker, February 15, 1950, RG 286, Acc. 53A177, box 88, folder: Eyes Only, Personal Correspondence, Jan.–Aug. 1950. See also Unsigned Note of Discussion, January 26, 1950, T232/185/EEC6/09C; Makins Record of Conversation of January 25, 1950, January 26, 1950, and Makins letter to R. E. Barclay, British Embassy in Italy, January 31, 1950, FO 371, 86970, UR104; Chadwick memorandum, February 13, 1950, FO 371, 87084, UR323; and Katz tel. to Acheson, February 18, 1950, Acheson tel. to Douglas, enclosing personal message for Bevin, February 22, 1950, and Acheson Memorandum of Conversation, March 1, 1950, *FRUS, 1950,* 3:631–2, 632–3, 634–8.

[30] Petsche message to Cripps, February 13, 1950, in Bevin letter to Ellis-Rees, February 14, 1950, FO 371, 87084, UR323; and Milward, *Reconstruction of Western Europe,* 316–19.

talux. The Germans were running a substantial deficit in trade with the sterling area, in part because Britain's decision to eliminate quantitative restrictions had not applied to imports from West Germany. This deficit fueled a serious drain on Germany's gold and dollar reserves, which the British would handle by permitting third countries to use their accumulated sterling to finance trade deficits with the Germans, who could then use the proceeds, rather than gold or dollars, to balance their accounts with the sterling area.

American officials saw this proposal as a blatant attempt to incorporate Germany – indeed, all of Western Europe – into the system of transferable accounts by which the British regulated payments and protected reserves. The British, they said, were trying to curry favor with those OEEC countries that feared the automatic and administrative regulators built into the ECA's scheme for an intra-European payments union and with those that might use the Federal Republic, rather than the union, as an outlet for accumulated sterling. If allowed to succeed, they worried, British strategy would wreck their efforts to break bilateral trading patterns and subject national economics to administrative coordination.[31] The ECA instructed Harriman to block action on the British proposal in Bonn. The State Department informed the British of its opposition as well, and both agencies suggested a temporary Anglo–German trade agreement that would last until the European payments union came into operation. According to their suggestion, gold settlements would be postponed without abandoning the principle of such settlements and Germany's deficit would be handled by eliminating some of the British restrictions on German imports or by granting the Germans additional drawing rights on sterling.[32] When the British turned their backs on this suggestion, the ECA again resorted to threats, this time warning that part of Britain's ERP allocation might be used to cover Germany's deficit until an acceptable trade agreement was negotiated.[33]

The American intervention in both the payments negotiations and the Anglo–German trade talks led to angry recriminations on both sides of the Atlantic. The British complained of " 'schoolboy' " lectures by the Americans and lamented the ECA's "attempt to set a long-range European pat-

[31] Hoffman torep 1497 to Harriman from State, ECA, and Treasury, February 21, 1950, RG 286, Acc. 53A177, box 112, folder: Inter-European; Acheson tel. to Douglas, February 22, 1950, *FRUS, 1950*, 3:632–3; and Katz reptos 1211, 1215, and 1258 to Hoffman, March 4 and 7, 1950, ECA Files, box 17.

[32] Hoffman torep 1497 to Harriman, February 21, 1950, RG 286, Acc. 53A177, box 112, folder: Inter-European; Webb tel. to Douglas, March 14, 1950, *FRUS, 1950*, 4:611–12; Foster torep 2400 to Harriman, March 23, 1950, ECA Files, box 64; Hoffman ecato 451 to W. John Kenney, Chief, ECA Mission, London, March 31, 1950, ECA Files, box 61; and Kenney toeca 470 to Hoffman, April 12, 1950, ECA Files, box 16.

[33] Foster torep 2400 to Harriman, March 23, 1950, ECA Files, box 64; and Kenney toeca 531 to Hoffman, April 26, 1950, ECA Files, box 16.

tern" at odds with their interests. As bankers for the sterling area, Cripps protested, the British could not "rush headlong into a scheme which may depreciate the value of sterling."[34] The Americans accused the British of basing policy "on narrow, short-term and almost petty self-interest," including a desire to shield the Labour government's full-employment policies against the adverse impact of competitive pressures. The "British brand of Socialism," added one ECA official, "does not dovetail with the increasing return to free enterprise on the continent" and, hence, with the ECA's plan to mesh the European economies into a single, integrated market.[35]

Anglo-American relations only worsened in late March, when the British circulated their new proposal for an intra-European payments union. Under the terms of this proposal, the sterling system and the European payments union would exist side by side, connected, in the State Department's words, "by a channel whose sluice gates" the British controlled.[36] The proposal would exempt sterling settlements from the automatic and multilateral offsetting of surpluses and deficits. It would leave Britain's bilateral agreements intact and protect its right to reimpose quantitative import restrictions unilaterally. Through these and other provisions, the British would eliminate the risk to their reserves and shelter their economy against the administrative controls of the managing board, even while they drew gold from the union, served on its board, and enjoyed the right to influence its policies and those of its members. The lack of automatic and administrative incentives made the British proposal an instrument of no value to the Americans. They said the proposal would do nothing to adjust the British economy in the interest of intra-European equilibrium. Nor would it lead to "a single, wide, competitive market" in Western Europe or encourage faster progress toward general convertibility between the dollar and nondollar areas.[37]

[34] Kenney torep 78 to Harriman, January 19, 1950, Harriman Papers, folder: United Kingdom; Holmes tel. to Acheson, February 28, 1950, *FRUS, 1950*, 4:605–6; and Cripps letter to Hoffman, March 7, 1950, Hoffman Papers, box 26, folder: Eminent Personages File – Cripps, Sir Stafford. See also Acheson tel. to McCloy, March 2, 1950, *FRUS, 1950*, 4:606–8.

[35] Harriman repto 371 to Hoffman, January 21, 1950, and Kenney torep 91 to Harriman, January 21, 1950, Harriman Papers, folder: United Kingdom.

[36] Acheson tel. to Harriman for Perkins, March 24, 1950, RG 286, Acc. 53A177, box 112, folder: Inter-European.

[37] The British proposal is summarized in Hoffman torep 2041 to Katz, March 11, 1950, ECA Files, box 64; and in a report the ECA prepared for the State Department, dated April 14, 1950, in *FRUS, 1950*, 3:646–52. See also Henry Tasca memorandum to Katz, March 13, 1950, Harriman Papers, folder: European Payments Union; Hebbard memorandum to Kenney, March 15, 1950, Hebbard memorandum to Douglas, March 16, 1950, and Willis memorandum to Assistant Secretary of the Treasury Martin, March 17, 1950, Treasury Records, Acc. 66A816, box 28, folder; European Payments and Clearing Union, Vol. I; Hoffman torep 2647 to Harriman, March 31, 1950, ECA Files, box 64; Katz repto 1880 to Hoffman, April 6, 1950, ECA Files, box 18, Foster torep 2904 to Hoffman, ECA Files, box 65; and ECA Memorandum

American policymakers saw the difference between the British proposal and their own as one "between economic nationalism and economic internationalism." According to the ECA, the British were unwilling to cooperate with the other participating countries in building the sort of "freely-trading area" that would bring "improvements in productivity and in the standard of living." They refused to make the "internal adjustments" required or "to accept limits on the exercise of national sovereignty, confining its absolute and arbitrary exercise to the legitimate field in which it would not conflict with the economic needs of Western Europe as a whole."[38] They would submit neither "to an international coordinating agency" with "real administrative powers," nor to the "automatic checks" on national policy that were inherent in the idea of partial gold settlements. Instead, the ECA concluded, the British sought "complete freedom to pursue [the] domestic policies they want on purely national grounds" and "to exploit all the benefits of their present bilateral trading arrangements."[39]

Under these circumstances, some European and American officials were thinking again of a strictly continental union linked to the sterling area, as the British had proposed, but without full British participation and voting rights. Nor would the British be eligible for part of the reserve fund that was being set aside to support the union or exempt from the unilateral imposition of quantitative restrictions by the continental group against sterling-area imports. As Harriman admitted, however, there was an "air of unreality" about a European union without Great Britain. The Scandinavians would refuse to participate and there was still the fear that Germany would dominate a strictly continental group. At the very least, "competitive jockeying" over Germany's position would deliver a "setback to Europe and [to] Atlantic community cooperation."[40]

III

By the end of March, earlier forecasts of an Anglo–American accommodation had given way to dismal predictions of a major break between the Atlantic powers. T. L. Rowan and Sydney Caine of the British Embassy in Washington warned of growing disillusionment in Congress and of the impact this could have on future appropriations for the Marshall Plan.[41]

for the Secretary of State, May 5, 1950, Harriman Papers, folder: European Payments Union.

[38] Report by the Economic Cooperation Administration, April 14, 1950, *FRUS, 1950*, 3:646–52.

[39] Hoffman torep 2647 to Harriman, March 31, 1950, ECA Files, box 64.

[40] Harriman repto 1816 to Hoffman, April 3, 1950, ECA Files, box 18. See also Hoffman torep 2041 to Katz, March 11, 1950, and Hoffman torep 2647 to Harriman, March 31, 1950, ECA Files, box 64.

[41] Caine letter to Sir Henry Wilson-Smith, February 11, 1950, FO 371, 87039, UR31113; and Rowan letter to Hitchman, February 24, 1950, FO 371, 81668, AU11156.

The ECA, as Hoffman and Harriman told the British, had shied away from the utopian idea of a Western European political federation. So had the State Department. Both agencies had tried to discourage such visionary dreams in Congress and to focus attention on the more realistic goal of economic integration. This limited program was identical to the Plan of Action that Britain and the other participating countries had ratified the previous November. If it now went further than the British were willing to go, Hoffman wrote Cripps on March 15, there was little hope of achieving the Anglo–American partnership that had been envisioned at the trilateral talks six months earlier.[42]

Hoffman's gloomy prognosis was one indication of the crisis of confidence that gripped the Western alliance in late 1949 and early 1950. He and other policymakers were convinced that the Western powers were losing the initiative in the Cold War to an increasingly confident Soviet Union. The deadlock in the payments negotiations had contributed to this feeling. So had the developments noted in the last chapter, including the "loss" of China to the Communists, the spread of revolutionary insurgency in Southeast Asia, and the premature end of America's atomic monopoly. In the background, too, was the delay in making the North Atlantic Treaty Organization (NATO) into an effective instrument of deterrence and the growing resentment of the Germans, who had yet to find a home in the Western community and were being wooed eastward with Soviet promises of reliable friends and markets stretching from the Oder to the Pacific. President Truman's decision to develop the hydrogen bomb also added to the air of crisis. Coming as it did on the heels of Russia's first atomic explosion, the decision triggered European fears of a third world war in which the continental countries would be hapless victims of a nuclear exchange between the super powers. The fear of war and the rumors that Washington was planning to rearm the Germans stirred a wave of anti-American sentiment in Western Europe and a powerful peace movement on which the Communists and Soviets were capitalizing. Giving extra force to these European reactions was the hyperbole of Republican Party leaders, who were busy denouncing the failures of American diplomacy, accusing the Truman administration of being soft on communism, and calling for a more aggressive foreign policy.

Political conditions in almost all of the Western countries offered little hope of reinvigorating the alliance. Adenauer's tenuous government still operated under Allied restrictions. It was neither a member of NATO nor an equal partner in Western European affairs. Political partisanship and wartime memories in France and Italy forced cautious governments to look to London for guidance. The British, however, were in no position to take

---

[42]   Hoffman letter to Cripps, March 15, 1950, FO 800/517/US/50/6; and Foreign Office Record of Conversation between Bevin and Harriman, March 8, 1950, FO 800/517/US/50/7.

the lead. The elections of late February had kept the Labour government in power, but with a margin of victory too narrow to support a confident diplomacy. Nor were Cripps and Bevin up to the challenge. Cripps was fatally ill and Bevin's increasingly severe attacks of angina required prolonged periods of hospital care.

Although the wreckage of bipartisanship in Washington and the angry fulminations of the Republican Party also left the Truman administration with little room to maneuver, these same conditions made Acheson and other policymakers anxious to recapture the initiative. So did their practical appreciation of the deteriorating position of the Western alliance. In 1950, as in 1947, fears that Soviet policy would gain from confusion and division in the West led to the conclusion that bold new measures were needed to restore the lost momentum. Franks drew this conclusion after a dinner meeting with Acheson on March 6 and an earlier talk with U.S. High Commissioner John J. McCloy. Acheson was ready to aid the French in Indochina, Franks reported, and both he and McCloy wanted to strengthen the North Atlantic alliance and take new steps to "link Western Germany more firmly to the West."[43]

Indeed, American policymakers were exploring several related strategies to revitalize the Western alliance. The escalation of Cold War tensions and new fears of Soviet aggression led in one direction to a greater stress on European rearmament. Prior to 1950, as we have seen, American leaders had relied on economic rather than military instruments to achieve their goals in Western Europe. They had given recovery priority over rearmament, settled for modest increases in European defense spending, and sought to offset the cost to participating governments through an American program of military assistance. By the spring of 1950, however, the revival of production and the new signs of financial stability had combined to accommodate a greater emphasis on rearmament. They made it possible to abandon the initial priority on recovery for a policy that gave *parity* to rearmament. The new policy also squared with President Truman's decision to develop the hydrogen bomb and with the deepening conviction, shared by key policymakers who were then at work on what would become National Security Council Paper No. 68, that the United States must devote a larger share of its national resources to defense. Nor did the policy raise objections in the ECA, where Hoffman, Harriman, and other officials agreed to take a balanced view giving due recognition both to the needs of defense and to those of recovery. In theory, at least, these needs could be harmonized by building balanced collective forces rather than separate national forces. Through shared expenditures, specialization, and more efficient use of resources, the NATO countries could ensure an adequate defense without

[43] Franks letter to Bevin, March 8, 1950, FO 800/517/US/50/8. See also Memorandum of Conversation by the Officer in Charge of United Kingdom and Ireland Affairs, March 7, 1950, *FRUS, 1950*, 3:638–42.

sacrificing the gains in economic growth and financial stability achieved
since 1947.[44]

At work here was the ERP model applied to the military sphere. Following
this model, the North Atlantic Treaty and the Mutual Defense Assistance
Act had stressed the importance of mutual self-help and had conditioned
American military aid on the development of plans for an integrated defense
of the North Atlantic. By early 1950, in addition, the Western powers had
approved a "strategic concept" that envisioned a collective defense based
on the principle of national specialization. But progress toward this goal
had been slow, in part because NATO lacked continuous machinery for
coordinating national policies and spurring the Europeans to greater self-
help. Not surprisingly, then, the second line of American policy aimed to
breathe new life into the organization by creating a permanent high-level
staff to coordinate defense planning and production. There was even talk
in Washington of using NATO to harmonize economic and political (as
well as military) policies across the North Atlantic area.[45]

Still another line of policy stressed the vital role that West Germany must
play in European security. Although some American and European leaders
were campaigning for Germany's immediate rearmament and full membership in NATO, most still considered both ideas premature. Their thinking
amounted to an extension of past policy. They wanted to give West Germany
greater control over its foreign affairs, use its industrial capacity to supply
NATO's rearmament program, and lift the remaining restrictions on its
economy and trade. These restrictions were alienating popular opinion in
the Federal Republic, fostering neutralist sentiment there, and robbing the
Western alliance of the benefits of Germany's industrial energy, which the

---

[44] Acheson, *Present at the Creation*, 397–9; Kaplan, *Community of Interests*, 80–2;
       Harriman repto 874 to Hoffman, February 14, 1950, ECA Files, box 17; Hoffman
       torep 1587 to Harriman, February 23, 1950, ECA Files, box 64; Under Secretary of
       the Army Tracy S. Voorhees letter, with enclosure, to Acheson, April 10, 1950, *FRUS,
       1950*, 3:43–8; and Paper Prepared in the Office of European Regional Affairs as
       Background for the May Foreign Ministers and North Atlantic Council Meetings,
       May 3, 1950, *FRUS, 1950*, 3:85–90. See also, Hoffman torep 3742 to Harriman,
       May 4, 1950, *FRUS, 1950*, 3:653–4. The State Department opposed any move in
       Europe "to freeze financial appropriations for military expenditures." See Acheson
       tel. to Douglas, April 15, 1950, *FRUS, 1950*, 3:53.
[45] Acheson, *Present at the Creation*, 352–3; Stebbins, *United States in World Affairs,
       1950*, 123; Kaplan, *Community of Interests*, 86–8; Memorandum of Conversation
       by the Officer in Charge of United Kingdom and Ireland Affairs, March 7, 1950,
       Perkins memorandum to Acheson, March 17, 1950, Summary Record of a Meeting
       of Ambassadors at Rome, March 22–24, 1950, Dunn tel. to Acheson, March 24,
       1950, Acheson tel. to Douglas, March 24, 1950, State Department Paper, "The
       Current Position in the Cold War," April 14, 1950, Paper Prepared in the Bureau
       of European Affairs as Background for the May Foreign Ministers Meetings, April
       25, 1950, and Paper Prepared in the Bureau of European Affairs, April 25, 1950, all
       in *FRUS, 1950*, 3:638–42, 828–30, 795–824, 824–6, 830–3, 857–60, 65–9, 70–1.

Americans thought could be tapped without risk by bringing the Germans within a larger Western European system.[46]

In American planning, then, all lines of policy led back to the idea of greater unity in Western Europe. This was the idea behind American support for liberalizing trade and payments, for central direction of defense planning and production, and for an integrated defense and balanced collective forces. For American leaders, European unity was the best way to achieve the gains in productivity needed to support rearmament without sacrificing recovery, and the only way to forge a collective framework "into which Germany can be 'integrated', by which Germany can be 'contained', [and] in which Germany can play a peaceful, constructive but not dictatorial role."[47] The problem was that attaining these goals still seemed to require a greater measure of British support for European unification and French support for German integration. These were two halves of the same walnut: Only an integrated system balanced between British and German power could reassure the French, clear a path to Germany's continued revival, and create a viable counterweight to the Soviet bloc.

Some European and American leaders would solve the problem by getting tough with the British. Paul-Henri Spaak told Acheson that only strong diplomatic pressure would force the British into line on European integration. Harriman made the same point, arguing on one occasion that the United States "should no longer tolerate interference and sabotage of Western European integration by [the] UK and should face Cripps with [a] clear statement of [the] US view that the Marshall Plan is breaking down because of British opposition."[48] But even Harriman thought a firm hand must carry concessions. Like others in the Truman administration, he sought some way to reconcile Britain's three-fold commitment to the United States, the Commonwealth, and Western Europe.

In the State Department, the basis of this search was the principle of British exceptionalism that had grown out of the trilateral talks and the great integration debate of late 1949. Mindful of the strategic and military implications of the Communist conquest of China and the atomic capability

---

[46] Memorandum Prepared in the Bureau of German Affairs, [February 11, 1950], McCloy tels. to Acheson, April 17 and 25, 1950, and Report to the National Security Council by the Secretary of Defense, June 8, 1950, *FRUS, 1950,* 4:597–602, 628–31, 633–5, 686–7; Acheson tel. to Certain Diplomatic Offices, March 13, 1950, Acheson tel. to Douglas for Bonesteel from Martin, March 23, 1950, Record of Ambassadors Meeting, March 22–24, 1950, and Dunn tel. to Acheson, March 24, 1950, *FRUS, 1950,* 3:30, 32–3, 795–824, 824–6.

[47] Memorandum Prepared in the Bureau of German Affairs, [February 11, 1950], *FRUS, 1950,* 4:597–602.

[48] McCloy memorandum of conversation, January 20, 1950, *FRUS, 1950,* 3:1608–9. See also, Acheson, memorandum of conversation, January 18, 1950, Acheson Papers, box 65, folder: Memoranda of Conversations; and Kennan memorandum of conversation, January 19, 1950, *FRUS, 1950,* 3:613–14.

of the Soviet Union, policymakers in that agency were unwilling to submerge Great Britain's sovereignty in a continental union at the risk of impairing its global position or ties to the United States. They now spoke of an Anglo–American "partnership," the preservation of which was "essential to the security, prosperity and expansion of the free world." Dissolving this partnership would be "a disaster involving the decline and eclipse of the whole Eastern Hemisphere and a policy of isolation for the Western Hemisphere or even perhaps for North America alone."[49] Even in the midst of widespread criticism of British foot dragging in Europe, these considerations had led more than one American official to see Britain not "as a battered and worn out veteran" but as "the only really reliable ally of the United States and therefore a country which must be strengthened." These officials believed in "the absolute necessity of firm Anglo–American partnership," Sydney Caine reported from Washington. T. L. Rowan reached the same conclusion, as did Ambassador Franks, who formed his opinion on the basis of his dinner meeting with Acheson on March 6. The secretary of state spoke of the need for new American initiatives in Western Europe and Southeast Asia and of his conviction that these initiatives could be formulated only "in partnership with Britain."[50]

Although British and American leaders divided over when and under what circumstances diplomatic recognition should be extended to the People's Republic of China, there were some indications that Anglo–American policies were beginning to run along parallel lines in Southeast Asia. This was particularly true of economic policies. Bevin had warned that revolutionary insurgencies could tip the balance of power in this region and had made a modest effort to hold the line at a Commonwealth conference that met in Colombo, Ceylon, in January 1950. The conference had prepared the ground for the "Colombo Plan" under which Britain and the older Dominions would begin to finance development projects in the newly emerging states of Southeast Asia. Modeled on President Truman's Point Four program, the Colombo Plan had support in Washington, where a long-standing ECA program of economic and technical aid to Nationalist China and Korea was followed in 1950 by an American economic mission to Southeast Asia and then by a more ambitious aid plan that got off the ground in 1951.[51]

Even in Southeast Asia, however, efforts to align Anglo–American policies fell victim to the same financial stringencies that blocked progress in Western

---

[49] State Department Paper, "Essential Elements of US–UK Relations," April 19, 1950, *FRUS, 1950*, 3:869–81.

[50] Caine letter to Wilson-Smith, February 11, 1950, FO 371, 87039, UR3113. See also Rowan letter to Hitchman, February 14, 1950, FO 371, 81668, AU1156/3; and Franks letter to Bevin, March 8, 1950, FO 800/517/US/50/8. For an account of American policy toward Mao Zedong's government and of Anglo–American differences prior to the Korean War, see Nancy B. Tucker, *Patterns in the Dust: Chinese–American Relations and the Recognition Controversy, 1949–1950* (New York, 1983).

[51] Bullock, *Bevin*, 743–7; and Williams, *Gaitskell*, 225.

Europe. Relations between the two countries turned on a cash nexus, as Acheson explained in his talk with Franks on March 6. The British surveyed every American proposal with an eye to its impact on their social programs, on sterling's position as an international currency, and on their chances for economic viability at the end of the Marshall Plan period.[52] So far as Western Europe was concerned, considerations of this sort had made them reluctant to liberalize trade and join a European payments union, with results, according to the Americans, that stymied progress and played into the hands of the Communists.

But if Britain's financial difficulties presented the main obstacle to Anglo–American cooperation, the State Department hoped to surmount them with what one position paper termed a " 'share-the-wealth' plan," what Charles Bohlen called an Anglo–American "partnership with respect to Britain's overseas problems." Under this plan, the British "would adopt a more positive approach to the Continent" in return for which the Americans would "assume unto ourselves at least the partial obligations of the sterling block [sic]," perhaps through continuing assistance to the British after the termination of Marshall aid in 1952.[53] Some policymakers questioned this strategy. Bissell doubted that promises of further aid would lead the British to cooperate. Kennan still thought in terms of an all-European union.[54] The strategy was nonetheless similar to Kennan's earlier emphasis on an Anglo–American grouping and would guide American policymakers during meetings in London of the Allied foreign ministers and NATO Council.

American leaders used these meetings in May and the preparatory talks preceding them to push the key elements of their integrationist strategy. They pressed for larger defense expenditures and balanced collective, rather than balanced national, forces. The British and French worried about overtaxing their economies and ignoring military commitments outside of Europe. But Acheson insisted that an integrated defense was the only way to eliminate waste and duplication, guarantee the most efficient use of limited resources, and thereby reconcile the needs of defense with those of recovery. His persistence led in mid-May to a compromise that satisfied most American requirements. It called for the progressive expansion of defense forces, urged member states to "concentrate" on balanced collective forces for the

---

[52] This was Acheson's opinion as well. See Franks letter to Bevin, March 8, 1950, FO 800/517/US/50/8.

[53] Memorandum Prepared in the Bureau of German Affairs [February 11, 1950], *FRUS, 1950,* 4:597–602; and Minutes of the Seventh Meeting of the Policy Planning Staff, January 24, 1950, *FRUS, 1950,* 3:617–22. See also State Department Paper, "Essential Elements of US–UK Relations," April 19, 1950, and Perkins memorandum to Acheson, January 24, 1950, *FRUS, 1950,* 3:869–81, 1610–14.

[54] Bissell memorandum to Henry A. Byroade, Bureau of German Affairs, State Department, February 21, 1950, RG 286, Acc. 53A405, box 60, folder: AAP Policy Series; and Minutes of the Seventh Meeting of the Policy Planning Staff, January 24, 1950, *FRUS, 1950,* 3:617–22.

North Atlantic area, and recognized the principle of parity between re-armament and recovery.[55]

Acheson also won support for a high-level standing committee of deputies who would represent their ministers between meetings of the NATO Council. Such a committee was necessary, he said, to oversee the work of NATO's various committees and harmonize the economic, military, and foreign policies of its members in matters relating to the organization's objectives. The British and French conceded this need but disagreed about how to organize the new committee and the powers it should command. The French wanted the committee to have a vigorous professional staff, strong secretary general, and broad "executive" authority to make recommendations and shape national policies. The British were opposed to the "superman" concept. Nor were they willing to entrust the committee with executive powers over national policies. In this case, as in others, the outcome was a compromise that favored the British while meeting American hopes for continuous direction. The compromise created a standing committee of deputies with a full-time professional staff to carry on the work of the NATO Council when it was not in session. Gone were the French concepts of executive authority and a strong secretariat. But as Acheson pointed out, the new committee would nonetheless exercise the full powers and responsibilities of the Council on a permanent basis.[56]

On the German question, the American strategy of integration collided with European self-interest in a way that made effective compromise more difficult. All sides agreed to further relax occupation controls and pave the way to West Germany's reintegration. The French had just announced the Schuman Plan for a European coal and steel community that would include the Germans; the British had decided that Germany's close association with the OEEC and the Council of Europe should serve as prelude to its membership in NATO and to "some measure of German rearmament."[57] Nevertheless, the British and the French sought to bring Germany into Western

---

[55]   US Delegation at the Tripartite Preparatory Meetings tels. to Acheson, April 28 and 29, 1950, Webb tel. to Acheson, May 12, 1950, Acheson tels. to Webb, May 14, 16 (2), and 18, 1950, and Acheson tel. to Truman, May 18, 1950, *FRUS, 1950*, 3:844–7, 896–8, 97–8, 98–9, 105–8, 108–12, 118–21, 123–5. See also Acheson, *Present at the Creation*, 398–9.

[56]   In addition to the last source cited in note 55, see US Delegation at the Tripartite Preparatory Meetings tels. to Acheson, April 27 and 28 and May 2 (2) and 4, 1950, Douglas tels. to Acheson from Jessup, April 30 and May 2, 1950, Paper Circulated by the Secretary General to the Delegates at the Foreign Ministers Meeting, May 12, 1950, Acheson tels. to Webb, May 14, 15, and 17 (2), 1950, and Acheson tel. to Truman, May 18, 1950, *FRUS, 1950*, 3:894–5, 844–7, 903–5, 905–6, 906–8, 77–8, 80–1, 1103–5, 1061–7, 103–5, 112–13, 114–18, 123–5; and "North Atlantic Council Resolution on Central Machinery," Department of State, *Bulletin* 22 (May 29, 1950): 831.

[57]   For the British decision, see CM (50) 29th Conclusion, May 8, 1950, CAB 128/17. The Schuman Plan is taken up in the next chapter.

Europe on terms that safeguarded their economies. The French would not lift the limits on Germany's steel production, saying that existing steel capacity was adequate and that further expansion would lead to German export pressure on European markets. The British would give priority to relaxing the restrictions on Germany's political affairs and foreign policy. They appeared indifferent to the American belief that some internal controls were necessary to safeguard the program of democratic education and reorientation in Germany. Like the French, moreover, they seemed to believe that economic rather than security considerations might require the retention of limits on German shipbuilding as well as on steel production.

These ideas did not fit with American thinking. The Americans wanted to tie Germany's economy to the West, not encourage the Germans to build economic bridges to the East. This meant loosening the restrictions on production in the Federal Republic and putting that production at the disposal of the North Atlantic alliance. With the Anglo–German trade talks in the background, the Americans were particularly suspicious of what they saw as a campaign by the British to enhance their influence in the Federal Republic at the expense of American plans. After all, the Americans said, the British proposal to terminate virtually all noneconomic controls over Germany's internal and external affairs would diminish the leverage that Washington could bring to bear on the direction of German policy. Still worse, it would do so without first creating the integrated Western European framework that American leaders thought essential to controlling the Germans and building a viable correlation of forces on the Continent.[58]

After days of debate, the ministers finally nailed down a compromise on the German question. They promised to "liberate" the Federal Republic from existing controls but conditioned the pace of liberation on Germany's progress toward "true democracy" and on the degree to which its association with the West safeguarded Allied security.[59] As we will see later in this chapter, the Americans were unable to secure an organizational mechanism for bringing Germany and Britain together in an integrated system. Nevertheless, the emphasis on "true democracy" and on safeguards geared to security rather than economic considerations suggested some gain for the American position. So did the agreements on balanced collective forces, parity for rearmament, and a new committee of deputies. During the course of the meetings, in addition, the Americans had also won British support

---

[58] Acheson tel. to US Delegation at the Tripartite Preparatory Meetings, May 2, 1950, US Delegation tels. to Acheson, May 3, 4, 5, and 6, 1950, Byroade memorandum to Acheson, May 6, 1950, Acheson tel. to Webb, May 9, 1950, US Delegation at the Tripartite Foreign Ministers Meetings tel. to Webb, May 10, 1950, Acheson tel. to Webb, May 14, 1950, *FRUS, 1950*, 3:913–14, 918–20, 923–6, 929–31, 932–3, 933–5, 1013–18, 1024–7, 1061–7.

[59] See the "Declaration for the Three Foreign Ministers on Germany," May 22, 1950, in *FRUS, 1950*, 3:1089–91, and *FRUS, 1950*, 3:1089, footnote 1.

for an informal understanding that finally broke the deadlock in the negotiations for a European payments union.

It was hard to see any room for accommodation when the Anglo–American discussions got underway. The talks revolved around the central issue of integration, with the Americans confusing matters by using the words "integration" and "unification" interchangeably, and with the British making a sharp distinction between "union" and "unity." Unity, said the British, involved conventional forms of cooperation and was desirable; union involved the surrender of sovereignty and was out of the question. Submerging Britain's sovereignty in a continental union, or even integrating the British and European economies, meant shelving the Labour government's welfare programs and subordinating its foreign policies to the collective control of a continental group. The British saw additional costs in the form of greater competition and the potential loss of markets, revenues, and reserves, all of which would make it difficult to shoulder their share of Europe's defense, maintain their position in other parts of the world, and reestablish sterling as a major reserve and trading currency. To avoid these difficulties, they wanted the Americans to slow the pace of trade and payments liberalization in Western Europe and curb the campaign to build central institutions of economic coordination and control. The Americans should also go slow with plans to re-create a fully multilateral system of world trade and should recognize the right of British officials, through bilateral agreements and trade restrictions, to safeguard their full-employment policies and leadership of the sterling area. What the British envisioned, in other words, was an Anglo–American partnership based on close cooperation and policies that protected the West by strengthening the British Empire.[60]

These were familiar arguments, as were the American rejoinders. There was a point, the Americans admitted, beyond which Britain's integration into Europe would adversely affect its commitments elsewhere. But they also threw Bevin's empirical approach back upon the British. The "point of no return" had to be determined on a case-by-case basis, they said, and nothing in the current American proposals threatened Britain's world position. Involved instead was a "middle position" that necessarily entailed some limits on the exercise of sovereign powers and cuts in social programs. To the American way of thinking, these sacrifices would be more than offset by the benefits to be derived from an integrated system in which British leadership balanced German power. In such a system, Germany would be tied securely to the Western alliance and gains in resource utilization, higher

[60] US Delegation at the Tripartite Preparatory Meetings tels. to Acheson, April 24 (2), 25, 26, 27, and 28, and May 3, 1950, US Delegation at the Tripartite Foreign Ministers Meetings tel. to Webb, May 9, 1950, and Acheson tel. to Webb, May 14, 1950, *FRUS, 1950*, 3:854–6, 856–7, 865–9, 881–3, 884–5, 886–90, 955–7, 1018–22, 1061–7.

productivity, and lower prices would strengthen Western Europe economically.[61]

Although nothing in this exchange suggested much progress since the bitter debates of late 1949 and early 1950, the exchange itself amounted to little more than hard bargaining between negotiators who were determined to strike a deal based on the share-the-wealth plan discussed in the State Department. Bevin planned to deal. By the time of the London Conference, the budget cuts of late 1949 and the devaluation of the pound had begun to correct Britain's trade imbalance with the dollar area. Britain's overall deficit in trade had given way to a surplus and hard-currency reserves had increased. As a result, Bevin thought the Labour government was in a stronger position to bid for an Anglo–American partnership. Others might still talk of this partnership as little more than a convenience, a way station on the road to economic viability and then to an independent third force under British leadership. But Bevin had buried such dreams long ago and was not about to disinter them now. Even "with the support of the Commonwealth," he explained in a statement ratified by the Cabinet, "Western Europe was not strong enough to contend with the military danger confronting it from the East." Security could be found only in the "wider conception of the Atlantic Community." And to make this community effective, British and American leaders had to bring their economic policies into line with the defense arrangements being organized under the North Atlantic Treaty. This did not mean that Britain should rush headlong into a multilateral world, only that British negotiators should adopt the same strategy they had followed in the trilateral talks of the previous September. They should make concessions and then seek the American support that would enable them to work toward multilateralism without impairing the Commonwealth connection or the strength of the British economy.[62]

British and American officials drafted an agreement along these lines during the preparatory talks leading up to the foreign ministers conference.[63]

---

[61] State Department Paper, "Essential Elements of US–UK Relations," April 19, 1950, US Delegation at the Tripartite Preparatory Meetings tels. to Acheson, April 24, 25, 26, and 28 and May 3 (2), 1950, and Agreed United Kingdom/United States Report, "The United Kingdom Relationship to Western Europe," [May 5, 1950], *FRUS, 1950*, 3:869–81, 854–6, 865–9, 881–3, 886–90, 955–7, 957–60, 967–70.

[62] CM (50) 29th Conclusion, May 8, 1950, CAB 128/17. See also Memorandum by the Councilor of Embassy for Economic Affairs in the United Kingdom to Ambassador Douglas, May 1, 1950, *FRUS, 1950*, 3:892–3; and Brook memorandum to Attlee, May 5, 1950, PREM 8/1204.

[63] American thinking is summarized in the State Department's paper "Essential Elements of US–UK Relations," April 19, 1950, *FRUS, 1950*, 3:869–81. Ambassador Jessup outlined the position in this paper for British officials during the Tripartite Preparatory Meetings in London. See US Delegation at the Tripartite Preparatory Meetings tel. to Acheson, April 25, 1950, *FRUS, 1950*, 3:865–9. For the informal Anglo–American agreement, see US Delegation at the Tripartite Preparatory Meetings tel. to Acheson, April 30, 1950, and Agreed United States/United Kingdom Report, "Continued Con-

According to his memoirs, Acheson was appalled to discover the draft when he arrived in London, and ordered all copies of the "wretched paper" destroyed. Not that he had doubts "about the genuineness of the special relationship." Mindful of the European reaction to the trilateral talks, he and others were naturally reluctant to approve a document that could make it more difficult to move the French toward greater cooperation with the Germans. Nor could Acheson have been anxious to ratify a commitment that would cut across the wave of anti-British sentiment in certain quarters of the American press and Congress. Bevin found his American colleague determined to avoid too many agreed papers and too much publicity. But he also informed the Cabinet that Acheson had "expressed agreement on the importance of maintaining the position of the sterling area" and had endorsed the recommendations embodied in the preparatory document. Indeed, Acheson still believed that British and American "interests were either the same or very close in all parts of the world" and that the policies of the two countries should therefore "be aligned as closely as possible." Although he thought it "quite impossible to allow it to be known" that the preparatory document "had been drawn up or that it had been agreed to," neither did he have the "wretched paper" destroyed. Instead, he insisted repeatedly that American measures in support of Britain's world position should make it easier for the British to play a more positive role in Western Europe.[64] This quid pro quo defined the terms for progress in the related negotiations for a European payments union.

IV

Basing its policy on the share-the-wealth plan, the ECA was now ready to negotiate a payments union that assured sterling's position as an international currency. It would limit the use of accumulated sterling to members in net deficit with the union and permit members in overall surplus to accept settlement in sterling, rather than in gold or dollars, and thus add to their sterling reserves. These concessions would keep Britain's gold payments to a minimum. Any unreasonable drain would be treated as a "structural" deficit subject to special assistance from the ECA. In addition, the ECA

sultation and Coordination of Policy," May 6, 1950, *FRUS, 1950,* 3:890–2, 1072–4.

[64] Acheson, *Present at the Creation,* 387–8; Foreign Office Record of Meeting at No. 1 Carlton Gardens, May 10, 1950, FO 800/517/US/50/19; and UK Record, Fourth Bipartite Ministerial Meeting, London Conference, May 10, 1950, PREM 8/1204. See also Bruce tel. to Jessup, May 4, 1950, *FRUS, 1950,* 3:960–1; Katz memorandum to Harriman, May 8, 1950, RG 286, Acc. 52A117, box 88, folder: Eyes Only, Personal Correspondence, Jan.–Aug. 1950; R. B. [Roderick Barclay, Bevin's Principal Private Secretary] note to Bevin, May 10, 1950, FO 800/517/US/50/18; and US Delegation at the Tripartite Foreign Ministers Meetings tels. to Webb, May 10 and 11, 1950, *FRUS, 1950,* 3:1024–31.

would support generous credit margins for debtors and permit the British to reimpose quantitative import restrictions if their gold and dollar payments became too great. In return, the British would have to bring the sterling area into an automatic and multilateral pattern of settlements and surrender the right to discriminate in the application of trade restrictions.[65]

This was a compromise that British and European leaders could accept. The Belgians, French, and Italians endorsed the American concessions. Ansiaux and the OEEC's Secretariat had urged similar but less substantial concessions earlier and the British had prepared a compromise plan that came close to what the ECA was suggesting. At the foreign ministers meeting in London, British and American negotiators hammered out an agreement that satisfied both sides. The British then handed a copy of the agreement to their colleagues in Paris while the Americans proclaimed it an "outstanding contribution" toward sterling's participation in "a multilateral trade and payments system" and thus toward "a single European market which is the heart of European integration."[66]

Yet this problem had no sooner been solved when another emerged, this one involving the ratio of gold to credits in settling intra-European imbalances. The Belgians were reluctant to advance additional credits or to participate in a plan that curbed their gold and dollar earnings. In their view, a scheme based on these terms would involve a substantial volume of unrequited Belgian exports, reduce the amount of hard currency available for their investment program, and inflate their economy. They still thought that debtors should accept the largest share of responsibility for financing deficits, which meant that credit margins should be kept to a minimum and hardcurrency payments should begin as quickly as possible. As an alternative,

[65] OSR memorandum, "Possible Reconciliation between the EPU System and the Sterling System," April 6, 1950, Treasury Records, Acc. 66A186, box 81, folder: EPU/21/300 – Original Negotiations and Drafting of EPU Agreement, Vol I. See also Hoffman toreps 1824, 2041, 2647 to Harriman, March 3, 11, and 31, 1950, ECA Files, box 64; Kenney toeca 475 to Hoffman, April 13, 1950, ECA Files, box 16; Foster toreps 3141 and 3142 to Harriman, both dated April 17, 1950, RG 286, Acc. 53A177, box 112, folder: Inter-European; Hoffman torep 3770 to Harriman, Katz, and Tasca, May 4, 1950, ECA Files, box 65; and Harriman repto 2441 to Hoffman, May 5, 1950, ECA Files, box 18.
[66] Harriman repto 2811 to Hoffman, May 24, 1950, ECA Files, box 18. See also ECA Memorandum for the Secretary of State, May 5, 1950, Harriman Papers, folder: European Payments Union; Record of UK–US Meeting on May 12, 1950, dated May 13, 1950, unsigned Treasury Department memorandum, May 13, 1950, T230/159/EAS81/01E; and Wilson-Smith memorandum, May 14, 1950, T230/159/EAS81/01E; Kenney toeca 581 to Hoffman, May 14, 1950, ECA Files, box 16; Harriman toeca 587 to Hoffman, May 15, 1950, *FRUS, 1950*, 3:658–69; unsigned Note by the UK Delegation of a Meeting of the Payments Committee [OEEC] on May 17, 1950, May 20, 1950, T230/159/EAS81/01E; and Hoffman torep 4435 to Harriman, May 25, 1950, ECA Files, box 65. See also CM (50) 30th Conclusion, May 11, 1950, CAB 128/17; and Williams, *Gaitskell Diary*, 185–6.

they proposed, debtors might draw additional credits from the IMF or the ECA might offset part of Belgium's credit liability with direct dollar aid beyond the conditional aid for "structural" surpluses already contemplated in the payments plan.[67]

ECA officials objected to the Belgian proposal. They still adhered to a middle ground between the "gold standard approach" and the lenient terms favored by the British. A balance between gold and credit settlements would, in their view, permit trade liberalization to proceed without alleviating the automatic incentive on creditors to maximize their exports to the dollar area and on debtors to adopt corrective internal policies when they were necessary to achieve equilibrium. The Americans had struck such a balance in their agreement with the British, promising, in effect, to support credit margins at least sufficient to cushion deflationary impacts. Nor were they anxious to abandon this agreement in order to appease the Belgians, whose proposal would work against the automatic incentives on creditors, violate the IMF's rules against automatic drawings, and involve the use of its resources for purposes other than those approved by the agency. The Belgians, according to the ECA, should stop looking for ways to escape their responsibilities as creditors. They should reduce their surplus on intra-European account by redirecting exports to the dollar area and increasing imports from the other OEEC countries.[68]

This dispute stalled the negotiations until mid-June, when a series of compromises finally permitted the OEEC countries to reach agreement on the principles of what became the European Payments Union (EPU). The agreement confirmed the special arrangements for sterling that had been made in London. The British were also pleased by provisions giving debtors generous credit margins and authorizing participating countries to substitute bilateral credits for those to and from the EPU. In addition, debtors that exhausted their credits would be permitted under certain circumstances to safeguard reserves by reimposing import restrictions on a nondiscriminatory basis. The Belgians were satisfied because the agreement reduced their credit

---

[67] Katz reptos 2305 and 3073 to Hoffman, April 27 and June 7, 1950, ECA Files, box 18; Chief, ECA Mission, Brussels, toreps 156, 166, and 198 to Harriman, May 6 and 13 and June 9, 1950, RG 286, Acc. 53A177, box 112, folder: Inter-European; Hoffman torep 4873 to Harriman, June 9, 1950, ECA Files, box 66; and Diebold, *Trade and Payments*, 90–1. See also Hall-Patch, "European Payments Union," June 4, 1950, T230/159/EAS81/01E; and Hall-Patch tel. to FO, June 19, 1950, in Records of the British Treasury, Marshall Aid Division, Record Class T237/87/OFM16/1/01 (hereafter cited as T237, with appropriate filing designation).

[68] In addition to the last two documents cited in note 67, see Harriman repto 2238 to Hoffman, April 29, 1950, ECA Files, box 18; Hoffman ecato 120 to the Embassy in Belgium, May 1, 1950, *FRUS, 1950*, 3:652–3; Hoffman toreps 3730 and 4332 to Harriman, May 4 and 23, 1950, ECA Files, box 65; Katz repto 2954 to Hoffman, Foster, and Bissell, June 1, 1950, ECA Files, box 18; and Hoffman torep 4659 to Katz, June 3, 1950, and Foster torep 4694 to Harriman, June 5, 1950, ECA Files, box 66.

liability and urged the ECA to offset part of this liability with both structural allowances and direct dollar aid. In return, the Belgians promised to reduce their surplus in intra-European trade and increase exports to the Western Hemisphere.[69]

As approved by the Europeans at an OEEC meeting on July 7, the agreement provided for automatic and multilateral offsettings of credits and debits among participating countries. Each country would then be left in net surplus or deficit to the group as a whole and net imbalances would be settled with the EPU rather than between members bilaterally. Each country would also receive an EPU "quota" for a two-year period beginning in July 1950. The quota would equal 15 percent of the country's aggregate trade with the group in 1949 and would determine the maximum deficit or surplus it could finance through the Union. Surplus and deficit countries respectively would grant or receive credits up to 20 percent of their quota, at which point residual imbalances would be financed according to a sliding scale of credits and gold payments. Under this scale, a debtor's gold payments would be limited until the debtor had used 60 percent of its quota, whereupon its payments to the Union would exceed the credits received. When its quota was exhausted, a debtor would have to settle entirely in gold unless special arrangements were made with the EPU. The settlement terms favored debtors over creditors but preserved the concept of automatic incentives on both. This arrangement is what the ECA had wanted and why it promised to set aside a fund of dollars as working capital for use by the EPU in covering the difference between the gold the union received and that it paid out.[70]

The ECA's support came only after opposition had been overcome in the Treasury Department and the NAC. Both agencies thought that the proposal went too far in shielding debtors against the competitive pressures of the market. The sliding scale of gold settlements was "too soft," they said. It would do little to drive participating countries toward intra-European equilibrium or toward full convertibility with the Western Hemisphere. On the contrary, the results might well be an integrated European market based on permanent discrimination against the dollar. ECA officials saw things

[69] See the exchange of letters between Katz and Hugh Gaitskell, British minister of state for economic affairs, quoted in Katz repto 3771 to Hoffman, July 7, 1950, and Katz repto 3318 to Hoffman, Foster, and Bissell, June 18, 1950, ECA Files, box 18; Harriman repto circular 136 to Hoffman, June 20, 1950, ECA Files, box 20; and Judd Polk and William B. Dale of the American Embassy, London, memorandum to Douglas, June 21, 1950, Treasury Records, Acc. 66A816, box 28, folder: European Payments and Clearing Union, Vol. II.

[70] The terms of the agreement are outlined in the documents cited in note 69. See also Harriman repto circular 155 to Hoffman, July 11, 1950, ECA Files, box 20; and ECA, *Ninth Report to Congress* (Washington, DC, 1950), 26–31. The reserve fund was in addition to the ECA's structural allowances to cover the initial debit or credit positions of participating states and its loans or grants to countries facing special difficulties.

differently. They argued that automatic inducements would increase after the first year of operation, that better terms were impossible to negotiate, and that agreement on the present basis was better than no agreement at all. The NAC finally concurred, but only on condition that nothing interfere with the progress of any participating country toward full convertibility with the dollar.[71]

There were few doubts in Hoffman's mind when he wrote a friend in London that the EPU would further "the trend from economic nationalism [to] economic unity" in Western Europe.[72] This it would do by alleviating the balance-of-payments difficulties that had led participating countries to protect reserves through bilateral bargaining and quantitative import quotas. The ECA, in fact, had wanted to liberalize trade and payments at the same time. It had conditioned its support for the payments plan on the elimination of quantitative import restrictions, calling specifically for the removal of restrictions on 75 percent of all private trade by the end of 1950 and on the remaining 25 percent by mid-1951. The only exceptions would be those due to security considerations, local or general shortages, or serious balance-of-payments difficulties. There would be no exceptions for purely protectionist purposes and the restrictions that remained would be applied on a multilateral, nondiscriminatory basis.[73] The goal, as the ECA kept repeating, was rapid progress toward a "single market" that would allow "full play for international specialization of production in accordance with comparative advantage."[74]

The OEEC's ambitions were less grand. Under the Plan of Action of November 1949, participating countries had pledged to remove quantitative restrictions on only 50 percent of their private imports. The OEEC promised to raise this to 60 percent by June 1950, 75 percent by December, but only if a new payments agreement reduced the risk to monetary reserves. It was this condition that had forced the Americans to concentrate their "main efforts" on the payments negotiations, the goal being an agreement that made it easier to liberalize trade but still retained the automatic inducements toward intra-European equilibrium.[75]

---

[71]   Hoffman torep 5091 to Katz, Tasca, and Gordon from Bissell, June 17, 1950, ECA Files, box 66. See also unsigned memorandum, "The Outcome of the EPU Negotiations," June 16, 1950, Snyder Papers, box 11, folder: ECA & International Trade Organization, 1950; Bissell torep 5798 to Harriman, July 8, 1950, ECA Files, box 66; and NAC, Minutes of 158th Meeting; June 29, 1950, RG 56, NAC Minutes.

[72]   Hoffman letter to H. G. Henly of Henlys Limited, London, June 21, 1950, Hoffman Papers, box 2, folder: Chronological File.

[73]   Harriman repto circular 7 to Hoffman, January 11, 1950, ECA Files, box 20; Foster torep 758 to Harriman, January 29, 1950, ECA Files, box 63; Hoffman torep 1588 to Harriman, February 23, 1950, ECA Files, box 64; and Diebold, *Trade and Payments*, 169.

[74]   Hoffman torep 33 to Harriman, January 3, 1950, ECA Files, box 63. See also Hoffman torep 174 to Harriman, January 6, 1950, ECA Files, box 63.

[75]   Harriman repto circular 70 to Hoffman, March 28, 1950, ECA Files, box 20. See

The EPU accord came close to this goal. While preserving the principle of gold settlements, it also provided partial credits. In addition, the offsetting arrangements now made it possible for members in net balance with the group to manage bilateral deficits without resorting to trade restrictions: A deficit with one country could be offset against a surplus with another. These provisions broke the dike that had been holding back progress in the area of trade liberalization. The OEEC countries immediately eliminated quantitative restrictions on 60 percent of their private imports from each other. They also agreed with the ECA that liberalization and nondiscrimination should go hand in hand. According to a set of trade rules embedded in the EPU agreement, all existing and future measures of liberalization were to be applied equally to imports from other members of the group, as were any restrictions that remained after January 1951. Members might be exempt from these rules under certain circumstances, particularly if they faced a serious drain on their reserves. But a special "Restricted Committee" would have to review these circumstances and only the EPU could authorize the reimposition of discriminatory restrictions.[76]

Although these rules could give real substance to the idea of Western Europe as a single market, applying them was not going to be easy. Each stage in the process of liberalization would require painful adjustments and guarantee opposition from a variety of vested interests who were busy rehearsing their arguments. Those in low-tariff countries were saying that tariffs should be raised to offset the reduction of import quotas. Those in free-market countries were complaining that government-controlled economies could use subsidies, rationing, and state trading to escape the consequences of liberalization. Those in regulated economies were arguing that liberalization could adversely affect their economic planning and full-employment policies. All agreed that liberalization and integration promised long-term benefits. But they also worried that the short-term results would include a wasteful dislocation of existing capital and high levels of unemployment. Concerns of this sort had already led participating states to concentrate their efforts in areas where initial restrictions were no longer practical or where additional imports would not compete with domestic production.[77]

The ECA understood that concerns about unemployment and its attendant political consequences could erode support for liberalization. This was one reason why Keynesians in that agency had been willing to accept "soft"

    also Harriman reptos 152, 217, and 642, January 10 and 13, and February 3, 1950, ECA Files, box 17; and Diebold, *Trade and Payments*, 162–9.

[76] Foster torep 5425 to Harriman, June 27, 1950, and Bissell torep 5657 to Harriman, ECA Files, box 66; Katz repto 3737 to Hoffman, June 6, 1950, and OSR to Hoffman, June 7, 1950, ECA Files, box 18; and OSR repto circular 155 to Hoffman, June 11, 1950, ECA Files, box 20. See also Diebold, *Trade and Payments*, 172–5.

[77] These "obstacles" to liberalization are discussed at some length in Diebold, *Trade and Payments*, 196–204.

terms that gave debtors larger credit margins than the Treasury Department thought desirable. Hugh Gaitskell, who negotiated the EPU accord for the British, drew a sharp contrast between policymakers in the two American agencies. Those in the ECA, he confided to his diary, were "economist new dealer types." They did not share the "banker outlook" of the Treasury Department, the IMF, and their allies among the Belgians, French, and Swiss, all of whom were more concerned with inflation than with unemployment and thus inclined to support credit terms more stringent than those agreed between the ECA and the Labour government.[78]

In addition to generous credit margins, Keynesians in the ECA relied on other elements of the New Deal synthesis to substitute the politics of growth for the redistributive battles of the past. They used part of their reserve fund to cushion the impact on national economies of measures to liberalize trade and integrate markets. These funds supplemented the counterpart accounts on which they drew to finance industrial and agricultural modernization projects in participating countries. Because secure employment and higher living standards depended on closing the dollar gap, the Keynesians also continued their efforts to promote European exports to the United States. They encouraged participating governments to organize dollar boards, target sales to the Western Hemisphere, and develop overseas territories as an indirect source of dollar income.

The technical-assistance program, productivity teams, and production councils formed another enduring element in the American policy synthesis. These schemes were still being used to build labor–management partnerships behind the Marshall Plan, including the trade-liberalization program, and to equip the Europeans with the technical, marketing, and production skills needed to raise productivity and ease the transition to a multilateral pattern of trade. The ECA thus far had expended $15.4 million on the technical-assistance program, with over half of this amount committed in the second quarter of 1950. Several hundred American "experts" were still working under the auspices of this program to overcome some of the barriers to greater growth in Europe. At the same time, both the ECA and the Anglo–American Council on Productivity continued to sponsor visits to American farms and factories by a steady stream of European managers and workers. The whole effort, according to the ECA, was beginning to transform the face of industrial relations in Western Europe. It was replacing the competitive zero-sum politics of an earlier day with a corporative collaboration similar to the labor–management teamwork that had brought greater growth, steady employment, and social harmony to the United States. It was doing so by pointing up the impressive gains that American industry had made through intensive competition in a large, internal market, through strict methods of product simplification, standardization, and cost account-

[78] Williams, *Gaitskell Diary*, 190–1.

ing, and through close cooperation with organized labor, which, "despite occasional differences with management over wages," generally agreed "that a high standard of living must be supported by a continuously increasing rate of output."[79]

In the midst of the EPU negotiations, the ECA also began a major campaign to refute charges that its policies sacrificed full employment to the idol of efficiency. The theme of its message was that strictly national strategies actually perpetuated the old trend toward economic fragmentation and the sort of inflationary policies and government controls that reduced employment and lowered living standards. The need, it said, was for a "regional" approach that raised employment by integrating markets.[80] To get this message out, the ECA extended its ties to farm, labor, and industry groups in the participating countries.[81] Harriman also went before the OEEC to explain how trade liberalization went hand in hand with "high and stable employment." Milton Katz, Harriman's deputy in Paris, struck the same theme in a speech to the European Trade Union Advisory Committee, telling its members that workers stood to gain in higher wages and better living standards from measures to liberalize trade and integrate markets. Any short-term dislocations, he and others said, could be handled through special assistance from the ECA and Keynesian strategies of aggregate economic management, including compensatory fiscal policies and new programs to retrain workers and relocate resources.[82]

The Europeans, of course, had their own ideas about how to integrate markets without causing serious short-term disruptions. The Italians favored a reciprocal reduction of tariffs on a commodity-by-commodity basis. The French suggested a "European Investment Bank" to finance transnational investment projects. Both proposals would set aside funds to relocate workers and capital resources displaced by the process of integration. This was also a central feature of the Stikker Plan proposed by the Netherlands, which called for an "Integration Fund" to modernize European industry on an industry-by-industry basis.[83] Still other plans would rely on government-

[79] ECA, *Ninth Report to Congress*, 65, 19, 60–6, 70–6. See also Harriman reptos 140 and 294 to Hoffman, January 10 and 17, 1950, and Katz reptos 912, 959, and 1640 to Hoffman, February 16 and 17, and March 25, 1950, ECA Files, box 17; Foster torep 750 to Harriman, January 25, 1950, ECA Files, box 63; Foster torep 2773 to Harriman, April 5, 1950, ECA Files, box 64; and Bissell torep 5554 to Harriman, June 30, 1950, ECA files, box 66.

[80] Hoffman torep 340 to Harriman, January 12, 1950, and Katz repto 1610 to Hoffman, March 24, 1950, ECA Files, box 17; and Hoffman torep 2637 to Harriman, March 31, 1950, ECA Files, box 64.

[81] See, for example, Harriman repto 2884 to Hoffman, May 26, 1950, ECA Files, box 18; and Katz repto circular 146 to Hoffman, June 30, 1950, ECA Files, box 20.

[82] Katz repto 2359 to Hoffman, May 1, 1950, ECA Files, box 18. See also Katz repto circular 87 to Hoffman, April 15, 1950, ECA Files, box 20.

[83] These European proposals are summarized in the ECA's *Ninth Report to Congress*, 33. On the Stikker Plan, see also Diebold, *Trade and Payments*, 204–8.

sanctioned agreements where private leaders, rather than market forces, would guide the process of integration. Such plans appealed particularly to private groups in protected sectors of the European economy, especially to French farm, labor, and industrial interests who feared losing markets to German competition. The French, for example, had hoped to include in the Fritalux project and in their new trade agreement with the Germans clauses that would limit imports above "abnormal" levels and allow ostensible competitors in different countries to negotiate national lines of economic specialization.

Arrangements of this sort had no appeal in Washington. They pointed to new cartels, said the Americans. They would frustrate the rule of comparative advantage and discourage the "rigorous competition" that was a "major cause of high productivity" in the United States. There was no reason to believe, the Americans concluded, that such arrangements would "yield desirable results approximating those attainable by competitive forces." Indeed, some in the ECA talked about using the technical-assistance program to acquaint European labor and management teams with the antitrust activities of the Justice Department and the Federal Trade Commission.[84]

V

If cartel-type agreements were out of the question, so was an approach that relied entirely on market incentives to promote integration. The ECA was not seeking to "impose [a] Hazlitt libertarianism" on Europe or following what Hoffman dismissed as a "policy [of] government non-intervention." Hoffman and others envisioned a European order superintended by central institutions with the power to coordinate national economies.[85] This was the organizational dimension of the ECA's policy as seen in its ongoing efforts to strengthen the OEEC, give positive powers to the EPU's managing board, and harmonize national policies across the North Atlantic area. In all cases, the results fell short of expectations, largely because of Britain's antipathy to central institutions that might compromise its social programs or break its ties to the Commonwealth and sterling area. Maintaining these ties was a central feature of Bevin's design for a North Atlantic system in which the British Empire operated as the balance wheel between two continents, occupying the pivotal position that for Bevin was the key to recapturing Britain's status as a world-class power. This design had its own

---

[84] Hoffman torep 33 to Harriman, January 3, 1950, ECA Files, box 63; and Katz repto 982 to Hoffman, February 18, 1950, ECA Files, box 17. See also Katz repto 73 to Hoffman, January 6, 1950, and Harriman repto 163 to Hoffman, January 10, 1950, ECA Files, box 17; Hoffman torep 317 to Harriman, January 11, 1950, ECA Files, box 63; and Hoffman torep 2637 to Harriman, March 31, 1950, ECA Files, box 64.

[85] Hoffman torep 340 to Harriman, January 12, 1950, ECA Files, box 63.

organizational imperatives and they continued to work at cross-purposes to those that guided the ECA.

So far as the EPU was concerned, the agreement on principles signed by the OEEC in July established a Managing Board of seven members with the right to make decisions by majority vote. But the board's powers were vaguely defined and its decisions subject to review by the OEEC, which could recommend changes in national policy only by the unanimous vote of its members. Nor did the ECA have voting membership on the Managing Board. These limitations were partly the result of opposition in the Treasury Department and the NAC to a strong European agency that might challenge the jurisdiction of the IMF in matters relating to the exchange rates or internal policies of its members. But they were also the result of opposition from some OEEC delegations, particularly the British delegation, to a truly independent board with considerable power to dictate national policies. Whatever the source, the outcome was the same. Although Hoffman and others would still try to make the board into a strong coordinating agency with an independent staff, the EPU would have to rely largely on automatic, not administrative, incentives to adjust national economies in the interest of European equilibrium and integration.[86]

Nor did the Americans enjoy much more success in their efforts to transform the OEEC into a strong agency of integration. The politics and diplomacy of organization in this case continued to center on the ECA's demand for the appointment of Paul-Henri Spaak to the new post of director general. The OEEC's Consultative Group had decided in December to establish such a position and Spaak seemed anxious to secure the appointment. In addition, Harriman was still hoping for an arrangement that would magnify the powers of the director general and enable Spaak to take this position while retaining his current office as president of the European Assembly. Both men wanted a director general who could deal with the large "political issues" of the day, not just the administrative and technical details that had occupied so much of the OEEC's time. In fact, Harriman's purpose was to harness the OEEC's administrative apparatus to the political objectives of American diplomacy. By investing the director general with considerable independence and executive authority, he and Spaak would transform the OEEC into a supranational "pressure mechanism" for disciplining member states and integrating economies.[87]

Whitehall's official line remained unchanged since the issue was last mooted at the end of 1949. The British would consent to a director gen-

---

[86]   See the documents cited in notes 71 and 72.
[87]   Hall-Patch letter to Berthoud, January 7, 1950, FO 371, 86973, UR1014; and Hall-Patch letter to Strang, January 8, 1950, FO 371, 87319, UR553. See also Hall-Patch tel. to FO, January 5, 1950, and Berthoud Note for the Meeting of the Consultative Group to be Held in Paris on January 26th, January 24, 1950, FO 371, 87319, UR553.

eralship, but only if the new position involved no alteration of the OEEC's constitution. This argument cloaked their strong opposition to the appointment of a supranational official and most of all to the appointment of Spaak, a robust supporter of European unity widely regarded in London as little more than an agent of American policy. Opposition to Spaak's appointment only hardened after he criticized Britain's policy toward European integration in an interview with the British press and in a major speech at the University of Pennsylvania. Coming on the eve of the British elections, these pronouncements looked at best like a "lamentable error of taste," at worst like a malicious intervention in the British elections on an issue that played into the hands of Winston Churchill and other Conservative Party champions of European unity. The pronouncements made Spaak persona non grata to policymakers in the Labour government, who were now completely convinced that he lacked the good judgment and impartiality required of a high official in the OEEC. The Economic Policy Committee decided on January 19 that Spaak had put himself "right out of court." Cripps conveyed this decision to John Kenney, who headed the ECA mission in London, while Bevin instructed Ambassador Franks to inform Acheson and Hoffman that his government could never accept Spaak's appointment.[88]

The Americans would not urge Spaak to withdraw his candidacy, as Franks requested, nor abandon their demand for the new position. But given the British opposition, they stopped pushing Spaak's appointment and made the Europeans primarily responsible for choosing a candidate.[89] So long as the new appointee gave "political direction" to the European agency, as Hoffman told Cripps, the participating countries could select the personality of their choice and define his responsibilities.[90] This softening of the American position made it possible for European leaders to implement the agreement of the previous December and to do so as part of a major reorganization of the OEEC in February and April 1950. Under this agreement, the Consultative Group of Ministers was to be abolished, the Council and its Executive Committee were to meet more frequently at the ministerial level, and top officials were to spend more time directing the work of the organization. Most important, the Council created the new post of "Political

[88]	FO tel. to Bevin on board H.M.S. *Birmingham*, January 18, 1950, and FO tel. to Franks, January 19, 1950, FO 371, 87319, UR553. See also Hall-Patch letter to Strang, January 18, 1950, and Bevin tel. to FO, January 19, 1950, FO 371, 87319, UR553; FO tel. to Franks, January 19, 1950, FO 371, 86969, UR103, Acheson tel. to Harriman, January 24, 1950, *FRUS, 1950*, 3:616–17; Berthoud memorandum to Jebb and Strang, January 27, 1950, FO 371, 87136, UR3211; and Harriman letter to Robert Murphy, American Ambassador to Belgium, February 10, 1950, Harriman Papers, folder: Belgium.

[89]	Acheson tel. to Harriman, January 24, 1950, *FRUS, 1950*, 3:616–17; and Franks tel. to FO, January 24, 1950, FO 371, 87319, UR553.

[90]	Makins, Record of Conversation of January 25th, 1950, dated January 26, 1950, FO 371, 86970, UR104.

Conciliator," rather than director general, and elected Dirk Stikker of the Netherlands to this position and to the chairmanship of the Council.[91]

Stikker was an advocate of European integration and Harriman considered his appointment a "constructive" step "in strengthening OEEC at [the] political level." Hoffman heralded it as the "single most hopeful move since [the] inception [of] OEEC."[92] In the weeks that followed Stikker's appointment, the Americans also tried their best to separate the political conciliator from other OEEC officials and to endow him with international status. The results humiliated Secretary General Robert Marjolin, who found himself ignored after years of faithful service to the OEEC, and led some Europeans to the conclusion that Stikker was acting more like a "Kaiser Bill" than a "constitutional monarch."[93] Yet neither these complaints nor Hoffman's hyperbole could conceal the fact that Stikker's authority was ill-defined or that real power still resided in the hands of individual governments. The reorganization of February and April had strengthened the OEEC as a vehicle of intergovernmental collaboration. But it had stopped short of creating the sort of independent, corporative authority that the ECA considered essential to European integration.

Nor did such an authority emerge from the London Foreign Ministers Conference in May. American policy planning for the conference had envisioned a more active role for the United States in European political and economic affairs. This new role could be achieved by enlarging NATO's responsibilities in these areas or by associating the United States with the OEEC. Either course would give the Americans a vehicle for maximizing their influence in Western Europe, something they considered necessary because Britain would not act except in tandem with the United States and because only ongoing American involvement would give the continental countries, particularly France, the assurances of security they needed to move ahead with Germany's revival and reintegration.[94]

[91] Hall-Patch tel. to FO, February 1, 1950, FO 371, 87319, UR553; Berthoud memorandum to Makins, February 2, 1950, FO 371, 86970, UR104; Harriman repto 616 to Hoffman, February 2, 1950, ECA Files, box 17; Berthoud letter to Sir Philip Nicholas, British Ambassador to the Netherlands, February 4, 1950, FO 371, 87319, UR553; Harriman repto circular 30 to Hoffman, February 4, 1950, ECA Files, box 20; Harriman repto 1646 to Hoffman, March 25, 1950, ECA Files, box 17; and Katz repto 1833 to Hoffman, April 4, 1950, ECA Files, box 18.

[92] Harriman repto circular 30 to Hoffman, February 4, 1950, ECA Files, box 20; and Hoffman torep 1053 to Harriman, February 3, 1950, ECA Files, box 63.

[93] Hall-Patch letter to Makins, March 25, 1950, FO 371, 87333, UR5519. See also Hall-Patch letter to Berthoud, March 10, 1950, FO 371, 87333, UR5519; and Hall-Patch, Report of Visit by OEEC Delegation to Washington, March 10, 1950, FO 371, 87050, UR3137.

[94] Memorandum Prepared in the Bureau of German Affairs, [February 11, 1950], *FRUS, 1950*, 4:597–602; Memorandum of Conversation by the Officer in Charge of United Kingdom and Ireland Affairs, March 7, 1950, *FRUS, 1950*, 3:638–42; and Joseph Jones letter to George Elsey, White House, March 3, 1950, with enclosed Jones

The difficulty came in reconciling British and French differences over which organizational framework to use. In this case, as in others, the politics of organization really involved a far more important struggle over the nature of the Western European system, specifically over how best to organize a balance of power that could control the Germans and contain the Soviets. As they had since 1947, the French wanted to centralize authority over national policies in the hands of a strong collective agency. They had first expressed this desire in a vague plan for an "Atlantic High Council" and had then gone on to more concrete proposals.[95] One of these was the Schuman Plan for a European coal and steel community that would blend German and French interests under the aegis of a supranational authority. Acheson later recalled how the prospect of such a community without Great Britain hung like a pall over the meetings.[96] According to the records, however, the ministers barely touched on the plan at London, where controversy turned instead on two other proposals tabled by the French. The first was their plan to give the NATO committee of deputies "executive powers"; the second was their call for a continental group that would be organized around the OEEC, would include Great Britain as a full member, and would cooperate with the United States in economic and political matters of common concern. This cooperation would be achieved by making the United States and Canada "associate members" of the OEEC. The OEEC would remain a "European organization for purely European affairs." But its transatlantic link would deepen the American commitment in Europe and this, together with Britain's active involvement in the continental group, would pave the way for Germany's further revitalization and reintegration.[97]

These proposals met with steadfast opposition from the British delegation to the London Conference. The British would not entrust "executive" power to the new committee of deputies, nor permit themselves to be incorporated into a purely European "zone." Although they had no objection to links between the OEEC and the United States, they much preferred a North Atlantic framework that embraced the United States, the United Kingdom, and "some European entity." This framework could be brought about, they said, by developing NATO as an "umbrella" organization with separate

memorandum of March 2, 1950, George M. Elsey Papers (Truman Library), box 62, folder: Foreign Policy Planning.
[95] Bruce tels. to Acheson, April 15 and 20, 1950, *FRUS, 1950*, 3:54–5, 57–8.
[96] Acheson, *Present at the Creation*, 393. The Schuman Plan is discussed in the following chapter.
[97] US Delegation at the Tripartite Foreign Ministers Meetings tel. to Webb, May 16, 1950, *FRUS, 1950*, 3:1069–71. See also US Delegation at the Tripartite Preparatory Meetings tel. to Acheson, May 6, 1950, Acheson tel. to Webb, May 9, 1950, US Delegation at the Tripartite Foreign Ministers Meetings tel. to Webb, May 11, 1950, and Acheson tel. to Webb, May 14, 1950, *FRUS, 1950*, 3:911–13, 1013–18, 1040–3, 1061–7. See also UK Record, Third Bipartite Ministerial Meeting, London Conference, May 10, 1950, PREM 8/1204.

arms for military and nonmilitary affairs. An arrangement like this would square with Britain's role as the balance wheel in a North Atlantic community, enabling the British to harmonize their commitments to the Continent with those to the Commonwealth and the United States. It also had the advantage of foreclosing West Germany's exclusive association with a strictly continental group. Germany would be brought instead into the nonmilitary affairs of the North Atlantic alliance, an association, according to the British, that would provide both the institutional mechanism and the Anglo–American military guarantees that were needed to reassure the French.[98]

The French, however, saw in such a proposal an alarming degree of British aloofness that virtually guaranteed Germany's predominance in an integrated European economy. Nor were they inclined to use NATO as an organizing framework, a course, they insisted, that would lead to Germany's rearmament and preclude participation by European neutrals. The result, according to French Foreign Minister Schuman, would be "new iron curtains on our side of [the] present Iron Curtain."[99] With this warning Acheson seemed to agree, telling his European associates that it would be better to develop separate organizations for military and economic matters and that the United States would be willing to establish a working association with the OEEC.[100]

The outcome was a compromise that pointed in all directions. Acheson pledged continuing American interest in European economic problems; Bevin and Schuman called for a "working relationship" between the United States and the OEEC. This relationship would be "informal" and would detract neither from the OEEC's role as an agency "devoted primarily to European economic problems" nor from NATO's general responsibility for economic and political issues affecting the North Atlantic area.[101] American leaders tried to put a good face on the compromise. The American delegation in London considered it the best one possible; Harriman thought it another step forward. The Europeans had at least agreed on the importance of

[98] US Delegation at the Tripartite Preparatory Meetings tels. to Acheson, April 25 and 26 and May 6, 1950, Acheson tel. to Certain Diplomatic Offices, April 27, 1950, US Delegation at the Tripartite Foreign Ministers Meetings tel. to Webb, May 9, 1950, and Acheson tel. to Webb, May 14, 1950, *FRUS, 1950*, 3:860–3, 881–3, 911–13, 71–2, 1018–22, 1061–7. For British records, see, in addition to the last document cited in note 97, CM (50) 29th Conclusion, May 8, 1950, CAB 128/17.

[99] Acheson tel. to Webb, May 9, 1950, *FRUS, 1950*, 3:1013–18. See also US Delegation at the Tripartite Preparatory Meetings tel. to Acheson, April 29, 1950, *FRUS, 1950*, 3:896–8.

[100] US Delegation at the Tripartite Foreign Ministers Meetings tel. to Webb, May 11, 1950, *FRUS, 1950*, 3:1040–3. See also Acheson tel. to Webb, May 9, 1950, *FRUS, 1950*, 3:1013–18.

[101] See the communiqué issued by the ministers on May 18, 1950, in Department of State, *Bulletin* 22 (May 29, 1950), 827. See also Acheson tel. to Webb, May 16, 1950, *FRUS, 1950*, 3:659–61.

continued economic collaboration and on the need to give this collaboration organizational expression. In June, moreover, they brought the United States and Canada into the OEEC as associate members.[102] Still, there was no hiding the fact that this arrangement fell short of what the ECA had wanted – a central institution that could transcend sovereignties and co-ordinate national policies across the ERP area.

VI

By mid-1950, American policymakers could add several important accomplishments to their balance sheet for Western Europe. Everyone conceded that the Old World would not achieve equilibrium with the New by the end of the ERP period. But Marshall Planners at least could claim to have set the participating countries on the road to this goal. The EPU agreement had committed the sterling area to a multilateral pattern of settlements, cutting the ground from under those who wanted to see Great Britain at the center of a soft-currency trading bloc or as the leader of an independent third force in world affairs. The level of production was still going up across most of Western Europe, the devaluations of late 1949 had narrowed the dollar gap, and the OEEC had made arrangements to liberalize intra-European trade. In line with those arrangements, the participating countries had begun to reduce quantitative import restrictions; some were eliminating other government controls; and Western Europe as a whole was far more responsive to the free-market forces that could work to hold down costs and integrate economies. On the security side of the coin, the NATO countries had created a new committee of deputies, agreed to parity between recovery and rearmament, and struck a compromise that further relaxed occupation controls and led in June to West Germany's accession to the Council of Europe. Taken together, these developments represented substantial progress toward an integrated Western European economic and security system of sufficient size and stability to corral the Germans, contain the Soviets, and achieve the long-term goal of viability.

Yet these gains could not conceal the central failure of American Marshall Planners. They had launched programs to expand output in critical sectors of the European economy, to improve production and marketing skills, to develop dependent territories, and to form partnerships among government, labor, and management. These were components of a larger formulation that aimed to create a Western European economic order similar to the American neo-capitalism that had taken shape under the New Deal. But

[102]   US Delegation at the Tripartite Foreign Ministers Meetings tel. to Webb, May 16, 1950, *FRUS, 1950*, 3:1069–71; Harriman tel. to Acheson, June 2, 1950, Harriman Papers, folder: O.E.E.C.; Harriman tel. to Acheson, June 15, 1950, *FRUS, 1950*, 3:662–3; *FRUS, 1950*, 3:662, footnote 3; and Katz repto 3669 to Hoffman, June 30, 1950, ECA Files, box 18.

the Marshall Planners had also urged the Europeans to build central institutions of economic coordination and control. This too was a central component of the American formulation, the key to an integrated single market and thus to the economies of scale that would adjourn redistributive battles and put Western Europe on a self-supporting basis. As it turned out, however, few of the participating countries would support the supranational ideal, and none gave less support than Britain. When it came to the debates over the EPU's Managing Board, the appointment of a director general, and the merits of a European or North Atlantic mechanism for coordinating national policies, the ECA's vision kept breaking down on the grand design that guided British policymakers, who found it impossible to square their membership in a European institution with their commitments at home and to the sterling area.

American leaders shared much of the responsibility for this failure. Opposition from the Treasury Department precluded a vigorous ECA campaign for a strong Managing Board. This development played into the hands of the British. So did the general preoccupation with defense and security considerations that led the State Department and the ECA to recognize the principle of British exceptionalism. American leaders were unable to reconcile the dualism in their diplomacy, that is, to harmonize their support for Britain's strategically important commitments around the world with their vision of an integrated Western Europe balanced between British and German power. They tried to do so by pressuring the British to play a role on the Continent that supposedly stopped short of merging sovereignties. But neither their pressure nor the bitter battles that resulted could overcome the restraints that operated on British policy. The British would go deeper into Europe, as they did with the EPU, when the Americans recognized (and subsidized) Britain's commitments to the sterling area and hence its claim to a special relationship with the United States. Otherwise, they forced the Americans into vague compromises that preserved their freedom to maneuver and exposed the two sides of American diplomacy.

Nor would the British reverse course in the second half of 1950. Then it would become clear that neither the OEEC nor NATO was to be the primary instrument of European economic integration, a choice now rendered moot by the Schuman Plan for a European coal and steel community. The developments that followed would point toward a "nuclear" Europe that incorporated the Germans but not the British. Together with the Korean War and the increasing demands of rearmament, they would further alter American priorities and bring the Marshall Plan to a premature ending. It is to these aspects of the story that we turn in the last chapters of this history.

8

Holding the line:
The ECA's efforts to reconcile
recovery and rearmament

I

THE TRUMAN ADMINISTRATION had asked Congress in January 1950 to renew the ERP for another year, the third of four years that had been planned from the start. Conservative opponents mounted the usual arguments. Pointing to an anticipated budget deficit of several billion dollars, they were now more convinced than ever that the ERP and other programs were paving the way to economic ruin and a regime of government controls. Senator Taft said the recovery of production and the restoration of financial stability in Western Europe made it possible to reduce the amount of American assistance by 16 percent. Others said that cuts in Marshall aid would encourage the Europeans to end "costly experiments with socialist devices" and to devote a greater share of their resources to productive investment. Complaints that American aid subsidized socialism in England mixed with charges that neither European nor American recovery planners had done enough to rebuild West Germany, where the new government was committed to private-enterprise capitalism and where the revival of production would do much to reduce the need for American dollars. As in 1948 and 1949, the conservatives also linked the Marshall Plan to the Reciprocal Trade Agreements Act, the International Trade Organization (ITO), and other measures that aimed to lower tariffs and organize a multilateral system of world trade. They identified these measures with the alliance of "internationalists" that had taken shape under the New Deal and went on to warn that "free trade" would destroy noncompetitive firms in the United States, throw workers off the job, and subject government policy to control by the ITO and other "super-states." It was no accident, according to Senator Malone, that the New Deal coalition also supported social welfare and aid to business, labor, and agriculture, since such programs would be needed to sustain the unfortunate victims of free trade.[1]

[1] U.S. Congress, Senators Kem, Malone, and Jenner speaking on S. 3304, 81st Cong.,

Despite the ferocity of their attacks, the conservatives were no match for "internationalists" who had supported the ERP from the beginning. Although the debate raged for nearly six months, it resembled nothing so much as a spectacular electrical storm – a brilliant display that lights up the sky but leaves the ground undisturbed. When the air cleared, the Marshall Plan had passed through both houses of Congress with comfortable majorities and only a modest reduction (from $2.95 billion to $2.7 billion) in the administration's original request. But this was on June 5, 1950. Less than three weeks later and half a world away, a storm broke that shattered the political landscape in Washington.

Almost overnight, the Korean War strengthened the hand of the conservative coalition in Congress and set the stage for a far more successful assault on the Marshall Plan. This assault would climax in 1951, but the general direction of policy had become clear much earlier. By the end of 1950, policymakers in Congress and in the executive branch had added nearly $13 billion to the Defense Department's original appropriation for fiscal year 1951. They doubled the size of the armed forces, vastly expanded the strategic stockpile, reimposed controls on the export of critical commodities, and diverted Marshall Plan dollars from civilian to military investment. As defense expenditures soared, conservatives on Capitol Hill found it much easier to convince their colleagues that the United States could no longer afford expensive foreign-aid programs. The principle of parity for recovery and rearmament gave way to a policy that subordinated economic to military requirements. While adding $4 billion to the military-assistance program, Congress slashed the ECA's budget by $208 million, just three days after the start of fighting in Korea.[2]

These wartime changes brought mixed economic blessings to the Marshall Plan countries. Additional defense expenditures and military assistance helped to boost production levels to a new high. By March 1951, industrial production in Western Europe had climbed 13 percent above the level of a year earlier, 39 percent above the prewar level. The American defense-production and stockpiling programs also led to the purchase of huge quantities of strategic raw materials from the overseas territories of the participating countries. These purchases swelled European gold and dollar reserves and narrowed the dollar gap to such an extent that Marshall aid to Great Britain could be suspended at the end of 1950. At the same time, however, the demands of defense and the controls that the Truman administration placed on the export of American commodities created a host of serious economic problems in Western Europe. Raw material shortages and defense expenditures unleashed inflationary pressures, driving the wholesale-price

2d sess., April 25 and 26 and May 1, 1950. *Congressional Record* 96, pt. 5: 5683–4, 5774, 6053. For a larger sampling of conservative opinion, see also in the same source 5685, 5769–74, 5883–6, 6048–52, 6060–71, 6128–39, 6217–24, 6439–40. Kaplan, *Community of Interests*, 104–5, 107–8; and Stebbins, *United States in World Affairs, 1950,* 252–3, 260–1.

index up between 20 percent and 30 percent in the nine months following the start of the Korean conflict. The shift from production for export to production for defense and the inflation of raw materials factors added to a marked deterioration in the terms of trade for many of the participating countries. The result was a growing deficit in Western Europe's overall trade with the rest of the world, which then combined with shortages and inflationary pressures to bring on new problems in the balance of payments. Unless resolved, these problems could reverse the gains in economic recovery, social stability, and European unity achieved since the inception of the Marshall Plan.[3]

The economic problems growing out of the Korean conflict deepened the crisis of confidence that still afflicted the Western alliance. So did the wave of anti-Communist hysteria that washed across the United States in the months following the start of hostilities, the Chinese intervention that came in November, and the inter-Allied disputes over how to bring the war to an early conclusion. All of these developments aroused European fears of a larger Asian conflict that would swallow up American resources and leave Western Europe vulnerable to Soviet attack. President Truman's decision to commit additional troops to the Continent assuaged these concerns to some extent. But it also heightened East–West tensions, spurred new fears of another world war, and underscored Western Europe's great dependence on the United States. American pressure to relax the restrictions on German industry added to the air of crisis, as did Washington's proposal to rearm the Germans and bring them into the North Atlantic alliance. The Americans saw these as measures of European self-help designed to guard against the prospect of Soviet aggression. The Europeans viewed them in the cold light of history; although fearful of a Soviet attack, neither did they want to fall victim to a resurgent German militarism.

Out of these concerns came renewed support for the idea of European unity, which many Europeans saw both as an end in itself and as an intermediate stop along a set of tracks that led to other destinations. One route led to Franco-German rapprochement via a European union that would "exorcise history," to use Monnet's compelling phrase.[4] Another path ended in military security and economic independence by way of a political and economic unit large enough to contain the Soviets and put Western Europe on a self-supporting basis. Still another pointed away from the barren plains of nationalism toward the fertile valley of a common market.

Steering any of these courses required careful directions, which the Europeans had begun to map out even before the Korean War gave new urgency to their efforts. The Italians planted signposts to a European trade

---

[3] ECA, *Twelfth Report to Congress* (Washington, DC, 1951), 20–5; Stebbins, *United States in World Affairs, 1950,* 279–80; and Stebbins, *The United States in World Affairs, 1951* (New York, 1952), 217–22.

[4] Monnet, *Memoirs,* 306.

zone, the Dutch to a sectorial integration of the European economy, and the French to a European coal and steel community that included the Germans. The Council of Europe drafted a blueprint for a European army, as did the French, who also drew up guidelines to the pooling of European resources in a common defense fund under the control of a collective authority. Most of these plans charted a course that cut across the commitments of the Labour government in London. Officials there preferred to elaborate Bevin's grand design for a Western consolidation that included a connection to the Commonwealth and a pathway to North America.

In Washington, meanwhile, policymakers blocked out their own plans to reconcile the needs of recovery with the burgeoning demands of defense. Integration remained the conceptual link between their economic and military goals, the way to forge a unit of power to sustain recovery and deter aggression. They had already stressed the importance of an integrated defense in their conception of NATO, in their demand for balanced collective forces, and in their support for the "strategic concept" that NATO adopted in 1950. Now they placed even more emphasis on military integration, renewing earlier efforts to give NATO greater coordinating power and urging the Allies to tap the latent military resources of the Federal Republic. While the Europeans worried that accelerated defense spending would lead to lower living standards and social unrest, the Americans argued that a collective pattern of defense, one including the Federal Republic, would reduce costs, put Germany's productive power at NATO's disposal, and lessen the impact of rearmament on the American and European economies.[5]

The Korean War and the rearmament program thus gave new impetus to the drive for European military integration and German reintegration, both of which promised greater efficiency and lower costs at a time when civilian and defense requirements were competing for limited resources. This was the same rationale behind demands for continued progress in the area of economic integration, where American leaders also made important gains in the months following the start of hostilities in Korea. They helped to manage a major German payments crisis, further liberalize intra-European trade, and engineer the Schuman Plan for a European coal and steel community. These gains capped the history of the Marshall Plan. They came

5 Kaplan, *Community of Interests*, 108–11, 124; and Stebbins, *United States in World Affairs, 1950*, 263, 267–78. According to officials in the Office of the Special Representative (OSR), "if Germany is admitted to partnership in [the] Western defense effort," it "would then undertake military expenditures on its own behalf" while also contributing to a "European force." German participation would require lifting the "restrictions that now limit [Germany's] economy," especially the restrictions on steel production. With these restrictions removed, Germany would "become an important civilian as well as military supplier for Europe and [the] need for supplementary aid from the US to support [the] European defense program would be reduced or eliminated." See Philip W. Bonsal, political advisor to the US Special Representative in Europe, repto 4548 to Hoffman, August 16, 1950, ECA Files, box 19.

despite the serious economic problems stemming from an expanded defense effort and at a time, as we will see in the next chapter, when that effort was bringing the ERP to a premature conclusion.

II

American leaders had decided even before the Korean War that rearmament and recovery must have equal claims on European and American resources. In addition to the strategic and geopolitical considerations noted earlier, the principle of parity was based on the assumption that European recovery had reached the point where governments could devote a larger share of their resources to the common defense. The goal, as it emerged from an ECA study,[6] was to enhance Western Europe's military strength without eroding living standards and making participating countries vulnerable to a resurgent Communist threat from "*within*." The way to achieve this goal was through accelerated efforts to tap underutilized resources in Germany, Italy, and Belgium, restrain inflationary pressures, and allocate scarce commodities efficiently. Most important, as the Americans told Robert Marjolin and other OEEC officials who visited Washington in late July, there must be no slackening of current efforts to liberalize trade and integrate economies. Integration was the best way "to develop the efficient production methods and production locations" required to meet the needs of both rearmament and recovery.[7]

Several weeks after the beginning of the Korean conflict, then, ECA policymakers in Washington still adhered to the principle of parity. In mid-August, they codified this principle in a draft circular to the ECA's overseas missions. American strategy, according to the draft, was to steer a "middle course" between the "twin objectives" of recovery and rearmament. Although this meant curtailing previously planned increases in civilian consumption and investment, it also meant that gains in both areas were to be preserved and even augmented slightly in order to maintain the public mo-

---

[6] For information on the ECA's national resource study, see Bissell letter to Harriman, May 26, 1950, RG 286, Acc. 53A177, box 96, folder: NATO–MDAP; Harriman repto 2899 to Hoffman, May 26, 1950, ECA Files, box 18; Hoffman toreps 4533 and 4582 to Harriman, May 31, and June 1, 1950, ECA Files, box 66; Katz repto 3032 to Hoffman, June 5, 1950, ECA Files, box 18; and Richard S. McCaffery, Jr., ECA Mission, London, letter to Lincoln Gordon of OSR, June 19, 1950, RG 286, Acc. 53A177, box 96, folder: NATO–MDAP.

[7] Foster toreps 6365 and 6465 to Katz, July 26 and 28, 1950, ECA Files, box 67. See also Foster letter to Senator Tom Connally, July 27, 1950, Hoffman Papers, box 22, folder: ECA – Letter to Senator Connally, Bonsal reptos 4223 and 4233 to Hoffman, July 29 and 31, 1950, ECA Files, box 19; Foster torep 6472 to Katz, July 29, 1950, and Hoffman torep 7420 to Katz, August 28, 1950, ECA Files, box 67; and Hitchman memorandum to Cripps, July 28, 1950, Hitchman memorandum to Bridges, July 31, 1950, and E.R.(L)(50)193, London Committee, Record of Meetings of 28th July, July 31, 1950, FO 371, 86979, UR1020.

rale and economic strength necessary for a sustained rearmament program. This goal could be accomplished through additional American aid, a "higher rate of productivity," and a "more equitable distribution of income."[8]

The last point added another wrinkle to the New Deal synthesis that had guided American recovery policy since the start of the Marshall Plan. In effect, the ECA admitted that rearmament constituted an additional claim on Western Europe's resources. Income shares might have to be adjusted in order to meet this claim without sacrificing hard-won gains in the political arena, particularly if the only alternative was to heap the economic burden of rearmament on the backs of the working classes. Taking the latter course could weaken public support for the defense effort, play into the hands of the Communists, and break the fragile political accommodations hammered out in France, Italy, and other participating countries. Seen in this light, the idea of income redistribution emerged as a variant of the species of Keynesian liberalism that had earlier led the ECA to channel counterpart funds into low-cost housing projects and balance its trade and payments goals against their cost to internal economic and political stability.

The emphasis on income redistribution was a less prominent feature of the ECA's policy than would be the case in 1951, when it became more apparent that Western Europe could not expand its resources fast enough to maintain a workable balance between recovery and rearmament. In the first months of the rearmament campaign, a "higher rate of productivity" assumed "central importance." Greater productivity was a relatively pain-less way to realize American policy objectives while keeping redistributive questions in the background. In the ECA's view, moreover, raising pro-ductivity simply required further progress down the road already taken, including further steps to liberalize trade, build "authoritative central in-stitutions," and forge a "single Western European market." A unified con-tinental economy, in the words of the draft circular, still promised the "most effective environmental influence for bringing about the increase in Euro-pean productivity upon which [the] simultaneous maintenance of economic progress and [the] acceleration of European rearmament depend."[9]

Although the ECA's "middle course" was in line with the principle of parity for recovery and rearmament, it was not long before American prior-ities pointed in a different direction. The NATO deputies meeting in July and August concluded that economic requirements had to be subordinated to the demands of rearmament.[10] A similar conclusion came from High Commissioner John J. McCloy, Ambassador Lewis Douglas, and other

---

[8] Foster torep 6849 to Katz, August 11, 1950, ECA Files, box 67. The "middle course" announced in the cable was in line with the policy that President Truman had artic-ulated in a message to Congress on July 19, 1950. See Stebbins, *United States in World Affairs, 1950,* 246.

[9] See the first source cited in note 8.

[10] Stebbins, *United States in World Affairs, 1950,* 259–60.

American officials in Europe, all of whom thought the ECA's approach was founded on "wishful thinking" and an "utter lack of appreciation" for current necessities. It was important, they admitted, to continue efforts to liberalize trade and strengthen European institutions. But these initiatives must now be "subordinated to immediate purposes," even if it meant turning some "old hobby horses . . . out to grass." These officials were particularly critical of the ECA's "misplaced" emphasis on maintaining, even increasing, current levels of European consumption. They assumed that civilian consumption could not be raised and that short-term sacrifices might be necessary. Any conclusion to the contrary, they argued, would undermine the resolve of European leaders to boost productivity and redistribute income. In their view, these measures, together with rearmament and the trend toward military integration, would do more to bolster European morale than the long-term prospect of economic unification.[11]

These criticisms signaled a basic change in American priorities, which the ECA embraced in its revised circular of September 16. The new circular anticipated a general shift in investment from the civilian to the military sector; inflationary pressures and raw material, manpower, and financial shortages; expansion of production in Germany, Belgium, and Italy; and some reduction of per capita consumption in Great Britain, Holland, and other full-employment economies. Gone was the emphasis on maintaining or increasing civilian investment and living standards across the ERP area as a whole. The revised circular gave rearmament priority over recovery. It stressed the need to use Marshall Plan dollars to support the European defense effort and talked about reconciling military and economic requirements in a way that prevented "serious inroads" on current consumption among "lower-income groups." Maintaining living standards was particularly important in connection with France and West Germany, where "social and political" unrest might otherwise result from the higher taxes and other sacrifices that would be needed to finance rearmament and restrain inflation.

Despite this change in priorities, the agents of reconciliation were still to be the old stratagems outlined in the draft circular of August. The revised circular of September stressed the need to control national economies and build supranational coordinators. It urged "tangible improvements in the distribution of national incomes." It emphasized the role that free trade unions should play in government programs to raise productivity. And to further enhance output and deploy resources more efficiently, it called again for "accelerated progress" in the area of trade liberalization and in other

[11]   McCloy tel. to Acheson, August 15, 1950, *FRUS, 1950*, 3:672–3; Bonsal repto circular 189 to Hoffman, August 19, 1950, ECA Files, box 20; and Douglas toeca 960 to Hoffman, August 22, 1950, ECA Files, box 16.

areas where the result would be "closer economic and political, as well as military, unification."[12]

Although the principle of parity was abandoned, the rearmament program had nonetheless provided new reasons to push ahead with old programs. With this strategy in mind, policymakers in the ECA liberalized the rules governing their Overseas Development Fund, hoping thereby to make the overseas territories less vulnerable to revolutionary nationalism while increasing the stockpile of critical raw materials available for civilian production and rearmament in Europe and the United States. They continued to gear their trade-promotion program to markets where European exports would earn more dollars and "evoke maximum supplies [of] scarce materials." And while pressing the Europeans to control inflation, they also launched new initiatives to boost production on the Continent, working, as they had in the past, through cooperating groups of farm, labor, and industrial leaders on both sides of the Atlantic.[13]

Most of these initiatives grew out of the ECA's enlarged technical-assistance program, which, in fact, was one of the few areas where expansion, rather than curtailment, was the norm. This was so because the diversion of resources from civilian investment to rearmament meant that greater productivity was the only way to sustain the economic gains of the past two years. "It is clear," as the ECA reported to Congress at the end of 1950, "that only increased productivity will make it possible for the Marshall Plan countries to make a contribution to defense production of the magnitude that is needed and at the same time maintain an acceptable standard of living for their peoples." For this reason, the ECA had committed nearly $20 million to over five hundred technical-assistance projects in the participating countries and their overseas territories. It maintained over three hundred American "experts" abroad, supported 124 European labor–management groups in the United States, sponsored "management seminars" and "in-plant and academic training" for European engineers and plant foremen, provided "industrial testing and research equipment," and distributed technical and scientific information through films, literature, and exhibits.[14]

American leaders thought that the OEEC must follow a similar approach if it wanted to remain a vital institution. Although NATO would fix defense

[12] Hoffman torep 7999 to Katz, September 16, 1950, ECA Files, box 68.
[13] Foster torep 222 to Douglas, February 28, 1951, ECA Files, box 79. See also Foster toreps 6333 and 6650 to Katz, July 25 and August 4, 1950, ECA Files, box 67; Foster toreps 8141 and 8798 to Katz, September 21 and October 10, 1950, and Bissell torep 8691 to Katz, October 10, 1950, ECA Files, box 68; Bissell torep 9660 to Katz, November 11, 1950, ECA Files, box 69; Foster torep 128 to Katz, January 5, 1951, ECA Files, box 83; and ECA, *Eleventh Report to Congress* (Washington, DC, 1951), 51.
[14] ECA, *Eleventh Report to Congress*, 49–54.

production plans and determine military manpower and resource requirements, the OEEC could assist by rededicating itself to the ERP's basic
objectives. It could investigate the economic consequences of an expanded
rearmament program, draw Germany's resources into that program, and
provide an institutional link between NATO and the neutral countries of
Western Europe, namely Sweden and Switzerland. It could also "influence"
national economic policies with a view to controlling inflation, mobilizing
resources, and allocating raw materials for civilian consumption. Through
these and related initiatives, according to calculations in Washington, the
OEEC could help to "accelerate rearmament" while minimizing its impact
on civilian economies.[15]

In effect, the Americans wanted the OEEC to function as the economic
arm of NATO. This organizational strategy had advantages that went beyond linking West Germany to the rearmament program. As the ECA
pointed out, NATO was still an embryonic organization. It could assemble
a group of economic experts only by draining talent from the OEEC, which
had a tested staff and well-established procedures for assessing national
resources and coordinating requirements. It seemed perfectly suited to perform NATO's economic work, and any lessening of its responsibilities would
dim the prospects for integrating Europe and promoting the gains in productivity that were now more important than ever. These were good reasons
for associating the OEEC with the economic aspects of the rearmament
program, another being that such an association would safeguard "civilian
economies from too serious an invasion by the demands of those responsible
for defense." This was Richard Bissell's estimation. It dovetailed with what
the ECA told Marjolin and other OEEC officials when they visited Washington in late July and with what the Europeans heard later from Walter
Salant of the President's Council of Economic Advisers, John Dickinson of
the Defense Department, and Paul Nitze of the State Department.[16]

An organizational arrangement of this sort had little to recommend it in
London. One of the salient features of British diplomacy, noted throughout
this narrative, was a decided opposition to organizational mechanisms that
scaled Great Britain to the dimensions of a continental power, the first

[15]   Foster torep 6470 to Katz, July 29, 1950, ECA Files, box 67. See also Bonsal repto
       4223 to Hoffman, July 29, 1950, ECA Files, box 19; Foster torep 6849 to Katz,
       August 11, 1950, ECA Files, box 67; Wood torep 6880 to Katz, August 11, 1950,
       and Bonsal to Hoffman, August 12, 1950, *FRUS, 1950*, 3:665–72; and Hoffman
       torep 7998 to Katz, September 16, 1950, ECA Files, box 68.
[16]   FO tel. to Franks, July 27, 1950, FO 371, 86979, UR1020. See also Hall-Patch letter
       to Strang, July 24, 1950, Hitchman memorandum to Cripps, July 28, 1950, Berthoud
       memorandum, "Impact of Korea on O.E.E.C.," July 29, 1950, E.R.(L)(50)193, Lon-
       don Committee, Record of Meetings on 28th July, July 31, 1950, and FO tel. to
       Franks, July 31, 1950, FO 371, 86979, UR1020; and Caine letter to Hitchman,
       August 1, 1950, and Hall-Patch letter to Berthoud, August 15, 1950, FO 371, 86980,
       UR1020.

among equals in a regional system of states that watered at the trough of American beneficence. The British were particularly adamant when it came to allocating scarce commodities and conducting the burden-sharing exercises by which the NATO powers were to assess their national resources and divide the economic burden of rearmament. They wanted the first task assigned to an international organization that would be dominated by Britain and the United States. The second task, that of burden sharing, would be assigned to NATO, in part because this arrangement suited Britain's position as a world power, in part because NATO provided a better forum than the OEEC for dealing on favorable terms with the Americans.

The OEEC, after all, remained essentially a European organization in which the United States was an associate member only and Britain a mere claimant of American aid. The two countries had an "unequal relationship," which the British were anxious to replace with the "Atlantic Pact relationship where we can sit at the table on a basis of equality." The British would "build up the status and authority of the Atlantic Treaty Organization" by making it, rather than the OEEC, responsible for the burden-sharing exercises. They would also use these exercises to subject American resources to collective control and would replace the ERP procedure, whereby Marshall aid was distributed to claimant states, with one in which America's contribution to the common defense was commensurate with American resources. So far as the OEEC was concerned, the British thought the organization might help by surveying resources and studying ways in which supplies could be utilized more effectively. But its role would be purely advisory. It would not act on its own authority nor formulate policy, even in areas where rearmament had a major impact on the Western European economy.[17]

These recommendations added up to a barely concealed assault on the OEEC, which the British saw withering away as its most important economic functions were taken over by a burgeoning staff of economic experts at NATO headquarters in London. They had no appeal to the Americans. The ECA admitted that a detailed division of functions had to be hammered out

---

[17] FO tel. to Franks, August 2, 1950, FO 371, 86979, UR1020. See also Williams, *Gaitskell Diary*, 207–10; FO tel. to Franks, July 26, 1950, Makins memorandum to Bevin, July 29, 1950, Berthoud memorandum, "Impact of Korea on O.E.E.C.," July 29, 1950, and E.R.(L)(50)193, London Committee, Record of Meetings Held on 28th July, July 31, 1950, FO 371, 86979, UR1020; FO tel. to Franks, September 21, 1950, and FO tel. to Hall-Patch, September 28, 1950, FO 371, 86980, UR1020; Makins memorandum, "Talk with Mr. Gaitskell," October 4, 1950, FO memorandum, "Relationship of O.E.E.C. and N.A.T.O. in Determination of Defence Aid," October 4, 1950, and Hall-Patch tel. to FO, October 7, 1950, FO 371, 86981, UR1020; and British Embassy, Washington, "Record of Meeting Held in the State Department," October 10, 1950, and British Embassy, Washington, "Record of Conversation between Harriman, Gordon, Rowan, Plowden, and Armstrong," October 10, 1950, T232/198/EEC7/1/013.

gradually. But it thought a tentative assignment of tasks to the OEEC, including much of the economic work relating to rearmament, was nonetheless imperative. Any delay, the ECA argued, could hold up the rearmament effort or lead participating countries to cope with its economic consequences through autarkic policies that reversed the trend toward integration. Nor did the ECA believe, as the British did, that the OEEC could perform its usual functions if denied a role in the allocation of raw materials and in the burden-sharing exercises, tasks that bore directly on its work in such areas as trade liberalization and intra-European payments.

Robert Marjolin, Dirk Stikker, and other European leaders repeated these American arguments. They, too, worried lest the OEEC's eclipse by NATO darken the chances for effective economic cooperation and exclude Sweden, Switzerland, and West Germany from the European community. They, too, wanted the OEEC to coordinate civilian and defense requirements. They did not trust NATO to consider civilian needs fairly, and they also thought it likely that British policymakers would use that organization to strike a deal with the Americans at Europe's expense. The smaller powers, along with France, were particularly alarmed by the prospect of NATO's allocating raw materials, and not just because it was dominated by great powers or inclined to give rearmament a higher priority than recovery. Like the ECA, they thought this task related directly to the balance of payments and internal financial position of participating countries. If NATO allocated raw materials, it would inevitably take charge in these areas as well. The OEEC would become an empty box, devoid of meaningful responsibilities.[18]

To avoid this possibility, Stikker had suggested that the OEEC delegates from the NATO countries constitute themselves as a Committee of Twelve in Paris. The committee would act as liaison between the two organizations and take primary responsibility for analyzing the economic impact of rearmament on Western Europe. The Swiss and the Swedes saw no conflict between this arrangement and their status as neutrals. The Americans had made a similar suggestion earlier. With their assistance, moreover, Stikker isolated the British and won support for his proposal from the NATO ministers and their Council of Deputies. By early November, the Committee of Twelve had been established and was making use of the OEEC's Secretariat in studies designed to harmonize military and civilian requirements

---

[18] The American and European positions are summarized in the following documents: Makins memorandum to Bevin, July 29, 1950, Berthoud memorandum, "Impact of Korea on O.E.E.C.," July 29, 1950, Hitchman memorandum to Bridges, July 31, 1950, and E.R.(L)(50)193, London Committee, Record of Meetings Held on 28th July, July 31, 1950, FO 371, 86979, UR1020; Franks tel. to FO, September 26, 1950, and Hall-Patch tels. (2) to FO, September 30, 1950, FO 371, 86980, UR1020; and Berthoud memorandum, "Views of M. Marjolin on Present United Kingdom Policy towards O.E.E.C.," November 30, 1950, FO 371, 87018, UR2852. See also Williams, *Gaitskell Diary*, 225.

and guide the distribution of rearmament burdens among the NATO countries.[19]

In the meantime, the British had locked horns with the Americans and Europeans on a related issue. The dispute in this case dated back to September, when Marjolin prepared a long memorandum enumerating solutions to the economic problems ahead. Marjolin had said earlier that European rearmament offered a "golden opportunity" to employ Germany's resources more fully, a view that dovetailed with the ECA's. He now urged the OEEC countries to make the most of resources elsewhere. They should push ahead with the OEEC's program to reduce import quotas and multilateralize intra-European trade. To cope with current or anticipated raw material shortages, they also should work through the OEEC to limit demand, increase supplies, and allocate commodities. And to contain inflationary pressures, they should establish appropriate internal controls, adjust civilian consumption in light of available resources, and direct investment into areas that yielded maximum gains in production.[20]

Marjolin's approach, like the ECA's, would rely on both administrative controls and market mechanisms to generate the gains in resource utilization, financial stability, and greater productivity that were required to achieve the "twin objectives" of recovery and rearmament. But while the British thought Marjolin went too far in this direction, the Americans wanted him to go still farther. At this point, of course, British and American policymakers were still wrangling over the division of functions between NATO and the OEEC. The British were naturally reluctant to jeopardize their position in this dispute by approving a memorandum that assigned a range of important tasks to the latter organization. Because Marjolin's memorandum had broad support among the other participating countries, they saw little to be gained from outright opposition and tried instead to render the document useless by appending a number of reservations. They urged the continental countries to respect the jurisdiction of other agencies, particularly NATO, to avoid specific agendas that committed governments prematurely, and to let time and practical experience set a course of action. Most of all, they warned, the OEEC must not act peremptorily to control

[19] Bonsal repto 4492 to Hoffman, August 12, 1950, *FRUS, 1950*, 3:668–72; Katz repto 4933 to Hoffman, September 7, 1950, ECA Files, box 19; Jebb tels. to FO, September 17 and 19, 1950, FO 371, 86980, UR1020; Katz repto 324 to American Embassy, Stockholm, September 22, 1950, RG 286, Acc. 53A177, box 88, folder: Eyes Only Personal, Outgoing, Sept.–Oct., 1950; Katz repto circular 248 to Hoffman, October 7, 1950, ECA Files, box 20; Katz repto 5499 to Hoffman, October 9, 1950, and Bruce repto 6023 to Foster, November 6, 1950, ECA Files, box 19; and Katz reptos 248 and 6214 to Hoffman and Foster, October 7 and November 14, 1950, ECA Files, box 20, See also Williams, *Gaitskell Diary*, 225.
[20] For Marjolin's views on Germany, see Foster torep 6472 to Katz, July 29, 1950, ECA Files, box 67. For his memorandum to the OEEC, see Katz reptos 5267, 5269, and 5270 to Hoffman, all dated September 26, 1950, ECA Files, box 19.

and allocate raw materials of which participating countries were neither major consumers nor producers.[21]

The ECA took a more positive position when the OEEC delegates attended an informal meeting on September 26. C. Tyler Wood, the ECA's assistant administrator in charge of operations, was on hand to warmly applaud Marjolin's memorandum. But he and other Americans also wanted the secretary general to draw up a timetable for progress and to include concrete recommendations for coordinating national monetary, financial, and commercial policies. The British had steadfastly resisted such measures as an encroachment on national sovereignty. As the ECA saw it, however, the time had come when "authoritative" coordination was the only way to guarantee the optimum use of available resources, prevent inflationary pressures and separate national controls from wrecking the trade-liberalization program, and safeguard the progress that Western Europe had made toward economic viability and integration.[22]

Marjolin subsequently reshaped his memorandum as a resolution for the OEEC's Council of Ministers, in the process strengthening its provisions on economic coordination and trade policy in the direction suggested by the ECA. The resolution would now authorize the OEEC to investigate ways to harmonize national economic controls and would instruct member states to maintain the freest possible trade.[23] The revisions struck a middle ground between the British, whose position remained unchanged, and some of the other delegations, who would tie further progress toward economic integration to specific arrangements for allocating critical materials, equalizing tariffs, and protecting the balance of payments. The compromise fell short of what the Americans had wanted. Still, the ECA considered it the best plan possible and decided to give it strong support when the Council met on October 6 and 7. The Office of the Special Representative endorsed the resolution during the early stages of the ministers meeting and Paul Hoffman, who was retiring after twenty-eight months as ECA administrator, used the occasion to articulate the ECA's new line of policy.[24] He told the

[21]   Hall-Patch tel. to FO, September 26, 1950, FO 371, 86980, UR1020; F. C. Everson of the Foreign Office, "O.E.E.C. Third Report and Relations with N.A.T.O.," September 29, 1950, FO 371, 86981, UR1020; and FO tel. Hall-Patch, October 3, 1950, and Hall-Patch tel. to FO, October 4, 1950, FO 371, 87058, UR3147.

[22]   Hoffman torep 7998 to Katz, September 16, 1950, ECA Files, box 68; Katz repto 5265 to Hoffman, September 26, 1950, ECA Files, box 19; Hall-Patch tel. to FO, September 26, 1950, FO 371, 86980, UR1020; Foster torep 8377 to Katz, September 28, 1950, ECA Files, box 68; and Hall-Patch tel. to FO, October 4, 1950, FO 371, 87058, UR3147.

[23]   Katz repto 5469 to Hoffman, October 7, 1950, ECA Files, box 19. See also Wood reptos 5417 and 5426 to Hoffman, October 3 and 5, 1950, ECA Files, box 19; and Hall-Patch tel. to FO, October 4, 1950, FO 371, 87058, UR3147.

[24]   Bissell torep 8570 to Katz, October 5, 1950, ECA Files, box 68; and Katz repto 5478 to Hoffman, October 7, 1950, ECA Files, box 19.

ministers that the burden of rearmament must not lead to a recrudescence of "economic nationalism" but rather to an economic integration that enabled participating countries to meet their defense requirements without compromising the gains achieved through the Marshall Plan. As he and others had done so often in the past, Hoffman urged the Europeans to follow the American example:

Here in Western Europe you have 270 million hard-working and resourceful people. Your gross national product last year was $160 billion. We in America have 150 million people, but our gross national product last year was $260 billion. If Western Europe had produced on the same per capita basis, her gross national production would have been $470 billion. I admit right away that Western Europe does not have all the natural resources that we possess. But there is one great resource we have and Europe does not, which Europe could possess – and that is a single great market. If that market is achieved through integration, and if a better use is made of the resources Europe already possesses . . . Western Europe can without any doubt increase her gross national product by $100 billion during the first decade of the second half of the 20th century. And within that $100 billion the free people of Europe can have both bread and guns in sufficiency.[25]

American pressure helped to ensure passage of Marjolin's resolution, but not without objections and reservations by the participating countries. The British objected to harmonizing national policies, particularly if it meant reducing social expenditures. Nor would they permit the OEEC to allocate critical raw materials. Other delegations were reluctant to reduce quantitative import restrictions without agreement on the allocation of scarce resources. Still others demanded measures to equalize tariffs in intra-European trade.[26] These objections and reservations, some of which grew out of the rearmament effort, pointed up the difficulties that American and European leaders would face in reconciling military and economic imperatives. They were already hampering the OEEC's program to liberalize trade. And because success in this area was one of the keys to greater growth and integration, on which recovery and rearmament seemed to depend, it is important to examine these difficulties in some detail.

III

After the OEEC agreed in July to the principles of the European Payments Union (EPU) and to a set of trade rules guaranteeing equality of treatment

[25] Hoffman's speech is quoted from Katz repto 5479 to Hoffman, October 7, 1950, ECA Files, box 19.
[26] For passage of the resolution, see Katz repto 5480 to Hoffman, October 7, 1950, ECA Files, box 19. On the European objections and reservations, see Katz repto 5478 to Hoffman, October 7, 1950, and Wood repto 5651 to Hoffman, October 16, 1950, ECA Files, box 19; and Hall-Patch tels. (3) to FO, October 7, 1950, FO 371, 87058, UR3147.

in the administration and removal of import quotas, a special trade committee had set to work translating the rules into a code of trade liberalization. The goal was an immediate reduction of quantitative restrictions on 60 percent of private, intra-European trade, whereupon additional steps would be taken to achieve 75-percent liberalization. Actual progress, however, awaited the trade committee's report and action by Congress in appropriating funds for the next year of the ERP.[27]

The delay gave time for second thoughts to percolate. These first came to the surface when the OEEC began debating the various proposals, noted earlier, to facilitate the formation of an integrated single market. One of these proposals, urged by Giuseppe Pella of Italy, envisioned the reduction of intra-European tariffs and the simultaneous elimination of import quotas on a common list of commodities. The result, according to Pella, would be a free-trade zone in which economies of scale would boost productivity and set the stage for Europe's return to a fully multilateral system of world trade. Another proposal, put forward by Maurice Petsche of France, called for a European Investment Bank to coordinate national investment policies and mobilize public and private capital behind new investment projects. And still another, this one by Dirk Stikker of the Netherlands, looked to the reduction of import quotas on an industry-by-industry basis, with the industries involved selected by a three-fourths vote of the OEEC countries. By making participation optional and basing action on a three-fourths vote, Stikker hoped for faster progress on a larger number of commodities than would be possible under the unanimity rule or through across-the-board reductions in quantitative restrictions. For similar reasons, he also called for a European Integration Fund to modernize industry, underwrite labor-retraining programs, and thus reassure business and labor interests who might feel threatened by the competitive pressures of a single market.[28]

Stikker's plan would apply the sectorial approach to integration captured in Schuman's proposal for a European coal and steel community, which is discussed later in this chapter. It also shared with Schuman's proposal, and with Petsche's plan, an emphasis on supranational regulation of investments, taxes, subsidies, and other internal policies in cases where national differences would impede integration. This strategy dovetailed with the growing reliance on economic planning in Dutch domestic policy and had the potential benefit of enabling the Dutch to steer integration down paths that

---

[27] Bonsal reptos 4596 and 4612 to Hoffman, August 18 and 19, 1950, ECA Files, box 19.

[28] Katz repto 3083 to Hoffman, June 7, 1950, ECA Files, box 18; Everson minute, "The Stikker Proposals," June 27, 1950, FO 371, 87161, UR3248; Stokes repto 3804 to Hoffman, July 8, 1950, ECA Files, box 18; Philip Broad memorandum, "Stikker, Pella, and Petsche Proposals," July 25, 1950, FO 371, 87162, UR3248; Foster torep 6601 to Katz, August 4, 1950, ECA Files, box 18; Bonsal repto 4626 to Foster, August 21, 1950, ECA Files, box 19; ECA, *Ninth Report to Congress*, 33; and Diebold, *Trade and Payments*, 204–11, 234–5.

avoided the random competitive impacts of the OEEC's percentage approach to the removal of import quotas. It had obvious appeal to the French, for whom supranationalism was a way to harness the Germans, but not to the Italians, whose plan for an integrated European trade zone aimed to limit internal dislocations, in part by maintaining tariff restrictions on imports from outside the area but also by permitting governments to retain differential tax rates, subsidies, and other devices that gave domestic producers a competitive advantage in the home market.[29]

These plans took on different shades of meaning at the time, as they have for historians ever since. Viewed from one angle, they appeared as shadowy expressions of the murderous struggle for national advantage. It was this aspect that made it difficult to harmonize their opposing features and prompted objections from Washington. But the same plans assumed a different appearance when refracted through the prism of the Cold War, emerging in the eyes of many Europeans as brilliant beams illuminating the path to safety in a European union. In truth, both perspectives were valid. However flawed their efforts, Stikker, Pella, and Petsche were trying to reconcile the dark realities of competitive struggle with the bright hopes of a collective future, combining them in a single plan as white light combines the colors of the spectrum.

This was how the British interpreted the plans and why consideration of them by the OEEC caused a tremor of concern in Whitehall. According to policymakers in the Foreign Office and the Treasury, the plans were "economic manifestations" of a larger tendency toward federation in Western Europe. This tendency was at odds with the policy of the British government, which could not "participate in a federated regime" or even support what Edwin Plowden of the Treasury called a "half-way house" on the road to European union. The Stikker and Petsche plans, with their emphasis on supranational regulation rather than on intergovernmental cooperation, amounted to an assault on the empirical approach and the principle known as "the point of no return" that guided British policy. They could not be reconciled with Labour's socialist program at home or with Bevin's search for security through a North Atlantic framework. Nor would it be easy to dovetail these plans, or Pella's proposal for a European trade zone, with Britain's system of imperial preferences or with a multilateral system of world trade, which still remained the ultimate economic goal of British diplomacy. These conclusions did not result in open opposition to the Stikker, Pella, and Petsche plans. Such a course could widen the dangerous gap between Britain and its allies on the Continent. Instead, the British used the same tactics they had in the Fritalux negotiations of the previous year. On the one hand, they threw their weight behind the OEEC's program to liberalize trade across the ERP area as a whole, hoping to head off support

[29] See the discussion in Milward, *Reconstruction of Western Europe*, 446–51.

for supranational strategies; on the other hand, they urged the Europeans to harmonize their schemes with the goal of a one-world system based on nondiscrimination and convertible currencies. The "world-wide approach," as the British called it, had the potential advantage of appealing to the Americans and being more in line with Bevin's plan "to make the U.K. a bridge between Western Europe, the Commonwealth and the North Atlantic Community."[30]

The British understood how difficult it would be to put the "world-wide approach" in an "attractive wrapping," by which they meant a package that had credibility in Washington. After all, they were hardly in a position to move quickly toward the goal of a fully multilateral system of world trade. Nor did the Americans view this goal as necessarily incompatible with the idea of economic regionalism in Western Europe.[31] On the contrary, policymakers in the ECA generally welcomed the Stikker, Pella, and Petsche plans. The various provisions for joint consultation on internal financial policies, for action by majority vote, and for a European investment bank or fund all gave hope of "advancing US objectives on European integration." A central financial institution could help to coordinate European investment policy, a task to which the OEEC had not been equal, and this coordination could be particularly effective if private financial experts and government authorities evaluated "projects on an international economic rather than [a] give-and-take political basis."[32] Indeed, such an approach would dovetail with the ECA's corporative formulations and with its earlier proposals for a European central bank and reserve fund.

These similarities should not be taken to mean that American leaders gave unqualified support to the European plans. On the investment side, it was not at all clear whether Stikker's investment fund would concentrate on new ventures, as the ECA hoped, or on cushioning the impact of trade

---

[30] "Note of a Meeting Held in the Chancellor's Room," July 19, 1950, FO 371, 87162, UR3248; Treasury memorandum, "Consequences of Contemporary Movements in Western Europe towards Forms of Economic Integration Having Federal Implications," July 19, 1950, T232/194/EEC30/03; and Playfair memorandum, "Notes on the Stikker Plan," June 15, 1950, FO 371, 87161, UR3248. See also Everson minute, "The Stikker Proposals," June 27, 1950, Berthoud memorandum, "The Stikker Plan," June 29, 1950, and unsigned Foreign Office memorandum, "The Stikker Proposals," June 30, 1950, FO 371, 87161, UR3248; Broad memorandum, "Stikker, Pella, and Petsche Proposals," July 25, 1950, FO 371, 87162, UR3248; and Treasury memorandum, "Notes of a Meeting Held in Sir Edward Bridges' Room, 14th July," July 20, 1950, T232/194/EEC30/03.

[31] "Note of a Meeting Held in the Chancellor's Room," July 19, 1950, FO 371, 87162, UR3248; and Treasury memorandum, "Consequences of Contemporary Movements in Western Europe towards Forms of Economic Integration Having Federal Implications," July 19, 1950, T232/194/EEC30/03.

[32] Foster toreps 6571 and 6601 to Katz, August 2 and 4, 1950, ECA Files, box 67. See also Hoffman torep 4952 to Harriman, June 14, 1950, ECA Files, box 66.

liberalization through financial subsidies to inefficient industries. Nor was it clear that Petsche's investment bank would be free of government domination or enjoy positive powers to mobilize private capital and prevent economically restrictive trade strategies. On the trade side, Stikker's proposal would permit low-tariff countries to discriminate against their high-tariff partners in the administration of residual import restrictions. Like Pella's plan, it also seemed to envision trade liberalization only in areas where the reduction of import quotas or the lowering of tariffs did not affect the "special economic structure" of each participating country. In addition, Pella's plan would result in a European trade zone based on tariff discrimination against dollar goods – a strategy, as we have seen, that the ECA would tolerate only if it led to the "ultimate achievement of global convertibility and multilateral trade."[33]

Given these problems, the ECA reserved its position on the Stikker, Pella, and Petsche plans. It urged the OEEC to review the proposals with a view to harmonizing their differences, to further reduce import quotas in the meantime, and to address tariff questions after this reduction had been achieved. The goal, it told the participating countries, should remain an "integrated European market" founded on supranational institutions and multilateral trade. The Europeans appointed a special committee to study and reconcile the three plans, with results that had not become apparent by the end of the recovery period, whereupon the spotlight shifted back to the OEEC's program to liberalize trade across the ERP area as a whole. This was what the British had wanted all along.[34]

As it turned out, some of the same issues raised in connection with the Stikker, Pella, and Petsche plans also hampered the OEEC's efforts to further reduce import quotas and multilateralize intra-European trade. In mid-August, the trade committee finished work on a draft code of trade liberalization that included a number of exemptions to the principle of nondiscrimination, one of which would permit low-tariff countries to discriminate against their high-tariff partners in the administration of residual import restrictions. The ECA took a "firm stand" against this and other "escape clauses," seeking to prevent the OEEC countries from "nibbling away" at the principles of trade liberalization. It insisted again that tariff discussions be postponed and that all participating countries support a 75-percent reduction of import quotas, apply residual restrictions in a nondis-

[33] Bonsal repto 4626 to Hoffman, August 21, 1950, and Foster torep 6571 to Katz, August 2, 1950, ECA Files, box 67. See also Hoffman torep 7817 to Katz, September 11, 1950, ECA Files, box 19.

[34] Katz repto 5511 to Hoffman, October 10, 1950, ECA Files, box 19. See also Hoffman torep 4952 to Harriman, June 14, 1950, ECA Files, box 66; Ellis-Rees tel. to FO, June 29, 1950, FO 371, 87161, UR3248; and Foster torep 6471 to Katz, July 29, 1950, and Hoffman torep 7420 to Katz, August 28, 1950, ECA Files, box 67.

criminatory fashion, and seek exemptions on a case-by-case basis from a "special restricted committee" of experts.[35]

American pressure led the trade committee to tighten some of the exemptions to the rule of nondiscrimination. The OEEC then approved the EPU accord and the code of trade liberalization at a meeting on September 19. Within weeks, twelve of the participating countries had achieved or exceeded a 60-percent reduction of their quotas on private imports. But the trade committee had been unable to agree on the timetable for achieving a 75-percent reduction or on the principle of nondiscrimination in the administration of residual restrictions. These issues had been referred to the Council of Ministers for decision in October, by which time the difficulties involved were further complicated by the problems growing out of the rearmament program.[36]

One such problem centered on the increasing shortage and rising price of critical raw materials, caused in part by the rapid increase in American stockpiling and the Truman administration's decision to regulate the export of American commodities in short supply. The French warned that raw material shortages and escalating prices, together with attendant national controls over domestic allocations and foreign exports, could fundamentally alter existing balance-of-payments relationships and wreck the OEEC's program to liberalize trade. Along with other OEEC representatives, they wanted the United States to take "self-sacrificing measures" to limit consumption, adjust its stockpiling program in the interest of European requirements, and form an international mechanism to allocate scarce commodities. The last step was especially important and had to be taken before participating countries eliminated additional import quotas that otherwise might be needed to defend the balance of payments.

Progress in this direction kept foundering on differences over the kind of allocation mechanism to be established. The British, who were major consumers and producers of raw materials from the sterling area, were just as anxious as the French to establish an allocation mechanism, particularly one that gave them access to American stockpiles. But they were reluctant

[35] Bissell torep 7600 to Katz, September 1, 1950, and Hoffman torep 7419 to Katz, August 28, 1950, ECA Files, box 67. See also Katz repto 3716 to Hoffman, July 4, 1950, ECA Files, box 18; Bonsal repto 4526 to Hoffman, August 15, 1950, and Wood reptos 4739 and 4751 to Hoffman, August 25, 1950, ECA Files, box 19; Hoffman torep 7420 to Katz, August 28, 1950, ECA Files, box 67; and Katz repto 5026 to Hoffman, September 13, 1950, ECA Files, box 19.
[36] Austria, Denmark, Turkey, and Iceland fell short of the 60-percent goal. Each had received a special exemption from the OEEC under terms permitted in the trade liberalization code. Taken together, moreover, these four countries accounted for only 10 percent of the total of intra-European imports. See ECA, *Eleventh Report to Congress*, 28–9; Bissell torep 7600 to Katz, September 1, 1950, ECA Files, box 67; and Wood repto 4891 to Hoffman, September 5, 1950, and Katz repto 4990 to Hoffman, September 11, 1950, ECA Files, box 19.

to use the OEEC for this purpose, which essentially meant giving that agency the authority to regulate sterling-area exports and British patterns of consumption. They preferred to work through ad hoc groups established by the major producing countries, a procedure that would exclude most of their OEEC colleagues, or through an international authority controlled by the American, British, and French governments. The French would support the last idea. They joined the British in talks with the American government looking to the formation of such an authority and to a joint policy on stockpiling. But the talks broke down when the Americans proposed an international allocation mechanism that would include such regional bodies as the OEEC and represent both producing and consuming countries. Nor were the Americans willing to give the British and French a voice in the administration of their export-control and stockpiling programs. Both programs, they insisted, were being administered with a view to the defense production efforts of the NATO countries.[37]

A related problem involved the Federal Republic's growing deficit with the EPU. West Germany's industrial production had risen dramatically in 1950, increasing the demand for imported raw materials and foodstuffs just as shortages were beginning to result from the rearmament program. Making matters worse were a decline in the growth of Germany's exports to other participating countries, an increase in raw material imports by German producers who were hedging against future shortages, a reduction in the volume of American aid, and a consequent shift in German purchases from the dollar area to Western Europe and the overseas territories of the OEEC countries. Nor did Germany benefit at this point from the rapid deregulation of its nonagricultural trade under the direction of Ludwig Erhard, the minister of economics, who was then emerging as the most prominent European champion of the free-trade policies associated with liberal economic doctrine. At the end of September, these and other factors had left the Federal Republic with an EPU deficit of approximately $172 million. Without remedial measures, Germany's EPU quota would soon be exhausted and the Germans would have to begin paying their deficits in gold or dollars.[38]

[37] Wood repto 5695 to Hoffman and Foster, October 18, 1950, ECA Files, box 19. See also Wood repto 4891 to Hoffman and Foster, September 5, 1950, and Katz repto 5843 to Foster, October 27, 1950, ECA Files, box 19; Foster toreps 9358 and 9045 to Katz, October 23 and November 2, 1950, ECA Files, box 68; Katz repto 6485 to Foster, November 25, 1950, ECA Files, box 20; Bissell torep 10134 to Katz, November 30, 1950, ECA Files, box 69; "Briefing Book for Prime Minister Attlee's Visit," December 1950, Section O, "Raw Materials Problem," Truman Papers, PSF, folder: Subject File – Conferences: Truman–Attlee Talks, Dec. 1950 – Briefing Book; Thorp memorandum of conversation, December 26, 1950, Acheson Papers, box 65, folder: Memoranda of Conversations; Summary of Meeting with the Under Secretary, January 4, 1951, RG 59, Secretary's Daily Meetings, box 1; Kaplan, *Community of Interests*, 124; and Williams, *Gaitskell Diary*, 206, 223–4.

[38] Diebold, *Trade and Payments*, 111–13; Katz repto 5532 to Hoffman, October 10,

Germany's EPU deficit brought to the fore certain differences that had long been a source of tension between the Federal Republic and the American officials responsible for the Marshall Plan, including John J. McCloy. McCloy was a Republican internationalist who had served as assistant secretary of the army and president of the World Bank before assuming his duties as American high commissioner. Despite his party affiliation and background on Wall Street, he was committed to the corporative neo-capitalism espoused by top policymakers in the ECA and just as determined as they were to get away from the conservative economic policies championed by General Clay. It was this determination that brought the Americans into conflict with the government in Bonn. German and American leaders had no trouble joining forces when it came to European integration and German reintegration. They collaborated to reduce the Allied restrictions on German industry, to eliminate import quotas, and to promote free trade. Policymakers on both sides were fiercely devoted to the free-enterprise system, disdainful of British socialism, and critical of the *dirigiste* policies pursued by the French. Nevertheless, McCloy, Hoffman, Harriman, and other American leaders had drawn certain lessons from the economic experiences of the interwar period that were not shared to the same extent by their counterparts in Germany. They viewed modern society as an organic unit and were convinced of the need for economic regulation, for Keynesian strategies of fiscal and monetary management, and for positive programs of social insurance and full employment. These were central elements in the New Deal synthesis as it evolved in the United States in the years after the First World War. If these elements were applied to Germany and other participating countries, or so McCloy and others believed, the result would be an organic community of prosperous and politically stable states.

Yet much of what the Americans had in mind exceeded the limits of Erhard's liberal economic doctrine. German and American leaders had been able to identify the same economic problems in Germany, including rising unemployment, a severe housing shortage, and a growing deficit in the balance of payments. But they were often at loggerheads when it came to solutions. The Germans blamed the Allies for restricting production, laid their problems in the lap of the High Commission, and asked the ECA for additional aid. The Americans poured a steady stream of criticism on the laissez-faire strategies of the government in Bonn. Much to the chagrin of Erhard, who saw himself as the champion of American capitalism in Western Europe, they urged the Germans to adopt a comprehensive economic plan that included the flexible use of monetary and fiscal instruments, stimulants to exports, restrictions on nonessential imports, higher wages, and progressive taxes. In their view, all of these measures would help to reduce

1950, ECA Files, box 19; and Foster torep 9136 to Katz, October 25, 1950, ECA Files, box 68.

Germany's deficit in trade. The last two would also distribute income more equitably, curb social unrest, and win support from the labor movement for collaborative programs to increase productivity.[39]

These differences had not been resolved when they were brought to a head by the crisis in Germany's balance of payments. The German government initially sought to deal with the crisis through modest measures to restrict credit, curb speculative purchases, and license imports. The ECA and the OEEC considered these measures inadequate. Both accused the Germans of following the "Schachtian policies" of the past; the Germans were deliberately incurring a payments deficit and then shifting the burden of adjustment by exchanging access to the German market for tariff concessions from their creditors and additional aid from the EPU. From the European point of view, an effective plan of action must put the burden of adjustment on the Germans and must not scuttle the OEEC's efforts to liberalize intra-European trade. ECA policymakers took a more balanced approach. Viewing the German crisis as a test of the EPU's ability to regulate national policies, they urged the Managing Board to insist on stronger German measures to limit credit and curb speculation and to persuade creditor countries to lower their barriers to German trade. They conditioned dollar assistance from the ECA's reserve fund on an effective plan drawn along these lines, and they wanted this plan to resolve the crisis without wrecking the trade-liberalization program, curtailing production in the Federal Republic, and limiting Germany's contribution to European recovery and rearmament.

The problem was how to force a program of self-help on West Germany that would not have debilitating economic and political repercussions in that country and across Western Europe. Both the British and the Americans worried that additional aid, either from the EPU or the ECA, would alleviate the pressure on Bonn to put its own house in order. But even an effective program of self-help could not reverse the deficit before the Federal Republic had exhausted its EPU quota and gold reserves, whereupon the Germans would have to deflate their economy and reimpose import quotas. These last steps could trigger a major political crisis in Bonn. They also could impact adversely on the trade of other participating countries and might well take Western Europe back down the road to bilateralism.

This view had support from the team of economic experts commissioned by the EPU, and from Denmark, Holland, and other participating countries that were dependent on the German market. These countries were more inclined to favor additional aid to the Germans. They also wanted Britain and France, as Germany's major creditors, to take primary responsibility

[39] For a discussion of McCloy and German–American differences, see Thomas Schwartz, "European Integration and the 'Special Relationship': Implementing the Marshall Plan in the Federal Republic of Germany, 1948–1951," in Charles S. Maier, ed., *The Marshall Plan in Germany* (forthcoming).

for solving the crisis, in part by increasing imports from the Federal Republic, in part by allowing the Germans to restrict imports from the sterling and franc areas. The last course would entail a measure of discrimination and violate the EPU's trade rules. It might also deflate the German economy and actually worsen the Federal Republic's balance of payments. This was the point of view of British policymakers and why they eventually supported the Managing Board's tentative decision to extend a further credit of $120 million, which the Germans could use to finance their deficit without reimposing import controls and disrupting the OEEC's trade program. The OEEC subsequently approved the new credit. It urged additional assistance from the ECA as well and tied both forms of aid to stringent corrective measures by the German government. These included measures to curb credit, raise taxes, avoid deficit spending, restrict long-term investment, and keep import licenses within the minimum permitted by the trade-liberalization program.

In approving this program, the OEEC effectively parted company with the ECA. The Americans agreed that Germany's Schachtian "gamble" must not succeed and that additional aid must be conditioned on stern measures of self-help by the Federal Republic. Throughout the crisis, McCloy and his ECA colleagues had continued to urge a program of government regulation on the Germans, including controls on wages, prices, and raw materials, consumer rationing, and curbs on an expansionary credit policy that American leaders no longer considered appropriate. In their view, however, the EPU's program focused on long-term restrictions that did not address the short-term causes of the German crisis, particularly the commodity and exchange speculation, which the Adenauer government had done little to discourage. On the contrary, the additional EPU credit would relax the pressure for more appropriate German reforms, while the long-term measures, particularly those restricting investment and requiring a balanced budget, would undermine Germany's recovery and lessen its contribution to the European defense effort. Despite these reservations, American officials were reluctant to block the European program and thereby weaken the authority of both the EPU and the OEEC. Yet neither would they throw good money after bad. They decided instead to withhold the additional aid that both the Germans and the OEEC had requested, hoping in this way to maintain the pressure for effective German self-help and escape responsibility if the European program failed.[40]

[40] The preceding three paragraphs are based on the following British and American documents: Foster toreps 9136 and 9336 to Katz, October 25 and November 1, 1950, ECA Files, box 68; Katz reptos 5836, 5870, 5878, 5916, 5985, and 6160 to Foster, October 27 and 30 (2) and November 1, 3, and 11, 1950, ECA Files, box 19; Ellis-Rees tels. to FO, November 2, 3, and 5, 1950, and FO tel. to Hall-Patch, November 4, 1950, T237/128/OFM16/2/05A; UK del. to the OEEC, tels. to FO, November 8 and 15, 1950, T237/129/OFM16/2/05B; Katz reptos 6247 and 6655 to Foster, November 15 and December 5, 1950, ECA Files, box 22; Bissell torep 9662 to Katz, November 11, 1950, and Foster torep 10305 to Katz, December 7,

The German problem, together with those involving tariffs and raw material shortages, hampered progress when the OEEC's Council and trade committee met in October to discuss the trade-liberalization code. The American position remained unchanged: The rapid elimination of quantitative import restrictions and the multilateralization of trade would integrate economies and bring the gains in productivity that were needed to meet the demands of recovery and rearmament. The British took a similar position. The devaluation of 1949 and the expansion of raw material exports from the sterling area had by this time greatly improved Britain's balance of payments. The British were emerging as major creditors on intra-European account, which made it easier for them to support the ECA's position. Indeed, measures to liberalize intra-European trade would further improve their balance of payments while reducing the incentive for other participating countries to integrate through such "dangerous" schemes as those proposed by Stikker, Pella, and Petsche. Due in part to British leadership and pressure applied by the Americans, the Council finally set February 1951 as the date for a 75-percent reduction of quotas on private imports.

But the Council's decision was hemmed with reservations that made its implementation by no means certain. Escape clauses were added to protect countries that traded largely in Europe and conducted most of their trade on private, as opposed to government, account. As in earlier discussions, the French demanded agreements on the distribution of scarce commodities and the coordination of national investment policies and trade controls. The Dutch, Danes, and Norwegians joined the French when it came to the allocation of raw materials in short supply. Along with the low-tariff countries as a group, they also threatened to retreat from the 75 percent goal unless the General Agreement on Tariffs and Trade (GATT) negotiations, then in progress in Torquay, England, led to the equalization of intra-European tariffs. In addition, the Dutch refused to apply residual trade restrictions in a nondiscriminatory fashion if doing so meant that greater competition would drive their exports from the German market. Other delegations took a similar position on this issue, in large part because they hoped to use residual restrictions as a bargaining chip to secure tariff concessions or a "fair share" of raw materials from their OEEC partners.[41]

1950, ECA Files, box 69; and Katz repto 6866 to Foster, December 15, 1950, ECA Files, box 20. See also Schwartz, "European Integration and the 'Special Relationship.' "

[41] Katz reptos 5146, 5527, 5533, and 5854 to Foster, September 20 and October 10 (2) and 28, 1950, ECA Files, box 19; UK del., "Note on the Next Steps in Liberalisation of Trade," September 27, 1950, and Hall-Patch tel. to FO, October 8, 1950, FO 371, 87080, UR322; Hall-Patch tel to FO, October 8, 1950, and UK del., "Urgent Economic Problems," October 9, 1950, FO 371, 87058, UR3147; UK del., "Ministerial Meeting, 7th October: Liberalisation of Trade," October 10, 1950, FO 371, 87081, UR322; Foster torep 8993 to Katz, October 20, 1950, ECA Files, box 68; Katz repto circular 237 and reptos 6748 and 6980 to Foster, October 12 and De-

It was not until 1951 that new developments broke the deadlock in the trade negotiations. In January, the American, British, and French governments finally reconciled their differences and formed the International Materials Conference to increase the production and improve the distribution of raw materials in short supply. The agreement grew out of Anglo–American discussions that had begun earlier and that formed part of an ongoing British effort to deal with raw material problems, indeed all economic problems, outside of the OEEC. Because the sterling area was a major producer and consumer of raw materials, the British did not want current shortages handled through a strictly continental organization. As they saw it, moreover, these shortages had been caused in large part by the Pentagon's buying spree and could be managed only by the NATO powers within the context of the defense program. This strategy had the extra advantage of putting the British on a more equal footing with the Americans, giving them a better chance to influence the Pentagon's stockpiling program and the allocation of American commodities in worldwide short supply. In addition, British strategy aimed to protect Bevin's grand design against very different dangers growing out of the Korean War. After the Chinese intervened in that conflict, the British had begun to worry that the whole focus of American foreign policy might shift from Europe to Asia. This possibility had made them more determined to cement the United States to the North Atlantic framework – a task, in their view, that could not be accomplished by the OEEC or by "any grouping or influence which excludes or discourages the Americans and Canadians from full participation." Armed with these arguments, the British had weaned the French away from their OEEC partners and had brought them first into the Anglo–American discussions and then into the International Materials Conference established in January.[42]

As it turned out, the conference did not quite fulfill the expectations of British policymakers, who apparently envisioned something akin to the inter-Allied control boards that Britain and the United States had dominated during the Second World War. The other OEEC countries had demanded representation, as had the Latin American states, and the Truman admin-

cember 8 and 21, 1950, ECA Files, box 20; Hall-Patch tels. (3) to FO, October 25, 1950, and I. D. Adams minute, October 26, 1950, FO 371, 87150, UR3238; and E. R.(L)(50)244, London Committee, "Note by the Board of Trade," October 18, 1950, Hall-Patch tel. to FO, October 27, 1950, Adams memorandum, "Meeting of the Council at Ministerial Level: Liberalisation of Trade," October 31, 1950, and UK del., "Record of Meeting of the Council on 26th and 27th October," November 6, 1950, FO 371, 87081, UR322.

42   Draft letter to Hall-Patch, November 24, 1950, FO 371, 86981, UR1020. See also Berthoud memoranda, November 6 and December 6, 1950, FO 371, 86981, UR1020; and Hitchman memorandum, December 15, 1950, with attached draft paper, FO 371, 86993, UR1051. For the formation of the International Materials Conference, see the documents in note 43, which also contain additional information on British policy.

istration had responded by urging a truly international mechanism of allocation and control. The outcome was a compromise. As finally organized, an Anglo–American–French control group dominated the conference. But the conference also established commodity committees representing the major producing and consumer countries. By the end of March, twenty-four countries were participating in these committees and the control group had been enlarged to include representatives from five additional countries and from both the OEEC and the Organization of American States.[43]

These arrangements made it possible for the French to withdraw their reservation against a further reduction of quantitative import quotas. So did an OEEC decision to draw up a common list of commodities on which all quotas would be removed, a strategy that France and Italy had supported for some time. Other countries followed the French lead. By the end of June, eight of them had met or exceeded the 75-percent target, the OEEC had appointed a special Steering Group to coordinate multilateral negotiations on a common list of liberalized commodities, and the Steering Group had reached a tentative agreement, which the Council approved in July. The agreement effectively created a "Europe wide market" for virtually all textiles, textile machinery, and chemicals, and for a list of industrial and agricultural products to which additions would be made by the end of 1951.[44]

Although the common list and the further reduction of import quotas were important steps toward European economic integration, they had been offset by reverses in other areas. Because the GATT negotiations in Torquay had been unable to equalize intra European tariffs, the low-tariff countries had refused to remove quotas that might be useful leverage in trade talks with their high-tariff partners. Similar motivations underlay the OEEC's failure to reach agreement on the principle of nondiscrimination in the administration of residual import restrictions. In this case, Switzerland and other countries had reserved the right to discriminate in their import policy

[43] Berthoud memorandum, "Views of M. Marjolin on Present United Kingdom Policy towards O.E.E.C.," November 30, 1950, FO 371, 87018, UR2852; Berthoud memorandum, "O.E.E.C., N.A.T.O., and the Atlantic Community," December 6, 1950, FO 371, 86981, UR1020; Foster toreps 260, 263, and 264 to Katz, all dated January 10, 1951, ECA Files, box 83; "Note of an Informal Meeting Held on 26th January 1951 in the Foreign Office," January 26, 1951, and E. R. Copleston letter to Ellis-Rees, February 2, 1951, FO 371, 93763, CE(W)113100/20; Thorp memorandum of conversation, February 13, 1951, Acheson Papers, box 66, folder: Memoranda of Conversations; and Summary of Meeting with the Secretary of State, February 13, 1951, RG 59, Secretary's Daily Meetings, box 1. See also ECA, *Twelfth Report to Congress*, 8.

[44] Wood repto circular 93 to Foster, July 31, 1951, ECA Files, box 33. See also Wood repto circular 16 to Foster, February 13, 1951, ECA Files, box 33; Wood repto 963 to Foster, March 1, 1950, Katz repto 1139 to Foster, March 12, 1950, and Stokes repto 1465 to Foster, April 3, 1951, ECA Files, box 30; and ECA, *Twelfth Report to Congress* and *Thirteenth Report to Congress* (Washington, DC, 1951), 31 and 36, respectively.

in order to gain favorable treatment for their exports or access to raw materials in short supply. Even more important, Germany's payments position had continued to deteriorate, forcing that country to suspend all import licenses in late February 1951. The EPU had sanctioned this action and had then prepared a report authorizing the Germans to reimpose import controls. The report also instructed the Germans to gear these controls to a planned allocation of import licenses and to implement a range of fiscal, monetary, and administrative measures to correct the internal causes of their deficit. In effect, the EPU exempted Germany from the 75-percent goal and from liberalizing controls on the common list of commodities, as it did Denmark and other countries that were dependent on the German market.[45]

Seen from another perspective, however, the EPU's handling of the German crisis was something of a victory for American and European efforts to protect the trade-liberalization program, build strong institutions of coordination and control, and bring the Federal Republic into an integrated economic and military framework. When the crisis resumed, the Americans reaffirmed their earlier position. They said the Germans had not honored their promise to implement an effective program of self-help in exchange for the EPU credit of the previous fall. Germany must "take her castor oil," as Ambassador Katz put it, or there was "the danger of getting on to the slippery slope of Schachtian policies." Katz and other ECA officials refused to provide additional assistance to the Federal Republic, while McCloy threatened to terminate existing lines of support unless the Germans put their house in order. The British took a similar stand, as did the Managing Board when it reported on the German crisis in February and March. But the problem remained exactly what it had been in late 1950: Well before a program of self-help could yield results, the Federal Republic would exhaust its gold and dollar reserves and be compelled to curtail production, suspend imports, and withdraw from the EPU. The last two steps could initiate a chain reaction across Western Europe. Other participating states might withdraw from the EPU and the OEEC's trade program would collapse. To circumvent these dangers, the ECA still sought a "balanced approach" that combined measures of German self-help, similar to those recommended in the EPU's report, with contributions from other participating countries.

This was the approach finally implemented after a long and acrimonious debate that ended with an OEEC decision in April. The debate centered on the allocation of German import licenses, that is, on how the burden of

---

[45] Diebold, *Trade and Payments*, 176–8, 225–30; ECA, *Twelfth Report to Congress* and *Thirteenth Report to Congress*, 29–32 and 36–7, respectively; Katz repto 119 to Foster, January 9, 1951, ECA Files, box 29; Katz reptos 777 and 863 to Foster, February 17 and 23, 1951, ECA Files, box 30; and Hall-Patch tel. to FO, February 23, 1951, and Ellis-Rees tel. to FO, February 23, 1951, FO 371, 93764, CE(W)113100.

corrective action would be distributed among the exports of the ERP countries. The Dutch and Swiss, with support from the Austrians, Danes, Greeks, and Turks, demanded the same share of the German market they had before the crisis. They thought that Germany should discriminate in their favor and against creditor countries in the allocation of import licenses. Their arguments echoed those of six months earlier, as did the British rebuttals, resulting in a deadlock that eventually forced concessions from all sides. Under the compromise hammered out in April, the OEEC made Germany's trade exemptions temporary and conditioned them on stern German efforts to curtail civilian consumption and expand exports. The Americans played a key role by pressuring the Germans into an effective program of self-help and by then agreeing to continue aid to the Federal Republic at a level approximating that of the previous year. Britain and France, as major creditors in the EPU, promised to limit their exports to the Federal Republic while increasing their imports from that country and from other OEEC countries whose balance of payments might be affected by Germany's reimposition of import controls. In addition, the Germans agreed to administer their import program in a way that minimized its impact on the same countries, and the OEEC established a special "mediation group" to oversee the program and resolve any disputes that might arise.[46]

These and other arrangements, together with a downturn in world commodity markets, set the stage for a sharp improvement in Germany's payments position. By the end of May, the Germans had repaid their initial EPU credit, were issuing additional import licenses, and were looking forward to an eventual return to trade liberalization.[47] This outcome seemed to reaffirm the ECA's faith in the efficacy of managerial approaches and supranational coordination. The EPU had withstood its first major test. With American aid and encouragement, its experts had engineered a solution to the payments crisis without seriously compromising the OEEC's trade program or hampering Germany's contribution to European recovery and rearmament.

The trade program, to be sure, had not gone as far or as fast as the ECA had wanted. Most of the participating governments had never favored a strictly free-trade approach to European integration. The Germans stood almost alone in their devotion to that strategy, and their payments crisis, as Alan Milward has noted, only reminded the other Europeans of the difficulties that could result if import quotas and other restrictions were removed too quickly.[48] They preferred a more controlled approach and invariably sought to curb the ECA's plans in order to limit the domestic

[46] For this part of the story, see the documents in FO 371, 93763–93771, CE(W)113100; ECA Files, boxes 30, 83, and 84. See also Diebold, *Trade and Payments*, 120–4.

[47] Diebold, *Trade and Payments*, 124–7.

[48] Milward, *Reconstruction of Western Europe*, 425.

impact of trade liberalization. But it would be a mistake to establish a strict dichotomy between the American and European positions, however appealing such a dichotomy might be to current revisionists. Aside from cushioning adverse impacts with additional aid, American policy had always combined the free-traders' and planners' approaches. Keynesians in the ECA had called for central institutions of economic coordination and control, as well as for trade liberalization, and thus had cause to celebrate the EPU's handling of the German crisis. Nor was this the only cause for celebration. The negotiations over the Schuman Plan came to a conclusion just as the OEEC and the EPU completed the trade-liberalization program and brought the German crisis to a successful resolution. Like these latter initiatives, the Schuman Plan seemed to combine the traders' and planners' approaches in a policy aimed at European integration and German reintegration. It amounted to another step down the road to a European neo-capitalism and to a workable balance of power between the Western states, and one we must therefore consider at some length.

IV

The French had consistently lost ground in their attempts to prevent the revival of Germany's economic and political power. American policymakers had succeeded in unifying the Western zones and replacing military government with a German administration and Allied High Commission of civilian officials. They had reduced the number of plants to be removed as reparations, lifted some of the constraints on German industry, and beaten back French proposals for international ownership of the Ruhr and permanent limits on German production. The French, of course, had won concessions in return. The Allies had agreed to safeguards against Germany's rearmament and remilitarization. They had created an International Authority to oversee the Ruhr. They had retained the limit on German steel production at approximately eleven million tons per year. But these gains were uncertain. The Ruhr Authority was turning out to be a feeble instrument of French policy. It was responsible to the Allied powers as a group, and there were no guarantees that it would command the allegiance of the Germans or put France's interests above those of the former Reich. Nor were there guarantees that it would retain its limited authority in the post-occupation period, or inherit from the Allied steel and coal boards the right to decartelize German industry and allocate German production between internal consumption and export. In addition, the Americans had been pressing relentlessly to expand German production. Even if they did not demand that Germany be rearmed, they would certainly escalate the pressure to eliminate residual restrictions and put Germany's industrial capacity at the disposal of NATO's defense effort.

The French were particularly concerned about restrictions on German steel production. An increase in Germany's steel output, together with a decline in its coal exports, could cripple the vastly expanded French steel industry. It could raise anew the danger of overproduction and the threat of cartelistic agreements similar to those that had failed to discipline competition and restrain German power in the interwar period. These dangers seemed real enough. By 1950, the demand for steel had slackened across Western Europe and gains in production had fallen off in France and Belgium. At the same time, however, pent-up demand and underutilized capacity had led to an expansion of steel production in West Germany and to the reentry of German steel exports into European markets, largely at the expense of French and Belgian producers.[49]

Coupled with the failure to prevent Germany's revival was the collapse of French efforts to build a European system that could safeguard their economic and security interests over the long term. The French had tried, in a fashion reminiscent of their strategy in the first postwar era, to contain Germany's power through offsetting arrangements with its neighbors. But their plans for a Franco–Italian tariff union and a merger of this union with the Benelux group had broken down in 1950, partly because of opposition from private interests but also because of Dutch demands that Germany be included. Nor had the French been able to build a supranational system in which Britain's power balanced that of a revitalized Germany. The British had refused to subordinate their economic planning to an international authority or to integrate into Europe at the expense of their commitment to a North Atlantic security system. They had joined the EPU, but only under terms that safeguarded their ties to the sterling area, and had torpedoed French plans to strengthen the Council of Europe, give the OEEC supranational powers, and centralize defense planning in the hands of a strong "executive" agency. Making matters worse, the United States had accepted the principle of British exceptionalism and had thus raised the haunting possibility that France would be left alone with Germany on the Continent.

By mid-1950, then, all lines of French policy had been stymied. The French had not been able to forge a European union balanced between Britain and Germany, nor a continental system that excluded the Germans. They were certain that Germany's power would continue to grow as the United States pushed forward with plans to loosen the remaining restrictions on German production. And they were equally convinced that the results would be a "Malthusian" system that restricted production, reversed the trend toward trade liberalization and economic integration, and led either to Germany's domination of the Continent or to a Soviet–German rapprochement.[50] Time was running out for the French. They had to strike a deal with the govern-

---

[49] On the Ruhr Authority and developments in the Western European coal and steel industry, see Milward, *Reconstruction of Western Europe*, 382–9, 367–72.

[50] Acheson tel. to Webb, May 12, 1950, *FRUS, 1950*, 3:697–701.

ment in Bonn while they still had the upper hand, and they had to do so even if it meant risking the future of Anglo–French cooperation on which they had earlier pinned their hopes for security against the Germans. The result was a dramatic reassertion of French leadership on the Continent.

Through the Schuman Plan, which Foreign Minister Robert Schuman announced on May 9, 1950, the French sought to break the deadlock in the debate over European integration and German reintegration. They sought to do so in a way that protected their economic and security interests by pooling European coal and steel production under a supranational authority in which France would participate and through which it would share in the development and direction of German industry. Such a pool, according to Schuman, would resolve the "age-old opposition between France and Germany," make war between the two countries "unthinkable" and materially impossible, and set the stage for economic expansion and political federation in Western Europe. The coal and steel community would operate under a high authority "composed of independent personalities" whose decisions were binding on governments. The authority would be empowered to improve working conditions, guarantee equal access to pooled resources, develop a joint export policy, and take other steps to create a common market for coal and steel. The first step would entail the elimination of tariff barriers and discriminatory transportation rates so as to ensure "automatically" the "fusion of markets and the expansion of production." A variety of transition measures, including a common production and development plan, a mechanism for equalizing prices, wages, and taxes, and a joint fund for modernizing industry, would simultaneously integrate markets, cushion the economic dislocations involved, and reassure private interests who might otherwise oppose the formation of a single, competitive market. But these measures were not intended, in the pattern of prewar cartels, to limit output, allocate markets, and fix prices.[51]

Schuman's plan built on a number of previous proposals, including French proposals for a customs union, for a stronger OEEC, for European military and political institutions, and for an international authority to oversee the Ruhr. The Council of Europe also had anticipated the French plan in a proposal of December 1949, which envisioned transnational economic planning between "European companies," government experts, and advisory panels representing industry, labor, and the public. In addition, Ambassador Douglas and High Commissioner McCloy had promoted the Ruhr Authority as the nucleus of a European regime with powers that went beyond the controls presently imposed on Germany. Chancellor Adenauer had suggested something similar, along with a variety of integrationist schemes that ranged from internationalization of the Saar, to Franco–German ownership

---

[51] The U.S. Charge in France tel. to Webb, May 9, 1950, *FRUS, 1950*, 3:692–4. See also the document cited in note 50.

of the Ruhr coal and steel industries, to full-fledged economic union between the two countries. To Adenauer and other Germans, European integration still offered the surest path to elimination of Allied occupation controls and West Germany's emergence as an equal member of the Western community.[52]

If the Schuman Plan evolved out of past policy, it was also nourished by a widespread conviction that economic integration and supranationalism pointed the way to a new day of peace and plenty in Western Europe. Unificationists considered it a step toward reconciling Franco–German differences and forming a European political federation. Socialists and trade unionists thought it meant greater public control of basic industries or a larger role for labor in economic decision making. Advocates of all stripes saw it as the route to higher living standards and security against the Soviets. So did the Americans, who greeted the French initiative with an enthusiasm that concealed their disappointment at not having been fully consulted in advance. Although some Americans worried that the high authority might be responsive to political rather than economic considerations or amount to a new cartel, most subscribed to the view expressed by John Foster Dulles, who saw the Schuman Plan as "brilliantly creative" and similar to the proposal that he and Marshall had discussed at the Moscow Foreign Ministers Conference of 1947. Secretary of State Acheson termed the plan a "major contribution toward the resolution of the pressing political and economic problems of Europe." President Truman called it "an act of constructive statesmanship."[53]

To American leaders, the Schuman Plan gave hope of the positive results to be gained from the more assertive role they had been urging on the French since the great integration debate of 1949. Policymakers in the State Department focused on the political advantages of the plan, and not simply on the prospects for relaxing industrial controls and increasing Germany's contribution to NATO's rearmament program. In a larger sense, the proposed community could help to reconcile the conflicting imperatives that had stalled a final German settlement. By providing a mechanism for harmonizing France's security with Germany's recovery, it could establish the conditions for a workable balance of power among the states of Western Europe ("without full British participation as a necessary pre-condition")

---

[52] Stebbins, *United States in World Affairs, 1950*, 118; William Diebold, Jr., *The Schuman Plan: A Study in Economic Cooperation, 1950–1959* (New York, 1959), 34–44; and Konrad Adenauer, *Memoirs, 1945–1953*, trans. by Beate Ruhm von Oppen (Chicago, 1966), 238, 244–8.

[53] Webb tel. to Acheson, May 10, 1950, *FRUS, 1950*, 3:695–6; and Acheson and Truman quoted in Stebbins, *United States in World Affairs, 1950*, 143. See also Webb torep 4049 to Harriman, May 13, 1950, and Hoffman torep 4492 to Harriman, May 27, 1950, ECA Files, box 65; and Acheson tels. to Webb, May 9 and 10, 1950, and Webb tels. to Acheson, May 10 and 11, 1950, *FRUS, 1950*, 3:691–2, 694–5, 695–6, 696–7.

and create a strategic unit of sufficient strength and coherence to countervail the Soviet bloc. Policymakers in the ECA noted how the plan dovetailed with their efforts to liberalize trade, harmonize national economic and investment policies, and build supranational institutions.[54] They were particularly pleased when the French added arrangements whereby cooperating private groups would advise the high authority. In all of these ways, the Schuman Plan seemed to combine the market incentives, administrative controls, and corporative collaboration that had become quintessential components in the ECA's formulation for a European neo-capitalism.

The British response was equally predictable. Five continental countries – Belgium, Germany, Italy, Luxembourg, and Holland – accepted Schuman's principles as preconditions for the so-called Conference of Six that opened in June. But Britain would not "buy a pig in a poke," as Bevin informed Acheson from his hospital bed in London.[55] The procedure proposed by Schuman was all wrong: Governments must not be asked to agree in principle before the conference convened. A committee of officials made the same point in a report commissioned by Prime Minister Attlee and subsequently approved by the Cabinet. It would be "wrong," the committee concluded, to abandon the empirical approach and give pledges "without knowing more precisely the nature of the commitments we are being invited to accept." The important point, of course, is that the British had no need to know "more precisely" the nature of the commitments involved. It was enough to know that Schuman's plan envisioned the "surrender of sovereignty in a European system." This did not square with Britain's "world position" or with its "settled policy" against committing itself "irrevocably to Europe."[56] Nor did it fit with the North Atlantic idea that Bevin saw as the key to Britain's security.

This aspect of British thinking is not easily discovered in the documents of the Foreign Office and Treasury. But Monnet, who was the prime architect of the Schuman Plan, got a sense of it in his discussions with the British. "Britain," he recorded in a note taken at the time,

54 Webb torep 4049 to Harriman, May 13, 1950, ECA Files, box 65. See also Harriman tel. to Acheson, May 20, 1950, Bruce tel. to Acheson, May 23, 1950, Acheson tel. to Certain Diplomatic Offices, June 2, 1950, and Douglas tel. to Acheson, June 6, 1950, *FRUS, 1950*, 3:702–4, 704–5, 714–15, 720–4; undated memorandum by Wayne Jackson of the State Department, "General Comments on Certain Aspects of the Schuman Coal and Steel Proposal," RG 43, box 298, folder: Schuman Plan, 1950–52; and Webb memorandum to President Truman, May 17, 1950, with enclosed State Department memorandum of May 16, 1950, Truman Papers, CF, folder: State Department, Correspondence, 1950.

55 Franks letter to Acheson, June 8, 1950, *FRUS, 1950*, 3:727.

56 CP (50) 120, Report by the Committee of Officials, "Integration of French and German Coal and Steel Industries," June 2, 1950, CAB 129/40. See also CP (50) 110, Attlee note to the Cabinet, May 12, 1950, CAB 129/40; and CM (50) 34th Conclusion, June 2, 1950, CAB 128/17.

has no confidence that France and the other countries of Europe have the ability or even the will effectively to resist a possible Russian invasion.... Britain believes that in this conflict continental Europe will be occupied but that she herself, with America, will be able to resist and finally conquer. She therefore does not wish to let her domestic life or the development or her resources be influenced by any views other than her own, and certainly not by continental views.[57]

Monnet understood that matters of procedure were linked inextricably to the goals pursued. This link was as true of the French as it was of the British. For the British, policy objectives ruled out a commitment to the principle of supranationalism in advance of the conference. They asked to be included on this basis. For the French, however, the principle had to be agreed before Germany regained the strength to resist their terms. This goal would be lost if Britain entered into the negotiations in a special position. The principle of supranationalism would be compromised and the British would be in a position to replace French schemes with plans of their own. As Monnet explained in a communication to his government: "To accept British participation on these terms – i.e., in a special capacity – would be to resign oneself in advance to the replacement of the French proposal by something that would merely travesty it.... There would be no common rules and no independent High Authority, but only some kind of OEEC." To avoid this danger, Monnet held Schuman to the original French proposal and then won support for this course from the Germans. Nor would he relent when the British suggested a meeting of ministers to consider the procedures by which the Schuman Plan might be examined. He and Schuman continued to demand prior commitment to the pooling of national resources and sovereignties. The British declined to participate on this basis, publishing their proposal for a ministerial meeting in a futile attempt to wean the other countries from the French initiative.[58]

The Labour government, as American officials surmised, was unwilling to impair its "programs for internal full employment" or its "ability to plan" by exposing either to "external forces" or the dictums of a supranational agency.[59] Cripps admitted as much when he explained the government's position to the House of Commons. So did Morrison when he heard the last version of the French proposal. "It's no good," he asserted, "we

---

[57] Monnet, *Memoirs*, 316–17.

[58] Monnet, *Memoirs*, 313. In addition to the documents cited in note 56, see Bruce tels. to Acheson, May 26 and 31 (2) and June 4, 1950, Douglas tel. to Acheson, June 5, 1950, and Bruce tel. to Acheson, June 28, 1950, *FRUS, 1950*, 3:709–11, 711–12, 712–14, 715–17, 717–20, 738–9; Great Britain, Foreign Office, *Anglo–French Discussions Regarding French Proposal for the Western European Coal, Iron, and Steel Industries, May–June, 1950*, Cmnd. 7970, 1950; Adenauer, *Memoirs*, 256–60, 263–4; and Bullock, *Bevin*, 778–80.

[59] Douglas tel. to Acheson, June 5, 1950, *FRUS, 1950*, 3:717–20. See also Bruce tels. to Acheson, May 3, and June 4, 1950, *FRUS, 1950*, 3:711–12, 715–17.

cannot do it, the Durham miners won't wear it."[60] That economic and ideological concerns reinforced security considerations also became clear in the pamphlet *European Unity*. Published in June by the Labour Party's Executive Committee, the pamphlet noted Britain's position as banker to the sterling area and leader of the Commonwealth, both of which precluded membership in a European union. But it went on to explain how the Labour government could scarcely enter a union with countries that did not share its commitment to full employment and fair shares for all. It attacked economic liberalism as a prescription for social injustice, warned that industrial planning without nationalization would serve private rather than public interests, and said that economic collaboration had to be arranged through intergovernmental agreement. The pamphlet left no doubt that such a course was the best way for the Labour government, which had nationalized the British coal industry and had similar plans for steel, to defend its programs against a supranational authority that would be dominated by capitalists from the Continent. Similar thinking lay behind its attack on the idea of an Anglo–European common market. The goal, as Prime Minister Attlee elaborated, should be the multilateralization of trade, not the integration of internal plans, which a common market required.[61]

"Every now and then," Douglas reported from London, "the British drop a brick and when they do it's a classic." Publication of *European Unity* raised a blizzard of criticism in the United States, where congressional leaders joined Douglas and Hoffman to denounce it as another indication of British isolationism. Most top policymakers took a more restrained view, perhaps because they thought that Anglo–American cooperation in other parts of the world precluded British participation in a unified Europe, perhaps because they welcomed Britain's decision to withdraw from the Schuman Plan negotiations. John Kenney, ECA mission chief in London, took the last position. He argued in a cable to Washington that the Labour government's support for "cartel arrangements" and for "Socialist principles of planning for full employment" would only wreck the chances for agreement.[62]

Although *European Unity* embarrassed the Labour government, it expressed in bold language what had been and would continue to be the position of British leaders. Those in the steel industry supported the government's decision to reject the Schuman Plan. They envisioned instead

[60] Morrison quoted in Bernard Donoughue and G. W. Jones, *Herbert Morrison: Portrait of a Politician* (London, 1973), 481.

[61] See the documents in *FRUS, 1950*, 3:1648–54. See also Kenney tocas 710 and 715 to Foster, June 15 and 16, 1950, ECA Files, box 16; Diebold, *Schuman Plan*, 55–7; and Bullock, *Bevin*, 781.

[62] Douglas tel. to Acheson, June 15, 1950, *FRUS, 1950*, 3:1648–51; and Kenney toeca 867 to Hoffman, July 31, 1950, ECA Files, box 16. See also Wood ecato 1018 to Kenney, August 11, 1950, ECA Files, box 61.

something like the prewar agreement between British producers and the European steel cartel, which prohibited dumping, protected domestic markets, and left British managers free to make their own production, wage, and investment decisions.[63] British socialists and trade unionists took a similar position. At meetings on the Schuman Plan sponsored by the International Conference of Socialists and the International Confederation of Free Trade Unions, they urged resolutions that echoed the rhetoric and recommendations of *European Unity*. When these resolutions failed, they refused to support majority reports that endorsed the French plan and that called for a high authority with labor representation and broad powers to control national policies.[64]

This also remained the position of policymakers in the Labour government following the collapse of their negotiations with the French. The British delegation to the Council of Europe, which reconvened in August and November, launched a ferocious assault against the French-led "federalists." Blocking a French campaign to make the council into an effective instrument of European political federation, they called instead for a "functional approach" that would begin with the formation of transnational authorities in such sectors as transportation, agriculture, and defense.[65] Support for this approach, however, did not extend to Britain's participation in the Schuman Plan. On the contrary, British policymakers had worked throughout the summer on an alternative proposal under which British and European production would be pooled through interindustrial agreements that did not involve a merger of sovereignties.[66] Like their industrial counter-

---

[63] See Douglas tel. to Acheson, June 15, 1950, *FRUS, 1950*, 3:1648–51, for information on preparation of the pamphlet and the embarrassment of the Labour government. See also Kenney's report of his conversations with representatives of British industry in Kenney toeca 799 to Hoffman, July 11, 1950, ECA Files, box 16.

[64] Kenney toeca 718 and Douglas toeca 719 to Hoffman, June 19, 1950, ECA files, box 16; Katz repto 3671 to Hoffman, July 1, 1950, ECA Files, box 18; and Wood repto 5753 to Katz, October 23, 1950, ECA Files, box 19.

[65] For developments at the Strasbourg meeting of the Council of Europe, see the documents in *FRUS, 1950*, 3:775–94. The State Department was reluctant to become involved in the struggle between the European "federalists" and "functionalists." Policymakers in that agency still considered the prospects for European political unification to be minimal. Progress in that direction, they said, must be gradual and must be brought about by European, rather than American, initiative. They saw the Council of Europe as a debating forum and worried that any expansion of its power would detract from the authority of the OEEC and other, more useful, European institutions. For thinking in the State Department, see, in addition to the sources cited at the beginning of this note, Webb tel. to Certain Diplomatic Offices, October 5, 1950, Bohlen tel. to Acheson, October 14, 1950, Douglas tel. to Acheson, October 17, 1950, and Murphy tel. to Acheson, October 20, 1950, *FRUS, 1950*, 3:674–5, 676–8, 678–81, 681–2.

[66] The plan took its name from Sir Edwin Plowden, chief planning officer in the British Treasury. See Diebold, *Schuman Plan*, 59–60; Bruce tel. to Acheson, July 31, 1950,

parts, British officials seemed to favor cartelistic arrangements that preserved Britain's autonomy while avoiding competition with the European pool.

There is no indication that British thinking influenced the Conference of Six that had opened at the Quai d'Orsay in Paris, where negotiations turned instead on a French working paper of June 24. The paper called for pooling coal and steel production under a "supranational" authority of "international civil servants." The authority's decisions would be taken by majority vote and would be binding unless appealed to an international court of arbitration or to a general assembly elected by parliaments. In response to demands for democratic control, particularly trade-union demands for labor participation, the authority would be advised by consultative committees of workers, consumers, and employers. It would also be pledged to equalize the working and living conditions of labor and to pursue policies aimed at full employment and higher living standards. In order to forge a common market for coal and steel, the authority and the participating countries were to guarantee equal access to pooled resources, eliminate barriers to competition, and abolish subsidies and restrictive practices. In addition, the authority would be empowered to engage in economic planning and research. It could recommend internal policies to member states, work through regional producer associations, and establish a compensation fund to modernize industry and help participating firms adapt to the competitive conditions of a single market.[67]

Because the working paper recapitulated principles that Schuman had announced on May 9, the ECA and the State Department decided to leave the negotiations to the Europeans. Some officials were not fully persuaded by British assurances of benign neutrality. Others wondered if Britain's refusal to participate would erode support for the Schuman Plan on the Continent. Still others worried that the authority's "supra-national character" might be impaired by a Dutch amendment that would reserve to a ministers council the right to make final decisions on matters relating to defense production and national economic and fiscal policies. One group favored an announcement of American financial support for the authority, seeing this as a way to counter potential British opposition and make the agency independent of national governments. A second group wanted to confine the ministers council to matters regarding defense production. Initially, however, policymakers found compelling reasons to set both ideas aside. Raising the issue of defense production would complicate the negotiations; suggestions of financial support would lessen the pressure for structural adjustments to the European economy, make the Schuman Plan look

    FRUS, 1950, 3:742–4; Reports by the Working Party of Officials, June 16 and 20, 1950, CAB 129/40; CM (50) 38th Conclusion, June 22, 1950, CAB 128/17; and Report by a Committee of Ministers, July 1, 1950, CAB 129/40.

67 Bruce tels. 3079, 3080, and 3081 to Acheson, June 24, 1950, *FRUS, 1950*, 3:727–34.

like an American initiative, and arouse opposition among Communists and nationalists.[68]

The ECA and the State Department decided to limit themselves to broad comments reaffirming the principles enumerated in Schuman's announcement and the French working paper. They reiterated the economic and political gains that would come from European integration. They stressed the importance of preserving the high authority. They urged European leaders to limit the transition period, minimize compensation to inefficient producers, and otherwise avoid an "excessive preoccupation" with cushioning competitive shocks.[69] This was the way to blend administrative controls with free-market forces. And so long as the Europeans adhered to this strategy, American policymakers were content to play the part of spectators cheering their team from the sidelines.

The Americans played this role until September, when new developments threatened to disrupt the negotiations in Paris or lead to an agreement that squared neither with Schuman's principles nor with their own expectations. They were alarmed when the negotiators began to expand the powers of the ministers council, supposedly to guarantee that actions by the high authority were consistent with national economic and political policies in areas beyond the scope of the common market. Such a course, the Americans warned, would destroy the high authority's supranational character and lead to "national bargaining" based on government vetoes and "autarchic considerations." Equally disturbing was the apparent eagerness of the negotiators to shield the coal and steel complex from the " 'anti-economic consequences of unruly competition.' " The negotiators would limit exports during periods of short supply, base import duties on the high Belgian tariff rather than on the low German tariff, and permit regional producer groups to fix prices and set production quotas.[70]

The goal, American leaders kept insisting, must be a single market organized by the forces of competition and founded on the principle of nondiscrimination. This did not mean that European leaders should be guided by the laissez-faire nostrums of an earlier day. Both the ECA and the State

---

[68]   U.S. Ambassador, The Hague, tel. to Acheson, July 18, 1950, *FRUS, 1950,* 3:740–1. See also Acheson tel. to Certain Diplomatic Offices, July 8, 1950, Acheson tel. to Certain Diplomatic Offices, July 25, 1950, Acheson tel. to Bruce, August 3, 1950, McCloy tel. to Acheson, August 24, 1950, Bruce tel. to Acheson, September 12, 1950, *FRUS, 1950,* 3:740, 741–2, 744–6, 746–7, 748; Hoffman torep 4492 to Harriman, May 27, 1950, ECA Files, box 65; Katz reptos 2923 and 3634 to Hoffman, May 31 and June 29, 1950, ECA Files, box 18; and Hoffman torep 8123 to Katz, September 20, 1950, ECA Files, box 48.

[69]   Hoffman torep 8123 to Katz, September 20, 1950, ECA Files, box 68. See also Acheson tel. to Certain Diplomatic Offices, June 2, 1950, *FRUS, 1950,* 3:714–15; and Foster torep 4695 to Harriman, June 5, 1950, ECA files, box 66.

[70]   Acheson tel. to Certain Diplomatic Offices, December 8, 1950, and Webb tel. to Bruce, October 3, 1950, *FRUS, 1950,* 3:761–5, 754–8.

Department had tailored their free-trade prescriptions to suit political realities and the need for central institutions of economic coordination and
control. They had been willing earlier to tolerate a European customs union
that discriminated temporarily against American exports and had written
rules to this effect into the ITO accord. They were now prepared to see the
coal and steel community evolve in a similar way. There should be a transitional stage, they agreed, in which restrictions were permitted and the high
authority would help producers adapt to the pressures of a single market.
In their view, however, the transition should be brief, assistance should
progressively decline, and marginal enterprises should give way eventually
to "efficient low cost production."[71]

Of particular concern to American officials was Belgium's demand for
substantial subsidies from the compensation fund. These would be used to
cover the price differential between Belgian and German coal and thereby
avert mine closings and widespread unemployment in the high-cost Belgian
coal industry. Under the Belgian proposal, moreover, German producers
would make the greatest contribution to the fund, with the result being an
increase in their coal prices and a weakening of their competitive position
in the common market. The Germans naturally sought to limit compensatory payments and even threatened to withhold support for the removal
of tariff barriers and quantitative import quotas unless Belgian concessions
were forthcoming. A long dispute ensued, with the negotiators at one point
considering a compromise that would exclude Belgium from the common
market during the transition period. The Americans thought this solution
would rob Belgian coal producers of the incentive to reduce costs and
become more productive. They urged the negotiators to incorporate Belgium
under terms that reduced current price differentials without eliminating
competitive pressures. In return, they promised to use dollar aid and counterpart funds to modernize the Belgian coal industry.[72]

The dispute over Belgian coal highlighted the aggressive posture of Germany's negotiators in the months following the outbreak of the Korean
War and the start of the rearmament program. So did disagreements over
policies that would perpetuate the Ruhr Authority, decartelize the German
steel industry, and tax imports from producers outside the common market
at rates set in the Belgian rather than the German tariff. Decartelization
was the most intractable issue. The French demanded limits on the amount
of steel produced by individual German firms and dissolution of the great

---

[71]   In additions to the sources cited in note 70, see Hoffman torep 7671 to Katz, Sep-
        tember 6, 1950, ECA Files, box 67; and Bissell torep 8645 to Katz, October 9, 1950,
        ECA Files, box 68.
[72]   Bruce tel. to Acheson, September 21, 1950, and Acheson tel. to Certain Diplomatic
        Offices, December 8, 1950, *FRUS, 1950*, 3:748–52, 761–5; Foster torep 10732 to
        Katz, December 26, 1950, ECA Files, box 69; and Katz repto 194 to Foster, January
        13, 1951, ECA Files, box 29.

German steel companies, their joint sales agency, and their control over the Ruhr coal mines. These demands, like those regarding compensation payments, aimed to weaken Germany's competitive position in the proposed complex. To the French, they were the price for Germany's reentry into the Western community; to the Germans, they promised the offsetting political and economic advantages that would come from reintegration and eventual removal of vestigial restrictions on the overall level of German production.[73]

But if this was a price that Germany was willing to pay in May, it had become too dear by September. By then, the rearmament program had increased the demand for coal and steel. The specter of overproduction had given way to the fear of shortages and the expectation that American leaders would move to lift the restrictions on German industry and bring the Federal Republic into the common defense. Expectation became reality at the September meetings of the Allied foreign ministers and NATO Council. On the eve of the meetings, President Truman decided to increase American troop levels in Europe, support a unified NATO staff, and appoint an American as commander-in-chief of the NATO army. The Europeans were delighted with the news. Truman's decision amounted to an American commitment to Europe's defense in advance of hostilities. This was a commitment without precedent in American history and additionally impressive in light of the burden the United States was then shouldering as a result of the military-assistance program, the Marshall Plan, and the war in Korea. But the weight of this burden added credibility to the quid pro quo that Truman and other policymakers demanded: the integration of German military units into NATO. Goaded by the Pentagon, Acheson announced this demand in the September meetings and in private talks with Bevin and Schuman, making it clear that European leaders had to take the American and German contributions as parts of the same prescription for a strong defense.

This demand was a bitter pill to swallow for European policymakers, who worried about a resurgent German militarism almost as much as they did about Soviet aggression. Bevin choked back his reservations and agreed in principle to the American position. It at least had the advantage of fleshing out the North Atlantic framework, to which he was committed. But Schuman claimed that no French government could agree to Germany's rearmament. American pressure for the impossible, he said, would only wreck the real prospects for a Franco–German rapprochement, then being explored in the negotiations for a European coal and steel community. Armed with these and other arguments, the French blocked the American proposal at the September meetings and then countered in October with the so-called Pleven Plan. This plan envisioned a European defense budget to which all participating countries would contribute, a European minister of defense

[73] Diebold, *Schuman Plan*, 68–73; Wexler, *Marshall Plan Revisited*, 242–3; and Bruce tel. to Acheson, September 21, 1950, Bohlen tel. to Acheson, October 25, 1950, and Thorp memorandum, December 14, 1950, *FRUS, 1950*, 3:748–52, 760–1, 765–6.

and defense council responsible to a common political authority, and a European army made up of troops drawn from national forces and integrated at the lowest unit possible. German troops would be included. But Germany would not have a separate national force or defense minister. Nor would German troops be included until after the European army had been established and the coal and steel negotiations had been brought to a successful conclusion. In effect, Germany's military contribution would be denationalized. Germany's troops would be integrated into a European army operating within NATO but responsible to European institutions under French leadership.[74]

The Pleven Plan was acceptable neither to the Germans, who said it would limit their sovereignty, nor to the British, who thought it would lock them out of Europe. Bevin wanted Britain to take the lead in a Western consolidation of overlapping blocs, not play second fiddle on the Continent (or in NATO) to a Franco–German group. He rejected the Pleven Plan on these grounds and also because both he and Acheson thought it would take months to hammer out the details and even longer to forge the European political institutions on which the French plan ultimately depended.[75]

The issue at stake in this debate was as old as the Marshall Plan. The French had consistently sought security within a unified Europe superintended by supranational institutions; the British had favored a North Atlantic framework founded on intergovernmental agreement; and the outcome had been a series of squabbles over the merits of a European customs union, over the power of the OEEC and the Council of Europe, and over the Schuman Plan for a European coal and steel community, on which the Pleven Plan was modeled. American pressure for Germany's rearmament had brought these differences to a head once again. The resulting disputes would tie up the NATO negotiations until the end of 1950, when a muddled compromise finally permitted discussions on the Pleven Plan and Germany's integration into NATO to go forward at the same time. But the course of these negotiations is less important to the purpose of this study than is the issue at stake, which involved nothing less than how to organize an economic and strategic unit that could reconcile Franco–German differences, create a workable balance of power among the states of Western Europe, and contain the Soviet Union.

The same issue was at stake in the parallel discussion regarding the Schuman Plan, on which American pressure for Germany's rearmament had a decided impact. The French had linked their support for Germany's military reintegration to the successful conclusion of these discussions. Indeed, given the American pressure and the British position, both of which made Ger-

---

[74] Diebold, *Schuman Plan*, 70; Wexler, *Marshall Plan Revisited*, 242; Mayne, *Recovery of Europe*, 194; Kaplan, *United States and NATO*, 159–62; Kaplan, *Community of Interests*, 114–15, 128–9; and Bullock, *Bevin*, 804–29.

[75] See the sources cited in note 74.

many's rearmament appear inevitable, French leaders may have intended the Pleven Plan to do little more than delay this outcome long enough to protect the leverage they could bring to bear in the negotiations for a European coal and steel agreement. Much to their chagrin, however, the United States had effectively surrendered this leverage to the Germans. Events in Korea and "talk of German rearmament," according to American officials in Paris, had stiffened Germany's position in the six-power negotiations. German politicians saw the prospects for increasing steel production "outside of the Schuman proposal framework," while German industrialists, many of whom had opposed the plan from the start, grew adamant in their opposition to compensatory payments and industrial deconcentration. Some were even talking of cartelistic agreements, similar to those in the prewar period, as a better way to organize a cooperative system that protected German interests. Given these developments, the German negotiators in Paris began "dragging their feet," convinced, as Charles Bohlen reported, that they could gain "the advantages and equality offered by the Schuman Proposal without accepting [its] commitments and limitations." The Germans, in the view of Ambassador Bruce, now sought "competitive advantage within [the] single market."[76]

The Germans used their leverage to win a variety of concessions, some of which had strong support in Washington. The French promised to abolish the Ruhr Authority. The Belgians accepted a compromise on the tariff question and agreed to join the common market with lower subsidies than originally demanded. In addition, the conferees preserved the supranational character of the high authority, in part by limiting the powers of the ministers council and making them more specific. They also dropped the French proposal for regional producer associations and included pledges to expand world trade, avoid protectionist policies, and consider the needs of producers and consumers outside the common market.[77] These changes were generally in line with what American leaders had been urging. But they were far more easily negotiated than the French demand for decartelization of the German steel industry.

The struggle over decartelization deadlocked the negotiations through December, by which time the Schuman Plan looked like a "dead duck" unless a quick solution was forthcoming. The solution finally came, however, only after American policymakers had intervened more directly than ever in the European negotiations. At the request of the French, who blamed the American rearmament initiative for Germany's intransigence, President

[76] Bruce tel. to Acheson, September 21, 1950, and Bohlen tel. to Acheson, October 25, 1950, *FRUS, 1950*, 3:748–52, 760–1. See also Thorp memorandum, December 14, 1950, *FRUS, 1950*, 3:765–6; Wexler, *Marshall Plan Revisited*, 242–3; and Diebold, *Schuman Plan*, 70–1.

[77] Thorp memorandum, December 14, 1950, *FRUS, 1950*, 3:765–6; and Diebold, *Schuman Plan*, 66, 78–80, 141–2, 202–5, 472–4.

Truman publicly reiterated his support for the Schuman Plan while High Commissioner McCloy worked behind the scenes to mediate a settlement. Meeting with French and German leaders during the winter of 1950–1, McCloy finally hammered out a compromise that satisfied both sides. The French abandoned their demand for limits on the amount of steel any German firm could produce. The Germans pledged to disband their joint sales agency, reorganize their steel industry into twenty-eight firms, and limit the amount of Ruhr coal production each firm controlled. On the whole, the final compromise came closer to French than to German expectations, in part because the French position dovetailed with Washington's opposition to industrial cartelization. That opposition helped bring forth the decisive American intervention that made a final settlement possible and set the stage for the Schuman Plan treaty, which European leaders signed in Paris on April 18, 1951.[78]

V

The Schuman Plan laid the political and economic bases for a final settlement between the Germans and their former enemies in the West. In a real sense, it amounted to the treaty of peace that had never been signed. Although not the by-product of American initiative, the plan had been inspired in part by American policy and brought to fruition with the help of American intervention. Politically, it reconciled Germany's recovery with France's economic and security concerns, brought both countries together in a unit of power equal to the Soviet challenge, and cleared a path for the Federal Republic's eventual participation in the common defense. Economically, it blended the traders' and planners' approaches, combining market incentives with administrative coordinators and using them to integrate economies and boost productivity. By leaving administrative controls in the hands of an international authority, and by linking this authority to a council of government ministers and a body of business and labor advisors, it also created a framework for a corporative collaboration similar to the public–private partnerships that revolved around the ECA. In these and other ways, the Schuman Plan pointed to a European neo-capitalism founded on the New Deal synthesis.

The successful efforts to reduce import quotas and organize a "single market" for a common list of commodities embodied a strategy similar to the one that European and American leaders followed in the Schuman Plan negotiations. They reflected a faith in the capacity of international experts, natural market forces, and supranational coordinators to reconcile national

---

[78] Summary of the Secretary's Daily Meeting, December 28, 1950, RG 59, Secretary's Daily Meetings, box 1. See also Diebold, *Schuman Plan*, 72–4; Wexler, *Marshall Plan Revisited*, 243; and George W. Ball, *The Past Has Another Pattern: Memoirs* (New York, 1982), 87–9.

aspirations and enhance productivity. Together with the EPU's handling of the German crisis, they also played a part in bringing the Federal Republic into the sort of integrated system that American Marshall Planners had always envisioned. These gains came just as the Korean War was altering American policy toward Western Europe. The war had influenced the outcome of the Schuman Plan negotiations, had been a cause of the German payments crisis, and had made progress in the field of trade liberalization more difficult and more limited than expected. In addition, the war had led American policymakers to assign rearmament priority over recovery and had strengthened the conservative bloc in Congress. Both of these developments would test the North Atlantic alliance. They would also bring the Marshall Plan to an end several months ahead of schedule.

9

Guns and butter:
politics and diplomacy at the end of
the Marshall Plan

I

THE END of the Marshall Plan began in November 1950, when Chinese armies intervened in the Korean War. Even more than the outbreak of hostilities in June, the Chinese intervention had the most far-reaching impact on the economic and political climate in the United States and on the foreign and domestic policies of the Truman administration. Earlier hopes that the war would end quickly gave way to plans for a long and costly struggle and to fears of Communist aggression in other parts of the world. American policymakers became more conscious of Western Europe's military vulnerability. As the White House laid plans to expand defense expenditures and mobilize the American economy behind the war effort, the Pentagon and the State Department intensified the pressure on European governments to strengthen NATO and bring West Germany into the common defense. Rearmament now had absolute priority in American policy, leading first to the transformation of Marshall aid into defense support and then to the demise of the Marshall Plan altogether.

These developments destabilized both the North Atlantic alliance and the political situation in participating countries. As the pace of rearmament outstripped the rate of economic growth in Western Europe, the price index shot up, the dollar gap widened, and the drain on reserves grew worse. The Europeans became more dependent on American economic assistance, just as priorities in Washington were shifting from Marshall aid to military support. Many Europeans resented the cuts in economic aid at a time when the United States was calling for a defense buildup that cost more than participating governments thought they could afford. Added to this source of tension between the United States and its allies was the pressure from Washington for Germany's rapid rearmament and what some Europeans saw as the reckless course of American policy in the Far East.

The source of internal tension in Western Europe could be found in the same issues. The dangers of German rearmament and the possibility that the United States might draw its allies into another world war fostered neutralist sentiment and sharpened political divisions in participating countries. So did the escalating cost of rearmament. The shift from civilian to defense production and the higher taxes, inflationary pressures, and cuts in social expenditures that accompanied the defense effort posed a serious threat to living standards and made more glaring than before the wide disparity of income between different social classes. In some of the participating countries, rearmament raised redistributive questions that had earlier been concealed by the politics of economic growth. Established governments began to falter, center parties lost ground to rivals on the Left and the Right, and class collaboration gave way to a dangerous trend toward political polarization.

Something similar transpired on the other side of the Atlantic. Prior to the Korean War, the Marshall Plan commanded substantial support in Congress. The Republican Party's electoral gains in 1946 had been dissipated two years later, when President Truman scored a surprising victory in the 1948 election and the Democrats captured both houses of Congress. These victories, together with bipartisan collaboration between the administration and the moderate, internationalist wing of the Republican Party, had set the stage for Truman's notable legislative triumphs in the field of foreign affairs. Opposition had been limited to a small bloc of conservatives. Composed largely of Republicans from the Midwest and Great Plains states, their ideology combined a commitment to orthodox economic doctrine and to the old tradition of isolationism with a conviction that the thrust of public policy under the New Deal and the Fair Deal was decidedly un-American.

These linkages were clear in the arguments that conservatives hurled against the ERP in the congressional debates between 1948 and 1950. It is worth repeating that Senators Kem, Jenner, and Malone, along with other conservatives, attacked the ERP as part of a broad program that also included free trade and New Deal strategies of social welfare, government regulation, and Keynesian economics. They associated this program with a bipartisan alliance of liberal internationalists drawn from both political parties, from the major trade unions, and from the multilateral bloc of capital-intensive firms and investment banks – what Malone had called "the very top of the manufacturing, producing, and investment groups." Malone and other conservatives said that smaller, less efficient firms would lose from rebuilding European competitors, lowering tariffs, and multilateralizing trade. They also insisted that free trade, together with expensive government programs at home, economic and military aid abroad, and such international "super-states" as the International Trade Organization (ITO), the IMF, and the World Bank, would lead to economic depression and fasten a "semisuper slave state" on the American people. These arguments were spiced with McCarthy-like charges that liberal internationalists were abetting Communist efforts to subvert the capitalist system. The internationalists, they said, were supporting "fellow-traveler[s]" in the British Labour government, hampering a capitalist revival in West Germany, and playing "directly into the hands of a communist strategy which is based upon encouraging the [American] private enterprise system to destroy itself." On the basis of this sweeping indictment, the conservatives had demanded that total Marshall aid be reduced, and terminated altogether in cases where it subsidized socialism or facilitated trade between Western Europe and the Soviet bloc.[1]

These demands had little support in Congress prior to 1950; the conservative coalition proved to be no match for the bipartisan alliance that marshaled majorities behind the ERP and other planks in the foreign-policy platform of the Truman administration. But the Korean War fanned the flames of McCarthyism and contributed to the Republican victory in the midterm elections of November. The Republicans picked up five seats in the Senate and twenty-eight in the House of Representatives. Although Democrats retained majorities in both houses, the elections reinvigorated the conservative coalition and led to the decline of bipartisanship in Congress. These developments then combined with the Chinese intervention of late November, the massive expansion of the Pentagon's budget, and the economic controls and dislocations that followed to produce a major economic and political crisis. The progressive alliance that supported the Truman administration was thrown on the defensive; the conservatives found themselves in a stronger position to block the Fair Deal's social agenda at home and the direction of American policy abroad.

This crisis led quickly to the triumph of military over economic diplomacy and eventually to the demise of the ECA. But it did not lead American Marshall Planners to abandon the New Deal synthesis as a guide to action. Their policy now combined such old themes as economic integration, greater productivity, and corporative collaboration between labor, business, and government with a more salient interest in "social justice." By moving forward along all of these routes, they hoped to reconcile civilian and military requirements and to point the way to a better day in which an integrated Western Europe could have guns and butter in sufficiency.

For the quotations not already documented in previous chapters, see U.S., Congress, Senate, Senator Jenner speaking on S. 3304, 81st Cong., 2d sess., May 1, 1950, *Congressional Record* 96, pt.5: 6053, 6051, 6050. For general background on what I call the conservative coalition, see also Justus D. Doenecke, *Not to the Swift: The Old Isolationists in the Cold War Era* (Lewisburg, PA, 1979). Doenecke focuses on the "isolationist" bloc in Congress and in the private sector. His work makes clear that the most substantial component of this bloc was composed of political conservatives who opposed the New Deal, came largely from the Midwest and Great Plains states, and drew support in the private sector from small business firms.

II

Prior to the Korean War, the Truman administration had waged a long and largely successful battle to hold the line on military expenditures. This policy fit neatly with the administration's initial decision to rely on economic diplomacy rather than military power to achieve its foreign-policy objectives, and with the determination of budget balancers to restrain inflationary pressures. Guided by these priorities, the administration had capped defense spending at $14.4 billion in 1950, had reduced this amount to $13.5 billion in the original budget for 1951, and had delayed action on National Security Council Paper No. 68 (NSC–68). This document envisioned a vast expansion of American military commitments around the world at an estimated cost in defense expenditures of approximately $40 billion a year. The price tag prompted strong objections from budget balancers in the Treasury Department, the Bureau of the Budget, and the Pentagon, where Secretary of Defense Louis A. Johnson held a presidential mandate to limit military expenditures. As it was, they said, the budget for 1951 anticipated a deficit of $5.1 billion, which would come on top of a similar deficit in 1950. Their determination to balance the budget might well have led to a freeze on defense expenditures had not the Korean War intervened. Under the weight of this event, however, the Truman administration approved NSC–68, doubled the defense budget by the end of 1950, and added several billion dollars to the original estimate for military assistance. In 1951, Congress appropriated over $50 billion for defense and international affairs, an amount that exceeded the wildest expectations of strategic planners two years earlier.[2]

Even with additional taxes, the jump in defense expenditures, the diversion of resources to defense production, and the worldwide shortage of critical materials combined to generate inflationary pressures in the United States. The price index climbed by more than five points in the three months following the Chinese intervention and the Truman administration was forced to put the American economy on what amounted to a war footing. Tentative steps in this direction had been taken as early as July, including controls over credit and the allocation and export of scarce commodities. These steps were followed in mid-December by a presidential proclamation of national emergency and new controls over rents, wages, and prices. Charles E. Wilson, president of the General Electric Company, took charge of the Office of Defense Mobilization, which President Truman established to superintend the work of the Defense Production Administration, the

[2] Donovan, *Tumultuous Years*, 132, 158–61, 242–7; Paul Y. Hammond, "NSC–68: Prologue to Rearmament," in Warner R. Schilling, Paul Y. Hammond, and Glenn H. Snyder, *Strategy, Politics, and Defense Budgets* (New York, 1962), 267–378; and Samuel F. Wells, Jr., "Sounding the Tocsin: NSC 68 and the Soviet Threat," *International Security* 4 (Fall 1979): 116–58.

Wage Stabilization Board, the Office of Price Administration, and other agencies that were leading the fight to control inflation and mobilize resources.[3]

The Truman administration did its best to win bipartisan support for these initiatives and to enlist the aid of private groups. To assuage conservatives in Congress, it offset hikes in defense spending with cuts in social expenditures and settled for new taxes that were less substantial than first recommended. So far as private groups were concerned, the administration would draw on their assistance through the network of private advisory committees that radiated from the Agriculture, Labor, and other departments. The Office of Defense Mobilization added another layer to this network of corporative collaboration, recruiting experts from the private sector, creating its own system of advisory committees, and trying, as it did with the Wage Stabilization Board, to bring government, labor, and industry together in a collective administration of the war economy. In the early months of the war, the administration could also count on support from the Business Advisory Council (BAC), the Committee for Economic Development (CED), and similar organs of progressive opinion in the business community. The CED reluctantly accepted the new system of wage–price controls, contributed key personnel, including Charles Wilson, to the war government, and joined the BAC in backing the administration's efforts to raise taxes, control credit, and effect government economies.[4]

The results hardly measured up to expectations. Although inflationary pressures abated after February, the cost of living climbed nearly 10 percent in 1950. Policymakers in the Treasury Department and the Federal Reserve System waged a divisive fight over interest rates on government securities while conservatives in Congress, strengthened by Republican gains in the midterm elections, launched an unrelenting assault on the administration's policies. The new mechanisms of collective regulation also began to break down almost as soon as they were established. Business leaders chafed under government price restrictions, as did farmers, and labor's representatives temporarily bolted the Wage Stabilization Board when it fixed a 10 percent limit on pay increases. In addition, liberals in the Democratic Party complained of cuts in social-welfare expenditures and conservatives in both parties joined forces with the Chamber of Commerce and the National Association of Manufacturers (NAM) to oppose the drift toward greater deficits, higher taxes, and government controls. The Korean truce talks that began in July gave incentive to this opposition. Conservatives in the business community, and most in Congress, became convinced that the war would remain limited and soon taper off, relieving pressure on the domestic econ-

[3]　Donovan, *Tumultuous Years*, 319–20, 324–7.
[4]　U.S., Congress, House, Committee on the Judiciary, *The Mobilization Program*, H. Rept. 1217, 82d Cong., 1st sess., 1951; and McQuaid, *Big Business and Presidential Power*, 161–7.

omy and reducing the need for economic controls. Even the BAC and CED jumped on the decontrol bandwagon. Bereft of old allies, the Truman administration had to stand by while Congress emasculated the system of government controls in a series of steps that began in the summer of 1951.[5]

A similar story unfolded in the area of foreign policy. In December 1950, the Republicans in Congress censured Secretary of State Dean Acheson, who was then in Brussels for a meeting of the North Atlantic Council.[6] The Republican action had been prompted in part by Truman's decision to contribute six American military divisions to a NATO army. Senator Taft, former President Hoover, and other Republican conservatives had opposed this decision, first accusing the president of exceeding his constitutional authority and then repudiating the very foundations of the administration's European policy. Pointing to the Soviet Union's atomic capability, they warned that American troops would be annihilated in the event of a European war. When the administration argued that atomic parity made the buildup of conventional forces imperative, the conservatives claimed that an American army large enough to deter the Soviets would cost more than the United States could afford. They denounced the NATO countries for not contributing enough to the American war effort in Korea and opposed the dispatch of additional troops to Europe, or the provision of additional aid, until the Europeans had united behind a strong system of self-defense. The last point had been a favorite of conservatives for several years. They backed the integrationist thrust of the administration's diplomacy, but only because a united Western Europe could stand without Marshall aid and military assistance, which the conservatives saw as trip wires to American involvement in the next European war.[7]

As an alternative to the administration's policy, which supposedly ran the risk of interring American troops in a European graveyard, the conservative bloc envisioned a system of defense based on air and sea power. This system would be centered on the Western Hemisphere, stretch from there across both oceans, but stop short of the Eurasian mainland. Hoover

---

[5] Donovan, *Tumultuous Years*, 326–8, 331, 368–9; McQuaid, *Big Business and Presidential Power*, 167–8; Karl Schriftgiesser, *Business Comes of Age: The Story of the Committee for Economic Development and Its Impact upon the Economic Policies of the United States, 1942–1960* (New York, 1960), 150–7; and Hamby, *Beyond the New Deal*, 449–52.

[6] Acheson, *Present at the Creation*, 365–6; and McLellan, *Acheson*, 300–1.

[7] Acheson, *Present at the Creation*, 488–95; McLellan, *Acheson*, 337–46; Donovan, *Tumultuous Years*, 322–4; Stebbins, *United States in World Affairs, 1951*, 48–56; Patterson, *Mr. Republican*, 476–82; Hoover, "Our National Policies in This Crisis," *Vital Speeches of the Day* 17 (January 1, 1951): 165–7; U.S., Congress, Senate, Senator Taft, "Constructive Criticism of Foreign Policy Is Essential to the Safety of the Nation," 82d Cong., 1st sess., January 5, 1951, *Congressional Record* 97, pt. 1: 54–61; and Doenecke, *Not to the Swift*, 196–201.

and Taft defended this strategy as militarily more prudent than Truman's decision to station ground forces in Europe and as the only way to avoid the internal consequences of total mobilization, which they tended to equate with a large standing army. Indeed, the "Great Debate," as it was called, revolved as much around the political economy of defense as it did around military strategy, with Hoover, Taft, and other conservatives drawing on the same arsenal of arguments they had earlier used to attack the Marshall Plan. Total mobilization, they said, would mean the end of private enterprise and democratic liberties in the United States. It would lead to perpetual deficits, permanent inflation, tremendous taxes, and rigid economic controls, all ending in what Taft called a "garrison state" choked by government regulations that inevitably became "more arbitrary and unreasonable."[8]

These economic arguments differed markedly from those spelled out by Leon Keyserling, chairman of the President's Council of Economic Advisers, and the other Keynesians who had worked on NSC–68. These men thought it possible to expand the rearmament program without serious economic dislocations or cuts in social expenditures, provided the administration raised taxes, controlled scarce commodities, and lived, at least temporarily, with larger budget deficits. By 1951, these Keynesians had negotiated a compromise with the economizers in the Truman administration, one that balanced cuts in social spending against a Keynesian regime of economic controls, higher taxes, and larger deficits. Although the compromise fell short of what Keyserling had wanted, it nonetheless made a reluctant Keynesian of the president. Wartime exigencies and national-security imperatives had forced Truman toward a liberal economic doctrine at odds with his cautious instincts, much as the requirements of depression had led Franklin Roosevelt to embrace the same economic theory in the 1930s.[9]

The Truman administration used this doctrine to counter conservative economic arguments in the Great Debate, which raged with unremitting fury until both sides struck a compromise in April 1951. Truman agreed to send four American divisions to Europe, instead of the six originally planned, and the conservatives settled for a Senate resolution that required congressional consent to commitments above this level.[10] The administration had been able to maintain its military pledges to Western Europe, but only

---

[8]   See the sources cited in note 7. The quotation is from Taft's speech to the Senate, January 5, 1951.

[9]   Hammond, "NSC–68: Prologue to Rearmament," 333–4; John Lewis Gaddis, *Strategies of Containment: A Critical Appraisal of Postwar American National Security Policy* (New York, 1982), 90–117; and Wells, "Sounding the Tocsin," Gaddis, "NSC 68 and the Problem of Ends and Means," and Paul Nitze, "The Development of NSC 68," in *International Security* 4 (Fall 1979): 116–58, 164–70, and 170–6, respectively.

[10] Acheson, *Present at the Creation*, 495–6; McLellan, *Acheson*, 346; and Donovan, *Tumultuous Years*, 324.

through a judicious step backward. It was less fortunate when it came to foreign aid and economic diplomacy. In these areas, when the domestic political situation zigged, the administration was left in the zag.

In the congressional debates of 1947–50, the Truman administration had argued that American resources were adequate to the task of European recovery, particularly if they were nourished by appropriate fiscal and budgetary policies and by enlightened cooperation between public policymakers and private elites. On each occasion, it said that measures of this sort would maintain living standards and a free economy at home. On each occasion, it offered the Marshall Plan as the only alternative to a massive expansion of defense expenditures and the collapse of European export markets, which together would bring economic depression and sweeping new controls over labor, industry, and agriculture. And on each occasion, it mobilized a coalition of farm, labor, and business groups powerful enough to overwhelm conservative opponents. This was the same coalition that defended the ITO and that won support in Congress for the Bretton Woods institutions, the General Agreement on Tariffs and Trade, the Reciprocal Trade Agreements Act, and the Point Four program.

But this impressive string of successes was broken after the opening of hostilities in Korea. In renewing the Reciprocal Trade Agreements Act, Congress inserted a peril-point provision that made it virtually impossible to reduce American tariffs below a level deemed harmful to domestic industry or agriculture. It mandated escape clauses in all trade agreements, withdrew trade concessions to the Soviet satellite states, limited exports of certain farm commodities, and refused to simplify American customs procedures as the administration had requested. In addition, the so-called cheese amendment to the Defense Production Act imposed quotas on imported dairy products while the Kem amendment and the Battle Act of 1951 instructed the president to suspend economic and military aid to countries exporting strategic commodities to the Soviet bloc.

All of these measures spelled a retreat toward economic nationalism, a course inspired in part by Cold War considerations but also by the revival of protectionist sentiment at a time when the Korean War and the rearmament program were putting a heavy strain on the American economy. The Truman administration had tried to forestall this retreat, but to no avail. As in the battle over wartime controls, the economic crisis had weakened the administration's leverage in Congress and played into the hands of a conservative coalition. Truman found it more difficult to defend the economic benefits of multilateralism against conservative critics, who turned this defense upside down. Having argued all along that multilateralism would wreck the domestic economy, conservatives now used the same argument to explain the current crisis and reverse what they saw as the dangerous trend toward "free trade" in American diplomacy. As if to acknowledge the power of conservatives on Capitol Hill, if not the force of their contention, the Truman administration finally suspended its long campaign to win Senate ratification of the ITO charter. [11]

The conservative resurgence in Washington also contributed to the shift from economic to military assistance in American foreign-aid policy. This shift occurred in three stages. The first stage came in 1949, when the Truman administration agreed to parity for rearmament and recovery and launched the military-assistance program. The second stage came after the outbreak of fighting in Korea, when policymakers subordinated the demands of recovery to those of defense and Congress shifted funds from the Marshall Plan to the military-assistance program. At this point, however, a gap began to widen between the executive and legislative branches. Truman had opposed the cut in Marshall aid and his defeat in Congress was another indication of how war and rearmament had reinvigorated the conservative bloc at the expense of multilateralists on whom the administration had anchored its economic diplomacy. The split set the stage for the third and decisive shift from economic to military assistance.

By the end of 1950, the Truman administration was targeting most of its economic aid on rearmament. The ECA was laying plans to divert counterpart funds from economic to military purposes and to replace the original formula for distributing ERP grants with one geared to European rearmament. [12] American policymakers announced the new priorities in speeches to their European colleagues. Richard Bissell told an OEEC meeting in November that recovery in Northern and Western Europe was complete and that future American aid would be channeled into defense production. A similar message came from William Foster, the new ECA administrator, and from President Truman, who declared in January that American aid would now be used to accelerate rearmament rather than raise living standards. [13]

At the same time, however, political and economic as well as defense considerations seemed to dictate the continuation of economic-aid programs, at least in the eyes of American policymakers and their allies in the peak associations, private foundations, and farm, labor, and business groups that had backed the Marshall Plan since its inception. Although the amount

[11]   Stebbins, *United States in World Affairs, 1951*, 226–32; and Stebbins, *United States in World Affairs, 1950*, 89–90.

[12]   On the use of counterpart funds for military purposes, which Congress finally authorized in the Mutual Security Act of 1951, see Foster ecato 958 to ECA Mission, London, July 28, 1950, ECA Files, box 61; Acheson memorandum, July 31, 1950, Acheson Papers, box 65, folder: Memoranda of Conversations; and the documentation in *FRUS, 1951*, 1:269, 346, 425–8, 1624. On the ECA's new system of allocating grants, see Foster torep 710 to Katz, January 30, 1951, ECA Files, box 83; and unsigned repto 618 to Foster, February 8, 1951, ECA Files, box 30.

[13]   Bissell toreps 9793 and 10095 to Katz, November 18 and 29, 1950, ECA Files, box 69; Katz repto 6524 to Foster, November 29, 1950, ECA Files, box 83; and Kaplan, *Community of Interests*, 148.

might be reduced and aimed at defense support, not civilian production, even a marginal volume of dollars would have what Foster called a "multiplier effect." It would enable the Europeans to utilize local resources that might otherwise remain idle. This would help to sustain rearmament without destabilizing economies and undermining the fragile political coalitions in such countries as France, Italy, and West Germany, where governments operated within a range of political choice that made it difficult to divert resources to military production at the expense of civilian living standards. Foster and the other ECA officials had begun to articulate this line of thinking shortly after the outbreak of fighting in Korea. Acheson and Harriman had called for continuing the Marshall Plan beyond 1952. President Truman had envisioned something similar when he told Congress that a "defense program of the size now being undertaken" in Western Europe, "must be supported by a strong and expanding economic base." Two presidential commissions, including the International Development Advisory Board of farm, labor, business, and professional leaders, reached the same conclusion, as did the CED, the National Planning Association (NPA), and the Brookings Institution.[14]

By 1951, however, the economic crisis growing out of the defense effort had eroded congressional and public support for foreign aid. Higher taxes, raw material shortages, burgeoning deficits, and inflationary pressures had strengthened the position of Taft and other conservatives who claimed that Europe was not doing enough to help itself, that American resources were limited, and that further drains would lead to economic disaster and political regimentation in the United States. Wielding these and other arguments, the conservative bloc opened a full-scale assault on the Marshall Plan. The battle opened in the spring and raged on two fronts throughout the summer and fall of 1951. On one front, conservatives engaged the administration over the amount and form of aid to be appropriated for the new fiscal year. The administration proposed a single, omnibus measure totaling approximately $8.5 billion in economic and military assistance to all regions of the globe,

---

[14] Foster letter to Senator Tom Connally, July 27, 1950, Hoffman Papers, box 22, folder: ECA – Letter to Senator Connally; and Price, *Marshall Plan and Its Meaning*, 359, for the remark by Truman. See also Price, *Marshall Plan and Its Meaning*, 360; McLellan, *Acheson*, 350; Richard M. Bissell, Jr., "The Impact of Rearmament on the Free World Economy," *Foreign Affairs* 29 (April 1951): 385–405; Committee for Economic Development, *Economic Aspects of North Atlantic Security: A Statement on National Policy by the Research and Policy Committee of the CED* (New York, 1951); Theodore Geiger and Harold Van B. Cleveland, *Making Western Europe Defensible* (Washington, DC, August 1951); The Brookings Institution, *Current Issues in Foreign Economic Assistance* (Washington, DC, 1951): 87–8; International Development Advisory Board, *Partners in Progress: A Report to the President*, by Nelson A. Rockefeller, chairman (Washington, DC, March 1951); and *Report to the President on Foreign Economic Policies*, by Gordon Gray (Washington, DC, November 10, 1950).

of which $2.5 billion would be earmarked for economic assistance. By making economic assistance part of a larger omnibus measure, by giving substantially greater emphasis to military aid, and by labeling economic aid as defense support, the administration had hoped to preclude opposition from conservatives in Congress. But this strategy failed miserably. The administration and its critics repeated the usual arguments, summarized previously, and the administration drew support from the CED, the NPA, and the Brookings Institution. In the end, however, conservatives combined to slash over a billion dollars from the original proposal and to reduce from $2.5 billion to $1.44 billion the amount earmarked for economic assistance. Of this latter amount, little more than a billion dollars was designated for Western Europe. The administration's only triumph came at the hands of General Eisenhower, whose intervention was credited with preventing even deeper cuts and preserving some flexibility for the president. [15]

Nor did the administration fare better on the second front, where the battle revolved around an organizational issue dating back to the start of the Marshall Plan. The issue had its immediate origins in bureaucratic struggles within the Truman administration. In late 1950, Truman had approved an interagency arrangement for coordinating military- and economic-aid programs. Growing out of the work of a special interdepartmental study group, the arrangement had confirmed the ECA's role as the operational agency responsible for economic-aid programs "required to support an adequate defense." The Defense Department retained primary responsibility for military assistance and both aspects of policy were to be coordinated by an International Security Affairs Committee (ISAC) representing the State, Treasury, and Defense departments, the ECA, and the Executive Office of the President. But a State Department representative chaired the committee as director of international security affairs. This assignment enhanced the department's authority at the expense of the ECA's autonomy, as did the organizational arrangements developed in Western Europe, where the ECA's mission chiefs and special representative became subordinate functionaries on a number of rearmament committees directed primarily by officials from the State and Defense departments. [16]

Despite these setbacks, the ECA had been content with the new arrangements. It remained an independent agency and still had primary authority in the field of economic aid. When the special representative noted how talk of curtailing the ECA's original functions had lowered morale at his office in Paris, Foster responded that planning for the next fiscal year did not envisage a significant reduction in staff or funding. Although the agency's responsibilities would be "reoriented from economic assistance for recovery

[15] Stebbins, *United States in World Affairs*, 1951, 233–6.
[16] Foster torep 143 to Katz, January 8, 1951, ECA Files, box 83. See also Foster torep 799 to Katz, February 3, 1951, ECA Files, box 83; and Kaplan, *Community of Interests*, 146–8.

purposes to economic assistance for building a military shield," Foster nonetheless expected the ECA to continue as an independent operation past the mid-1952 deadline originally set for terminating Marshall aid. [17]

Shortly thereafter, the ECA suffered a more serious setback in the Truman administration and then a fatal defeat at the hands of Congress. According to the administration's original drafts of the 1951 foreign-aid bill, the secretary of state, with the advice of the ISAC, would be empowered to allocate foreign-aid funds among the various agencies involved, including the ECA and the Pentagon. The bill would reduce the ECA to the level of a "country desk" in the State Department, as Foster complained, and spell the end of its life "as an independent agency." Similar complaints came from the Defense Department, resulting in another round of bureaucratic negotiations that nonetheless ended in something of a victory for the State Department. Under the final compromise as submitted to Congress, the ECA would continue to administer the shrunken economic-assistance program. But the ISAC would remain the primary coordinating mechanism, would continue to be housed in the State Department, and would have ultimate control in matters of policy and a voice in operational decisions. [18]

By granting additional authority to the State Department, the administration set itself on a collision course with Congress. Conservatives in both parties were just as suspicious of the State Department as they had been in 1948 and just as determined to clip its wings in favor of an independent agency under a single administrator of cabinet rank. In this case, moreover, conservatives could count on support from the CED, the NPA, the Brookings Institution, and similar private agencies that continued to favor a unified and businesslike administration of American foreign-aid programs. Influenced by these considerations, Congress torpedoed the administration's proposal, created a new agency, the Mutual Security Administration, and gave it, not the State Department, the responsibility for coordinating foreign-aid programs. The State and Defense departments continued to operate the Point Four and military-assistance programs, respectively, albeit under the coordinating eye of the Mutual Security Administration.. But the ECA fell victim to congressional concerns about economy and efficiency, including, ironically, some of the same concerns that had inspired its creation three years earlier. Under congressional mandate, it was to cease operations within sixty days of the appointment of a director of mutual security. Truman gave this post to Averell Harriman, who had resigned as special representative to become the president's foreign-aid coordinator. Harriman assumed his

[17] Foster torep 351 to Katz, January 15, 1951, ECA Files, box 83. See also Katz repto 195 to Foster, January 13, 1951, ECA Files, box 29; and Foster torep 375 to Katz, January 17, 1951, ECA Files, box 83.
[18] See the documentation in *FRUS, 1951*, 1:270–317, 329–35. The quote is from Lucius D. Battle, Special Assistant to the Secretary of State, Memorandum of Telephone Conversation, April 3, 1951, *FRUS, 1951*, 1:287–8.

duties on October 31, 1951 and the ECA closed its doors two days before the start of the new year.[19]

The financial provisions of the Mutual Security Act, as the new measure was entitled, sorely disappointed policymakers in the Truman administration. The administration had been willing as a last resort to curtail the State Department's responsibility for economic and military assistance, hoping thereby to appease congressional critics and avoid a substantial reduction of the funds appropriated for economic aid.[20] But this gamble had failed and Acheson had reacted by accusing Congress of overemphasizing military assistance at the expense of economic aid.[21] Truman told the cabinet that Congress must not be allowed to "sabotage" the Marshall Plan.[22] The "economic and social health of the participating countries," Richard Bissell elaborated in a speech to the NPA, was vital to the success of the rearmament program.[23] Donald Stone, the ECA's director of administration, made a similar point in a letter to Paul Hoffman. The Mutual Security Act, he wrote, threatened to "destroy...the economic foundation of our foreign policy." It was based on the erroneous assumption "that security and peace can be assured by military might" and thus consigned to the "junk pile" the doctrine, developed since 1947, that both must ultimately rest on a "sound economic foundation."[24]

Hoffman, Bissell, and other policymakers operated on the assumption that American resources were adequate to wage war, support social-welfare programs, and contribute to European recovery and rearmament, so long as the American people were prepared to live with higher taxes, larger deficits, and economic controls. To conservatives, on the other hand, the economic consequences of the Korean War had confirmed the thesis that the United States could not afford guns and butter both. Invigorated by the red-baiting tactics of Senator Joseph McCarthy and by Republican gains in the November elections, conservatives were in a stronger position to overturn the domestic and foreign policies of the Truman administration. Social-welfare programs were curtailed or put in cold storage, notably the program for public housing and the plan for national health insurance.[25] Wartime economic controls were trimmed, foreign aid was reduced, and some of the

[19] See the documentation in *FRUS, 1951*, 1:338–43, 347–9, 425–8; and Kaplan, *Community of Interests*, 159–60.

[20] Memoranda of telephone conversations, June 27, July 12, and August 6, 1951, Acheson Papers, box 66, folder: Memoranda of Conversations.

[21] Meeting with the Secretary of State, December 13, 1951, RG 59, Secretary's Daily Meetings, 1949–1952, box 1.

[22] Notes on Cabinet Meeting, December 1951, Connelly Papers, box 1, folder: Notes on Cabinet Meetings, Post-presidential File.

[23] Bissell's remarks are quoted from *New York Times*, December 4, 1951, 15.

[24] Stone letter to Hoffman, October 19, 1951, Hoffman Papers, box 22, folder: Economic Cooperation Administration, Correspondence, 1951.

[25] Donovan, *Tumultuous Years*, 365; and Hamby, *Beyond the New Deal*, 444–5.

props were cut from under the multilateral edifice constructed by the Truman administration.

Something similar was happening in many of the Western European countries. Here the defense effort taxed available resources to the limit, dislocated economies, and shook political coalitions. To some European leaders, these developments required more effective cooperation to preserve the economic gains of the past three years and avoid a dangerous political disintegration that could play into the hands of the Communists. But these same developments also generated new tensions in the North Atlantic alliance and made cooperation more difficult, as did old disputes over the German question and new ones resulting from American policy in Korea and cuts in American aid.

III

The European NATO countries increased their defense expenditures from $4.4 billion in 1949 to $8 billion in 1951. Partly because of this stimulus, industrial production in Western Europe climbed 62 percent above the level for 1947. At the same time, however, the enormous expenditures for defense combined with the high price of commodity imports and the shortage of raw materials to generate inflation and erode Western Europe's overall trade balance. Between July 1950 and June 1951, the cost of living increased 20 percent in France and between 9 percent and 10 percent in Great Britain, West Germany, and Italy. In the second quarter of 1951, Western Europe's commodity deficit averaged $650 million a month. The dollar gap started to widen again and the gold and dollar reserves of participating countries began to decline, after having grown by $2.4 billion in the fifteen months following the devaluations of September 1949. Industrial production also began to taper off in the summer of 1951, due in large part to raw material shortages. The shortage of coal was particularly important. It operated as a major bottleneck to production in the steel industry and forced the Europeans to spend their precious reserves on coal imports from the United States.[26]

Participating countries were taking a variety of steps to defend the balance of payments and control inflation. Besides reducing nonmilitary expenditures, governments were controlling wages and prices and establishing new programs to curb credit, regulate trade, and allocate materials.[27] The ECA generally applauded these measures. But it was also quick to admit the risk

---

[26] ECA, *Thirteenth Report to Congress* (Washington, DC, 1951), 27–33; Stebbins, *United States in World Affairs, 1951*, 218–22; Price, *Marshall Plan and Its Meaning*, 137–42; and OEEC, *Economic Progress and Problems of Western Europe: Third Annual Report to the Economic Co-operation Administration* (Paris, June 1951), 23–31. On the European coal crisis, see also *FRUS, 1951*, 4:141–4.

[27] ECA, *Thirteenth Report to Congress*, 5–6, 9.

of untoward repercussions. On the one hand, measures to prohibit exports and limit imports "could conceivably lead to a revival of bilateralism and restrictive trade practices," with results that prevented the most efficient use of resources and stifled further efforts to integrate economies.[28] On the other hand, the diversion of investment from civilian to defense production, the higher taxes, and the reduction of nonmilitary expenditures could easily endanger economic and political stability in participating countries. Industrial workers in most of Western Europe had just begun to recapture prewar levels of real earnings and standards of living were still dangerously low in France, Italy, West Germany, and other countries where inflationary pressures and political fragmentation tended to be the greatest. According to the ECA, workers had "great difficulty in providing adequate diets for their families." Inflation added to this difficulty, as did the maldistribution of income, the inequitable system of taxation, and the cuts in social expenditures. All of these factors put the burden of rearmament on those least able to bear it. Taken together, they could weaken support for the defense effort, play into the hands of the Communists, and threaten the tenuous centrist governments that the United States supported.[29]

According to Dirk Stikker of the Netherlands, these factors had led to discouraging results in the French and Italian elections of May and June 1951, respectively. Three years after the start of the Marshall Plan, the Communist parties in both countries showed enduring vitality. Although the elections witnessed a decline in their voting strength and direct representation in public administration, the Communists captured a third of the electorate in Italy and remained the largest single party in France. Still worse, the elections pointed toward a dangerous political polarization in both countries: Parties on the Left and the Right maintained or improved their position at the expense of those in the center. In France, the Communists captured 26 percent of the vote and de Gaulle's party 22 percent. The "third force" of center parties marshaled a majority, but the margin of victory was narrow and the group itself was badly split into left-wing, center, and right-wing factions. The same was true of West Germany, where state elections in Lower Saxony saw gains for the neo-Nazi party and losses for Adenauer's coalition.[30]

The economic crisis growing out of the rearmament program thus seemed to be altering the balance of political forces in France, Italy, and West Germany, just as a similar crisis in the United States was strengthening the

[28]   Ibid., 6.
[29]   ECA, *Tenth Report to Congress*, 13. See also Price, *Marshall Plan and Its Meaning*, 153–4.
[30]   Katz repto 3411 to Foster, July 16, 1951, ECA Files, box 31; and Stebbins, *United States in World Affairs, 1951*, 67–8, 165–6. For American analyses of the political situation in France and Italy, see the documents in *FRUS, 1951*, 4:349–62, 380–3, 395–7, 616–20.

conservatives at the expense of Truman's liberal coalition. The same was true of Great Britain. In this case, war and rearmament led Attlee's government to revise its budgetary priorities, caused a major split in the Labour Party, and paved the way to a victory for the Tories in the elections of October 1951. This part of the story has been told so often that only a brief summary is needed here.[31] Britain's defense expenditures jumped dramatically in the months following the outbreak of hostilities in Korea, climbing from an anticipated $8.16 billion over a four-year period, to $8.64 billion over three years, to $11.28 billion over the same period. The last figure, although still short of what the Americans expected, tripled the increase in defense spending that had been anticipated prior to the start of the Korean War. Such a fantastic increase was bound to cause economic problems, which Hugh Gaitskell, who had succeeded Cripps as chancellor of the exchequer, spelled out in a Cabinet meeting on January 25. According to Gaitskell, the expansion of defense expenditures would aggravate raw material shortages and worsen the terms of trade for Great Britain. Civilian investment would also suffer, as would exports; living standards would decline; and new controls would be needed to curb inflation and redirect manpower and materials from civilian to military production.

Despite these problems, the defense plan had strong support from Gaitskell and the majority of his colleagues, but not from Aneurin Bevan, who was then a member of the Cabinet and a prominent figure on the left wing of the Labour Party. From the first Cabinet debates of August, Bevan and other dissidents, notably Harold Wilson of the Board of Trade, had questioned the size of the defense program. They said it exaggerated the Soviet Union's military capabilities and plans for aggression, exceeded resource availabilities, and would lead, unless bridled, to cuts in social spending. At this point, dissent was confined to the cabinet and generally muted. Bevan went so far as to support the defense plan in the House of Commons on February 15. Nevertheless, battle lines were being drawn on whether guns or butter would have first claim on Britain's resources.

These differences burst into the open when the Cabinet debated the budget for fiscal 1951–2. Gaitskell told his colleagues in March that escalating defense expenditures made it necessary to keep the budget for health services at the current level of $941 million and to impose charges for dentures, spectacles, and prescriptions. The Ministry of Health reluctantly agreed. So did most of the ministers serving on a special committee that Attlee had appointed to review the cost of health services. Bevan was the outstanding

---

[31]   This and the next three paragraphs in the text are based on the following accounts: Williams, *Gaitskell*, 249–62; Kenneth O. Morgan, *Labour in Power, 1945–1951* (Oxford, England, 1984), 441–61; Henry Pelling, *The Labour Governments, 1945–1951* (New York, 1984), 248–50; and Michael Foot, *Aneurin Bevan: A Biography*, Vol. 2 (London, 1973), 319–39. For an interesting firsthand account, see also Williams, *Gaitskell Diary*, 238–59.

exception, although he later won a measure of support from Ernest Bevin, who had been forced by ill health to give up the Foreign Office for the less taxing post of lord privy seal. At a meeting of the Cabinet on March 22, just days before his death, Bevin proposed a compromise that would raise the ceiling on health expenditures to $960 million, eliminate the levy on prescriptions, but retain the charges on eyeglasses and dentures. The majority supported the compromise, Gaitskell included. Bevan and Wilson did not. Both men devoted themselves instead to overturning the decision when the Cabinet reconvened for two long and tortuous meetings on April 9. Bevan repeated his earlier charges. He charged his opponents with caving in to American pressure and with devising a defense plan that cost more than Britain could afford. He accused Gaitskell of dismantling the "welfare state" in favor of a warfare state, branded the charges on false teeth and spectacles a "serious breach of Socialist principles," and threatened to resign if the outcome went against him.[32] Gaitskell delivered a similar ultimatum, whereupon Attlee sided with the chancellor and a divided Cabinet voted to reaffirm the decision of March 22.

The following day, April 10, Gaitskell delivered his budget speech to the House of Commons. The budget envisioned another increase in defense expenditures, to be covered by eliminating previous budget surpluses, curbing personal consumption, and raising taxes. It would not reduce the previous level of social expenditures. But neither would it provide for much expansion, which meant an effective reduction in light of rising costs. Even then, the level of expenditures would be maintained by imposing charges on false teeth and eyeglasses. Bevan listened silently and red-faced to Gaitskell's speech, stormed out of the Commons immediately thereafter, and quit the government less than two weeks later. Wilson followed suit, as did John Freeman, parliamentary secretary to the Ministry of Supply.

No one would claim that the Labour government broke down on the miserable issues of false teeth and spectacles. The new charges were expected to raise no more than $60 million of additional revenue in a full year, barely $32 million in fiscal year 1951–2. At stake were larger issues summed up in Bevan's resignation speech of April 23, in a broadside issued earlier by the left-wing journal *Tribune*, and in a pamphlet entitled *One Way Only* subsequently published by so-called Bevanites on the back bench of the Labour Party. The *Tribune* attacked Gaitskell as a latter-day Philip Snowden. It said the new budget was taking the Labour government down the same road its predecessor had trod in 1931. Bevan accused his former colleagues of being "dragged behind the wheels of American diplomacy." He denounced the budget figures as the "arithmetic of Bedlam," said the charges on health services amounted to cracks in the dike of the welfare state, and claimed the dike would burst unless government relieved the

---

[32]   Bevan quoted in Morgan, *Labour in Power*, 450, 449.

pressure of mounting defense expenditures. The Bevanites repeated these accusations, along with the rest of Bevan's litany, in *One Way Only*. The pamphlet played down the Soviet threat and attacked the tendency, in Britain and the United States, to seek military rather than economic and political solutions to outstanding problems. This tendency, it said, was feeding a fantastic arms race that actually increased the danger of world war. It was also generating inflation, reducing social expenditures, and widening political cleavages, not only between rich and poor in Western Europe but also between developed and underdeveloped countries. These trends posed a far greater threat than Soviet aggression to economic growth and political stability, at least according to the Bevanites, who urged the Labour government to curb the arms race, redirect Western Europe's resources into the war against poverty, and apply the doctrine of fair shares to the world at large.[33]

If the budget battle caused a serious rift in the Labour Party, the gloomy economic news that followed only widened the breach and gave the Tories a leg up in the election of October. It had become clear as early as July that personal consumption was increasing, contrary to expectations. Competition for resources between the civilian and military sectors drove the price index up still further and led inevitably to the collapse of the Labour government's policy of wage restraint. Trade-union unrest opened new rifts in the Labour Party, as did debates over the future of the nationalization program, while the upward pressure on wages, the raw material shortages, and the jump in dollar purchases by the rest of the sterling area all combined to fuel a rampant inflation, a substantial trade deficit, and a serious drain on Britain's reserves. These economic developments, which eventually led to cutbacks in the defense program, vindicated the Bevanites and sharpened the attacks of Conservative Party leaders who had earlier promised to "harry the life out" of the government. "The storm is blowing up harder," Gaitskell had confided to his diary as early as February 1951. The "general feeling is that we should suffer a pretty heavy defeat if there was to be an Election now." The election came later, in October, but Gaitskell's prediction proved right: The Conservatives captured a majority and the Labour government resigned.[34]

The problems that divided the Labour government and set the stage for its defeat went beyond the realm of economic policy. They included major issues of diplomacy as well, most notably the direction of American policy in Korea, the question of Germany's rearmament, and the decision by the government in Iran to nationalize the Anglo-Iranian Oil Company. In ad-

[33] Bevan's resignation speech is quoted at length in Foot, *Bevan*, 336–9. See also Morgan, *Labour in Power*, 454; and Foot, *Bevan*, 344–6.

[34] Pelling, *Labour Governments*, 247; and Williams, *Gaitskell Diary*, 229. See also Morgan, *Labour in Power*, 435–41, 456–60, 477–80; Pelling, *Labour Governments*, 237–40, 246–7, 259; and Williams, *Gaitskell Diary*, 266–8, 275, 289–90. For American reports on the British economic crisis, see *FRUS, 1951*, 4:952–61.

dition to setting a dangerous precedent with potential ramifications elsewhere, Iran's decision could weaken Britain's strategic position in the Middle East, cut off a major source of nondollar oil, and worsen an already serious drain on the Treasury's reserves. It divided the Labour government into two broad factions, one calling for a diplomatic settlement, the other for a show of force. It also threatened to drive a wedge between the British and their allies in Washington, where policymakers were loath to see an Anglo–Iranian conflict that could open the door to Soviet expansion in the area of the Persian Gulf.[35]

The German negotiations were a bed of roses with many thorns. The new year saw important strides toward the reintegration of West Germany into Western Europe, which the Truman administration still saw as one of the keys to containment. The Allied occupying powers gave the Federal Republic control over its foreign affairs, officially terminated the state of war with Germany, and further reduced the restrictions on German industry. They also abandoned some of the powers reserved under the Occupation Statute and opened negotiations with the government in Bonn to replace the statute with a contractual agreement more appropriate to the Federal Republic's growing autonomy. In addition, the Adenauer government conducted negotiations with the Allied High Commission regarding Germany's military integration into NATO and with the European NATO countries regarding the Pleven Plan for a European Defense Community (EDC) that would include German units. The first set of negotiations produced the "Petersberg Plan," which looked to the integration of twelve German divisions into a NATO force. The second set, that for the EDC, opened in Paris in February and received a boost five months later when the American government reversed course, threw its weight behind the EDC concept, and urged the negotiators to mesh this concept with the Petersberg Plan.[36]

At the same time, however, the German negotiations strained political coalitions and provoked new controversies among the Western powers. Despite the pressure exerted by Washington, the EDC negotiators had failed to reach agreement by the end of 1951. The talks had stalled on a number of controversial issues. The negotiators could not agree on the size of the German units to be included in a European army or on the level at which they should be integrated. Nor could they agree on the division of financial responsibilities involved and the powers of the supranational political institutions that would preside over the community. These differences pointed up again how difficult it was to reconcile national ambitions with supranational goals on terms that were politically acceptable to participating governments. The Germans wanted full equality in both the EDC and NATO.

---

[35] Acheson, *Present at the Creation*, 505–11; Pelling, *Labour Governments*, 251–2; Morgan, *Labour in Power*, 465–71; and Williams, *Gaitskell Diary*, 259–65.

[36] Acheson, *Present at the Creation*, 557–9, 585–6, 590; McLellan, *Acheson*, 347–9, 355–63; and Stebbins, *United States in World Affairs*, 1951, 61–73, 344–53.

They demanded financial support for Germany's rearmament and resolution of the Saar dispute, as well as a contractual agreement under which the Allies would remove the constraints on Germany's sovereignty and abandon virtually all economic and security controls. The German negotiators thought these and other concessions would be needed to sell rearmament at home, where the whole idea divided popular opinion and threatened Adenauer's coalition. The Social Democrats were bitterly opposed to Germany's rearmament. So was a large bloc of pacifists. Incited in part by the Communist-inspired World Peace Council, pacifists worried that rearmament might trigger a Soviet attack or wreck the chances for unifying their homeland.[37]

Similar constraints operated on other governments. Although the French government had invented the EDC concept and had made numerous concessions to the Germans, there were definite limits to how far it could go without alienating large segments of French opinion that remained virulently opposed to Germany's rearmament. This limit had been reached by the end of 1951. There were even signs that the French wanted to back away from earlier concessions. They would not consent to a military high command in West Germany or to the integration of autonomous German units into the European force. Nor would they join without Anglo–American military guarantees against Germany's withdrawal. They also continued to insist on supranational political institutions to regulate the proposed community, even though this idea went much further than other delegations were prepared to go. The Benelux and Italian delegates were unwilling to see their military forces merged under a supranational authority that might be dominated by France. The British had been reluctant to embrace the EDC concept and were disappointed when the Americans threw their support behind the French project. Although the Cabinet endorsed the idea at a meeting in September 1951, it was not inclined to back this endorsement by joining a supranational authority, moving NATO's headquarters from London to Paris, or giving military guarantees of the kind demanded by the French.[38]

In addition, the British were as put off as the French by Washington's incessant pressure for Germany's speedy rearmament and just as divided over how to respond. One faction of the Cabinet, led by Aneurin Bevan and Hugh Dalton (who "hates the Germans"), opposed Germany's rearmament in principle. Another, including Hugh Gaitskell and Ernest Bevin, supported the American position but with strong reservations. They wanted Germany's rearmament to proceed at a slower pace than the Americans considered necessary. They were also far more anxious than their colleagues in Washington to assuage the French, placate the Social Democrats in Germany, and avoid provoking the Russians. Gaitskell and Bevin eventually

[37]   See the sources cited in note 36.
[38]   In addition to the sources cited in note 36, see Morgan, *Labour in Power*, 463–4.

prevailed over their Cabinet opponents. But victory came at a steep price. In this case, as in the budget battles, it divided the government and added another grievance to the list on which the Bevanites would capitalize in the years ahead.[39]

As the preceding discussion suggests, the acrimonious debates over Germany's military reintegration and over the cost of national defense had a divisive impact on the political parties and governing coalitions that had dominated Western Europe and the United States since the start of the Marshall Plan. Gaitskell recorded these developments in his diary, writing despairingly of the bitter controversies that split the British Cabinet and of the anti-Americanism that led certain quarters of the Labour Party "to oppose a lot of things which the Americans want to do." Gaitskell made this comment in connection with a cabinet discussion of the German question. But he could have been talking about similar discussions in the French government or about comparable debates over the cost of Western Europe's defense – debates that brought forth from Bevan and like-minded critics the steady complaint that peace and prosperity were being squashed under the "wheels of American diplomacy."[40]

Nothing contributed more to anti-American sentiment, or to the strains that racked the North Atlantic community and the participating governments alike, than what the Europeans saw as the ruinous course of American policy in Korea. Led by Britain, the European NATO countries had given strong support to the United States in the weeks following the outbreak of fighting in Korea. But support began to fade when United Nations troops under General Douglas MacArthur launched their fateful march into North Korea. The offensive raised the prospect of drawing China into the conflict. This possibility was a matter of great concern to European leaders, who worried that a wider war would undercut the American commitment to Europe and alienate nationalist elements in Asia, notably the Indians, who had joined the British in urging a conciliatory policy toward the new regime in Beijing. The Chinese intervention of late November heightened these fears, as did the sabre-rattling of General MacArthur, the demands for total victory coming from the conservative bloc on Capitol Hill, and the intimation by President Truman that atomic bombs might be used to end the conflict. A mood close to paranoia swept across Western Europe. British Prime Minister Attlee promptly left for Washington to convey his own concerns and those of other European leaders with whom he conferred.[41]

[39] Williams, *Gaitskell Diary*, 232–3. See also Morgan, *Labour in Power*, 430–1; and Williams, *Gaitskell*, 245–6.
[40] Williams, *Gaitskell Diary*, 232–3.
[41] Bullock, *Bevin*, 791–5, 821–2; Morgan, *Labour in Power*, 422–7; Pelling, *Labour Governments*, 242–5; and McLellan, *Acheson*, 296. See also Memorandum of Conversation by the First Secretary of the Embassy in the United Kingdom, January 4,

The Truman-Attlee talks of late December ended without resolving major issues of controversy. Truman and Acheson said that neither they nor Congress could tolerate a policy of containing communism in Western Europe while appeasing it in Asia. They turned a deaf ear to Attlee's proposals to recognize the new government in Beijing and to open negotiations with the Chinese regarding Korea, Formosa, and other outstanding issues. Nor would they give Attlee and other NATO leaders greater control over the direction of American military strategy, any more than the British would give in to American pressure for even faster rearmament in Western Europe.

Nevertheless, the talks cleared the air somewhat. Attlee won assurances regarding the use of atomic weapons and had other reasons to believe that American leaders would pursue a more cautious policy in Korea. The two sides also discussed the critical shortage of raw materials and the so-called Spofford Plan, under which German troops would be integrated into NATO. The British, who still wanted to get "out of the queue with Denmark and Luxembourg," came away from the talks reassured. Acheson and Truman had seemed to accept the notion of a special Anglo–American relationship and the view that Britain should be the linchpin in a North Atlantic alliance. Acheson told Attlee that Britain was "the only ally on whom they could rely." Attlee cabled Bevin that Britain had been "lifted out of the European queue." Britain was being treated as a real partner, he said, "unequal no doubt in power but still equal in counsel."[42]

This verdict helped to steady opinion in Britain temporarily, but in less than a month Anglo–American relations would be strained again by a nasty dispute involving the "brand-China" resolution that American policymakers introduced in the United Nations General Assembly. The resolution would condemn China as the aggressor in Korea and authorize a blockade and other sanctions against her. Virtually all British leaders worried that such a course would wreck the chance of containing the conflict and plunge the United States, and perhaps its allies as well, into a larger Asian war. The "international outlook gets gloomier and gloomier," Gaitskell wrote in his diary. The Americans talked "of a limited war but we all feel there is no such thing, and the worst of it is that the Chinese would probably retaliate, if [a] blockade is organized against them or if the Americans bomb them, by occupying Hong Kong and moving south through Indo-China to Malaya." The "awful dilemma," said Gaitskell, "is that if we cannot restrain

1951, and Walter S. Gifford, United States Ambassador to the United Kingdom, tel. to Acheson, January 20, 1951, *FRUS, 1951*, 4:891–4, 894–9.

[42] Holmes tel. to Acheson, December 3, 1950, *FRUS, 1950*, 3:1698–1703; and Attlee tel. to Bevin, December 10, 1950, FO 800/517/US/50/57. See also Morgan, *Labour in Power*, 428–30; Bullock, *Bevin*, 822–3; McLellan, *Acheson*, 298–9; Donovan, *Tumultuous Years*, 316–18; and Acheson, *Present at the Creation*, 480–5. The details of the Truman–Attlee talks can be followed in *FRUS, 1950*, 3:1706–88.

the Americans then we have to go in with them in China, which nobody wants, or desert them," which could have "very serious consequences in their participating in European defense."[43]

The Cabinet divided over which of these options to take. Bevin, who did not like the brand-China resolution, was nevertheless resigned to support it rather than risk the Anglo–American partnership on which much of his grand design was based. He wrote Attlee: "We have to imagine what it would be like to live in a world with a hostile Communist bloc, an uncooperative America, a Commonwealth pulled in two directions and a disillusioned Europe deprived of American support."[44] Gaitskell agreed, and the two men initially won Cabinet support for a policy that aimed to soften the American resolution "but in the last [resort] to accept it."[45] At a Cabinet meeting on January 24, however – the very meeting at which Aneurin Bevan launched his powerful attack on Britain's defense plan – the majority reversed course and agreed to stand against the Americans. Bevin was in the hospital and his minister of state, Kenneth Younger, spoke strongly against the American resolution, quite contrary to the views of the Foreign Office. Nor would Younger and others agree when Gaitskell proposed that Britain merely abstain from the United Nations vote. The discussion was adjourned to the following day.

Gaitskell used the interval to mobilize support from the Foreign Office, from Ambassador Franks in Washington, and from other officials, all of whom agreed with the chancellor that a vote against the Americans would "have the most fatal consequences on Anglo–American relations." It would "enormously strengthen the anti-European block in the U.S.A.," Gaitskell told William Strang of the Foreign Office. It might even lead the Americans to withdraw from Europe, "which would, in my opinion, be the end for us." Armed with these opinions and threats of resignation, Gaitskell met privately with Attlee and won his support just hours before the Cabinet reconvened on January 26. At the meeting itself, the prime minister overruled objections from Bevan, Dalton, and other dissenters and the Cabinet reaffirmed the position that Bevin and Gaitskell had staked out earlier. The outcome was aided immeasurably by hints that a United Nations compromise was in the offing. As it turned out, the Americans eventually agreed to modify their resolution along lines that made it possible to win votes from Britain and the other NATO countries.[46]

43   Williams, *Gaitskell Diary*, 225–6.
44   Bevin cited in Bullock, *Bevin*, 826.
45   Williams, *Gaitskell Diary*, 229.
46   Gaitskell recorded the story in some detail in his diary. See Williams, *Gaitskell Diary*, 229–32. See also Acheson tel. to Gifford, January 27, 1951, Gifford tel. to Acheson, January 29, 1951, and the United States Attaché to the United Kingdom tel. to Acheson, January 29, 1951, *FRUS, 1951*, 4:902–3, 903–5, 906–11; Bullock, *Bevin*, 826–7; Morgan, *Labour in Power*, 431–3; and Foot, *Bevan*, 313–14.

The United Nations compromise, together with Truman's subsequent dismissal of General MacArthur, helped to mollify the Europeans somewhat, but it could not undo the damage already wrought by the Korean War on the North Atlantic alliance and on participating governments. Other sources of tension persisted throughout 1951, most notably those stemming from the costly effort to rebuild Western Europe's defenses at a time when Marshall aid was coming to an end. The problem in this case was how to rearm Western Europe and still preserve the gains in economic and political stability that had been won since 1947. To American leaders, the solution was to be found in Keynesian strategies of economic management and in new initiatives to unify economies, raise productivity, and build corporative patterns of collaboration between business, labor, and government. Even as the ECA neared the end of its history, American recovery planners continued to see these and other elements of the New Deal synthesis as keys to an ever-expanding abundance that would enable the Europeans to have guns and butter in sufficiency. The initiatives that followed are thus important less because of their short-term success than because they point out the persistence of themes that had characterized American policy from the start of the Marshall Plan – just as the response from London highlighted the equally persistent themes in British diplomacy.

IV

In the OEEC, the most recent effort to reconcile civilian and military requirements began in February 1951, six months after Secretary General Robert Marjolin had first sought to refocus the OEEC's work on the economic problems growing out of rearmament. Little had come of this initiative and the pressure for more effective action had begun to mount after China's intervention in Korea. That event had dashed all hopes of a quick settlement in Korea and thus of some abatement in the pace of American and European rearmament. It had become clear that current economic problems, most of which were related to rearmament, would grow worse unless the Western Europeans took remedial action. This was the conclusion coming from Marjolin and others in the OEEC's Secretariat, who were then conducting a major review of economic trends with the aid of John H. Williams, a distinguished American economist with close ties to the Council on Foreign Relations and other private agencies that had long supported the ERP. Marjolin and Williams were particularly concerned about inflationary pressures in the participating countries and Western Europe's deteriorating terms of trade, both of which they blamed on commodity shortages resulting from the American defense buildup and the stockpiling and export-control programs inaugurated by the Truman administration. They thought the situation serious enough to call to the attention of policymakers in Washington and proposed, for this purpose, a special OEEC memorandum urging the Truman administration to dampen worldwide commodity prices by curbing the Pentagon's buying spree, relaxing export controls, and restraining civilian consumption.[47]

In addition, Marjolin had convinced himself that "European morale [would] not stand for a large rearmament program" unless the OEEC captured the popular imagination with a bold new program based on "the conception of European unity" and including a "social charter." The program he had in mind would reduce tariffs, further liberalize trade, harness inflation, raise productivity, and redistribute wealth on a more equitable basis. Although a "painless rearmament" was impossible, Marjolin and his colleagues thought that a European program based on these initiatives would at least limit the sacrifices involved. It would also raise hopes of a brighter future, inspire greater support for the rearmament program, and make that program look more like a European than an American initiative. Marjolin and other European officials put these arguments to the British in early February, stressing in their brief that Britain must become "the spokesman of Europe in America." Only Britain, they said, had the clout to influence American policy on such matters as the stockpiling of critical materials and the pace of rearmament.[48]

It is difficult to imagine what the Europeans were thinking when they asked the British to take the lead in such a program. It was as if amnesia had wiped all memory of past British policy from their minds, only to have it rudely restored by Whitehall's response. The British saw the need to improve production and they were just as anxious as the Europeans to avert shortages, control prices, and defend the balance of payments. Nor were they averse to taking up these matters with the Americans. But they doubted the OEEC's ability to influence policy in Washington and the wisdom of urging the American government to curb civilian consumption at a time when many European countries were reluctant to make similar sacrifices on behalf of rearmament. Indeed, British leaders were less inclined than most of their OEEC colleagues to slow the pace of rearmament and extremely reluctant to deal with its economic impacts through an OEEC program. Using that body would promote the French ideal of European unity over the British vision of a North Atlantic community. It also would give the OEEC greater authority to regulate national policies, including trade and tariff policies, and this gain would come at the expense of Britain's economic sovereignty and system of imperial preferences. The British urged Marjolin to reconsider his proposals. They said that national efforts to increase production were already underway and that other problems were being dealt with through the GATT negotiations, the International Materials Conference, and the North Atlantic Council.[49]

[47] Hall-Patch letter to Berthoud, February 4, 1951, T232/230/EEC78/11/07.
[48] Rumbler minute, February 7, 1951, FO 371, 94135, M107.
[49] Makins Record of Conversation, January 16, 1951, and Makins Record of Conversation, January 17, 1951, FO 371, 94135, M107; and Hall-Patch letter to Berthoud,

But Marjolin thought that the economic crisis facing the West was as great as the one that had produced the Marshall Plan; it required cooperative action on a scale comparable to the Paris Conference of 1947.[50] He therefore ignored the advice coming from London and issued a major paper in late February entitled "Immediate Tasks of Economic Cooperation between the Members of OEEC, the United States, and Canada." The paper identified inflation, trade deficits, and raw material shortages as the most serious economic difficulties confronting participating countries. Of these, Marjolin said, only the last had been tackled through the International Materials Conference established in Washington. Inflation and Europe's worsening trade balance still loomed as major problems that must be addressed lest they "endanger the social and political fabric of the whole western world, . . . undo much of the recovery which has been achieved, [and] frustrate the rearmament effort itself." To avert such dangers, Marjolin urged member governments to control raw material allocations, restrict credit, expand exports, and increase production, particularly in such bottleneck areas as coal, steel, and foodstuffs. He also wanted these measures coordinated on an intra-European basis, the better to safeguard existing payments relationships, protect gains in the field of trade liberalization, and utilize existing resources efficiently. The whole program, Marjolin told his colleagues, must raise the overall level of European output dramatically if participating governments were going to combat inflation, defend the balance of payments, and guarantee social and political stability.[51]

American and European leaders discussed Marjolin's paper at meetings in February and March. The British gave tepid support to a study of current economic problems. But they reserved their position when it came to concrete action, particularly in the area of intra-European tariffs, where adjustments might open the British economy to external pressures or collide with the system of imperial preferences. The French wanted to liberalize trade and coordinate national economic controls. Together with the Dutch and the Italians, they also saw current economic problems as "common problems" that required "collective action" in a "common forum." The Europeans left no doubt that the OEEC was the forum they had in mind; the French went so far as to urge Marjolin to couple his paper with an OEEC "program of concrete action." ECA officials took the same position. They were "extremely favorable" to Marjolin's paper and considered the OEEC perfectly competent to coordinate national efforts to restrain inflation, boost production, and stimulate exports.[52]

February 4, 1951, Berthoud letter to E. A. Hitchman of the Treasury, February 6, 1951, Robert Hall, Director, Economic Section, Cabinet Office, letter to Hitchman, February 7, 1951, Berthoud letters to Hall-Patch, February 8 and 21, 1951, T232/230/EEC78/11/07.

50   Katz repto 880 to Foster, February 23, 1951, ECA Files, box 30.
51   Katz tel. to Foster, February 22, 1951, *FRUS, 1951,* 4:5–12.
52   Hall-Patch tel. to FO, February 22, 1951, T232/230/EEC78/11/07; and Foster torep

The problem was that the OEEC could not act without the support and cooperation of NATO, which retained exclusive authority in the field of defense planning and production. In late 1950, it will be recalled, the participating governments had hoped to coordinate the work of these two agencies through the Committee of Twelve, established in Paris and made up of NATO delegates who also represented their governments in the OEEC. But the committee had not been particularly successful. The OEEC had withered as rearmament played a larger role in the economic policies of member states and the Western Europeans had become convinced that a new arrangement would be needed to coordinate civilian and military requirements effectively. In their talks with the British earlier, Marjolin and other European leaders had complained bitterly about the "inanition" of the OEEC.[53] Similar complaints and calls for a new arrangement had come from Washington, where the State Department and the ECA envisioned a "*de facto* consolidation" of the OEEC and NATO. To achieve this consolidation, thinking in both agencies revolved around proposals to make Paris the permanent headquarters of the North Atlantic Council, the Council's Defense Production Board, or the Finance and Economic Board that was then being organized.[54]

The British had the same concerns about these proposals as they had about Marjolin's bold new program. They would neither move the Defense Production Board from London to Paris nor make Paris the permanent seat of the NATO Council. The furthest they would go was a decision to locate the Finance and Economic Board in the French capital. The Americans had reached a similar decision in March. They had opened negotiations with the OEEC looking to a working relationship under which personnel and information from the OEEC's Secretariat would be made available to the new board and Secretary General Marjolin would act as liaison between the two agencies. The British continued to delay progress, however. They refused to appoint a delegate of real stature to the board, as proposed by the Americans. Nor were they happy when the French nominated as chairman an economist whose commitment to "classical" economic theory did not square with the socialist doctrine of the Labour government. In American eyes, the negotiations revealed again the reluctance of the Labour government to support any scheme that would give central institutions

1313 to Katz, February 24, 1951, ECA Files, box 84. See also Acting ECA Administrator Paul Porter torep 1336 to Katz, February 26, 1951, ECA Files, box 30.

[53] Rumbler minute, February 7, 1951, FO 371, 94135, M107. See also Katz tel. to Foster, February 22, 1951, *FRUS, 1951*, 4:5–12.

[54] Acheson tel. to Charles Spofford, United States Deputy Representative on the North Atlantic Council, December 16, 1950, *FRUS, 1950*, 3:682–5. See also Summaries of Secretary's Daily Meetings, December 14, 1950, February 13 and March 6, 1951, RG 59, Secretary's Daily Meetings, box 1. As the last documents point out, the Pentagon generally opposed moving the NATO Council from London to Paris.

greater authority over the British economy or spoil their plan to build NATO into an "Anglo–American partnership with others also participating."[55]

For similar reasons, the British raised the strongest possible objections to a Swedish proposal that would merge the OEEC and the Council of Europe into a single body with extensive economic and political powers. The Foreign Office rejected the proposal in February, subsequently discouraged the OEEC from investigating it, and insisted again that international cooperation be organized through ad hoc arrangements appropriate to each task. The British took the same position in opposing a French proposal, launched in the Council of Europe, for a high authority that would integrate European agricultural markets and reach decisions by majority vote. In both cases, they reasserted the empirical approach and stopped short of what many in the OEEC and the Council of Europe had in mind. As a result, according to Dirk Stikker, the British were increasingly regarded as the major "stumbling block" to European cooperation and were "losing ground accordingly on the continent."[56]

This perception may help to explain why British leaders eventually supported the American plan for closer liaison between the OEEC and NATO's Finance and Economic Board. The plan was modest by comparison with the Swedish proposal and might actually undercut more sweeping schemes that posed a real danger to British interests. The State Department and the ECA had also eased the way with important assurances embodied in a telegram to American officials in London, who promptly conveyed its contents to the Foreign Office. The telegram began by assuming support for cooperative arrangements that did not put Britain on the "slippery slope toward union with the continent." It then went on to distinguish between Western European "market integration," which the United States supported, and political federation, which it did not. Until "the North Atlantic framework had been further developed," it said, a Western European union without Great Britain would only "increase the risk both of German domination and of encouragement of a 'third force.'" For these reasons, and because the most pressing problems were those related to the defense effort, the

---

[55] Katz repto 1522 to Foster, April 5, 1951, ECA Files, box 30. See also Katz reptos 1387, 1605, 1833, 1840, 2017, and 2440 to Foster, March 30, April 10 and 21 (2), and May 1 and 25, 1951, ECA Files, box 30.

[56] British Embassy, The Hague, "Notes of a Conversation with the Minister of Foreign Affairs," April 4, 1951, FO 371, 94136, M107. On the Swedish proposal, see W. Walton Butterworth, United States Ambassador to Sweden, tel. to Acheson, January 5, 1951, *FRUS, 1951*, 4:1–4; CP (51) 101, Foreign Secretary Herbert Morrison, "Swedish Proposal for the Amalgamation of the Organisation for European Economic Co-operation and the Council of Europe," April 19, 1951, PREM 8/1434; CM (51) 30th Conclusion, April 23, 1951, CAB 128/19; and Katz repto 1977 to Foster, April 28, 1951, ECA Files, box 30. On the French proposal, see George Andrews, United States Consul at Strasbourg, tel. to Acheson, February 28, 1951, *FRUS, 1951*, 4:13–17.

"primary United States interests" would be "in the North Atlantic Treaty Organization," in "those functions of the OEEC which directly support the attainment of NATO objectives," and in "ad hoc" arrangements to coordinate the work of these bodies.[57]

Although the British already knew that economic integration was much higher on the American agenda than political federation, it is nonetheless easy to understand why they were pleased by this elaboration of policy. The State Department and the ECA had reaffirmed the principle of British exceptionalism, put the North Atlantic community over the goal of European *political* union, and adopted the empirical approach to relations between the OEEC and NATO. Slight wonder that the Foreign Office could conclude that British and American thinking was running along similar lines or that it could now throw support behind the plan for cooperation between the OEEC and NATO's Finance and Economic Board. By mid-June, the Board had been established in Paris, national representatives had been appointed, and the neutral countries had agreed to link the OEEC and the Board through the exchange of personnel and information.[58]

The new arrangement facilitated a closer coordination of the defense and civilian aspects of European economic policy. So did the participation of a top ECA official in meetings of the Finance and Economic Board.[59] Together with the ECA's involvement in the work of the ISAC and the OEEC's membership on the central group of the International Materials Conference, these developments completed the first round of organizational adjustments growing out of the rearmament program. On the European side, they also set the stage for new initiatives to integrate markets, boost production, and reconcile rearmament and recovery imperatives. This had been Marjolin's goal in February, and the subsequent elections in France and Italy had only strengthened his conviction that initiatives of this sort were necessary.

The same view emerged from another round of meetings between top American and European policymakers in July 1951. According to Ambassador Milton Katz, who had succeeded Harriman as special representative, those involved were deeply distressed by the "morale and psychological" crisis that gripped Europe. The source of this crisis lay less in specific economic problems than in the fact that NATO's "defense build-up" had assumed a "negative character in [the] minds of Europeans." They saw it "as a kind of castor oil which has to be taken" but worried about its impact on economic stability and living standards. NATO's policies and purposes had to be cast in a more positive light, or so Katz assumed, and this could

---

[57] Summary of State Department telegram given by the U.S. Embassy to the Foreign Office, April 19, 1951, PREM 8/1434.

[58] Private Secretary to the Secretary of State letter to W. Armstrong, Private Secretary to the Chancellor of the Exchequer, April 28, 1951, PREM 8/1434; and Katz repto 3109 to Foster, June 30, 1951, ECA Files, box 31.

[59] ECA, *Thirteenth Report to Congress*, 11.

be done by reminding the Europeans that military and economic strength were "mutually consistent" and "mutually necessary." According to this line of argument, military security required a temporary diversion of Western Europe's resources from civilian to defense production. But security against aggression would guarantee investment security as well and the expanded production created would be used to enhance Western Europe's "economic strength and standard of living" once military requirements had been satisfied.[60]

Marjolin made some of the same points in a talk with British officials in London on July 5, as did he, Stikker, and other European leaders when they met in Paris on July 11 with Ambassador Katz and British Chancellor of the Exchequer Gaitskell. In their view, rearmament had not encouraged production but rather discouraged it. Workers were reluctant to work harder unless "assured of some amelioration in their standard of living." Investors refused to invest without guarantees that additional capacity could be utilized once the stimulus of rearmament had been removed. The result was a "general apathy" that made it virtually impossible to strengthen Western Europe's defense without seriously compromising civilian investment and consumption. According to Stikker, the diversion of resources to defense, together with raw material shortages, higher taxes, and inflationary pressures, already had fueled charges that rearmament meant "all guns and no butter." It had led to a virulent anti-Americanism in Western Europe, played into the hands of the Communists, and set the stage for a major political crisis, of which the French and Italian elections were harbingers. Stikker and others agreed with Katz that it was physically possible to expand production sufficiently to meet civilian and military requirements. But there was no "will" to do so, nor would there be without a dramatic political initiative and a concrete plan to raise production by 25 percent over a five-year period. As Katz told the meeting in Paris on July 11, a plan like this would permit "guns and butter" over the long term, thereby alleviating the despair that paralyzed workers and fed Communist propaganda.[61]

As had been true since the start of the Marshall Plan, economic growth was the American solution to the problems that afflicted Western Europe. But despite what seemed to be a general consensus on the productionist philosophy, there were important differences over where to sound the clarion call for greater productivity and over the specific economic program to be prescribed. Keynesians in the ECA had been urging the Europeans to

[60] Katz repto 3411 to Foster, July 16, 1951, ECA Files, box 31.
[61] UK del. to the OEEC, "Note of Discussion at a Dinner Party Given by Dr. Stikker on July 11th 1951," July 15, 1951, FO 371, 94136, M107. See also, in addition to the document cited in note 60, F. C. Everson, "European Productivity: The Stikker Plan of Action," July 2, 1951, FO 371, 94155, M1026; and Treasury memorandum, "Note of a Meeting with Monsieur Marjolin in Sir Edwin Plowden's Room, Treasury, Thursday, 5th July 1951," July 5, 1951, T232/231/EEC78/11/09.

adopt a program similar to the one they were trying to implement in the United States. They endorsed government controls over prices, wages, and allocations so long as these controls were coordinated on a transnational basis. They considered budgetary deficits permissible if productivity increased at an acceptable rate. They wanted strict fiscal and monetary policies to curb inflation, but they also warned that an "exclusive preoccupation with the tightness of the budget and inflationary danger" could discourage growth, lead to unemployment, and alienate workers at a time when their cooperation in government programs to increase production was more important than ever. As the Keynesians saw it, moreover, fiscal prudence need not preclude "comprehensive social programs" to combat "internal aggression in the field of labor."[62]

New social programs were hardly necessary in the Scandinavian countries or Great Britain, where the ECA faced the opposite problem of persuading public officials to curtail social expenditures for the sake of productive investment. Ambassador Douglas had repeatedly urged that ERP aid be limited to amounts that would force the Labour government to curb what he saw as extravagant public expenditures. He was therefore pleased with the decision to terminate Marshall aid to Great Britain in late 1950, claiming that additional aid would only make "it easier for [the] British Government to avoid taking steps, including budgetary non-defense retrenchment, which I consider fundamentally essential to [the] long-range economic stability of [the] UK."[63] But while American leaders attacked the British from the Right, they mounted a Keynesian critique of public policy in France, West Germany, and Italy. They complained the governments there were too concerned with the balance of payments, put stable currencies ahead of economic growth, adhered to antiquated tax systems, or neglected social programs. In France, the ECA even threatened to tie counterpart funding to the development of a positive social program, calling in particular for larger public expenditures on low-cost housing for defense workers.[64]

Sir Edmund Hall-Patch captured the reformist streak in the ECA's policy in a letter to Roger Makins on August 6, just as European and American policymakers were negotiating the details of the production plan that Marjolin had proposed. Hall-Patch had been the only British guest at an American dinner party in Paris the previous evening. All of the "American swells" were there, including General Eisenhower and Milton Katz. Paul Hoffman, who now headed the Ford Foundation, was also on hand. So was his deputy,

---

[62] C. Tyler Wood, Deputy U.S. Special Representative, repto 431 to Foster, January 26, 1951, ECA Files, box 29. See also Foster torep 6849 to Katz, August 11, 1950, ECA Files, box 67; and Hoffman torep 7999 to Katz, September 16, 1950, ECA Files; box 68.

[63] Douglas tel. to Acheson, October 24, 1950, *FRUS, 1950*, 3:1684–5.

[64] Foster toreps 193, 739, and 624 to Katz, January 9, 14, and 25, 1951, ECA Files, box 83; and Wood repto 431 to Foster, January 26, 1951, ECA Files, box 29.

Robert Hutchins, former president of the University of Chicago and, with Hoffman, one of the founders of the American Policy Commission, a group of academic and business leaders established in 1941 to promote the sort of progressive public policies later associated with the CED. Dinner talk turned on the "low state of European morale," which the Americans attributed to the "most glaring social injustices." The British earned high marks for their progressive social policies. "We are supposed to be 'doing our bit,' " Hall-Patch reported. But the French, Germans, and Italians ended up at the bottom of the American scorecard. The Americans thought they "had been led down the garden path" in these countries, particularly in France, and were "fully resolved that 'social justice' must figure largely in any future programme" financed by the United States. They believed, Hall-Patch concluded, "that really strenuous efforts... from the masses cannot be expected unless 'social justice' figured as part and parcel" of the OEEC's plan to raise production.[65]

ECA policymakers made their views perfectly clear in the negotiations leading up to the European production plan. At the meeting in Paris on July 11 and in the drafting process that followed, they urged language that expressed confidence in Europe's ability to reconcile rearmament and recovery, portrayed defense expenditures as an "antidote" to the fear of Soviet aggression, and blamed this fear for impeding economic progress. But they also called for production targets, particularly in such bottleneck areas as coal, steel, and electrical power; for harmonizing national economic controls and investment decisions; for additional progress in the field of trade liberalization; and for other measures to increase production and integrate markets. In their view, moreover, European governments should address the serious shortage of housing for industrial workers and pledge progressive tax policies and other economic reforms to correct the maldistribution of national income. In addition to stimulating growth over the long term, reforms of this sort had the short-term advantage of distributing the economic burden of rearmament more equitably, rallying workers behind the defense effort, and strengthening governments against political challenges on the Right and the Left.

Despite Marjolin's call for a "social charter," only the British seemed enamored of the economic reforms that appealed to Keynesians in the ECA. The other Europeans were fixated on the problem of inflation, which they said discouraged investment, led to trade restrictions, and eroded living standards. They stressed the need to protect savings and the importance of American aid to stabilize currencies and defend the balance of payments. The Italians took this position, arguing that such a program must come before governments tackled the housing problem or the maldistribution of income. The French tended to agree, although they also joined the Americans

---

[65] Hall-Patch letter to Makins, August 6, 1951, FO 371, 94136, M107.

in urging further efforts to reduce tariffs, coordinate national policies, and devise a collective program to raise production by 5 percent per annum over a five-year period. The British objected to this part of the plan. They said that economic coordination smacked of cartelization, that tariff matters should be left to the GATT negotiations, and that economic cooperation should be organized on an intergovernmental basis.[66]

As the talks in Paris suggest, whereas European–American differences centered on the merits of economic reform, those between the British and their American and European colleagues revolved around issues as old as the recovery program. The British were reluctant to support a strictly European initiative launched through the OEEC. They claimed that current economic problems stemmed directly from the rearmament effort and could be addressed only "within the N.A.T.O. context." In their opinion, NATO also provided a far better vehicle than the OEEC for influencing the Truman administration's stockpiling and export-control programs, both of which contributed markedly to inflationary pressures in the participating countries and to Western Europe's deteriorating terms of trade. Behind these arguments lay the deep-seated reluctance of British officials to reconstitute the OEEC as a "major economic forum" or to subject themselves to a comprehensive plan that would reduce tariffs and set national production targets. Such a plan implied a substantial degree of supranational direction and economic integration, neither of which was acceptable to policymakers in London. Nor did the Labour government think it possible to raise production in certain British industries by more than 3 or 4 percent a year or to eliminate trade controls at a time when they might be needed to defend the balance of payments.[67]

Little of what the British had to say won support in France, Italy, West Germany, and other continental countries, where there was almost uniform support for a comprehensive production plan. What "was needed was action rather than words," explained the French, by which they meant a plan that included production targets for particular industries and pledges of 5 percent growth each year over a five-year period. This kind of plan gave hope of reconciling civilian and military requirements. Anything less, said the Europeans, would do nothing to inspire European opinion. Similar thinking explained their determination to make the OEEC the springboard for action. In Western Europe, they argued, NATO was widely regarded as a "tool of

[66] Wood tel. to Foster, August 7, 1951, *FRUS, 1951*, 4:44–5. See also UK del. to the
     OEEC, "Note of Discussion at a Dinner Party Given by Dr. Stikker on July 11th
     1951," July 15, 1951, FO 371, 94136, M107; and Porter reptos 4074, 4075, 4099,
     4124, 4188, 4218, 4219, and 4243 to Foster, August 18 (2), 20, 21, 23, 25 (2), and
     28, 1951, ECA Files, box 31.
[67] UK del. to the OEEC, "Record of Conversation," July 15, 1951, FO 371, 94136,
     M107; and Berthoud minute, July 27, 1951, FO 371, 94199, M1068. In addition
     to the sources cited in note 68, see UK del. to the OEEC, "Note[s] of Discussion[s]
     on July 12 and 14, 1951," July 15, 1951, FO 371, 94136, M107.

the Pentagon" and as far "too military a forum" to take charge of a production plan that aimed to reconcile civilian and military requirements. A plan launched in that arena would be perceived as an American ploy, not a European initiative, and might actually strengthen "communist minorities" in such countries as France and Italy. Nor did this exhaust the list of European arguments. The Europeans also pointed out that a NATO initiative would exclude West Germany, Sweden, and Switzerland, weaken the OEEC, and wreck the chances for integrating Europe. The French were particularly adamant on the last two points. They apparently saw the European production plan, much as they did the Schuman and Pleven plans, as a device for guaranteeing France's economic and military security within the framework of a unified and supranational system.[68]

This tangled web of arguments tied up the negotiations until late August, at which time the parties finally reached a compromise that came closer to the British than to the French position. The compromise put civilian and military requirements on an equal footing, as both the Americans and the British had wanted, and used flexible language to obfuscate the issue of specific production targets in particular industries. It did not include a detailed production plan or assign a wide range of new tasks to the OEEC. In addition, the French had to publish their demand for a "unitary market" in a separate statement and both they and the Americans reluctantly approved a provision that called for consolidating gains, not additional progress, in the field of trade liberalization. These were concessions to the British, who in turn accepted language mandating a vast expansion of overall production. They also agreed to launch the European initiative in the OEEC, after which it would go to the North Atlantic Council for approval and support. With these details ironed out, the OEEC's Council of Ministers formally issued the "European Manifesto" at a meeting in Paris on August 29, 1951.[69]

---

[68] Hall-Patch tel. to FO, August 16, 1951, and Foreign Office, "Record of a Meeting in Sir Roger Makins' Room, Foreign Office, 1st August 1951, " August 1, 1951, FO 371, 94199, M1068; Hall-Patch tel. to FO, July 28, 1951, T232/231/EEC78/11/09; and Hall-Patch, "Note of Conversation," August 3, 1951, FO 371, 94199, M1068. See also Hall-Patch letter to Makins, July 25, 1951, FO tel. to Hall-Patch, July 27, 1951, UK del. to the Council of Europe, Strasbourg, tel. to FO, August 3, 1951, and FO tel. to Hall-Patch, August 16, 1951, FO 371, 94199, M1068; Hall-Patch tels. (2) to FO, August 20, 1951, FO tel. to Hall-Patch, August 21, 1951, and Berthoud memorandum, "European Initiative," August 23, 1951, FO 371, 94200, M1068; and Berthoud memorandum, "European Initiative," August 25, 1951, FO 371, 94201, M1068.

[69] Berthoud memorandum, "European Initiative," August 30, 1951, FO 371, 94201, M1068. For the American records on the last round of negotiations leading up to the compromise, see *FRUS, 1951*, 4:49–54. For the British records, see FO tel. to Hall-Patch, August 8, 1951, and Hall-Patch tel. to FO, August 16, 1951, FO 371 94199, M1068; Hall-Patch tel. to FO, August 20, 1951, FO tel. to Hall-Patch, August

The manifesto boldly proclaimed a 25 percent expansion of Western Europe's total production as a goal to be achieved over the next five years. This expansion would enable the Europeans to have guns and butter both. Although increments to production would go first to strengthen Western Europe's defenses, the manifesto promised "that the present need for restraint is temporary," that accelerated defense spending would level off, and that "progressively a growing surplus will be available to raise supplies of consumer's goods." To achieve the desired expansion, the manifesto urged participating governments to establish and coordinate production targets, particularly in bottleneck industries, to utilize unemployed manpower in West Germany and Italy, to curb inflationary pressures, and to avoid new restrictions on trade. Because existing resources were limited and the volume of American aid was declining, it focused particular attention on the need to expand production by increasing the productivity of labor. This was the "most essential" element in the program. It could be accomplished, the manifesto stated, by modernizing plant and equipment, improving production methods, and winning labor's support by distributing the cost of rearmament and the benefits of production more equitably.[70]

Despite its shortcomings, particularly the lack of a concrete production plan, the manifesto had at least endorsed the principles that American leaders thought important. Acheson called it a "sound and constructive" statement.[71] Foster congratulated the OEEC on identifying "the real answer to many of Europe's difficulties – to expand production and to increase productivity."[72] By stressing the need to distribute the benefits of productivity more evenly, the manifesto also underscored what had gradually become a salient theme in American recovery policy. The ECA's draft circular of August 1950 had called for "a more equitable distribution of income," as had the revised circular of mid-September, and the ECA had pushed the same idea aggressively in the negotiations leading up to the European manifesto. Greater productivity and "social justice," together with economic integration and corporative collaboration, made up central themes in what I have called the New Deal synthesis. They came together in the European manifesto, as they did in the ECA's revitalized technical assistance program, which is worth examining for that reason.

V

The great bulk of American aid, approximately $12 billion by mid–1951, had gone to help participating countries finance essential imports of fuel

21, 1951, and Berthoud memoranda (2), "European Initiative," August 23 and 25, 1951, FO 371, 94200 and 94201, M1068.

[70] Porter tel. to Foster, August 29, 1951, *FRUS, 1951*, 4:54–7.
[71] Acheson quoted in Hall-Patch tel. to FO, September 1, 1951, FO 371, 94201, M1068.
[72] Foster quoted in Porter tel. to Foster, August 30, 1951, *FRUS, 1951*, 4:58–9.

($1.567 billion); food, feed, and fertilizers ($3.192 billion); raw materials and semimanufactured products ($3.430 billion); and machines, vehicles, and equipment ($1.853 billion). These imports brought steady increments to European output that would not have been possible otherwise. By July 1951, industrial and agricultural production had climbed 43 percent and 10 percent, respectively, above prewar levels. But expanding prewar production could not by itself open the door to Western Europe's entry into a multilateral system. Productivity was the key to this goal, at least in the eyes of American leaders. Only by raising the productivity of labor could participating countries break their dependence on American aid and become truly competitive. Counterpart funds played a part here, in that the ECA was earmarking 60 percent of these funds for industrial modernization projects such as the Monnet Plan in France, the remainder being used for financial stabilization or to underwrite land-reclamation plans, low-cost housing schemes, and a variety of other relief and social-welfare projects. The ECA's Industrial Projects Program expended additional dollars to expand and modernize industrial facilities on the Continent.[73] For the most part, however, raising European productivity had been and remained the special mission of the Technical Assistance Program.

The significance of the Technical Assistance Program cannot be measured in terms of dollars. The ECA had never invested a large portion of its budget in the program, in part because restoring production had top priority for sound economic and political reasons, but also because technical assistance was a low-overhead item. Technical assistance involved the transfer not of commodities and resources but of knowledge, skill, and other services of great importance but little cost. In the most profound sense, it involved the transfer of attitudes, habits, and values as well, indeed, of a whole way of life that Marshall Planners associated with progress in the marketplace of politics and social relationships as much as they did with greater output in industry and agriculture. This was the American way of life. Through the technical-assistance program, in other words, the Marshall Planners aimed to implant in Western Europe the seeds of a democratic neo-capitalism that had flourished in the United States.

With economic aid now limited and increasingly targeted for defense support, technical assistance was one of the last areas in which the ECA could pursue its own initiative. By mid–1951, the ECA had expended nearly $30 million on the technical-assistance program, with most of this amount allocated after the outbreak of the Korean War and nearly $8 million in the period between March and July 1951. Under the auspices of this program, the first German productivity team of labor and management leaders

[73]   ECA, *Thirteenth Report to Congress*, ix, x, 15, 53–5, 56–60, 110–11. The cumulative allocation figures noted in the text include those for military assistance (from July 1, 1950) as well as Marshall aid (from April 3, 1948). The balance not accounted for in the text was expended on miscellaneous and unclassified commodities and services.

visited the United States to study coal-mining practices. Other teams gave special attention to the capital-goods industries that were critical to the success of European rearmament and continued economic growth. Italian, British, Danish, and French teams studied American methods of smelting and refining nonferrous metals; iron, steel, and machine-tool production; foundry practices; and railway-equipment manufacturing. All told, 145 European productivity teams visited the United States between March and July 1951, involving over a thousand European labor, management, and agricultural representatives. The ECA also maintained 372 technical experts overseas and continued, in collaboration with the National Management Council, to sponsor management seminars in which American experts "lectured" European executives on the gains in productivity to be derived by emulating American engineering, marketing, and research techniques, American methods of product simplification and standardization, and American programs of labor–management training.[74]

With the same gains in mind, the ECA had also used technical-assistance funds to support the ongoing work of the Anglo–American Council on Productivity and to establish so-called production centers in participating countries. By the end of 1951, the Council on Productivity had sponsored visits to the United States by sixty-six British productivity teams, disseminated over five hundred thousand copies of the council's reports, and published major studies on standardization and simplification in industry.[75] Other participating countries had organized their own production centers and the OEEC had launched an intra-European technical-assistance program under which national groups of cooperating labor, management, and professional leaders had begun to exchange technical information and production data. The whole process, as a Dutch manufacturer said of the technical-assistance program, had brought about "a change in attitude among [European] industrialists." It had made them willing for the first time "to offer competitors hospitality and information" and had opened the door to "a most promising and fertile dissemination of American experience in handling productivity problems."[76] Indeed, the ECA took great pains to crowd its latest report to Congress with examples of how technical assistance had led to real gains in the productivity of European industries.[77]

The goal of greater productivity also inspired the ECA's "Production Assistance Drive," which got underway in 1951. The new program was a response to the additional burden of rearmament on the European economies, the declining volume of American aid, and the consequent need to

[74] ECA, *Thirteenth Report to Congress*, 50–3.
[75] Anglo–American Council on Productivity, *Final Report of the Council* (September 1952), Hoffman Papers, box 24, folder: Economic Cooperation Administration, Publications.
[76] ECA, *Twelfth Report to Congress*, 53.
[77] ECA, *Thirteenth Report to Congress*, 51.

multiply the productive output of available resources. To accomplish this task, it focused "on technical factors such as investment in new or improved machinery and the development of improved techniques and methods of organization." Like the technical-assistance program, out of which it grew, the Production Assistance Drive also envisioned the dissemination of technical information, the provision of "expert assistance" to "plant owners, managers and union groups," and the formation in participating countries of "production assistance boards" representing government, industry, agriculture, and labor.[78]

Once again, the ECA saw the secret to Europe's success in the example of the United States, where labor productivity was nearly three times greater than on the Continent and was "the core of America's industrial strength." The Europeans, according to this line of thinking, must adopt the "advanced" American production techniques and the American pattern of labor–management teamwork if they hoped to enhance the output of existing capacity and ensure "adequate and equitable living standards to all levels of [the] population." In this case, moreover, the ECA also aimed "to improve business and labor practices so as to bring about an equitable distribution of the fruits of greater productivity among labor, management and owners." As the ECA explained in a telegram to its missions, the Production Assistance Drive was "based on the theory that it is both desirable and necessary for the benefits of expanded productivity to be divided fairly among those responsible for its creation," specifically that greater productivity "should provide higher wages for workers, a fair profit for owners and lower prices for consumers."[79]

To facilitate this work, the ECA increased funding for the full range of technical-assistance programs. It reorganized its industry division, as did the Office of the Special Representative, appointed new assistant administrators for production in Washington and Paris, and gave them greater authority over programming decisions. The country missions also expanded their contacts with local trade and labor associations, appointed directors of production, and "plumped" themselves with men of "industrial experience and background," what one official called " 'know-how' and 'do-how' men" who were able to pass "judgment as to plant capacities, labor security, financial stability and management capabilities."[80]

The principal figure behind the Production Assistance Drive was William H. Joyce, Jr., the new assistant administrator for production in Washington and a leading advocate of the corporative neo-capitalism that ECA officials

[78] Ibid., 2–4.
[79] Ibid., 2–3; and Wood repto circular 95 to Foster, August 1, 1951, ECA Files, box 33.
[80] William H. Joyce letter to John A. Stephens, Vice President, United States Steel Corporation, May 21, 1951, RG 286, Acc. 53A441, box 264, folder: Chronological File – May 1951. See also ECA, *Thirteenth Report to Congress*, 4.

had been promoting in Western Europe. Joyce wanted participating countries to "accept the American definition of the social and economic desirabilities of productivity," the conviction, in other words, that the "benefits" of increased productivity must be shared "amongst the three basic groups – labor, stockholders and the consumers." In his view, and that of William Foster, this had become "the accepted philosophy" among enlightened American business elites in the wake of the New Deal. Britain and the Scandinavian countries had also moved well down the road "toward a true industrial evolution." But capitalism remained "more feudalistic than capitalistic" in France, Italy, and West Germany, countries where industrial elites were often to blame for Communist domination of the leading trade unions. As Joyce bluntly wrote the president of Fiat enterprises, European capitalism had not given "the working man a reasonable standard of living," which was the surest antidote "to the appeal of Communist doctrines." In these countries, the productivity councils and production-assistance boards would serve as vehicles for conveying the new "ideas developed in the United States during the past fifteen years." Around them would form a "progressive" alliance of European labor and business leaders who had "a direct interest in overcoming tariff barriers, restrictive trade practices and the other inhibiting forces to trade and higher standards of living." And through them, "productivity, American style" would be translated into European terms. European leaders would then learn what their American counterparts knew already, that "sharing of the benefits of productivity amongst employees, stockholders and consumers is one of the underlying solutions to the Communist problem."[81]

Joyce echoed the sentiments of those public and private leaders who had reconciled themselves to the New Deal and Fair Deal and had thrown their weight behind the internationalist and multilateralist foreign policies of the Roosevelt and Truman administrations. His views had support from other officials in the ECA, the Pentagon, the State Department, and the Office of Defense Mobilization; from key figures in the trade-union movement; from spokesmen for the capital-intensive bloc of firms that had joined organized labor at the center of the New Deal coalition; and from such organs of progressive opinion in the business and professional community as the CED, the Brookings Institution, the Ford Foundation, and the NPA. The AFL's

[81]   Joyce letter to Katz, May 1, 1951, RG 286, Acc. 53A441, box 264, folder: Chronological File – May 1951; Foster letter to Senator William Benton, August 23, 1951, and Joyce letters to Charles Hook, Armco Steel Corporation, and Mr. V. Valletta, August 17 and 16, 1951, RG 286, Acc. 53A441, box 264, folder: Chronological File – August 1951; Joyce letter to Stephens, May 21, 1951, RG 286, Acc. 53A441, box 264, folder: Chronological File – May 1951; Joyce letter to Senator Henry Cabot Lodge, August 22, 1951, RG 286, Acc. 53A441, box 264, folder: Chronological File – August 1951; and *New York Times*, September 5, 1951, 14. See also Foster letter to Philip Cortney of the International Chamber of Commerce, August 31, 1951, RG 286, Acc. 53A441, box 264, folder: Chronological File – August 1951.

Committee on Resolutions, Philip Murray of the CIO, Walter Reuther of the United Automobile Workers, and other trade-union leaders reaffirmed their support for the Marshall Plan, the Schuman Plan, the North Atlantic Treaty, and other efforts to integrate Europe and strengthen defense. They called higher living standards and a more equitable distribution of income essential to the success of these efforts and said that both must be defended by the "democratic middle" against "reactionaries from the right as well as from the left."[82] The CED also reaffirmed its support of the Marshall Plan in a major statement in May 1951. It called the plan a great success, urged further efforts to integrate economies, raise productivity, and reform tax systems, and went on to argue that rearmament should be financed so far as possible by expanding productivity rather than cutting exports or reducing living standards.[83] The Brookings Institution and the NPA issued similar statements, while the Ford Foundation, under Paul Hoffman's leadership, was laying plans to use a third of its budget to support the State Department's foreign-policy programs, particularly those aimed at "increasing the ability of people to produce."[84]

By 1951, however, the economic and political crisis growing out of the Korean War and the rearmament program had made it more difficult for this alliance of progressive labor, business, and government leaders to translate its views into effective public policy. Conservative forces had grown stronger and the Truman administration had suffered a reversal of fortunes in Congress. The administration itself was a house divided. When it came to international policy, all of the agencies involved were committed to European recovery and rearmament and to the development of a multilateral system of world trade. But within this consensus, the Treasury Department had taken a consistently tougher position whenever the Europeans asked the United States to finance the difference between European capabilities and American objectives. Hugh Gaitskell had remarked on this difference in late 1950, explaining in his diary how much easier it was to get along with the "new-dealer types" in the ECA, the State Department, and other agencies than with their conservative colleagues in the Treasury Department.[85]

Nor did the chancellor's opinion change when he visited Washington in September 1951 to argue that additional American support would be needed if the Labour government was going to rearm Britain without restricting

[82] The views of American labor leaders are quoted from Bissell toreps 8551 and 9924 to Katz, October 5 and November 22, 1950, ECA Files, boxes 68 and 69, respectively.

[83] Committee for Economic Development, *Economic Aspects of North Atlantic Security.*

[84] Donald Kennedy, State Department, memorandum of conversation between Secretary Acheson and various State Department and Ford Foundation officials, July 16, 1951, Acheson Papers, box 66, folder: Memoranda of Conversations. See also Brookings Institution, *Current Issues in Foreign Economic Assistance*, especially 81–8; and Geiger and Cleveland, *Making Western Europe Defensible.*

[85] Williams, *Gaitskell Diary*, 190, 181–2.

dollar imports and wrecking its economy. Gaitskell was especially anxious to get a waiver of interest payments on the American loan of 1946 and some agreement to stabilize world commodity prices. He had "very pleasant" talks on these subjects with Secretary of the Air Force and former ECA Chief in London Thomas Finletter, "who remains as cultured and charming as ever"; Secretary of State Dean Acheson, "an impressive personality"; former Special Representative Averell Harriman, "an old friend" who could "be trusted as somebody who will try and solve the problem for us"; Secretary of Commerce Charles Sawyer, who was "reasonably friendly"; Defense Mobilization Director Charles Wilson, who was "very co-operative and obviously anxious to do his best"; and Assistant ECA Administrator Richard Bissell, "who grasped more quickly than anybody what we were up against." Talks with this group of officials always took place in what the chancellor considered "an atmosphere of real friendship in which everybody was trying to help."[86]

Gaitskell could not say the same about his talks with Secretary Snyder, other officials in the Treasury Department, or their allies in the IMF. These men "took a very laissez-faire view," always "pressing for freedom from exchange restrictions" and always trying "to bully or bribe countries into getting rid of restrictions." Snyder personified this outlook, according to Gaitskell. Whereas the ECA and State Department negotiators appreciated Britain's "economic plight" and were anxious to help, Snyder complained repeatedly "that the American taxpayers had to pay for everything." He revealed himself in Gaitskell's book as a "rather ridiculous man," very much a "small minded, small town, semi-isolationist." "Why do we have to put up the money?" Snyder asked the embarrassed guests at a dinner party of finance ministers and central bankers. "Americans were always the milch cow."[87]

The differences between the Treasury Department, on the one hand, and the ECA and State Department, on the other, paralleled in some ways the disagreements between economizers and Keynesians concerning domestic policy. These disagreements flared up again in the last months of 1951, as did those between the American and European approaches to economic recovery. The occasion came at a series of conferences organized by William Joyce as part of the ECA's Production Assistance Drive. One of these conferences, the International Congress on Productivity, brought together several hundred European and American business leaders. The Council of European Federations, a peak association representing the leading industrial federations of Western Europe, selected the European participants. At the ECA's suggestion, the council organized advisory committees in each par-

[86] Ibid., 276–82.
[87] Ibid. On the British economic situation at this point and Gaitskell's talks in Washington, see also the documents in *FRUS, 1951*, 4:955–70; and Acheson, *Present at the Creation*, 560.

ticipating country. The committees were headed by a national spokesman for the council and charged with compiling a list of conference participants, each of whom was to be a "top man in an important company in a major industry" and "a person having wide influence in the business community." The NAM selected the American participants and then coordinated the International Congress on Productivity with two related conferences convened under its own auspices.[88]

The conferences opened in November and December with approximately three hundred Europeans in attendance. The guests were promptly treated to major speeches by American government, business, and labor leaders who supported the ECA's productivity program and the ideology behind it. Charles Wilson joined other government spokesmen to argue that new programs to boost productivity, together with current wage and price controls, would enable the American and European economies to restrain inflation, stimulate growth, and absorb the cost of rearmament. Although "guns and butter" would have to give way to "guns and margarine" in the short run, Wilson predicted that civilian investment and consumption would resume as defense goals were attained. Success in Western Europe depended on the modernization of plant and equipment, the application of American production, management, and marketing techniques, and the elimination of trade restrictions and other barriers to competition and economies of scale. Wilson also made it clear that mass production required mass consumption, which in turn required that workers share more fully in the material benefits of economic growth. A more equitable distribution of the fruits of greater productivity, he and Joyce told the conferees, would also bring such ancillary advantages as encouraging workers to work harder and making them less hostile to technological innovation and managerial direction. Similar messages came from Clinton Golden, who still played an important role in the ECA's Office of Labor Advisers; William Foster, who had just assumed the post of deputy secretary of defense; Michael DiSalle, who directed the Office of Price Stabilization; Manly Fleischmann, who headed the Defense Production Board; Harold G. Moulton, who presided over the Brookings Institution; and Paul Hoffman, who led the Ford Foundation.[89]

Many of those assembled found it difficult to accept every aspect of the ECA's message. Sir Norman Kipping, director of the Federation of British

---

[88] Katz repto circular 73 to Foster, June 25, 1951, ECA Files, box 33. See also Joyce letter to William L. Batt, ECA Mission Chief, United Kingdom, August 18, 1951, RG 286, Acc. 53A441, box 264, folder: Chronological File – August 1951.

[89] *New York Times*, December 1, 1951, 4; *New York Times*, December 4, 1951, 1 and 12; *New York Times*, December 6, 1951, 1 and 14; *Commercial and Financial Chronicle*, December 13, 1951, 10 and 87; and William H. Joyce, Jr., "Participation: America's Real Secret Weapon," *Vital Speeches of the Day* 18 (January 1, 1952): 176–8.

Industries, agreed that the Marshall Plan had given European businessmen a keener appreciation of the importance of productivity to higher living standards. But he and other European business leaders, including George Villiers, president of the Council of European Federations, also insisted that raw material shortages, balance-of-payments difficulties, and fears of unemployment made it difficult to apply all parts of the American program on the Continent. The British took exception to the American emphasis on eliminating trade restrictions; the French defended cartels as a way to integrate economies without ruinous and wasteful dislocations.[90] Nor were many of the European conferees sympathetic to the social gospel being preached by the ECA. They did not want that agency to disturb existing social arrangements in participating countries and had earlier demanded, and received, what amounted to a government veto over the ECA's contacts with European trade unions, business associations, and other private groups.[91]

There were similar differences between the ECA and business leaders on the American side. Spokesmen for the NAM and the Chamber of Commerce were less inclined than the ECA to believe that resources were sufficient to provide guns and butter both. Nor did they agree that Keynesian strategies of economic management, including government controls, higher taxes, and larger deficits, would permit a painless reconciliation of military and civilian requirements. They opposed wage and price controls, called instead for voluntary restraint by business and labor, and urged government to reduce nonmilitary expenditures and balance the budget.[92]

The International Congress on Productivity thus ended in a dialogue between conservatives and Keynesians on the American side, with both groups mobilizing some of the arguments heard in the Great Debate and in the subsequent battles over the economics of rearmament and the merits of Truman's program for regulating the war economy. The fault line in all of these squabbles ran along the same range of issues: government economy versus deficit spending, voluntary restraints versus government controls, guns versus butter. On the other hand, it is important to remember that arguments coming from both groups intersected at key points. Conservatives and liberals alike gave full backing to the technical-assistance program, the export of American production, marketing, and engineering skills, and the comparable efforts to modernize plant and equipment. In their view, the Americanization of European business was one way to generate the gains in output that were needed to defray the cost of rearmament and put the

---

[90] *New York Times*, December 4, 1951, 1 and 12; *New York Times*, December 6, 1951, 1 and 14; and Ugo Stille, "European vs. U.S. Industrialists," *The Reporter* 6 (January 8, 1952):28–30.

[91] *New York Times*, September 3, 1951, 1; and Wood repto 3648 to Foster, July 27, 1951, ECA Files, box 31.

[92] *New York Times*, December 6, 1951, 1 and 14.

Continent on a self-supporting basis. For similar reasons, individuals on both sides of the ideological divide gave strong support to the formation of a single European market. Out of this, too, would come the gains in competition, resource utilization, and economies of scale that held the secret to productive abundance in Western Europe.

Like the concept of productivity, to which it was linked, the idea of integration remained an enduring component in the American formula for peace and prosperity in Western Europe. It continued to connect the strategic and economic goals being pursued and had the support of military leaders and recovery planners, of liberals and conservatives, of Congress and the executive branch. This support made it possible for American policymakers to push for greater progress in the direction of integration, even as the Marshall Plan was coming to an end. And on the front involving military integration, they had made substantial headway by the end of 1951. As we have seen, the Truman administration had thrown its weight behind the French proposal for a European Defense Community. The North Atlantic Council had endorsed the American proposal for a Defense Production Board that was to expand and coordinate military production across the European and North Atlantic areas. This action had been followed in May 1951 by the Finance and Economic Board, which was to supervise the economic mobilization for defense, and in September by the Temporary Council Committee, which was to draw up a common plan for financing rearmament and dividing the burden involved.[93] In theory at least, the coordination of defense production and financial planning would be one more step along Western Europe's road to economic and military integration, Germany's reintegration, and the goal of permanent recovery.

These initiatives paralleled ongoing American efforts to stimulate interest in an integrated market. Gains in this area were slow to materialize in the second half of 1951, a lull between the OEEC's springtime successes in the field of trade liberalization and the formation of the European Coal and Steel Community in 1952. Indeed, the economic problems growing out of rearmament actually resulted in setbacks, the most glaring being the deterioration of Britain's payments position, the subsequent decision in November to reduce British imports by 10 percent, and the resulting cuts by France and other OEEC countries.[94] But given the connection that American leaders made between economic integration and greater productivity and between productivity and rearmament, it was not long before they took concrete steps to protect the gains that had been made in the liberalization of intra-European trade. In the fall of 1951, the Truman administration relaxed its rearmament program to lessen the strain on both the American and Eu-

[93] Kaplan, *Community of Interests*, 129–31, 136–7, 162–6; and Stebbins, *United States in World Affairs, 1951*, 62–6, 347.

[94] Stebbins, *United States in World Affairs, 1951*, 356; and Diebold, *Trade and Payments*, 134–5, 426–7.

ropean economies. It also agreed to slow the pace of European rearmament, curb the Pentagon's stockpiling program, permit the International Materials Conference to allocate some American commodities in short supply, and increase aid to Britain and France in hopes of relieving the strain on their balance of payments.[95]

At the same time, European and American leaders joined in a host of new pronouncements designed to revive the trend toward European integration. In July, General Eisenhower called for a "workable European federation" as the best way to "build adequate security" without compromising living standards.[96] The same thinking was incorporated in the OEEC's manifesto of August. William Foster then drove the point home when he explained, in responding to the manifesto, how the "crippling effects on production of national trade barriers and cartels need to be eliminated if our European friends, by moving in the direction of a single market, are to achieve the goals they have set for themselves."[97] A month later, the NATO Council endorsed the manifesto and established a special committee to recommend further steps to coordinate economic, financial, and social policies in Western Europe.[98] A group of American congressmen who visited Europe in the fall also called for progress in the same direction, while Congress made it clear in the preamble to the Mutual Security Act that European "economic unification," even "political federation," remained cardinal goals of American diplomacy.[99]

VI

So it was that the end of the Marshall Plan saw no slackening of American enthusiasm for European integration. Nor could it have been otherwise. For American Marshall Planners, European integration had always been a goal in itself and a means to other enduring objectives. Together with the export of American techniques, American patterns of labor–capital collaboration, and American strategies of economic management and social welfare, European integration held the key to boosting productivity, closing the dollar gap, and bringing participating countries into a fully multilateral system of world trade. By generating abundance and raising living standards, integration would also help to cut the economic ground from under political radicals on the Left and the Right. And if capped by institutional coordi-

[95] Acheson, *Present at the Creation*, 559; and Stebbins, *United States in World Affairs, 1951*, 152, 212, 224, 364.
[96] Eisenhower, "The Challenge of Our Time," a speech delivered before the English Speaking Union, London, July 3, 1951, *Vital Speeches of the Day* 17 (August 1, 1951): 613–14. See also Eisenhower letter to Truman, January 4, 1952, Truman Papers, box 118, PSF, folder: Eisenhower, Dwight D. (NATO).
[97] Foster quoted in Porter tel. to Foster, August 30, 1951, *FRUS, 1951*, 4:58–9.
[98] Stebbins, *United States in World Affairs, 1951*, 358–9.
[99] Ibid., 360–1.

nators and regulators, it would create a framework into which Germany could be incorporated and by which it could be controlled. The final result, or so the Americans believed, would be a unit of economic and political power large and strong enough to restore confidence to all Western Europeans that a new day of peace and plenty had arrived to stay.

The Americans had made progress toward these interrelated goals in the four years since Secretary of State Marshall's commencement address at Harvard University in June 1947. Intra-European payments had been liberalized and trade barriers reduced. New mechanisms had been established to promote American management strategies and bring different functional groups into corporative collaboration with one another and with government. In addition, the Schuman Plan looked to the integration of an important sector of the European economy, and both the Schuman Plan and the European Payments Union envisioned a major role for central institutions of economic coordination and control. The British had been exempted from the trend toward integration. But the Germans were being included and their participation pointed to a final settlement between the former Reich and its enemies in the West. To this list of accomplishments could be added other important gains, notably the reconstruction of Western Europe's economic infrastructure, the recovery of production, and the headway made in the area of military integration.

Even if these gains fell short of original targets, which was the case, they were substantial when measured against the situation that American and European leaders had confronted in the aftermath of the Second World War. The outbreak of fighting in Korea and the urgent drive to strengthen Western Europe's defenses forestalled additional progress in 1951, even wiping out some of the gains in financial stability and trade liberalization that had been achieved in previous years. At the same time, the economic and political crisis growing out of rearmament tended to destabilize European political coalitions and undermine the Labour government in Britain. In the United States, the same crisis weakened the liberal coalition that had backed the New Deal at home and multilateralism abroad. It strengthened the alliance of conservatives in Congress and in the private sector, with one result being a retreat from the principles of multilateralism and from the commitment to foreign aid, on which European stability still depended.

By the end of 1951, however, the same crisis had brought key policymakers back to the conclusion that continued progress toward the stated goals of the Marshall Plan was now more imperative than ever if participating countries were going to fortify themselves against Soviet aggression and Communist subversion – if they were going to have guns and butter both. General Eisenhower's speech was in some ways the most important expression of this conviction. It elaborated the familiar economic and security objectives of American policy and then used the concept of integration to link them, much as American leaders had been doing since the start of the recovery program. Eisenhower's address read like an ECA pamphlet on the benefits in greater growth and permanent peace to be derived from a "workable European federation." It thus articulated ideas that Marshall Planners had done so much to promote, and on which Eisenhower would build in the decade ahead.

Conclusion

America made the European way

I

"The Americans want an integrated Europe looking like the United States of America – 'God's own country.' "[1] This assessment, offered by Robert Hall of the British Treasury, sums up the central theme of the preceding chapters. Of course, the "Americans" to whom Hall referred did not include Henry Wallace, Henry Hazlitt, and other critics who accused the Truman administration of leading the nation down the garden path to economic ruin and world war. The Marshall Plan, as these critics understood, was the brainchild of a particular political coalition, the so-called New Deal coalition, which was strong enough to prevail against opponents on the Left and the Right. The outgrowth of underlying changes in the industrial structure and the concomitant political realignment of the 1930s, the New Deal coalition included at its core a bloc of capital-intensive firms and their allies among labor, farm, financial, and professional groups. Its leadership combined the technocorporative formulations of the 1920s with the ideological adaptations of the 1930s in a policy synthesis that envisioned a neo-capitalist reorganization of the American and world systems. It was this synthesis, what I have called the New Deal synthesis, that inspired the Marshall Plan to remake Western Europe in the image of " 'God's own country.' "

At the center of the New Deal synthesis was the vision of an integrated Western European economy much like the large internal market that had taken shape in the United States under the Constitution of 1787. An integrated single market promised the benefits that inhered in economies of scale, with the ultimate result being a prosperous and stable European community secure against the dangers of Communist subversion and able to join the United States in a multilateral system of world trade. To achieve this goal, Marshall Planners blended what the preceding chapters call the

[1] Hall quoted in Kaplan, *United States and NATO*, 131.

427

free-traders' and planners' approaches. They aimed to reduce barriers to the free flow of goods, services, and capital, put intra-European trade and payments on a multilateral basis, and permit natural market mechanisms to promote a rational integration. But they also sought to organize European institutions with the power to transcend sovereignties and coordinate policies so that normal market forces could operate. If led by qualified experts and civil servants of international status, institutions of this sort could help to depoliticize divisive issues, discipline the selfish pursuit of national interests, and weld once rival states into an organic unit of economic and political power.

Similar benefits would come from re-creating in Western Europe the patterns of corporative collaboration that had become a standard feature of public administration in the United States, the ECA being a notable example. By organizing national and transnational networks of power sharing between private functional groups and between these groups and government authorities, Marshall Planners hoped to create a framework for integration while at the same time protecting private enterprise and public order against the dual dangers of bureaucratic statism and class conflict. With these goals in mind, they promoted institutional links between the Trade Union Advisory Committee and the OEEC. They encouraged participating governments to bring trade unionists together with business, agricultural, and professional leaders in national recovery planning. And through the technical-assistance program, the productivity teams, and the national production centers, they tried to unite the same groups around a common political and economic agenda.

The agenda that Marshall Planners had in mind was a shared commitment to economic growth. The idea of growth made up another component of the New Deal synthesis. For Marshall Planners, it was both a goal in its own right and the key to social harmony, to the survival of private-enterprise capitalism, and to the preservation of political democracy. By focusing on growth, it seemed possible to widen the area of collaboration and shrink the area of conflict between ostensibly competing groups, particularly organized labor and organized capital. And by generating growth, it seemed possible to avoid the redistributive contests and the excessive expansion of state power that might otherwise result from economic stagnation and retrenchment.

Actually generating growth, however, required more than corporative collaboration between different functional groups or the integration of economies, the formation of supranational institutions, the liberation of natural market forces, and the organization of transnational networks. It also required the modernization of production, the assimilation of American technical and business acumen, the reform of fiscal and tax policies, and the willingness of the European business and government elites to raise the productivity of labor by sharing the benefits of growth more equitably with the working classes. These requirements, too, were parts of the New Deal synthesis by which Marshall Planners steered, the keys to a neo-capitalism in Western Europe similar to the one that supposedly had led to a new era of economic growth and social stability in the United States. Through American aid, and particularly through the use of counterpart funds, Marshall Planners tried to underwrite industrial modernization projects, promote Keynesian strategies of aggregate economic management, overhaul antiquated systems of public administration, and encourage progressive tax policies, low-cost housing programs, and other measures of economic and social reform. Through the production centers and productivity teams, they sought to build an alliance of labor, business, and professional leaders behind these reforms. And through the technical-assistance program, of which the productivity campaign was a part, they hoped to transform distributive battles into the search for a shared abundance and political problems into technical ones that were soluble, they said, by adopting American engineering, production, and marketing techniques and American methods of labor–management teamwork.

If these and related initiatives would fashion an organic economic order in Western Europe, one able to pay its way in a multilateral world, the same initiatives would also help to achieve the political and strategic objectives of American diplomacy. Economic growth, modest social programs, and a more equitable distribution of production would immunize participating countries against Communist subversion while generating the resources and mobilizing the public support necessary to sustain a major rearmament program. In addition, economic integration, supranational coordinating mechanisms, and transnational patterns of corporative collaboration would create an interdependent unit large enough to reconcile Germany's recovery with France's economic and military security. Such a unit could forge a viable balance of power among the states of Western Europe, establish a favorable correlation of forces on the Continent, and play an active role in the global containment of Soviet expansion. It is in this sense, as the chapters argue, that integration operated as an interlocking concept in the minds of American policymakers, the link that connected the economic and strategic goals on their agenda for Western Europe.

As this summary suggests, it would be an error to argue, as Lawrence Kaplan does, that American leaders merely manipulated the rhetoric of unification to entangle the United States in the defense of Europe. Kaplan, whose pioneering work on NATO informs much of this book, is right to claim that top policymakers had no truck with those who nourished hopes of immediate political federation among the states of Western Europe.[2] They viewed these "Europeanists" as dreamers whose enthusiastic eruptions could play into the hands of isolationists in Congress and nationalists in the

[2] Kaplan, *United States and NATO*, 57–8, 63, 78–9, 89.

participating countries, both of whom thought that a unified Western Europe might stand without American props. To Marshall Planners, on the other hand, even a unified Western Europe would be vulnerable to Soviet attack, particularly a Western European third force beyond the protective embrace of American arms. This was reason enough to dampen their ardor for the unificationist movements that shot up like hothouse plants on both sides of the Atlantic, and much the same reason why they dismissed Kennan's proposal for an all-European union from which the United States and the Soviet Union might withdraw.

But it does not follow from the preceding that policymakers in Washington were less than sincere in their conviction that unification promised the best future for Western Europe. Nor were they less than determined to bring unification about by liberalizing trade and harmonizing economies, coordinating military-production and supply programs, and promoting what even Kaplan calls a "supranational defense plan" and a "genuine military interdependence."[3] It would be more accurate to say that American leaders viewed European unification as a gradual process that had to begin with limited but realizable plans for a functional integration of economic and defense systems. In operation, these plans would make participating countries self-supporting, harness the Federal Republic to the cause of European recovery and security, and lay the foundation on which a political federation might then be constructed. Given this view, the ECA paid perfunctory attention to blueprints that would erect the superstructure of a federal system before the foundation had been finished. Policymakers in that agency concentrated on an economic integration of Western Europe, although in this case as well, European schemes rivaled American designs, so that the final edifice differed from the one laid out in the Marshall Plan.

II

The Marshall Plan was a success if judged simply as a program to control inflation, revive trade, and restore production. By 1950, inflation had been contained in most of the participating countries, France being a notable exception, and both intra-European and extra-European trade had recovered to levels well above those anticipated at the start of the Marshall Plan. The Korean War undercut these gains and also dashed already faint hopes that participating countries might balance accounts with the Western Hemisphere by the end of the ERP period. This is Imanuel Wexler's assessment. But it is also true, as Wexler notes, that these were temporary reversals in an established pattern of recovery that would resume in the early 1950s, continue unabated over the next decade, and lead to the restoration of European currency convertibility and the formation of a "free-

---

[3]   Ibid., 79, 172.

world" trading system comparable to the one envisioned in the Bretton Woods agreements of 1944.[4]

Something similar can be said of the recovery of Western European production. During the Marshall Plan period, Western Europe's aggregate gross national product jumped by more than 32 percent, from $120 billion to $159 billion; agricultural production climbed 11 percent above the prewar level, just slightly less than the target set in 1948; and industrial output increased by 40 percent against the same bench mark, greatly exceeding the OEEC's original projection.[5] As a new generation of European revisionists has reminded us, American Marshall Planners cannot take all of the credit for this remarkable record of success. Alan Milward makes this point in his penetrating economic history of postwar reconstruction. Arguing that the crisis of 1947 was not a crisis of production but a payments crisis brought on by the speed at which production had revived, Milward concludes that Marshall aid merely enabled participating countries to cover deficits with the dollar area and thus continue the recovery that had begun earlier.[6] Charles Maier constructs a different version of the same argument. Repeating a point noted earlier in this text, he concludes that local resources accounted for 80–90 percent of capital formation in the major European economies during the first two years of the Marshall Plan. The American contribution was marginal, measured in quantitative terms, and actually declined in the years after 1949.[7]

Although this sort of revisionism is a healthy corrective to earlier American paeans to the Marshall Plan, it succeeds through a feat of analytical legerdemain that denigrates the American contribution and leads to conclusions almost as unbalanced as those it seeks to refute. The payments crisis, after all, portended a serious crisis in production that would come with the collapse of critical dollar imports. Signs of this were apparent early in 1947, and it is impossible to get around them by arguing, as Milward does, that most participating countries might have managed their balance of payments and achieved sustained rates of growth by simply limiting imports to capital goods. This option was not available to the fragile coalitions that presided over many of the participating countries, none of which could retreat from already low levels of consumption and hope to survive.[8] Marshall aid enabled these coalitions to operate within a range of political choice that precluded vigorously deflationary policies, promised higher living standards, and thus closed the door to extremist elements on the Left and the Right. To put it in a way that balances contemporary European

4   Wexler, *Marshall Plan Revisited*, 250–5.
5   Ibid., 250–1.
6   Milward, *Reconstruction of Western Europe*, 465–6.
7   Maier, "The Two Postwar Eras and the Conditions for Stability in Twentieth-Century Western Europe," 341–2.
8   Milward, *Reconstruction of Western Europe*, 466, 469–70.

revisionism against the encomiums of an earlier day, the Marshall Plan provided what Stephen A. Schuker calls the "crucial margin" that made European self-help possible.[9] It facilitated essential imports, eased production bottlenecks, encouraged higher rates of capital formation, and helped to suppress inflation, all of which led to gains in productivity, to improvements in trade, and to an era of social peace and prosperity more durable than any other in modern European history.

The same judgment, one that weighs American initiative against European self-help, applies to other aspects of the recovery program as well. There is little doubt that the Marshall Plan helped to modernize budgetary systems in Western Europe or that it encouraged the spread of indicative economic planning, the rationalization of production, the development of corporative patterns of public–private power sharing, and the conviction that economic growth was the way to ameliorate social divisions. These had been American goals from the start. They were parts of the New Deal synthesis and were pursued with particular vigor through the technical-assistance program, the productivity teams, and the national production centers that Marshall aid helped to establish.

Because of the emphasis on self-help, however, and because the ECA's leverage was less than absolute, the new era that dawned in Western Europe was neither solely the result of American initiative nor fully in line with American thinking. During the course of this century, virtually all of the participating countries had begun to move from the liberal economic order of a bygone day toward what some have called a mixed economic system, others an organized capitalism, still others a corporative political economy. Industry had begun to organize and adopt scientific management techniques. Labor had shown a willingness to abandon redistributive political prescriptions for a labor–management partnership that tied wage gains to productivity rates. Government had assumed new responsibilities for coordinating national economic policy, stimulating growth, and performing other tasks once entrusted to private initiative and automatic market regulators. The Second World War accelerated these transformations, as did the nationalizations of the early postwar period, although neither development displaced the private sector, which remained largely intact, nor fully erased all elements of the liberal ideology. The outcome instead was a European synthesis somewhat similar to its New Deal counterpart.

France provides a good example of this outcome. The rapid defeat of 1940 convinced important public and private elites that the nation's long-term economic decline had to be reversed. They blamed this decline for France's defeat and saw a program of modernization as the only way for

[9]   See Schuker's commentary on the article by Maier, cited in note 7, in *American Historical Review* 86 (April 1981): 353–8.

the country to redeem itself, deal on favorable terms with the Germans, retain its status as a major European power, and avoid the internecine social divisions of the interwar period. Both Vichy and the Resistance promoted this notion, just as they elaborated somewhat overlapping economic agendas that anticipated the modernization strategies of the postwar era. Although Vichy's ideology celebrated the virtues of a limited state, of capitalist hegemony, and of economic decentralization and rugged individualism, in practice Pétain's regime added weight to the government's economic authority, institutionalized collaboration between industry and the state, and pioneered in measures of social welfare. These developments dovetailed in many ways with the thinking of the Resistance leaders, particularly with their conviction that social democracy depended on economic modernization, which in turn depended on centralized planning, more aggressive state direction, and a greater degree of collaboration between the public and private sectors.[10]

In charting a course to modernization, Vichy and the Resistance also drew much of their inspiration from abroad. Vichyites were thrown into close contact with the Germans, from whom they learned the benefits of industrial organization, central direction, and close collaboration between industry and the state. The Resistance drew similar lessons from the wartime mobilizations in Britain and America. Georges Boris, Pierre Mèndes-France, Robert Marjolin, and Jean Monnet, to name a few, spent all or part of the war years in London or Washington, where they imbibed the Anglo–American faith in the healing power of productivity and studied Anglo–American methods of controlling inflation, mobilizing investment, organizing production, analyzing data, and forecasting economic trends. Monnet later recruited Robert Nathan, a former wartime planner in Washington, to help draft the French modernization plan of 1946 and outline the organizational arrangements that would characterize economic planning in the Fourth Republic.[11]

This summary is not intended to deny the important ideological and political differences between Vichy and the Resistance, nor those between the Communists, Socialists, Catholics, and Gaullists during the *Libération* and the early years of the Fourth Republic. It is intended instead to highlight common denominators; the common commitment to a productionist ideology, to the positive use of state power, and to the benefits of industrial organization, indicative planning, and public–private collaboration – all of which were seen as keys to economic modernization and growth. These

---

[10]   Stanley Hoffmann, "Paradoxes of the French Political Community," in Hoffmann et al., *In Search of France* (Cambridge, MA, 1963), 1–117; and Philip M. Williams, *Crisis and Compromise: Politics in the Fourth Republic* (Hamden, CT, 1964), 13.

[11]   Hoffmann, "Paradoxes of the French Political Community," 53–4; and Kuisel, *Capitalism and the State in Modern France*, 191, 200, 220–1, 230.

common denominators operated like sluice gates to channel public policy toward a neo-liberal reorganization of the French economy, just as differences between the parties dammed up other possibilities.

Economic planning is a case in point. The differences in this case were those between Mèndes-France and Monnet. Mèndes-France and other Socialists envisioned a mixed economy of public and private sectors, but one geared to a comprehensive plan drawn up by a central state planning authority and used to promote both modernization and socialism. Catholics and Gaullists were not inclined to centralize planning in the state or to give it a socialist content. Nor were government ministries anxious to see their prerogatives sacrificed to a planning commissariat. These opponents combined to defeat Mèndes-France in 1945, but not the notion of planning, which was resuscitated within a year by Monnet and his colleagues. Monnet succeeded where Mèndes-France had failed precisely because he conceptualized planning in a way that proved acceptable to all of the parties involved. He delimited the planners' role so as to protect established ministries, brought public and private elites together in the planning process, limited the scope of planning, and linked it to the goals of modernization and growth, which even the Socialists saw as preconditions to political reform and social democracy.[12]

Many of the same themes recapitulated themselves when it came to the nationalization of industry, to cite one last example. The parties of the Left, notably the Socialists, saw nationalization as the first step toward a socialist overhaul. They envisioned a vast public sector and wanted public enterprises held accountable to syndicates representing government, business, and labor. The Catholics saw nationalization as the exception to the rule of private-enterprise capitalism. They aimed to limit the number of industries nationalized and guard the managers of these firms against intrusions by both the state and the trade unions. The Gaullists took a similar position, although they were more inclined to see nationalized industries as instruments of state power responsible to the dictates of technocrats in the public ministries rather than to the rule of autonomous managers or corporative syndicates.

These differences were substantial, but running through the debate were lines of agreement that made progress possible. All sides saw nationalization as a way to punish the big-business collaborators of the Vichy period, to bust the trusts that corrupted politics in the Third Republic, to overcome the Malthusian outlook that dominated much of the business community in the prewar period, and to set the stage for a new era of economic modernization and growth. The commitment to modernization was the most salient plank in the platform of all three parties, with the Socialists again giving it priority over a socialist reconstruction of the French economy.

---

[12] Kuisel, *Capitalism and the State in Modern France*, 190–201, 219–46; and Williams, *Crisis and Compromise*, 26–7.

Because of this, and because none of the parties had a mandate, the program drawn up followed lines that overlapped their respective agendas. Nationalization went further than the Catholics and the Gaullists would have liked, but not nearly so far as the Socialists had hoped, while the arrangements for managing the nationalized industries tended to amalgamate the technocratic, statist, and syndicalist prescriptions urged by Catholics, Gaullists, and Socialists, respectively.[13]

In France, then, political compromise and common lines of thinking led neither to the economic liberalism of the past nor to a statism of the Left or Right, but to a mixed economic system that had much in common with the neo-liberal synthesis developed in America. Nor was France the only participating country to move in this direction. The war and postwar emergencies accelerated similar trends in Britain. As we have seen, British policymakers won labor's support for voluntary wage restraints, negotiated industry's compliance with government production plans, and brought labor and industry representatives together in such agencies as the National Production Advisory Council and the National Joint Advisory Board. A similar system eventually took shape in Italy and West Germany, a system, that is, in which economic planning and more assertive state direction reinforced normal market regulators, organized concerts of group action supplemented private initiative, and traditional political forums lost ground both to administrative agencies and to corporative networks of public–private power sharing.[14]

The Marshall Plan reinforced these similarities; it neither invented them nor prevented European elites from tailoring American initiatives to their own specifications when they diverged from the New Deal synthesis. In Italy, for example, the technical-assistance and productivity programs were reformulated to square with government policies that aimed to suppress inflation, consolidate reserves, and expand trade. In France, they were absorbed into the Monnet Plan for industrial modernization. In West Germany, they accelerated earlier trends toward Taylorism and Fordism in industry. In Britain, they facilitated the Labour government's experiment in socialist planning. In each case, they led to important technological adaptations, to improved engineering and marketing methods, and to the spread of industrial planning, the growth of automation, and the better

---

[13] Kuisel, *Capitalism and the State in Modern France*, 202–11.

[14] Unsigned memorandum of meeting between Cripps, Hoffman, and other British and American officials, Paris, July 26, 1948, T232/27/EEC16/8/010. Also see, in addition to the sources cited in note 15, Dow, *Management of the British Economy;* Hildebrand, *Growth and Structure in the Economy of Modern Italy;* Andrew Shonfield, *Modern Capitalism: The Changing Balance of Public and Private Power* (London, 1965); Sidney Pollard, *The Development of the British Economy, 1914–1967,* 2d ed. (London, 1969); François Caron, *An Economic History of Modern France* (New York, 1979); Leslie Hannah, *The Rise of the Corporate Economy,* 2d ed. (New York, 1983); and Rogow, *Labour Government and British Industry.*

organization of production. These and other changes contributed substantially to the high rate of productivity that persisted through the 1950s. But the outlet for productivity was often found in the expansion of exports, not, as the ECA had hoped, in the expansion of internal demand.

As this suggests, public and private leaders in key continental countries successfully blunted the reformist impulse behind the ECA's policy. Nor was it simply that Keynesian strategies of aggregate internal management never took hold in Italy and Germany, where conservative governments ignored American advice and pursued an orthodox stabilization that curtailed public spending, curbed consumption, and restrained inflation. In these and other countries, France being a good example, profit takers appropriated the fruits of greater productivity and governments refused to overhaul antiquated tax systems. Industry benefitted from public subsidies while wages remained stable and unemployment persisted. In addition, managers retained their previous hegemony over shop-floor issues, codetermination in Germany notwithstanding, and technocrats from government and business dominated the corporative mechanisms of economic planning that proliferated after 1947. Although organized labor practiced what Maier calls the "politics of productivity," it is also true that divisions in the trade-union movement, divisions the ECA had encouraged, left workers with little choice but to forfeit immediate gains for a share of future growth, which their sacrifices helped to make possible.[15]

As evident from the persistence of unemployment, not to mention the restraints on consumption, the low wages, and the maldistribution of wealth, government and business elites divested the Marshall Plan of its social-democratic dimensions. In the end, as Pier D'Attorre has said of Italy, Western Europe was only "half-Americanized."[16] Much the same assessment pertains to the coordination of national policies, the liberalization of trade and payments, and the integration of markets. In these areas as well, American initiatives generally succeeded only to the extent that they accorded with the interests and aspirations of key participating countries.

It is important to begin this part of our assessment by recalling that

[15] Maier, "The Politics of Productivity"; Maier, "The Two Postwar Eras and the Conditions for Stability in Twentieth-Century Western Europe"; and Maier, "Between Taylorism and Technocracy: European Ideologies and the Vision of Industrial Productivity in the 1920s," *Journal of Contemporary History* 5 (April 1970): 27–61. See also Lieberman, *Growth of European Mixed Economies, 13,* 15, 53, 57, 58, 107–9; Kuisel, *Capitalism and the State in Modern France,* 248–59; Karl Hardach, *The Political Economy of Germany in the Twentieth Century* (Berkeley, CA, 1980), 140–85; Pier Paolo D'Attorre, *ERP Aid and the Politics of Productivity in Italy during the 1950s* (Florence, Italy, 1985); Raymond J. Raymond, "The Marshall Plan and Ireland, 1947–1952," in P. J. Drudy, ed., *The Irish in America: Emigration, Assimilation, and Impact* (Cambridge, England, 1985), 312–16; and James Edward Miller, *The United States and Italy, 1940–1950* (Chapel Hill, NC, 1986), 251–66.

[16] D'Attorre, *ERP Aid and the Politics of Productivity in Italy,* 37.

Marshall Planners did not seek a strictly "liberal" reconstruction in Western Europe, in the sense that Milward uses that term.[17] Top officials in the Treasury Department espoused a free-trade approach to European recovery and integration, as had William L. Clayton at the start of the Marshall Plan, and this approach also found support in the Belgian government and the IMF. But even Treasury officials tempered conviction with realism, as was revealed in the debates over intra-European payments, whereas those in the ECA and many in the State Department completely rejected what Hoffman called a "Hazlitt libertarianism." Marshall Planners repudiated French schemes to cartelize the European economy, arguing that such schemes would stifle competition and prevent the most efficient use of resources. But they also conceded that institutional regulators were needed to control the Germans and harmonize national policies so that markets might be integrated. To their way of thinking, as evident in the ECA's proposals for a European reserve board and trade commission, the Marshall Plan should seek to transpose on Western Europe as a whole the sort of mixed economic system that existed in the United States.

Evaluating the success of this effort is a bit like asking whether the glass is half empty or half full. The trade and payments agreements of 1948 and 1949 removed some of the barriers that had grown out of the interwar period. But they did not end the pattern of bilateralism in Western Europe. The Americans settled for less than they had wanted, in part because of European opposition but also because the revival of production had top priority. Once this objective was achieved, the ECA launched a concerted campaign to adjust European exchange rates, remove import quotas, and make currencies transferable, out of which came the devaluation of sterling, the realignment of other European currencies, and the EPU accord of 1950. The EPU agreement liberalized intra-European payments, lessened the pressure for discrimination, and substantially reduced trade restrictions. Although many restrictions remained and new ones would be added, it nonetheless put intra-European trade on a multilateral basis, thereby unleashing market forces that would drive participating countries toward a greater degree of integration.

As Milward has noted, moreover, the multilateralization of intra-European trade, no matter how imperfect, placed limits on the internal and external policy choices available to participating countries.[18] To this extent, it promoted the sort of transnational economic coordination that many Americans saw as one of the keys to a single, integrated market. Participating governments, to be sure, refused to go as far in this direction as expected in Washington, where Keynesians in the ECA believed that economic integration also required the centralization of authority in European institu-

---

[17] Milward, *Reconstruction of Western Europe*, 10. As Milward uses it, the term "liberal" is synonymous with "free-trade."

[18] Ibid., 474.

tions with the power to harmonize national policies. Despite the pressure they exerted, both the OEEC and the EPU remained vehicles of intergovernmental cooperation, not supranational institutions, and the post of political conciliator, established in 1950, was devoid of real status and executive authority. This is not to say that American officials scored no gains. They helped to spawn a new class of European civil servants and deserve some credit for the international authority established under the Schuman Plan. In addition, under their prodding, the EPU exerted considerable influence over the economic policies of participating countries, as the German payments crisis makes clear, and thus contributed to what even Milward describes as a "pattern of institutionalized interdependence" in Western Europe.[19]

The American drive to liberate market forces, build institutional coordinators, and integrate economies fell short of the mark set at the inception of the Marshall Plan. But if viewed against the pattern of bilateralism that existed in 1947, or from the perspective of the Treaty of Rome concluded a decade later, it seems clear that American recovery policy helped to set the Europeans on a road that led from the economic autarky of the 1930s to the Common Market of the 1960s. Still more might have been accomplished had the Korean War not intervened and had the Europeans been more cooperative. Although Milward exaggerates when he claims that European leaders defeated the integrationist thrust of American diplomacy, they did throw up barriers that forced the ECA to detour down paths different from those originally charted.[20]

It should be obvious from the narrative that economic recovery was essentially an avenue over which the main actors in our story maneuvered to protect their economic and strategic interests. Britain and France traveled in the same direction as the United States, but to destinations other than the one mapped out in Washington. The French saw recovery as a highway to hegemony in Western Europe. Reaching this destination depended on modernizing industry under the Monnet Plan and replacing German with French exports in European markets. These gains would shield France against a renascent Reich while at the same time generating an internal growth that could adjourn the redistributive struggles of the interwar period. The success of the Monnet Plan, however, depended on France's recovery taking precedence over that of her former enemy, on guaranteed access to the resources of the Ruhr, and on some measure of French control over Germany's revival and reintegration. These imperatives led the French to resist Anglo–American demands for a higher level of industry in the Allied occupation zones and American pressure to relax the restrictions on German

[19] Ibid.
[20] Ibid., 476.

trade, both of which had to follow, not precede, durable guarantees regarding France's economic and military security.

The same imperatives also prompted France's search for an integrated Western European framework in which these guarantees would be institutionalized. This search followed a tortuous course, its pace and direction directly connected to American pressures for Germany's revival and to the squabbles between economic planners and economic liberals in Paris. Despite these differences, however, or perhaps because of them, French diplomacy displayed a discernible continuity when it came to anchoring national security in an institutionalized system of integration. The French proposal for a customs union, and the Fritalux and Finebel proposals that followed, pointed to a European trade zone in which Germany's power would be regulated through cartelistic agreements, selective trade restrictions, and the offsetting power of France and other participating countries. Nothing came of these initiatives. Nor were the French initially able to regulate Germany's development through a supranational institution that they controlled. The Ruhr Authority was too weak to support their ambitions and the Council of Europe, the OEEC, and the North Atlantic Council were never endowed with supranational power. Yet these failures eventually combined with London's obstructionism and pressure from Washington to produce the Schuman Plan, under which the gradual liberalization of trade and the regulation of markets would integrate the French and German economies on terms that ensured France's economic and military security. In this way, the Schuman Plan created an economic framework that stood in lieu of a final peace settlement. It set the stage for a historic rapprochement between ancient enemies and led to West Germany's reintegration into Western Europe.

Although the Schuman Plan looked to an integrated Europe smaller than the Americans had envisioned at the start of the ERP, neither this nor the fact that it was a French initiative should belittle the American contribution or conceal the similarity between French and American thinking. It is inaccurate to argue, as Milward does, that Schuman's plan amounted to a repudiation of American policy.[21] After all, American leaders had always seen a "nuclear" Europe as one step toward a wider, more thorough integration of the kind that began to take shape with the Treaty of Rome. Their decision to exempt Great Britain from the process of integration and demands for Germany's revival had combined to prompt the French initiative. And through their aid to Western Europe and support for an integrated market, not to mention their last-minute intervention in the Franco–German negotiations, the Americans had played a part in creating the conditions under which the Schuman Plan could succeed. None of these assertions is intended to grasp all of the credit for American Marshall Planners, only to

---

[21] Ibid., 475–6.

redress the imbalance embedded in revisionist writing. Nor should they be taken to mean that Schuman's plan perfectly coincided with what the Americans had in mind. Policymakers in the ECA were prepared to tolerate something less than a free-trade area in Western Europe. They accepted preferential arrangements so long as these arrangements led to economic integration and multilateralism. They lived with trade restrictions, especially those against the dollar. They appreciated the economic and political need to balance free-market forces against central institutions of economic coordination and control. In the integrated community as it evolved under the Schuman Plan, however, the balance nonetheless tilted more toward the regulation of markets than was envisioned in the New Deal synthesis. In this sense as well, Western Europe was only "half-Americanized."

This outcome was due as much to British as to French diplomacy. Bevin and others in the Foreign Office had promoted the idea of an Anglo–Western European customs union in 1947 and early 1948, seeing this as a way to retain Britain's status as a world power and as the route to an economic and security system able to control Germany and survive without excessive dependence on the United States. But this idea had no support from Stafford Cripps and his colleagues in the economic ministries. By the end of 1948, even the Foreign Office had come to the conclusion that an Anglo–Western European union could not be reconciled with socialist planning at home or Britain's ties to the Commonwealth and the sterling area. In addition, the Foreign Office was convinced that unstable political conditions made the continental countries unreliable allies and that neither the Commonwealth nor the Western European states had the resources to erect an adequate defense. These convictions strengthened Bevin's determination to prevent Britain's integration into Western Europe beyond the "point of no return." Bevin still aimed to restore Britain's position as a great world power and to do so in a way that preserved the Commonwealth connection, resolved the German problem, and contained the Soviet Union. But in the grand design of British diplomacy, summed up in Bevin's metaphor of the table with four legs, these objectives were to be realized within a North Atlantic framework in which Britain functioned as the linchpin between two continents.

For the British, in other words, the cost of an Anglo–European condominium was prohibitive. They preferred their own room with connecting doors to the United States and the Continent and protested when the Americans suggested a suite with the Europeans. Although the British saw nothing improper in a "special relationship" with their transatlantic relatives, they were appalled at the prospect of sharing close and continuous quarters with the Italians, the French, and the Germans. So intimate a union, particularly if licensed by supranational authority and joined by free-market forces, could diminish their sterling dowry, compromise their socialist virtue, and alienate the affection of their offspring in the Commonwealth, who might well desert them. Still worse, once such a union was consummated it would be difficult for the British to annul, even if their European partner succumbed to the ravaging embrace of a suitor from the East. So coupling with the Continent was out of the question, although a liaison of sorts was possible provided the other ERP countries followed an "empirical" approach that enabled the British to fend off improper advances.

Guided by this approach, the British insisted on intergovernmental collaboration, not supranationalism, and sought to shield the sterling area and the welfare state against the integrating powers of the market. They demanded special consideration for sterling in the intra-European payments negotiations, undermined French efforts to strengthen the Council of Europe, and raised one obstacle after another to American plans to endow the OEEC with the authority to coordinate national economies. Anglo–American differences came to a head during the second sterling crisis of 1949, when American pressure to liberalize intra-European trade, create a European monetary union, and devalue currencies prompted British threats of a closed sterling bloc that would wreck the chances for an integrated Western Europe and a multilateral system of world trade.

Yet the sterling crisis also led in short order to a major reformulation of American policy. Coinciding as it did with an economic recession in the United States, the crisis alerted the State Department and the ECA to the connection between Britain's recovery and fluctuations in the American business cycle. At the same time, the defeat of the nationalist regime in China and the spread of revolutionary insurgency in Southeast Asia made Kennan and others more aware of how economic dislocations in the sterling bloc might endanger the geopolitical aspirations of the United States in areas of the world outside of Western Europe. These considerations, together with similar thinking in London, laid the basis for an Anglo–American understanding negotiated first at the Washington Conference of 1949 and then in the EPU accord of 1950. The Americans agreed to support the pound as an international reserve and to exempt Great Britain from the process of European integration. The British agreed to devalue the pound, renew their commitment to the principles of multilateralism, and thereby avert a dangerous division of the nonruble world into sterling and dollar blocs.

The reformulation of American policy grew as much out of European considerations as it did out of concerns over the strategic value of the sterling area. As Kennan pointed out in the great integration debate of 1949, the British had been a persistent obstacle to a Western European integration that could control the Germans and contain the Soviets. Recognizing the principle of British exceptionalism removed this obstacle. It put the burden of European integration and German reintegration on the French. But it also gave the French greater incentive to rapprochement with the Germans and permitted faster progress toward a more coherent integration than would have been possible with British participation. One result was a European coal and steel community that included the Germans but not the British. Another, less apparent at the time, was the triumph of French over British diplomacy. The French realized their dream of a Western European system in which they played a pivotal role; the British compromised their position on the Continent, and the welfare state as well, in an elusive effort to retain the Empire and refurbish Britain's status as a great world power.

The Schuman Plan, taken together with the EPU, the Council of Europe, and the OEEC, made up the organizational framework of the postwar order in Western Europe. For all practical purposes, these arrangements completed the process of peacemaking in the West and institutionalized the division of the Continent into hostile blocs. Three years earlier, junior officials in the State Department had hoped to avoid this division through an all-European recovery program. Kennan had scoffed at this idea in 1947, but changed his mind in 1948. By the time of the North Atlantic Treaty negotiations, he had come to believe that the division of Europe into Soviet and American "military zones" was not a "viable" strategy. Such a division would make it difficult to wean the Eastern European satellites from Soviet control, would lay the basis for future war, and would put an undue burden on the backs of American taxpayers, who were clearly reluctant "to support western Europe indefinitely as a military appendage." To Kennan's way of thinking, the better course was one that held out the prospect of bringing Western and Eastern Europe into a single union. This course might lead to a third force under German leadership, as he admitted. But it would also create a solid barrier to Soviet expansion, preclude irredentist claims, and permit the superpowers to disengage from the Continent.[22]

Kennan's recommendations found little support among top policymakers in Washington or in the Western European capitals. They considered the division of Europe to be inevitable and concentrated their efforts on building a continental correlation of forces that could forestall Soviet encroachments. But if this is a commonplace conclusion in the literature on the Cold War, it is less well known that a viable correlation of forces required a workable balance of power among the states of Western Europe. Forging an integrated and supranational system was the key to these related objectives, the way to defuse ancient tensions, mobilize the entire region behind a countervailing unit of power, and ensure that the Soviets would not be tempted to advance, nor the Americans to withdraw. Integration and supranationalism thus were woven into a single thread that ran throughout the fabric of American diplomacy. They linked the economic and strategic goals that American leaders pursued through the EPU, the Schuman Plan, and the other instruments of integration coming out of the ERP.

Collective security arrangements were to complement these instruments

---

[22] Kennan quoted in Gaddis, "The United States and the Question of a Sphere of Influence in Europe," 76.

of integration. They were to encourage the economic and military integration of Western Europe while at the same time creating a North Atlantic security system that had not existed before. These were not parallel directions, however, as the British pointed out from the start. So did Kennan, who predicted in 1948 that the North Atlantic Treaty "would come to overshadow, and probably to replace, any development in the direction of European union."[23] Most dismissed this prediction or saw no alternative. The Europeans made American military guarantees the sine qua non of their diplomacy. The Americans thought an adequate defense ruled out a strictly European security system, as it did the so-called dumbbell plan for separate but linked Western European and North American alliances. To this extent, as Kaplan rightly observes, strategic considerations cut across the economic and political goals that American leaders had in mind. They relieved the pressure on participating countries to seek their security through a full-fledged economic and political, as well as military, unification of Western Europe, perhaps, as Gladwyn Jebb suggested later, through an arrangement whereby the Brussels Treaty Organization would be transformed into a strong political authority. Collective security arrangements did not "replace" the trend toward greater unity in Western Europe. But they did "overshadow" that trend, with results in NATO that came closer to Bevin's grand design than they did to early American plans for a Western European system balanced between British and German power."[24]

III

The preceding summary puts the conclusions of Joyce and Gabriel Kolko and other New Left historians in proper perspective.[25] Although the Marshall Plan projected American power into Western Europe on a scale far greater than ever before, it did so to protect what policymakers in Washington regarded as important economic and strategic assets and in a way that was far less heavy-handed than the concurrent interventions in Greece or the subsequent interventions in Central America, Southeast Asia, and other parts of the globe. In these interventions, the United States often slighted indigenous economic and political problems, relied primarily on military solutions, and acted more or less unilaterally. By comparison, the Marshall Plan amounted to a reasonable defense of American interests, one in which the means used were largely positive, largely scaled to the interests involved, and largely applied in collaboration with reliable local elites.

Indeed, American interests coincided to a high degree with how the Europeans defined their own interests. Policymakers on both sides saw the

---

[23] Ibid.
[24] Kaplan, *United States and NATO*, 78–9.
[25] Kolko and Kolko, *Limits of Power*. See also Block, *Origins of International Economic Disorder*.

need to rehabilitate the European economies, stabilize political systems, and discourage Communist aggression. Bevin and Bidault took the initiative in responding to Marshall's speech at Harvard University in June 1947. They joined other European leaders to draft a recovery plan, issued what amounted to an invitation to intervention by the United States, and then collaborated with their American and European colleagues in the transnational system of elite management that arose from the Marshall Plan and NATO. Viewed in this light, the outcome came closer to what Geir Lundestad calls "empire by invitation" and what Maier terms "consensual American hegemony" than it does to the naked imperialism described by some New Left writers – and not simply because the Europeans invited American aid but also because the Marshall Plan tended to buttress an established pattern of European politics. As European revisionists have argued, for example, it is probably the case that American aid did not fundamentally alter the political fortunes in countries like France and Italy. Communist parties, though large, would have remained minority factions outweighed by "centrist" coalitions at once too conservative for the Communists and too hidebound, statist, or socialist for the Americans.[26]

In addition, the principle of self-help, to which the Americans generally adhered, gave the Europeans a good deal of control over their own destinies and a good deal of leverage over the Americans. So did the fact that American leaders needed their allies as much as their allies needed them. The British capitalized on this mutual dependence, specifically on concerns about the strategic importance of the sterling area, to deflate American pressure for convertible currencies and negotiate a special position for themselves in the ERP. By warning of socialist gains, of a new Rapallo, and of a dangerous neutralism or a resurgent nationalism, the Germans pried support from Washington even while turning their backs on many of the social reforms and Keynesian strategies urged by the ECA. Likewise, the Americans found it difficult to exert too much pressure on the Italian government, pressure for more aggressive industrial development and for housing reform, income redistribution, and social welfare, lest this pressure strengthen the Communists and tilt a precarious political balance in the wrong direction. Much the same was true in France, where local political and economic elites used threats of a Communist resurgence or a Gaullist triumph to deflect American demands for social reform and faster progress on the German front.

By manipulating American dependence and the principle of self-help, participating governments were able to exercise a considerable degree of autonomy within the framework of the ERP. Recovery continued in the years ahead, as did American aid of a largely military nature, so that Western Europe was able to enter the multilateral world envisioned at Bretton

[26] Geir Lundestad, "Empire by Invitation? The United States and Western Europe, 1945–1952," SHAFR *Newsletter* 15 (September 1984): 1–21; and Maier, "The Politics of Productivity," 630.

Woods. Measured against this and other gains – against the resolution of the German problem, the containment of Soviet expansion, the stabilization of politics, the revival of production, and the progress made toward industrial reorganization and economic integration – the Marshall Plan must be judged as one of the most successful peacetime foreign policies launched by the United States in this century. But participating countries were not clay in the hands of American potters, these impressive gains notwithstanding. They resisted the social-democratic elements in the New Deal synthesis, adapted other elements to their own needs and traditions, and thus retained much of their original form. In the beginning, the Marshall Plan had aimed to remake Europe in an American mode. In the end, America was made the European way.

Bibliography

Primary sources

Private manuscript collections
Bentley Historical Library, University of Michigan, Ann Arbor, MI
   Arthur H. Vandenberg Papers
W. Averell Harriman Residence, Washington, DC
   W. Averell Harriman Papers
Harry S Truman Library, Independence, MO
   Dean G. Acheson Papers
   Clinton P. Anderson Papers
   William L. Batt Papers
   Everett H. Bellows Papers
   Thomas C. Blaisdell, Jr. Papers
   William L. Clayton Papers
   Clark M. Clifford Papers
   Matthew Connelly Papers
   George M. Elsey Papers
   Thomas K. Finletter Papers
   Ellen Clayton Garwood Papers
   Paul G. Hoffman Papers
   Lou E. Holland Papers
   Joseph M. Jones Papers
   Philip M. Kaiser Papers
   Milton Katz Papers
   Charles P. Kindleberger Papers
   Frederick J. Lawton Papers
   J. Howard McGrath Papers
   Charles Murphy Papers
   Edwin G. Nourse Papers
   Walter S. Salant Papers
   John W. Snyder Papers
   John D. Sumner Papers
   Harry S Truman Papers
     President's Confidential File
     President's Official File
     President's Secretary's File

James E. Webb Papers
A. L. M. Wiggins Papers
Clayton-Thorp Office Files
Phillip Brook, Oral History Interviews on the European Recovery Program
Harry B. Price, Oral History Interviews on the Marshall Plan
Records of the President's Committee on Foreign Aid, 1947 (Harriman Committee)
Records of the Committee for the Marshall Plan

Government archives

Great Britain
Public Record Office, Kew, England
  CAB 128, Cabinet Minutes, Conclusions, and Confidential Annexes
  CAB 129, Cabinet Papers
  Record Class FO 371, General Records of the British Foreign Office
  Record Class FO 800, General Records of the British Foreign Office (Ernest Bevin Papers)
  Record Class PREM 8, Records of the Prime Ministers' Office (Clement R. Attlee Papers)
  Record Class T229, Records of the British Treasury, Central Economic Planning Division
  Record Class T230, Records of the British Treasury, Economic Advisory Section
  Record Class T232, Records of the British Treasury, Economic Co-operation Committee
      (London Committee)
  Record Class T236, Records of the British Treasury, Overseas Finance Division
  Record Class T237, Records of the British Treasury, Marshall Aid Division

United States
Agency for International Development, Washington, DC
  Records of the Agency for International Development
    Accession 53A278 (ECA Telegram Files)
Department of the Treasury, Washington, DC
  Records of the Department of the Treasury
    Accessions: 66A816
               66A1039
               66A1804
               66A2809
National Archives of the United States, Washington, DC
  Record Group 43, Records of International Conferences, Commissions, and Expositions
    Records of the Post-CFM 1949 Meetings
    Records Relating to the US–UK–Canadian Financial Talks, September 7–12, 1949 (tri-
      lateral talks)
  Record Group 56, General Records of the Department of the Treasury
    Office of the Secretary of the Treasury, Records of the National Advisory Council on
      International Monetary and Financial Policies
    NAC Actions
    NAC Minutes
    NAC Staff Committee Minutes
  Record Group 59, General Records of the Department of State
    Decimal Files
    Memoranda to the President
    Records of Charles E. Bohlen, 1942–1952
    Records of the Office of European Affairs, 1934–1947 (John D. Hickerson and H.
      Freeman Matthews Files)
    Records of the Office of the Executive Secretariat, Summaries of Secretary's Daily
      Meetings, 1949–1952
    Records of the Policy Planning Staff

Record Group 353, Records of Interdepartmental and Intradepartmental Committees (State Department Lot 122)
   European Recovery Program Subject File
   Records of the Advisory Steering Committee on the European Recovery Program
   Records of the Committee for the Marshall Plan
   Records of the Committee on the European Recovery Program
   Records of the Committee on the Extension of U.S. Aid to Foreign Governments
   Records of the European Recovery Program Coordinating Committee
   Records of the Executive Committee on Commercial Policy
   Records of the Executive Committee on Economic Foreign Policy
Washington National Records Center, Suitland, MD
   Record Group 84, Records of the Foreign Service Posts of the Department of State
   London Embassy Records
      Files: 710 Western Bloc
             850 Marshall Plan
   Record Group 286, Records of the Agency for International Development
      Records of the Economic Cooperation Administration
         Accessions: 53A177
                     53A405
                     53A441
                     63A405

Published government documents

Great Britain

Great Britain, Foreign Office. *Anglo–French Discussions regarding French Proposal for the Western European Coal, Iron, and Steel Industries, May–June, 1950.* Cmnd. 7970, 1950.
Great Britain, Parliament. *Parliamentary Debates* (Commons), 5th series, Vol. 466 (1947–8).

United States

U.S. Congress. *Congressional Record*, 1947–51.
U.S. Congress, House. Committee on Foreign Affairs. *Emergency Foreign Aid, Hearings*, 80th Cong., 1st sess., 1947.
   United States Foreign Policy for a Postwar Recovery Program, Hearings, 80th Cong., 1st and 2d sess., 1947–8.
   Extension of European Recovery Program, Hearings on H. R. 2362, in 2 parts, 81st Cong., 1st sess., 1949.
   Mutual Defense Assistance Act of 1949, Hearings on H. R. 5748 and H. R. 5895, 81st Cong., 1st sess., 1949.
   Extension of European Recovery Program, Hearings on H. R. 7378 and H. R. 7797, in 2 parts, 81st Cong., 2d sess., 1950.
   Committee on International Relations. *Foreign Assistance Act of 1948 (Public Law 472)*, 80th Cong., 2d sess., 1948. Historical Series, *Selected Executive Hearings, Foreign Economic Assistance Programs*, Part 1.
   Committee on the Judiciary. *The Mobilization Program.* H. Rept. 1217, 82d Cong., 1st sess., 1951.
U.S. Congress, Senate. Committee on Foreign Relations. *Interim Aid for Europe, Hearings*, 80th Cong., 1st sess., 1947.
   Foreign Relief Aid: 1947, Hearings Held in Executive Session on S. 1774, 80th Cong., 1st sess., 1947.
   European Recovery Program, Hearings, in 2 parts, 80th Cong., 2d sess., 1948.

European Recovery Program, Hearings Held in Executive Session, 80th Cong., 2d sess., 1948.

Extension of European Recovery, Hearings on S. 833, 81st Cong., 1st sess., 1949.

Extension of the European Recovery Program, Hearings Held in Executive Session on S. 833, 81st Cong., 1st sess., 1949.

Extension of European Recovery, Hearings on S. 3101, 81st Cong., 2d sess., 1950.

United States Foreign-Aid Programs in Europe, Hearings before a Subcommittee of the Committee on Foreign Relations on United States Economic and Military Assistance to Free Europe, 82d Cong., 1st sess., 1951.

Committee on Foreign Relations and Committee on Armed Services. *Military Assistance Program, Joint Hearings on S. 2388,* 81st Cong., 1st sess., 1949.

Mutual Defense Assistance Program: 1950, Joint Hearings, 81st Cong., 2d sess., 1950.

Mutual Security Act of 1951, Joint Hearings on S. 1762, 82d Cong., 1st sess., 1951.

U.S. Council of Economic Advisers. *The Impact of Foreign Aid upon the Domestic Economy.* Washington, DC: Government Printing Office, 1947.

U.S. Department of Commerce. *Thirty-Sixth Annual Report of the Secretary of Commerce, 1948.* Washington, DC: Government Printing Office, 1948.

U.S. Department of State. *Bulletin.* Washington, DC: Government Printing Office, 1947–51.

Foreign Relations of the United States, 1947. Vols. 2, 3. Washington, DC: Government Printing Office, 1972.

Foreign Relations of the United States, 1948. Vols. 2, 3. Washington, DC: Government Printing Office, 1973, 1974.

Foreign Relations of the United States, 1949. Vols. 1, 3, 4. Washington, DC: Government Printing Office, 1976, 1974, 1975.

Foreign Relations of the United States, 1950. Vols. 3, 4. Washington, DC: Government Printing Office, 1977, 1980.

Foreign Relations of the United States, 1951. Vols. 1, 4. Washington, DC: Government Printing Office, 1979, 1985.

Germany, 1947–1949: The Story in Documents. Washington, DC: Government Printing Office, 1950.

U.S. Economic Cooperation Administration. *American Business and European Recovery.* Washington, DC: Government Printing Office, 1948.

Quarterly Reports to Congress. 13 reports. Washington, DC: Government Printing Office, 1948–51.

A Report on Recovery Progress and United States Aid. Washington, DC: Government Printing Office, February 1949.

Country Data Book: [All Participating Countries]. Washington, DC: Government Printing Office, March 1950.

Local Currency Counterpart Funds: Midpoint Review. Washington, DC: Government Printing Office, April 1950.

U.S. High Commissioner for Germany. *Quarterly Reports on Germany.* 5 reports. Washington, DC: Government Printing Office, March–December 1950.

International Development Advisory Board. *Partners in Progress: A Report to the President.* By Nelson A. Rockefeller, Chairman. Washington, DC: Government Printing Office, March 1951.

U.S. Office of the Federal Register. *Public Papers of the Presidents of the United States: Harry S Truman, 1947–1950.* Washington, DC: Government Printing Office, 1963–5.

President's Committee on Foreign Aid [Harriman Committee]. *A Report on European Recovery and American Aid.* Washington, DC: Government Printing Office, November 7, 1947.

Report to the President on Foreign Economic Policies. By Gordon Gray. Washington, DC: Government Printing Office, November 10, 1950.

Other official publications

Committee on European Economic Co-operation. *General Report.* Vol. 1. London, 1947. *Technical Reports.* Vol. 2. London, 1947.

Organisation for European Economic Co-operation. *Interim Report on the European Recovery Programme.* Vol. 1: *Report of the Council of the O.E.E.C. to the United States Economic Co-operation Administration on the First Stages of the European Recovery Programme.* Paris, December 30, 1948.

Interim Report on the European Recovery Programme. Vol. 2: *National Programmes of Members for the Recovery Period Ending 30th June 1952.* Paris, December 30, 1948.

Interim Report on the European Recovery Programme. Vol. 3: *Technical Reports.* Paris, 1949.

Report to the Economic Co-operation Administration on the First Annual Programme, July 1, 1948–June 30, 1949. Paris, 1949.

Report to the Economic Co-operation Administration on the Second Annual Programme, July 1, 1949–June 30, 1950. Paris, 1950.

Report to the Economic Co-operation Administration on the 1949–1950 Programme, July 1, 1949–June 30, 1950: Country Programmes. Paris, 1950.

Economic Progress and Problems of Western Europe: Third Annual Report to the Economic Co-operation Administration. Paris, June 1951.

Europe – The Way Ahead: Fourth Annual Report to the Economic Co-operation Administration. Paris, June 1952.

United Nations. General Assembly. Official Records of the Second Part of the First Session of the General Assembly. Supplement No. 3. *Preliminary Report of the Temporary Sub-commission on Economic Reconstruction of Devastated Areas* (A/147), October 26, 1946.

Economic Commission for Europe. *Economic Survey of Europe in 1948.* Geneva, 1949.

Memoirs, diaries, and contemporary accounts

Acheson, Dean G. *Present at the Creation: My Years in the State Department.* New York: Norton, 1969.

Sketches from Life of Men I Have Known. New York: Harper & Bros., 1961.

Adenauer, Konrad. *Memoirs, 1945–1953.* Translated by Beate Ruhm von Oppen. Chicago: Regnery, 1966.

Attlee, Clement R. *As It Happened.* New York: Viking, 1954.

Twilight of Empire: Memoirs of Prime Minister Clement Attlee. New York: Barnes, 1962.

Ball, George W. *The Past Has Another Pattern: Memoirs.* New York: Norton, 1982.

Bidault, Georges. *Resistance: The Political Autobiography of Georges Bidault.* Translated by Marianne Sinclair. New York: Praeger, 1967.

Bissell, Richard M. "The Impact of Rearmament on the Free World Economy," *Foreign Affairs* 29 (April 1951): 385–405.

"European Recovery and the Problems Ahead," *American Economic Association, Papers and Proceedings* 42 (May 1952): 306–26.

Blaisdell, Thomas C., Jr. "The European Recovery Program – Phase Two," *International Organization* 2 (September 1948): 443–54.

Blum, John M. *From the Morgenthau Diaries: Years of War, 1941–1945.* Boston: Houghton Mifflin, 1967.

Bohlen, Charles E. *The Transformation of American Foreign Policy.* New York: Norton, 1969.

Witness to History, 1929–1969. New York: Norton, 1973.

The Brookings Institution. *Major Problems of United States Foreign Policy, 1948–1949.* Washington, DC: The Brookings Institution, 1948.

Major Problems of United States Foreign Policy, 1949–1950. Washington, DC: The Brookings Institution, 1949.

Major Problems of United States Foreign Policy, 1950–1951. Washington, DC: The Brookings Institution, 1950.

Current Issues in Foreign Economic Assistance. Washington, DC: The Brookings Institution, 1951.

Brown, William A. *The United States and the Restoration of World Trade.* Washington, DC: The Brookings Institution, 1950.

Brown, William A., and Opie, Redvers. *American Foreign Assistance.* Washington, DC: The Brookings Institution, 1953.

Campbell, John C. *The United States in World Affairs, 1945–1947.* New York: Harper & Bros. (for the Council on Foreign Relations), 1947.

The United States in World Affairs, 1947–1948. New York: Harper & Bros. (for the Council on Foreign Relations), 1948.

The United States in World Affairs, 1948–1949. New York: Harper & Bros. (for the Council on Foreign Relations), 1949.

Carlyle, Margaret, ed. *Documents on International Affairs, 1949–1950.* London: Oxford University, 1953.

Clay, Lucius D. *Decision in Germany.* Garden City, NY: Doubleday, 1950.

Committee for Economic Development. *An American Program of European Economic Cooperation.* New York: Committee for Economic Development, February 1948.

Economic Aspects of North Atlantic Security: A Statement on National Policy by the Research and Policy Committee of the CED. New York: Committee for Economic Development, 1951.

Cooper, Duff. *Old Men Forget: The Autobiography of Duff Cooper.* New York: Dutton, 1954.

Dalton, Hugh. *High Tide and After: Memoirs, 1945–1960.* London: Frederick Muller, 1962.

Dobney, Frederick J., Jr., ed. *Selected Papers of Will Clayton.* Baltimore: Johns Hopkins University, 1971.

Ellis, Howard S. *The Economics of Freedom: The Progress and Future of Aid to Europe.* New York: Harper & Bros. (for the Council on Foreign Relations), 1950.

"European Proposals for a Recovery Program," *International Conciliation* 436 (December 1947): 803–27.

Ferrell, Robert H., ed. *The Autobiography of Harry S Truman.* Boulder, CO: Associated University Press, 1980.

Off the Record: The Private Papers of Harry S Truman. New York: Harper & Row, 1980.

Dear Bess: The Letters from Harry to Bess Truman, 1910–1959. New York: Norton, 1983.

Galbraith, John K. "European Recovery: The Longer View," *Review of Politics* 12 (April 1950): 165–74.

Geiger, Theodore, and Cleveland, Harold Van B. *Making Western Europe Defensible.* Washington, DC: National Planning Association, August 1951.

Gordon, Lincoln. "ERP in Operation," *Harvard Business Review* 27 (March 1949): 129–50.

Harris, Seymour, ed. *The European Recovery Program.* Cambridge: Harvard University, 1948.

Hirschman, A. O. "The European Payments Union: Negotiations and Issues," *Review of Economics and Statistics* 33 (February 1951): 49–55.

Hoffman, Paul G. *Peace Can Be Won.* Garden City, NY: Doubleday, 1951.

Hoover, Herbert C. *An American Epic.* 4 vols. Chicago: Regnery, 1959–64.

Hull, Cordell. *The Memoirs of Cordell Hull.* 2 vols. New York: Macmillan, 1948.

Jebb, Gladwyn, *The Memoirs of Lord Gladwyn.* New York: Weybright and Talley, 1972.

Kennan, George F. *Memoirs (1925–1950).* New York: Bantam paperback, 1969.

Lutz, Frederick A. *The Marshall Plan and European Economic Policy*. Princeton: Princeton University, 1948.

Marjolin, Robert. *Europe and the United States in the World Economy*. Durham, NC: Duke University, 1953.

Millis, Walter, ed. *The Forrestal Diaries: The Inner History of the Cold War*. New York: Viking, 1951.

Monnet, Jean. *Memoirs*. Translated by Richard Mayne. Garden City, NY: Doubleday, 1978.

Morrison, Herbert. *Herbert Morrison: An Autobiography*. London: Odhams, 1960.

Patterson, Gardner. *Survey of United States International Finance, 1949*. Princeton: Princeton University, 1950.

Patterson, Gardner, and Behrman, Jack. *Survey of United States International Finance, 1950*. Princeton: Princeton University, 1951.

Survey of United States International Finance, 1951. Princeton: Princeton University, 1952.

Patterson, Gardner, and Gunn, John, Jr. *Survey of United States International Finance, 1952*. Princeton: Princeton University, 1953.

Smith, Jean E., ed. *The Papers of General Lucius D. Clay*. Vol. 1: *Germany, 1945–1949*. Bloomington: Indiana University, 1974.

Spaak, Paul-Henri. *The Continuing Battle: Memoirs of a European, 1936–1966*. Translated by Henry Fox. Boston: Little, Brown, 1971.

Stebbins, Richard P. *The United States in World Affairs, 1949*. New York: Harper & Bros. (for the Council on Foreign Relations), 1950.

The United States in World Affairs, 1950. New York: Harper & Bros. (for the Council on Foreign Relations), 1951.

The United States in World Affairs, 1951. New York: Harper & Bros. (for the Council on Foreign Relations), 1952.

Stikker, Dirk U. *Men of Responsibility: A Memoire*. New York: Harper & Row, 1966.

Stille, Ugo. "European vs. U.S. Industrialists," *The Reporter* 6 (January 8, 1952): 28–30.

Strang, Lord William. *Home and Abroad*. London: Andre Deutsch, 1956.

Streit, Clarence K. *Union Now: A Proposal for a Federal Union of the Democracies of the North Atlantic*. New York: Harper & Bros., 1939.

Truman, Harry S. *Memoirs*. 2 vols. Garden City, NY: Doubleday, 1955–6.

Vandenberg, Arthur, Jr., ed. *The Private Papers of Senator Vandenberg*. Boston: Houghton Mifflin, 1952.

White, Theodore H. *Fire in the Ashes: Europe in Mid-century*. New York: Sloane, 1953.

J. H. W. [Williams, John H.] "The Revision of the Intra-European Payments Plan," *Foreign Affairs* 28 (October 1949): 153–5.

Williams, Philip M., ed. *The Diary of Hugh Gaitskell, 1945–1956*. London: Jonathan Cape, 1983.

Contemporary periodicals and biographical directories
Commercial and Financial Chronicle
Economist (London)
Monthly Review (Federal Reserve Bank of New York)
New York Times
Vital Speeches of the Day
Wall Street Journal
Washington Post
Washington Star

Current Biography: Who's News and Why. New York: H. W. Wilson, 1940–.

Fink, Gary M., ed. *Biographical Dictionary of American Labor Leaders*. Westport, CT: Greenwood, 1974.

The International Who's Who. London: Europa, 1935–.

National Cyclopaedia of American Biography. Clifton, NJ: J. T. White, 1926–.

Who's Who in America. Chicago: Marquis Who's Who, 1899–.

Who Was Who in America. Chicago: Marquis Who's Who, 1963–.

Secondary sources

Articles

Baylis, John. "Britain, the Brussels Pact, and the Continental Commitment," *International Affairs* 60 (Autumn 1984): 615–29.

Burnham, Walter Dean. "The System of 1896: An Analysis." In *The Evolution of American Electoral Systems*, pp. 147–202. Paul Kleppner et al. Westport, CT: Greenwood, 1981.

Clayton, William L. "GATT, the Marshall Plan, and OECD," *Political Science Quarterly* 78 (December 1963): 493–503.

Collins, Robert M. "Positive Business Responses to the New Deal: The Roots of the Committee for Economic Development,"*Business History Review* 12 (Autumn 1978): 369–91.

Costigliola, Frank. "The Other Side of Isolationism: The Establishment of the First World Bank, 1929–1930," *Journal of American History* 59 (December 1972): 602–20.

"Anglo–American Financial Rivalry in the 1920s," *Journal of Economic History* 37 (December 1977): 911–34.

Cromwell, William C. "The Marshall Non-plan: Congress and the Soviet Union," *Western Political Quarterly* 32 (December 1979): 422–43.

Cuff, Robert D. "Herbert Hoover, the Ideology of Voluntarism, and the War Organization during the Great War," *Journal of American History* 64 (September 1977): 358–72.

Ferguson, Thomas. "From Normalcy to New Deal: Industrial Structure, Party Competition, and American Public Policy in the Great Depression," *International Organization* 38 (Winter 1984): 41–94.

Gaddis, John Lewis, "NSC 68 and the Problem of Ends and Means," *International Security* 4 (Fall 1979): 164–70.

"The United States and the Question of a Sphere of Influence in Europe, 1945–1949." In *Western Security: The Formative Years. European and Atlantic Defence, 1947–1953*, pp. 60–91. Edited by Olav Riste. New York: Columbia University, 1985.

Gomberg, William. "Labor's Participation in the European Productivity Program: A Study in Frustration," *Political Science Quarterly* 74 (June 1959): 240–55.

Gordon, Lincoln. "The Organization for European Economic Cooperation," *International Organization* 10 (February 1956). 1–11.

Greenwood, Sean. "Ernest Bevin, France, and 'Western Union': August 1945–February 1946," *European History Quarterly* 14 (July 1984): 319–38.

Griffith, Robert. "Dwight D. Eisenhower and the Corporate Commonwealth," *American Historical Review* 87 (February 1982): 87–122.

Hammond, Paul Y. "NSC 68: Prologue to Rearmament." In *Strategy, Politics, and Defense Budgets*, pp. 267–388. Warner R. Schilling, Paul Y. Hammond, and Glenn H. Snyder. New York: Columbia University, 1962.

Hawley, Ellis W. "Herbert Hoover and American Corporatism, 1929–1933." In *The Hoover Presidency: A Reappraisal,* pp. 101–19. Edited by Martin L. Fausold and George T. Mazuzan. Albany: State University of New York, 1974.

"Herbert Hoover, the Commerce Secretariat, and the Vision of an 'Associate State,' " *Journal of American History* 61 (June 1974): 116–40.

"The Discovery and Study of a 'Corporate Liberalism,' " *Business History Review* 52 (Autumn 1978): 309–30.

Hitchens, Harold L. "Influences on the Congressional Decision to Pass the Marshall Plan," *Western Political Quarterly* 21 (March 1968): 51–68.

Hogan, Michael J."Thomas W. Lamont and European Recovery: The Diplomacy of Privatism in a Corporatist Age." In *U.S. Diplomats in Europe, 1919–1941*, pp. 5–22. Edited by Kenneth Paul Jones. Santa Barbara, CA: ABC-Clio, 1981.

"The Search for a 'Creative Peace': The United States, European Unity, and the Origins of the Marshall Plan," *Diplomatic History* 6 (Summer 1982): 267–85.

"Revival and Reform: America's Twentieth-Century Search for a New Economic Order Abroad," *Diplomatic History* 8 (Fall 1984): 287–310.

"American Marshall Planners and the Search for a European Neocapitalism," *American Historical Review* 90 (February 1985): 44–72.

Jackson, Scott. "Prologue to the Marshall Plan: The Origins of the American Commitment for a European Recovery Program," *Journal of American History* 65 (March 1979): 1043–68.

Kindleberger, Charles P. "The Marshall Plan and the Cold War," *International Journal* 23 (Summer 1968): 369–82.

Koistinen, Paul A. C. "Mobilizing the World War II Economy: Labor and the Industrial–Military Alliance," *Pacific Historical Review* 42 (November 1973): 443–78.

Leffler, Melvyn P. "American Policy Making and European Stability, 1921–1933," *Pacific Historical Review* 46 (May 1977): 201–28.

"The American Conception of National Security and the Beginnings of the Cold War, 1945–1948," *American Historical Review* 89 (April 1984): 346–81.

Lundestad, Geir. "Empire by Invitation? The United States and Western Europe, 1945–1952," *SHAFR Newsletter* 15 (September 1984): 1–21.

Lynch, Frances M. B. "Resolving the Paradox of the Monnet Plan: National and International Planning in French Reconstruction," *Economic History Review* 37 (May 1984): 229–43.

Maier, Charles S. "Between Taylorism and Technocracy: European Ideologies and the Vision of Industrial Productivity in the 1920s," *Journal of Contemporary History* 5 (April 1970): 27–61.

"The Politics of Productivity: Foundations of American International Economic Policy after World War II," *International Organization* 31 (Autumn 1977): 607–33.

"The Two Postwar Eras and the Conditions for Stability in Twentieth-Century Western Europe," *American Historical Review* 86 (April 1981): 327–52.

Mallalieu, William C. "Origins of the Marshall Plan: A Study in Policy Formulation and National Leadership," *Political Science Quarterly* 73 (December 1958): 481–504.

McCormick, Thomas J. "Drift or Mastery? A Corporatist Synthesis for American Diplomatic History," *Reviews in American History* 10 (December 1982): 318–30.

McHale, James M. "National Planning and Reciprocal Trade: The New Deal Origins of Government Guarantees for Private Exporters," *Prologue* 6 (Fall 1974): 189–99.

McQuaid, Kim. "Corporate Liberalism in the American Business Community, 1920–1940," *Business History Review* 52 (Autumn 1978): 342–68.

Moore, James R. "Sources of New Deal Economic Policy: The International Dimension," *Journal of American History* 41 (December 1974): 728–68.

Newton, C. C. S. "The Sterling Crisis of 1947 and the British Response to the Marshall Plan," *Economic History Review* 37 (August 1984): 391–408.

Nitze, Paul. "The Development of NSC 68," *International Security* 4 (Fall 1979): 170–6.

Paterson, Thomas G. "Foreign Aid under Wraps: The Point Four Program," *Wisconsin Magazine of History* 56 (Winter 1972/1973): 119–26.

Prowe, Diethelm. "Economic Democracy in Post-World War II Germany: Corporatist Crisis Response, 1945–1948," *Journal of Modern History* 57 (September 1985): 451–82.

Radosh, Ronald. "The Corporate Ideology of American Labor Leaders from Gompers to Hillman," *Studies on the Left* 6, no. 2 (1966): 66–88.

Rappaport, Armin. "The United States and European Integration: The First Phase," *Diplomatic History* 5 (Spring 1981): 121–49.

Raymond, Raymond J. "The Marshall Plan and Ireland, 1947–1952." In *The Irish in America: Emigration, Assimilation, and Impact*, pp. 295–328. Edited by P. J. Drudy. Cambridge: Cambridge University, 1985.

Rowen, Hobart. "America's Most Powerful Private Club," *Harper's Magazine* 221 (September 1960): 79–84.

Rowland, Benjamin M. "Preparing the American Ascendancy: The Transfer of Economic Power from Britain to the United States, 1933–1944." In *Balance of Power or Hegemony: The Interwar Monetary System*, pp. 195–224. Edited by Benjamin M. Rowland. New York: New York University, 1976.

Schuker, Stephen A. "Comment on Charles S. Maier's 'The Two Postwar Eras and the Conditions for Stability in Twentieth-Century Western Europe,' " *American Historical Review* 86 (April 1981): 353–8.

Schwartz, Thomas. "The Case of German Rearmament: Alliance Crisis in the 'Golden Age,' " *The Fletcher Forum* 8 (Summer 1984): 295–309.

"European Integration and the 'Special Relationship': Implementing the Marshall Plan in the Federal Republic of Germany, 1948–1951." In *The Marshall Plan in Germany*. Edited by Charles S. Maier. (forthcoming).

Weiler, Peter. "The United States, International Labor, and the Cold War: The Breakup of the World Federation of Trade Unions," *Diplomatic History* 5 (Winter 1981): 1–22.

Wells, Samuel F., Jr. "Sounding the Tocsin: NSC 68 and the Soviet Threat," *International Security* 4 (Fall 1979): 116–58.

Zieger, Robert H. "Labor, Progressivism, and Herbert Hoover," *Wisconsin Magazine of History* 58 (Spring 1975): 196–208.

Books

Adams, Frederick C. *Economic Diplomacy: The Export Import Bank and American Foreign Policy, 1934–1939*. Columbia: University of Missouri, 1976.

Ardagh, John. *The New French Revolution: A Social and Economic Survey of France, 1945–1967*. London: Secker & Warburg, 1968.

Arkes, Hadley. *Bureaucracy, the Marshall Plan, and the National Interest*. Princeton: Princeton University, 1972.

Backer, John H. *Priming the German Economy: American Occupational Policies, 1945–1948*. Durham, NC: Duke University, 1971.

The Decision to Divide Germany: American Foreign Policy in Transition. Durham, NC: Duke University, 1978.

Winds of History. The German Years of Lucius DuBignon Clay. New York: Van Nostrand Reinhold, 1983.

Barclay, Sir Roderick. *Ernest Bevin and the Foreign Office, 1932–1969*. London: Latimer, 1975.

Barker, Elisabeth. *Britain in a Divided Europe, 1945–1970*. London: Weidenfeld & Nicolson, 1971.

Bartlett, C. J. *A History of Postwar Britain, 1945–1974*. New York: Longman, 1977.

Baum, Warren C. *The French Economy and the State*. Princeton: Princeton University, 1958.

Becker, William H. *The Dynamics of Business–Government Relations: Industry and Exports, 1893–1921*. Chicago: University of Chicago, 1982.

Becker, William H., and Wells, Samuel F., Jr., eds. *Economics and World Power: An Assessment of American Diplomacy since 1789*. New York: Columbia University, 1984.

Beer, Samuel H. *Britain against Itself: The Political Contradictions of Collectivism*. New York: Norton, 1982.

Beloff, Max. *The United States and the Unity of Europe*. Washington, DC: The Brookings Institution, 1963.

Bernstein, Barton J., ed. *Towards a New Past: Dissenting Essays in American History.* New York: Pantheon, 1968.

Politics and Policies of the Truman Administration. Chicago: Quadrangle, 1972.

Best, Gary Dean. *Herbert Hoover: The Postpresidential Years, 1933–1964.* 2 vols. Stanford: The Hoover Institution, 1983.

Blank, Stephen. *Industry and Government in Britain: The Federation of British Industries in Politics, 1945–1965.* Lexington, MA: Lexington Books, 1973.

Block, Fred L. *The Origins of International Economic Disorder: A Study of United States International Monetary Policy from World War II to the Present.* Berkeley: University of California, 1977.

Borden, William S. *The Pacific Alliance: United States Foreign Economic Policy and Japanese Trade Recovery, 1947–1955.* Madison: University of Wisconsin, 1984.

Brandes, Joseph. *Herbert Hoover and Economic Diplomacy: Department of Commerce Policy, 1921–1928.* Pittsburgh: University of Pittsburgh, 1962.

Brody, David. *Workers in Industrial America: Essays on the Twentieth-Century Struggle.* New York: Oxford University, 1980.

Bromberger, Merry, and Bromberger, Serge. *Jean Monnet and the United States of Europe.* Translated by Elaine P. Halperin. New York: Coward-McCann, 1969.

Brown, A. J. *The Great Inflation, 1939–1951.* London: Oxford University, 1955.

Bullock, Alan. *Ernest Bevin, Foreign Secretary, 1945–1951.* New York: Norton, 1983.

Burner, David. *Herbert Hoover: A Public Life.* New York: Knopf, 1978.

Cairncross, Alec. *Years of Recovery: British Economic Policy, 1945–1951.* London: Methuen, 1985.

Calleo, David P. *The Imperious Economy.* Cambridge: Harvard University, 1982.

Caron, François. *An Economic History of Modern France.* Translated by Barbara Bray. New York: Columbia University, 1979.

Carré, Jean-Jacques; Dubois, P.; and Malinvaud, E. *French Economic Growth.* Translated by John P. Hatfield. Stanford: Stanford University, 1975.

Case, Josephine Y., and Case, Everett N. *Owen D. Young and American Enterprise: A Biography.* Boston: David R. Godine, 1982.

Chandler, Lester V. *Benjamin Strong, Central Banker.* Washington, DC: The Brookings Institution, 1958.

Clarke, Sir Richard. *Anglo–American Economic Collaboration in War and Peace, 1942–1949.* Edited by Alec Cairncross. Oxford, England: Clarendon, 1982.

Clarke, Stephen V. O. *Central Bank Cooperation, 1924–1931.* New York: Federal Reserve Bank of New York, 1967.

Coffin, Tristram. *Senator Fulbright: Portrait of a Public Philosopher.* New York: Dutton, 1966.

Collins, Robert M. *The Business Response to Keynes, 1929–1964.* New York: Columbia University, 1981.

Cooke, Colin. *The Life of Richard Stafford Cripps.* London: Hodder & Stoughton, 1957.

Crozier, Michel. *The Stalled Society.* A Viking translation. New York: Viking, 1973.

Cuff, Robert D. *The War Industries Board: Business–Government Relations during World War I.* Baltimore: Johns Hopkins University, 1973.

Curtis, Michael. *Western European Integration.* New York: Harper & Row, 1965.

D'Attorre, Pier Paolo. *ERP Aid and the Politics of Productivity in Italy during the 1950s.* EUI Working Paper No. 85/159. Florence, Italy: European University Institute, 1985.

Diebold, William, Jr. *Trade and Payments in Western Europe: A Study in European Economic Cooperation.* New York: Harper & Bros. (for the Council on Foreign Relations), 1952.

The Schuman Plan: A Study in Economic Cooperation, 1950–1959. New York: Praeger (for the Council on Foreign Relations), 1959.

Doenecke, Justus D. *Not to the Swift: The Old Isolationists in the Cold War Era.* Lewisburg, PA: Bucknell University, 1979.

Donoughue, Bernard, and Jones, G. W. *Herbert Morrison: Portrait of a Politician.* London: Weidenfeld & Nicolson, 1973.

Donovan, Robert J. *Conflict and Crisis: The Presidency of Harry S Truman, 1945–1948.* New York: Norton, 1977.

  Tumultuous Years: The Presidency of Harry S Truman, 1949–1953. New York: Norton, 1982.

Dow, J. C. R. *The Management of the British Economy, 1945–1960.* Cambridge: Cambridge University, 1964.

Eckes, Alfred E., Jr. *A Search for Solvency: Bretton Woods and the International Monetary System, 1941–1947.* Austin: University of Texas, 1975.

Ehrmann, Henry W. *Organized Business in France.* Princeton: Princeton University, 1957.

Feis, Herbert. *The Diplomacy of the Dollar: First Era, 1919–1932.* Baltimore: Johns Hopkins University, 1950.

Ferrell, Robert H. *George C. Marshall.* New York: Cooper Square, 1966.

  Harry S Truman and the Modern American Presidency. Boston: Little, Brown, 1983.

Fitzsimons, Matthew A. *The Foreign Policy of the British Labour Government, 1945–1951.* Notre Dame: University of Notre Dame, 1953.

Foot, Michael. *Aneurin Bevan: A Biography.* Vol. 2. New York: Atheneum, 1973.

Frankel, Joseph. *British Foreign Policy, 1945–1973.* New York: Oxford University (for the Royal Institute of International Affairs), 1975.

Gaddis, John Lewis. *The United States and the Origins of the Cold War, 1941–1947.* New York: Columbia University, 1972.

  Strategies of Containment: A Critical Appraisal of Postwar American National Security Policy. New York: Oxford University paperback, 1982.

Gardner, Lloyd C. *Architects of Illusion: Men and Ideas in American Foreign Policy, 1941–1949.* Chicago: Quadrangle, 1970.

  Economic Aspects of New Deal Diplomacy. 2d ed. Boston: Beacon, 1971.

Gardner, Richard N. *Sterling–Dollar Diplomacy: The Origins and Prospects of Our International Economic Order.* 2d ed. New York: McGraw-Hill, 1969.

Gatzke, Hanz W. *Germany and the United States: A "Special Relationship"?* Cambridge: Harvard University, 1980.

Gilbert, James. *Designing the Industrial State: The Intellectual Pursuit of Collectivism in America, 1880–1940.* Chicago: Quadrangle, 1972.

Gimbel, John. *The American Occupation of Germany: Politics and Military, 1945–1949.* Stanford: Stanford University, 1968.

  The Origins of the Marshall Plan. Stanford: Stanford University, 1976.

Godson, Roy. *American Labor and European Politics: The AFL as a Transnational Force.* New York: Crane-Russak, 1976.

Golob, Eugene O. *The "ISMS": A History and Evaluation.* New York: Harper & Bros., 1954.

Gordon, Michael R. *Conflict and Consensus in Labour's Foreign Policy, 1914–1965.* Stanford: Stanford University, 1969.

Goulden, Joseph C. *Meany.* New York: Atheneum, 1972.

Griffiths, Richard T., and Lynch, Frances. *The Fritalux/Finebel Negotiations, 1949–1950.* EUI Working Paper No. 84/117. Florence, Italy: European University Institute, 1984.

Grindrod, Muriel. *The Rebuilding of Italy: Politics and Economics, 1945–1955.* New York: Oxford University (for the Royal Institute of International Affairs), 1955.

Guhin, Michael A. *John Foster Dulles: A Statesman and His Times.* New York: Columbia University, 1972.

Haines, Gerald K., and Walker, J. Samuel, eds. *American Foreign Relations: A Historiographical Review.* Westport, CT: Greenwood, 1981.

Halle, Louis J. *The Cold War as History.* New York: Harper & Row, 1967.

Hamby, Alonzo L. *Beyond the New Deal: Harry S Truman and American Liberalism.* New York: Columbia University, 1973.

Hannah, Leslie. *The Rise of the Corporate Economy.* 2d ed. London: Methuen, 1983.

Hardach, Karl. *The Political Economy of Germany in the Twentieth Century.* Berkeley: University of California, 1980.

Harris, Kenneth. *Attlee.* London: Weidenfeld & Nicolson, 1982.

Harris, Nigel. *Competition and the Corporate Society: British Conservatives, the State, and Industry, 1945–1964.* London: Methuen, 1972.

Harris, Seymour E. *The European Recovery Program.* Cambridge: Harvard University, 1948.

Hartmann, Susan M. *The Marshall Plan.* Columbus, OH: Charles E. Merrill, 1968.

Truman and the 80th Congress. Columbia: University of Missouri, 1971.

Hathaway, Robert M. *Ambiguous Partnership: Britain and America, 1944–1947.* New York: Columbia University, 1981.

Hawley, Ellis W. *The New Deal and the Problem of Monopoly.* Princeton: Princeton University, 1966.

The Great War and the Search for a Modern Order: A History of the American People and Their Institutions, 1917–1933. New York: St. Martin's, 1979.

Hawley, Ellis W. et al. *Herbert Hoover and the Crisis of American Capitalism.* Cambridge, MA: Schenkman, 1973.

Hawley, Ellis W., ed. *Herbert Hoover as Secretary of Commerce: Studies in New Era Thought and Practice.* Iowa City: University of Iowa, 1981.

Hayward, Jack, and Watson, Michael, eds. *Planning, Politics, and Public Policy: The British, French, and Italian Experience.* New York: Cambridge University, 1975.

Heller, Francis H., ed. *Economics and the Truman Administration.* Lawrence, KS: Regents Press of Kansas (for the Harry S Truman Institute for National and International Affairs), 1981.

Hildebrand, George H. *Growth and Structure in the Economy of Modern Italy.* Cambridge: Harvard University, 1965.

Hoffman, John D. *The Conservative Party in Opposition, 1945–1951.* London: MacGibbon & Kee, 1964.

Hoffmann, Stanley. *Decline or Renewal? France since the 1930s.* New York: Viking, 1974.

Hoffmann, Stanley, and Maier, Charles S., eds. *The Marshall Plan: A Retrospective.* Boulder, CO: Westview, 1984.

Hoffmann, Stanley, et al. *In Search of France.* Cambridge: Harvard University, 1963.

Hogan, Michael J. *Informal Entente: The Private Structure of Cooperation in Anglo–American Economic Diplomacy, 1918–1928.* Columbia: University of Missouri, 1977.

Horowitz, Daniel L. *The Italian Labor Movement.* Cambridge: Harvard University, 1963.

Horowitz, David, ed. *Corporations and the Cold War.* New York: Monthly Review Press, 1969.

Horsefield, J. Keith. *The International Monetary Fund, 1945–1965: Twenty Years of International Monetary Cooperation.* Vol. 1. Washington, DC: The International Monetary Fund, 1969.

Howarth, T. E. B. *Prospect and Reality: Great Britain, 1945–1955.* London: William Collins' Sons, 1985.

Hughes, H. Stuart. *The United States and Italy.* 3d ed. Cambridge: Harvard University, 1979.

Ireland, Timothy P. *Creating the Entangling Alliance: The Origins of the North Atlantic Treaty Organization.* Westport, CT: Greenwood, 1981.

Jacobson, Jon. *Locarno Diplomacy: Germany and the West, 1925–1929.* Princeton: Princeton University, 1972.

Jones, Joseph M. *The Fifteen Weeks (February 21–June 5, 1947).* New York: Viking, 1955.

Kaplan, Lawrence S. *A Community of Interests: NATO and the Military Assistance Program, 1948–1951.* Washington, DC: Government Printing Office (for the Office of the Secretary of Defense, Historical Office), 1980.

The United States and NATO: The Formative Years. Lexington: University of Kentucky, 1984.

Kindleberger, Charles P. *Economic Growth in France and Britain, 1951–1960*. Cambridge: Harvard University, 1964.
    Power and Money. New York: Basic Books, 1960.
Klein, Lawrence R. *The Keynesian Revolution*. 2d ed. New York: Macmillan, 1966.
Kogan, Norman. *A Political History of Italy: The Postwar Years*. New York: Praeger, 1983.
Kolko, Joyce, and Kolko, Gabriel. *The Limits of Power: The World and United States Foreign Policy, 1945–1954*. New York: Harper & Row, 1972.
Krause, Lawrence B. *European Economic Integration and the United States*. Washington, DC: The Brookings Institution, 1968.
Kuisel, Richard F. *Capitalism and the State in Modern France: Renovation and Economic Management in the Twentieth Century*. Cambridge: Cambridge University, 1981.
Kuklick, Bruce. *American Policy and the Division of Germany: The Clash with Russia over Reparations*. Ithaca: Cornell University, 1972.
LaFeber, Walter F. *America, Russia, and the Cold War, 1945–1975*. 3d ed. New York: Wiley & Sons, 1976.
Leffler, Melvyn P. *The Elusive Quest: America's Pursuit of European Stability and French Security, 1919 1933*. Chapel Hill. University of North Carolina, 1979.
Lichtheim, George. *Europe and America: The Future of the Atlantic Community*. London: Thames & Hudson, 1963.
Lieberman, Sima. *The Growth of European Mixed Economies, 1945–1970: A Concise Study of the Economic Evolution of Six Countries*. Cambridge, MA: Schenkman, 1977.
Lipgens, Walter. *A History of European Integration*. Vol. 1: *1945–1947: The Formation of the European Unity Movement*. Translated by P. S. Falla and A. J. Ryder. New York: Oxford University, 1982.
Lochner, Louis P. *Herbert Hoover and Germany*. New York: Macmillan, 1960.
Lorwin, Lewis L. *The International Labor Movement: History, Policies, Outlook*. New York: Harper & Bros., 1953.
Lorwin, Val R. *The French Labor Movement*. Cambridge: Harvard University, 1954.
Louis, William Roger. *Imperialism at Bay: The United States and the Decolonization of the British Empire, 1941–1945*. New York: Oxford University, 1977.
    The British Empire in the Middle East, 1945–1951: Arab Nationalism, the United States, and Postwar Imperialism. New York: Oxford University, 1984.
Lundestad, Geir. *The American Non-policy towards Eastern Europe, 1943–1947: Universalism in an Area Not of Essential Interest to the United States*. New York: Humanities, 1975.
    America, Scandinavia, and the Cold War, 1945–1949. New York: Columbia University, 1980.
Lynch, Frances. *French Reconstruction in a European Context*. EUI Working Paper No. 86. Florence, Italy: European University Institute, 1984.
MacLennan, Malcolm; Forsyth, Murray; and Denton, Geoffrey. *Economic Planning and Policies in Britain, France, and Germany*. New York: Praeger, 1968.
Maier, Charles S. *Recasting Bourgeois Europe: Stabilization in France, Germany, and Italy in the Decade after World War I*. Princeton: Princeton University, 1975.
Mallalieu, William C. *British Reconstruction and American Policy, 1945–1955*. New York: Scarecrow, 1956.
Manderson-Jones, R. B. *The Special Relationship: Anglo–American Relations and Western European Unity, 1947–1956*. London: Weidenfeld & Nicolson, 1972.
Markowitz, Norman. *The Rise and Fall of the People's Century: Henry A. Wallace and American Liberalism*. New York: Free Press, 1973.
Mayer, Herbert C. *German Recovery and the Marshall Plan*. New York: Atlantic Edition Forum, 1969.
Mayne, Richard. *The Recovery of Europe: From Devastation to Unity*. New York: Harper & Row, 1970.

McArthur, John H., and Scott, Bruce R. *Industrial Planning in France*. Boston: Harvard University, 1969.

McConnell, Grant. *Private Power and American Democracy*. New York: Knopf, 1966.

McDonald, Ian S., ed. *Anglo–American Relations since the Second World War*. New York: St. Martin's, 1974.

McGeehan, Robert. *The German Rearmament Question: American Diplomacy and European Defense after World War II*. Urbana: University of Illinois, 1971.

McLellan, David S. *Dean Acheson: The State Department Years*. New York: Dodd, Mead, 1976.

McNeill, William H. *America, Britain, and Russia: Their Cooperation and Conflict, 1941–1946*. London: Oxford University, 1953.

McQuaid, Kim. *Big Business and Presidential Power: From FDR to Reagan*. New York: William Morrow, 1982.

Mee, Charles L., Jr. *The Marshall Plan: The Launching of the Pax Americana*. New York: Simon & Schuster, 1984.

Meehan, Eugene, Jr. *The British Left Wing and Foreign Policy: A Study of the Influence of Ideology*. New Brunswick, NJ: Rutgers University, 1960.

Merkl, Peter H. *The Origin of the West German Republic*. New York: Oxford University, 1963.

Miller, James Edward. *The United States and Italy, 1940–1950*. Chapel Hill: University of North Carolina, 1986.

Milward, Alan S. *The Reconstruction of Western Europe, 1945–1951*. London: Methuen, 1984.

Morgan, Kenneth O. *Labour in Power, 1945–1951*. Oxford, England: Clarendon, 1984.

Morgan, Roger. *West European Politics since 1945: The Shaping of the European Community*. London: Batsford, 1972.

   The United States and West Germany, 1945–1973. New York: Oxford University, 1974.

Mosley, Leonard. *Marshall: Hero for Our Times*. New York: Hearst Books, 1982.

Mowat, Robert C. *Creating the European Community*. London: Blandford, 1973.

Newman, Michael. *Socialism and European Unity: The Dilemma of the Left in Britain and France*. London: Junction Books, 1983.

Nicholas, H. G. *The United States and Britain*. Chicago: University of Chicago, 1975.

Northedge, Frank S. *Descent from Power: British Foreign Policy, 1945–1973*. London: Allen & Unwin, 1974.

Paterson, Thomas G. *Soviet–American Confrontation: Postwar Reconstruction and the Origins of the Cold War*. Baltimore: Johns Hopkins University, 1973.

   On Every Front: The Making of the Cold War. New York: Norton, 1979.

Patterson, James T. *Mr. Republican: A Biography of Robert A. Taft*. Boston: Houghton Mifflin, 1972.

Pelling, Henry. *The Labour Governments, 1945–1951*. New York: St. Martin's, 1984.

Pells, Richard H. *The Liberal Mind in a Conservative Age: American Intellectuals in the 1940s and 1950s*. New York: Harper & Row, 1985.

Penrose, Ernest F. *Economic Planning for the Peace*. Princeton: Princeton University, 1953.

Pimlott, Ben. *Hugh Dalton*. London: Jonathan Cape, 1985.

Pollard, Robert A. *Economic Security and the Origins of the Cold War, 1945–1950*. New York: Columbia University, 1985.

Pollard, Sidney. *The Development of the British Economy, 1914–1967*. 2d ed. London: Edward Arnold, 1969.

   The Integration of the European Economy since 1815. London: University Association for Contemporary European Studies, 1981.

Postan, M. M. *An Economic History of Western Europe, 1945–1964*. London: Methuen, 1967.

Price, Harry B. *The Marshall Plan and Its Meaning*. Ithaca: Cornell University, 1955.

Pritt, D. N. *The Labour Government, 1945–1951*. London: Lawrence & Wishart, 1963.

Pruessen, Ronald W. *John Foster Dulles: The Road to Power*. New York: Free Press, 1982.

Radosh, Ronald. *American Labor and United States Foreign Policy*. New York: Random House, 1969.

Radosh, Ronald, and Rothbard, Murray N., eds. *A New History of Leviathan: Essays on the Rise of the American Corporate State*. New York: Dutton, 1972.

Raucher, Alan R. *Paul G. Hoffman: Architect of Foreign Aid*. Lexington: University Press of Kentucky, 1985.

Rearden, Steven L. *History of the Office of the Secretary of Defense*. Vol. 1: *The Formative Years, 1947–1950*. Washington, DC: Government Printing Office (for the Office of the Secretary of Defense, Historical Office), 1984.

Ridley, F., and Blondel, J. *Public Administration in France*. London: Routledge & Kegan Paul, 1964.

Rogow, Arnold A. *The Labour Government and British Industry, 1945–1951*. Oxford, England: Blackwell, 1955.

Rostow, Walt W. *The Division of Europe after World War II: 1946*. Austin: University of Texas, 1981.

Roth, Andrew. *Sir Harold Wilson: Yorkshire Walter Mitty*. London: Macdonald and Jane's, 1977.

Rothwell, Victor. *Britain and the Cold War, 1941–1947*. London: Jonathan Cape, 1982.

Rowland, Benjamin M., ed. *Balance of Power or Hegemony: The Interwar Monetary System*. New York: New York University, 1976.

Schilling, Warner R.; Hammond, Paul Y.; and Snyder, Glenn H. *Strategy, Politics, and Defense Budgets*. New York: Columbia University, 1962.

Schmitt, Hans A. *The Path to European Union: From the Marshall Plan to the Common Market*. Baton Rouge: Louisiana State University, 1962.

Schriftgiesser, Karl. *Business Comes of Age: The Story of the Committee for Economic Development and Its Impact upon the Economic Policies of the United States. 1942–1960*. New York: Harper & Row, 1960.

Schuker, Stephen A. *The End of French Predominance in Europe: The Financial Crisis of 1924 and the Adoption of the Dawes Plan*. Chapel Hill: University of North Carolina, 1976.

Schulzinger, Robert D. *The Wise Men of Foreign Affairs: The History of the Council on Foreign Relations*. New York: Columbia University, 1984.

Shlaim, Avi. *The United States and the Berlin Blockade, 1948–1949: A Study in Crisis Decision-Making*. Berkeley: University of California, 1983.

Shonfield, Andrew. *British Economic Policy since the War*. Harmondsworth, England: Penguin paperback, 1959.

   Modern Capitalism: The Changing Balance of Public and Private Power. London: Oxford University (for the Royal Institute of International Affairs), 1965.

Shoup, Laurence H., and Minter, William. *Imperial Brain Trust: The Council on Foreign Relations and United States Foreign Policy*. New York: Monthly Review Press, 1977.

Silverman, Dan P. *Reconstructing Europe after the Great War*. Cambridge: Harvard University, 1982.

Smith, Gaddis. *Dean Acheson*. Vol 16. *The American Secretaries of State and Their Diplomacy*. Edited by Robert H. Ferrell. New York: Cooper Square, 1972.

Smith, Leslie. *Harold Wilson: The Authentic Portrait*. New York: Scribner's, 1964.

Steel, Ronald. *Walter Lippmann and the American Century*. New York: Vintage, 1980.

Stein, Herbert. *The Fiscal Revolution in America*. Chicago: University of Chicago, 1969.

Steward, Dick. *Trade and Hemisphere: The Good Neighbor Policy and Reciprocal Trade*. Columbia: University of Missouri, 1975.

Strange, Susan. *Sterling and British Policy: A Political Study of an International Currency in Decline*. New York: Oxford University, 1971.

Stueck, William W. *The Road to Confrontation: American Policy toward China and Korea, 1947–1950.* Chapel Hill: University of North Carolina, 1981.

Tew, Brian. *International Monetary Cooperation, 1945–1967.* 9th rev. ed. London: Hutchison, 1967.

Thorne, Christopher. *Allies of a Kind: The United States, Britain, and the War against Japan, 1941–1945.* London: Hamish Hamilton, 1978.

Triffin, Robert. *Europe and the Money Muddle: From Bilateralism to Near-Convertibility, 1947–1956.* New Haven: Yale University, 1957.

Tucker, Nancy B. *Patterns in the Dust: Chinese–American Relations and the Recognition Controversy, 1949–1950.* New York: Columbia University, 1983.

Ulam, Adam B. *Expansion and Coexistence: Soviet Foreign Policy, 1917–1973.* 2d ed. New York: Praeger, 1974.

Van Der Beugel, Ernst H. *From Marshall Aid to Atlantic Partnership: European Integration as a Concern of American Foreign Policy.* New York: Elsevier, 1966.

Vaughan, Richard. *Twentieth-Century Europe: Paths to Unity.* London: Croom Helm, 1979.

Vital, David. *The Making of British Foreign Policy.* London: Allen & Unwin, 1968.

Wallich, Henry C. *Mainsprings of the German Revival.* New Haven: Yale University, 1955.

Watt, Donald C. *Britain Looks to Germany: A Study of British Opinion and Policy towards Germany since 1945.* London: O. Wolff, 1965.

——— *Personalities and Policies: Studies in the Formulation of British Foreign Policy in the Twentieth Century.* Notre Dame: University of Notre Dame, 1965.

——— *Succeeding John Bull: America in Britain's Place, 1900–1975.* Cambridge: Cambridge University, 1984.

Weinstein, James. *The Corporate Ideal in the Liberal State, 1900–1918.* Boston: Beacon, 1969.

Wexler, Imanuel. *The Marshall Plan Revisited: The European Recovery Program in Economic Perspective.* Westport, CT: Greenwood, 1983.

Wiebe, Robert. *The Search for Order, 1877–1920.* New York: Hill & Wang, 1967.

Wilkins, Mira. *The Maturing of Multinational Enterprise: American Business Abroad from 1914 to 1970.* Cambridge: Harvard University, 1974.

Williams, Francis. *A Prime Minister Remembers: The War and Post-war Memoirs of the Rt. Hon. Earl Attlee.* London: Heinemann, 1961.

Williams, Philip M. *Crisis and Compromise: Politics in the Fourth Republic.* Hamden, CT: Archon Books, 1964.

——— *Hugh Gaitskell: A Political Biography.* London: Jonathan Cape, 1979.

Willis, Frank R. *France, Germany, and the New Europe, 1945–1967.* rev. ed. Stanford: Stanford University, 1968.

Wilson, Joan Hoff. *American Business and Foreign Policy, 1920–1933.* Lexington: University of Kentucky, 1971.

——— *Herbert Hoover: Forgotten Progressive.* Boston: Little, Brown, 1975.

Wilson, Theodore A. *The Marshall Plan: An Atlantic Venture of 1947–1951 and How It Shaped Our World.* Headline Series, No. 236. New York: Foreign Policy Association, June 1977.

Windmuller, John P. *American Labor and the International Labor Movement, 1940–1953.* Ithaca: Cornell University, 1954.

Windrich, Elaine. *British Labour's Foreign Policy.* Stanford: Stanford University, 1952.

Winks, Robin W. *The Marshall Plan and the American Economy.* New York: Holt, Rinehart, 1960.

Wittner, Lawrence S. *American Intervention in Greece, 1943–1949.* New York: Columbia University, 1981.

Woodhouse, Christopher M. *British Foreign Policy since the Second World War.* New York: Praeger, 1962.

Worswick, George, and Ady, P. H., eds. *The British Economy, 1945–1950.* Oxford, England: Clarendon, 1952.

The British Economy in the Nineteen-Fifties. Oxford, England: Clarendon, 1962.

Yergin, Daniel. *Shattered Peace: The Origins of the Cold War and the National Security State.* Boston: Houghton Mifflin, 1978.

Young, John W. *Britain, France, and the Unity of Europe, 1945–1951.* Leicester, England: Leicester University, 1984.

Zurcher, Arnold J. *The Struggle to Unite Europe, 1940–1958.* Washington Square, NY: New York University, 1958.

Unpublished material

Harriman, W. Averell. Interview by author on January 6, 1982. (Author's Files)

Hawley, Ellis W. "Neo-institutional History and the Understanding of Herbert Hoover." (Author's Files)

   "Techno-corporatist Formulas in the Liberal State, 1920–1960: A Neglected Aspect of America's Search for a New Order." Paper presented at the Conference on Twentieth-Century Capitalism, Harvard University, Cambridge, September 1974.

Hitchens, Harold Lee. "Congress and the Adoption of the Marshall Plan." Ph.D. dissertation, University of Chicago, 1949.

Leffler, Melvyn P. "Standing Tough: The Strategic and Diplomatic Aftermath of the Iranian Crisis of March 1946." Paper presented at The Lehrman Institute, New York, April 1985.

Maier, Charles S. "Western Europe and American Foreign Policy in the Truman Years." Paper presented at the Truman Centennial Conference, Woodrow Wilson International Center for Scholars, Washington, DC, September 7–8, 1984.

Schwartz, Thomas. "From Occupation to Alliance: John J. McCloy and the Allied High Commission in the Federal Republic of Germany, 1949–1952." Ph.D. dissertation, Harvard University, 1985.

Index

Acheson, Dean G., 37, 41, 45, 108, 200, 249; orders studies of European aid needs, 40; urges integrated Europe, 42, 273; as member of Marshall Plan Committee, 98; Vandenberg vetoes appointment of, as ECA administrator, 108; calls for intergovernmental agreement on German policy, 197; and Washington Foreign Ministers Meeting of 1949, 198–9; and State Department relations with organized labor, 203; praises formation of Council of Europe, 216–17; views of, on British proposal to liberalize trade and payments, 234; and Kennan's talks with British and French, 260; political philosophy of, 262; and U.S.–U.K.–Canada financial talks of September 1949, 262; on Anglo–American relations, 262, 311, 314–15, 320, 401; on European reaction to U.S.–U.K.–Canada financial talks of September 1949, 268; on role of Britain and France in European integration, 269–70, 271; rules out Anglo–Western European unification, 276; criticizes British policy toward Europe, 279, 284, 306, 310; urges strengthening of OEEC, 283–4; and appointment of director general of OEEC, 284, 289, 290–1; urges concessions to appease the Germans, 287; on American policy toward European integration and German reintegration, 288, 289, 291; urges integrated defense of North Atlantic area, 315; on Schuman Plan, 332, 367; demands German integration into NATO, 375; criticizes Pleven Plan, 376; calls for continuing Marshall Plan beyond 1952, 389; criticizes Mutual Security Act, 392; praises "European Manifesto," 414

Adenauer, Konrad: urges elimination of Allied restrictions on German industry, 287; as advocate of European integration, 304, 366–7
Advisory Steering Committee, 84–5, 100; formation and work of, 75–6
Agent General for Reparations, 7
Agriculture Department, U.S.: role of, in ERP, 107; liaisons of, with private sector, 137; and EPU negotiations, 297
Aldrich, Winthrop, 256
Allied High Commission: established, 199; negotiates Petersberg Protocol, 287–8
Alphand, Hervé: views of, on European unification, 64
Alsop, Joseph and Stewart, 260
American Federation of Labor, 201; and Harriman Committee, 141; seeks to mobilize European labor behind Marshall Plan, 146–7; and TUAC, 147; disagreements of, with TUC and CIO, 202–3; reaffirms support for the Marshall Plan, 418–19
American Policy Commission, 13
Anderson, Clinton, 101
Anderson, Samuel, 138
Anglo–American Council on Productivity, 138, 151; labor representation on, 142; formation and work of, 143–5, 204, 256–7, 326–7, 416
Anglo–American Loan Agreement of 1946, 29, 31, 48, 50; and sterling crisis of 1947, 68, 82–3
Ansiaux, Hubert, 165, 296
Army Department, U.S.: criticizes reparation payments, coal transfers, and 1946 level-of-industry plan, 31; and bizonal share of ERP aid, 163–4; complains

465